Kuala Lumpur, Melaka & Penang

Joe Bindloss
Celeste Brash

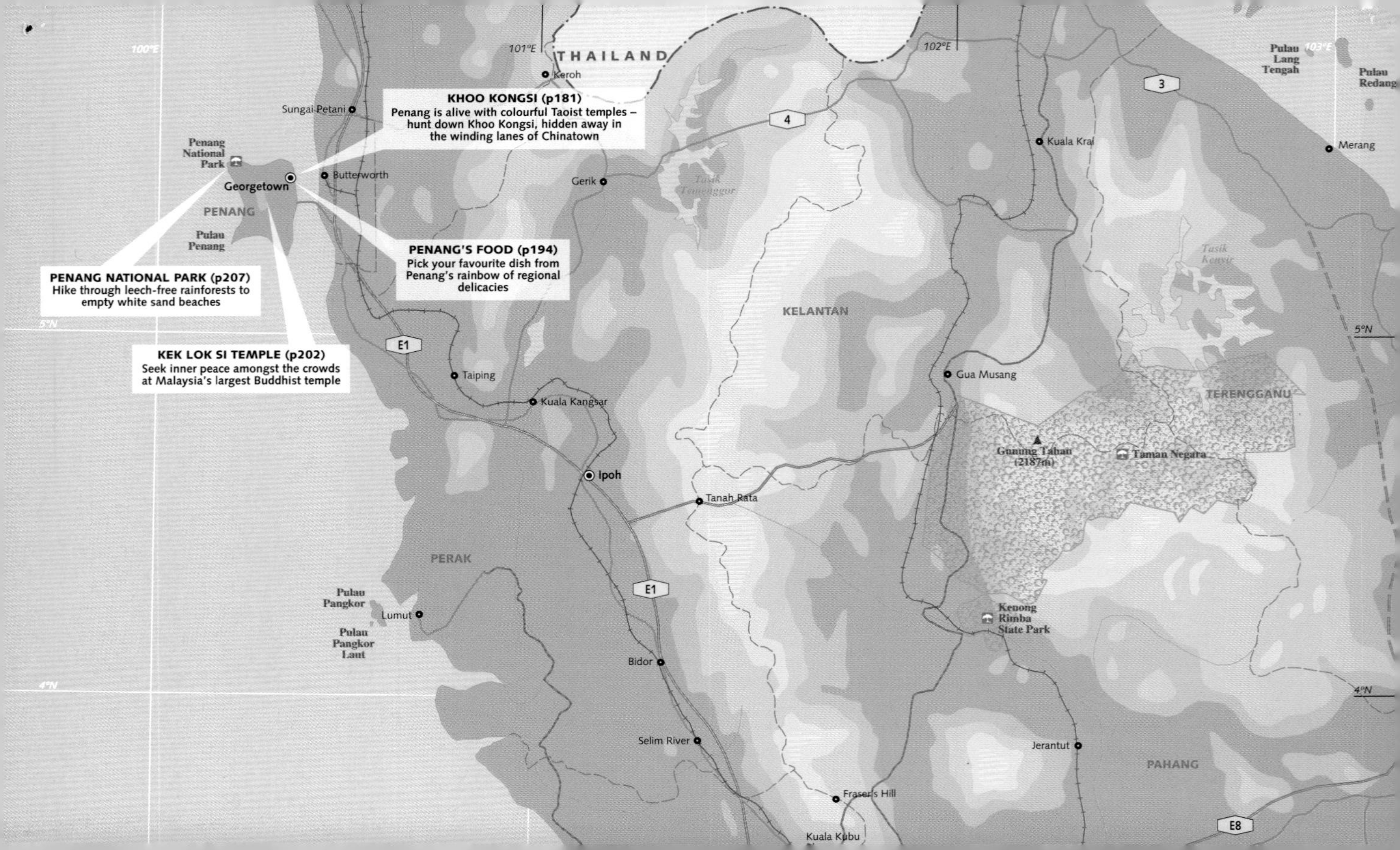

KHOO KONGSI (p181)
Penang is alive with colourful Taoist temples – hunt down Khoo Kongsi, hidden away in the winding lanes of Chinatown
PENANG'S FOOD (p194)
Pick your favourite dish from Penang's rainbow of regional delicacies
PENANG NATIONAL PARK (p207)
Hike through leech-free rainforests to empty white sand beaches
KEK LOK SI TEMPLE (p202)
Seek inner peace amongst the crowds at Malaysia's largest Buddhist temple
THAILAND
100°E
101°E
102°E
103°E
5°N
4°N
Keroh
Sungai Petani
Penang National Park
Georgetown
Butterworth
PENANG
Pulau Penang
Gerik
Tasik Temenggor
KELANTAN
Kuala Kral
Pulau Lang Tengah
Pulau Redang
Merang
Tasik Kenyir
TERENGGANU
Gua Musang
Gunung Tahan (2187m)
Taman Negara
Taiping
Kuala Kangsar
Ipoh
Tanah Rata
PERAK
Pulau Pangkor
Lumut
Pulau Pangkor Laut
Bidor
Selim River
Fraser's Hill
Kuala Kubu
Kenong Rimba State Park
Jerantut
PAHANG
E1
E8
3
4

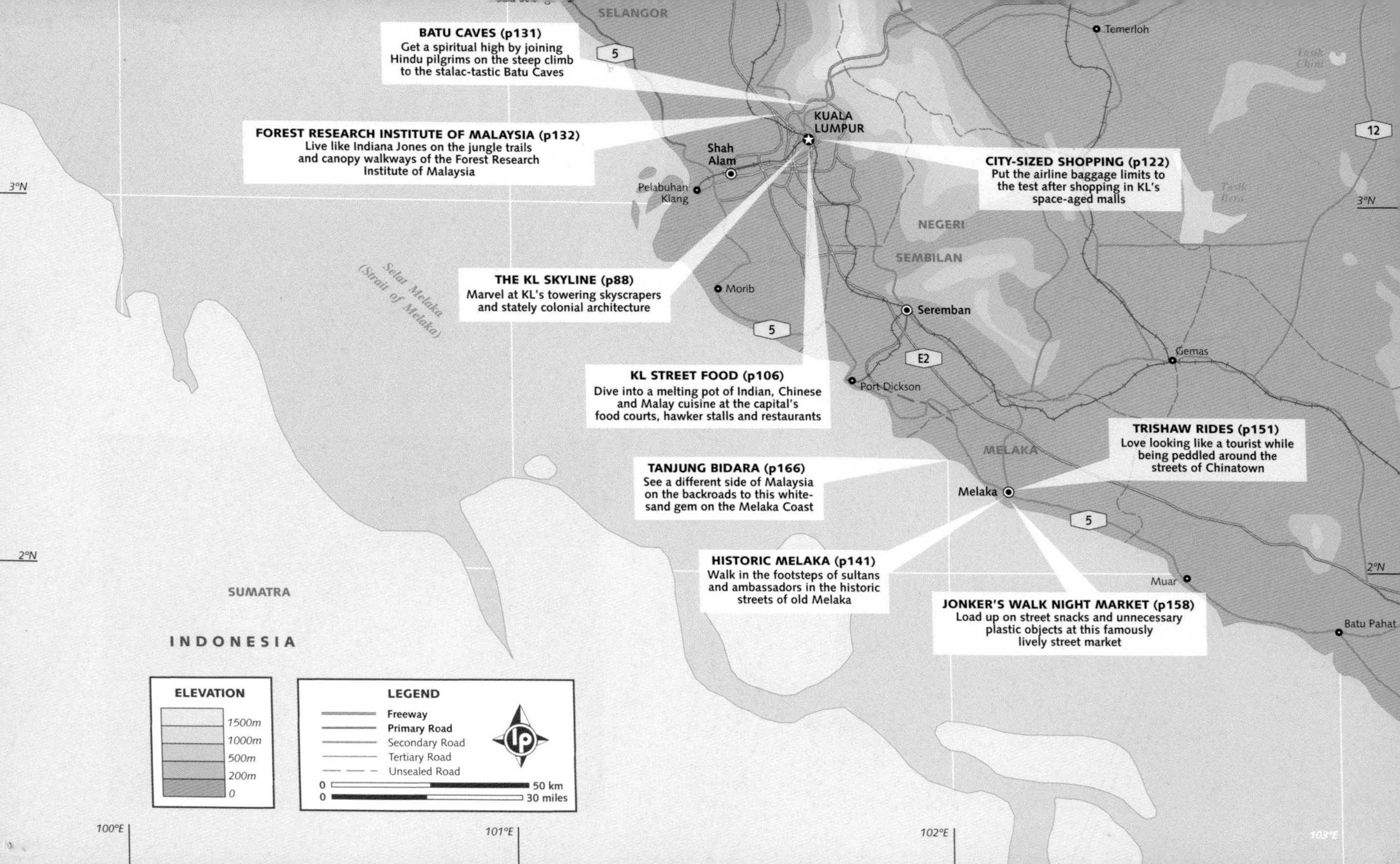
BATU CAVES (p131)
Get a spiritual high by joining Hindu pilgrims on the steep climb to the stalac-tastic Batu Caves
FOREST RESEARCH INSTITUTE OF MALAYSIA (p132)
Live like Indiana Jones on the jungle trails and canopy walkways of the Forest Research Institute of Malaysia
THE KL SKYLINE (p88)
Marvel at KL's towering skyscrapers and stately colonial architecture
KL STREET FOOD (p106)
Dive into a melting pot of Indian, Chinese and Malay cuisine at the capital's food courts, hawker stalls and restaurants
TANJUNG BIDARA (p166)
See a different side of Malaysia on the backroads to this white-sand gem on the Melaka Coast
HISTORIC MELAKA (p141)
Walk in the footsteps of sultans and ambassadors in the historic streets of old Melaka
JONKER'S WALK NIGHT MARKET (p158)
Load up on street snacks and unnecessary plastic objects at this famously lively street market
TRISHAW RIDES (p151)
Love looking like a tourist while being peddled around the streets of Chinatown
CITY-SIZED SHOPPING (p122)
Put the airline baggage limits to the test after shopping in KL's space-aged malls
SELANGOR
KUALA LUMPUR
Shah Alam
Pelabuhan Klang
Morib
Seremban
Port Dickson
Temerloh
Gemas
Melaka
Muar
Batu Pahat
NEGERI SEMBILAN
MELAKA
Selat Melaka (Strait of Melaka)
SUMATRA
INDONESIA
5
12
E2
3°N
2°N
100°E
101°E
102°E
103°E
ELEVATION
1500m
1000m
500m
200m
0
LEGEND
Freeway
Primary Road
Secondary Road
Tertiary Road
Unsealed Road
0
50 km
0
30 miles

On the Road

JOE BINDLOSS Coordinating author
This wasn't what I was used to in the wet tropics. Perfect blue skies, brilliant sunshine overhead, ducking into the shade of palm trees to escape the glare. In fact, Kuala Lumpur (KL) probably has the best weather of all the Southeast Asian capitals. In five weeks I saw only half a dozen rain showers; although, admittedly, one left me knee-deep in black murky water, the origins of which I didn't want to speculate about. The sunny days provided perfect opportunities to try and capture the space-age magnificence of the Petronas Towers on film – I just wish I'd packed a wider lens.

CELESTE BRASH Notice the giant cicada blending perfectly into my wrinkled brown shirt? My son found this guy dying in a gutter so we kept him for the day and named him Chirpy. He (or she?) seemed happy just clinging onto one of our shirts and if you touched his back gently he would sing beautifully. Cicada nymphs live underground for several years, then survive only a few weeks in this adult stage. They do bite (not poisonous) but Chirpy never bit us. If any Malaysians thought we were strange carrying around a giant bug, they kept it to themselves.

For full author biographies, see page 254

Highlights

Kuala Lumpur (KL), Melaka and Penang are simmering melting pots of Chinese, Indian and Malay culture, best experienced through the fragrantly exotic cuisine served at street stalls, and the historic temples, mosques and Chinese clan-houses dotted around the streets. Some people come here for the history, others for the space-age shopping malls and the buzz of future Asia. What impresses most about these captivating cities is their cultural diversity – in a single street, you can visit Chinese temples and snack on South Indian street food while the call to prayer rings out from the minarets of a Malay mosque.

MANFRED GOTTSCHALK

1 PETRONAS TOWERS

No visit to KL would be complete without a stop at the Petronas Towers, the tallest buildings in the world. I wanted to go to the Skybridge (p86) on the 41st floor to get a view of the city, but it was closed that day, so I headed to Menara KL instead. Menara KL (p88) is a 421m-tall communications tower that offers wonderful views of Kuala Lumpur and beyond.

Adrien Stoloff, traveller

© NEIL MCALLISTER / ALA

2 COLONIAL DISTRICT

At Merdeka Square (p80) the flag of independent Malaysia flies commandingly over the playing fields of the Royal Selangor Club, founded as a retreat for civil servants in the days of British Malaya. On all sides the onion domes and gothic towers of Malaysia's finest colonial buildings rise against a backdrop of soaring skyscrapers.

Joe Bindloss, author

PAUL BEINSSE

3 BATU CAVES

I had no expectations of the Batu Caves (p131) but was totally blown away by them. The 272 stairs at the entrance looked easy enough to climb, but in the sweltering heat I found myself struggling and being over taken by hoards of elderly women. The caves themselves are stunning – some are full of very cheeky monkeys, others garish Hindu décor. When I was there I saw very few tourists: this is a place for locals and so it feels like you're getting an authentic insight into Malaysian life.

Heather Carswell, Lonely Planet staff

DAVID HAGERMAN

DAVID HAGERMAN

4 NONYA FOOD

Nonya food headlines in Melaka and is everywhere. Stop at food stalls, food courts, restaurants, you name it. Trying something different each time makes you realise how vast this Chinese-Malay repertoire is – but a laksa followed by an iced *cendol* (sweet dessert with shaved ice, coconut milk, palm-sugar syrup, and condensed milk; p45) is hard to beat.

Celeste Brash, author

DAVID HAGERMAN

© LAURIE STRACHAN / ALA

5 EASTERN & ORIENTAL HOTEL

Step out of the balmy heat and into the fan-spun cool of Penang's still-grand hotel (p193), and the heady exoticism of Somerset Maugham's colonial days doesn't seem so far away – you half expect to find him on the terrace, drinking gin-and-tonics as the sun sets.

emgibbs1, traveller

TOM COCK

6 KHOO KONGSI

My first experience with Khoo Kongsi (p181) was finding it by accident when I followed the screeching sounds of Chinese opera one balmy August night – unforgettable. But there's also a quiet side to the temple, one that requires thoughtful lingering to savour each detail of the intricate stonework, woodwork and opulent paintings. Like a fine wine, you can't rush through this place.

Celeste Brash, author

7 MOSQUES & TEMPLES

In KL's Chinatown (p76), plumes of smoke curl upwards from smouldering incense sticks and flower garlands hang like pearls from the necks of Hindu statues. The temples and mosques of the city's Hindus, Muslims and Chinese Buddhists are crammed shoulder-to-shoulder in this atmospheric neighbourhood along the River Klang

Joe Bindloss, author

PAUL BEINSSEN

© ROB WALLS / ALAMY

8

THAIPUSAM

Thaipusam (p221) is a Hindu festival that falls in January or February. It's an eye-opener, with pierced devotees to Lord Muruga paying homage, by carrying structures called *kavadi* up 200-plus steps, to a temple located in Batu Caves.

Leong Mun Yi, traveller

AUN KOH

9 PANCAKES IN PENANG

The one thing you have to do in Penang is to have an *apam balik* (peanut pancake; p43), which seems to be a local speciality, from a street stall. Crunchy, sweet, salty, soft, mmmm…I haven't had one since that trip, but I could do with one now.

Alex Holland, Lonely Planet staff

GREG ELMS

10 THE MALLS OF KUALA LUMPUR

Vast, gleaming malls (p122) dot KL – come for the air-conditioning, stay for the designer bargains! Suria KLCC (under the Petronas Towers) will have you hyperventilating over Armani and Escada (the sales, darling, and in ringgit it costs practically nothing…). Food courts suddenly become a viable dining option, with hawker stalls brought undercover and tidied up but serving up the same delicious chicken rice. But it's the unexpected finds – the kids who finished their industrial-design degrees in Melbourne and went back to KL to make jewellery, or the celebrity hairdresser who used to coif the stars of *Eastenders* – that really set these malls apart from their American cousins.

Janet Brunckhorst, Lonely Planet staff

OH WHAT A NIGHT

Where to begin? Maybe with a mysterious looking herbal drink to sip while taking a first lap through the low street stalls. Sniff some incense, try on some fancy flip-flops or cheap sunglasses, then get your fortune read – all at the Jonker's Walk Night Market (p158). Make your way to the bottom of the street where a crowd is cheering on street performer Dr Ho Eng Hui as he shoves his finger into a coconut (p151). Everyone is smiling and nibbling on something delicious. The night ends at a streetside bar with cold beer and live music.

Celeste Brash, author

11

PETER PTSCHELIN

GEORGETOWN

As you stroll down the streets of Georgetown (p175) in Penang, you can experience a spiritual journey. See all of the Hindu gods in the temple; smell the incense as you pass the Buddhist temple; and experience the call to prayer as you see people devoutly bow to Allah.

Jeff King, traveller

12

RICHARD I'ANS

Contents

Regional Map Contents

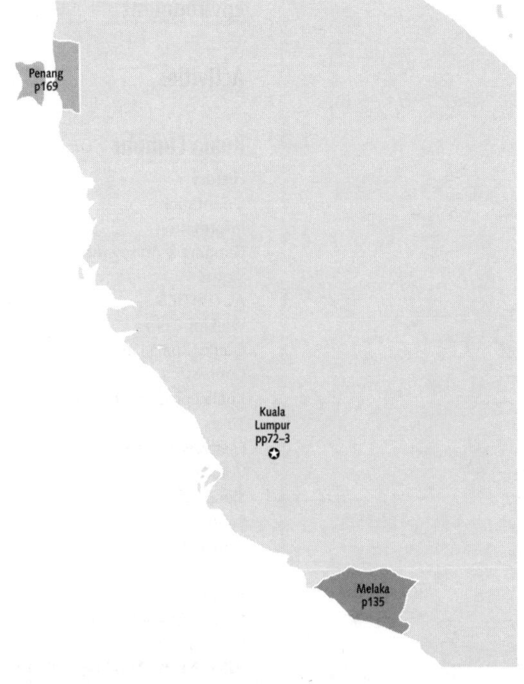

Destination Kuala Lumpur, Melaka & Penang

The story of Peninsular Malaysia is painted large in the historic cities of Kuala Lumpur (KL), Melaka and Penang. Many of the pivotal events in Malaysian history – the first Chinese settlements, the rise of the Melaka sultans, the arrival of the British, the declaration of Malaysian independence in 1957 – took place in these three fascinating cities. Here, the stories of Malaysia's diverse ethnic groups and colonial empires are intertwined – South Indian cooks serve fiery curries from the doorways of Sino-Portuguese houses built as part of trade deals between European powers and the sultans of Melaka. The diversity of the peninsula is perhaps Malaysia's biggest drawcard – this is not one country but three, the best of Malay, Indian and Chinese culture united under one flag.

In April 2007 the rulers of the nine Malaysian states selected Sultan Mizan Zainal Abidin as the 13th king of Malaysia – the first king to be born after independence from colonial rule. Later the same year Malaysia celebrated 50 years of independence with a string of festivals and special events. However, Malaysia's famous policy of unity in diversity is showing signs of strain. Ever since independence, the Malay community has been strengthening its control over the government, police and military, and Indian, Chinese and tribal Malaysians are facing increasing marginalisation and discrimination. Simultaneously, the *syariah* (Islamic) courts are growing in power, threatening the secular foundation of Malaysian democracy.

In recent years Malaysia's sedition laws have been used to detain growing numbers of bloggers, journalists and other critics of the Malay-dominated government. In late 2007 police used tear gas and water cannons to break up antidiscrimination protests by thousands of Malaysian Indians in KL – the ringleaders were even charged with attempted murder before the government backed down under local and international pressure. The same year Malaysian Chinese student Wee Meng Chee (aka Namewee) caused a major political storm by posting a satirical rap criticising the government to the tune of the Malay national anthem on the video website YouTube (see p38).

Malaysia's increasingly strict stance on public morality has also caused a few casualties – Malaysia's first reality-TV pop star, Faizal Tahir, was censured for exposing his chest at a concert in early 2008, and the organisers of a concert by the Pussycat Dolls faced a massive fine in 2006 for allowing the public performance of 'suggestive dance routines'. Malaysia's censors also cited public decency as an excuse for banning Ang Lee's award-winning gay love story *Brokeback Mountain*. All of which is a little ironic considering that the Malaysian health minister, Chua Soi Lek, was forced to step down in 2008 after appearing in an amateur pornographic DVD.

Another hot potato in Malaysian politics is economic migration. Migrant workers are one of the main causes of population growth in Peninsular Malaysia, placing a growing strain on jobs and resources; the government is taking an increasingly hard line on illegal workers from India, Thailand, Indonesia and the Philippines. There's an inevitable ethnic angle to the

FAST FACTS

Population: Malaysia 27.17 million; Kuala Lumpur 1.8 million; Melaka 688,694; Penang 1.31 million

Rate of population increase: one person every 56 seconds

Rate of population increase due to international migration: one person every five minutes.

GDP: US$12,900

Rate of inflation: 3.2%

Literacy rate: 89%

Private car ownership: 195 cars per 1000 citizens

Average noise level in Kuala Lumpur: 70 decibels

Hokkien (Fujian Chinese) speakers in Penang: 638,900

Kristang (pidgin Portuguese) speakers in Melaka: 5000

debate – as part of its immigration crackdown, the government introduced new restrictions on visas for Indian migrant workers, widely perceived as a punishment for Indian protests against discrimination in 2007.

But the prognosis is not entirely gloomy. Malaysia continues to ride a wave of economic optimism, despite declining profits at some of the big state corporations. In a bid to revitalise the ailing fortunes of the Proton – the first Malaysian car – local designers have come up with a new concept in driving: the Muslim automobile. Built to appeal to drivers from Islamic countries, the revamped Proton features a compass pointing to Mecca and other must-have religious accessories. And Malaysia continues to embrace the digital age with aplomb – KL is already one of the most connected cities in Southeast Asia and free wi-fi hotspots are due to blossom across Penang in 2008.

Meanwhile, Malaysia's new administrative capital continues to rise at Putrajaya, 20km south of Kuala Lumpur. Budgeted at US$60 billion, this futuristic enclave is slowly filling with politicians and civil servants, though the much touted Putrajaya monorail is years away from being completed. On one level, the glistening federal capital is a perfect symbol for the aspirations of the nation, but many see parallels with Malaysia's wider ethnic crisis. The new inhabitants of Putrajaya are overwhelmingly Malay and the new city features numerous Islamic institutions, but few concessions to Malaysia's other ethnic groups.

Communal relations seem less strained in Melaka, where Malaysians from all backgrounds are injecting new money into old rubble as part of an ambitious project to resurrect the ruined fort, Porta de Santiago (A'Famosa). This is positive news considering the damage caused by the floods that hit Melaka in 2006 and 2007, leaving thousands homeless. With more heavy rainfall predicted, the municipality voted to replace the official 2008 New Year celebrations with special prayers for divine intervention to prevent a repeat of the floods.

It may take more than divine intervention to prevent sparks flying in the new Malaysian parliament. The 2009 elections saw a massive drop in support for Prime Minister Abdullah Ahmad Badawi and the ruling National Front coalition. Returning to politics after a four-year political ban, former deputy prime minister Anwar Ibrahim has emerged as the effective leader of the opposition, in charge of a coalition of Islamic, Chinese and secular parties. The new Chinese-dominated administration in Penang has already announced its intention to abandon the policy of positive discrimination towards Malays – the next few years are likely to see some radical changes to the Malaysian political system...

Nevertheless, from a visitor's perspective, Malaysia continues to more than satisfy the tourism department slogan: *Malaysia, Truly Asia*. Kuala Lumpur is the same captivating theme park of historic monuments and city-sized shopping malls; Penang remains a fascinating hodgepodge of British-era monuments and Chinese temples; and Melaka is the museum of Malaysia, preserving not just the buildings but the culture of the diverse groups who helped found the nation. Factor in some of the best food and retail therapy in Southeast Asia and there's only one question left: what are you waiting for?

Getting Started

Malaysia is one of the easiest countries in Southeast Asia for international travellers – English is widely spoken, good accommodation is easy to find, restaurants serve up some of the finest food in Asia and locals are used to dealing with people from all over the world. Kuala Lumpur (KL), Melaka and Penang have hotels, restaurants, attractions and transport options to suit all budgets. KL is the main international hub for Malaysia, though a few international flights go directly to Penang. Getting from KL to Melaka or Penang is a breeze with plentiful and inexpensive buses, trains and flights.

WHEN TO GO

Peninsular Malaysia is part of the wet tropics, but the monsoon is only a minor obstacle to travel: rain falls fairly evenly throughout the year and the October-to-April rainy season is only marginally wetter than the rest of the year. As a general rule, the lowest rainfall is from May to August. Temperatures rarely dip below 30°C so bring plenty of loose-fitting cotton clothes. Note that the peninsula is periodically affected by haze from fires in Indonesia (see p60), particularly in September and October. The haze can trigger respiratory complaints and asthma, as well as creating a pall of urban smog.

Malaysia's diverse ethnic groups hold celebrations throughout the year. The festivals can be a great spectacle, particularly Thaipusam and Chinese New Year in January or February (p219). Many locals travel to visit friends and relatives during this period, so hotels and seats on buses, trains and planes can be in short supply. Most things run as normal during the Muslim holy month of Ramadan, but Hari Raya Puasa (see p220 for dates) and Christmas can get very busy. Beach and hill resorts get crowded at weekends throughout the year but are generally quiet during the week.

See Climate (p217) for more information.

COSTS & MONEY

KL, Melaka and Penang have hotels, restaurants and transport options to suit all budgets. At the bottom of the accommodation scale, cheap backpacker hostels offer dorm beds with hot and cold running bedbugs for as little as RM9 per night. Considering the exchange rates, it's usually worth upgrading to a cheap hotel or trying one of the new breed of upmarket traveller guesthouses – double rooms with bathroom start from RM60. In the midrange category, RM70 to RM200 will get you a clean room with a TV and air-con plus a hot shower in the bathroom. Top-end hotels can be bona fide bargains, with promotional rates as low as RM250.

Cheap food is one of the delights of Malaysia. Don't be afraid to step out of your comfort zone and sample the excellent street food and local restaurants – a meal that costs RM10 can be just as delicious as a meal that costs RM300. The top-end hotels offer world-class cooking at prices that bring tears to the eyes. Soft drinks, juices, tea and coffee are the local quaffs of choice. Beer, wine and spirits are widely available but much more expensive – if cost is an issue, buy your beers from convenience stores rather than restaurants.

Getting from A to B will never cost a fortune. KL has an extensive public transport system, and Melaka and Penang have inexpensive buses, taxis and rickshaws. With persistence you can usually get drivers to use the meter or bargain to a reasonable fixed fare. Buses, trains, long-distance taxis and international flights are all excellent value.

HOW MUCH?

Double room at a midrange hotel RM70-200

Cup of *kopi* (coffee) or *teh tarik* (hot tea) RM2-4

Bowl of laksa RM5

Restaurant meal RM20

Designer label shirt RM70

TOP 10

FESTIVALS & EVENTS

Malaysia has loads of fast-paced festivals and special events (see p219). Plan your travels around the following, but remember to book ahead during peak holiday seasons.

1 Thaipusam, Batu Caves and Penang, January/February
2 Chinese New Year, countrywide, January/February
3 KL International Tower Jump, KL, March
4 Malaysian Grand Prix Formula, Sepang near KL, April
5 Dragon Boat Festival, Penang, June to August
6 Por Thor (Hungry Ghosts Festival), Penang and Melaka, August
7 Hari Kebangsaan (Malaysian National Day), countrywide, 31 August
8 Lantern Festival, countrywide, particularly Penang, September
9 Hari Raya Puasa, countrywide, September/October
10 Deepavali, countrywide, October/November

EATING & DRINKING

Junk the diet – eating is a reason to come to KL, Melaka and Penang all by itself. Allow your appetite to steer you towards the following taste sensations:

1 Start the day with *roti canai* (unleavened bread and curry) and *teh tarik* (tea with condensed milk), the classic Malay **tiffin** (p106).
2 KL's food streets offer dozens of restaurants crammed into one location – try **Jalan Alor** (p106) for top-notch Malay-Chinese food.
3 Looking for somewhere to take a date? Try the restaurants on the **Starhill Gallery Feast Level** (p107).
4 Drink in the view as well as your cocktail at one of KL's **skyscraper bars** (p116).
5 Make a night of it at KL's food-tastic **night markets** (p91).
6 Fancy a midnight snack? Many of KL's excellent **mamak restaurants** (see p110) are open 24/7.
7 Slurp some spicy sour **asam laksa** (p194), the renowned speciality of Penang.
8 Learn to make your own Nonya cuisine on a **cooking course** (p150) in Melaka.
9 No meal is complete without pudding – make time for shaved ice desserts such as **cendol** (p45) and **air batu campur** (p45).
10 Hold your nose and discover what all the fuss over **durian** (p81) is about.

UNIQUE EXPERIENCES

Asia is never predictable. Here are some of the quirkier experiences on offer in Kuala Lumpur, Melaka and Penang:

1 Crossing the **Skybridge** (p86) between the Petronas Towers.
2 Riding a roller coaster through a shopping mall at KL's **Berjaya Times Square** (p96).
3 Walking in the rainforest canopy at the **Forest Research Institute of Malaysia** (p132).
4 Climbing the 272 steps to the **Batu Caves** (p131) beside a 43m-tall statue of Muruga.
5 Witnessing gruesome acts of religious devotion at **Thaipusam** (p221).
6 Lighting a 2m-long stick of incense at Penang's **Kuan Yin Teng** (p181) temple.
7 Riding the **cable car** (p203) to Kek Lok Si, Malaysia's biggest Buddhist temple.
8 Trekking though the jungle to empty beaches at **Penang National Park** (p207).
9 Touring old Melaka in an outrageously dolled-up **trishaw** (p151).
10 Running the gauntlet of fortune tellers and snack vendors at **Jonker's Walk Night Market** (p158).

DON'T LEAVE HOME WITHOUT...

- Checking the visa situation (p225). Note that citizens of Israel can only enter Malaysia with a visa – which is granted at the discretion of the Malaysian embassy in the country where you apply.
- Checking government travel advice (see p219).
- Your credit card – major cards are accepted at many shops, restaurants and hotels, but keep the emergency lost-or-stolen number handy.
- An umbrella for sudden showers.
- A torch or headlamp, a pair of binoculars, mosquito net and leech-proof socks – essential gear for jungle treks.
- A fleece or light jacket to beat the air-con on chilly bus journeys.
- A swimming costume (Malaysian pool rules: one-piece for women, tight shorts for men).
- A sheet, blanket or sleeping bag liner – many cheap hotels do not provide a top sheet.
- An appetite – Malaysia is heaven for foodies!

Besides the travel essentials, luxuries are very moderately priced. Your money will go a lot further here than in most Western countries, particularly when shopping for clothes and electronics.

TRAVEL LITERATURE

The Consumption of Kuala Lumpur by Ziauddin Sardar is an evocative meditation on the once-sleepy capital evolving into a technological marvel. Incisive comment on modern Malaysia can be found in *The Other Malaysia* and *From Majapahit to Putrajaya – Searching for the Other Malaysia* by Malaysian journalist Farish A Noor.

Malaysia's complex relationship with religion is explored in the Malaysia chapter of Ian Buruma's *God's Dust,* based on a visit to a hard-line Islamic commune near KL in the 1980s. Although the commune has since been disbanded, many of the issues raised are still pertinent today. Literary knight VS Naipaul offered his own insights into Malaysian Islam in *The Believers* (1982) and *Beyond Belief* (1999).

For a more historical perspective, try *The Golden Chersonese and the Way Thither,* written by Isabella Bird in 1883 after a stiff-upper-lip journey through the jungles of Peninsular Malaysia. A less romantic take on jungle life is given in *The Jungle is Neutral* by Spencer Chapman, a British soldier who helped train Malayan forces to resist the Japanese invasion.

INTERNET RESOURCES

Kuala Lumpur Tourism (www.kualalumpur.gov.my) KL-centric website from the Kuala Lumpur Tourism Action Council.
Lonely Planet (www.lonelyplanet.com) Succinct summaries on travel to Malaysia, the Thorn Tree forum and much more.
Malaysiakini (www.malaysiakini.com) Malaysia's best online news site.
Tourism Malaysia (www.tourismmalaysia.gov.my) Official government tourism site, with listings of domestic and international tourist offices.
Tourism Melaka (www.melaka.gov.my) State information portal for Melaka.
Tourism Penang (www.tourismpenang.gov.my) Government tourism site for Penang.
Virtual Malaysia (www.virtualmalaysia.com) Government portal for tourism in Malaysia.

History

As a modern independent nation, Malaysia has only been around since 1963, though the peninsula became independent of British colonial rule in 1957. The early history of the peninsula is hazy because of a lack of written records but events from the rise of the Melaka Sultanate in the 16th century were well documented by the nations which came here to trade with, and later rule over, the Malay peninsula. The following sections sketch in the main events – see the history sections of Kuala Lumpur (KL), Melaka and Penang for details of the rise of these destinations.

ORIGINAL PEOPLE

The first evidence of human life in the region was a 40,000-year-old skull found in Sarawak in 1958, but the oldest human relics found on the peninsula date back about 13,000 years. 'Perak Man' was genetically similar to the Negrito people who still live in the north of the peninsula. The Negritos were joined by Malaysia's first immigrants, the Senoi, from southern Thailand, and later by the Proto-Malay, ancestors of today's Malays, who came by sea from Indonesia between 1500BC and 500 BC. For more information on Malaysia's indigenous people see p25.

There are estimated to be 560 Christian missionaries striving to convert the Orang Asli (Original People; indigenous Malaysians) in Malaysia. Muslim groups are working just as hard to convert Orang Asli to Islam – several state governments have allegedly offered cash rewards for every Orang Asli converted.

EARLY TRADE & EMPIRES

By the 2nd century AD, Malaya was known as far away as India and Europe. Ptolemy, the Greek geographer, labelled it Aurea Chersonesus (Golden Chersonese) and Indian traders referred to the land as Savarnadvipa (Land of Gold). Malaya soon became a trading stop for Indian merchants in search of precious metals, tin and aromatic jungle woods. The first formalised religions on the peninsula – Hinduism and Buddhism – arrived with Indian traders, giving rise to the first recorded Hindu kingdom on the peninsula,

THE LOST KINGDOM OF LANGKASUKA

We should not really be surprised that the early kingdom of Langkasuka was lost. Even at the time, people were unable to agree on its exact location. Chinese explorers claimed it was on the east coast, while Malay histories place it on the west coast near Penang. Probably there was just one kingdom extending right across the peninsula. Between the 3rd and 6th centuries, Langkasuka's power dwindled and the Funan Kingdom, centred in what is now Cambodia, took over control of the region, before they were in turn supplanted by the Srivijaya Empire. The kingdom of Langkasuka disappeared from the map, though part of its name lives in on in the islands of Langkawi.

TIMELINE

2nd century AD

First trade recorded between Malaya and the ancient world.

700

The Buddhist Srivijaya Empire dominates Malaya, Singapore, Indonesia and Borneo for six centuries.

1400

Foundation of Melaka, the most successful Malay sultanate.

A HISTORY OF PIRACY

From the start of maritime trade to the present day, the Strait of Melaka has provided rich pickings for pirates. The earliest recorded seafaring pirates were the Orang Laut (Sea Gypsies), who were employed to police the trade routes by the Srivijaya Empire, but soon turned to piracy themselves. Parameswara, the founder of Melaka, also staged daring raids on traders from his temporary base of Temasek (Singapore); see p136. A millennium later and piracy is still a problem in the Strait of Melaka. There were 50 attacks in 2006, down from 79 in 2005, despite coordinated sea patrols by the Malaysian, Singaporean and Indonesian coast guards.

The tradition of piracy continues on land. Malaysia is one of the world's most notorious centres for pirate goods – clothes, software, DVDs, auto parts, you name it. For many visitors, this makes Malaysia a shopping mecca. Convincing fakes of big name brands cost a fraction of the price of the real thing. Unfortunately, it's not just big business that suffers – the trade in pirate software, films and music increases the price of legitimate goods for everyone and reduces the amount of money available to new artists and film makers. In response to international pressure, the government is slowly starting to crack down on the counterfeiting industry; take a walk around Chinatown's Petaling Street Market (p77) and judge for yourself how successful this has been…

Langkasuka (from the Sanskrit for 'resplendent land'); see opposite. Many key Malay words such as *bahasa* (language), *raja* (ruler) and *jaya* (success) are also Sanskrit terms.

From the 7th century to the 13th century, Malaya become dominated by the Srivijaya Empire, based in southern Sumatra. This Buddhist empire controlled the entire Malacca Straits, Java and southern Borneo and became fabulously rich from trade with India and China. Under the protection of the Srivijayans, a significant Malay trading state grew up in the Bujang Valley area in the far northwest of the Thai-Malay peninsula. The growing power of the southern Thai kingdom of Ligor and the Hindu Majapahit Empire of Java finally led to the demise of the Srivijayans in the 14th century.

The Other Malaysia by Farish A Noor is a collection of articles in which the writer uses forgotten gems of Malaysia's history to comment on and critique contemporary Malaysian politics.

THE MELAKA EMPIRE

Founded around the 14th century, Malaya's greatest empire was the brainchild of the renegade Hindu prince Parameswara (see p136), from Sumatra, who declared himself independent from the Javanese Majapahit Empire and was forced to flee to Temasek (Singapore). On arrival, Parameswara befriended the local chieftain, then killed him and pronounced himself ruler over the peninsula. From his base at Temasek, Parameswara and his pirate army wrought havoc on shipping and trade, until a huge Thai force drove Parameswara north to Melaka. As a seafarer, Parameswara recognised a good port when he saw it and he immediately lobbied the Ming emperor of China for protection from the Thais in exchange for generous trade deals.

14th century

The Srivijaya Empire comes to an end.

1445

Islam becomes Melaka's state religion and spreads throughout Southeast Asia.

1509

The Portuguese land on the Malay Coast.

Thus the Chinese came to Malaysia. Equidistant between India and China, Melaka became a major stop for freighters from India loaded with pepper and cloth, and junks from China loaded with porcelain and silks, which were traded for local metal and spices. The Indian ships sailed in on the southwest monsoon, berthed in Melaka and waited for the northeast monsoon, which blew in the Chinese junks; both then sailed home when the winds reversed. Business boomed as regional ships and *perahu* (Malay-style sampans) arrived to take advantage of trading opportunities.

Peninsular Malaysia was Buddhist and Hindu for a thousand years before the local rulers converted to Islam in the 15th century.

EARLY ISLAM

The first record of Islam on the peninsula was a stone plaque dated 1303 found in Terengganu. Islam came to Malaysia with Indian-Muslim traders and was quickly adopted by locals. In the mid-15th century, the third ruler of Melaka, Maharaja Mohammed Shah (1424–44) converted and his son, Mudzaffar Shah, took the title of sultan and made Islam the state religion. With its global trade links, Melaka became a hub for the dissemination of Islam and the Malay language across the region. The Melaka sultans soon ruled over the greatest empire in Malaysia's history, successfully repelling Siamese attacks.

THE PORTUGUESE ERA

By the 15th century, Europe had developed an insatiable appetite for spices, ostensibly to the mask the flavour of rotten meat in the days before refrigeration. At the time spices were conveyed via a convoluted trade route through India and Arabia, but the Portuguese decided to cut out the middle man and go directly to the source. They quickly established fortified depots along the sea route to Malaya, reaching the Malay coast in 1509. At first, the Portuguese were greeted warmly by the local sultan, but relations soon soured and the Portuguese laid siege to Melaka in 1511 under Viceroy Alfonso de Albuquerque, capturing the city and driving the sultans back to Johor.

A government-sanctioned version of Malaysian history is given on the website Sejarah Malaysia (sejarahmalaysia.pnm .my).

The Portuguese secured Melaka by building the robust Porta de Santiago (A'Famosa fortress; see p142), and expeditions were sent to the Moluccas to secure trade deals for Moluccan spices. The Portuguese domination of Melaka lasted 130 years, though the entire period was marked by skirmishes with local sultans. Compared with Indian-Muslim traders, the Portuguese contributed little to Malay culture; attempts to introduce Christianity and the Portuguese language were never a big success, though a dialect of Portuguese, Kristang (see p147), is still spoken in Melaka.

THE DUTCH PERIOD

Vying with the Portuguese for control of the spice trade, the Dutch formed an allegiance with the sultans of Johor to drive the Portuguese from Melaka. The Dutch East India Company had no interest in God or national glory; they

1511

The Portuguese conquer Melaka.

1641

The Dutch wrest Melaka from the Portuguese.

1786

The British open a free-trading port in Penang.

MEANWHILE IN BORNEO...

While the East India Company was furthering its interests on the peninsula, Borneo was left largely to its own devices, until the arrival of British adventurer James Brooke. In 1835 Brooke inherited £30,000, bought a ship and sailed from London to Borneo, where he helped the local sultan suppress a tribal rebellion and took personal control of part of the island, founding his capital at Kuching. Through a combination of force and negotiation, Brooke gained control of large parts of Sarawak, founding his own dynasty of 'white Rajas', which ruled right up until 1941. The British obtained Sabah as down-payment on a debt from the Sultan of Brunei in 1865, though Brunei itself was preserved as a British protectorate.

came to Malaya to make money and negotiated directly for spices with the sultans of the local spice islands from their new base at Batavia (now Jakarta).

A joint force of Dutch and Johor soldiers and sailors besieged Melaka in 1641 and wrested the city from the Portuguese. In return for its cooperation, Johor was made exempt from most of the tariffs and trade restrictions imposed on other vassal states. Despite maintaining control of Melaka for about 150 years, the Dutch never really realised the full potential of the city. High taxes forced merchants to seek out other ports and the Dutch focused their main attention on Batavia as their regional headquarters.

EAST INDIA COMPANY

Britain entered the fray in the 18th century. With increasing British involvement in trade between India and China, the East India Company (EIC) needed a depot in Southeast Asia, and Francis Light negotiated a deal with the sultan of Kedah in 1786 to establish a settlement on the largely uninhabited island of Penang. Light immediately instituted a free-trade policy, which attracted massive trade from across the region.

A History of Malaya by Barbara and Leonard Andaya brilliantly explores the evolution of 'Malayness' in Malaysia's history and the challenges of building a multiracial, post-independence nation.

Meanwhile, events in Europe were conspiring to consolidate British interests on the Malay peninsula. When Napoleon overran the Netherlands in 1795, the British, fearing French influence in the region, took over Dutch Java and Melaka. When Napoleon was defeated in 1818, the British handed the Dutch colonies back – but not before leaving the fortress of A'Famosa beyond use.

The British lieutenant-governor of Java, Stamford Raffles – yes, *that* Stamford Raffles – soon persuaded the EIC that a settlement south of the Malay peninsula was crucial to the India–China maritime route. In 1819, he landed in Singapore and negotiated a trade deal that saw the island ceded to Britain in perpetuity, in exchange for a significant cash tribute. In 1824, Britain and the Netherlands signed the Anglo-Dutch Treaty dividing the region into two distinct spheres of influence. The Dutch controlled what is now Indonesia, and the British controlled Penang, Melaka, Dinding and Singapore, which were soon combined to create the 'Straits Settlements'.

1795

The British take over Dutch Java and Melaka before returning them after the defeat of Napoleon in 1818.

1824

Britain assumes control of Melaka as part of the Anglo-Dutch Treaty.

1841

James Brook becomes the first White Raja of Sarawak.

BRITISH MALAYA

The British enterprise in Malaya had always focused on trade, rather than territory, but the start of the civil wars between the sultans of Negeri Sembilan, Selangor, Pahang and Perak began to threaten British trade, leading to the first serious territorial expansion. In 1874 the British appointed the first colonial governor of Perak and, in 1896, Perak, Selangor, Negeri Sembilan and Pahang were united under the banner of the Federated Malay States, each governed by a British Resident.

Kelantan, Terengganu, Perlis and Kedah were then purchased from the Thais, in exchange for the construction of the southern Thai railway, much to the dismay of local sultans. The 'Unfederated Malay States' eventually accepted British 'advisers', though the sultan of Terengganu held out till 1919. As a result, these states received far fewer migrant workers from India and China. To this day, the states of the northeast peninsula form the heartland of the strident and increasingly fundamentalist Malay Muslim nationalist movement.

ECONOMIC DEVELOPMENT

As elsewhere in the empire, the British created massive social change in Malaya. Tin mines, rubber plantations and trading companies were created to swell the empire's coffers, but ethnic Malays were marginalised in favour of Indian and Chinese migrant workers who shared a similar economic agenda and had less nationalist grievance against the colonial administration. Malays were pushed from the cities to the countryside, while the Chinese were encouraged to work the mines, the Indians to tap the rubber trees and build the railways, the Ceylonese to be clerks in the civil service, and Sikhs to man the police force.

Founded by Chinese miners, Kuala Lumpur became the capital of the Federated Malay States in 1896 (for more on KL's history, see p70). By the time the Singapore Malay Union was formed in 1926, the ethnic balance of Malaya had changed dramatically. The 1931 census revealed that the Chinese numbered 1.7 million and the Malays 1.6 million. The Chinese came to dominate the capital and most towns on the coast, forming a new wealthy elite, and resentment among the Malay population grew. By the outbreak of WWII, Malays were vocally demanding independence.

F Spencer Chapman's *The Jungle is Neutral* follows a British guerrilla force based in the Malaysian jungles during the Japanese occupation of Malaya.

WWII PERIOD

WWII came to Malaya just hours before the Japanese bombed Pearl Harbor in December 1941. The Japanese surged over the peninsula and captured Kuala Lumpur within a month. A month later they surged into Singapore. With its guns pointing uselessly out to sea, Singapore capitulated in February 1942. The popular perception that the British left Malaya to its fate is not quite accurate. Although Britain quickly ceded Malaya and Singapore, this

1896

Kuala Lumpur becomes capital of the Federated Malay States.

1926

The Malay states and Singapore are united as the Singapore Malay Union.

1941–45

The Japanese invade and lay siege to Malaya and Singapore, ushering in a brutal five-year occupation.

ORANG ASLI

Throughout the history of Malaysia, settlers have jostled for control of the Malay peninsula. In the process, the indigenous people of Malaysia have emerged as the most marginalised people of all. According to data published by the **Department of Orang Asli Affairs** (JHEOA; www.jheoa.gov.my), in December 2004 Peninsular Malaysia had just under 150,000 Orang Asli (Original People); 80% live below the poverty line, compared with an 8.5% national average. The tribes are generally classified into three groups: the Negrito; the Senoi; and the Proto-Malays, who are subdivided into 18 tribes, the smallest being the Orang Kanak with just 87 members. In Borneo, Orang Asli make up about around 50% to 60% of the population but they face similar obstacles of poverty and neglect. There are dozens of different tribal languages and most Orang Asli follow animist beliefs, though there are vigorous attempts to convert them to Islam or Christianity.

The Orang Asli played an important role in early trade, teaching the colonialists about forest products and guiding prospectors to outcrops of tin and precious metals. They also played a vital role during the communist Emergency in the 1950s, acting as scouts and guides for anti-insurgent forces. After the communists were thwarted, 'guardianship' of the Orang Asli passed to the JHEOA, which has spectacularly failed to uphold Orang Asli rights in the face of exploitation by the government. Whenever logging, mining, agricultural or development projects infringe on Orang Asli land, native land rights are routinely ignored, usually for reasons of 'national interest'. JHEOA is also spearheading the campaign to convert the Orang Asli to Islam.

For an excellent introduction to the customs and culture of Malaysia's indigenous people, visit the Orang Asli Museum (p131), just north of Kuala Lumpur. A number of international NGOs are now campaigning for Orang Asli land rights and freedom of religious expression – see the sidebar, below.

was more through poor strategy than neglect. Many British soldiers were captured or killed and others stayed on and fought with the Malayan People's Anti-Japanese Army (MPAJA) in a jungle-based guerrilla war throughout the occupation.

The Japanese achieved very little in Malaya. The British had destroyed most of the tin-mining equipment before their retreat, and the rubber plantations were neglected. However, Chinese Malaysians faced brutal persecution – the atrocities of the occupation were horrific even by the standards of WWII. The Japanese surrendered to the British in Singapore in 1945, after the devastating atom bombs dropped over Hiroshima and Nagasaki.

For more information on the plight of Orang Asli people in Peninsular Malaysia, visit the websites of Temier Web (www.temiar.com), the Centre for Orang Asli Concerns (www.coac.org.my) or the Borneo Project (www.borneoproject.org).

FEDERATION OF MALAYA

In 1946 the British persuaded the sultans to agree to the Malayan Union, which amalgamated all the peninsular Malayan states into a central authority and came with the offer of citizenship to all residents regardless of race. In the process, the sultans were reduced to the level of paid advisers, the system of special privileges for Malays was abandoned and ultimate sovereignty passed

1946

Creation of the Malayan Union, which is subsequently dissolved two years later, and replaced by the Federation of Malaya.

1948

Communist rebellion leads to the declaration of the Emergency in Malaya.

1951

British High Commissioner Sir Henry Gurney is assassinated in the Malayan Communist Party's guerrilla war against the British.

to the king of England. Bankrupted by the war, the third Raja Brooke allowed North Borneo and Sarawak to become the crown colony of British Borneo, while Singapore was granted a separate administration.

The normally acquiescent Malay population were less enthusiastic about the venture than the sultans. Rowdy protest meetings were held throughout the country, and the first Malay political party, the United Malays National Organisation (UMNO), was formed, leading to the dissolution of the Malayan Union, and the creation of the Federation of Malaya in 1948, which reinstated the sovereignty of the sultans and the special privileges of the Malays.

Anthony Burgess's *A Malayan Trilogy* is based on his experiences as an information officer during the Malayan Emergency.

THE EMERGENCY

While the creation of the Federation of Malaya appeased Malays, the Chinese felt betrayed, particularly after their massive contribution to the war effort. Many joined the Malayan Communist Party (MCP), which promised an equitable and just society. In 1948 the MCP took to the jungles and embarked on a 12-year guerrilla war against the British. Even though the insurrection was on par with the Malay civil wars of the 19th century, it was classified as an 'Emergency' for insurance purposes, so that claims could still be made on policies that didn't cover riots and civil commotions.

Noel Barber's *The War of the Running Dogs* is a classic account of the 12-year Malayan Emergency.

The effects of the Emergency were felt most strongly in the countryside, where villages and plantation owners were repeatedly targeted by rebels. In 1951 the British high commissioner was assassinated on the road to Fraser's Hill. His successor, General Sir Gerald Templer, set out to 'win the hearts and minds of the people'. Almost 500,000 rural Chinese were resettled into protected 'new villages', restrictions were lifted on guerrilla-free areas and the jungle-dwelling Orang Asli (see p25) were bought into the fight to help the police track down the insurgents.

In 1960 the Emergency was declared over, although sporadic fighting continued and the formal surrender was signed only in 1989.

MERDEKA & MALAYSIA

Malaysia's march to independence from British rule was led by UMNO, which formed a strategic alliance with the Malayan Chinese Association (MCA) and the Malayan Indian Congress (MIC). The new Alliance Party led by Tunku Abdul Rahman won a landslide victory in the 1955 election and, on 31 August 1957, Merdeka (Independence) was declared. A unique solution was found for the problem of having nine state sultans eligible for the ceremonial position of paramount ruler – they would take turns once every five years (the current king is the Sultan of Terengganu).

Communism is a thorny issue in Malaysia – Amir Muhammad's film *The Last Communist* was banned in 2006 for allegedly glorifying communism.

In 1961 Tunku Abdul Rahman put forward a proposal suggesting a merger of Singapore, Malaya, Sabah and Sarawak, and modern Malaysia was born in July 1963. The new nation immediately faced a diplomatic crisis. The

1957

Merdeka (Independence) in Malaya; Tunku Abdul Rahman becomes the first prime minister. Malaysia comes into being in 1963.

1960

Sir Gerald Temple, successor to Sir Henry Gurney, declares the Emergency over.

1965

Singapore is formally expelled from Malaysia.

Philippines broke off relations, claiming that Sabah was part of its territory (a claim upheld to this day), while Indonesia laid claim to the whole of Borneo, invading parts of Sabah and Sarawak before finally giving up its claim in 1966. The Malay-majority kingdom of Brunei, buoyed by wealth from its considerable oilfields, opted to leave Malaya and remain a British protectorate, finally becoming an independent nation in 1984.

ETHNIC TENSIONS

The marriage between Singapore and Malaya was doomed from the start. Ethnic Chinese outnumbered Malays in both Malaysia and Singapore and the new ruler of the island-state, Lee Kuan Yew, refused to extend constitutional privileges to the Malays in Singapore. Riots broke out in Singapore in 1964 and in August 1965 Tunku Abdul Rahman bowed to the inevitable and booted Singapore out of the federation. Over the following decades, the Chinese created a dynamic and prosperous city-state in Singapore, while Malaysia remained wracked by ethnic tensions.

Explore the politics and ethos of Barisan Nasional (National Front) at www.bn.org.my.

Impoverished Malays became increasingly resentful of the economic success of Chinese Malaysians, while the Chinese grew resentful of the political privileges granted to Malays. Things reached breaking point when the Malay-dominated government attempted to suppress all languages except Malay and introduced a national policy of education that ignored Chinese and Indian history, language and culture.

In the 1969 general elections, the Alliance Party lost its two-thirds majority in parliament and a celebration march by the opposition Democratic Action Party (DAP) and Gerakan (The People's Movement) in Kuala Lumpur led to a full-scale riot, which Malay gangs used as a pretext to loot Chinese businesses, killing hundreds of Chinese in the process. Stunned by the savageness of the riots the Malaysian government decided that the Malay community needed to achieve economic parity if there was ever going to be harmony between the races.

The Indian and Chinese communities have their own organisations campaigning on minority issues – see the websites of the Malaysian Indian Congress (www.mic.org.my) and Malaysian Chinese Association (www.mca.org.my).

NEW ECONOMIC POLICY

In 1970 the government introduced the New Economic Policy (NEP) with the aim that 30% of Malaysia's corporate wealth be in the hands of indigenous Malays, or *bumiputra* (literally 'sons of the land'), within 20 years. A massive campaign of positive discrimination began which handed majority control over the army, police, civil service and government to Malays. The rules extended to education, scholarships, share deals, corporate management and even the right to import a car.

On one level, the policy was a success – it increased the wealth and political voice of Malays and quietened nationalist violence by Malay extremists. However, it also heralded an increase in complaints of cronyism, as well as discrmination against Indians and Chinese. Ever since the introduction of

1969
In 1969 race riots in Malaysia result in a national policy of positive discrimination for Malays.

1970
Malaysia introduces the New Economic Policy – positive discrimination for ethnic Malays.

1981
Dr Mahathir becomes prime minister of Malaysia.

the NEP, Malaysia has been ruled by Barisan Nasional (the National Front), a coalition of the Alliance Party and other pro-Malay parties, including the ultranationalist UMNO.

ENTER MAHATHIR

In 1981 former UMNO member Mahathir Mohamad became prime minister, despite a rocky political past where he was accused of failing to stand up for the Malay nationalist cause. Under Mahathir, Malaysia started to look away from Britain and Europe and model itself on Asian economies such as Japan, South Korea and Taiwan. Malaysia's economy went into overdrive, shifting almost overnight from commodities such as rubber and tin to industry and manufacturing.

Read about the Malaysian politics in the words of a former prime minister in *The Malay Dilemma* by Mahathir Mohamad.

Government monopolies were privatised, and massive investment was funnelled into state enterprises such as Petronas and the manufacture of the Proton, the first Malaysian car. Simultaneously, multinational corporations invested heavily in infrastructure and Malaysia embarked on a series of ostentatious civic schemes including the creation of a huge new political and technological enclave at Putrajaya (see p130). This wealth came at the cost of liberty – the government began a massive crackdown on dissent, ruling the sultans out of the legislative process and curbing the freedom of the judiciary and the press.

ECONOMIC & POLITICAL CRISIS

Things took a turn for the worse in 1997, when Malaysia was caught up in a region-wide recession triggered by the Thai currency crisis. Riding a growing wave of anti-Western sentiment, Mahathir shifted all the blame to the West. His own remedies for the ailing economy involved pegging the Malaysian ringgit to the US dollar, bailing out companies run by cronies, forcing banks to merge and preventing foreign investors from removing money from Malaysia's stock exchange. Mahathir was opposed by his deputy prime minister and heir apparent, Anwar Ibrahim, a fierce opponent of corruption.

Malaysia has two judicial systems: the federal court system rules on secular matters while the *syariah* (Islamic) courts have jurisdiction over Islamic affairs.

In September 1998 Anwar was sacked and then arrested on dubious charges of corruption and sodomy, during which time he was assaulted in prison by the inspector general of police. Opposition marches calling for his release were harshly suppressed and Anwar was summarily sentenced to 15 years. In the 1999 general elections Barisan Nasional suffered huge losses to the new, radical Islamic party PAS (which stands for Parti Islam se-Malaysia), and Keadilan (People's Justice Party), the party headed by Anwar's wife.

The rise of PAS was just one sign of growing Islamic influence in Malaysia; the *syariah* (Islamic) courts also began to wield increasing influence over secular affairs.

1997

Malaysian economy hit by recession.

1998

Deputy prime minister Anwar Ibrahim arrested and imprisoned on charges of corruption and sodomy.

2003

Dr Mahathir steps down as prime minister; Abdullah Badawi takes over.

Laws that used to cover only Muslim Malays were extended to non-Muslims, women's rights were suppressed (see p35) and projects for new mosques and Islamic schools were initiated all over the country, while churches, temples and minority schools were closed down. At the same time, the government has cracked down on Islamic extremists, who have been implicated in violence from southern Thailand to Indonesia and the Philippines.

Read about Anwar Ibrahim in his own words on the politician's official website – www.anwaribrahim.com.

MALAYSIA TODAY

In 2003, Mahathir was replaced as prime minister by Abdullah Badawi, a former Islamic scholar. Abdullah shifted the focus of government from urban development to education and wealth redistribution, and promoted a new policy of Islam Hadhari, a progressive concept of Islam where religious values are enshrined within a secular state. PAS has seen a fall in support and Anwar Ibrahim was released from prison on appeal in 2004, though the courts refused to clear his name on any of the charges. Although banned from politics until 2008, Anwar continues to play an active role in the battle against corruption both in Malaysia and overseas.

Despite many positive developments, discrimination against minorities continues to rise and Islamic law is increasingly taking precedence over secular law, as in the recent apostasy ruling against Lina Joy (see p31). Many commentators now fear that Malaysia is creeping towards becoming a fully fledged Islamic republic, with implications for social stability and minority rights.

The news website www.malaysiakini.com has uncensored news and comment on current events in Malaysia.

A particularly worrying development has been the widespread banning of films, songs and websites that allegedly 'present Malaysia in a bad light' (see boxed text, p38) and a spate of arrests of journalists, bloggers and website editors on spurious sedition charges, in most cases over comments criticising the NEP. See p32 for more on the issue of minority rights.

The elections in 2008 saw a massive drop in support for Prime Minister Badawi and the ruling coalition. The National Front lost its two-thirds parliamentary majority for the first time since 1969 and opposition parties gained control of five state assemblies, including Penang, which has already announced plans to abandon the New Economic Policy. Whatever happens, the next few years will see some radical changes in the Malaysian status quo.

2004

Anwar Ibrahim is released from prison.

2007

Police crack down on anti-discrimination rallies by Indian Malaysians in Kuala Lumpur.

2008

The 2008 elections saw a massive drop in support for Prime Minister Abdullah Ahmad Badawi and the ruling National Front coalition.

The Culture

REGIONAL IDENTITY

You don't have to spend long in Malaysia to realise that this is not one country, but three – although bound by a strong sense of shared experience and national identity, Malay, Chinese and Indian Malaysians identify most strongly with their own ethnic and religious communities. For the most part, despite their differences, everyone gets along, partly because they have to and partly because of the generous spirit of the country and its relative wealth compared with its immediate neighbours.

The Malay surname is the child's father's first name. This is why Malaysians will use your Christian name after the Mr or Miss; to use your surname would be to address your father.

Making up around 60% of the population, Muslim Malays have traditionally dominated the countryside as farmers and *kampung* (village) dwellers, while the Chinese minority have traditionally formed the wealthy, urban elite. The roots of this go back to the European colonial period and the marginalisation of Malays in favour of more pro-European Chinese settlers. The Indian population also arrived in Malaysia during the colonial period, but Indians were employed as indentured labourers and many still find themselves at the bottom of the social heap, particularly in the cities.

Between these clearly defined ethnic groups are smaller mixed communities such as the Baba-Nonya (Peranakans) of Melaka, descendants of 15th-century Chinese immigrants who married Malay women (see p144), and the Chitty, descended from 14th-century Indian traders who married local women. Malaysia also has large numbers of tribal people – around 5% of the population – who make up the majority in Malaysian Borneo.

Perhaps the most important shift in the social structure of Malaysia has been the rise of the Malay community since independence. Following the departure of the British in 1957, Malaysia introduced the New Economic Policy (NEP), a nationwide programme of positive discrimination to bring marginalised Muslim Malays and certain groups of tribal people – known collectively as *bumiputra* – into the political and economic mainstream. The policy was nothing if not successful; Malays now form the overwhelming majority in the police force, army, civil service and government, and the *syariah* (Islamic) courts are taking an increasingly active role in political affairs, with implications for the future of secular democracy.

Some Indian and Chinese Malaysians have reported growing discrimination at all levels of government. The Hindu Rights Action Force, which is campaigning for better representation for Malaysian Indians, has accused the government of giving preferential treatment to social projects that benefit the Muslim community.

The underlying religious and ethnic tension is a fact of life in Malaysia, but as a rule it is less noticeable in the cities, particularly in historically mixed communities such as Kuala Lumpur (KL), Melaka and Penang. For foreign visitors, the most obvious sign of growing religious conservatism is the national obsession with propriety, which extends to newspaper polemics on female modesty and raids by the police on 'immoral' public establishments.

The website www.bangkit.net is a portal for civil liberties groups across Malaysia.

LIFESTYLE

By global standards most Malaysians lead relatively comfortable lives. The average monthly salary in Malaysia is around RM1750 (US$500), less than in Singapore but more than in Thailand. With the low cost of most items, Malaysians manage to enjoy a reasonably high standard of living. However, many people in rural areas earn less than RM300 a month, well below the

A MALAYSIAN CATCH-22

Officially, the Malaysian government is committed to the principle of Islam Hadhari (progressive Islam), which enshrines the right to freedom of religion. However since 1988, the secular courts have been unable to overrule decisions made by the *syariah* courts (which have jurisdiction only over matters of Islamic law).

Campaigners against the 1988 decision, hoping for a ruling that returned power to the secular authorities, backed the case of Lina Joy, a Christian Malay and a convert from Islam. Joy's case, in Malaysia's High Court and then Federal Court, may seem at face value to be simple enough: to change her official designation from Muslim to Christian More serious legally was that in having this decision made by the secular courts, Joy was circumventing the *syariah* courts.

Under Malaysian law all ethnic Malays are classified as Muslims, which makes them subject to the jurisdiction of the *syariah* courts and a system of laws that only apply to Muslims, including a ban on marriage to people of other faiths. One of Lina Joy's aims in having her change of religion recognised was to gain permission to marry her Christian fiancée.

One area that is deemed to fall within the remit of the *syariah* courts is granting permission for Muslims to change religion. However, Joy and others who want to convert from Islam are caught in something of a catch-22 situation: to convert from Islam, and thus avoid any restrictions of Islamic law, a Muslim must apply for permission from the *syariah* courts, who have only once granted such permission (to a woman already dead). It was this paradox that Joy hoped to escape by taking her case to the secular courts.

In 2007 the Federal Court, supporting the High Court in 1999, ruled that Lina Joy could not change her religion outside of the *syariah* court system.

official poverty line. Unemployment is a growing problem, with local workers being undercut by migrant workers from Indonesia, Thailand, the Philippines and Myanmar (Burma).

Although Western attitudes are gaining ground, particularly when it comes to wealth and material possessions, traditional customs and religious values still form the backbone of Malaysian society. Malays follow Islam devoutly, as well as adhering to older spiritual beliefs and *adat* (the village-based social system). With its roots in the Hindu period, *adat* places great emphasis on collective responsibility and on maintaining harmony within the community – almost certainly a factor in the general goodwill between the different ethnic groups in Malaysia. Many city-dwellers still hanker for this *kampung* spirit, despite the perks of city life.

The Muslim religious leader, the imam, holds a position of great importance in the community as the keeper of Islamic knowledge and the leader of prayer, but even educated urban Malaysians periodically turn to *pawang* (shamans who possess a supernatural knowledge of harvests and nature) or *bomoh* (spiritual healers with knowledge of curative plants and the ability to harness the power of the spirit world), for advice before making any life-changing decisions.

Religious customs govern much of the Chinese community's home life, from the moment of birth (which is carefully recorded for astrological consultations later in life) to funerals (with many rites and rituals). Most Indians in the region originally come from Tamil Nadu in India, so the Hindu and Muslim traditions of South India hold a powerful sway.

The cartoonist and artist Lat is a national institution in Malaysia. His most famous character is *Kampung Boy,* whose village experiences mirror events in public life. Look out for his strip in the *New Straits Times*.

ECONOMY

The Malaysian economy has grown steadily since independence. Old earners such as rubber, tin and timber exports have been replaced by manufacturing, particularly electronics and electrical machinery, which accounts for 67.7% of exports. However, palm oil production still forms a significant part of the rural economy, as well as being the main engine driving deforestation; see p59.

THE POWER OF PETRONAS

Oil was first discovered by the British Resident of the Baran district of Sarawak in 1882, but it was nearly a century before Malaysia started extracting oil and natural gas under the banner of Petroliam Nasional Bhd – better known as **Petronas** (www.petronas.com.my). Founded in 1974, the national oil and gas company continues to have the sole rights to develop oil- and gas-fields across Malaysia, the bulk of which lie between Peninsular Malaysia and Borneo.

Today Petronas is one of the world's largest corporations, with assets valued at RM239 billion and 30,000 employees in 31 different countries. Despite global concerns about peak oil, profits continue to rise – in 2007, Petronas earned a record pretax profit of RM76 billion, 10% up from 2006.

The phenomenal success of Petronas is all the more surprising considering the way that past earnings have been spent by the Malaysian government. The Petronas board is accountable directly to the prime minister, ensuring financial backing for a string of white elephant projects such as the construction of Putrajaya – a glimmering but so far mostly uninhabited new capital just south of Kuala Lumpur (KL) – and the similarly underutilised 'cyber-city' at Cyberjaya. Of course, some Petronas projects have widespread popular support – Petronas is the main sponsor of the Malaysian Formula One Grand Prix.

Multinational corporations invested heavily in the Malaysian economy in the Mahathir years, leading to an upsurge in construction and urban expansion. Simultaneously, soaring profits at Petronas, the national oil and gas company (see above), provided revenue for a string of grand civic projects such as Cyberjaya, planned as Malaysia's answer to Silicon Valley but still lying mostly dormant in the hills south of KL.

Under Abdullah Badawi, the nation has taken a more cautious approach to the economy. The ringgit was allowed to float freely in December 2005, and the government has pulled back on expensive construction programmes in favour of practical policies to improve education and reduce poverty. The government also seems less willing to plough money into overblown civic projects, and is more circumspect about bailing out ailing national enterprises such as the car manufacturer Proton, which saw a 40% drop in sales in 2006.

POPULATION

Malaysia's population is currently 27.17 million, with approximately 85% living in Peninsular Malaysia. Malays, including indigenous groups, make up 61.7% of the population, Chinese 23.8%, Indians 7.1% and the remaining 7.4% are mainly expat workers from Europe, Japan, Korea and other parts of Asia.

Until the 1970s Penang had a small but active Jewish community, descended from refugees from China and Iraq. Most have now moved to Singapore, but funerals are still carried out at the Jewish cemetery in Penang.

ETHNIC MINORITIES

Malaysia has always been a multicultural country, but the problem of balancing the needs of all these different religions and ethnic communities was thrown into sharp relief by the interracial riots of 1969. In the aftermath of the riots, the government introduced a programme to redistribute wealth and opportunities to the marginalised Malays, and promoted Bahasa Malaysia as the national language, which ushered in the broadly tolerant Malaysia of today.

Positive discrimination has been a partial, although unsurprisingly not a total, success (for further information, see p27). Increased representation of Malays has been achieved at the cost of under-representation of Chinese and Indians, and relations between the main ethnic communities remain strained.

In the past the government has been careful to show even-handedness in cultural issues and keep the Chinese and Indian communities on side in the interests of social stability. Political decisions seen to be influenced by Islamic thinking have been viewed as an erosion of this principle – for example, the banning, and then unbanning, of translations of the Bible, and the decision to make all Malaysian policewomen wear the *tudong* (headscarf), regardless of their religion.

MEDIA

The press in Malaysia has to be circumspect about what it says. Some journalists who have criticised government policies have been arrested on charges such as 'inciting racial tension', 'harming national unity' and 'revealing official secrets'. Self-censorship is commonplace and editorials take care not delve too deeply into stories of religious persecution and discrimination against Indians and Chinese.

The online news site Malaysiakini (www.malaysiakini.com) continues to be the leading voice of uncensored journalism in Malaysia, despite intimidation by the police and the youth wing of United Malays National Organisation (UMNO), the largest Malaysian political party.

Blogs Malaysia (www.blogsmalaysia.com) acts like an anarchic clearing house for many of Malaysia's leading blogs.

The government's decision not to censor the internet has created a fertile breeding ground for 'seditious' blogs that explore all the taboo subjects in Malaysian society (now you know what all those people tapping away at laptops in Malaysian cafés are doing!).

The government makes periodic noises about clamping down on bloggers and there have been a number of high-profile arrests, but there are still dozens of vocal online commentators – for example you'll find that there's always something interesting being said by Kenny Sia (www.kennysia.com) and Jeff Ooi (www.jeffooi.com).

TALKING THE TALK

As a former British colony Malaysia is an easy place to travel for English-speakers, but it's still worth learning a few words of the local language – Bahasa Malaysia or Malay (see p246 for some useful phrases).

Although all Malaysians speak Malay, many are fluent in at least two other languages. Commonly spoken languages include Tamil, Hokkien, Cantonese and Mandarin, but there are many other Chinese dialects, various Indian and Orang Asli (Original People) languages, and even a form of 16th-century Portuguese known as Kristang (p147).

Even if you stick to English, you'll have to get used to the local patois – Manglish – which includes plenty of Mandarin and Cantonese words and short phrases from text messages and online chat. Many words are used solely to add emphasis and have no formal meaning, which can make things a little confusing. Used incorrectly, Manglish can come across as quite rude, so get a local to show you the ropes before trying it out in polite company. Some common Manglish terms to look out for:

Ah Used for questions, eg 'Why late ah?'
Got Used for all tenses of the verb 'to have', eg 'Got milk ah?'
Lah Used to affirm a statement, eg 'Don't be stupid lah!'
Liao Similar to 'already', eg 'All done liao.'
Le Used to make an order less harsh, eg 'Give le.'
Lor Used for explanations, eg 'Just is lor.'
Meh Used for sceptical questions, eg 'Really meh?'
One Used to add emphasis to the end of a sentence, eg 'That car so fast one.'
Reddie Another form of already, eg 'No thanks, eat reddie.'

RELIGION

The variety of religions found in Malaysia is a direct reflection of the diversity of races living there. Although Islam is the state religion, freedom of religion is guaranteed by law (see the boxed text, p31).

Islam

Islam came to Malaysia with South Indian traders, who practised a less strict form of the faith than the orthodox Islamic traditions of Arabia. It was adopted peacefully by the coastal trading ports of Malaysia and Indonesia, absorbing rather than conquering existing beliefs. Islamic sultanates replaced Hindu kingdoms, but the Hindu concept of kings remained. The social structure of *adat* remained in place, though decisions were made according to Islamic law.

Islam is a monotheistic religion. Muslims believe that the will of Allah was revealed on earth to the prophet Mohammed through the Quran. Religious scholars known as imams have the job of interpreting Islamic teachings, but there is no equivalent to the hierarchy of the Catholic or Anglican churches. Muslims draw divine inspiration directly from the Quran.

Muslim Malays are banned by law from gambling and buying alcohol.

Most Malaysian Muslims are Sunnis, but all Muslims share a common belief in the Five Pillars of Islam: *shahadah* (the declaration of faith) – 'There is no God but Allah; Mohammed is his Prophet'; prayer, ideally five times a day, in which the muezzin (prayer leader) calls the faithful to prayer from the minarets of every mosque; *zakat* (tax) usually taking the form of a charitable donation; fasting, including observing the fasting month of Ramadan, although the sick, children, pregnant women, the elderly and travellers are usually exempt; and hajj (the ritual pilgrimage to Mecca), which every Muslim aspires to do at least once in their lifetime.

Pre-Islamic ceremonies and beliefs are still widespread, but most Malays are ardent Muslims to the point that the history of Malaysia before Islam is rarely discussed or even acknowledged.

Chinese Religions

Chinese in the region usually follow a mix of Buddhism, Confucianism and Taoism. Buddhism takes care of the afterlife, Confucianism looks after the political and moral aspects of life, while Taoism contributes animistic beliefs to teach people to maintain harmony with the universe. Chinese religion upholds a belief in the innate vital energy in rocks, trees, rivers and springs. At the same time, people from the distant past, both real and mythological, are worshipped as deities. Ancestor worship is particularly important to the Chinese in Malaysia.

For a handy introduction to the core teachings of Taoism visit www.taopage.org.

On a day-to-day level most Chinese are much less concerned with the high-minded philosophies and asceticism of Buddha, Confucius or Lao Zi than they are with the pursuit of worldly success, the appeasement of the dead and the spirits, and the seeking of knowledge about the future. Like Hinduism, Chinese religion is polytheistic – as well as Buddha, Lao Zi and Confucius, there are a host of house gods, auspicious deities and gods and goddesses for particular professions.

The most popular gods and *shen* (local deities) are Kuan Yin, the goddess of mercy, and Toh Peh Kong, a local deity representing the spirit of pioneers, found only outside China. Kuan Ti, the god of war, is also very popular and is also regarded as the god of wealth.

Hinduism

Hinduism has been practised in Malaysia for 1500 years and there are clear Hindu influences in many Malay cultural traditions, such as *wayang kulit* (shadow puppetry) and the wedding ceremony. Most practising Hindus today are the descendants of Indian contract labourers and settlers who came to Malaysia in the colonial era.

Hinduism has three core practices: *puja* (worship); the cremation of the dead; and the rules and regulations of the caste system. Although still very strong in India, the caste system has never been that significant in Malaysia, mainly because most Indian migrants came from the lower castes.

There are said to be 330 million deities in the Hindu pantheon!

Hindus worship a vast pantheon of gods, some derived from real historical figures and others representing different forces and human characteristics, but all worshipped as attributes of one omnipresent divine force. This force usually has three physical representations: Brahma, the creator; Vishnu, the preserver; and Shiva, the destroyer or reproducer.

Hindus fall into various sects depending on which deity they most revere – most Malaysian Hindus are devotees of Shiva, represented by various South Indian incarnations, including Muruga/Murugan, Subramaniam, the Great Mother Mariamman and Kali. There are also large numbers of Vaishnavites who follow Vishnu, particularly his earthly incarnation as Krishna.

Hindu deities are frequently represented with multiple arms and faces showing different aspects of the divine character, most famously on the ornate *gopuram* (gateway towers) on Hindu temples. The four Vedas (Hindu books of divine knowledge), which are the foundation of Hindu philosophy, are believed to have emanated from the multiple mouths of Brahma.

Animism & Christianity

The religions of indigenous tribal people in Malaysia can broadly be described as animism. Natural phenomena are perceived to be animated by various spirits or deities, and a complex system of practices are used to propitiate these spirits. Ancestor worship is also a common feature of animist societies and departed souls are often considered to be intermediaries between this world and the next. Animism is only followed by a few communities in Peninsular Malaysia, but it remains widespread in Borneo.

Christianity has a small following, though numbers are growing in Borneo. Kuala Lumpur, Melaka and Penang all have small Christian minorities.

Robert Wolff takes an esoteric look at Malaysia's tribal religions in his partly autobiographical book *Original Wisdom*.

WOMEN IN MALAYSIA

As you travel through Malaysia, you'll see women taking part in all aspects of society, from politics and big business through to academia and family life. However, women in all communities, particularly those with conservative religious values, face restrictions on their behaviour despite the general openness of Malaysian society. Arranged marriage is common among Muslim and Hindu families and the concept of 'honour' is still a powerful force in internal family politics.

Although the wearing of the *tudong* (headscarf) is encouraged, women are permitted to work, drive and go out unchaperoned, though the religious authorities frequently crack down on *khalwat* (close proximity) – ie couples who get too intimate in public – which is considered immoral. Full purdah (the practice of screening women from men or strangers by means of a curtain or all-enveloping clothes) is rare. For many Muslim women from the Persian Gulf, a holiday to Malaysia represents a chance to throw off some of the restrictions of home and dress up in Western fashions.

Recent changes to Islamic family law have made it easier for men to marry and divorce multiple wives and claim a share of their property. Religious parties are also campaigning to remove the crime of marital rape from the statute books and bring in new laws requiring four male witnesses before a rape case can come to trial.

In response to these moves, Marina Mahathir, the daughter of the former prime minister, compared the lot of Malaysia's Muslim women to that of blacks under apartheid in South Africa. **Sisters in Islam** (sistersinislam.org.my), run by professional Malaysian Muslim women, is campaigning to change patriarchal interpretations of Islam in Malay society.

The Women's Aid Organisation (www.wao.org.my) is campaigning for increased protection from violence for Malaysian women.

ARTS

Despite the rush towards modernisation, traditional art forms such as *wayang kulit* (shadow puppetry) and *mak yong* (traditional dance) still have a popular following in Malaysia, alongside contemporary art, drama and film making. Each of Malaysia's diverse ethnic groups has its own artforms and traditions, which are experiencing something of a revival inside Malaysia.

Sadly, the government has a history of underperforming when it comes to promoting the arts. Under the Ninth Malaysia Plan, introduced in 2006, the government has shifted RM11.6 million in funding from the arts to new projects in education and development. Two notable events supporting the arts in Malaysia are the Boh Cameronian Arts Awards and the annual Amazing Malaysians award sponsored by the phone company Digi.

Literature

The oldest formal piece of Malay literature is *Sejarah Melayu* (Malay Annals), a history of the Melaka sultanate written in the 16th century. During the colonial period, Malaysia attracted writers such as W Somerset Maugham and Joseph Conrad. The classic colonial expat experience is recounted by Anthony Burgess in *The Malayan Trilogy* written in the 1950s. In the 1960s Paul Theroux used Malaysia as the backdrop to his short story collection, *The Consul's File.*

The current bright light of the Malaysian literary scene is Tash Aw. His debut novel *The Harmony Silk Factory,* set deep in the heart of Peninsular Malaysia during part of WWII, won the 2005 Whitbread First Novel award. The harsh years of the Japanese occupation are vividly described by expat Malaysian Rani Manicka in *The Rice Mother,* the tale of a Sri Lankan bride who moves to Malaysia just before the outbreak of WWII. KS Maniam's *The Return* (1994) shines a light on the Indian Malaysian experience from the perspective of a student returning home after studying abroad.

Peter Carey's *My Life As A Fake* is a great reworking of Frankenstein, set partly in Malaysia and evoking wonderfully the sultry side of Kuala Lumpur (KL).

If you want to find out more about what people are reading in Malaysia a couple of good places to start are the website of local publisher Silverfish (www.silverfishbooks.com); and Bibliobibuli (http://thebookaholic.blogspot.com) – the erudite blog of Sharon Bakar, a Malaysian-based British expat.

Architecture

Malaysia has been producing noteworthy architecture since before the colonial period, but the country gained international attention with the construction of the Petronas Towers (p83) in KL in 1998. The towers have become the symbol of KL and a major drawcard for tourists, though you can only climb to the level of the Skybridge that connects the two towers.

The Petronas Towers is just one of a number of futuristic skyscrapers in the capital (see boxed text, p88), but perhaps the most striking buildings in KL are the administrative buildings around Merdeka Square (p80) designed by British architect AC Norman, who drew his inspiration from the Mughal architecture of India.

The Dutch and British were jointly responsible for distinctive colonial architecture of Melaka, but the real geniuses of architecture on the coast were the Chinese, who built distinctive stucco-fronted shophouses, ornate temples, regal mansions and stately clan houses (see boxed text, p182) in Melaka, Penang and later in KL.

Malay architecture reached its peak under the sultans of Melaka – the traditional Malay house is built on stilts with high peaked roofs, large windows and lattice-like grilles in the walls to maximise the cooling effect of breezes. The layout of a traditional Malay house reflects Muslim sensibilities, with separate areas for men and women, as well as areas where guests of either sex may be entertained.

Edited by Chen Voon Fee, the *Encyclopaedia of Malaysia: Architecture* will tell you everything you need to know about Malay architecture.

The best places to see traditional Malay houses are the *kampung* along the coast – for some of the finest examples, take a wander around Melaka's Kampung Morten and check out Villa Sentosa (p147). There are reconstructed *kampung* houses in KL at the Badan Warisan Malaysia (see boxed text, p89) and the National Museum (p89), and more traditional Malay homes in the city's Kampung Baru district (p93).

Drama & Dance

Traditional dramatic forms are still popular in Malaysia, particularly *wayang kulit,* shadow-puppet performances which tell tales from the Hindu epic the *Ramayana,* a distant link to Malaysia's Hindu past. The Tok Dalang (Father of the Mysteries) manipulates the buffalo-hide puppets behind a semitransparent screen, casting shadows onto the screen. The authentic shadow-plays at weddings and harvest festivals can last for many hours, though shorter performances are often laid on for visitors.

A number of traditional dances are still practised on the peninsula. Similar to Thai folk dances, the masked *menora* dance (performed only by men) and female-only *mak yong* dance are used to mark Buddhist festivals. Malay dances include *rodat,* traditionally performed by fishermen to encourage a good catch, and *joget,* an upbeat dance with Portuguese origins, often performed at weddings. In Melaka it's better known as *chakunchak.*

Visit www.kakiseni.com for up-to-date information on what's currently going on in the Malaysian arts scene.

Malaysia's premier traditional dance troupe is the Petronas Performing Art Group (PPAG). Its repertoire includes more than 100 ethnic dances from across the country, including Chinese and Indian dances. Various professional troupes perform in KL (see p121 for the main venues), or there are several tourist-oriented dance shows (see p121). Theatre in Penang and Melaka tends to be restricted to shows at community theatres and traditional shows at festivals.

Musicals about national heroes are very popular – recent names to get the full stage treatment include sultanate-era warrior Hang Tuah and independence hero Tan Cheng Lock. There is also a growing interest in modern theatre in English, as well as in Malay, Indian and Chinese languages, though playwrights have to tread carefully when dealing with controversial topics such as race and religion. A growing phenomenon is the reinterpretation of the classics – director Sabera Shaik recently staged Shakespeare's *The Tempest* in KL, with the characters and story shifted to a mythical medieval Balinese kingdom.

SILAT

Properly known as *bersilat,* this Malay martial art originated in Melaka in the 15th century. Originally designed as an art of war, *silat* has evolved into a highly refined and stylised activity, more akin to a choreographed dance than self defence. The best places to see *silat* in Malaysia are at weddings and Malay festivals, where ritualised bouts are accompanied by music from drums and gongs.

BE CAREFUL WHAT YOU RAP FOR: IT MIGHT COME TRUE...

A major musical controversy ensued in 2007 when a Malaysian student rapper known as 'Namewee' was featured on the video site YouTube rapping about discrimination against Chinese Malaysians over the Malaysian national anthem. The rap provoked a national outcry from Malays, with some even calling for the student to be executed. The government initially pursued Namewee under Malaysia's sedition laws, but has since taken a more reconciliatory tone and for now, Namewee is continuing his studies in Taipei.

CHINESE OPERA

Cantonese-style *wayang* (Chinese opera) is popular among the Chinese community. Shows feature clanging gongs, high-pitched romantic songs and outrageous dances in spectacular costumes. Performances can go for an entire evening, but plots are fairly self-explanatory and you don't have to speak Cantonese to follow the story. Street performances are held during important festivals such as Chinese New Year (January/February), the Festival of the Hungry Ghosts (August/September) and the Festival of the Nine Emperor Gods (September/October) – head to KL's Chinatown, Melaka or Penang's Georgetown for the best chance of seeing performances.

Music

Traditional Malay music is based largely on *gendang* (drums), but other percussion instruments include the gong and various tribal instruments made from seashells, coconut shells and bamboo. The Indonesian-style *gamelan* (a traditional orchestra of drums, gongs and wooden xylophones), also crops up on ceremonial occasions. The Malay *nobat* uses a mixture of percussion and wind instruments to create formal court music. For Western-style orchestration, attend a performance at the Dewan Filharmonik Petronas (p120), inside the Petronas Towers.

The KL-based Dama Orchestra combines modern and traditional Chinese instruments and play songs that conjure up the mood of 1920s and 1930s Malaysia.

Islamic and Chinese influences are felt in the music of *dondang sayang* (Chinese-influenced romantic songs), and *hadrah* (Islamic chants, sometimes accompanied by dance and music). The KL-based **Dama Orchestra** (www.damaorchestra.com) combines modern and traditional Chinese instruments and play songs that conjure up the mood of 1920s and 1930s Malaysia.

On the popular music scene the Malaysian queen of pop remains the demure Siti Nurhaliza; her recent live album was recorded at London's Albert Hall. The poster boy of every good Muslim girl (and her eternally grateful family) is the devout Mawi. A more mainstream Malay artist is Reshmonu, who sings sprightly pop songs in English and Malay; you can catch him on Lonely Planet's *Six Degrees: Kuala Lumpur* DVD. Other local artists to keep an ear out for include jazz singer Shelia Majid, surf rockers Kugiran, R&B–influenced songstress Adibah Noor, and environmentally conscious world-music singer Zainal Abidin.

Crafts

Although Malaysia is modernising rapidly, many traditional crafts are still practised in KL, Melaka and Penang. Handmade fabrics, wood-carvings and other traditional crafts are popular souvenirs – here are some things to look out for.

TEXTILES

Produced by drawing or printing a pattern on fabric with wax and then dyeing the material, batik came to Malaysia with seafaring traders from

Indonesia. Batik fabrics can be made into clothes, cushion covers, tablecloths, placemats or simply displayed as works of art, but traditional abstract patterns have largely been replaced by figurative designs inspired by nature. Originally from Borneo, *pua kumbu* is a colourful weaving technique where the threads are first tie-dyed on a wooden frame using a traditional process known as ikat.

Another textile to look out for is *kain songket* (a luxurious fabric with gold and silver threads woven throughout the material). Clothes made from this beautiful fabric are usually reserved for the most important festivals and occasions. Another unusual art from the region, still practised in Melaka, is the traditional beadwork used to decorate Nonya shoes (see Wan Aik Shoemaker, p161).

Malaysian crafts get the full coffee-table treatment in the informative *Crafts of Malaysia* by Leo Haks and Dato Haji S Othman.

BASKETRY & MENGKUANG

Basketry is a living art in Malaysia. Local people make all sorts of useful household items using rattan, bamboo, swamp nipah grass and pandanus leaves. Basketware from Borneo has the best reputation, but you can find lots of appealing items at souvenir shops in KL, Melaka and Penang. *Mengkuang* (a local form of weaving) uses pandanus leaves and strips of bamboo to make baskets, bags and mats.

For more information on popular Malaysian crafts visit the website of Karyaneka (www.malaysiancraft.com).

KITES & PUPPETS

Eye-catching Malay kites and traditional *wayang kulit* (shadow puppets) are produced in the north of Peninsular Malaysia. Shadow puppets are made from buffalo hide to portray characters from epic Hindu legends, while kites are made from paper and bamboo strips in a variety of traditional designs. The crescent-shaped *wau bulan* (moon kite) of Kelantan can reach 3m in

DJ GABRIEL

Gabriel is a top club DJ and producer in Kuala Lumpur (KL), famed for his soulful House mixes. He lives in Bangsar and spins the decks regularly at KL's Zouk (p120).

What's the low-down on the KL club scene? The global dance scene used to look towards Europe and America but the world is getting smaller. DJs from this part of the world are starting to get noticed. I'm flying off to other countries several times a month to do sets – an Asian flavour is what the West is looking for right now. Zouk is the heart of the KL club scene. As most places close around 3am, there isn't time to keep hopping from club to club. I have a regular night upstairs at Zouk called Grown-Up Music where I play techno for purists. Most of my sets are at bigger venues but I prefer playing in a small room that's packed and intimate. There's a village culture in KL – all the DJs know each other and we work together to share ideas. We have a culture here called *lepak* – it means chilled out, laid-back. That's the defining feature of the club scene.

Is there a distinctive KL sound? I don't know – dance music in KL is so varied now. People are listening to lots of hip-hop, techno, House, R&B. A lot of influences are coming from Europe: Berlin is providing that pure electronic sound, and London provides the best of every genre. That said, educated clubbers are still in the minority in KL. People here are quite traditional and they don't like to do anything too different – you often find that all the radio stations play the same song at the same time.

What do you miss from KL when you play overseas? The food. KL is so diverse for food. And where else in the world can you find so many restaurants open 24 hours? In Malaysia, you never go hungry. If there's one dish I crave when I go overseas it's *nasi lemak* (rice steamed in coconut milk, served with *ikan bilis*, fried peanuts, egg, sambal or curries). It's like a meal in a packet, but so much better than McDonald's.

length and breadth, while the *wau kucing* (cat kite) from Terengganu is the logo of Malaysia Airlines.

KRIS

The wavy-bladed daggers traditionally carried by Malays make popular souvenirs. Good-quality kris are marked out by the distinctive *pamor* (water pattern) on the blade, where various metal ores have mixed and fused. These days, kris are purely ceremonial – the king of Malaysia is normally photographed with a number of ornate, gold-handled kris, equivalent to the crown jewels of the British royal family.

Over the centuries the Malays have forged their kris (wavy-bladed daggers) from such diverse materials as meteorite iron, railway tracks, captured Dutch cannons and bicycle chains.

METALWORK

Peninsular Malaysia has many skilled silversmiths who specialise in filigree and repoussé work, where designs are hammered through the silver from the underside. Objects crafted out of pewter (an alloy of tin) are synonymous with Selangor – the Royal Selangor Pewter Factory (p123) near KL is the largest pewter manufacturer in the world. Penang also has a number of pewter makers (see p200).

WOODCARVING

The most famous wood carvers in Malaysia are the Kenyah and Kayan peoples of Borneo, but the Orang Asli (Original People) of Peninsular Malaysia are also gifted carvers. The Mah Meri tribe from Pulau Carey (off the coast of Selangor) are particularly renowned for their sinuous carvings of animist spirits – you can see and buy some of their work at the Orang Asli Museum (p131) near KL.

The big film event of 2006 was the release of Oliver Knott's *The Red Kebaya* (www.theredkebaya.com), a sumptuous period drama filmed partly in Penang's Cheong Fatt Tze Mansion (p181).

Cinema

Although Malaysia's film industry dates back to the 1930s, its heyday was the 1950s, when P Ramlee took to the silver screen. Malaysia's answer to Douglas Fairbanks Jr acted in 66 films, recorded 300 songs, and even became a successful film director – his directorial debut *Penarik Becha* (The Trishaw Man; 1955) remains an enduring icon of Malay cinema. Malaysia's best known modern acting star is Michelle Yeo, the agile, Ipoh-born star of *Crouching Tiger, Hidden Dragon,* though most of her work has been for the Hong Kong film industry.

More recently Yasmin Ahmad set a benchmark in Malaysian cinema by broaching the controversial subject of interracial relationships in her multiaward winning 2005 film *Sepet.* The film upset many religious Malays, as did her follow up *Gubra* (2006), which dared to take a sympathetic approach to prostitutes. Perhaps the best known Malaysian director is Taiwan resident Tsai Ming Liang. His latest film, the haunting interracial romance *I Don't Want to Sleep Alone,* was filmed entirely in KL's Chinatown but it was banned and later released with massive cuts for presenting an allegedly 'negative depiction of Malaysia'.

In recent years Malaysian censors have banned such diverse films and TV shows as *Saving Private Ryan, South Park, The Family Guy, Scary Movie, Zoolander,* George Clooney's *Good Night & Good Luck* and *Babe*!

Other directors of note include Ho Yu-Hang and James Lee, who picked up the Best Asean Feature award for his surreal 2005 comedy *The Beautiful Washing Machine,* set in KL. See www.doghouse73pictures.com for more films by James Lee. The production company **Red Films** (www.redfilms.com.my) has also produced some striking work, including Amir Muhammad's compelling *The Last Communist* (2006), banned by the Malaysian government for 'glorifying communism' before any government ministers had seen the film! For a local take on Malaysian film makers, see boxed text, p118.

Visual Arts

Among the most interesting and internationally successful contemporary Malaysian artists are Jalaini Abu Hassan (aka Jai), Wong Hoy Cheong, Bornean artist Ramsay Ong, landscape painter Wong Perng Fey, and Australian-trained multimedia artist Yee I-Lann. Amron Omar has focussed for nearly 30 years on *silat* (a Malay martial art; see p37) as a source of inspiration for his paintings – a couple are in the National Art Gallery in KL (p93).

You can also find work by contemporary Malaysian artists in KL's upmarket commercial galleries (see p123) and at Penang's Alpha Utara Gallery (p183), Pinang Gallery (p186) and Muzium & Galeri Tuanku Fauziah (p203). Malaysia Airlines commissioned several contemporary artists, including Jai and the children's book illustrator Yusof Gajah to provide the interior and exterior decoration for KL's monorail trains.

Food & Drink

Robyn Eckhardt

Malaysia is a hungry traveller's dream destination – a multi-ethnic nation boasting a wide-ranging cuisine shaped over the centuries by the European, Indonesian, Indian and Chinese traders, colonisers and labourers who have landed on its shores. Come mealtime you'll find yourself spoilt for choice. Fancy breakfasting on Chinese dim sum? How about an Indian *dosa* (savoury pancakes) for lunch, followed by a selection of rich Malay curries for dinner? If the thought of choosing from the innumerable options is a bit overwhelming, seek advice from a local. Malaysians, opinionated but affable gourmets, love nothing more than to introduce outsiders to the joys of their cuisine. The traveller who partakes of the nation's edible delights will leave with delicious memories, as well as make a few *makan kaki* (food friends) along the way. In Malaysia it's not 'How are you?' but '*Sudah makan?*' (Have you eaten yet?).

Writer Robyn Eckhardt has lived in Asia for more than 12 years and collaborated on food-focused articles for publications such as *Travel + Leisure*, the *Chicago Tribune*, *Wall Street Journal Asia* and *Time Out Kuala Lumpur*.

FLAVOURS

Though chillies are a mainstay of Malaysian cuisine few dishes are prohibitively spicy. Curries start with *rempah*, a pounded paste of chillies and aromatics such as garlic, shallots, *serai* (lemongrass), *kunyit* (tumeric), and *lengkuas* (galangal). Dried spices – coriander, fennel seeds, cumin, fenugreek – might also be included, especially if the dish is Indian-influenced. Capsicum also plays a starring role in the Malaysian condiment known as *sambal:* mild to fiery, made with fresh or dried chillies, and incorporating ingredients from dried fish to fruit, this cross between a dip and a relish accompanies simple soup noodles, lavish feasts, and every meal in between. There are as many variations of *sambal* as there are Malaysian cooks, but the most common is *sambal belacan*, made from fresh or dried red chillies pounded with dried *belacan* (shrimp paste). If its pungent punch puts you off initially, try, try again – *sambal belacan* is rarely loved at first bite but often proves addictive in the long run.

Fresh herbs such as cilantro, mint, *daun kesom* (polygonum), turmeric, *pandan* (screwpine leaves), lime- and curry-leaves impart a fresh liveliness to curries and noodle dishes. Malaysians prefer their food on the sweet side, but tartness is also key to the cuisine. *Asam* (sour) curries derive their piquancy from fresh tamarind, *belimbi* (a sour relative of the carambola or starfruit), and *asam keping* (the dried flesh of a tart fruit related to the mangosteen, also known as *gelugor*). Fresh *kalamansi* (a tiny, sour lime) juice dresses salads and is squeezed into *sambal belacan* just before it's served.

Belacan is the embodiment of the Malaysian love of fishy flavours. A Penang variation is *hae ko* (a black, sticky-sweet shrimp paste) that dresses *rojak* (vegetable-and-fruit salad). Other well-loved condiments from the sea include *budu* (a long-fermented anchovy sauce favoured by Malay cooks), and *cincalok* (tiny shrimps treated with brine). *Ikan bilis* (dried anchovies) are deep-fried and incorporated into *sambal* or sprinkled atop noodle and rice dishes, while salted fish finds its way into stir-fries.

The Star Guide to Malaysian Street Food lists worthy eateries in most Malaysian cities and towns. Entries include maps, information on what to order and hours of operation.

No Malaysian kitchen is without soy sauce, and its sweetened cousin *kecap manis*. Other seasonings and sauces integral to the cuisine are oyster sauce, hoisin sauce, and *taucu* (fermented, salted bean paste).

Many Malaysian curries contain coconut milk and the fruit's flesh is grated and dry-fried to make *kerisik* (a garnish for rice dishes). Grated coconut also features in many Malaysian sweets, where it is often paired with *gula melaka* (a distinctive dark sugar made from the sap collected from the flower stalks of the coconut palm).

HEAD CHEF ZULKIFLI RAZALI

Zulkifli Razali is head chef at Bijan (p112), one of the most respected Malay restaurants in Kuala Lumpur (KL).

What are the must-try Malay dishes? One of my personal favourites is *udang masak lemak nenas* (prawns cooked with pineapple and coconut). We locals like it hot, with lots of chilli. *Rendang daging* (beef rendang) is another classic Malay dish. Kampung people love it because the lime leaves and coconuts grow in the villages. And everyone should try *rojak* (Malay-style salad). It comes in two styles: *rojak buah* (with fruit) and *rojak pasembor* (with prawn fritters, coconut dumplings, tofu and morsels of cucumber and turnip). Different parts of Malaysia have their own specialities, but there isn't really a KL-specific dish. The city is a real melting pot so you can find dishes from all over Malaysia in one spot. Of course, the different communities have their own cooking styles – Muslims won't eat pork or dishes cooked with wine, Hindus won't eat beef and some Chinese avoid beef and lamb. One dish everyone likes is *ayam panggang* (grilled chicken with chilli) – it's fast and tasty, which suits the hectic lifestyles of people in KL. If you're feeling brave, try *tempoyak* (fermented durian). It has all the flavour of durian without the strong smell.

What makes Malay cooking stand out from the crowd? It's the way we use spices and coconut. It's quite different from Chinese, Indian or Thai cooking. And sharing is a major part of eating in Malaysia – we like to put lots of dishes in the centre and share it around *hidang*-style, like a big buffet.

Where is the best place to sample Malay food? On the streets at hawker stalls! The street food is so good because the chefs focus on one dish. They make the same dish every day so they learn to make it perfectly. They're real experts!

STAPLES & SPECIALITIES

Malaysians would be hard-pressed to choose between *nasi* (rice) and *mee* (noodles) – one or the other figures in almost every meal. *Nasi lemak*, an unofficial 'national dish' and popular breakfast food, is rice steamed in coconut milk and served with *ikan bilis*, fried peanuts, sliced cucumber, *sambal* and half a hard-boiled egg – curry optional. Rice is also boiled with meat or seafood stock to make *bubur* (porridge), *nasi goreng* (rice fried with shallots and topped with an egg) and *lontong* (rice packed into banana leaf–lined bamboo tubes, cooked over wood, then sliced and doused with coconut milk gravy). Tinted blue with the butterfly or blue-pea flower *(bunga telung)* and adorned with fresh herbs, bean sprouts and *kerisik*, rice becomes the Malay favourite *nasi kerabu*. Glutinous, or sticky, rice is a common ingredient in Malaysian sweets.

Rice flour, mixed with water and allowed to ferment slightly, becomes the batter for *idli* (Indian steamed cakes) and *apam* (pan-fried pancakes). It goes into the making of noodles for dishes such as laksa: *asam* laksa is served in a fish-based sour and spicy broth, while curry laksa (also known as laksa *lemak*) comes in a chilli coconut gravy. Wide rice noodles known as *kway teow* are stir-fried with prawns, cockles, egg and bean sprouts to make the country's other 'national dish': *char kway teow*. Other rice noodles include *beehoon* (vermicelli) and *loh see fun* (stubby 'rat tail' noodles). *Chee cheong fun* are steamed rice-flour sheets sliced into strips and topped with meat gravy or chilli and black shrimp sauces.

Mee (round yellow noodles) are served in soup; stir-fried with curry leaves and chilli sauce for the Indian Muslim speciality *mee mamak*; or smothered in a sweet potato–based gravy for the Malay dish *mee rebus*. A favourite Chinese noodle dish is *won ton mee* – egg vermicelli floated in broth with pork dumplings, a few leaves of Chinese mustard greens and sliced pork – it can also be served 'dry', with the broth on the side.

Given Malaysia's multiple coastlines, it's no surprise that seafood plays a major role in the national diet. Quality is high and the options endless.

NOODLES, WET OR DRY

If the thought of hanging your head over a steaming bowl in Malaysia's withering heat puts you off soupy noodle dishes, consider adding the word *'konlo'* to your order. You'll end up getting a bowl of warm noodles tossed in light or dark soy sauce and a bit of oil, with the hot broth served on the side. Many Malaysians order their noodles 'dry' to protect the pasta's *al dente* integrity. As any *won ton mee* (egg vermicelli floated in broth with pork dumplings) connoisseur will tell you, a noodle that doesn't offer a bit of resistance to the tooth is hopelessly overcooked.

Favourites for *ikan bakar* (grilled fish; also known as *ikan panggang*) include *ikan tenggiri* (Spanish mackerel) and *ikan pari* (stingray), while pomfret and *garoupa* (a Southeast Asian white fish)are usually steamed Chinese-style with garlic, ginger and soy sauce. The whole head and 'shoulders' of large fish such as *ikan merah* (red snapper) and sea bass feature in the delectable Indian-Malay *kari ikan kepala* (fish-head curry). *Sotong* (squid) is battered and deep-fried, stirred into curries, and griddled on a banana leaf with *sambal.* Malaysians adore shellfish: from prawns to 'top shell' (a snail-like saltwater creature with sweet, snow-white flesh), and it isn't an authentic *char kway teow* unless it includes plump blood-red cockles. Crab is steamed or stir-fried with curry, and in Penang its meat is rolled into an extravagant soft spring roll *popiah* (spring roll).

Babi (pork) is *haram* (forbidden) to Malaysia's Muslims but is the meat of choice for the Chinese, who prefer fatty cuts such as the belly and shoulder; they even dress cooked dishes with lard oil. Crispy-skinned *char yoke* (roast pork), sweet glazed *char siew* (barbecued pork), and pork cracklings are eaten on their own and incorporated into noodle dishes and snacks. *Bak kut teh* (literally 'meat-bone tea') is a comforting dish of pork ribs (innards optional) stewed in a claypot with medicinal herbs, mushrooms and bean curd, and eaten with Chinese crullers. Malaysia's Hakka (a Chinese dialect group) are renowned for their succulent, long-cooked pork dishes such as sliced belly stewed with *khaw yoke* (taro).

Ayam (chicken) is tremendously popular in Malaysia; locals prefer flavourful *ayam kampong* (free-range birds) Nearly every coffee shop houses a stall selling *nasi ayam* (Hainan-style chicken rice; poached and sliced breast served with broth-infused rice, sliced cucumber and tomato, and chilli sauce). Most Malay eateries serve a variety of chicken curries, and the bird makes for Malaysia's most popular satay meat, where it's skewered, grilled and dipped in peanut-chilli sauce. Another oft-eaten fowl is *itik* (duck), roasted or simmered in star anise–scented broth and eaten with noodles, or stewed in a spicy *mamak* (Indian Muslim) curry.

Tough Malaysian *daging* (beef) is best in long, slow-cooked dishes such as Indonesian-influenced rendang (an aromatic dry-cooked coconut-milk curry). Lamb is a favourite of Malaysia's *mamak,* who stew ribs to tenderness in a spicy soup stew *(sup kambing)* that's served with sliced white bread.

Tau (soy beans) are consumed in many forms. *Tuahu fa* (soy-bean milk and warm, fresh bean curd), eaten plain or doused with palm-sugar syrup, are sold from white trucks. *Yong tauhu* is a healthy Hakka dish of firm bean curd and vegetables stuffed with ground fish paste. The chewy skin that forms on the surface of vats of boiling soy milk is fried golden or eaten fresh in noodle dishes, and *tauhu pok* (flavour-absorbent deep-fried bean curd 'puffs') are added to noodles and stews. Malaysians even barbecue bean curd, then stuff it with sliced cucumber and top it with sweet shrimp paste and peanuts. Malays stew *tempeh* (nutty-tasting 'cakes' of soybeans mixed with starter yeast and allowed to ferment) with vegetables in mild coconut gravy or stir-fry it with *kecap manis* and chillies.

Vegetables are an important part of the Malaysian table. A full Malay meal includes *ulam* (a selection of fresh vegetables and herbs)to eat with *sambal*. Eggplant, okra and cauliflower are cooked into curries and leafy greens like *daun ubi* (sweet potato leaves), *kangkong* (water spinach) and *choy sum* (yellow-flowered mustard) are stir-fried with garlic or *sambal belacan*. The humble yam bean or jicama *(sengkuang)* is particularly versatile: it's sliced and added raw to *rojak;* grated, steamed, and rolled into *popiah*; and mashed, formed into a savoury cake and topped with deep-fried shallots and chillies *(oh kuih)*. Sweet yellow corn is sold as a snack, on or off the cob, from mobile carts.

In Malaysia a sugar high is never far away. Vendors selling sweets *kuih muih* (sweets) lie in wait in front of stores, on street corners and at markets. Many *kuih* incorporate freshly grated coconut and palm sugar – among the best are *ketayap* (*pandan* leaf–flavoured rice-flour 'pancakes' rolled around a mix of the two; also known as *kuih dadar*) and *putu piring* (steamed rice-flour 'flapjacks' filled with palm sugar and topped with coconut). *Cendol* is a heat-beating mound of shaved ice and chewy mung-bean 'pasta' doused in fresh coconut milk, palm-sugar syrup and condensed milk. The more elaborate *ais kacang* or ABC (the initials stand for *air batu campur* – mixed ice) combines flavoured syrups, jellies, red beans, palm seeds and sweet corn. Sweet coconut-milk porridges made with *gandum* (wheat) or *bubur kacang hijau* (mung bean) are an afternoon treat, and Chinese *tong sui* (warm sweet soups) featuring ingredients such as peanuts and winter melon are said to be as healthy as they are tasty. Don't leave Malaysia without sampling the subcontinental sweets stacked in colourful pyramids in Little India shop windows.

Those who have overindulged in *kuih* might repent with a dose of healthy tropical fruits. *Nenas* (pineapple), watermelon, *jambu* (rose apple), papaya and green guava are year-round choices, with more unusual fruits available seasonally. The dull brown skin of the sopadilla *ciku* (sopadilla) hides super-sweet flesh that tastes a bit like a date. Strip away the yellowish peel of the *duku* to find segmented, perfumed pearlescent flesh with a lycheelike flavour. April and May are mango months, and come December to January and June to July, follow your nose to sample notoriously odiferous love-it-or-hate-it durian. Should the king of fruits prove too repellent, consider the slightly smelly but wonderfully sweet yellow flesh of the young *nangka* (jackfruit).

Ever wondered why many durian stalls also sell mangosteens? The latter is thought to be a 'cooling fruit' that, eaten on the heels of 'heaty' durian, brings the body back into balance.

DRINKS

Half the fun of taking breakfast in one of Malaysia's Little Indias is watching the tea wallah toss-pour an order of *teh tarik* (literally, 'pulled' tea) from one pitcher to another. Malaysians, who rank among the world's largest tea consumers, brew the leaf with ginger *(teh halia)*, drink it hot or iced, with or without milk *(teh ais/teh-o-ais)*, and tart it up with lime. For an especially rich cuppa head for an Indian café and ask for *teh susu kerabau* (hot tea with boiled fresh milk). Coffee is also popular – the dark, thick brew served in Chinese coffee shops is an excellent antidote to a case of jetlag. Caffeine-free alternatives include freshly blended fruit and vegetable juices; sticky-sweet green sugar-cane juice; and coconut water, drunk straight from the fruit with a straw. Other, more unusual, drinks include *barley peng* or *ee bee chui* (barley boiled with water, *pandan* leaf, and rock sugar served over ice); *air mata kucing* (sweet dried longan beverage); and *cincau* (a herbal grass-jelly drink; to add a splash of soy milk ask for a 'Michael Jackson'). Sweetened *kalamansi* juice and Chinese salted plums may sound a strange combination but make for a thoroughly refreshing potion *(kak cai shin mooi)*.

Sky-high duties on alcohol can make a boozy night out awfully expensive. The cheapest beers are those brewed locally, such as Tiger and Carlsberg, and Chinese liquor shops stock less expensive, if not always palatable, hard liquors.

REGIONAL SPECIALITIES

Mention Penang and Malaysians swoon. The island's reputation as gastronomic ground zero lures foodies from Kuala Lumpur, Singapore and beyond, who come to partake of its stellar hawker fare. Must-eats include the iconic *asam* laksa (round rice noodles in a hot and sour fish-based gravy topped with slivered torch ginger flower, chopped pineapple and mint leaves) and laksa *lemak* (comes with a curry broth that's spicier and lighter on the coconut milk than versions served elsewhere).

Hokkien *mee* (yellow noodles, bean sprouts, and shrimp in a rich prawn and pork stock), is another signature dish of the Pearl of the Orient, as is its *rojak* (fruit salad doused in Penang's unique sweet and gooey-black shrimp paste and topped with ground nuts). One food found all over Malaysia but firmly entrenched in the island's food history is *nasi kandar* (rice eaten with a variety of curries). A speciality of Penang's *mamak* community, the dish is named for the *kandar* (shoulder pole) from which, originally, ambulant vendors suspended pots of rice and curry. Drinks specific to Penang include nutmeg juice *lau hao* (nutmeg juice) and an iced infusion of eight Chinese medicinal herbs sweetened with rock and brown sugar *(pat poh peng)*.

The word laksa derives from the Persian word for noodle, *lakhsha* (slippery). *The Oxford Companion to Food* speculates that pasta was introduced to Indonesia (from where it migrated to Malaysia) by Arab traders or Indian Muslims in perhaps the 13th century.

Penang and Melaka are known for Nonya (also spelled Nyonya), or Peranakan, cuisine, a fusion of Chinese and Malay ingredients and cooking techniques. The Malay word *'nonya'* refers to prominent women in the Baba-Nonya community, descendants of early Chinese male immigrants who settled in Penang, Melaka and Singapore, and intermarried with locals (*'baba'* is the male counterpart). Penang Nonya food is influenced by the cuisine of nearby Thailand and tends to be spicier and more sour than that of Melaka. The preparation of Nonya dishes is laborious and time-consuming and, Malaysians say, best left to home kitchens. Still, there are a couple of Penang Nonya hawker specialities worth seeking out: *kerabu beehoon* (rice vermicelli tossed with fiery *sambal* and garnished with toasted coconut and herbs), and *lorbak* (a crispy treat of pork seasoned with Chinese five-spice powder, wrapped in bean curd sheets and deep-fried). See p193 for Penang's eating options.

Melaka boasts a number of sit-down restaurants serving local Nonya favourites such as *ikan cili garam* (fish curry) and chicken cooked with *taucu,*

MALAYSIA'S TOP TASTES

Don't even think about leaving Malaysia without sampling these much-loved specialities:

- *Nasi lemak* – rice steamed in coconut milk and served with *ikan bilis* (deep-fried anchovies), fried peanuts, half a hard-boiled egg, *sambal* (chilli sauce) and a selection of curries, often eaten for breakfast.
- *Char kway teow* – wide rice noodles stir-fried with prawns, cockles, bean sprouts and egg; it vies with *nasi lemak* for the title of 'national dish'.
- *Roti canai* – flaky unleavened bread griddled with ghee until crisp and eaten with curry or dhal. It is another breakfast favourite.
- *Asam* laksa – Penang's iconic dish is a sour and chilli-hot bowlful of round rice noodles in a fish-based soup, garnished with slivered torch ginger flower, chopped pineapple and mint.
- *Cendol* – a wonderfully refreshing sweet of shaved ice mounded over toothsome mung bean noodles, all doused in fresh coconut milk and luscious palm-sugar syrup.

A DISH BY ANY OTHER NAME

Be sure to keep your nomenclature straight when city-hopping. Penangites are justifiably proud of their Hokkien *mee,* a spicy dish of yellow noodles, bean sprouts and shrimp in a pork-and-prawn-based broth. Order Hokkien *mee* anywhere else in Malaysia, however, and you'll end up with a plate of deliciously greasy thick noodles stir-fried with pork and egg in a dark, soy-based gravy. In Penang *otak-otak* is a curried coconut-milk-and-fish 'mousse' steamed in a banana leaf, but in Melaka and other parts of the southern peninsula it takes the form of a grilled coconut leaf–wrapped fish paste and chilli sausage.

dark soy sauce, and sugar *(ayam pong teh)*. In addition to its Nonya fare, Melaka is known for its unique take on Hainan chicken, which is served with a particularly zesty chilli sauce and ping pong–sized rice balls, rather than a mound of rice. A favourite evening snack is *satay celup,* skewered vegetables, meat, and seafood that diners cook themselves in a pot at the center of the table, which they then dip into a spicy, peanut-based sauce. Pork fans shouldn't miss the Melaka version of *popiah,* which includes bits of crackling and a splash of lard oil. Though *cendol* isn't unique to Melaka it's thought to be especially delicious there because vendors douse their ice with locally-produced palm-sugar syrup. For Melaka's food-scene recommendations, see p156.

Kuala Lumpur doesn't really lay claim to any dishes in particular, but there are some wonderful foods more easily found there than in Penang or Melaka. *Pan meen* (literally, 'board noodles') are substantial hand-cut or hand-torn wheat noodles tossed with dark soy and garlic oil, garnished with chopped pork and crispy *ikan bilis,* and served with soup on the side. Some versions include a poached egg. More expensive than your average noodle dish but well worth it are *sang har meen* (literally 'fresh sea noodles') huge freshwater prawns in gravy flavoured with Chinese rice wine and the fat from the shellfish heads, served over *yee mee* (crispy fried noodles).

Head to the city's Malay enclave of Kampung Baru to sample the specialities of Malaysia's eastern states, such as Kelantanese *nasi kerabu* and *ayam percik* (barbecued chicken smothered in chilli-coconut sauce) and, from Terengganu, *nasi dagang* (nutty, coconut milk–cooked red rice).

Food website Fried Chillies (friedchillies.com) is a goldmine of unbiased Kuala Lumpur food reviews.

Kuala Lumpur also boasts a notable range of regional Chinese cuisines. Choose from eateries serving authentic Cantonese, Sichuanese, Dongbei (northeastern), Xinjiang, Guizhou, Teowchew, Hokkien and Hakka fare.

Need a break from Malaysian? Kuala Lumpur has a cosmopolitan dining scene and you needn't look far to find – thanks to Malaysia's huge migrant workforce – inexpensive Thai, Burmese, Nepalese, Indonesian, Bangladeshi and Pakistani fare. Restaurants serving Italian, French, fusion, Japanese and pan-Asian cuisine and ranging in style from casual to white-tablecloth are among its more upmarket dining options. For KL's eating recommendations, see p106.

FESTIVALS & CELEBRATIONS

It's no surprise that a people as consumed with food and its pleasures as Malaysians mark every occasion with edible delights.

Securing a restaurant reservation in the weeks leading to Chinese New Year can be tricky, as friends, colleagues and family gather over endless banquets. Each table is sure to be graced with *yee sang* (literally, 'fresh fish'), a Cantonese raw-fish dish believed to bring luck in the coming year. Other foods special to this time of the year (look for them in Chinese groceries) include pineapple tarts, snow-white melt-in-the-mouth cookies called *kuih bangkit,* deep-fried

FASTING & FEASTING

Don't be deterred from visiting Malaysia during Ramadan (see the boxed text, p220), the Muslim holy month of sunrise-to-sunset fasting. Indian and Chinese eateries remain open during the day to cater to the country's sizeable non-Muslim population and, come late afternoon, Ramadan bazaars pop up all over the country. These prepared-food markets offer a rare chance to sample Malay specialities from all over the country, some of which are specific to the festive season or rarely found outside private homes. One of the country's biggest Ramadan markets is held in Kuala Lumpur's Malay enclave of Kampung Baru (p114). Cruise the stalls and pick up provisions for an evening meal – but don't snack in public until the cry of the muezzin tells believers it's time to *buka puasa* (break the fast).

Chinese arrowroot chips *nga ku* (deep-fried Chinese arrowroot chips) and *ti kuih* (glutinous rice cakes wrapped in banana leaf).

For several weeks before the Indian festival Deepavali Malaysia's Little Indias are awash in food stalls selling clothing, textiles, and household goods. Vendors also offer special sweets and savoury snacks, as well as foodstuffs shipped over from the subcontinent, such as hand-patted pappadams and kulfi.

Malaysia's Ramadan bazaars are reason in themselves to visit Malaysia during the Muslim holy month. In Kuala Lumpur vendors compete every year to secure a lucrative spot at one of the city's Ramadan markets, which swing into action late in the afternoon to serve those breaking the fast at sunset. They offer an excellent opportunity to sample home-cooked, otherwise hard-to-find Malay dishes; see the boxed text, above.

WHERE TO EAT & DRINK

Malaysians argue that the tastiest and best-value food is found at hawker stalls, and they are fiercely loyal to their favourite vendors. Many hawkers have been in business for decades or operate a business inherited from their parents or even grandparents; the best enjoy reputations that exceed their geographical reach. To sample Malaysian hawker food simply head to a stand-alone streetside kitchen-on-wheels or a coffee shop or food court. Place your order with one or multiple vendors, find a seat (shared tables are common), and pay for each dish as it's delivered to your table. You'll be approached by someone taking drink orders after you've sat down – pay for these separately as well.

The term *kopi tiam* generally refers to old-style, single-owner coffee shops. These are simple, fan-cooled establishments that serve noodle and rice dishes, strong coffee and other drinks, and all-day breakfast fare such as half-boiled eggs and toast spread with *kaya* (coconut jam).

Famous Street Food of Penang, a guide to the island's most well-known hawkers and their specialities, includes, along with maps and hours of operation, recipes.

Intrepid eaters shouldn't overlook *pasar* (markets). Morning markets include stalls selling coffee and other beverages, as well as vendors preparing foods such as freshly griddled roti and curry and *chee cheong fun*. Takeaway *(ta pao)* or eat 'in' – most can offer at least a stool. Night markets are also excellent places to graze. The larger ones include Kuala Lumpur's Saturday market in the Malay enclave of Kampung Baru (p114); Penang's Pulau Tikus market on Jln Pasar, the market at the corner of Jln Macalister and Lorong Baru, as well as Gurney Dr (p194); and Melaka's Jonker's Walk (p158).

The word *restoran* (restaurant) applies to eateries ranging from the casual, decades-old Teowchew, Cantonese and Nonya places dotting Penang's Georgetown and small, family-run Malay restaurants in KL's Kampung Baru, to upscale establishments boasting international fare, slick décor and a full bar. Between the two extremes lie Chinese seafood restaurants (where the main course can be chosen live, from a tank on the premises), as well as the numerous eateries found in Malaysia's many shopping malls.

While they often serve indifferent fare, a few chains rise above the pack. Keep an eye out for Penang-origin Kayu Nasi Kandar, named for the speciality of the house; Saravana Bavan, serving delicious Keralan (South Indian) delights; Little Penang, offering excellent versions of Nonya specialities; and Madam Kwan's, known for *nasi lemak* and authentically sour-spicy *asam* laksa.

VEGETARIANS & VEGANS

Given the inclusion of shrimp paste and fish in many dishes, vegetarians and vegans will find it difficult to negotiate their way around most menus. Chinese vegetarian restaurants and hawker stalls (signage will include the words *'makanan sayur-sayuran'*) are safe bets – they are especially busy on the 1st and 15th of the lunar month, when many Buddhists adopt a vegetarian diet for 24 hours. Indian vegetarian restaurants are another haven, for snacks such as steamed *idli* served with dhal and *dosa,* as well as *thali* (full set meals consisting of rice or bread with numerous side dishes).

Justlife, a chain of organic groceries with attached cafés, serves Western and local vegetarian fare and has stores in all major west coast cities, including Melaka and Penang.

Food From the Heart: Malaysia's Culinary Heritage (Cross Time Matrix, 2004) is a collection of mouth-watering family recipes, culinary remembrances and kitchen counsel from 86 Malaysians; the proceeds from the book benefit seven Malaysian charities.

EATING WITH KIDS

Travellers toting tots will do well at hawker centres and food courts, where the wide selection of dishes offers the best chance of satisfying fussy appetites. If familiar flavours are in order, head to one of the many Western fast-food outlets, pizza shops and restaurant chains dotting Malaysia's larger cities. Should the little ones crave a good old hamburger, stalls selling Ramly Burgers – thin-meat-patty sandwiches that enjoy cult status in Malaysia – are a local alternative to the Golden Arches.

HABITS & CUSTOMS

To those of us used to 'three square meals' it might seem as if Malaysians are always eating. In fact, five or six meals or snacks is more the order of the day than strict adherence to the breakfast-lunch-dinner trilogy. Breakfast is often something that can be grabbed on the run: *nasi lemak* wrapped to go *(bungkus)* in a banana leaf or brown waxed paper, a quick bowl of noodles, toast and eggs, or griddled Indian bread. Come late morning a snack might be in order, perhaps a *karipap* (deep-fried pastry filled with spiced meat or fish and potatoes). Lunch generally starts from 12:30pm, something to keep in mind if you plan to eat at a popular establishment. In the late afternoon, stalls offering teatime treats – sweet porridge, *vadai* (Indian deep-fried pulse

MALAYSIA'S WESTERN CONNECTION

Dine at enough Malaysian coffee shops and you're bound to run into lamb chops and mushroom soup. Though these may seem out of place on a menu that also features *belacan* (fermented prawn paste) fried rice and fish in sour curry, these dishes are as much a part of the Malaysian culinary universe as laksa *lemak* (curry laksa). Introduced by the British but popularised in the early decades of the 20th century by Hainanese immigrants who served as their private cooks – and later became known throughout the country for their prowess in the kitchen – Western classics such as chops (pork and chicken, in addition to lamb) and fish and chips are Malaysia's intergenerational comfort food. The best versions – found in old-time *kopi tiam* (coffee shops) sporting original floor tiles and peeling paint – are astoundingly authentic. Seek them out when a break from local fare is in order and eat a bit of history.

'donuts'), and battered and fried slices of cassava, sweet potato, and banana – pop up on street corners. *Mamak* stalls and hawker areas see a jump in business a few hours after dinner (which is eaten around 6:30pm or 7pm) as Malaysians head out in search of a treat to tide them over until morning.

EatingAsia (eatingasia.typepad.com) is a lovingly photographed source of hawker- and street-food reviews, information on Malaysian wet markets, out-of-the-way gastronomic hotspots, ingredients and culinary culture.

You'll rarely find a knife on the Malaysian table – fork and spoon are the cutlery of choice. Forks aren't used to carry food to the mouth, but to nudge food onto the spoon. Chinese noodles and dishes served in Chinese restaurants are usually eaten with chopsticks (Westerners are offered a fork and a spoon as a courtesy). Malays and Indians eat rice-based meals with their right hand (the left is reserved for unclean tasks), using their thumbs to manoeuvre rice onto the balls of their fingers and then transferring the lot to their mouth. Moistening your rice with curries and side dishes helps things along and, as with any new skill, practice makes perfect. Before and after eating, wash your hands with water from the teapotlike container on your table (Malay eateries) or at a communal sink to the rear or side of the room. Napkins on the table (and a towel to wipe your wet hands) aren't a given, so it's always a good idea to carry along a pack of tissues when heading out to graze.

In some Chinese eateries a server will bring a basin of hot water containing saucers, chopsticks, bowls and cutlery to the table after you've placed your order. This is meant to allay hygiene concerns – remove the items from the water and dry them off with a napkin (or shake them dry).

COOKING COURSES

Enrolling in a cooking class is a great way to meet locals. Kuala Lumpur offers the best range; see p99.

EAT YOUR WORDS

Useful Phrases

These Malay phrases may help in off-the-beaten-track eating adventures – at most places in Malaysia English will be understood. For guidelines on pronunciation see p246.

Where's a ...?	*... di mana?*
restaurant	*kedai makan/restoran*
coffee shop	*kedai kopi/kopi tiam*
hawker centre	*pusat penjaja*
Can I see the menu?	*Minta senarai makanan?*
I'd like ...	*Saya mahu...*
What's in this dish?	*Ini termasuk apa?*
Is this dish spicy/sweet/sour?	*Makanan ini pedas/manis/asam?*
Not too spicy, please.	*Kurang pedas.*
I like it hot and spicy!	*Saya suka pedas lagi!*
Please add extra chilli.	*Tolong letak cili lebih.*
The bill/cheque, please.	*Minta bon.*
Thank you, that was delicious.	*Sedap sekali, terima kasih.*
I don't want any meat at all.	*Saya tak mahu daging.*
I'm a vegetarian.	*Saya makan sayur-sayuran sahaja.*

Menu Decoder

ABC – a sweet colourful dish of shaved ice, red beans, agar jelly, palm-sugar seeds, chewy mung-bean-flour noodles, and sweet corn doused with palm sugar and other flavoured syrups, coconut milk and condensed milk
acar – sweet, sour and spicy fruit-and-vegetable pickle
air buah – fruit juice
ais kacang – see *ABC*
aloo gobi – Indian potato-and-cauliflower dish

apam – spongy, sourish Indian rice-flour 'pancake', usually eaten for breakfast, accompanied with coconut and chilli chutney
apam balik – sweet, crispy pancake filled with sugar and chopped peanuts; in Penang, a soft pancake filled with sliced banana
asam laksa – round rice noodles in a fish-based sour-and-spicy broth, topped with chopped pineapple and mint and served with *hae ko*
ayam goreng – fried chicken
ayam percik – barbecued chicken slathered in coconut milk gravy; from Kelantan, on the east coast of the peninsula
ayam pong the – Melaka Nonya dish of chicken cooked with preserved, salted soy beans, dark soy sauce and sugar
bak chang – steamed, leaf-wrapped glutinous rice dumpling with a sweet or savoury filling
bak kut teh – pork ribs stewed in a claypot with Chinese medicinal herbs, mushrooms and bean curd
barley peng – an iced drink of water boiled with barley and rock sugar, sometimes served with a squeeze of *kalamansi*
belacan kangkong – water convolvulus stir-fried with chillies and shrimp paste
biryani – steamed basmati rice with spices and meat, seafood or vegetables
bubur – sweet porridge made with coconut milk and dried beans or barley, or a savoury Ramadan dish of rice porridge with meat and herbs
bubur sumsum – smooth rice-porridge topped with *pandan*-coconut custard and doused with palm-sugar syrup
cendol – sweet dish of chewy mung-bean-flour noodles topped with shaved ice and doused in coconut milk, palm-sugar syrup and condensed milk
char kway teow – rice noodles stir-fried with egg, cockles, prawns, bean sprouts, chilli sauce and, sometimes, pork
char siew – sweet barbecued pork
char siew pao – steamed wheat-flour dumpling filled with chopped, sweet barbecued pork
char yoke – roasted pork with three layers: meat, fat and skin
chee cheong fun – in Penang, steamed rice-flour rolls topped with black shrimp paste, chilli sauce and sesame seeds; elsewhere, steamed rice-flour rolls topped with meat sauce
clay-pot rice – rice cooked in a claypot with chicken, mushroom, Chinese sausage and soy sauce
congee – rice porridge
curry laksa – round rice noodles, deep-fried soy bean pieces, bean sprouts, long beans and meat or seafood in a spicy chilli-coconut soup
dadar – see *ketayap*
dhal – Indian dish of seasoned stewed lentils
dim sum – Chinese sweet and savoury minidishes served at breakfast and lunch; also known as *dian xin* or *yum cha*
dosa – large, light, crispy pancake
fish-head curry – fish head and shoulders in spicy Malay-Indian red coconut curry with tomatoes and okra
gado gado – cold dish of bean sprouts, potatoes, long beans, bean curd, rice cakes and prawn crackers, topped with a spicy peanut sauce
Hainan chicken rice – poached or roasted chicken served with broth-infused rice, sliced cucumber and a variety of dipping sauces
Hakka mee – thin wheat noodles tossed with soy sauce and lard oil, topped with minced pork, slices of *char siew* and chopped scallions
Hokkien mee – in Penang, yellow noodles, bean sprouts and prawns in a prawn-and-pork stock; elsewhere, thick yellow noodles stir-fried with pork and dark soy sauce
idli – slightly sour steamed cakes made from a fermented rice-flour batter, usually eaten with thin curry or *dhal*
ikan asam – fish, tomatoes and okra in a thin red curry soured with tamarind
ikan bakar – grilled fish
ikan cili garam – Melaka Nonya dish of fish in a spicy, red curry sauce

ikan gulai tumis – Penang Nonya dish of fish (usually pomfret) in a spicy sour curry
ikan panggang – see *ikan bakar*
kari ayam – curried chicken
kari ikan kepala – Indian-Malay coconut milk-based fish-head curry with tomatoes and okra
karipap – deep-fried pastry filled with curried meat or seafood and potatoes
kaya – rich egg-and-coconut jam
keema – spicy minced meat
kerabu beehoon – rice vermicelli tossed with spicy *sambal*, toasted coconut, and herbs
ketayap – green, sweet *pandan*-flavoured pancakes filled with grated coconut and palm sugar
kofta – minced-meat or vegetable ball
korma – mild Indian yogurt-based curry
kulfi – Indian ice cream
laksa – one of a number of noodle dishes with soup; see *asam laksa, laksa lemak*, and curry laksa
laksa lemak – see curry laksa; Penang-style has a lighter, slightly sour broth
laksam – a Malay dish of wide, thick rice-flour 'noodles' topped with bean sprouts and fresh herbs, doused with mild coconut gravy
lassi – yogurt-based drink
lau hu – nutmeg juice
lontong – pressed rice cakes in spicy coconut-milk gravy topped with fried *tempeh*, long beans, hard-boiled egg, *sambal* and toasted grated coconut
lorbak – a Nonya snack of pork seasoned in five-spice powder, wrapped in bean curd sheets and deep-fried
masala dosa – thin rice-flour pancake rolled around spicy curried potatoes and vegetables
mee goreng – fried noodles
mee mamak – yellow noodles fried with chicken, tofu pieces, scallion, tomato and chilli sauce
mee rebus – yellow noodles served in a thick, sweetish sauce made from sweet potatoes and garnished with sliced hard-boiled eggs and green chillies
mee siam – white thin noodles in a sweet-and-sour gravy made with tamarind
mee soto – noodle soup with shredded chicken
mee sua – thin white rice noodles stir-fried with meat, bean sprouts and seaweed
murtabak – *roti canai* filled with pieces of mutton, chicken or vegetables
nasi air – Malay-style *congee;* a brothy rice soup with fresh herbs and sliced chicken
nasi biryani – saffron rice flavoured with spices and garnished with cashew nuts, almonds and raisins
nasi campur – buffet of curried meats, fish and vegetables, served with rice
nasi dagang – dish of unpolished rice steamed with coconut milk and served with a variety of curries; from Terengganu, on the east coast of the peninsula
nasi goreng – fried rice, often topped with a fried egg and served with prawn crackers
nasi kandar – a *mamak* (Indian Muslim) speciality of rice served with a selection of curries
nasi kerabu – a Malay dish of blue-tinted rice topped with bean sprouts, fresh herbs and toasted grated coconut
nasi kunyit – rice soaked in water with turmeric, cooked with coconut milk
nasi lemak – rice boiled in coconut milk, served with fried *ikan bilis*, peanuts, half a hard-boiled egg, *sambal* and an optional curry dish
nasi minyak – 'oil rice', or rice cooked with *ghee*, margarine and dry spices, topped with raisins and nuts
nasi padang – Indonesian meal of rice accompanied by a selection of curries, vegetables and *sambal*
onde-onde – *pandan*-scented glutinous rice-flour balls filled with palm sugar and rolled in fresh grated coconut
pan meen – wheat-flour pasta cut into thick strips or torn by hand into pieces; served 'dry' topped with chopped pork and *ikan bilis*, or 'wet' in meat broth with green vegetables
pat poh peng – iced infusion of Chinese medicinal herbs sweetened with rock and brown sugar
pecel jawa – see *gado gado*

popiah – fresh, or fried, spring roll made with wheat-flour wrappers and filled with boiled yam bean, tofu, bean sprouts, and chilli and sweet sauces
pulut panggang – glutinous-rice rolls stuffed with a filling of grated coconut, chopped dried prawns and chilli, and grilled in a banana leaf
putu piring – steamed rice-flour cakes filled with palm sugar and topped with fresh grated coconut
otak-otak – in Penang, a spicy, coconut fish 'mousse' steamed in a banana leaf; in southern Malaysia, a spicy fish sausage grilled in a coconut leaf
raita – side dish of cucumber, yogurt and mint
rasam – spicy-and-sour soup to accompany a *thali* meal
rendang – spicy, aromatic dry coconut curry of beef or chicken
rogan josh – stewed mutton in a rich sauce
rojak – Penang-style, a fruit-and-vegetable salad dressed with chilli sauce and black shrimp paste and topped with peanuts; Indian *rojak* is a salad of cucumber and assorted fritters doused in a peanut-based sauce
roti canai – unleavened flaky bread cooked with *ghee* on a hotplate; eaten dipped in *dhal* or curry
roti bakar – toast, usually eaten with butter and *kaya* and a half-boiled egg
saag – spicy chopped-spinach dish
sambal belacan – essential Malaysian spicy and fishy dipping sauce made from chillies and shrimp paste
sambal udang – hot curried prawns
sambar – fiery mixture of vegetables, lentils and split peas
samosa – pastry filled with curried vegetables or meat
sang har meen – large freshwater prawns cooked in a gravy flavoured with Chinese rice wine and prawn heads, served over deep-fried noodles
satay – skewered pieces of chicken, beef or mutton grilled and served with a peanut-based dipping sauce
soto ayam – spicy chicken soup with vegetables and potatoes
steamboat – meats, seafood and vegetables cooked at the table by being dipped into a pot of boiling clear stock
sup kambing – mutton ribs (innards and tongue optional) in a spicy, herby broth
tauhu bakar – firm bean curd grilled, split, stuffed with slivered cucumber and bean sprouts and topped with dark sweet sauce and peanuts
teh ais – iced tea with evaporated milk
teh halia – ginger tea
teh kosong – tea without milk or sugar
teh-o – tea without milk
teh tarik – tea made with evaporated milk, which is literally pulled or stretched *(tarik)* from one glass to another
Thali – Indian full set meals consisting of rice or bread with numerous side dishes
tikka – small pieces of meat or fish served off the bone and marinated in yogurt before baking
tong sui – Chinese sweet soups eaten warm, said to be good for the health
tom yam – red chilli–based hot-sour-sweet seafood soup
ulam – selection of raw herbs and vegetables eaten with *sambal*, to accompany a Malay meal
vadai – Indian snack of deep-fried pulse 'donuts' seasoned with chillies and curry leaves
won ton mee – egg vermicelli served with pork dumplings in soup; or 'dry', tossed with dark soy and topped with sliced *char siew*
yee sang – 'lucky' raw-fish salad dressed with sweet sauce, eaten in the weeks leading up to Chinese New Year
yong tau fu – bean curd and vegetables stuffed with fish paste and, sometimes, served in fish-based gravy
yu char kway – Chinese deep-fried crullers, often eaten with *congee*
yu yuan mian – fish-ball soup

Food Glossary

asam – sour
ayam – chicken
ayam kampong – free-range chicken, small and sinewy but preferred over intensively farmed birds for its superior flavour
babi – pork
belacan – fermented prawn paste
brinjal – aubergine (eggplant)
budu – pungent long-fermented anchovy sauce
bhindi – okra (lady's fingers)
bungkus – wrapped (in banana leaf or paper), to go
chapati – griddle-fried wholewheat bread
chilli padi – extremely hot small chilli
choy sum – Chinese mustard greens served steamed with oyster sauce or added to noodle soups
daging – beef
daun kesom – polygonum or 'Vietnamese mint'; a pungent, spicy herb used in Malaysian cooking
daun kunyit – turmeric leaf
daun pisang – banana leaf, often used as a plate in Malaysia
daun salam – fresh herb native to Indonesia, used in some Malay dishes
daun ubi – cassava leaves, usually eaten stir-fried with garlic or cooked with *tempoyak*
Dongbei – northeastern Chinese provinces, known for wheat noodles, dumplings and hearty stir-fries
dow see – fermented, salted black beans
duku – round, yellowish brown-skinned fruits with pearlescent perfumed flesh and a lycheelike flavour
fish sauce – liquid made from fermented anchovies and salt
galangal – gingerlike root used to flavour various dishes
garam – salt
garam masala – sweet, mild mixture of freshly ground spices
garoupa – white fish popular in Southeast Asia, usually steamed Chinese-style with ginger, garlic and soy sauce
ghee – clarified butter
gula melaka – dark sugar made from the sap of the coconut palm flower stalk, usually sold in flat disks or short tubes
hae ko – black sticky-sweet shrimp paste native to Penang
Hainan – southern Chinese island province, origin of many immigrants to Malaysia; Hainanese are known for their skill in the kitchen
Hakka – Chinese dialect group known for their hearty, rustic foods and pork dishes
halal – food prepared according to Muslim dietary laws
haram – forbidden to Muslims
hoisin sauce – thick sweet-spicy sauce made from soya beans, red beans, sugar, flour, vinegar, salt, garlic, sesame, chillies and spices
Hokkien – immigrants from China's Fujian province, known for their seafood dishes; the same word is used to describe their language
ikan bilis – deep-fried anchovies
ikan merah – red snapper
ikan pari – stingray, a popular fish for barbecuing
ikan tenggiri – mackerel, usually used to make the broth for *asam laksa*
itik – duck
jambu – rose apple
kalamansi – tiny, sour lime
kambing – lamb
kangkong – water convolvulus or morning glory; thick-stemmed type of spinach
kecap – soy sauce
kecap manis – sweet soy sauce

kelapa – coconut
kepala ikan – fish-head, usually in curry
kuih muih – Malay sweets
kway teow – flat broad rice noodles
lala – clams
lemak – fatty or rich; often used to describe dishes made with coconut milk or cream
loh see fun – 'rat tail noodles'; short, stubby and chewy rice flour noodles often used in claypot dishes
lombok – type of hot chilli
makanan sayur-sayuran – vegetarian food
mamak – Indian Muslims; *'mamak'* comes from the word for 'uncle' in Tamil
manis – sweet
mee pok – flat noodles made with egg and wheat
mee – noodles
naan – tear-shaped leavened bread baked in a clay oven
nangka – jackfruit, can be eaten as a vegetable in curries and stews
nasi – cooked rice
nenas – pineapple
Nonya – prominent women in the Baba-Nonya community, the descendants of early Chinese male immigrants who settled in Penang, Melaka and Singapore and intermarried with locals (also spelled Nyonya); their cuisine is a fusion of Chinese and Malay ingredients and cooking techniques
pakora – vegetable fritter
pandan – screwpine
pappadam – Indian cracker
pisang goreng – banana fritter
pudina – mint sauce
rempah – pounded paste of chillies and aromatics that is the basis of a Malaysian curry
sambal – a variety of chilli-based sauces
santan – coconut milk
sengkuang – yam bean or jicama
Sichuan – region in south central China famous for its spicy cuisine; also spelt Szechuan
sotong – squid
susu – milk; fresh cow's milk is 'susu kerabau'
tamarind – large bean from the tamarind tree with a brittle shell and a dark brown, sticky pulp; used for its sweet-sour taste
tandoori – Indian style of cooking in which marinated meat is baked in a clay oven
taro – vegetable with leaves like spinach, stalks like asparagus, and a starchy root similar in size and taste to the potato
tau – soy bean
taucu – fermented, salted bean paste
tauhu fa – fresh, smooth bean curd, eaten warm, plain or with sugar syrup
tauhu pok – deep-fried bean curd
tempeh – nutty-tasting 'cakes' of soybeans mixed with starter yeast and allowed to ferment, usually sliced and fried with ingredients such as chillies and *ikan bilis* or stewed in coconut milk with vegetables
tempoyak – fermented durian paste, usually mixed with *budu* and chillies for a dip or cooked with leafy green vegetables
yee mee – crispy deep-fried noodles

Environment

THE LAND

Covering a total of 329,758 sq km, Malaysia consists of two distinct regions. Peninsular Malaysia is the long finger of land extending south from Thailand towards Indonesia. Most large cities – including Kuala Lumpur (KL), Melaka and Penang – are found on the west coast where the land is flat and the soil fertile. The interior is made up of densely forested hills, descending steeply to the sparsely populated east coast.

The other part of the country, comprising over half its area, is Malaysian Borneo, which shares the island of Borneo with the Indonesian state of Kalimantan and the tiny Sultanate of Brunei. Malaysian Borneo is made up of Sabah and Sarawak, and is characterised by dense jungle, with many large river systems. Mt Kinabalu (4101m), in Sabah, is the highest mountain between the Himalayas and New Guinea.

The Encyclopedia of Malaysia: The Environment by Professor Sham Sani Dato, one volume of an excellent series of illustrated encyclopedias, covers everything you need to know about Malaysia's environment.

WILDLIFE

Malaysia is one of the world's so called 'mega-diversity' areas. The Malaysian jungle is believed to be 130 million years old and tropical rainforest covers around 40% of the country (although official figures dispute this). The forests support a staggering amount of life: around 14,500 species of flowering plants and trees, 210 species of mammal, 650 species of bird, 150 species of frog, 80 species of lizard and thousands of types of insect. Although vast tracts of forests have been cleared, some magnificent areas remain mostly protected by a nationwide system of reserves and parks (opposite).

The word orang-utan comes from the Malay phrase for 'Wild Man' or 'Man of the Forest'.

Animals

MAMMALS

Sadly, Malaysia's signature animal, the charismatic orang-utan, is only found in the jungles of Sabah and Sarawak, along with the unique proboscis monkey, a curious creature with a pot belly and (on males) a dangling, pendulous nose. Commonly seen monkeys in Peninsular Malaysia include graceful gibbons; various species of tree-dwelling langurs (leaf monkeys); and pugnacious macaques, the stocky, aggressive monkeys that solicit snacks from tourists at temples and nature reserves. If you are carrying food, watch out for daring raids and be wary of bites – remember these are wild animals and rabies is a potential hazard.

Malaysia has several species of wild cat, most endangered because of hunting and the trade in body parts for traditional medicines. Tigers are now extremely rare, and leopards and black panthers (actually black leopards) are only occasionally spotted on the peninsula. Smaller bay cats, leopard cats and marbled cats are faring slightly better, in part because they need less territory and eat smaller prey (birds and small mammals). You may also run into various species of civet cats, a separate family of predators with vaguely catlike features but longer snouts and shaggier coats.

The Malaysian Nature Society (www.mns.org.my) runs various nature-related projects across the country; see the website for details.

Big herbivores to look out for include rare tapirs, something between a wild pig and a hippo, with a curving snout and a distinctive two-tone colour scheme. Pangolins, also known as scaly anteaters, feed exclusively on ants and termites, and roll into a ball as a form of self defence, making them very vulnerable to hunters. Numerous species of bat flit around the peninsula – most distinctive is the doglike fruit bat, a huge but harmless fruit-eater often seen taking wing from caves and trees at dusk.

BIRDS

Malaysia has a number of distinctive birds – 650 species live on the peninsula alone. Keep an eye out for colourful pittas, kingfishers, trogons and flycatchers, various species of bulbul, handsome long-tailed great arguses (a species of pheasant) and regal hornbills, with their huge, toucanlike beak. You can spot exotic species in many urban parks, but for rarer birds you'll have to head to the jungle – see p61 for some excellent birding hotspots. Another must-see is KL's Bird Park (p82).

REPTILES & AMPHIBIANS

Some 250 species of reptile have been recorded in Malaysia, including 140 species of snake. Cobras and vipers pose a potential risk to trekkers, although the chances of encountering them are low – see p244 for tips for treating snake bites. Large pythons are sometimes seen in national parks and you may also encounter 'flying' snakes, lizards and frogs (all these species glide using wide flaps of skin). Even in city parks, you stand a good chance of running into a monitor lizard, a primitive-looking carrion feeder notorious for consuming domestic cats.

Tropical Marine Life of Malaysia & Singapore, Tropical Birds of Malaysia & Singapore and *Tropical Plants of Malaysia & Singapore* are some of the titles in Periplus Editions' great series of field guides to the plants and animals of Malaysia.

Four species of marine turtle are native to Malaysia: hawksbills, green turtles, olive-ridleys and giant leatherbacks. Although they nest on many Malaysian beaches, all four species are currently listed as endangered (see p58) because of coastal development and the harvesting of turtle eggs for food. To help preserve these magnificent creatures, avoid buying any products made from turtles. You may be able to see turtles nesting near Melaka (p164) but take care to avoid creating bright lights or loud noises that could disturb laying females.

Plants

The wet, tropical climate of this region produces an amazing range of trees, plants and flowers, including such signature species as the carnivorous pitcher plant, numerous orchids and the parasitic rafflesia (or 'corpse flower'), which produces the world's largest flower – a whopping 1m across when fully open. However, vast tracts of rainforests have been cleared to make way for plantations of cash crops such as rubber and palm oil. Just look out of the window on the flight into Kuala Lumpur International Airport and you'll see endless rows of oil palms, introduced by the British from West Africa in the 20th century – see p59 for the environmental implications of palm oil cultivation.

Rafflesia is the world's largest flower – this monster bloom has no stem, leaves or true roots and it gives off a smell of rotten meat to attract flies to carry its pollen to other rafflesia.

NATIONAL PARKS & OTHER PROTECTED AREAS

The British established Malaysia's first national park in 1938 – it now forms part of the Taman Negara National Park at the northern end of the peninsula (see p100 for tours from KL). There are 26 other national parks across the country along with numerous government-protected reserves and sanctuaries for forests, birds, mammals and marine life – however, these conservation areas protect less than 5% of the country's natural habitats.

Parks and reserves to look out for in the area covered by this book include Penang National Park (p207) and Teluk Bahang Forest Reserve (p206) near Penang, the Forest Research Institute of Malaysia (p132) and Templer Park (p132) near KL, and Hutan Rekreasi Air Keroh (p163) near Melaka. Accommodation or camping sites are provided at most reserves and national parks but transport and accommodation is increasingly being handled by private tour companies. There are also several marine parks, including the reef conservation area at Pulau Payer, accessible on snorkelling and diving trips from Penang – see p185.

LAST CHANCE TO SEE...

Habitat loss is pushing several of Malaysia's best-loved species towards extinction. The **Malaysian Nature Society** (www.mns.org.my) has extensive resources on endangered species in the region. The following animals are among the most at risk:

- Around 11,300 orang-utans are thought to live in the forests of Sabah and Sarawak, but their future is threatened by habitat loss; the population has declined by 40% in the last 20 years. The **Orangutan Foundation** (www.orangutan.org.uk) supports conservation projects in Malaysia and Borneo.
- The Sumatran rhinoceros is found only in a few isolated areas of Sabah and Peninsular Malaysia. The last survey by the **World Wildlife Fund** (WWF; www.wwfmalaysia.org) in Sabah found evidence of just 13 individuals. The nonprofit organisation **SOS Rhino** (www.sosrhino.org) is campaigning to save the species from extinction.
- Malaysia's 1200 Asian elephants are severely threatened by habitat loss and competition with farmers for land. This competition frequently leads to elephants being shot. Tours run from Kuala Lumpur (KL) to the Kuala Gandah Elephant Conservation Centre (see p100) where you can see some of these wonderfully intelligent creatures up close.
- Indo-Chinese (Malaysian) tigers were only given legal protection in 1976, and today just 500 are thought to remain in the forests of Peninsular Malaysia. Hunting for pelts and body parts for traditional medicines and competition for land with humans (where tigers are invariably the loser) are the main threats facing the tiger. **WWF Malaysia** (www.wwfmalaysia.org) is working in several areas of Peninsular Malaysia to reduce the risk of conflict between humans and tigers. You can also find information on the **Save the Tiger Fund** (www.savethetigerfund.org) website.
- The clouded leopard is even rarer than the Malaysian tiger, but for broadly the same reasons. A US-based project aimed at raising awareness about the endangered status of this beautiful big cat is the **Clouded Leopard Project** (www.cloudedleopard.org).
- All of Malaysia's turtle species are threatened by marine pollution, accidental (and deliberate) capture in drift nets and massive harvesting of turtle eggs in coastal villages. The number of giant leatherback turtles is believed to have fallen by a shocking 98% since the 1950s. To make a donation or volunteer to help sea turtle conservation, check out the website of **Turtle Aid Malaysia** (www.umt.edu.my/turtle/).
- Dugongs are found off the southern end of the peninsula; these rare marine herbivores are threatened by the destruction of the sea grass beds they feed on, as well as hunting and injury from fishing nets and boat propellers. The UN is now working with local oil companies to help conserve the dugong, in conjunction with WWF Malaysia and other organisations.

ENVIRONMENTAL ISSUES

Malaysia treads a delicate line when it comes to the environment. On one level the government wants to appear to be doing something, particularly with the growing concern about atmospheric pollution caused by forest fires in neighbouring Indonesia. At the same time, the government has promised the population a certain standard of development. Malaysia's big problem has always been balancing development with environmental protection. Ever since the colonial era, the Malaysian economy has depended on plantation crops such as palm oil and rubber, and on destructive industries such as mining, logging and petroleum extraction. Big business still has the ear of government when it comes to environmental decisions.

Forest Management & Logging

Logging in Malaysia is reckoned to generate at least US$4.5 billion a year, employing hundreds of thousands of Malaysians. It also wreaks untold ecological damage. The **World Rainforest Information Portal** (www.rainforestweb.org) reports that Malaysia's deforestation rate is over 2.4% annually. The government produces more favourable statistics, but the scientific consensus is that 60% of Malaysia's rainforests have already been logged. In the process, dozens of species have been driven towards extinction and hundreds of thousands of tribal peoples have been displaced from their ancestral lands.

Wild Malaysia: The Wildlife & Scenery of Peninsular Malaysia by Junaidi Payne and Gerald Cubitt is a lavishly illustrated, large-format coffee-table guide to Malaysian wildlife and habitats.

Government initiatives such as the National Forestry Policy have reduced deforestation by a third to 900 sq km a year, and the long-term aim is to reduce the timber harvest by 10% year on year. However, this still means that Malaysia is losing an area of forest three times larger than Kuala Lumpur every year. One positive development has been the creation of several new national parks in Sarawak and Sabah.

Close to KL, the Forestry Research Institute of Malaysia (p132) is pioneering work into new ways of preserving and regenerating Malaysia's rainforests. You can visit in person and help support its work on a day trip from KL. For more information on government forestry projects visit the **Forestry Department** (www.forestry.gov.my) website.

Overdevelopment

During the Mahathir era, Malaysia embarked on a massive campaign of construction and industrialisation. Huge swathes of countryside were sacrificed to make space for housing estates, factories and highways, displacing many indigenous communities from their ancestral lands. KL developers are increasingly setting their sights on cheap rural land in Selangor – the new capital in Putrajaya has gobbled up 4932 hectares of prime agricultural land. Although the national desire for construction shows some signs of slowing down, new projects are still getting the green light with little concern for the environmental impact.

Proving every argument has two sides, the Palm Oil Truth Foundation (www.palmoiltruthfoundation.com) is campaigning to debunk accepted theories on climate change and the environment, including the alleged negative effects of palm oil production.

The construction of new hydroelectric dams is another worrying issue. Although the new dams have the capacity to generate huge amounts of electricity, this has to be balanced against the social and environmental impact. Problems have been most acute on Borneo, but large numbers of Orang Asli

PALM OIL: ONE STEP FORWARD, TWO STEPS BACK?

When scientists first discovered that palm oil could be refined into biodiesel, it looked like a massive environmental breakthrough. A bright future loomed, where cars would run on environmentally friendly palm-oil diesel instead of fossil fuels, significantly reducing the amount of CO_2 being released into the atmosphere. This was particularly good news for Malaysia, the world's largest producer of palm oil and also a major global supplier of crude oil. Unfortunately, nothing environmental is ever quite as simple as it seems.

The Malaysian government seized on biodiesel as a way to bring down fuel prices, and dramatically increased the area of land approved for palm-oil plantations. In 2003 the campaigning organisation **Friends of the Earth** (www.foe.org) reported that palm-oil production was responsible for 87% of deforestation in Malaysia. The idea that biodiesel is a 'clean fuel' is further undermined by the massive use of pesticides and fertilisers in palm-oil production. In Indonesia, land clearance for palm-oil plantations is thought to be responsible for 75% of forest fires (see p60) and palm-oil production also produces thousands of tonnes of polluting sludge, which is dumped unceremoniously into rivers or the sea, disrupting aquatic ecosystems.

Unfortunately, consumers around the world are unwittingly contributing to the problem by buying palm-oil derivatives – it crops up in products as diverse as chocolate, crisps and toothpaste. Various environmental organisations, including Friends of the Earth, are lobbying Asian governments to adopt sustainable farming practices for palm-oil production, but with the current enthusiasm for biofuels, this may be too little, too late for Malaysia's rainforests.

(original people) have been displaced by the dam project at Kuala Kubu Baru, north of KL. For the latest information check www.xlibris.de/magickriver, the website of writer, cartoonist and activist Antares.

Another side effect of forest clearing for development has been an increase in flooding and landslides. Construction rules were tightened in 1993 after a 12-storey building collapsed in Selangor, but development continues unabated in the cooler highlands close to KL. The community-based organisation **Regional Environmental Awareness Cameron Highlands** (Reach; www.reach.org.my) is campaigning to protect the threatened Cameron Highlands from the concrete trucks.

The local Friends of the Earth organisation is Sahabat Alam Malaysia (SAM); check out its various campaigns on www.foe-malaysia.org.my.

Haze

Large parts of Southeast Asia face an ongoing threat from 'haze' – the polluting smoke from fires created as a result of slash-and-burn architecture in the Indonesian states of Kalimantan and Sumatra. The haze has been linked to an increase in respiratory disease and other health complaints, leading the government to declare a state of emergency in parts of the Klang Valley in 2005. The haze is at its worst in southern parts of Malaysia, usually around September and October, just before the rainy season.

Activities

Kuala Lumpur (KL), Melaka and Penang have no shortage of interesting ways to keep you amused during your stay. For nature buffs, there are jungle treks and bird-spotting tours. Thrill-seekers can go rock climbing, mountain biking or white-water rafting, while grown-up waterbabies can don masks and fins to explore the underwater world on the coral reefs near Penang. More sedate activities include golf and boat cruises on rivers and lakes. Then there are more esoteric activities for the mind and body – meditation, yoga and a host of pampering spa treatments.

OUTDOOR ACTIVITIES

It's hard to ignore the great outdoors in Malaysia – at points the rainforest extends right into the city. This is great news for nature fans and adrenaline junkies. Within an hour's drive of central KL, you can rock climb, mountain bike, trek and swim in jungle pools. Penang is another excellent centre for wilderness activities – the surrounding waters are teeming with fish and half the island is covered by jungle. There are also more leisurely outdoor activities – bird-watching, river cruises and golf. Here are some of the top ways to connect with the great outdoors.

Bird-Watching

Peninsular Malaysia is home to an incredible range of weird and wonderful birdlife, from iridescent flycatchers to the huge Malaysian hornbill. Most tour agents can arrange on-demand bird-watching tours with a guide. Top spots for a bit of birding are listed below.

A good pocket-sized companion for bird-watchers in Malaysia is *A Photographic Guide to Birds of Peninsular Malaysia and Singapore* by GWH Davison and Chew Yen Fook.

KUALA LUMPUR

Numerous wild bird species can be spotted at Bukit Nanas Forest Reserve (p88) in central KL and the Forest Research Institute of Malaysia (FRIM; p132) and Templer Park (p132) just north of the capital. If you don't fancy heading out into the wild unknown, you can see an impressive range of species at KL's excellent Bird Park (p82).

PENANG

Track down white-bellied eagles and 48 other species of bird in Penang National Park (p207) and Teluk Bahang Forest Reserve (p206), both easily accessible from Georgetown. You can also spot many exotic birds on forest walks atop Penang Hill (p202), accessible by the funicular railway. For birding more on-the-beaten-track, try the Penang Bird Park (p213) in Butterworth.

Peninsular Malaysia is home to more than 600 species of birds.

Boating

Boat cruises along the Melaka River are a popular diversion for visitors to Melaka – see p152 for details. The lakes at Putrajaya near KL are another popular spot for cruises (see p131) – take your pick from luxury cruise boats or gondala-like *perahu*. More leisurely boating is possible in many city recreational parks, including Lake Gardens Park (p82) and Taman Tasik Titiwangsa (p93) in KL.

An interesting time to be in Penang is during the annual Penang International Dragon Boat Festival (p171) held in May/June, which is attended by teams from around the world.

The Penang dragon boat races have taken place every year since 1976 – see www.penangdragonboat.com for details.

Diving, Snorkelling & Watersports

Malaysia is famed for its fabulous coral reefs, attracting scuba divers from around the world. Unfortunately, the Strait of Melaka is often too murky for snorkelling or diving. Things are much better over on the east coast of the peninsula, but the west coast does have some good places to witness the underwater world. By far the best snorkelling and diving in the area is at Pulau Payer Marine Park, accessible by boat between Penang and Langkawi – see p185 for details.

Kurt Svrcula's *Diving in Malaysia* is the definitive Malaysia diving guide.

Various beach resort watersports – jet skiing, waterskiing, parasailing – are possible at Batu Ferringhi (p209) on Penang. Freshwater kayaking is possible at the Wetland Park (p131) in Putrajaya near KL.

SAFE & RESPONSIBLE DIVING

Before embarking on a scuba-diving, skin-diving or snorkelling trip, carefully consider the following points to ensure a safe and enjoyable experience:

- If you're scuba diving, obtain a current diving certification card from a recognised scuba diving instructional agency before heading out.
- Be sure you are healthy and feel comfortable diving.
- Obtain reliable information about physical and environmental conditions at the dive site (eg from a reputable local dive operation).
- Be aware of local laws, regulations and etiquette about marine life and the environment.
- Dive only at sites within your realm of experience; if available, engage the services of a competent, professionally trained dive instructor or dive master.
- Be aware that underwater conditions vary significantly from one region, or even site, to another. Seasonal changes can significantly alter any site and dive conditions. These differences influence the way divers dress for a dive and what diving techniques they use.
- Ask about the environmental characteristics that can affect your diving and how locally trained divers deal with these.

Please also consider the following tips when diving and help preserve the ecology and beauty of reefs:

- Never use anchors on the reef, and take care not to ground boats on coral.
- Avoid touching or standing on living marine organisms or dragging equipment across the reef. Polyps can be damaged by even the gentlest contact. If you must hold on to the reef, only touch exposed rock or dead coral.
- Be conscious of your fins. Even without contact, the surge from fin strokes near the reef can damage delicate organisms. Take care not to kick up clouds of sand, which can smother organisms.
- Practise and maintain proper buoyancy control. Major damage can be done by divers descending too fast and colliding with the reef.
- Take great care in underwater caves. Spend as little time within them as possible as your air bubbles may be caught within the roof and thereby leave organisms high and dry. Take turns to inspect the interior of a small cave.
- Do not collect or buy corals or shells or loot marine archaeological sites (mainly shipwrecks).
- Ensure that you take home all your rubbish and any litter you may find as well. Plastics in particular are a serious threat to marine life.
- Do not feed fish.
- Minimise your disturbance of marine animals. Never ride on the backs of turtles.

Golf

Golf is becoming an obsession for the Malaysian middle classes and new courses are springing up all over the country, frequently as part of exclusive private clubs. In fact, clearing land for golf clubs has become a serious environmental issue – golf courses contribute heavily to soil erosion and rainwater run-off, as well as increasing fertiliser and pesticide levels in the local water table.

Many of Malaysia's golf clubs are reserved for members of exclusive country clubs or hotel guests, but there are still some great places for visitors to tee off. Good options to consider include Titiwangsa Golf Club and Kelab Darul Ehsan in KL (p94), the A'Famosa Resort (p165) near Melaka and Bukit Jambul Country Club (p184) near Penang. Club hire is usually available and green fees start at around RM50 for nine holes.

See the website of Golf Malaysia magazine (www.golfmalaysia.com.my) for the low-down on golfing on the peninsula.

Mountain Biking

If the only thing you fear is a flat planet, you can find some wonderfully rugged wilderness trails in the countryside around KL, Melaka and Penang. Visit the website **KL Bike Hash** (www.bikehash.freeservers.com) for tips on mountain biking around Malaysia (including places to rent bikes) and details of upcoming cycle 'hashes' in the hills around Kuala Lumpur.

The most serious bikers bring their own wheels from home, but good-quality mountain bikes are available locally if you'll be sticking around for a while – see p232. The following wilderness areas offer some fantastic opportunities for mountain biking.

KUALA LUMPUR

The best places to ride near KL are Templer Park (p132) and the Forest Research Institute of Malaysia (p132) – both have rugged jungle trails where you can slip and slide, bounce and charge to your heart's content. The parks lie outside the city limits but you can take a commuter train to the edge of town and cycle from there.

MELAKA

In Melaka, Eco Bike Tour (p152) offers interesting guided cycle trips to local *kampung* (villages).

PENANG

Bikes can be hired for local rambles in Penang (see p174) – the Penang International Mountain Bike Challenge in September attracts bikers from across the region. The best places to cycle near Georgetown are the forest trails of Penang National Park (p207), Teluk Bahang Forest Reserve (p206) and Penang Hill (see p202).

Rock Climbing

The limestone cliffs that rise around Kuala Lumpur offer some excellent opportunities for rock climbing, particularly the exposed massifs around the Batu Caves (see p131). Most routes here are bolted, but there's no harm bringing a selection of nuts, hexes, cams and slings and some rigging biners as disposable anchors. Carry plenty of chalk – climbing in the tropics is a sweaty business. See the websites following for information on routes and grades.

Tour operators in KL offer day trips to the Batu Caves area for around RM150 including lunch and climbing gear – see p99 for some suggestions.

For first timers, wall-climbing day trips can be arranged at Pulau Jerejak (p204) near Penang.

Useful climbing web resources:

rockclimbing.com (www.rockclimbing.com/routes/Asia/Malaysia/Kuala_Lumpur)
Wild Asia (www.wildasia.net/main.cfm?page=article&articleID=213)

The World Club Climbing Malaysia website (www.climbingmalaysia.org) has information on indoor and outdoor climbing in Malaysia.

Swimming

Most hotel pools are reserved for guests, but Peninsular Malaysia has some fabulous wet-and-wild theme parks where you can ride the slides and surge the wave pools to your heart's content. All are great for children and most are easily accessible on public transport. In KL, the best choices are Sunway Lagoon (p129) and Desa Waterpark (p130). As well as the water parks, you can splash around in natural jungle pools at the Forest Research Institute of Malaysia (FRIM; p132) and Templer Park (see p132) near KL.

The best places to swim on Penang are the tourist beach at Batu Ferringhi (p209) and the wild beaches and jungle waterholes at Penang National Park (p207). However, note that jellyfish can be a problem for sea swimming. There's also the family-friendly water park at Midlands Park Centre (p188).

Theme Parks

If the moment of anticipation before a roller coaster thunders into the abyss has you reaching for your rosary, skip this section. If not, read on. Peninsular Malaysia has some world-class theme parks with all the usual goofy mascots, fast-food franchises, booths selling tacky souvenirs and vertiginous thrill rides. Malaysian theme parks are well maintained and most offer all-day passes and a good selection of gentle rides for younger children.

KL has the best options. Cosmo's World (p96) has an adrenaline-focused set of rides squeezed into the Berjaya Times Square mall and there are more good theme parks at Sunway Lagoon (p129), Mines Resort City (p130) and Genting Highlands (p133).

For information on water parks, see above.

Walking & Trekking

The jungle encroaches almost into the middle of both KL and Penang, providing some excellent opportunities for old-fashioned jungle trekking. Most of the parks have clearly marked walking trails, picnic areas and waterfalls

SAFETY GUIDELINES FOR WALKING

Before embarking on a walking trip, consider the following points to ensure a safe and enjoyable experience:

- Pay any fees and possess any permits required by local authorities.
- Be sure you are healthy and feel comfortable walking for a sustained period.
- Obtain reliable information about physical and environmental conditions along your intended route (eg from park authorities).
- Be aware of local laws, regulations and etiquette about wildlife and the environment.
- Walk only in regions, and on trails, within your realm of experience.
- Be aware that weather conditions and terrain vary significantly from one region, or even from one trail, to another. Seasonal changes can significantly alter any trails. These differences influence the way walkers dress and the equipment they carry.
- Ask before you set out about the environmental characteristics that can affect your walk and how local, experienced walkers deal with these considerations.

where you can take a dip (suitably clothed of course). Many people just visit on day trips, but some parks allow camping and almost all are easily accessible by public transport. Here are some top spots for trekking.

KUALA LUMPUR

Some of the best places for walks are north of the capital. FRIM (p132) has a huge network of forestry trails and a fabulous suspended walkway in the forest canopy, and there are more rugged jungle tracks in Templer Park (p132).

If you don't have the energy or inclination to carve your own way through the virgin jungle, there are plenty of more leisurely walks. In KL, the Bukit Nanas Forest Reserve (see p88) sits right in the middle of the city, with a series of nature trails that will give you a taste of the jungle without having to leave the city limits.

You might also consider arranging a tour to Taman Negara National Park in the far north of the Peninsula – several agents in KL offer overnight packages (see p99).

MELAKA

Melaka has less unspoiled rainforest than KL or Penang, but you can take a leisurely walk along paved forest trails in Hutan Rekreasi Air Keroh (p163), which also has a treetop canopy walk.

For an introduction to the walking trails of Penang island consult the website http://trails.forestexplorers.com/index.shtml, run by local naturalist Forest Ang.

PENANG

Penang Island has large areas of pristine jungle to explore. Strap on your hiking boots and head to Penang National Park (p207) or Teluk Bahang Forest Reserve (p206), both near the village of Teluk Bahang at the northwest tip of the island. If you don't feel up to the full jungle-Jim experience, a network of easier forest trails snakes over Penang Hill (p202), accessible from Georgetown by funicular railway.

White-Water Rafting

Malaysia has some excellent rivers for white-water rafting but only a handful are accessible from KL, Melaka and Penang. Tour operators in KL offer full-day rafting trips on the Grade I to Grade III waters of the Sungai Kampar (Kampar River) in Perak for around RM255 per person – see p99 for details.

INDOOR ACTIVITIES

As well as enjoying the great outdoors, don't overlook the relaxing effects of the great indoors. Spa treatments, yoga and meditation are popular all over Asia and Malaysia is no exception. KL has by far the biggest selection of spas and therapy centres, but you can also find some deliciously indulgent spas at luxury hotels in Melaka and Penang.

Meditation & Yoga

First introduced by Indian migrants in the colonial era, yoga is a popular leisure activity in Malaysia. As well as the traditional yoga centres attached to ashrams and Hindu religious centres, you'll find numerous spas offering yoga and meditation classes, often modified to appeal to first-time yoga practitioners. Here are the best places to try.

Several cultural centres in KL offer courses in traditional forms of meditation, yoga and t'ai chi (p99). There are also a number of modern yoga centres offering various styles of yoga for beginners as well as for more advanced practitioners (p95).

RESPONSIBLE TREKKING

To help preserve the ecology and beauty of Malaysia's countryside, consider the following tips when trekking.

Rubbish

- Carry out all your rubbish. Don't overlook easily forgotten items, such as silver paper, orange peel, cigarette butts and plastic wrappers. Empty packaging should be stored in a dedicated rubbish bag. Make an effort to carry out rubbish left by others.
- Never bury your rubbish: digging disturbs soil and ground cover and encourages erosion. Buried rubbish will likely be dug up by animals, who may be injured or poisoned by it. It may also take years to decompose.
- Minimise waste by taking minimal packaging and no more food than you will need. Take reusable containers or stuff sacks.
- Sanitary napkins, tampons, condoms and toilet paper should be carried out despite the inconvenience. They burn and decompose poorly.

Human Waste Disposal

- Contamination of water sources by human faeces can lead to the transmission of all sorts of nasties. Where there is a toilet, please use it. Where there is none, bury your waste. Dig a small hole 15cm (6in) deep and at least 100m (320ft) from any watercourse. Cover the waste with soil and a rock.
- Ensure that these guidelines are applied to a portable toilet tent if one is being used by your trekking party. Encourage all party members, including porters, to use the site.

Washing

- Don't use detergents or toothpaste in or near watercourses, even if they are biodegradable.
- For personal washing, use biodegradable soap and a water container (or even a lightweight, portable basin) at least 50m (160ft) away from the watercourse. Disperse the waste water widely to allow the soil to filter it fully.
- Wash cooking utensils 50m (160ft) from watercourses using a scourer or sand instead of detergent.

Erosion

- Hillsides and mountain slopes, especially at high altitudes, are prone to erosion. Stick to existing trails and avoid short-cuts.

Penang's Trisula Yoga school (p187) offers well-respected six-week training courses in hatha yoga and reiki. In Melaka, the Renaissance Melaka Hotel (p156) is one of several upmarket hotels offering yoga classes for guests.

The website www.yogabasics.com is an excellent online guide to the basics of yoga practice.

Spa Treatments

Riding an international wave of enthusiasm for wellness and traditional therapies, Malaysia is going spa crazy. Most big hotels and resorts have upmarket spas offering the full range of massages, rubs and marinades, and many malls have their own private spas where you can escape for an dose of self-indulgence. Each of Malaysia's ethnic groups has introduced its own forms of traditional medicine, so local spas offer everything from Chinese reflexology to Indian Ayurveda (herbal medicine) and Malay traditional massage. Wellness is no longer a girls-only affair; many of the big resort

- If a well-used trail passes through a mud patch, walk through the mud so as not to increase the size of the patch.
- Avoid removing the plant life that keeps topsoil in place.

Fires & Low-Impact Cooking

- Don't depend on open fires for cooking. Cutting wood for fires in popular trekking areas can cause rapid deforestation. Cook on a light-weight kerosene, alcohol or Shellite (white gas) stove and avoid those powered by disposable butane gas canisters.
- If you are trekking with a guide and porters, supply stoves for the whole team. In alpine areas, ensure that all members are outfitted with enough clothing so that fires are not a necessity for warmth.
- If you patronise local accommodation, select those places that do not use wood fires to heat water or cook food.
- Fires may be acceptable below the tree line in areas that get very few visitors. If you light a fire, use an existing fireplace. Don't surround fires with rocks. Use only dead, fallen wood. Remember the adage 'the bigger the fool, the bigger the fire'. Use minimal wood, just what you need for cooking. In huts, leave wood for the next person.
- Ensure that you fully extinguish a fire after use. Spread the embers and flood them with water.

Wildlife Conservation

- Do not engage in or encourage hunting. It is illegal in all parks and reserves unless you are a member of an indigenous tribal community in the area.
- Don't buy items made from endangered species; if in doubt, avoid all products made from wild animals.
- Don't attempt to exterminate animals in huts. In wild places, they are likely to be protected native animals.
- Discourage the presence of wildlife by not leaving food scraps behind you. Place gear out of reach and tie packs to rafters or trees.
- Do not feed the wildlife as this can lead to animals becoming dependent on hand-outs, and can create unbalanced populations and problems with disease.

Environmental Organisations

- The **Malaysian Nature Society** (www.mns.org.my) is the main organisation promoting conservation in Malaysia – see the website for details of current environmental issues to consider.

and hotel spas offer dedicated spa treatments for men as well as women. Here are some of the options.

Malay traditional massage came to Malaysia from Java. Unlike Thai or Chinese massage, Malay massage makes extensive use of *minyak* (herbal oils).

KUALA LUMPUR

The capital has a fabulous selection of luxury spas, plus plenty of more accessible massage and reflexology centres that won't cost you an arm and a leg. Another interesting option here is to visit a blind masseur at one of the rehabilitation centres for the blind in Brickfields. For more on all these options, see the boxed text on p95.

MELAKA

Melaka has a number of spas and therapy centres offering reflexology, traditional Chinese treatments and massages – see p148.

PENANG

There are spas are several resorts on Penang Island, including the Jerejak Resort & Spa (p204) on Pulau Jerejak and the Grand Plaza Park Royal (p211) and Shangri-La Rasa Sayang Resort (p211). There are also a few reflexology/massage places in Batu Ferringhi (p209).

Kuala Lumpur

Kuala Lumpur – KL to its friends – is more than just a capital city: it is a monument to Malaysian ingenuity and determination. From humble beginnings as a tin-mining shanty town, KL has evolved into a 21st-century metropolis, dominated by the tallest skyscrapers in Southeast Asia and flush with the proceeds of international trade and commerce. Over the years, KL has faced its share of challenges but nothing has succeeded in suppressing the determination of locals to make KL, and Malaysia, a leader among Asian tiger economies.

The marketing slogan for the Malaysian tourist board is 'truly Asia' and nowhere is this more true than in the capital. KL is every inch the Asian cyber-city: historic temples and mosques rub shoulders with space-age towers and shopping malls; traders' stalls are piled high with pungent durians and counterfeit DVDs; and locals sip cappuccino in wi-fi–enabled coffee hops or feast at bustling streetside hawker stalls serving food from across the continent.

The most striking thing about KL from a visitor's perspective is its remarkable cultural diversity. Ethnic Malays, Chinese prospectors, Indian migrants and British colonials all helped carve the city out of the virgin jungle, and each group has left its indelible mark on the capital. Eating, shopping and nightlife are undeniable highlights of any visit to KL, but don't restrict yourself to the city – there are numerous parks and monuments dotted around KL that make easy day trips for a break from the hustle and bustle.

HIGHLIGHTS

- Giddying views from the **Skybridge** (p86) at the Petronas Towers or the **Menara KL** (p88)
- Feasting in KL's fabulous **mamak restaurants** (p110)
- Shopping till you drop at KL's city-sized **shopping malls** (p122) – bring the platinum card!
- Taking in the temples and markets of **Chinatown** (p76) and the colonial architecture of **Merdeka Square** (p80)
- Exploring the peaceful Lake Gardens – don't miss the **Bird Park** (p82) and the **Islamic Arts Museum** (p83)
- Hiking up the 272 steps to the **Batu Caves** (p131)

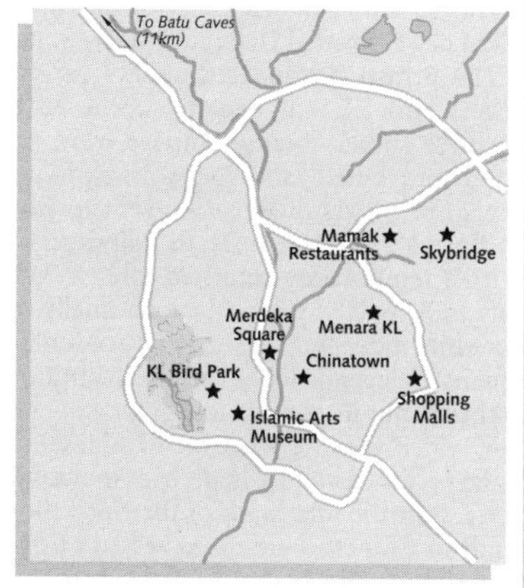

TELEPHONE CODE: 03	POPULATION: 1.8 MILLION	AREA: 243 SQ KM

HISTORY

The founding of KL was almost an accident. In 1857, 87 Chinese prospectors in search of tin landed at the meeting point of the Klang and Gombak rivers and set up camp, naming the spot Kuala Lumpur, meaning 'muddy confluence'. Within a month all but 17 of the prospectors had died of malaria and other tropical diseases, but the tin they discovered in Ampang attracted more miners and KL quickly became a brawling, noisy, violent boomtown, ruled over by so-called 'secret societies', a network of Chinese criminal gangs.

As in other parts of the Malay peninsula, the local sultan appointed a proxy (known as Kapitan China) to bring the unruly Chinese fortune-seekers and their secret societies into line. The successful candidate, Yap Ah Loy (Kapitan China from 1868 to '85), took on the task with such ruthless relish that he's now credited as the founder of KL. According to legend, Yap Ah Loy was able to keep the peace with just six policemen, such was the respect for his authority in the Chinese community.

Loy had only just established control when local sultans went to war over the throne of Perak and its tin mines, marking the start of the Malay Civil War. KL was swept up in the conflict and burnt to the ground in 1881. This allowed the British government representative, Frank Swettenham, to push through a radical new town plan which transferred the central government from Klang to KL. By 1886 a railway line linked KL to Klang. A year later a new city was constructed in fire-resistant brick, and in 1896 KL became the capital of the newly formed Federated Malay States.

The British surrendered Malaya early in WWII and KL was brutally occupied by Japanese forces. Many Chinese were tortured and killed, and many Indians and British prisoners of war were sent to work on Burma's notorious 'Death Railway'. The British temporarily returned after WWII, only to be ousted when Malaysia finally declared its independence in 1957 at Merdeka Square (Independence Square). KL continued to thrive, but its confidence took a knock in 1969 when race riots between Chinese and Malays claimed hundreds, perhaps thousands, of lives. In the aftermath of the riots, thousands of Chinese were dispossessed of their homes and the Muslim Malay community consolidated its control over the army, police and political administration.

The city officially became the Federal Territory of Kuala Lumpur when it was ceded by the sultan of Selangor in 1974. Its mayor and councillors are appointed on the recommendation of the government, which is dominated by Malay politicians. There's little accountability and a job on the council is largely seen by locals as license to print money, not least because KL is Malaysia's most prosperous and populous city.

In 1996, Prime Minister Mahathir Mohammed approved the construction of a new political capital 20km south of KL at Putrajaya (p130). Although only 50,000 of the 330,000 residents planned for Putrajaya have moved into their new homes, the budget for the project has already exceeded US$5 billion. Putrajaya was made the official seat of the Malaysian government in 1999. Since the turn of the millennium, Kuala Lumpur has been in the news more for demonstrations than innovation – city police used tear gas and water cannons to disperse antidiscrimination protests by thousands of ethnic Indians in 2007 and 2008, arresting many protesters under Malaysia's draconian security laws.

ORIENTATION

Although this is one of the more manageable Asian capitals, KL is divided into a series of separate neighbourhoods by a network of multilane highways and railway lines. As a result, getting from A to B can involve numerous underpasses, bridges and road crossings. You may find that it's easier to travel by public transport, even over short distances. One exception to this rule is the built-up area around the Kuala Lumpur City Centre (KLCC) – walking is often quicker than changing lines on KL's poorly integrated rapid transit system (see p126).

The colonial heart of KL is Merdeka Square, near the confluence of the two rivers from which the city takes its name. Just northeast of Merdeka Square is Little India, a bustling neighbourhood of Indian-owned shops and restaurants, while further south is Chinatown, noteworthy for its cheap accommodation, night market, temples and long-distance bus station. West of Chinatown (across a maze of flyovers and railway tracks) are the peaceful Lake Gardens, home to many of KL's best-known tourist attractions. South of the Lake Gardens is the ethnically mixed neighbourhood of Brickfields, where you'll find KL Sentral, the main long-distance train station (which replaced the historic old train station on the eastern edge of Lake Gardens). This is the place to come for trains to Melaka, Penang and Singapore, and for local buses and trains to the international airport and low-cost carrier terminal.

New KL is a space-age jumble of skyscrapers, shopping centres and monorail tracks, centred on the KLCC development and Petronas Towers. The business district is loosely bound by Jln Ampang, Jln Sultan Ismail, Jln Bukit Bintang and Jln Tun Razak. The main area for accommodation downtown is the Golden Triangle, which has long since expanded from its original boundaries of Jln Imbi, Jln Raja Chulan and Jln Sultan Ismail. On the eastern edge of the business district, Jln Tun Razak provides access to the National Library, National Theatre, National Art Gallery and Taman Tasik Titiwangsa. North of the centre is Kampung Baru, a Malay neighbourhood dominated by traditional wooden houses, and further west is Chow Kit, a sprawling district of markets and shophouses, strung out along Jln Tuanku A Rahman (commonly called Jln TAR). Nearby Asian Heritage Row (Jln Doraiswamy) is crammed with restaurants and clubs.

The relatively small central area is surrounded by burgeoning suburbs, some of which are becoming tourist attractions in their own right for their excellent restaurants and nightlife. Two places to clock for a lively night out are Bangsar Baru, southwest from KL Sentral, and Desa Sri Hartamas, 7km west (a half-hour taxi or bus ride) from the centre.

20km south of KL is Putrajaya, the new administrative capital of Malaysia, worth a visit for its parks and modern architecture. Between Putrajaya and the centre are the Mines and Sunway Lagoon, two ostentatious entertainment resorts built on reclaimed industrial land. Kuala Lumpur International Airport (KLIA) and the Low Cost Carrier-Terminal (LCC-T) are about 73km south of KL, while Berjaya Air operates a handful of flights from Sultan Abdul Aziz Shah Airport, 20km west of the centre.

North of KL are the famous Batu Caves, a major pilgrimage destination for Malaysian

KUALA LUMPUR (KL) IN...

Two Days

With just two days, you'll need to move fast. Get to the Kuala Lumpur City Centre (KLCC) early to queue for one of the limited free tickets for the **skybridge** (p86) of the Petronas Towers. Get in some retail therapy at the **Suria KLCC mall** (p86) then head to the **Menara KL** (p88) for even better views and a stroll through the surrounding forest reserve. Next, head over to Chinatown to pay your respects at the **Masjid Jamek** (p76) and see the colonial buildings around **Merdeka Square** (p80). Drop in on some of the Hindu and Taoist temples in **Chinatown** (p76), then browse the boisterous Jalan Petaling **street market** (p77) and the craft stalls in **Central Market** (p77). In the evening, dive into **Jalan Alor** (p106) for some tasty Chinese street food, then sample one of the bars or pubs near the Golden Triangle along **Changkat Bukit Bintang** (p116).

On day two, gaze in awe at exquisite Islamic artworks housed in the **Islamic Arts Museum** (p83) and be deafened by the avian orchestra in the Lake Garden's **Bird Park** (p82). Grab an Indian vegetarian lunch in **Little India** (p108), then get a dose of history at the **National Museum** (p89). Next, head over Jln Bukit Bintang to see the extravagant **Starhill Gallery** (p122). Finish up with a fabulous hawker-style dinner at **Nasi Kandar Pelita** (p110), located by the KLCC.

One Week

With more time to spare, take three days to explore the sights listed above. On day four, head out to the **Batu Caves** (p131) and **Zoo Negara** (p131) or **Orang Asli Museum** (p131). On day five, visit the **Pudu Market** (p91) or Chow Kit's **Bazaar Baru** (p93), and explore the sleepy backstreets of **Kampung Baru** (p93). Start day six at a theme park – **Sunway Lagoon** (p129) is the best of the bunch. Use the afternoon for a stroll around **Taman Tasik Titiwangsa** (p93), then head out to **Bangsar Baru** (p113) or **Desa Sri Hartamas** (p114) for an extravagant supper. On day seven, visit the striking **Masjid Negara** (p82) and squeeze in some last-minute shopping at KL's malls (p122). In the evening, go all out at the clubs and bars on **Asian Heritage Row** (p120).

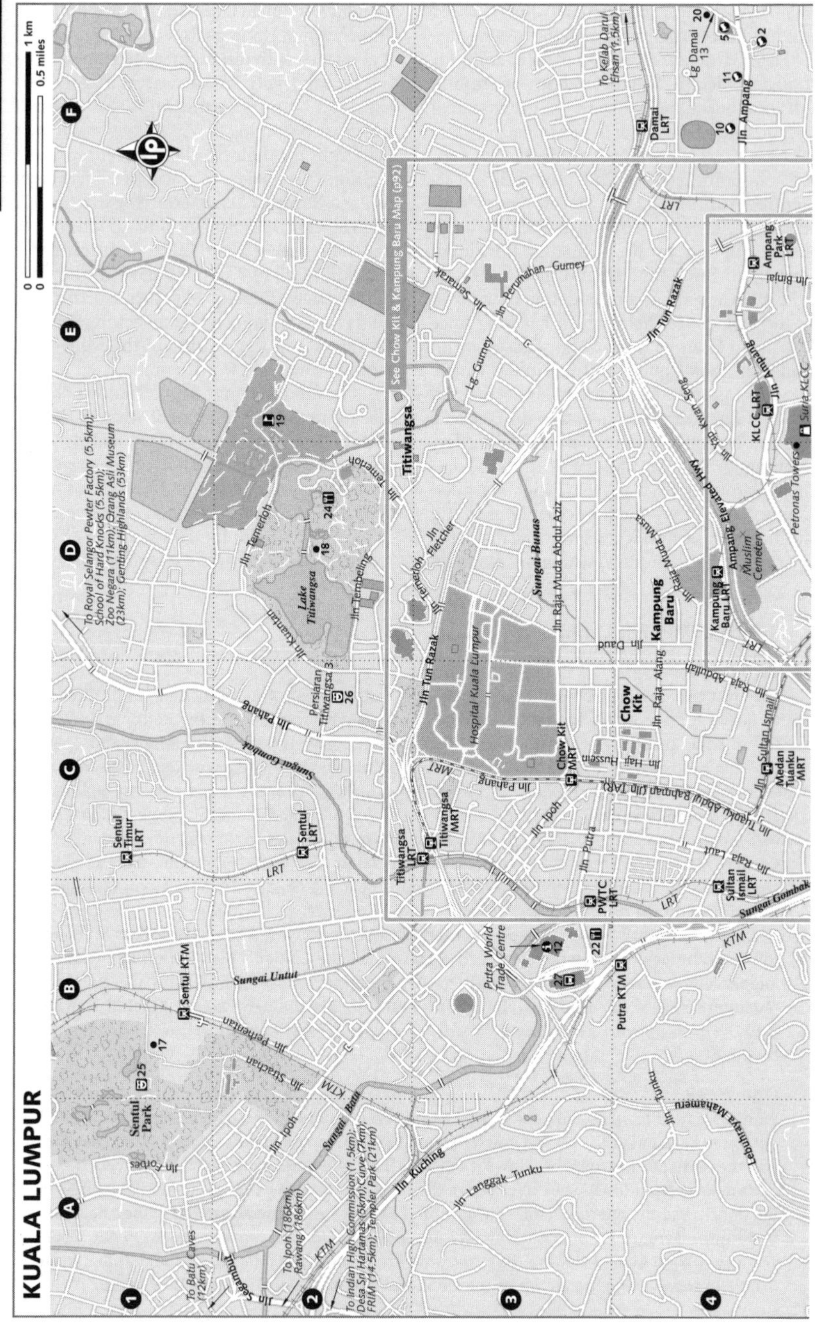
KUALA LUMPUR
See Chow Kit & Kampung Baru Map (p92)
Sentul Park
Sentul KTM
Sentul Timur LRT
Sentul LRT
Lake Titiwangsa
Titiwangsa
Titiwangsa LRT
Titiwangsa MRT
Hospital Kuala Lumpur
Chow Kit
Chow Kit MRT
Kampung Baru
Kampung Baru LRT
Sungai Bunus
Muslim Cemetery
Petronas Towers
Suria KLCC
KLCC LRT
Ampang Park LRT
Damai LRT
Putra World Trade Centre
PWTC LRT
Putra KTM
Sultan Ismail LRT
Medan Tuanku MRT
Jln Tun Razak
Jln Pahang
Jln Ipoh
Jln Kuching
Jln Ampang
Ampang Elevated Hwy
Jln Tuanku Abdul Rahman (Jln TAR)
To Royal Selangor Pewter Factory (5.5km); School of Hard Knocks (5.5km); Zoo Negara (11km); Orang Asli Museum (23km); Genting Highlands (53km)
To Batu Caves (12km)
To Ipoh (186km); Rawang (186km)
To Indian High Commission (1.5km); Desa Sri Hartamas (5km); Curve (7km); FRIM (14.5km); Templer Park (21km)
To Kelab Darul Ehsan (1.5km)
0 1 km
0 0.5 miles

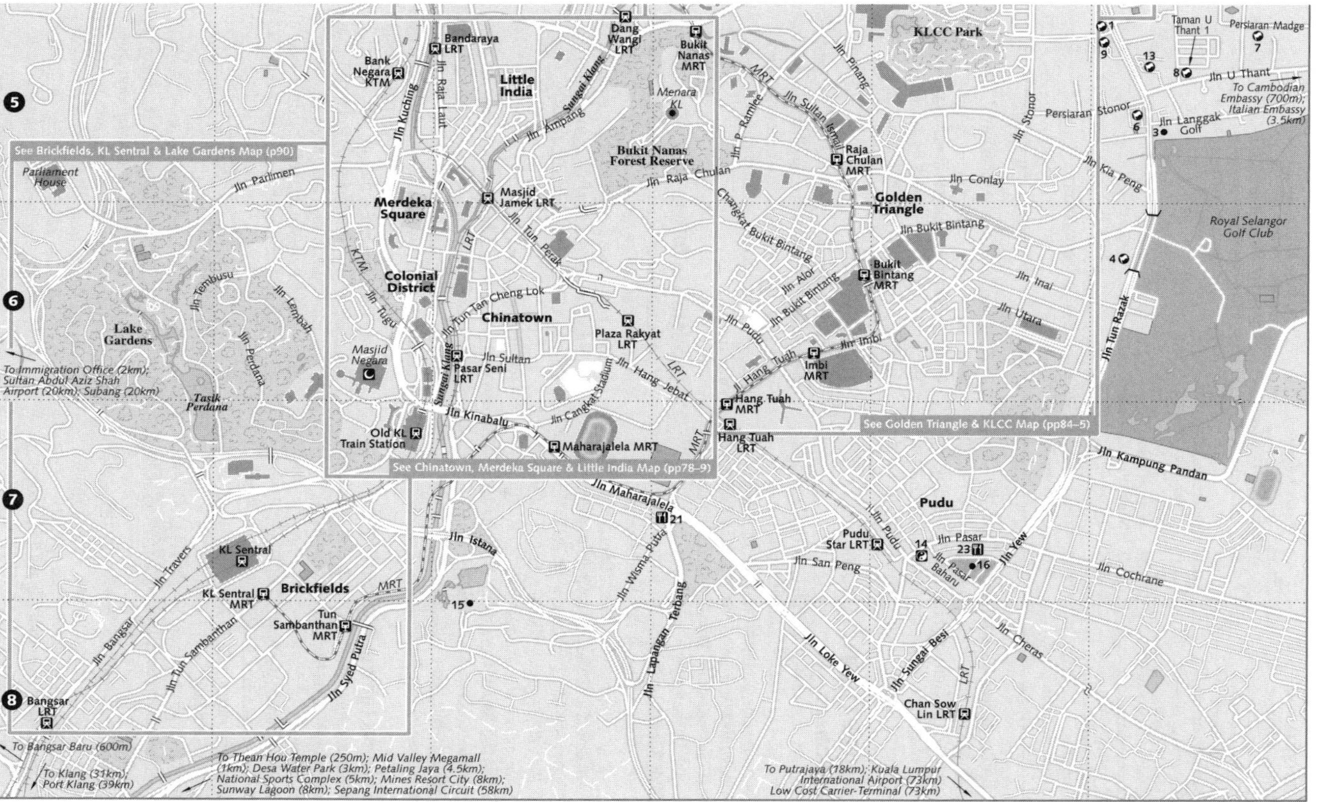

KLCC Park
Golden Triangle
Little India
Merdeka Square
Colonial District
Chinatown
Pudu
Brickfields
Lake Gardens
Royal Selangor Golf Club
Bukit Nanas Forest Reserve
Menara KL
Masjid Negara
Tasik Perdana
Parliament House
KL Sentral
Raja Chulan MRT
Bukit Bintang MRT
Imbi MRT
Hang Tuah MRT
Hang Tuah LRT
Bukit Nanas MRT
Dang Wangi LRT
Bandaraya LRT
Bank Negara KTM
Masjid Jamek LRT
Plaza Rakyat LRT
Pasar Seni LRT
Maharajalela MRT
Old KL Train Station
KL Sentral MRT
Tun Sambanthan MRT
Bangsar LRT
Pudu Star LRT
Chan Sow Lin LRT
Jln Tun Razak
Jln Kampung Pandan
Jln Cochrane
Jln Yew
Jln Cheras
Jln Sungai Besi
Jln Loke Yew
Jln Pudu
Jln Pasar
Jln Pasar Baharu
Jln San Peng
Jln Lapangan Terbang
Jln Wisma Putra
Jln Maharajalela
Jln Istana
Jln Syed Putra
Jln Tun Sambanthan
Jln Travers
Jln Bangsar
Jln Kuching
Jln Raja Laut
Jln Tugu
Jln Parlimen
Jln Lembah
Jln Perdana
Jln Tembusu
Jln Kinabalu
Jln Tun Tan Cheng Lok
Jln Sultan
Jln Hang Jebat
Jln Cangkat Stadium
Jln Tun Perak
Jln Ampang
Sungai Klang
Jln Raja Chulan
Changkat Bukit Bintang
Jln Bukit Bintang
Jln Alor
Jln Hang Tuah
Jln Imbi
Jln P Ramlee
Jln Sultan Ismail
Jln Pinang
Jln Conlay
Jln Utara
Jln Inai
Jln Stonor
Persiaran Stonor
Jln Kia Peng
Jln Langgak Golf
Jln U Thant
Taman U Thant 1
Persiaran Madge
MRT
LRT
KTM
To Cambodian Embassy (700m); Italian Embassy (3.5km)
To Putrajaya (18km); Kuala Lumpur International Airport (73km); Low Cost Carrier-Terminal (73km)
To Thean Hou Temple (250m); Mid Valley Megamall (1km); Desa Water Park (3km); Petaling Jaya (4.5km); National Sports Complex (5km); Mines Resort City (8km); Sunway Lagoon (8km); Sepang International Circuit (58km)
To Bangsar Baru (600m)
To Klang (31km); Port Klang (39km)
To Immigration Office (2km); Sultan Abdul Aziz Shah Airport (20km); Subang (20km)
See Golden Triangle & KLCC Map (pp84–5)
See Chinatown, Merdeka Square & Little India Map (pp78–9)
See Brickfields, KL Sentral & Lake Gardens Map (p90)
5
6
7
8

INFORMATION

- Brunei Embassy....1 F5
- Canadian Embassy....(see 1)
- Chinese Embassy....2 F4
- German Embassy....(see 1)
- Goethe Institut....3 F5
- Indonesian Embassy....4 F6
- Irish Embassy....5 F4
- Japanese Embassy....6 F5
- Laos Embassy....7 F5
- Myanmar Embassy....8 F5
- Netherlands Embassy....(see 5)
- Singapore Embassy....9 F5
- Spanish Embassy....10 F4
- Thai Embassy....11 F4
- Tourism Malaysia....12 B3
- USA Embassy....13 F5

SIGHTS & ACTIVITIES

- Choon Wan Kong....14 E7
- Istana Negara....15 C8
- Pudu Market....16 E7
- Sentul Park Koi Centre....17 B1
- Taman Tasik Titiwangsa....18 D2
- Titiwangsa Golf Club....19 E2
- Yogshakti....20 F4

EATING

- Café Café....21 D7
- Medan Hang Tuah....22 B3
- Pusat Makanan Peng Hwa....23 E7
- Restoran Nelayan Titiwangsa....24 D2
- Yu Ri Tei....(see 17)

ENTERTAINMENT

- Kuala Lumpur Performing Arts Centre....25 B1
- Sutra Dance Theatre....26 C2

TRANSPORT

- Putra Bus Station....27 B3

Hindus as well as Zoo Negara and the Orang Asli Museum. Shuttle buses run even further north to the Genting Highlands, a gaudy complex of casinos, shopping malls and theme parks on a cool hilltop about 54km from the capital.

INFORMATION

Bookshops

Borders (Map pp84-5; ☎ 2141 0288; Level 2, Berjaya Times Sq, 1 Jln Imbi; 10am-10pm) Huge English-language range. Another branch in the Curve (p122).

Kinokuniya (Map pp84-5; ☎ 2164 8133; Level 4, Suria KLCC, Jln Ampang; 10am-10pm) Excellent range of English-language titles.

MPH Bookstores Bangsar (Map p94; ☎ 2287 3600; Level 2, Bangsar Village II, Jln Telawi 1, Bangsar Baru; 9.30am-10pm); Golden Triangle (Map pp84-5; ☎ 2142 8231; Ground fl, BB Plaza, Jln Bukit Bintang; 10.30am-9.30pm); Mid Valley (off Map p94; ☎ 2938 3818; Ground fl, Mid Valley Megamall, Mid Valley City; 10am-10pm) Strong on local titles and magazines.

Silverfish Books (Map p94; ☎ 2284 4837; www.silverfishbooks.com; 67-1 Jln Telawi 3, Bangsar Baru; 10am-8pm Mon-Fri, 10am-6pm Sat) Publisher of contemporary Malaysian literature.

Cultural Centres & Libraries

Alliance Française (Map p92; ☎ 2694 7880; www.alliancefrancaise.org.my; 15 Lorong Gurney; 10am-6pm Thu-Sat)

British Council (Map pp84-5; ☎ 2723 7900; www.britishcouncil.org.my; Ground fl, West Block, Wisma Selangor Dredging, 142C Jln Ampang; 9am-9pm Mon-Fri, 9am-6pm Sat)

Goethe Institut (Map pp72-3; ☎ 2142 2011; www.goethe.de/ins/my/kua/; 1 Jln Langgak Golf, off Jln Tun Razak; 8.30am-6pm Mon-Fri)

Japan Foundation (Map pp84-5; 2161 2104; www.jfkl.org.my; Level 30, Menara Citibank, 165 Jln Ampang; 10.30am-6.30pm Tue-Fri, 10am-6pm Sat)

Kuala Lumpur Memorial Library (Perpustakaan Kuala Lumpur; Map pp78-9; ☎ 2612 3508; Jln Raja; 2-6.45pm Mon, 9.30am-6.45pm Tue-Fri, 11am-5pm Sat & Sun)

National Library of Malaysia (Perpustakaan Negara Malaysia; Map p92; ☎ 2694 3488; www.pnm.my; 232 Jln Tun Razak, Titiwangsa; 10am-7pm Tue-Sat, to 6pm Sun)

Emergency

The **tourist police** (Map pp84-5; ☎ 2163 4422; Malaysian Tourism Centre, 109 Jln Ampang) handles minor crimes affecting tourists. For other emergencies, call ☎ 999 for police or an ambulance and ☎ 994 for fire.

Immigration Offices

Visa extensions can be arranged at the **Immigration Office** (off Map pp72-3; ☎ 2095 5077; Aras 1-5, Block I, Pusat Bandar Damansara; 8.30am-5pm Mon-Fri, closed 12.15-2.45pm Fri), 2km west of Lake Gardens. See p225 for more details.

Internet Access

Most hostels and hotels offer internet access to guests and there are numerous 24-hour internet cafés in Chinatown and the Golden Triangle – see following for recommendations. The going rate for internet access is around RM3 per hour, though rates are higher in some of the upmarket hotels and malls. Most top-end hotels offer wi-fi access in the lobby; travellers on tighter budgets should head to any branch of Starbucks – fast wi-fi

VISA SHOPPING

Kuala Lumpur (KL) is a good place to stock up on visas for other parts of Asia. The exchange rates are favourable, embassies tend to be fast and efficient, and there are regular flights from KL to countries across the region. See p219 for listings of embassies and p227 for listings of airlines.

access is free if you buy a drink and contribute to the Seattle coffee-chain's campaign for world domination.

21st Century Internet (Map pp84-5; Jln Alor, Golden Triangle; per hr RM2.50; 24hr)

Net Youth Resources (Map pp78-9; Jln Sultan, Chinatown; per hr RM2.50; 24hr) Near the KFC; fast connections and air-con.

Yoshi Connection (Map pp84-5; Lower ground fl, Suria KLCC; per hr RM8; 10am-10pm)

Laundry

Most hotels offer a laundry service, but you'll have to drop your clothes off first thing in the morning if you want them back the same day. Alternatively, there are private laundries in the main tourist areas.

Dry Point (Map pp84-5; 2143 3845; 73 Changkat Bukit Bintang; 9am-9pm Mon-Sat, 10am-10pm Sun) A handy option in the Golden Triangle.

Left Luggage

The train and bus stations have luggage offices where you can leave padlocked luggage. These places are reasonably secure but carry any important valuables with you and be sure to check the opening and closing times. The KL Sentral **left luggage office** (bag storage per hr/day RM2/6; 7.30am-10pm) is near the Air Asia office. There's a similar **luggage office** (bag storage per day RM3; 7am-midnight) at the Puduraya Bus Station.

Media

KL has a number of good listings and lifestyle magazines, available from most bookshops and news vendors.

Juice (www.juiceonline.com; free) Trendy mag that covers the local club scene; available in upmarket clubs and bars.

KL Lifestyle (www.kl-lifestyle.com.my; RM4.80) Covers activities and attractions in the city, including nightlife options; comes with a useful list and map of airline offices.

KLue (www.klue.com.my; RM5) A glossy monthly with good nightlife listings and plenty of upbeat features about things to do in and around the city.

Medical Services

Pharmacy chains Watsons and Guardian have branches all over KL selling toiletries, healthcare products, prescription medicines and, curiously, ladies' underwear and men's boxers. Opticians are found in most shopping centres. KL is an increasingly popular destination for health tourism, from cosmetic surgery to dental veneers. Medical centres and dentists are found in all the big malls and a private consultation will cost around RM35 – try the following.

DENTISTS

Dental Pro (off Map p94; 2287 3333; www.dentalpro.org; 8 Lengkok Abdullah, Bangsar Utama; 10am-6pm Mon-Sat)

Pristine Dental Centre (off Map p94; 2287 3782; 2nd fl, Mid Valley Megamall, Mid Valley City; 10am-6pm)

HEALTH CENTRES

Klinik Medicare (off Map p94; 2287 7180; 2nd fl, Mid Valley Megamall, Mid Valley City; 10am-10pm)

Twin Towers Medical Centre KLCC (Map pp84-5; 2382 3500; www.ttmcklcc.com.my; Level 4, Suria KLCC; 8.30am-6pm Mon-Sat)

HOSPITALS

Hospital Kuala Lumpur (Map p92; 2615 5555; www.hkl.gov.my; Jln Pahang)

Tung Shin Hospital (Map pp78-9; 2072 1655; www.tungshinhospital.com.my; 102 Jln Pudu)

Money

Moneychangers and banks are found on every other corner in KL. Rates are fairly consistent, though private moneychangers sometimes offer slightly better rates for cash than banks. Most banks and shopping malls provide international ATMs (typically on the ground floor or basement level) but see the warning, p223.

Useful places to change money include the following:

Maybank Forex Counter (Map pp78-9; Jln Hang Lekir, Chinatown; 10am-6pm)

RHB Bank (Map pp84-5; Ground fl, Suria KLCC; 10am-7pm)

Post

For international postal services, go to **Pos Malaysia** (Map pp78-9; Jln Raja Laut; 8.30am-6pm Mon-Sat, closed first Sat of month) in the Dayabumi complex. Stamps and the poste restante service are handled in the main hall upstairs, registered letters and small parcels are handled next door, and the office for large parcels is down in the basement. There's also a **philately museum** (admission free; 8.30m-5pm Mon-Fri, closed 12.30pm-2.30pm Fri) on the same level as the main entrance. Branch post offices are open 8.30am to 5pm Monday to Saturday (closed first Saturday of the month) and are found all over KL, including inside the Sungei Wang (Map pp84–5) and Suria KLCC (Map pp84–5) shopping centres.

See p223 for more information on sending letters and parcels in Malaysia. Other postal options include the following:

DHL (Map p94; ☎ 2283 6504; 60 Jln Telawi, Bangsar Baru; ⏰ 9am-9pm Mon-Sat, 9am-5pm Sun) Good for urgent parcels.

Post office Jln TAR (Map p92); Jln Telawi (Map p94)

Telephone & Fax

Payphones abound in the capital and most take coins, credit cards and phonecards (available from convenience stores). Alternatively, street-side phone counters sell prepaid SIM cards for mobile phones (see p224). Most internet cafés offer Skype and other net-phone services.

Telekom Malaysia (Map pp78-9; Jln Raja Chulan; ⏰ 8.30am-5pm Mon-Fri, 8.30am-1pm Sat) Quiet booths for international calls and a desk where you can send and receive faxes.

Tourist Information

KL has a number of tourist information offices, run by various tourist associations. There are also small information booths at many tourist attractions.

KL Information Centre (Map pp78-9; ☎ 2691 0285; www.kualalumpur.gov.my; Lorong Tuanku Abdul Rahman; ⏰ 10am-6pm) Run by the KL administration; has general information on the city.

KL Tourist Association (Map p90; ☎ 2287 1831; www.klta.org.my; National Museum, Jln Damansara; ⏰ 9am-5pm Mon-Fri, till 1pm Sat) Good for brochures and general information on the city.

Malaysian Tourism Centre (MTC; Map pp84-5; ☎ 2163 3664, info line 1300-885050; www.mtc.gov.my; 109 Jln Ampang; ⏰ 7am-10pm) Housed in a mansion built in 1935 for rubber and tin tycoon Eu Tong Seng; a useful office with a restaurant, tour agent, moneychanger and ATM, plus daily cultural performances (see p121).

Tourism Malaysia (www.tourismmalaysia.gov.my) Kuala Lumpur International Airport (off Map pp72-3; ☎ 8776 5651; International Arrival Hall, KLIA, Sepang; ⏰ 9am-midnight); KL Sentral (Map p90; ☎ 2274 5823; KL Sentral, Brickfields; ⏰ 9am-6pm); Putra World Trade Centre (Map pp72-3; ☎ 4041 1295; Level 2, Putra World Trade Centre, 45 Jln Tun Ismail; ⏰ 9am-6pm Mon-Sat) Well-informed offices providing information on all of Malaysia, plus free maps of KL.

Travel Agencies

The agencies listed here are reliable for discount fares. See p99 for companies offering tours inside Malaysia.

MSL Travel (Map p92; ☎ 4042 4722; www.msltravel.com; 66 Jln Putra; ⏰ 9am-5pm Mon-Fri, to 1pm Sat)

Sri Sutra Travel (Map pp84-5; ☎ 3282 7575; www.srisutra.com.my; Level 3, Suria KLCC, Jln Ampang; ⏰ 9am-9.30pm Mon-Fri, 10am-9.30pm Sat & Sun)

STA Travel (Map pp84-5; ☎ 2148 9800; www.statravel.com.my; Lot 506, 5th fl, Magnum Plaza, 128 Jln Pudu; ⏰ 9am-5pm Mon-Fri, 9am-noon Sat)

DANGERS & ANNOYANCES

KL is generally very safe, but it pays to watch for pickpockets on crowded public transport. One ongoing irritation in KL is the state of the pavements. The temporary covers thrown over drains can give way suddenly, dumping you in the drink or worse, so walk around them. Flooding can also a be problem, particularly during the monsoon – carry an umbrella and be prepared to roll up your trousers to wade through giant puddles.

SIGHTS

Because of KL's disjointed layout and convoluted road network, walking between the sights can be quite an undertaking. It's often better to use public transport or taxis, even over short distances. That said, the city centre is smaller than you might expect – from Chinatown, you can walk to Little India in five minutes, Bukit Bintang in 10 to 15 minutes and the KLCC in half an hour. Some districts have a huge concentration of sights in a small geographical area – see p96 for recommended walking tours.

Chinatown

SRI MAHA MARIAMMAN TEMPLE

The most striking religious monument in old KL, this **Hindu shrine** (Map pp78-9; 163 Jln Tun HS Lee; ⏰ 6am-8.30pm, to 9pm Fri & Sat) was founded by migrant workers from the Indian state of Tamil Nadu in 1873. Flower-garland vendors crowd the entrance and the temple is crowned by a huge *gopuram* (temple tower) covered in riotously colourful statues of Hindu deities. Locals leave incense, flowers, coconuts and strings of limes as offerings to Mariamman, the South Indian mother goddess, an incarnation of Durga. The idol from the temple is paraded to the Batu Caves (p131) in a silver chariot during the Thaipusam festival in January or February each year. Non-Hindus are welcome to visit but leave your shoes at the entrance.

MASJID JAMEK

Chinatown's Muslim population prays at the historic **mosque** (Friday Mosque; Map pp78-9; off Jln Tun

Perak; 8.30am-12.30pm & 2.30-4pm, closed Fri 11am-2.30pm). Constructed in 1907 on an island at the confluence of the Klang and Gombak rivers, the mosque is an island of serenity, with airy open pavilions shaded by palm trees. Although the architecture looks traditional, the mosque was actually designed by a British architect, AB Hubbock, who sought inspiration from the Mughal mosques of northern India. Visitors are welcome outside of prayer times, but shoes should be removed and female visitors should cover their heads, legs and shoulders (scarves and sarongs are available at the entrance).

OTHER TEMPLES

On a narrow alleyway near the Central Market, the Taoist **Sze Ya Temple** (Map pp78-9; Jln Tun HS Lee; 7am-5pm) is probably the most atmospheric Chinese temple in KL. The temple was constructed in 1864 on the instructions of Yap Ah Loy, the semi-official founder of Kuala Lumpur (see p70). You can see a statue of Yap Ah Loy just left of the main altar. The slightly odd position, squished between rows of shophouses, was determined by feng shui. Fortune-telling sticks are provided for devotees; just rattle the pot until a stick falls out, then find the paper slip corresponding to the number on the stick. Staff will translate the fortune on the slip for RM1. On your way out, note the two gilded sedan chairs used to carry the deity statues during religious processions. You can enter the temple through the stucco gatehouse on Jln Tun HS Lee or the back gate on the next alley west.

Around the corner is the similarly atmospheric 1886 **Guandi Temple** (Kwong Siew Free School; Map pp78-9; Jln Tun HS Lee; 7am-5pm). The main hall is hung with fragrant coils of spiral incense, paper clothes and money that are burned to bring good fortune to the ancestors. The temple is dedicated to Kwan Ti, a historical Chinese general revered by Taoists as the god of war.

There are two more interesting temples further south, facing the Bulatan Merdeka roundabout. **Chan She Shu Yuen Temple** (Map pp78-9; ☎ 2078 1461; Jln Petaling; admission free; 9am-6pm) features a stunning tiled roof with dioramas of celestial scenes and dramatic woodcarvings inside the main shrine. There's also a **library** (1-7pm Thu-Sat, 10am-5pm Sun) with 4000 Chinese books. Across the road is the less dramatic **Guan Yin Temple** (Koon Yam Temple; Map pp78-9; cnr Jln Stadium & Jln Maharajalela; 7am-5pm), which displays golden Chinese Buddhist statues.

CENTRAL MARKET

Housed in a glorious Art Deco building that looks more Miami than Southeast Asia, the **Central Market** (Pasar Seni; Map pp78-9; ☎ 2031 0399; Jln Hang Kasturi; 10am-9.30pm) was the wet market for the miners of old Kuala Lumpur. The market was constructed by the British in 1888 and was nearly demolished in the 1970s before the Malaysian Heritage Society intervened to save it for future generations. Today, it houses a touristy but colourful market with some good handicrafts – batiks, wood carvings, kris (Malay daggers), durian candies – and Malay fabrics on sale. Prices are often elevated so bargain hard.

PETALING STREET MARKET

Traders start to fill covered Jln Petaling from midmorning until the whole street is jammed with market stalls selling everything from fake Gucci handbags and pirate DVDs to *nasi lemak* (coconut rice) and bunches of lychees. The **market** (Map pp78-9; Jln Petaling; noon-11pm) really comes into its own at night, when hordes of tourists scour the stalls for convincing fakes of brand-name clothes, perfumes, watches and luggage. The fact that there is a police station in the middle of the market is evidence of the rather relaxed Malaysian attitude towards counterfeit goods. If you do buy fakes, the risks include poor stitching on bags, and DVDs of current releases recorded on grainy hand-held video cameras smuggled into KL's cinemas. Running west of the main market towards Jln Tun HS Lee is Chinatown's pungent **wet market**, where locals shop for fresh fish, vegetables and gruesomely anatomical cuts of meat.

KOMPLEKS DAYABUMI

The former headquarters of Petronas, Malaysia's national oil and gas company, the **Kompleks Dayabumi** (Map pp78-9; Jln Sultan Hishamuddin) was built in 1981 on land formerly occupied by the workshops for the Malayan Railway. The landmark feature here is a tall marble tower, cloaked in delicate fretwork screens. In profile, the tower forms a four-pointed star intersected by a square, a reoccurring symbol in Islamic art. Despite being one of the older buildings in KL, the tower is notable for its clean lines and purity of form. To get here, walk over the footbridge behind Central Market.

OTHER SIGHTS

On the ground floor of the Menara Maybank (p88), the **Numismatic Museum** (Map pp78-9; ☎ 2690

CHINATOWN, MERDEKA SQUARE & LITTLE INDIA

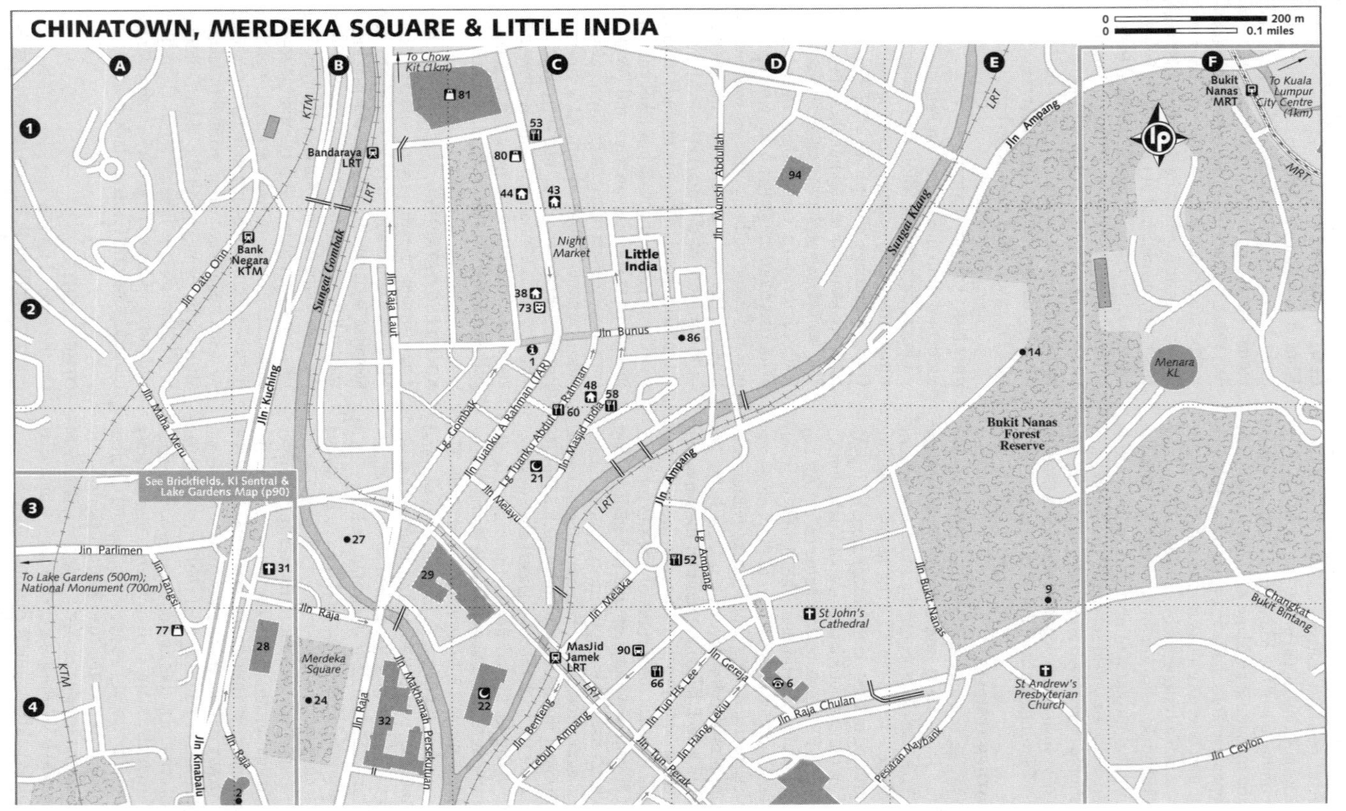

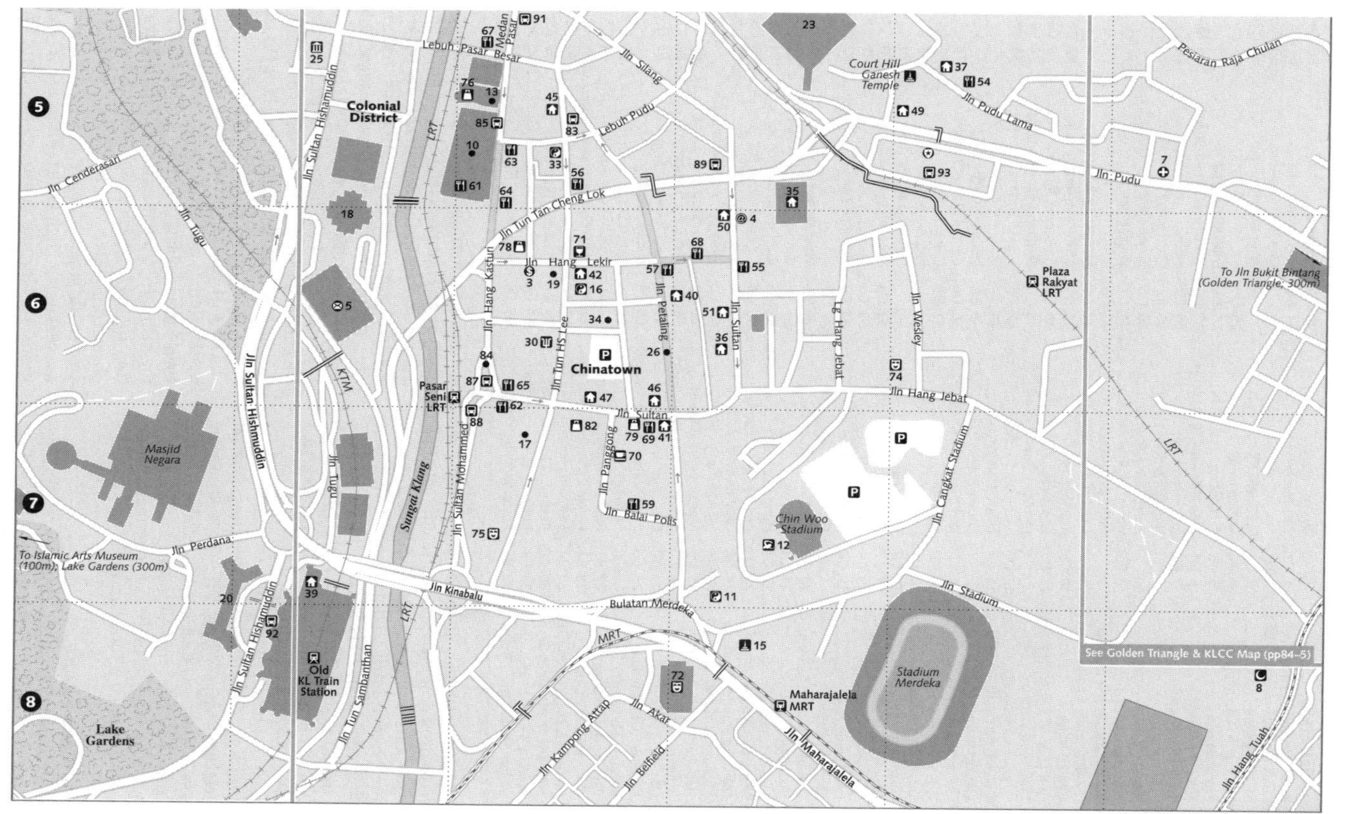
Lebuh Pasar Besar
Medan Pasar
Colonial District
Jln Sultan Hishamuddin
Jln Cenderasari
Jln Tugu
Jln Silang
Lebuh Pudu
Court Hill Ganesh Temple
Jln Pudu Lama
Pesiaran Raja Chulan
Jln Pudu
Jln Tun Tan Cheng Lok
Jln Hang Lekir
Jln Hang Kasturi
Jln Tun HS Lee
Jln Petaling
Jln Sultan
Lg Hang Jebat
Jln Wesley
Jln Hang Jebat
Chinatown
Plaza Rakyat LRT
To Jln Bukit Bintang (Golden Triangle; 300m)
LRT
KTM
Pasar Seni LRT
Jln Sultan Mohammed
Jln Panggong
Jln Balai Polis
Sungai Klang
Masjid Negara
Jln Sultan Hishmuddin
Jln Perdana
To Islamic Arts Museum (100m); Lake Gardens (300m)
Chin Woo Stadium
Jln Cangkat Stadium
Jln Kinabalu
Bulatan Merdeka
Jln Stadium
MRT
Old KL Train Station
Jln Tun Sambanthan
Stadium Merdeka
Maharajalela MRT
Jln Akar
Jln Kampong Attap
Jln Belfield
Jln Maharajalela
See Golden Triangle & KLCC Map (pp84–5)
Jln Hang Tuah
Lake Gardens

INFORMATION

KL Information Centre 1 C2
Kuala Lumpur Memorial Library 2 B4
Maybank Forex Booth 3 C6
Net Youth Resources 4 D6
Pos Malaysia 5 B6
Telekom Malaysia 6 D4
Tung Shin Hospital 7 F5

SIGHTS & ACTIVITIES

Albukhary Masjid 8 F8
Bukit Nanas Forest Reserve Information Centre 9 E3
Central Market 10 C5
Chan She Shu Yuen Temple 11 D7
Chin Woo Stadium Swimming Pool 12 D7
Gajah Gajah Gallery 13 C5
Gate to Bukit Nanas Forest Reserve 14 E2
Going Places Tours (see 36)
Guan Yin Temple 15 D8
Guandi Temple 16 C6
Impressions 17 C7
Kompleks Dayabumi 18 B6
Lee Rubber Building 19 C6
Malayan Railway Administration Building 20 A7
Masjid India 21 C3
Masjid Jamek 22 C4
Menara Maybank 23 D5
Merdeka Square 24 B4
Muzium Telekom (see 6)
National History Museum 25 B5
Numismatic Museum (see 23)
Old Asia (see 10)
Petaling Street Market 26 C6
Philately Museum (see 5)
Pitcherplant Fountain 27 B3
Royal Selangor Club 28 B4
Sessions & Magistrates Court 29 B3
Sri Maha Mariamman Temple 30 C6
St Mary's Cathedral 31 B3
Sultan Abdul Samad Building 32 B4
Sze Ya Temple 33 C5
Wet Market 34 C6

SLEEPING

Ancasa Hotel 35 D5
Backpackers Travellers Inn 36 D6
Casa Villa Travellers Lodge 37 E5
Coliseum Hotel 38 C2
Heritage Station Hotel 39 B7
Hotel China Town Inn 40 D6
Hotel Lok Ann 41 C7
Hotel Malaya 42 C6
Hotel Noble 43 C1
Kowloon Hotel 44 C1
Le Village 45 C5
Lee Mun Guest House 46 C6
Mandarin Pacific Hotel 47 C6
Palace Hotel 48 C2
Pudu Hostel 49 E5
Red Dragon Hostel 50 D6
Swiss-Inn 51 D6

EATING

Bilal Restoran 52 D3
Capital Café 53 C1
Coconut House 54 E5
Coliseum Café (see 38)
Food Court (see 93)
Gin Ger (see 61)
Hong Kee Stall 55 D6
Kedai Kopi Lai Foong 56 C5
Lakshmi Vilas (see 66)
Madam Tang's Stall 57 C6
Mangrove Food Court (see 61)
Masjid India Hawker Court 58 C2
Old China Café 59 C7
Pasar Malam (Night Market) 60 C3
Precious 61 C5
Puduraya Hawker Court (see 93)
Purple Cane Tea Restaurant (see 72)
Restoran Hameed's 62 C6
Restoran Oriental Bowl 63 C5
Restoran Yusoof dan Zakhir 64 C5
Restoran Zhing Kong 65 C6
Sangeetha 66 C4
Sing Seng Nam 67 C5
Streetside Restaurants 68 D6
West Lake Restoran 69 C7

DRINKING

Chinatown Liquor Shop (see 46)
Ikopi 70 C7
Old Town Kopitiam (see 61)
Purple Cane Tea House (see 70)
Reggae Bar 71 C6

ENTERTAINMENT

Chinese Assembly Hall 72 D8
Coliseum Cinema 73 C2
Stadium Bola Keranjang 74 E6
Taman Budaya 75 C7

SHOPPING

Central Market Annexe 76 C5
Galeri Tangsi 77 A4
Peter Hoe Evolution 78 C6
Purple Cane Tea Arts 79 C7
Silk Street 80 C1
Sogo 81 C1
UO Superstore 82 C7

TRANSPORT

Bangkok Bank Bus Stop 83 C5
Bus Information Booth 84 C6
Central Market Bus Stop 85 C5
Indian Airlines 86 D2
Jalan Sultan Mohammed Bus Stop 87 C6
Klang Bus Station 88 C7
Kota Raya Bus Stop 89 D5
Lebuh Ampang Bus Stop 90 C4
Medan Pasar Bus Stop 91 C5
NiCE Coaches (see 92)
Plusliner 92 B8
Puduraya Bus Station 93 E5
Royal Nepal Airlines (see 86)
Singapore Airlines 94 D1

7461; Menara Maybank, 100 Jln Tun Perak; 10am-6pm) has a display of Malaysian currency, including early Chinese 'coin trees'. While Europeans preferred to strike coins, the Chinese cast their coins in moulds, leaving a tree of washer-shaped coins attached to metal 'branches'. The coins were then snapped off and carried around looped on strings.

A few blocks north, in a striking colonial building, the reasonably diverting **Muzium Telekom** (Map pp78-9; ☎ 2031 9966; Jln Raja Chulan; admission free; 9.30am-5pm) has exhibits on the history of telecommunications in Malaysia, with an English or Bahasa commentary on old-fashioned phone handsets.

Merdeka Square

The huge open square (Map pp78–9) where Malaysian independence was declared in 1957 is ringed by heritage buildings and dominated by an enormous flagpole and fluttering Malaysian flag. In the British era, the square was used as a cricket pitch. Along its western edge is the mock-Tudor **Royal Selangor Club** (Map pp78-9; www.rscweb.org.my; Jln Raja), founded in 1884 and still an exclusive social club for the KL elite. It's also the place where world-wide running-and-drinking club the Hash House Harriers kicked off in 1938 (On, On!).

The east side of the square is dominated by the domes and clocktower of the **Sultan Abdul Samad Building** (Map pp78-9; Jln Raja), built as the secretariat for the colonial administration in 1897. It was designed by the India-obsessed architect AC Norman – who also created the Jamek Masjid – and it now houses the Malaysian High Court. There are several more AC Norman constructions along the east side of the square, providing a striking counterpoint to the looming Menara KL and Petronas Towers.

At the south end of the square is the **National History Museum** (Muzium Sejarah Nasional; Map pp78-9; ☎ 2694 4590; 29 Jln Raja; admission RM1; 9am-6pm), which covers Malaysian history from prehistoric times to the present day. The building was constructed in 1888 and originally housed the first bank in Kuala Lumpur. Inside you can see relics and treasures from the various cultures that preceded the British colonial administration, including the Hindu and Buddhist kingdoms that existed here before the rise of Islam.

Nearby is the Kuala Lumpur Memorial Library (see p74), a modern building that uses traditional features to blend into its

ORANGES ARE NOT THE ONLY FRUIT...

One of the highlights of KL is the fantastic variety of tropical fruit sold at markets and street stalls. Modified motorcycles piled high with lychees and mangoes loiter outside bus and train stations. Elderly ladies sit by the roadside selling bunches of rambutans. Vendors set up plastic tables beside food markets for the (some would say immoral) trade in durians, perhaps the world's stinkiest fruit. With a spiky armoured shell and soft, slimy flesh that smells vaguely like rotting meat, durian is definitely an acquired taste – though locals regard it as the king of fruits – and seeing as durian is the most expensive fruit on the market, many are happy not to acquire it. Should you feel tempted, be warned that durians are banned from most hotels, shopping malls and cinemas. Heed this advice – you may be asked to leave if your durian is upsetting other patrons. There is a host of other fruit to look out for, all coming into season at different times of year. Keep an eye out for the following sweet delights:

Buah nona The custard apple; a knobbly green skin conceals hard black seeds and sweet gloopy flesh with a granular texture.

Buah salak Known as the snakeskin fruit because of its scaly skin; the exterior looks like a mutant strawberry and the soft flesh tastes like unripe bananas.

Cempedak The Malaysian breadfruit; a huge green fruit with skin like the Thing from the *Fantastic Four*; the seeds and flesh are often curried or fried.

Chikoo The sapota or sapodilla; a brown, plum-shaped fruit with soft orange flesh that tastes vaguely of dates.

Dragon fruit An alien-looking red pod with tonguelike flanges, hiding fragrant, kiwi fruit–like flesh with lots of tiny edible seeds.

Duku Also known as *dokong* and *langsat;* a small, soft-skinned ball containinging sweet segments, some with bitter seeds. Squeeze from the bottom to pop the shell and avoid the bitter sap from the skin.

Guava A green, applelike ball containing sweet pink or white flesh with seeds you can eat.

Jambu merah Malay apple; elongated pink or red fruit with a smooth shiny skin and pale watery flesh. A good thirst quencher on hot days.

Longan A tiny hard ball like a mini lychee with sweet, perfumed flesh; peel it, eat the flesh and spit out the hard seeds.

Lychee Has a thin scaly shell that makes it look like a reptile egg; clear flesh that melts in the mouth, wrapped around hard black seeds.

Mango Many varieties of this fruit, all with succulent yellow flesh surrounding a hairy seed that mirrors the shape of the fruit.

Mangosteen A hard purple shell conceals delightfully fragrant white segments, some containing a tough seed that you can spit out or swallow.

Pomelo Like a grapefruit on steroids, with a thick pithy green skin hiding sweet, tangy segments; cut into the skin, peel off the pith then break open the segments and munch on the flesh inside.

Rambutan People have different theories about what rambutans look like, not all repeatable in polite company; the hairy shell contains sweet, translucent flesh that you scrape off the seed with your teeth.

Soursop A shapeless, sacklike fruit, with tasty but tart granular flesh and hard black seeds; it's only ripe when soft and it goes off within days so eat it quickly.

Starfruit The star-shaped cross-section is the giveaway; the yellow flesh is sweet and tangy and believed by many to lower blood pressure.

Tamarind Fresh tamarind comes in a curved brown pod; the hard seeds are hidden inside the delicious, tart flesh.

surroundings. There's a small **gallery** (admission free; 10am-9pm) with artworks by local student artists and displays on the history of KL.

At the end of the square is **St Mary's Cathedral** (2692 8672; www.stmaryscathedral.org.my; Jln Raja), looking every inch the white-washed English country church. The church was built in 1894 by the colonial administration and it still maintains a small Anglican congregation. The best time to visit is during the 5pm Sunday service.

Lake Gardens

Just a few hundred metres from busy Chinatown, the urban landscape gives way to sculpted parks and dense tropical jungle. Covering 92 hectares, the Lake Gardens were created during the colonial era as an urban retreat where the British administrators could escape the hurly burly of downtown (as well as people of other races). On the top of the tallest hill, the official residence of British government representative Frank Swettenham is now the swanky hotel Carcosa Seri Negara (p105), while on the northern fringes of the Lake Gardens is the striking honeycomb tower containing the Malaysian Parliament.

As well as the pleasantly restful Lake Gardens Park, the hills are dotted with interesting attractions, including two of KL's best: the Islamic Arts Museum and Kuala Lumpur Bird Park. The dense foliage creates a lot of humidity so strolling around can be a sweaty experience – a drier way to see the gardens is to hire a taxi and ask the driver to wait while you explore each of the sights. At weekends, a tourist tram rolls between the main gardens for a nominal charge.

KUALA LUMPUR BIRD PARK

The undisputed highlight of the gardens is this fabulous **aviary** (Taman Burung; Map p90; 2272 1010; Jln Cenderawasih; adult/child RM30/22; 9am-7pm), where 160 species of (mostly) Asian birds fly free beneath an enormous canopy. Star attractions include ostriches, hornbills, eagles, flamingos and parrots. It's worth getting to the park for feeding times (eagles 2.30pm, ostriches 2pm and 4pm) or the child-friendly bird shows (12.30pm and 3.30pm), which feature plenty of parrot tricks to keep youngsters amused. The park's Hornbill Restaurant is the best place in the gardens for an inexpensive feed.

BUTTERFLY PARK

Flying creatures of a different sort are showcased at the interesting **butterfly reserve** (Taman Rama Rama; Map p90; 2693 4799; Jln Cenderasari; adult/child RM15/8, camera/video RM1/4; 9am-6pm) near the Bird Park. Some of the iridescent butterflies fluttering around the covered grounds are real monsters, and there's a bug gallery where you can shudder at the size of Malaysia's giant centipedes and spiders. The park shop sells mounted butterflies and other giant insects, but it's best not to encourage the trade in these increasingly endangered creatures.

OTHER PARKS & GARDENS

The Lake Gardens are centred on the pretty **Lake Gardens Park** (Taman Tasik Perdana; Map p90; Jln Tembusu; admission free; daylight hours). The park covers a huge area, planted with a variety of native plants, trees and shrubs – it's hard to believe that this calm open space exists just a few hundred metres from the main train station. In the middle is a huge children's adventure playground and nearby is the sprawling lake for which the gardens are named. You can rent boats for RM6 per hour and watch t'ai chi practitioners in the early morning.

Close to the children's play area is the small **Deer Park** (Taman Rusa & Kancil; Map p90; Jln Perdana; admission free; 10am-6pm, closed noon-2pm weekdays), which has a collection of tame Malaysia deer, including the tiny *kancil* (lesser mouse deer), the world's smallest hoofed mammal.

Malaysia's fabulous orchids are collected together at the handsome **Orchid Garden** (Taman Orkid; Map p90; Jln Cenderawasih; weekdays admission free, Sat & Sun RM1; 9am-6pm), uphill from the lake. The adjacent **Hibiscus Garden** (Taman Bunga Raya; Jln Cenderawasih; free weekdays admission free, Sat & Sun RM1; 9am-6pm) is a riot of hibiscus blooms, surrounding a small art gallery. Both are places to stroll and contemplate. Several small shops sell live and cut orchids.

MASJID NEGARA

The principle place of worship for KL's Malay Muslim population is the gigantic **Masjid Negara** (National Mosque; Map p90; Jln Lembah Perdana; 9am-noon, 3-4pm & 5.30-6.30pm, closed Fri morning). The mosque was inspired by the Grand Mosque in Mecca. Its umbrella-like blue-tile roof has 18 points symbolising the 13 states of Malaysia and the five pillars of Islam. Rising above the mosque, a 74m-high minaret issues the call to prayer that can be heard across Chinatown. Non-Muslims are welcome to visit outside of prayer times but dress appropriately and remove your shoes before entering.

ISLAMIC ARTS MUSEUM

Malaysia's fascinating Islamic history is showcased at this **museum** (Muzium Kesenian Islam Malaysia; Map p90; ☎ 2274 2020; www.iamm.org.my; Jln Lembah Perdana; adult/child RM12/6; 🕑 10am-6pm), which houses one of the best collections of Islamic art in the world. The building itself is full of striking Islamic architectural details and the galleries contain carpets, costumes, textiles, tiles, ceramics, jewellery, weapons and religious manuscripts. Highlights include a stunning recreation of an Ottoman room and a collection of miniature models of famous mosques from around the world. The complex also includes an upmarket restaurant serving Middle Eastern buffet lunches at weekends (RM45 plus tax) and an excellent shop selling high-quality Islamic arts and crafts.

NATIONAL PLANETARIUM

Looking more like a mosque than a centre for scientific research, this **planetarium** (Map p90; ☎ 2273 4303; www.angkasa.gov.my/planetarium; 53 Jln Perdana; admission RM1; 🕑 9.30am-4.30pm Tue-Sun) is a short walk uphill from the Islamic Arts Museum. The planetarium is part of the National Space Agency, and parts of the rocket that launched Malaysia's first satellite are displayed in the main gallery. Planetarium shows (RM2 to RM6 depending on the programme) take place throughout the day in English and Bahasa. In the grounds are models of famous historic observatories, including Jai Singh's Delhi observatory and Stonehenge.

OTHER ATTRACTIONS

At the northern end of the Lake Gardens, the **National Monument** (Plaza Tugu Negara; Map p90; Jln Parlimen; admission free; 🕑 7am-6pm) commemorates the defeat of the Communists in 1950. The militaristic bronze sculpture was created in 1966 by Felix de Weldon, the artist behind the Iwo Jima monument in Washington, DC. Nearby is a monument to the Malay fighters who died in WWI and WWII. Creating an interesting juxtaposition to the triumphalism of the monument, members of the **Tugu Drum Circle** (http://tugudrumcircle.blogspot.com/) meet here every Sunday from 5.30pm for some therapeutic drumming.

Between the Islamic Arts Museum and the Planetarium is the surprisingly interesting **Royal Malaysia Police Museum** (Map p90; 5 Jln Perdana; admission free; 🕑 10am-6pm Tue-Sun, closed noon-3pm Sun). Inside you can see police uniforms and vehicles, a collection of old swords, cannons and kris, plus some sinister-looking handmade guns and knives seized from members of Malaysia's shady 'secret societies'.

Other sights in the park include the **Civil Service Memorial** (Map p90; Jln Cenderawasih; admission free; 🕑 10am-5pm Tue-Sun, closed 12.15-3pm Fri), dedicated to the work of the Malaysian Civil Service, and the **Tun Abdul Razak Memorial** (Map p90; Jln Perdana; admission free; 🕑 10am-5.30pm Tue-Sun, closed noon-3pm Fri), containing the personal effects, speed boat and golf cart of the second prime minister of Malaysia.

Golden Triangle & KLCC

PETRONAS TOWERS & KLCC

There could be no better symbol of KL than the iconic **Petronas Towers** (Map pp84-5; ☎ 2331 8080; www.petronastwintowers.com.my; KLCC, cnr Jln Ampang & Jln P Ramlee), the headquarters of the national oil and gas company Petronas (see boxed text, p32). These shimmering chrome towers rise above the city like twin silver rockets plucked from an early episode of *Flash Gordon*, a perfect allegory for the meteoric rise of KL from tin mine to space-age metropolis. The towers are the focal point of the enormous KLCC development, which includes a sprawling tropical

SECRET SOCIETIES

Although nominally loyal to the local sultans, the Chinese prospectors who founded Kuala Lumpur maintained their own network of 'secret societies', responsible for most of the organised crime in Malaysia. These forerunners to the modern-day Triads accumulated vast fortunes from smuggling and racketeering, carrying out robberies and assassinations, stage-managing strikes and riots, and pushing forward the political agenda of the Hokkien and Hakka communities. Their reach extended across Malaya and Singapore. During the 1860s, Penang faced all-out war between the Hai San and Gheen Hin gangs over the Perak Mines, triggering a massive crackdown on gang membership by the colonial police. The power of the secret societies waned as the Malay community took control of Malaysian politics. You can see some of the brutal weapons confiscated from gang members in the Royal Malaysia Police Museum (above).

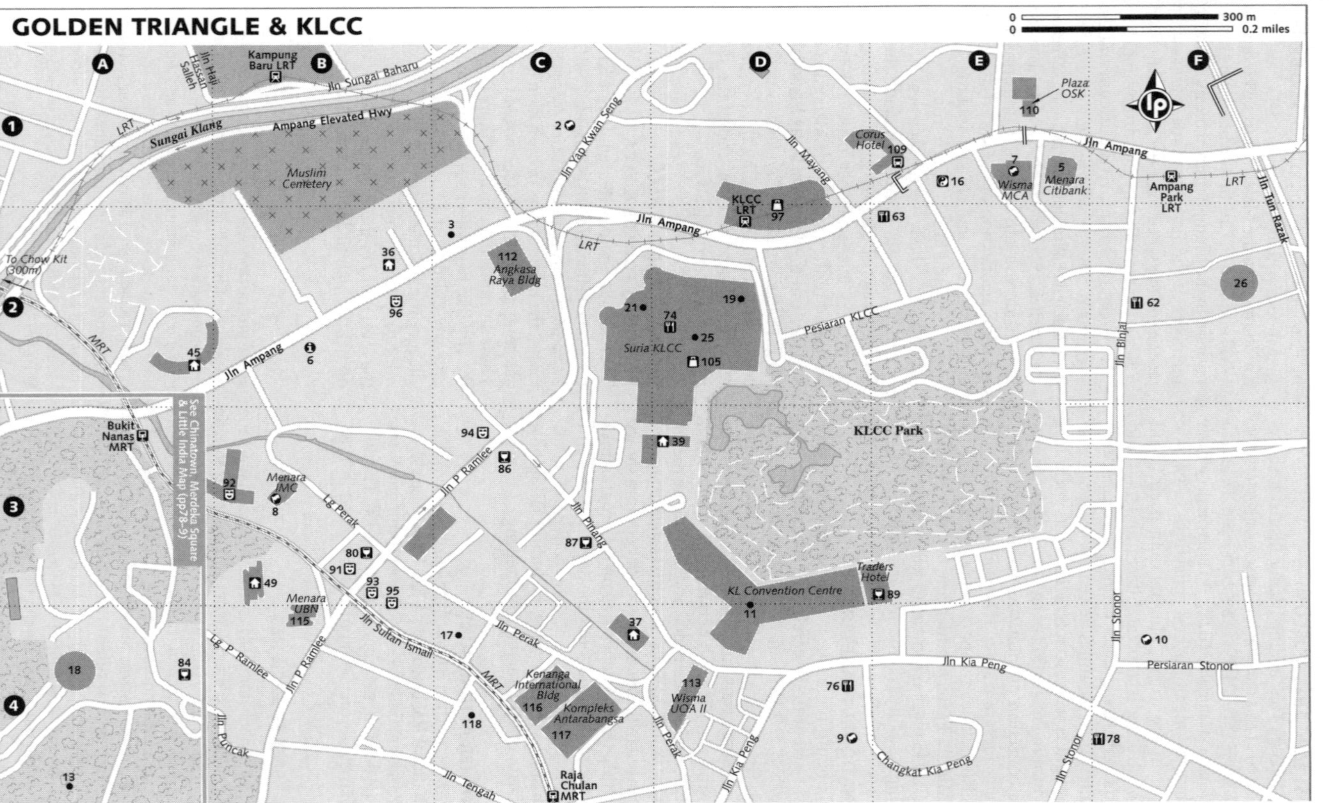
GOLDEN TRIANGLE & KLCC
0 300 m
0 0.2 miles
A
B
C
D
E
F
1
2
3
4
Kampung Baru LRT
Jln Sungai Baharu
Jln Haji Hassan Salleh
Ampang Elevated Hwy
Sungai Klang
Muslim Cemetery
LRT
MRT
To Chow Kit (300m)
Jln Ampang
Angkasa Raya Bldg
Jln Yap Kwan Seng
Suria KLCC
KLCC LRT
Jln Mayang
Corus Hotel
Pesiaran KLCC
KLCC Park
Traders Hotel
KL Convention Centre
Wisma MCA
Menara Citibank
Plaza OSK
Ampang Park LRT
Jln Tun Razak
Jln Binjai
Jln Stonor
Persiaran Stonor
Jln Kia Peng
Changkat Kia Peng
Wisma UOA II
Jln Perak
Jln Pinang
Jln P Ramlee
Kenanga International Bldg
Kompleks Antarabangsa
Raja Chulan MRT
Jln Tengah
Jln Sultan Ismail
Lg Perak
Menara IMC
Menara UBN
Lg P Ramlee
Jln Puncak
Bukit Nanas MRT
See Chinatown, Merdeka Square & Little India Map (pp78–9)

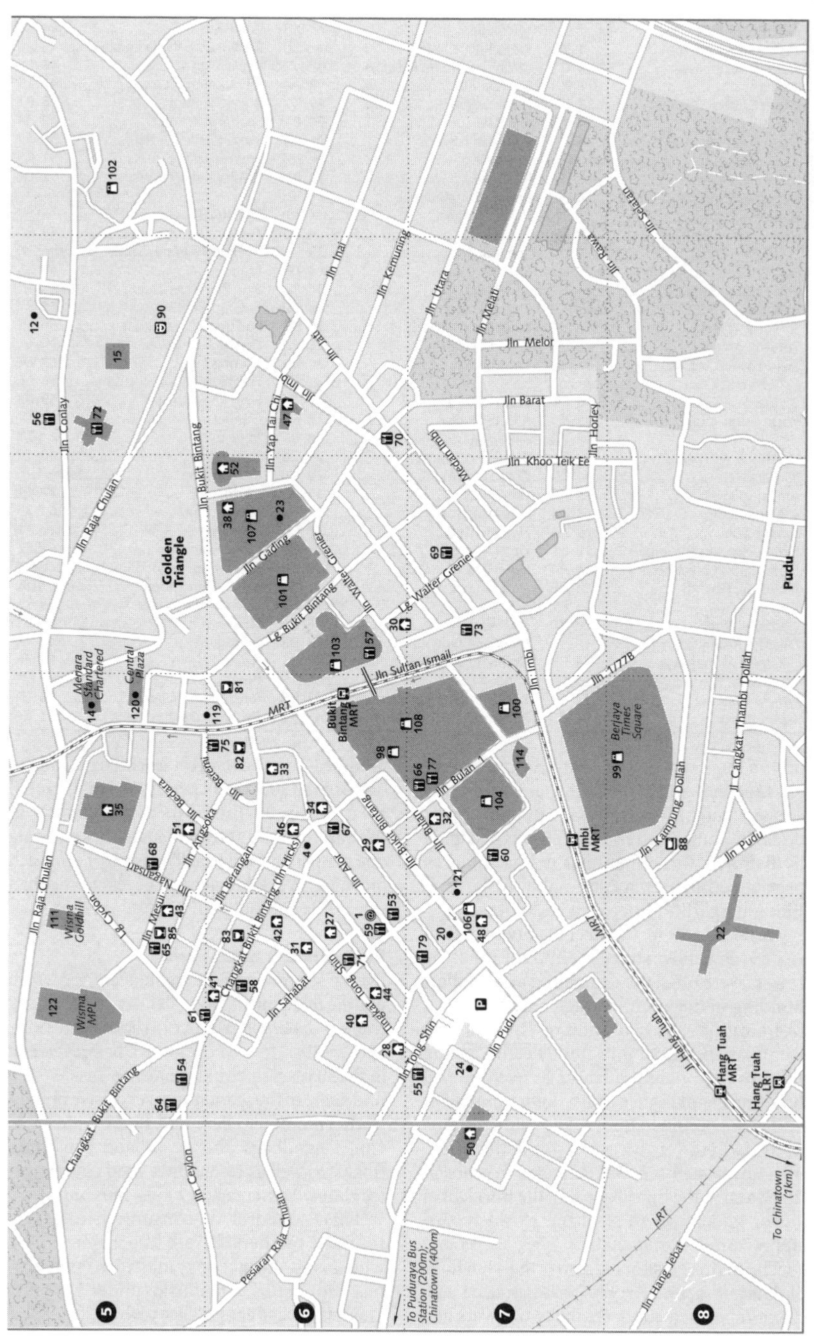
Golden Triangle
Pudu
Jln Raja Chulan
Jln Conlay
Jln Bukit Bintang
Jln Yap Tai Chi
Jln Imbi
Jln Inai
Jln Kemuning
Jln Utara
Jln Melati
Jln Melor
Jln Barat
Jln Khoo Teik Ee
Jln Horley
Medan Imbi
Jln Rawa
Jln Selatan
Jln Gading
Lg Bukit Bintang
Jln Walter Grenier
Lg Walter Grenier
Jln Sultan Ismail
MRT
Bukit Bintang MRT
Menara Standard Chartered
Central Plaza
Jln 1/77B
Berjaya Times Square
Jln Bulan 1
Jln Bulan
Imbi MRT
Jln Kampung Dollah
Jl Cangkat Thambi Dollah
Jln Pudu
Jln Bedara
Jln Berangan
Jln Angsoka
Jln Nagasari
Jln Mesui
Lg Ceylon
Wisma Goldhill
Jln Alor
Changkat Bukit Bintang (Jln Hicks)
Jln Sahabat
Tengkat Tong Shin
Jln Tong Shin
Wisma MPL
Changkat Bukit Bintang
Jln Ceylon
Pesiaran Raja Chulan
To Puduraya Bus Station (200m); Chinatown (400m)
Jl Hang Tuah
Hang Tuah MRT
Hang Tuah LRT
LRT
Jln Hang Jebat
To Chinatown (1km)

INFORMATION

Name	Ref	Grid
21st Century Internet	1	B6
Australian Embassy	2	C1
Borders	(see 99)	
British Council	3	C2
Dry Point	4	C6
Japan Foundation	5	E1
Kinokuniya	(see 105)	
MPH Bookstores	(see 98)	
Malaysian Tourism Centre	6	B2
Nepalese Embassy	7	E1
New Zealand Embassy	8	B3
Philippines Embassy	9	D4
Post Office	(see 108)	
Post Office (Suria KLCC)	(see 25)	
RHB Bank	(see 25)	
Sri Sutra Travel	(see 25)	
Tourist Police	(see 6)	
Twin Towers Medical Centre KLCC	(see 25)	
Vietnamese Embassy	10	F4
Yoshi Connection	(see 25)	

SIGHTS & ACTIVITIES

Name	Ref	Grid
AJ Hackett	(see 18)	
Ampang Bowl	(see 99)	
Aquaria KLCC	11	D4
Ayurvedium	(see 23)	
Badan Warisan Malaysia	12	E5
Bukit Nanas Forest Reserve	13	A4
California Fitness	14	C5
Chulan Tower	15	E5
Cosmo's World	(see 99)	
Dharma Realm Guan Yin Sagely Monastery	16	E1
Escentials	(see 23)	
Fitness First	17	C4
Galeri Petronas	(see 25)	
JoJoBa Spa	(see 99)	
Kings Kitchen Klub	(see 52)	
Malaysian Travel Business	(see 6)	
Menara KL	18	A4
Menara Maxis	19	D2
Old Asia	20	B7
Petronas Towers	21	C2
Petrosains	(see 25)	
Pudu Jail	22	B8
Rumah Penghulu	(see 12)	
Rustic Nirvana	(see 70)	
Skybridge	(see 21)	
Spa Indrani	23	D6
Spa Village	(see 47)	
STA Travel	24	B7
Starhill Spa	(see 38)	
Suria KLCC	25	D2
Tabung Haji	26	F2
Travel Han	(see 42)	

SLEEPING

Name	Ref	Grid
Allson Genesis	27	B6
Bintang Guesthouse	28	B6
Bintang Warisan Hotel	29	C6
Coronade Hotel	30	D6
Green Hut	31	B6
Hotel Capitol	32	C7
Hotel Fortuna	33	C6
Hotel Imperial	34	C6
Hotel Istana	35	C5
Hotel Maya	36	B2
Impiana	37	C4
JW Marriott	38	D6
Mandarin Oriental	39	D3
Number Eight Guesthouse	40	B6
Pondok Lodge	41	B6
Radius International Hotel	42	B6
Rainforest Bed & Breakfast	43	B5
Red Palm	44	B6
Renaissance Kuala Lumpur	45	A2
Replica Inn	46	C6
Ritz Carlton	47	E6
Royale Bintang	48	B7
Shangri-La Hotel	49	B3
Swiss-Garden Hotel	50	A7
Trekker Lodge	51	C5
Westin Kuala Lumpur	52	D6

EATING

Name	Ref	Grid
1+1	53	B6
Avenue 10 Food Court	(see 99)	
Bijan	54	B5
Blue Boy Vegetarian Food Centre	55	B7
Bon Ton	56	E5
Crystal Jade La Mian Xiao Long Bao	57	D6
Frangipani	58	B6
Frog Porridge Stall	59	B6
Gonbei	(see 107)	
Jogoya	(see 107)	
Kameya Restoran Jepun	60	C7
KoRyo-Won	(see 107)	
Lafite	(see 49)	
Le Bouchon	61	B5
Little Penang Kafé	(see 74)	
Lotus Hotel	62	F2
Medan Selera Food Court	(see 57)	
Mythai Jim Thompson	(see 107)	
Nasi Kandar Pelita	63	E2
Nerovivo	64	B5
Old Siam	(see 71)	
Palate Palette	65	B5
Prego	(see 52)	
Restoran de Kitaro	66	C7
Restoran Dragon View	67	C6

park, a huge convention centre, an aquarium, an excellent kids' museum, a world-class concert hall and one of KL's most ostentatious shopping centres. One tower is occupied by Petronas while the other is leased out to private companies, most notably Al Jazeera, Bloomberg, IBM, Microsoft and Boeing.

Opened in 1998, the steel-clad twin towers rise 451.9m above street level. At the time, the towers were officially recognised as the tallest building in the world, though only through a technicality – the two spires on the roof tops were classified as 'architectural details', giving the towers a height advantage over several buildings with higher roofs, higher pinnacles and more occupied floors. The exulted status of the twin towers was short-lived: the Taipei 101 tower eclipsed the Petronas Towers in 2003, and at the time of writing the Burj Dubai tower looked set to steal the world record upon completion in 2008.

The highest visitors can go is the 41st-floor **Skybridge** (Map pp84-5; 9am-7pm Tue-Sun, closed 12.30-2.30pm Fri), which connects the two towers at a modest 170m above street level. To get hold of one of the 1200 free tickets issued daily, you'll need to join the line at the ticket counter in the basement by at least 8.30am; tickets (only one per person) are usually gone by 11am each morning. Weekdays tend to be less hectic than weekends and public holidays.

Suria KLCC & KLCC Park

Even if shopping bores you to tears, it's worth visiting the futuristic **Suria KLCC** (Map pp84-5; ☎ 2382 2828; www.suriaklcc.com.my; KLCC, cnr Jln Ampang & Jln P Ramlee; 10am-10pm) to see how fast KL has developed in the 50 years since independence. Inside you'll find some of the world's most exclusive brands, from Tiffany jewellery and Rolex watches to Gucci handbags and Prada and Moschino frocks, as well as restaurants, food courts, coffee shops, a cinema and a kids' museum.

This cathedral to consumerism is surrounded by the **KLCC Park** (Map pp84-5; 24hr), with a soft-surface jogging track, synchronised fountains, a fantastic (under 12s only) kids' **playground and paddling pool** (10am-7.30pm

Restoran Nagansari Curry House........................**68** C5
Restoran Oversea........................**69** D7
Restoran Sahara Tent..............(see 33)
Restoran Sakura........................**70** E6
Sagar........................(see 35)
Sao Nam........................**71** B6
Sentidos Tapas........................(see 107)
Seri Angkasa........................(see 18)
Seri Melayu........................**72** E5
Shang Palace........................(see 49)
Shook!........................(see 107)
Si Chuan Dou Hua........................**73** D7
Signatures Food Court..............**74** D2
Spice of India........................(see 74)
Srirekha........................**75** C6
Tai Thong Grand Restaurant.....(see 3)
Top Hat........................**76** D4
U Village........................**77** C7
Vansh........................(see 107)
Wa-Raku........................**78** F4
Wong Ah Wah........................**79** B7

DRINKING

Beach Club Café........................**80** B3
Blue Boy........................**81** C6
Ceylon Bar........................(see 41)
Finnegan's........................**82** C6
Green Man........................**83** B6
Legends........................(see 95)
Luna........................**84** A4
No Black Tie........................**85** B5
Old Town Kopitiam..............(see 104)
Olé Café........................(see 83)
Rum Jungle........................**86** C3
SevenAteNine........................**87** C3
Sixty Nine Bistro........................**88** C8
Skybar........................**89** E3
Tiffin Bay/Tiff's Jazz Lounge..(see 107)
Village Bar........................(see 107)
Wings........................(see 88)

ENTERTAINMENT

Bangkok Jazz........................**90** E5
Dewan Filharmonik Petronas..(see 21)
DiGi Imax Theatre........................(see 99)
Espanda........................**91** B3
Frangipani Bar........................(see 58)
Golden Screen Cinema...........(see 99)
Hard Rock Café........................**92** B3
La Queen........................**93** B3
Neway........................(see 99)
Passion........................**94** C3
Planet Hollywood..................(see 101)
Ruums........................**95** B3
Saloma........................(see 6)
Tanjung Golden Village..........(see 25)
Top Room @ Top Hat.............(see 76)
Zouk........................**96** B2

SHOPPING

Art Seni........................(see 107)
Avenue K........................**97** D2
BB Plaza........................**98** C6
Berjaya Times Square................**99** C8
House of Suzie Wong...........(see 107)
Imbi Plazqa........................**100** C7
Jim Thompson Silk................(see 107)
KL Plaza........................**101** D6
Kompleks Budaya Kraf...........**102** F5
Lot 10........................**103** D6
Plaza Low Yat........................**104** C7
Pucuk Rebung........................**105** D2
Sarawak Paradise in Borneo....**106** B7
Starhill Gallery........................**107** D6
Sungei Wang Plaza................**108** C6
Tear Proof........................(see 105)
Tenmoku Pottery..................(see 105)
Teratei........................(see 103)
Yogini Mystical Treasures.....(see 103)

TRANSPORT

Aeroline........................**109** E1
Air China........................**110** E1
Air France........................(see 73)
Air India........................(see 112)
All-Nippon Airways................**111** B5
Avis........................**112** C2
Berjaya Air........................(see 99)
British Airways (Agent)...........**113** D4
Cathay Pacific........................(see 8)
China Airlines........................**114** C7
China Eastern........................(see 110)
Emirates........................**115** B4
Etihad........................(see 14)
EVA Air........................**116** C4
Garuda Indonesian Airlines.......(see 5)
Hertz........................**117** C4
Japan Airlines........................(see 5)
Jet Airways........................(see 112)
KLM Royal Dutch Airlines.......(see 73)
Kuwait Airways....................(see 115)
Lufthansa........................(see 116)
Malaysia Airlines....................**118** C4
Mayflower........................**119** C6
Myanmar International Airways (Agent).................**120** C5
Orix........................**121** C7
Philippine Airlines (Agent).....(see 112)
Qatar Airways........................(see 120)
Royal Brunei Airlines............(see 115)
Sri Lankan Airlines................(see 117)
Thai Airways........................(see 111)
Vietnam Airlines......................**122** B5

Tue-Sat) and – of course – great views of the Petronas Towers. In the early evening, it can seem like everyone in town has come down here to watch the glowing towers punching up into the night sky.

Kids and kidults can fill an educational few hours at **Petrosains** (Map pp84-5; ☎ 2331 8181; www.petrosains.com.my; Level 4, Suria KLCC; adult/child RM12/7; 9.30am-4pm Tue-Thu, 1.30-4pm Fri, 9.30am-5pm Sat, Sun & holidays), an interactive science discovery centre in Suria KLCC. Many of the science-oriented displays and activities focus on the wonderful things that petrol has bought to Malaysia – no prizes for guessing who sponsors the museum. There are all sorts of buttons to press and levers to pull; you don't have to be a boy to enjoy it, but it probably helps.

The impressive **Aquaria KLCC** (Map pp84-5; ☎ 2333 1888; www.klaquaria.com; Concourse level, KL Convention Centre; adult/child RM38/26; 11am-8pm) is a short stroll from Suria KLCC, in the basement of the KL Convention Centre. As well as tanks of colourful fish and touch-a-starfish type activities, you can walk through a 90m underwater tunnel to view sinister-looking (but mostly harmless) sand tiger sharks and giant gropers. If possible, time your trip to coincide with the shark feeding (3pm on Monday, Wednesday and Saturday).

You can swap consumerism for culture at the interesting **Galeri Petronas** (Map pp84-5; ☎ 2051 7770; www.galeripetronas.com; 3rd fl, Suria KLCC; admission free; 10am-8pm Tue-Sun), an art gallery which showcases contemporary photography and paintings. It's a bright, modern space and the work on display often delves deep into Malaysian history and culture. Check the website for details of upcoming shows.

DHARMA REALM GUAN YIN SAGELY MONASTERY

Just down the road from the consumer excesses of Suria KLCC, you can retreat into quiet meditation at this expansive **Buddhist temple** (Map pp84-5; 161 Jln Ampang; 7am-4pm). Although modern, the calm spaces, potted bonsai, mandala ceilings and giant gilded statues create an appropriately contemplative mood. The shrine is dedicated to Guan Yin, the Buddhist goddess of compassion, represented by the central statue in the main shrine.

MENARA KL & BUKIT NANAS FOREST RESERVE

Although the Petronas Towers are taller, the 421m **Menara KL** (KL Tower; Map pp84-5; ☎ 2020 5448; www.menarakl.com.my; 2 Jln Punchak) offers the best views over the city. Surrounded by a dense area of pristine jungle, this lofty spire is KL's answer to Seattle's Space Needle or Auckland's Sky Tower. This is the world's fourth-highest telecommunications tower – the bulb at the top contains the revolving restaurant Seri Angkasa (p112) and an **observation deck** (adult/child RM20/10; 9am-10pm) with soaring views over KL. This is the best place to appreciate the phenomenal growth of the city – on clear days you can see planes taking off from Sultan Abdul Aziz Shah Airport, 20km from the town centre. A free shuttle bus runs between the tower and Jln P Ramlee.

The Menara KL stands atop the **Bukit Nanas Forest Reserve** (Map pp84-5; 7am-6pm), gazetted in 1906. A series of nature trails snake through the jungle, which contains a variety of animals and plants typical of lowland dipterocarp forests. You can access the park from Jln Raja Chulan, Jln Bukit Nanas or from the Menara KL. Free guided tours leave from the base of the Menara KL at 11am, 12.30pm, 2.30pm and 4.30pm daily lasting around 45 minutes. Drop into the **information centre** (Map pp78-9; ☎ 2698 8244; www.forestry.gov.my; 9am-5pm) on Jln Raja Chulan to see displays on the wildlife inside the park.

Near the base of the tower, **AJ Hackett** (☎ 2141 0822; www.aj-hackett.com; adult/child RM30/15; 11am-7pm) operates the Flying Fox, a giant,

OBJECTS IN THE ARCHITECTURE

For reasons best known to themselves, the British decided that Indian Mughal architecture was the perfect look for colonial KL. In more recent years, Malaysians have had their own ideas, creating buildings with a distinct local identity inspired by traditional ceremonial objects and motifs from Islamic art. The most famous example of this is the Petronas Towers (see p83) by the Argentinean architect Cesar Pelli. The cross-section of each tower is an eight-sided star that echoes the patterns from Arabic tiles, the five tiers represent the five pillars of Islam and the crowning masts call to mind two gigantic minarets.

Other striking buildings to look out for include the following:

- Chulan Tower (Map pp84–5; 3 Jln Conlay) – completed in 2006, this new skyscraper on the edge of the Golden Triangle resembles a vast Chinese pagoda, jacked up on top of a red-marble tower.
- Istana Budaya (p121) – designed by Mohammed Kamar Ya'akub, the building's soaring roof is based on a traditional Malay floral decoration of betel leaves, while its footprint resembles a *wau bulan* (Malay moon kite).
- Kompleks Dayabumi (p77) – this 35-storey marble-clad tower is one of KL's most graceful buildings. It was designed by Nik Mohammed and the hanging marble screens pay tribute to the pierced screens on medieval mosques.
- Menara KL (above) – the tower's bulbous pinnacle is inspired by a Malaysian spinning top, and the interior features Arabic inscriptions and stucco work that recalls a mosque mihrab (the niche that points towards Mecca).
- Menara Maybank (Map pp78–9; 100 Jln Tun Perak) – designed by Hijas Kasturi, this was one of KL's first skyscrapers but it still stands out today for its chunky design inspired by the handle of a kris, the traditional Malay dagger.
- National Library of Malaysia (p74) – one of the city's most striking buildings, created by architect Shamsuddin Mohammed; traditional motifs from Malay fabrics are incorporated into both the roof and interior walls.
- Tabung Haji (Map pp84–5; 201 Jln Tun Abdul Razak) – another of Kasturi's creations, this striking tower houses the Haj pilgrimage funding body. The five main exterior columns represent the five pillars of Islam while the overall structure recalls the drum used to summon pilgrims to the Haj and the shape of a traditional Arabic perfume vessel.

HERITAGE UNDER THREAT

Once upon a time, the entire business district of Kuala Lumpur (KL) was dominated by elegant colonial-era mansions belonging to tin and rubber tycoons. One by one, these stately homes have been bulldozed in the name of progress and profit, replaced by sky-piercing office blocks and aircraft hangar–sized shopping malls. The few mansions that remain face an uncertain future. Some – like the MTC (see p76) – have been saved by becoming embassies or government offices but many are abandoned, used as car parks until developers find the money to start the concrete pouring. You can witness one of these sad stories just behind the (ironically named) Asian Heritage Row: **Wisma Loke** (Map p92; Jln Medan Tuanku), the fading former home of tin and rubber mogul Loke Yew, is slowly falling into ruin. Similarly threatened are the wooden Malay houses of Kampung Baru, where permission for development is already being granted.

In 2005 the government passed the National Heritage Bill which allows the authorities to protect properties of historic note by declaring them heritage buildings. The Malay version of the UK National Trust, **Badan Warisan Malaysia** (Heritage of Malaysia Trust; Map pp84-5; ☎ 2144 9273; www.badanwarisan.org.my; 2 Jln Stonor; 9am-5.30pm Mon-Sat) is itself housed in a restored colonial mansion. Trustees are campaigning to save similar historic buildings around Malaysia. One of the trust's big success stories was the **Rumah Penghulu** (Map pp84-5; Badan Warisan Malaysia, 2 Jln Stonor; suggested donation RM5; tours 11am & 3pm Mon-Sat), a glorious wooden stilt-house saved from dereliction and moved to the trust headquarters from Kedah. The Trust also holds exhibitions in the mansion, which has a good shop selling antiques, crafts and books on Malay architecture and history.

high-speed death-slide, one of several thrill rides dotted around the city.

OTHER SIGHTS

Immediately southwest of Berjaya Times Sq is the looming hulk of **Pudu Jail** (Map pp84–5). The star-shaped building was constructed by the British in 1895 and hundreds of prisoners were executed here (many for drug offences) before the prison was closed in 1996. Painted around the perimeter wall is the world's longest mural, a frieze of tropical trees and islands created by prisoners with 2000L of paint. Many locals believe that the prison is haunted and local travel agents occasionally organise ghost tours of the decaying cells and corridors. See p99 for a list of agents, and contact them to see if any tours are currently running.

A short stroll east is the gleaming modern **Masjid Albukhary** (Map pp78-9; Jln Hang Tuah; 6am-midnight). Its dome features stunning blue tile work outside and detailed stucco work inside. Visitors are welcome outside of prayer times.

Brickfields, KL Sentral & Around

The following attractions are best reached from KL Sentral.

NATIONAL MUSEUM

Housed in a striking 1960s building styled after a Sarawak longhouse, this **musem** (Muzium Negara; Map p90; ☎ 2282 6255; www.museum.gov.my; Jln Damansara; adult/child RM2/free; 9am-6pm) has an extensive but musty collection of exhibits on the history, economy, arts, crafts and culture of Malaysia. The galleries are slowly being renovated but most of the new displays seem to concentrate on the achievements of modern Malay royals and politicians. Probably the most interesting exhibits are the cultural displays in the main building, the treasures from Malay shipwrecks in the annexe and the 19th-century stilt house in the garden (formerly owned by the Sultan of Terengganu). The KL Tourist Association (p76) office occupies a wooden pavilion in the grounds. Free museum tours (in English and French) leave the ticket desk at 10am on Tuesday and 11am on Thursday – contact **Museum Volunteers Malaysia** (☎ 2282 6255; mvmenquiries@yahoo.com) for more information.

Although the museum is very close to KL Sentral station, it's surrounded by a snarl of spaghetti junctions – the easiest way to get here is by taxi, or via the walkway over the highway south of the Lake Gardens.

OLD KL TRAIN STATION

Midway between Chinatown and KL Sentral is another of AB Hubbock's Moorish-inspired fantasies. **KL Train Station** (Map pp78-9; Jln Sultan Hishamuddin) opened with much pomp and circumstance in 1911 to receive trains from Butterworth and Singapore. This wonderful

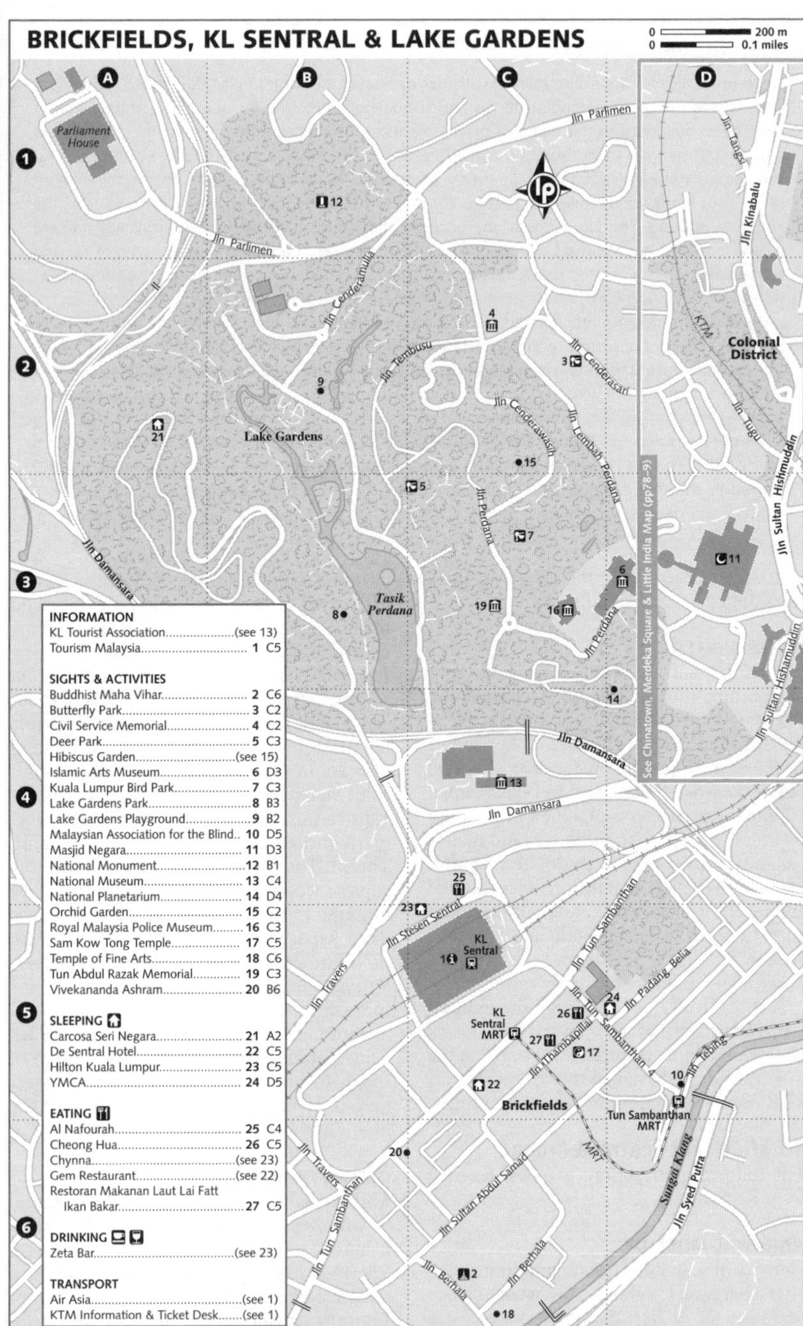
BRICKFIELDS, KL SENTRAL & LAKE GARDENS
0 200 m
0 0.1 miles
A
B
C
D
1
2
3
4
5
6
Parliament House
Jln Parlimen
Jln Parlimen
Jln Tangsi
Jln Kinabalu
Jln Cenderamulia
Jln Tembusu
Jln Cenderasari
KTM
Colonial District
Jln Tugu
Jln Cenderawasih
Jln Lembah Perdana
Lake Gardens
Jln Perdana
Jln Sultan Hishmuddin
Jln Damansara
Tasik Perdana
Jln Perdana
Jln Sultan Hishamuddin
See Chinatown, Merdeka Square & Little India Map (pp78-9)
Jln Damansara
Jln Damansara
Jln Tun Sambanthan
Jln Stesen Sentral
KL Sentral
Jln Travers
Jln Padang Belia
KL Sentral MRT
Jln Tun Sambanthan
Jln Thambapillai
Jln Tun Sambanthan 4
Jln Tebing
Brickfields
Tun Sambanthan MRT
MRT
Sungai Klang
Jln Travers
Jln Sultan Abdul Samad
Jln Syed Putra
Jln Tun Sambanthan
Jln Berhala
Jln Berhala
INFORMATION
KL Tourist Association (see 13)
Tourism Malaysia 1 C5
SIGHTS & ACTIVITIES
Buddhist Maha Vihar 2 C6
Butterfly Park 3 C2
Civil Service Memorial 4 C2
Deer Park 5 C3
Hibiscus Garden (see 15)
Islamic Arts Museum 6 D3
Kuala Lumpur Bird Park 7 C3
Lake Gardens Park 8 B3
Lake Gardens Playground 9 B2
Malaysian Association for the Blind 10 D5
Masjid Negara 11 D3
National Monument 12 B1
National Museum 13 C4
National Planetarium 14 D4
Orchid Garden 15 C2
Royal Malaysia Police Museum 16 C3
Sam Kow Tong Temple 17 C5
Temple of Fine Arts 18 C6
Tun Abdul Razak Memorial 19 C3
Vivekananda Ashram 20 B6
SLEEPING
Carcosa Seri Negara 21 A2
De Sentral Hotel 22 C5
Hilton Kuala Lumpur 23 C5
YMCA 24 D5
EATING
Al Nafourah 25 C4
Cheong Hua 26 C5
Chynna (see 23)
Gem Restaurant (see 22)
Restoran Makanan Laut Lai Fatt Ikan Bakar 27 C5
DRINKING
Zeta Bar (see 23)
TRANSPORT
Air Asia (see 1)
KTM Information & Ticket Desk (see 1)

confection of turrets and towers looks particularly impressive in the golden afternoon sunlight – half close your eyes and you can imagine the old *Orient Express* steaming in from Singapore. The soaring domes and arches were skilfully restored in the 1980s, but the station was replaced by the new KL Sentral station in 2001. Today the platforms are only used for KTM Komuter trains to the suburbs. Although it's looking a bit dishevelled these days, it's still worth coming here to imagine the glory days.

The station is mirrored by the equally handsome **Malayan Railway Administration Building** (Map pp78–9) across the road. Walking here from Chinatown, the best route to follow is to take the pedestrian bridge across from the Central Market to Kompleks Dayabumi and then head south around the back of the post office to the underpass leading to the Masjid Negara.

THEAN HOU TEMPLE

The Chinese community has created some impressive modern temples around KL, including this ornate **temple** (off Map pp72-3; ☎ 2274 7088; www.hainannet.com; Persiaran Endah, admission free; 🕑 8am-10pm), off Jln Syed Putra, just south of Brickfields. Crowning a forested hilltop, this towering shrine is full of gaudy statuary and topped by a soaring dragon roof. The main shrine is dedicated to the Heavenly Mother, Thean Hou, flanked by Guan Yin (the Buddhist Goddess of Mercy) on the right and Shuiwei Shengniang (the Goddess of the Waterfront) to her left.

There are great views from the temple's upper decks, while the basement level houses hawker stalls and stalls selling prayer beads and other religious bric-a-brac. To reach the temple, take a taxi or catch bus 27 or 52 from Klang bus station and then walk up the hill (ask to be dropped off near the temple). Another option is to take the monorail to Tun Sambanthan station, cross Jln Syed Putra using the overpass and walk up the hill.

OTHER SIGHTS

There are several other interesting religious monuments in Brickfields. The small **Sam Kow Tong Temple** (Map p90; 16 Jln Thambapillai; 🕑 7am-5pm) has an impressive dragon roof but a slightly sterile interior. Nearby you'll find the redeveloped **Temple of Fine Arts** (Map p90; ☎ 2274 3709; 114 Jln Berhala) and the huge **Buddhist Maha Vihar** (Map p90; ☎ 2274 1141; www.buddhistmahavihara.com; 123 Jln Berhala), centred on a stucco Buddhist shrine dating from 1895, founded by Sinhalese Buddhists.

On the far side of the river, off Jln Istana, is the **Istana Negara** (Map pp72–3), the official residence of the Sultan of Malaysia. The palace itself is only distantly visible through the trees, but locals flock here to see the hourly changing of the palace guard (from 8am to 4pm weekdays).

Pudu

PUDU MARKET

South of the Golden Triangle, accessible by LRT from Hang Tuah station, **Pudu Market** (Map pp72-3; Jln Pasar Baru; 🕑 6am-2pm) is KL's biggest wet and dry market. It's a frenetic place, full of squawking chickens, frantic shoppers and porters forcing their way through the crowds with outrageous loads. Stalls here sell everything from goldfish in bowls to pig heads, cows tongues and durians in baskets. Arrive early in the morning to experience the market at its most lively and pungent. You can recover from the sensory overload at the attached hawker court – see p113. Pudu Market

NIGHT MARKETS

As well as the permanent markets dotted around KL, atmospheric *pasar malam* (night markets) are held once a week at several different locations around the city. The night markets are quite a spectacle – whole streets vanish suddenly under a sea of hawker stalls, traders' tables and motorcycles modified into mobile kitchens. Stalls are piled high with grilled fish, fragrant curries in tin pots and mysterious rice cakes bundled up in banana leaves. Rice and noodles swish around in giant woks, roti and *dosa* (paper-thin Indian pancakes) sizzle on oily hot plates, and locals gather in their hundreds to feast until the early hours of the morning. The top *pasar malam* in KL are the Saturday night markets on Jln Raja Muda Musa in Kampung Baru (see p114) and Lorong Tuanku Abdul Rahman in Little India (p113), and the Sunday night market on Jln Telawi in Bangsar (p113).

CHOW KIT & KAMPUNG BARU
400 m
0.2 miles
To Lake Titiwangsa (300m)
Titiwangsa
Titiwangsa LRT
Titiwangsa MRT
Hospital Kuala Lumpur
Chow Kit
Chow Kit MRT
Kampung Baru
Kampung Baru LRT
Medan Tuanku MRT
Sultan Ismail LRT
PWTC LRT
Dang Wangi LRT
KLCC LRT
Ampang Park LRT
Muslim Cemetery
Petronas Towers
Suria KLCC Shopping Complex
KLCC Park
See Golden Triangle & KLCC Map (pp84–5)
Jln Tun Razak
Jln Tuanku Abdul Rahman (Jln TAR)
Jln Raja Muda Abdul Aziz
Jln Raja Abdullah
Jln Raja Laut
Jln Sultan Ismail
Jln Ampang
Ampang Elevated Hwy
Jln Gurney
Jln Semarak
Jln Perumahan Gurney
Jln Yap Kwan Seng
Jln Sungai Baharu
Jln Raja Alang
Jln Raja Mahmud
Jln Raja Uda
Jln Hamzah
Jln Haji Sheik Ahmad
Jln Daud
Jln Haji Hussein
Jln Haji Taib
Jln Tiong Nam
Jln Putra
Jln Ipoh
Jln Pahang
Jln Fletcher
Jln Temerloh
Jln Mayang
Jln Binjai
Jln Doraisamy
Jln Medan Tuanku
Jln Yap Ahshak
Jln D S Sulaiman
Jln Raja Muda Musa
Jln Haji Hassan Salleh
Lg Gurney
Sungai Gombak
Sungai Klang
Sungai Bunas
MRT
LRT

INFORMATION
- Alliance Française 1 E1
- British Embassy 2 F4
- French Embassy 3 F4
- Hospital Kuala Lumpur 4 B1
- MSL Travel 5 A2
- National Library of Malaysia 6 D1
- Post Office 7 A4

SIGHTS & ACTIVITIES
- Bazaar Baru Market 8 B3
- Imperial Spa (see 14)
- Kampung Baru Mosque 9 C3
- Kuala Lumpur Craft Market (see 10)
- National Art Gallery 10 C1
- Tatt Khalsa Diwan Gurdwara 11 B3
- Wisma Loke 12 A4

SLEEPING
- Ben Soo Homestay 13 A3
- Sheraton Imperial 14 B4
- Tune Hotel 15 A4

EATING
- Bujang Lapok 16 C3
- Chop 'n' Steak 17 C3
- CoChine by Indochine 18 B4
- D'Istana Jalamas Café (see 28)
- Hawker Court (see 8)
- Ikan Bakar Berempah 19 C3
- Lotus Hotel 20 A4
- Pasar Malam (Night Market) 21 C3
- Pesona Food Court (see 31)
- Restoran Buharry 22 B4
- That Indian Thing 23 B4
- Warong Perasan 24 C3
- Yé Chine (see 27)

DRINKING
- Bed 25 B4
- Ivy 26 B4
- SaVanh (see 18)

ENTERTAINMENT
- Cynna 27 B4
- Garçon (see 29)
- Istana Budaya 28 C1
- Loft (see 27)
- Maison 29 B4

SHOPPING
- Clothes Market 30 A3
- Maju Junction 31 A4
- UO Superstore 32 B3

TRANSPORT
- AAM (Automobile Association Malaysia) 33 E3
- Long-Distance Taxi Station (see 34)
- Pekeliling Bus Station 34 A1

is five minutes' walk from Pudu LRT station; go south along Jln Pudu, right onto Jln Pasar, then right down Jln Pasar Baharu, passing the colourful temple **Choon Wan Kong** (Map pp72-3; Jln Pasar Baharu) dating from 1879.

Chow Kit & Titiwangsa

Access the following sights from Chow Kit or Titiwangsa monorail station.

BAZAAR BARU MARKET

This lively **market** (Map p92; 469-473 Jln TAR, Chow Kit; 8am-9pm) sells clothes, toys, buckets, stationery, noodles, spices, fresh meat and live, flapping catfish, as well as a staggering array of weird and wonderful tropical fruit (see p81). Overweight cats loiter around the wet market looking for scraps, and locals struggle through the narrow aisles with huge bags of shopping. Just wandering round is a heady, sensory experience, particularly for the sense of smell. Stroll east along Jln Raja Alang to peek at the **Tatt Khalsa Diwan Gurdwara** (Map p92; 24 Jln Raja Alang), the largest Sikh Temple in Southeast Asia and spiritual home for KL's 75,000 Sikhs.

TAMAN TASIK TITIWANGSA

Head to relaxing **Taman Tasik Titiwangsa** (Map pp72-3; daylight hours), a recreational park surrounding Lake Titiwangsa, for a picture-postcard view of the city skyline. As well as relaxing walking paths and jolly boating on the lake (from RM3 per hour), there are tennis courts, squash courts and a remote-controlled car racing track where enthusiasts stage miniature Formula Ones. The park is a favourite spot for courting Malaysian couples (and the religious police on the lookout for improper behaviour). Temporary attractions are often set up on the lakeshore – in 2007, the park played host to the Eye on Malaysia, an oversized big wheel styled after the London Eye.

Taman Tasik Titiwangsa is a 10-minute walk east of the Titiwangsa monorail station. Rapid KL bus B101 runs between Titiwangsa and KL Sentral, via Jln Cheng Lock in Chinatown. Bus B102 runs here from Jln Bukit Bintang and bus B103 runs here from the KLCC.

NATIONAL ART GALLERY

Housed in a striking pyramid-shaped block between Jln Tun Razak and the park is KL's main **art gallery** (Balai Seni Lukis Negara; Map p92; 4025 4990; www.artgallery.gov.my; 2 Jln Temerloh), showcasing the best of contemporary Malaysian art. The gallery was closed for renovation at the time of writing, but it's set to reopen in 2008 – check locally for the latest information on opening times and entry fees. Next door to the gallery is the Istana Budaya (see p121), built according to traditional principles of Malay architecture but almost certainly influenced by the Sydney Opera House.

Kampung Baru

Just a few hundred metres from the high-rise business district, the Malay neighbourhood of Kampung Baru looks like a rural Malaysian village smuggled into the heart of the city. Despite overwhelming pressure to develop this area, the streets are lined with old-fashioned wooden houses and people go quietly about their business on the leafy residential streets – except on Saturday night when a bustling *pasar malam* (night market) takes over the area around Jln Raja Muda Musa (see p114).

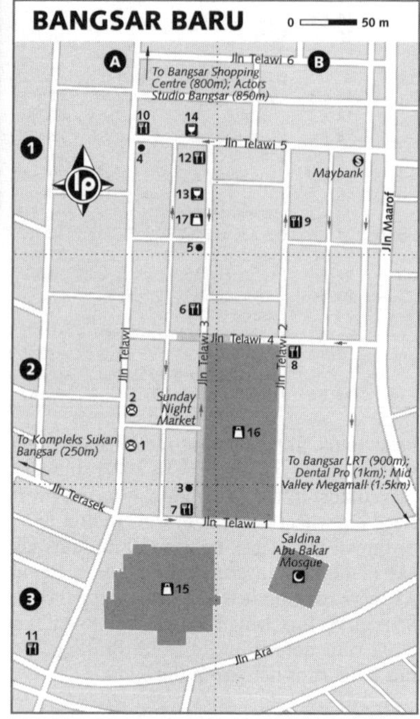

INFORMATION
DHL 1 A2
MPH Bookstores Bangsar .... (see 16)
Post Office 2 A2
Silverfish Books 3 A3

SIGHTS & ACTIVITIES
Celebrity Fitness .... (see 16)
Touches de Siam 4 A1
Yoga 2 Health 5 A1

EATING
Alexis Bistro 6 A2
Bangsar Seafood Garden Restaurant .... (see 11)
Country Farm Organics .... (see 15)
Cungdinh .... (see 11)
Delicious .... (see 16)
Devi's Corner 7 A3
Hawker Court 8 B2
La Bodega 9 B1
Nasi Kandar Pelita 10 A1
One Bangsar 11 A3
Saffron .... (see 11)
Sagar .... (see 11)
Telawi Street Bistro 12 A1

DRINKING
Bakerzin .... (see 15)
Bar Flam 13 A1
Bar Upstairs .... (see 6)
Finnegan's 14 A1

SHOPPING
Bangsar Village I 15 A3
Bangsar Village II 16 B2
Mumbai Sé .... (see 16)
Planet Scuba .... (see 10)
Valentine Willie Fine Art 17 A1

This is a place to just come and soak up the sleepy village atmosphere. The Kampung Baru LRT station provides easy access to the backstreets and it's worth coming here for lunch any day of the week. Jln Raja Muda Musa is lined with hawker-style restaurants serving excellent Malay food to hordes of hungry city workers – see p114 for some recommendations.

Nearby on Jln Raja Alang is the **Kampung Baru Mosque**, built in 1924, with a handsome gateway decorated with eye-catching tiles in traditional Islamic patterns. Stalls around the mosque sell religious paraphernalia, including white *kopia* and black songkok, the traditional head coverings for Malay Muslim men. It's a short stroll west from here to Chow Kit and the Bazaar Baru market.

ACTIVITIES

Bowling & Pool

Pool halls are a popular diversion for folk in the city and most of the big malls. Most of the big malls also have enormous bowling alleys – the going rate is around RM5 per game plus RM2 for shoe hire. Good places to send balls and pins flying include the following:

Ampang Bowl (Map pp84-5; ☎ 2144 8323; 5th fl, Berjaya Times Sq, 1 Jln Imbi; 10am-1am, to 3am Fri & Sat)

Brewbull Pool (off Map p94; ☎ 2938 3893; 3rd fl, Mid Valley Megamall, Mid Valley City; noon-2am, to 3am Fri & Sat) Pool tables cost RM3/12 per game/hour.

Cosmic Bowl (off Map p94; ☎ 2287 8280; 3rd fl, Mid Valley Megamall, Mid Valley City; 10am-1am, to 2am Fri & Sat)

Golf

KL has a half a dozen world-class golf courses, but most are only open to paid-up members or guests from affiliated international clubs. The following clubs welcome visitors without the rigmarole of being nominated by an existing member. Call ahead to check club rules and rates.

Kelab Darul Ehsan (off Map pp72-3; ☎ 4257 2333; www.berjayaclubs.com/kde/; Taman Tun Abdul Razak, Jln Kerja Air Lama; 9/18 holes from RM50/80; 10am-7pm, to 8.30pm Sat & Sun) Respected nine-hole course on the northeast city limits.

Titiwangsa Golf Club (Map pp72-3; ☎ 2693 4903; Aras 17172, Taman Tasik Titiwangsa; 9 holes RM31.50; 7am-6pm Tue-Sun, 2-6pm Mon) Nine-hole course behind Taman Tasik Titiwangsa.

Gyms & Yoga

All the top-end hotels have gyms, and there are several chains dotted around the city. Note that most places require you to have an interview with a personal trainer to draw up an exercise regimen – a bit of a hassle if you just want a workout. Ask about short-term membership deals – these can work out far cheaper than the usual admission charge of RM50.

California Fitness (Map pp84-5; ☎ 2145 1000; www.californiafitness.com; Menara Standard Chartered, Jln Sultan Ismail; 6.30am-11pm Mon-Fri, 7am-9pm Sat, 10am-9pm Sun)

Celebrity Fitness (Map p94; ☎ 2092 8000; Bangsar Village II, Jln Telawi 1, Bangsar Baru; 6am-midnight)

Fitness First (Map pp84-5; ☎ 2711 3299; www.fitnessfirst.com.my; Wisma SPK, 22 Jln Sultan Ismail; 6.30am-11pm Mon-Fri, 7am-7pm Sat & Sun)

A KUALA LUMPUR PAMPERING

Spa treatments are all the rage in KL and even men are getting in on the act with dedicated treatments for male wellness at many of the city's exclusive spas. The best spas are generally found in big five-star hotels, but more accessible spas are appearing all over the city. KL's spas draw on traditional therapies from India, China and Southeast Asia, reflecting the diverse ethnic groups who inhabit the city – a perfect way to unwind after a cramped flight or the train ride from Thailand or Singapore.

The best place to start your quest for indulgence is the swish Starhill Gallery (see p122) on Jln Bukit Bintang. The 'Pamper' floor is dedicated to exclusive spa and beauty treatments: **Spa Indrani** (Map pp84-5; ☎ 2782 3868; www.spaindrani.com; 10am-10pm) offers Asian therapies for men and women; **Ayurvedium** (Map pp84-5; ☎ 2142 2202; www.ayurvedium.com; 10am-9.30pm) specialises in traditional Indian herbal treatments; and **Escentials** (Map pp84-5; ☎ 2148 3288; 10am-9.30pm) specialises in facial treatments.

Next door at the JW Marriott, the award-winning **Starhill Spa** (Map pp84-5; ☎ 2715 9000; JW Marriott, 183 Jln Bukit Bintang; 10am-9pm Mon-Sat, 9.45am-7pm Sun) offers aromatherapy baths, exfoliating scrubs and various styles of massage, plus steam rooms and plunge pools. Nearby at the Ritz Carlton, **Spa Village** (Map pp84-5; ☎ 2782 9090; Ritz Carlton, 168 Jln Imbi; 9am-9pm) offers a similarly indulgent menu of Chinese, Indian and Southeast Asian healing and toning therapies.

There are many more upmarket spas in the Jln Bukit Bintang area. At Berjaya Times Square, **JoJoBa Spa** (Map pp84-5; ☎ 2141 7766; www.jojoba.com.my; 15th fl, East Wing, Berjaya Times Square Hotel, 1 Jln Imbi; 11am-12.30pm) claims to be Malaysia's largest tourist spa – come for seaweed wraps, coffee scrubs and ginger tea. Around the corner on Jln Imbi, **Rustic Nirvana** (Map pp84-5; www.rusticnirvana.com; 173-175a Jln Imbi; 11am-8.30pm Mon-Fri, 10am-7pm Sat) offers a host of health pampering and holistic treatments for women only.

Chinatown is only just getting the spa bug, but **Old Asia** (Map pp78-9; ☎ 2273 9888; 1st fl, Central Market; 10am-9pm) in the Central Market offers a full range of rubs and scrubs. Bangsar Baru has half a dozen exclusive spas. **Touches de Siam** (Map p94; ☎ 2287 2866; www.touchesdesiam.com.my; 2a Jln Telawi; 10am-10pm) specialises in Thai massage, which focuses on the entire skeletomuscular system. Another spa worth the trip across town is the **Imperial Spa** (Map p92; Sheraton Imperial, Jln Sultan Ismail, Dang Wangi; 10am-10pm) at the Sheraton Imperial.

If the top-end spas seem out of reach, there are numerous Chinese massage and reflexology centres strung out along Jln Bukit Bintang. Pricing is fairly consistent – around RM65 per hour for a full body massage and RM25 for 30 minutes of foot reflexology, though you can bargain down – but standards vary and some places are slightly seedy. One reliable option on the strip is the local branch of **Old Asia** (Map pp84-5; ☎ 2143 9888; 14 Jln Bukit Bintang; 10am-10pm); as well as massages and reflexology, you can try ear candle and hot stone treatments.

Another interesting option is to visit one of the blind masseurs in Brickfields. There are numerous massage centres here, employing blind people who might otherwise be forced to beg for a living. Contact the **Malaysian Association for the Blind** (Map p90; ☎ 2272 2677; www.mab.org.my; Kompleks MAB, Jln Tebing, Brickfields) for recommendations.

Yoga 2 Health (Map p94; ☎ 2282 3866; www.yoga2health.com.my; 1st fl, 21A Jln Telawi 3, Bangsar Baru; nonmembers RM45-50; 🕑 11am-7pm Tue-Sun) Conveniently located yoga centre in Bangsar Baru.

Yogshakti (off Map pp72-3; ☎ 4252 4714; www.yogshakti.com; 1 Lorong Damai 13; classes RM45; 🕑 beginners 7pm Mon-Wed, intermediate 7pm Thu, Sat & Sun) Hatha yoga centre in the embassy district east of Jln Tun Razak, off Jln Ampang.

Swimming & Other Sports

Hotel pools in KL are generally only open to guests, but there are some excellent water parks, including the Desa Waterpark (p130) and Sunway Lagoon (p129). As well as the following sports centres, you can rent tennis courts at the YMCA (see p104) provided you have your own racket.

Chin Woo Stadium (Map pp78-9; ☎ 2072 4602; admission RM4; 🕑 2-8pm Mon-Fri, 9am-8pm Sat & Sun) Great city views at this 50m outdoor pool. All swim suits must be tight fitting. Located off Jln Hang Jebat.

Kompleks Sukan Bangsar (off Map p94; ☎ 2284 6065; 3 Jln Terasek 3, Bangsar Baru; entry adult/child RM1.50/60 sen 🕑 9.30am-noon, 2pm-4.30pm & 6-8.30pm) Entry fee covers one 2½-hour session. You can also rent courts for badminton from 8am to 2am (per hour RM4) and tennis from 7am to 11pm (per hour RM4).

Theme Parks

There are numerous theme parks and water parks dotted around KL. The most convenient is **Cosmo's World** (Map pp84-5; ☎ 2117 3118; Berjaya Times Sq, 1 Jln Imbi; adult/child RM25/15; 🕑 10am-10pm), located inside the Berjaya Times Square shopping centre. Despite the mall location, there's a full-sized looping coaster plus a good selection of thrill rides for teenagers and gentler rides for families. (Avoid the DNA Mixer unless you want too see your *nasi lemak* a second time.) You'll find more thrill rides and wet and wild activities at Sunway Lagoon (see p129), Mines Wonderland (see p130) and Genting Highlands (p133).

WALKING TOURS

Although KL places many obstacles in the path of walkers, Chinatown and Little India are great places to explore on foot. The following walking tours will take you to the best of the sights.

Chinatown Walk

This tour starts at **Pasar Seni LRT station (1)** and explores the temples and sights of Chinatown. Walk along Jln Cheng Lock to **Central Market** (**2**; p77) on the corner of Jln Hang Kasturi.

WALK FACTS

Start Pasar Seni LRT Station
Finish Maharajalela Monorail Station
Distance 2km
Duration 1½ hours

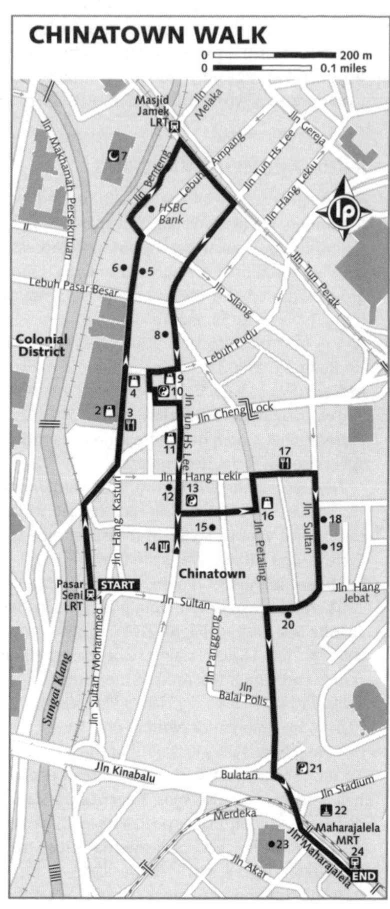

Browse the craft stalls, then pop over the road for a top-notch *roti canai* (flat bread with curry sauce) and a mug of *teh tarik* (tea with evaporated milk) at **Restoran Yusoof Dan Zakhir** (**3**; p110). Continue north on Jln Hang Kasturi and take a peek at the aromatic **Soon Hing Cheong Ginseng shop (4)** on the corner of Lebuh Pudu, a popular centre for traditional Chinese medicine. Next, cross Lebuh Pasar Besar into

Medan Pasar (5), the site of KL's original market, marked by a clock tower built in 1937 to commemorate the coronation of King George VI. Note the striking **painted shophouses (6)** along both sides of the road.

Continue north behind the HSBC Bank along Jln Benteng for the best view of the colonial-era **Masjid Jamek** (**7**; p76), KL's most atmospheric mosque. If dressed appropriately, you can peek inside, except during the weekly Friday prayers. Next cut back along Jln Tun Perak and turn right into Jln Tun HS Lee. Stroll south until you reach the bus stand at Lebuh Pudu, then look right to see the glorious but time-ravaged frontage of the **Bank Simpanan Building (8)**, built in 1914 (it now houses Le Village hostel, p101). Cross over Lebuh Pudu and duck into **Thin Yee (9)**, a Chinese store selling incense, spirit money and crockery.

Continue west along Lebuh Pudu then duck down the next alley to the back gate of the historic **Sze Ya Temple** (**10**; p77). Exit via the gatehouse on Jln Tun HS Lee and cross over busy Jln Cheng Lock. Note the pint-sized pines in the **bonsai shops (11)** to your right then cross Jln Hang Lekir, passing the four-storey Art Deco **Lee Rubber Building (12)**, the tallest building in KL when it was constructed in the 1930s (the bookstore on the ground floor is good for postcards and stationery).

Further along Jln Tun HS Lee on the right is the **Guandi Temple** (**13**; p77), another Taoist temple filled with the scent of incense smoke. On the other side of the road is the 22m-high *gopuram* (temple tower) of the **Sri Maha Mariamman Temple** (**14**; p76) – step inside to see devotees making fragrant offerings of jasmine flowers and carnations. Cross the road again and duck down **Jln Sang Guna (15)**, the covered arcade housing Chinatown's pungent wet and dry market.

Beyond is the famous **Petaling Market** (**16**; p77) – if you arrive any time after midday, the whole street will be crowded with stalls selling fake everything. Head north through the market and turn right Jln Hang Lekir, passing several **streetside restaurants (17)** where you can grab a quick satay. Next, turn right along Jln Sultan – as you head south, grab some tropical fruit from the well-stocked **fruit stall (18)** opposite Swiss-Inn and pop into **Shanghai Books** (**19**; ☎ 2078 4642; 63C Jln Sultan; 🕑 10am-7pm) to check out the *chop* (Chinese seals) and calligraphy materials.

Follow the road round to the right, passing a string of creature-crammed **pet shops (20)**, then turn south down Jln Petaling. Turn left at the end of the road to reach the ornate **Chan She Shu Yuen Temple** (**21**; p77) and **Guan Yin Temple** (**22**; p77). Over the footbridge is the **Chinese Assembly Hall** (**23**; p121), built during the British era and now a focal point for the campaign to stop discrimination against Indian and Chinese Malaysians. Finish your walk at **Maharajalela monorail station (24)** and let the air-conditioned monorail whisk you to your next destination.

Colonial KL & Little India Walk

Starting from the **Sultan Abdul Samad Building** (**1**; p80), this walk takes in the highlights of colonial Kuala Lumpur and Little India.

WALK FACTS

Start Sultan Abdul Samad Building
Finish Medan Tuanku
Distance 2km
Duration Three hours

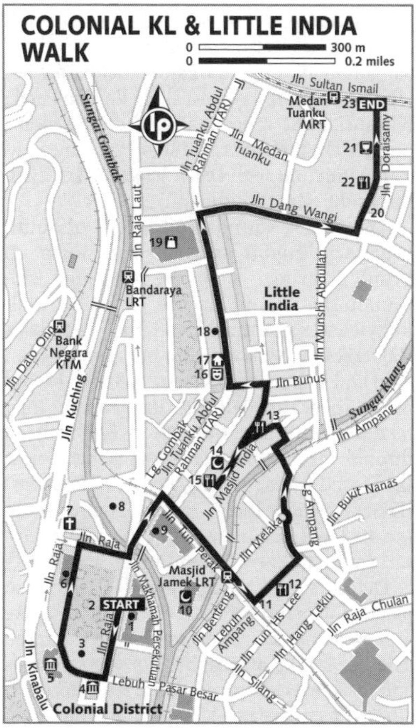

COLONIAL KL & LITTLE INDIA WALK

0 — 300 m
0 — 0.2 miles

Begin your walk by examining the handsome frontage of this outrageous Victorian Mughal fantasy, formerly the Secretariat of the British colonial government and now home to one of Malaysia's highest courts. The building looks even better from across the road in **Merdeka Square** (**2**; p80), which used to resound to the thwack of leather on willow during cricket matches held by the British administration.

After pausing to note the enormous **flagpole (3)** where the Malaysian flag was first raised on 31 August 1957, take a circuit around the cricket field, ducking into the **National History Museum** (**4**; p81) to swot up on Malaysian history. Next, check out the gallery at the **Kuala Lumpur Memorial Library** (**5**; p74) and stroll past the front of the mock-Tudor **Royal Selangor Club** (**6**; p80), still a meeting point for KL high society. Cross Jln Raja and pop into **St Mary's Cathedral** (**7**; p82), a white-washed British colonial church from 1894.

Returning to Jln Raja Laut, head north, passing the bizarre **pitcherplant fountain (8)**, a theme-park creation set in a small garden marooned by a cat's cradle of roads. Turn right at the next major junction onto Jln Tun Perak, passing another mock-Mughal building – the **Sessions & Magistrates Courts** (**9**; Jln Tun Razak), designed by AB Hubbock, who also created the Sultan Abdul Samad Building and the landmark **Masjid Jamek** (**10**; p76), a short walk east along Jln Tun Perak. Nip inside the mosque if you're dressed appropriately, then continue along the same road to the junction with **Lebuh Ampang (11)**, which marks the edge of Little India.

The sights, sounds and smells of South India will engulf as you stroll north up Lebuh Ampang – shops are piled high with Ganesh statues and incense, radios blast out Bollywood soundtracks and busy **restaurants (12)** serve inexpensive South Indian vegetarian food and Indian sweets (see p109). At the end of the road, turn left into Jln Ampang then take the footbridge over the river and stroll through the bustling alleyways to emerge near Jln Masjid India, passing a covered **food court (13)** serving tasty Indian snacks. You're now in the thick of Little India – note the goldsmiths, sari shops and flower vendors on all sides.

Detour south to **Masjid India (14)**, the main place of worship for local Muslims, and take a peek at the surrounding covered market. The bazaarlike atmosphere of the streets is enhanced every Saturday from late afternoon when a **pasar malam** (**15**; p108) sets up along Lorong Tuanku Abdul Rahman – the narrow alley sandwiched between Jln Tuanku Abdul Rahman (Jln TAR) and Jln Masjid India. Stroll north to Jln Bunus and cross Jln TAR to the historic **Coliseum Cinema (16**; ☎ 2692 5995; Jln TAR), which now screens nonstop Tamil and Bollywood blockbusters. Next door is the similarly historic **Coliseum Hotel** (**17**; p103) – although faded, this colonial relic is a great spot to eat or drink or even sleep.

Continue north along Jln TAR passing the fabulously renovated frontages of a string of chichi silk shops – the Art Deco beauty containing **Euro Moda** (**18**; ☎ 2694-0805; 126 Jln TAR; 🕓 10am-8pm) at No 126 is particularly striking. Continue past **Sogo** (**19**; p122), one of KL's better department stores, then turn right onto Jln Dang Wangi. Head east until you reach Jln Doraisamy, aka **Asian Heritage Row (20)**. Don't expect too much heritage – this renovated street is all about upmarket restaurants and trendy bars and clubs. If you don't have the energy to party, opt instead for a relaxing pint at the **Ivy** (**21**; p117) or a mango smoothie at **Buharry** (**22**; p110) before finishing up at the nearby monorail stop **Medan Tuanku (23)**.

QUIRKY KUALA LUMPUR

Berjaya Times Square Attend a manga comics expo or an Ultraman convention, then ride a rollercoaster above the milling crowds (p122).

Istana Negara Join the locals marvelling at the changing of the guards at the home of the King of Malaysia (p91).

National Planetarium Indulge a few *Spinal Tap* memories at the scale model of Stonehenge by this planetarium in the Lake Gardens (p83).

Sentul Park Koi Centre (Map pp72-3; ☎ 4045 1311; www.ytlcommunity.com; Jln Strachan) Discover a little piece of Japan and pools of giant koi carp.

Sze Ya Temple Let wooden sticks tell your fortune at this Chinatown temple (p77).

Tugu Drum Circle Bang your drum on Sunday afternoons with this drum circle at the National Monument in the Lake Gardens (p83).

COURSES

There are some unusual cultural courses on offer if you'll be staying in KL for a while.

Arts & Crafts

Gajah Gajah Gallery (Map pp78-9; ☎ 2164 2100; Central Market Annexe, Jln Hang Kasturi; painting classes RM50; 🕓 10am-9pm) This small art studio offers informal classes in Malaysian tribal painting; children will love the bright colours and hands-on painting style.

Kompleks Budaya Kraf Kids and adults can try traditional Malay crafts such as batik or pottery at the craft village in the grounds of this one-stop crafts complex. Check with the information desk for prices (p123).

School of Hard Knocks (off Map pp72-3; ☎ 4145 6122; visitorcentre.royalselangor.com; 4 Jln Usahawan 6, Setapak Jaya; classes RM50; 9am-5pm) This famous pewter centre offers entertaining 30-minute classes where you make your own pewter bowl; advance booking required.

Music & Dance

Kuala Lumpur Performing Arts Centre A variety of performing arts courses are offered here, including courses in traditional instruments such as the *gamelan* (traditional orchestra). Contact the centre for prices and timings (p121).

Sutra Dance Theatre Courses in Odissi and other forms of classical Indian dance are offered at this cultural centre near Taman Tasik Titiwangsa. Contact the theatre for prices and timings (p121).

Temple of Fine Arts This Indian cultural centre was under renovation at the time of writing, but the courses in classical Indian dance, song and music were due to resume when it reopens. Stage shows take place here throughout the year. The temple also runs the Annalakshmi restaurant (p114) in Bangsar. Contact the centre for prices and timings (p91).

Meditation, Yoga & T'ai Chi

Buddhist Maha Vihar This Brickfields landmark offers a variety of courses. Meditation and chanting classes plus dharma talks take place most days. Contact the centre for timings; classes are run on a donation basis (p91).

Chan She Shu Yuen Temple Runs t'ai chi classes at various locations around Chinatown and Brickfields (p77). Contact Mr Eng on ☎ 2274 3246 for details.

Vivekananda Ashram (Map p90; ☎ 2272 5051; 220 Jln Tun Sambanthan, Brickfields) This historic Indian ashram is part of the global Ramakrishna movement. Classes in *kundalini* yoga take place at 6.30pm on Tuesday – call for details.

Cooking

International School of Home Cookery (☎ 2274 1571; 9 Jln Teluk Pulai, Taman Seputeh) Lim Bian conducts classes on Nyonya, Chinese, Thai and Indian cuisine.

Kings Kitchen Klub (Map pp84-5; ☎ 2773 8689; www.westindining.com.my; Westin Kuala Lumpur, 199 Jln Bukit Bintang; classes incl lunch RM168) On fixed Saturday and Sunday mornings throughout the year, the chefs at the Westin's prestigious restaurants offer 12-person cooking classes covering everything from Indian and Malay cooking to Italian pasta and Chinese dim sum.

Norrizan Bakers (☎ 7876-3336; 22 Jln 22/49 Len Seng Garden, Petaling Jaya) Occasional courses in Malay cooking are offerred here. Phone for details.

Rohani Jelani (www.rohanijelani.com) Cookbook author Rohani Jelani offers hands-on courses in her KL kitchen. Classes are small (you need to book ahead) and end with a sit-down meal of the dishes prepared that day.

Languages

YMCA (p104) Want to learn the local lingo? Go to the YMCA for its Bahasa Malaysia classes. Other languages include Thai, Mandarin/Cantonese and Japanese, as well as courses in martial arts and different dancing types.

KUALA LUMPUR FOR CHILDREN

KL is probably the most child-friendly city in Southeast Asia. Malaysians love children and there are dozens of attractions around the city set up specifically to keep little ones entertained.

A good starting point is the Lake Gardens, particularly the Bird Park (p82), Butterfly Park (p82) and the playground and boating pond in the Lake Gardens Park (p82). The waterfall splash pool (p86) in the KLCC Park is great for waterbabies, as is the adjacent adventure playground and the Aquaria KLCC (p87).

Kids will also enjoy KL's malls. Berjaya Times Square (p122) has shops for kids of all ages plus a boisterous indoor theme park. Most big malls have bowling alleys (see p94) and cinemas (see p119) showing blockbuster kids' films. For younger kids, try Megakidz (off Map p94; ☎ 2282 9300; www.megakidz.com.my; 3rd fl, Mid Valley Megamall; entry weekday/weekend RM17/21) in the Mid Valley Megamall – there are storytelling sessions, art activities and an indoor adventure playground, and the centre provides a crèche service (RM30 to RM35 for two hours) for kids aged four and over.

There are more theme parks dotted around KL, including the indoor and outdoor parks at Genting Highlands (p133) and the wet-and-wild park at Sunway Lagoon (p129). Close to Sunway, the Pyramid shopping centre has a popular ice rink (p130). For nature activities, head to Zoo Negara (p131) or the canopy walkway at the Forest Research Institute of Malaysia (p132). The splash pools at Templer Park (p132) are also fun for a family picnic.

As well as these sights and attractions, there are plenty of child-friendly courses available in KL – see opposite.

TOURS

Local agencies offer various tours of the city and attractions around KL. Probably the easiest city tour is the **KL Hop-On Hop-Off** (☎ 2691 1382; www.myhoponhopoff.com; adult/child RM38/17; 🕑 8.30am-8.30pm), an air-con tourist bus that does a circuit of the main tourist sites half-hourly throughout the day. Stops include the KLCC, Jln Bukit Bintang, Menara KL, the Malaysian Tourism Centre, Chinatown, Merdeka Sq and the attractions of Lake Gardens. The ticket lasts all day and you can get on and off as often as you like.

Based at the Malaysian Tourism Centre (p76), **Malaysian Travel Business** (Map pp84-5; ☎ 2163 0162; MTC, 109 Jln Ampang) runs a decent selection of tours: half-day city tours and trips to the Batu Caves (RM50), day tours of Putrajaya (RM150), evening trips to see the fireflies at Kuala Selangor (RM180) and day tours to the Kuala Gandah elephant sanctuary (RM190 including an elephant ride). Cheaper rates apply for children under 12. Similar tours are offered by **Impressions** (Leisure & Incentive Tours; Map pp78-9; ☎ 2070 8667; www.impressions.com.my; 4th fl, Plaza Warisan, Jln Tun HS Lee, Chinatown), located inside the Plaza Warisan shopping arcade.

Based at the Backpackers Travellers Inn (opposite), **Going Places Tours** (☎ 2078 4008; www.goingplaces-kl.com; 60a Jln Sultan, Chinatown) runs a huge range tours to sights around KL tailored to the backpacker market. Popular tours include trips to the Forest Research Institute of Malaysia (RM130), firefly-spotting tours near Kuala Selangor (RM180) and trips to the Batu Caves (RM85). It also offers city tours (RM50), rock-climbing days at the Batu Caves (RM150) and rafting trips to Perak (RM255).

Several agents specialise in overnight trips to Taman Negara National Park in the north of Peninsular Malaysia, a 4343-sq-km reserve protecting one of the world's oldest tropical rainforests. **Travel Han** (Map pp84-5; ☎ 2144 0899; www.taman-negara.com; Ground fl, Radius International Hotel, Changkat Bukit Bintang) offers three-day, two-night packages from KL from RM350 to RM500 per person, including park fees, accommodation and meals.

FESTIVALS & EVENTS

The capital is a good venue for Malaysia's major holidays and festivals, including Chinese New Year, Deepavali and Thaipusam; see p219 for more information. Dates for nonreligious events shift from year to year so check the exact dates of the following festivals locally.

Flora Fest KL goes flower-crazy in January/February with exhibitions and the international Floral Parade.

City Day KL commemorates becoming a federal territory on 1 February each year with celebrations at Tasik Perdana and Lake Titiwangsa gardens.

KL International Tower Jump (www.kltowerjump.com) Adrenaline junkies descend on KL in March for the one day they can legally Base jump off the Menara KL.

Malaysian Grand Prix (www.malaysiangp.com.my) Special shopping promotions accompany the annual Formula One race at Sepang International Circuit in March/April.

Malaysia Fest (Colours of Malaysia) Two weeks in May – a celebration with exhibits of traditional arts and special cultural performances around town.

Shopping Carnival Shopping in KL becomes even more of a bargain as prices plummet during this annual June sale.

KL Festival (www.klfestival.org.my) July is a month of events showcasing Malaysian art, dance, theatre and music.

National Day Join the crowds in Merdeka Sq at midnight on 31 August to celebrate the anniversary of Malaysia's independence in 1957. There are parades and festivities the next morning – check with the MTC (p76) for this year's venue.

KL International Buskers Festival (www.malaysiabuskers.com) The streets fill with performers for nine days of musical and acrobatic fun during December.

VOLUNTEERING

Volunteering opportunities in KL are mainly geared towards Malaysians and Bahasa speakers. Most travellers who volunteer in the capital arrange a placement with a volunteering agency in their home country. Placements can be arranged in all sorts of fields, from community work with disadvantaged youngsters to local environmental projects – contact volunteering organisations before you leave home to secure a placement. One volunteer opportunity you can arrange after arrival is a day helping out at Zoo Negara (p131). You can volunteer any day of the week (minimum of four hours). See www.zoonegara.org.my/volunteer.html for details.

Another good place to find information on volunteering opportunities is your national embassy in KL – most diplomatic offices are involved with local community projects and can point you in the right direction. People with experience in development or community work could try contacting non-government organisations (NGOs) directly – there are useful listings of locally based NGOs on www.mycen.com.my/malaysia/ngo.html and www.msc.com.my/expatriate/volunteer_service.html.

SLEEPING

KL has accommodation to suit all budgets, from ultracheap backpacker hostels to tow-

TRANSITTING THROUGH KUALA LUMPUR?

If you arrive at the international airport (see p124) in the early hours of the morning, you might find the **Airside Transit Hotel** (☎ 8787 4848; Satellite Bldg, KLIA; d for 6 hours RM140-200;) useful. There's a fitness centre, business centre, spa and sauna, and all rooms come with attached bathroom and TV.

Alternatively, treat yourself to the overnight package at the luxurious **Pan Pacific KLIA** (☎ 8787 3333; www.panpacific.com/klairport; r from RM400;), linked by a bridge to the main terminal. Rooms are extravagantly appointed, there are three restaurants, a bar, a pool, tennis courts and a fitness centre, and there's a check-in desk by the luggage carousel in the airport so you can go straight to your room on arrival.

ering five-star palaces. One thing to note is that top end hotel rates in KL are fantastically good value for what you get – a five-star hotel room can be had for as little as RM250. At the other end of the spectrum, you can find a backpacker dorm bed for as little as RM9, though you may end up sharing it with unwelcome blood-sucking companions (itch, itch). Midrange hotels have traditionally been a little thin on the ground, but new places are now opening up to plug this gap in the market.

The main area for midrange and budget accommodation is the Golden Triangle, particularly the area around Jln Bukit Bintang. Hotels here range from basic hostels to big tower-block hotels at midrange prices. There's another group of budget hotels – some pretty grimy – in Chinatown, KL's original traveller centre. However, you need to watch your step as some hotels here are fronts for prostitution (targeting locals rather than foreigners). There are more inexpensive hotels in Little India and Chow Kit, though the same caveats apply. Top-end hotels are largely concentrated in the Golden Triangle – particularly along Jln Ampang and Jln Sultan Ismail – and above KL Sentral.

Rates quoted here are official rack rates, but most midrange and top-end places offer endless promotions which slash rates by up to 50% – always ask about special deals. Advance booking is a sensible precaution during the peak tourist season and on big public holidays. We have three categories for hotels in KL: budget (double room or dorm bed for RM70 or less); midrange (doubles from RM71 to RM250); and top end (doubles for RM251 plus).

Budget

CHINATOWN & LITTLE INDIA

Chinatown is awash with cheap backpacker hostels and budget hotels. However, some of the cheap hotels are basically brothels – not the most wholesome places to stay. Hotels in Little India mainly cater to visiting traders; rooms have decent facilities but little character. The following options are legit.

Lee Mun Guest House (Map pp78-9; ☎ 2078 0639; 5th fl, 109 Jln Petaling; dm/s/d RM9/22/27;) Don't expect the Ritz; this small boxy guesthouse is elevated above the competition by a cheerful collage of pictures cut out of magazines and plastered all over the walls. The super-cheap rooms share bathrooms, but you have a choice of fan or air-con (for about RM20 extra). The entrance is via an anonymous lift on Jln Sultan.

Backpackers Travellers Inn (Map pp78-9; ☎ 2078 2473; www.backpackerskl.com; 60B Jln Sultan; dm RM10, d without RM25-28; d RM50-60;) Travellers have been pulling up at this original Chinatown backpacker inn for decades. Although small and sparsely furnished, the rooms are clean, bedbug free and excellent value. There's a left-luggage service, a roof-top bar and café and a travel agent offering backpacker tours around Malaysia (see opposite). Considering the temperatures in KL, it's worth paying extra for an air-conditioned room.

Le Village (Map pp78-9; ☎ 019-278 9677; numa7777777@yahoo.co.uk; 99A Jln Tun HS Lee; dm/s RM12/20, d RM30-35) A bohemian air hangs over this shabby yet atmospheric hostel in a fading colonial building (the 1914 Bank Simpanan Building). Rooms are so-so but the communal spaces are livened up by colourful artworks created by the owner. Clean bathrooms, cooking facilities and free coffee and tea add to the appeal.

Pudu Hostel (Map pp78-9; ☎ 2078 9600; www.puduhostel.com; 3rd fl, Wisma Lai Choon, 10 Jln Pudu; dm/s/d RM12/30/40;) This big, institutional hostel has a huge open lounge area and pokey box rooms with a shared bathroom. It's opposite the Puduraya Bus Station, so the bus to your next destination is just minutes away. To get here, take the lift on Jln Pudu to the 3rd floor.

Red Dragon Hostel (Map pp78-9; ☎ 2078 9366; www.hostelreddragon.com; 80 Jln Sultan; dm RM20, s/d/tr RM40/50/60;) A hostel in an old cinema sounds like a great idea – the reality is rather less exciting. The rooms don't have much character but are a decent size and everything is clean, plus it's cheap and centrally located. There's an internet centre and a simple café for breakfast.

our pick **Coliseum Hotel** (Map pp78-9; ☎ 2692 6270; 98-100 Jln TAR; r RM35-45;) A real KL institution, the Coliseum has hardly changed since the 1920s. The same could be said of the bedsheets, but the fading wood-panel rooms still manage to exude a tangible colonial charm. Bathrooms are shared, but there's a delightfully timeless bar and Indian-style restaurant (p109) downstairs serving old-fashioned cocktails and nice fat steaks.

Casa Villa Travellers Lodge (Map pp78-9; ☎ 2031 1971; 24 Jln Pudu Lama; d without bathroom RM40, d with bathroom RM60-70;) A simple Indian-run guesthouse that benefits from being quiet and cheap. Box rooms have high ceilings which helps air circulation and there's a shaded patio with a pool table and darts. A two-minute stroll from the Puduraya bus stand.

Hotel Lok Ann (Map pp78-9; ☎ 2078 9544; 113A Jln Petaling; d from RM60;) It doesn't look like much from the outside but Lok Ann is a bright light among the gloomy cheap hotels of Chinatown. It's run by elderly Chinese staff who live on-site and keep the rooms brushed, cleaned and polished. All rooms have air-con and hot water. Rates are discounted by RM10 for single occupancy.

GOLDEN TRIANGLE & KLCC

There are numerous small guesthouses in the alleys north of Jln Bukit Bintang.

Red Palm (Map pp84-5; ☎ 2143 1279; www.redpalm-kl.com; 5 Tingkat Tong Shin; dm/s/d/tr incl breakfast RM25/40/65/90;) There's no sign outside this cosy shophouse hostel, which ensures a pleasantly informal atmosphere inside. Rooms are typical for the area – small and thin-walled with shared bathrooms – but the communal areas are great and the owners charming.

Pondok Lodge (Map pp84-5; ☎ 2142 8449; www.pondoklodge.com; 3rd fl, 20 Changkat Bukit Bintang; dm/s/d from RM25/50/55;) This cheerful little guesthouse above the Ceylon Bar (p117) makes more effort than most. The spacious rooms are kept in tip-top shape and there are several airy guest lounges and a magnificent rooftop sitting area with chairs under plant-covered pergolas. Shoes should be left at the door. Rooms with windows cost extra.

Green Hut (Map pp84-5; ☎ 2142 3339; www.thegreenhut.com; 48 Tingkat Tong Shin; dm/s/d incl breakfast RM25/50/65;) The ever-popular Green Hut is a wholesome travellers' choice with a varied selection of rooms and lots of communal spaces to relax in. It's bright and inviting and the air-conditioned rooms are a bargain. You can check your email and play pool. Pay more if you want a private bathroom.

Trekker Lodge (Map pp84-5; ☎ 2142 4633; www.thetrekkerlodge.com; 1-1 Jln Angsoka; dm/s/d withoutbathroom RM25/50/70;) Owned by the same team as Green Hut, the Trekker Lodge is another popular traveller-oriented place, with clean, brightly painted rooms, plus free internet access for guests and a relaxing TV lounge. The best rooms are the doubles without bathroom – the en-suite rooms (which cost extra) can be slightly musty.

Bintang Guesthouse (Map pp84-5; ☎ 2144 3398; 27 Jln Tong Shin; s/d/q RM30/50/90;) Located inside an old shophouse, this simple guesthouse attracts locals as well as foreigners, a rarity in this area. Rooms are the usual boxy wooden affairs with shared bathrooms, but the place has central air-con and a few rooms have tiny TVs. You can pay RM5 extra for a doubles with private bathroom and air-con.

our pick **Number Eight Guesthouse** (Map pp84-5; ☎ 2144 2050; www.numbereight.com.my; 8-10 Tingkat Tong Shin; dm/tw without bathroom from RM30/85, d from RM95-135;) Head and shoulders above the competition, Number Eight is a beautifully conceived guesthouse spread over two shophouses. We love the tea-lit tables on the patio, the comfy sofas in the TV lounge and the fact that the rooms are laid out like real hotel rooms, with wooden furniture, eccentric ornaments and old B&W photos on the walls. The rooms with bathroom have TVs; other rooms share an immaculate shower block at the back. Breakfast is included.

Rainforest Bed & Breakfast (Map pp84-5; ☎ 2145 1466; rainforest_kl@hotmail.com; 27 Jln Mesui; d incl breakfast/without bathroom RM80/70;) Lush greenery cascades down the front of this tasteful guesthouse. The wood-panel rooms are as clean as an Ikea showroom (you can pay extra if you want windows) and there are several TV rooms, terraces and balconies where guests can unwind. Rates go up by RM10 at weekends.

CHOW KIT

Ben Soo Homestay (Map p92; ☎ 012-675 6110; bensoohome@yahoo.com; 2nd fl, 61B Jln Tiong Nam; s/d RM30/35; ❄ 💻) Off Jln Raja Laut, this long-established homestay has just two rooms. Staying here is like visiting a family home – quite a different experience from the other guesthouses in town. The owners are very welcoming and the location quiet. Rooms with air-con cost extra.

Midrange

CHINATOWN & LITTLE INDIA

Hotel China Town Inn (Map pp78-9; ☎ 2070 4008; www.chinatowninn.com; 52-54 Jln Petaling; d RM80-100, tr RM130; ❄ 💻) The better of the two China Town Inns on Jln Petaling, this place offers cool, carpeted rooms and a calm escape from the hectic market outside. All rooms have attached showers and TV but only deluxe rooms have windows.

Palace Hotel (Map pp78-9; ☎ 2698 6122; www.palacehotel.com.my; 40-46 Jln Masjid India; d from RM120; ❄) Indian tourists favour this neat hotel arranged around a central atrium, right in the thick of things in Little India. Superior rooms have windows overlooking the bustle of Jln Sultan Masjid.

Mandarin Pacific Hotel (Map pp78-9; ☎ 2070 3000; mandpac@tm.net.my; 2-8 Jln Sultan; r from RM128; ❄) A decent, well-run place close to Pasar Seni LRT station. Rooms have been improved by a recent renovation – all have mosaic-tile bathrooms with tubs. We recommend paying the extra RM20 for a deluxe room with fridge and an external window.

Hotel Noble (Map pp78-9; ☎ 2691 7111; nobelkl@po.jaring.my; 4th fl, 165 Jln TAR; d incl breakfast with/without window RM180/150; ❄) One of the better Little India hotels, Hotel Noble is reached by an anonymous door behind a silk store. Rooms have bathrooms, minibars, safes, coffee- and tea-making facilities and TVs. To preserve the freshly cleaned aroma and clean white sheets, durians and mangosteens are banned.

Swiss-Inn (Map pp78-9; ☎ 2072 3333; www.swissgarden.com/hotels/sikl/; 62 Jln Sultan; d RM155-200; ❄ 💻) The Swiss connection is pretty vague, but facilities at this centrally located hotel are good for the price. Rooms with windows are worth the extra investment and there's an internet centre and a pleasant patio café. Enter from Jln Sultan rather than busy Jln Petaling.

Ancasa Hotel (Map pp78-9; ☎ 2026 6060; www.ancasa-hotel.com; Jln Tun Tan Cheng Lock; d RM165-265, q RM416; ❄ 💻) A tower hotel beside the Puduraya Bus Station offering big-hotel ambience at midrange prices. The above-average rooms have TVs, fridges, coffee- and tea-making facilities and in-room safes, and some have good views out over the city.

Also recommended:

Kowloon Hotel (Map pp78-9; ☎ 2693 4246; www.kowloonhotelkl.com; 142-6 Jln TAR; s/d from RM90/115; ❄) A decent midrange hotel with chintzy furnishings but a handy location in Little India.

Hotel Malaya (Map pp78-9; ☎ 2072 7722; www.hotelmalaya.com.my; cnr Jln Hang Lekir & Jln Tun HS Lee; d with/without window from RM161/138; ❄) Off from the Petaling Market; offers worn but comfortable rooms with fridges, TVs and tubs.

GOLDEN TRIANGLE & KLCC

Replica Inn (Map pp84-5; ☎ 2142 1771; www.replicainn.com; Changkat Bukit Bintang; s/d/tr from RM128/138/178; ❄ 💻) Curious name but a good hotel. The striking modern exterior conceals immaculately clean rooms that look like they received their first guests yesterday. The pricier rooms are bigger and face the front, admitting more natural light.

Hotel Imperial (Map pp84-5; ☎ 2148 1422; h.imperial@hotmail.com; 76-80 Changkat Bukit Bintang; s/d from RM128/168; ❄) The bright entrance promises much but the design ethos doesn't extend far beyond the lobby at this small tower hotel just off the main strip. Still, it's a decent choice, and very handy for Jln Alor food street (p106). Rooms have TVs, air-con, fridges and phones.

Hotel Fortuna (Map pp84-5; ☎ 2141 8310; www.fortunakl.com; 87 Jln Berangan; d RM148-270; ❄) A friendly place in the alley behind Jln Bukit Bintang. Rooms are excellent value and there's a good Middle Eastern restaurant downstairs, Restoran Sahara Tent (p112), where you can suck on a shisha. It's worth paying extra for the superior rooms with tasteful Chinese-style wood panels and screens.

Allson Genesis (Map pp84-5; ☎ 2141 2000; www.allson-genesis.com; 45 Tingkat Tong Shin; r from RM150, ste from RM255; ❄ 💻) Another hotel offering top-end facilities without the steep price tag. Although small, rooms are very contemporary. The main difference between the standard and deluxe rooms is the view – go deluxe for a glimpse of the Petronas Towers.

Bintang Warisan Hotel (Map pp84-5; ☎ 2148 8111; www.bintangwarisanhotel.com; 68 Jln Bukit Bintang; s/d from

RM173/196;) A pre-independence façade adds character to this small hotel in the thick of things on Jln Bukit Bintang. There's a pub and coffee shop, and the rooms in the tower behind are thoroughly modern.

Radius International Hotel (Map pp84-5; ☎ 2715 3888; www.radius-international.com; 51A Changkat Bukit Bintang; d RM202-260, ste from RM374;) Slightly out of scale with its surroundings, this big tower hotel has all the facilities of an international chain hotel but at lower prices. Rates are almost always on promotion and the tasteful 'premier' rooms have kettles, safes, tubs and LAN (Local Area Network) internet access.

Hotel Capitol (Map pp84-5; ☎ 2143 7000; www.fhihotels.com; Jln Bulan; d from RM207;) Hemmed in by shopping malls, the Capitol shares a pool with the flashier Federal Hotel but charges slightly less stratospheric rates. Uncluttered, well-laid out rooms have safes, kettles, LAN internet access (RM24 per day) and 24-hour room service.

Swiss-Garden Hotel (Map pp84-5; ☎ 2141 3333; www.swissgarden.com; 117 Jln Pudu; d from RM242;) Around the corner from the other Bukit Bintang hotels, with upscale rooms and a full suite of facilities, including a fitness centre.

BRICKFIELDS

De Sentral (Map p90; ☎ 2272 3748; 128 Jln Tun Sambanthan; s/d 60/75;) Extremely handy for KL Sentral – just across the road in fact – this small, tidy hotel has pocket-sized rooms with showers, TV and air-con. If you just want to freshen up before jumping on the train, the day rate is RM50 for four hours.

YMCA (Map p90; ☎ 2274 1439; www.ymcakl.com; 95 Jln Padang Belia; d/tw RM80/80, tr without bathroom RM100;) A great cheap choice near KL Sentral, the YMCA offers spic-and-span rooms with TVs, telephones and proper wardrobes for hanging up your clothes. There's an internet café, laundry, shop and café, and also tennis courts for hire. The education centre offers a broad programme of language courses (see p99).

Heritage Station Hotel (Map pp78-9; ☎ 2272 1688; Old KL Train Station, Jln Sultan Hishamuddin; s/d/tr RM98/108/128;) Offering a chance to stay in a piece of KL history, the hotel at Old KL Train Station (p89) has an evocative lobby but rather shabby, dated rooms. You can get here by KTM Komuter train and it's just a short walk to Chinatown or the Lake Gardens.

CHOW KIT

our pick **Tune Hotel** (Map p92; ☎ 7962 5888; www.tunehotels.com; 316 Jln TAR; r RM10-100;) Midway between Little India and Chow Kit, and not far from Medan Tuanku monorail station, this bright red-and-white hotel takes the Air Asia principle and applies it to hotel rooms. The ultraminimalist rooms can only be booked online and prices decrease the further ahead of time you book (down to a minimum of just RM10!). The basic rate just gets you the room – air-con, toiletries and other perks are extra.

Top End

Most top end hotels in KL offer heavily discounted promotional rates, so ask when you check in. Note that breakfast is usually extra.

GOLDEN TRIANGLE & KLCC

Hotel Istana (Map pp84-5; ☎ 2141 9988; www.hotelistana.com.my; 73 Jln Raja Chulan; r from RM375;) An outrageously ostentatious lobby gives way to more restrained styling in the rooms. Tasteful colours and ethnic fabrics create relaxing feng shui and there are fine city views. The outside pool is pleasantly cloaked in greenery and in-room amenities include LAN internet access, tea- and coffee-making facilities, safes, TVs, minibars and your own personal prayer rug.

Royale Bintang (Map pp84-5; ☎ 2143 9898; www.royale-bintang-hotel.com.my; 17-21 Jln Bukit Bintang; d from RM400;) Bright décor and tasteful details score points for this towering hotel on the Bukit Bintang strip. There's a lovely palm-shaded pool area, and rooms have all the expected mod cons, including minibars, safes and everything you need to make tea and coffee. Room service is 24-hour and rooms from the 15th floor up have LAN internet access. Promotional rates can slash the listed prices to almost midrange levels.

Impiana (Map pp84-5; ☎ 2141 1111; www.impiana.com; 13 Jln Pinang; d from RM437;) A sleek hotel that benefits from a great location (just metres from the KLCC) and a boutique design sensibility. Rooms have parquet floors and all the usual top-end amenities. The well-regarded spa has an infinity pool that seems to run right to the base of the Petronas Towers. There's wi-fi in the lobby and LAN internet access in the rooms.

JW Marriott (Map pp84-5; ☎ 2715 9000; www.ytlhotels.com.my; 183 Jln Bukit Bintang; d from RM460;) Linked to Starhill Gallery (p122) by a shimmering hall of lights, the Marriott is the first choice for travellers with big bank accounts and expensive tastes. Rooms have real grandeur and the overall mood is classical and refined. Several huge ballrooms host conferences and showy weddings. Business travellers will appreciate the work station with broadband internet access.

Shangri-La Hotel (Map pp84-5; 2032 2388; www.shangri-la.com; 11 Jln Sultan Ismail; r from RM520;) Opulence verging on decadence is the stock in trade of the Shangri-La. The glitzy rooms are almost as extravagant as the lobby and the gold-trimmed elevators. The restaurants here are highly regarded and there's a fair-sized pool and a gorgeous tropical garden. Laptop users will find wi-fi in the lobby and LAN internet access in the rooms.

Westin Kuala Lumpur (Map pp84-5; 2731 8333; www.westin.com/kualalumpur; 199 Jln Bukit Bintang; r from RM563;) Service is the watchword at the Westin – staff here are courteous and extremely professional. The tasteful rooms feature huge windows – some with grand views towards the Petronas Towers – and famously powerful showers. Commendably, children under 18 can sleep free in the same room as their parents.

our pick Hotel Maya (Map pp84-5; 2711 8866; www.hotelmaya.com.my; 138 Jln Ampang; r from RM575;) A designer hotel in every sense of the word, the Maya is full of polished stone and timber, unusual textiles and funky designer furniture. In case you can't be without your cappuccino and email, rooms have espresso machines and LAN internet access. The Maya has several chichi restaurants and the decadent glass-walled bathrooms have power showers and tubs. To seal the deal, the hotel is just a 200m stroll from the KLCC. Look out for discount promotional rates at weekends.

Mandarin Oriental (2380 8888; www.mandarinoriental.com/kualalumpur; KLCC, Jln Pinang; d from RM780;) Backing onto the greenery of KLCC Park in the shade of the Petronas Towers, the Mandarin is unashamedly luxurious. Silks and batiks lend an Asian feel to the rooms, which have every conceivable amenity: slippers and robes, ironing boards, internet access, the works. There's a spa and infinity pool that seems to merge into the parkland beyond.

Ritz Carlton (Map pp84-5; 2142 8000; www.ritzcarlton.com; 168 Jln Imbi; d from RM1000;) Only a handful of hotels in Asia offer this degree of sophistication. Dark wood and marble create an nostalgic old-world atmosphere, and rooms are extravagantly appointed. Ceramic tiffin pots and other pieces of Asian bric-a-brac add a hint of colonial grandeur. The on-site Spa Village (p95) is highly recommended. Promotional rates bring the room prices into the range of ordinary mortals.

Also recommended:

Coronade Hotel (Map pp84-5; 2148 6888; www.coronade.com; Jln Walter Grenier; d from RM255;) Well-equipped modern hotel behind Lot 10, with good views from upper floors.

Renaissance Kuala Lumpur (Map pp84-5; 2162 2233; www.klrenaissance.com; cnr Jln Sultan Ismail & Jln Ampang; r from RM385;) Notable for its excellent facilities and huge landscaped pool.

ELSEWHERE

Sheraton Imperial (Map p92; 2717 9900; www.starwood.com/kualalumpur; Jln Sultan Ismail, Dang Wangi; r from RM350;) An elegant and sophisticated hotel that combines top-end amenities with the illusion of antiquity. Rooms are extremely well appointed and the hotel is right on the doorstep of Asian Heritage Row. Work out some tension at the opulent spa (see p95) before supper.

Hilton Kuala Lumpur (Map p90; 2264 2264; www.hilton.com; 3 Jln Stesen Sentral; r from R385;) Sharing a fabulous landscaped pool and spa with the Meridien next door, the Hilton is a design diva's dream. Sliding doors open to join the bathroom to the bedroom, picture windows present soaring city views and rooms are decked out from floor to ceiling in eye-catching materials. It's almost on top of KL Sentral and there are five respected restaurants and two bars on-site.

our pick Carcosa Seri Negara (Map p90; 2295 0888; www.ghmhotels.com; Taman Tasik Perdana; ste RM1100-3500;) Scents of jasmine and lemongrass waft around the airy corridors of this colonial-era retreat in the heart of the Lake Gardens. Spread over two mansions – Carcosa and Seri Negara – this was once the residence of British Government representative Sir Frank Swettenham. When the hotel opened in 1989 the very first guests were Queen Elizabeth II and Prince Phillip of England. Staff are courteous and discrete, and the only sound to disturb your privacy will be the chirp of insects and the chatter of jungle birds. Facilities are luxurious and there are two excellent restaurants – Gu Lei House (serving great Chinese food) and the Dining Room (one of KL's most exclusive French restaurants).

EATING

KL is a world -class place to chow down. Every cuisine under the sun is represented here, from Malay and Nonya cooking to Chinese, Indian, Japanese, Korean and Thai food, plus dishes from across Europe and the Middle East. You can start the evening with tapas and finish with tamarind ice-cream – indeed, many restaurants deliberately combine cuisines, creating curious hybrid dishes such as spaghetti korma. And the best thing about eating in KL is the price – you can get as tasty a meal from a RM5 *mamak* (Indian Muslim) stand (see the boxed text, p110) as you can from a RM300-per-head fine-dining restaurant.

To some degree, food is localised to the areas where the different ethnic minorities live. Chinatown, Bukit Bintang and, to a lesser extent, Chow Kit are good places for Chinese food, while Little India has excellent South Indian vegetarian food. Kampung Baru shows off the pinnacle of Malay home cooking. See boxed text, below, for some essential KL snacks.

For international food, make a beeline for the five-star hotels or the big shopping malls. Starhill Gallery has a whole floor devoted to swish restaurants (an update on the traditional Asian idea of 'food streets') and Asian Heritage Row (Jln Doriaswamy) is awash with upmarket eateries and bars. Some whole districts are being taken over by restaurants – you'll find an incredible range of food on offer in Bangsar, Desa Sri Hartamas and on the alleyways north of Jln Bukit Bintang.

As well as the following recommendations, it pays to consult **Friedchillies** (www.friedchillies.com), a great website blog written by KL foodies. Two other useful sources of dining inspiration are the *Malaysia Tatler's Malaysia's Best Restaurants* (RM30; updated annually) and the *Star* newspaper's *Star Guide to Malaysian Street Food* (RM38).

Unless otherwise stated, the restaurants listed are open daily for lunch from noon to 2.30pm and dinner from 6pm to 10.30pm.

Food Streets

The grouping of restaurants onto 'food streets' has a long history in Asia, and this tradition has been continued by the builders of modern KL. Although some old-fashioned food streets remain – most notably Jln Alor – the concept has been updated in swish developments such as Asian Heritage Row, One Bangsar and the Starhill Gallery.

JALAN ALOR

KL's biggest collection of roadside restaurants sprawls along Jln Alor, just north of Jln Bukit Bintang. From around 5pm till late every evening, the street transforms into a continuous open-air restaurant, with hundreds of plastic tables and chairs and rival caterers shouting out to passers-by to drum up business. Most places serve alcohol and you can sample pretty much every Malay Chinese dish imaginable, from grilled fish and satay to *kai-lan* (Chinese greens) in oyster sauce and fried noodles with frogs' legs. The best way to experience the food street is to stroll along looking at the signs and the dishes on the tables to see what takes your fancy.

Stalls to look out for include: 1+1 (Map pp84–5), good for 'drunken' chicken *mee* (noodles)

MALAYSIAN TIFFIN

When the British came to Malaysia, they brought with them the Indian concept of tiffin – in simple terms, snacking between meals, which is now an integral part of Malaysian food culture – you'll see locals stopping off for a quick snack at any time of day. The undisputed king of tiffin snacks is *roti canai* ('ro-tee cha-nai'), fried unleavened bread served with several rich and spicy dipping sauces. Originally a South Indian creation, *roti canai* has been adopted by all communities in Malaysia. Some restaurants serve plain roti while others mix in onion and egg, but few places charge more than RM2 for this delicious snack. If you've been to southern Thailand, you may recognise roti as the basis for Thai-style chocolate pancakes. Another Malay favourite is *nasi lemak* – rice cooked in coconut cream, typically wrapped in banana leaves in a pyramid-shaped bundle with dried anchovies and peanuts.

The standard accompaniment to either dish is Malay-style tea, which comes in several forms – *teh tarik* is hot tea with condensed milk; *teh o* is hot black tea; *teh ais* is iced tea with milk; and *teh o ais* is iced black tea, usually with sugar and lemon. *Kopi* (coffee) is available in similar configurations.

with rice wine, dim sum and wontons; Wong Ah Wah (Map pp84–5), good for spicy chicken wings, grilled seafood, tofu and satay; and the unnamed but ever-popular frog porridge stall (Map pp84–5; bowl RM7) – you can choose to have 'spicy' where the frogs legs are served separate or 'nonspicy' where they're mixed in with the tasty rice gruel (per bowl RM7).

ONE BANGSAR

Jln Ara in Bangsar Baru has recently been redeveloped as 'One Bangsar' – an upmarket food street with a diverse collection of restaurants catering to Bangsar foodies. There are some great places to eat here – just stroll up and down the strip and pick a restaurant to match your mood.

Cungdinh (Map p94; ☎ 2283 5088; www.cungdinh.com; 63D-G Jln Ara; mains from RM30; lunch & dinner) Steaming bowls of *pho* (rice-noodle soup) and imperial dishes from Hue roll out of the kitchen at this popular Vietnamese restaurant. There's live traditional music from 8pm most evenings.

Saffron (Map p94; ☎ 2287 1158; www.saffron.com.my; 63G Jln Ara; mains from RM30; lunch & dinner) Saffron offers summer colours and Mediterranean food – tapas, salads, grilled scallops and the like. Food is good but it can get busy here at weekends.

Sagar (Map p94; ☎ 2284 2532; www.sagarrestaurant.com; 63A Jln Ara; mains RM30-100; lunch & dinner) The Bangsar branch of Sagar serves artfully prepared North Indian food in convivial surroundings. There's a sister restaurant in the Hotel Istana (see p112).

Bangsar Seafood Garden Restaurant (Map p94; ☎ 2282 2555; 63 Jln Ara; mains RM40-100; lunch & dinner) A huge, hangarlike seafood restaurant with tanks full of fish and crustaceans, and chefs on hand to cook them any way you fancy. It's popular at weekends for big family lunches.

STARHILL GALLERY FEAST LEVEL

The entire Feast (ie lower ground) Floor of the Starhill Gallery (p122) is given over to upmarket, themed restaurants, creating an underground food street. You'll need a healthy wallet but the food is some of the best in town. There are more choices away from the other Starhill restaurants on the Relish Floor.

Sentidos Tapas (Map pp84-5; ☎ 2145 3385; Feast Fl, Starhill Gallery; tapas RM5-20) A stylishly designed tapas bar, with a casual ambience and a huge range of authentic tapas on offer. There's an excellent-value tapas buffet on Sunday, with all-you-can-drink wine and sangria (RM60) or champagne (RM150).

our pick **Mythai Jim Thompson** (Map pp84-5; ☎ 2148 6151; www.jimthompson.com; Feast Fl, Starhill Gallery; mains RM15-60) Silk cushions and drapes abound at this Thai place that aims to create the colonial mood of Jim Thompson's villa in Bangkok. Refreshingly, style does not triumph over substance – the Thai food is excellent, with numerous regional dishes from around Thailand.

Vansh (Map pp84-5; ☎ 2142 6162; Feast Fl, Starhill Gallery; mains from RM30) This place offers high-quality Indian cuisine at prices that match the posh surroundings. Look out for imaginative fusion dishes such as tandoori-marinated lobster.

Gonbei (Map pp84-5; ☎ 2782 3801; Relish Fl, Starhill Gallery; mains RM30-100) This brilliantly conceived Japanese restaurant is entered through a Zen walkway of leaning beams. There's a broad sushi and sashimi menu, including seasonal *fugu* (blowfish) for the brave. Diners sit around a series of open kitchens.

Shook! (Map pp84-5; ☎ 2719 8535; Feast Fl, Starhill Gallery; mains RM80-100) A huge sprawling place with open kitchens and dedicated chefs preparing Pacific Rim, Japanese, Italian and Chinese food. The wine cellar is fabulously well stocked and the menu features loads of fresh seafood. Evening reservations advised.

Also recommended:

KoRyo-Won (Map pp84-5; ☎ 2143 2189; Feast Fl, Starhill Gallery; mains RM20-60) Excellent Korean barbecue dishes prepared at the table.

Jogoya (Map pp84-5; ☎ 2142 1268; Feast Fl, Starhill Gallery; lunch/dinner RM78/88) Huge family-friendly Japanese buffet restaurant.

ASIAN HERITAGE ROW

As well as trendy bars, Asian Heritage Row (aka Jln Doraisamy) is lined with upmarket restaurants, perfect for a preparty feast. As well as the following choices, there's great hawker-style food at Buharry (see boxed text, p110).

Yé Chine (Map p92; ☎ 2694 1888; 28-40 Jln Doriaswamy; meals RM30-80; lunch & dinner) Round Chinese doorways create a suitably imperial mood at the restaurant downstairs from Loft (p120) and Cynna (p120). Come for dim sum at lunchtime or filling claypot casseroles after a night on the dancefloor upstairs.

That Indian Thing (Map p92; ☎ 2698 6357; 52 Jln Doraisamy; mains RM60-100; 11am-3pm & 6-11pm) The

Indian choice on the strip serves very good North and South Indian food, with some curious fusion dishes such as spaghetti korma.

our pick **CoChine by IndoChine** (Map p92; ☎ 2721 2811; 62-66 Jln Doriaswamy; mains RM60-200; 🕑 11am-2.30pm & 6.30-11pm) The KL branch of a famous Singapore restaurant, Cochine serves dishes from Vietnam, Laos and Cambodia, subtly spiced and full of flavour. The décor plays tribute to Khmer temples and there's a popular bar, SaVanh (p117), downstairs.

Chinatown, Little India & Around

HAWKER STALLS & FOOD COURTS

Chinatown has some of the best street food in KL. From late afternoon the pavements along Jln Sultan and Jln Tun HS Lee fill with plastic chairs and tables, and mobile kitchens are set up in the street, serving an astonishing array of Malay and Chinese dishes. Many of the food stalls stay open till midnight or later and you can get a filling meal of rice and spicy stir-fried beef with a cold beer for as little as RM20. Everything is prepared fresh so the food is almost always safe to eat. To be absolutely safe, stick to stalls with lots of customers.

The best time to visit Little India is during the Saturday *pasar malam* on Lorong Tuanku Abdul Rahman, the alley between Jln TAR and Jln Masjid India. From midafternoon, this narrow lane becomes crammed with food stalls serving excellent Malaysian Indian food, as well as favourite dishes of the Chinese and Indian communities.

Masjid India Hawker Court (Map pp78-9; Jln Masjid India; meals RM2-10; 🕑 8am-9pm) A bustling covered hawker court serving all the usual Malay, Indian and Chinese favourites. Good to visit if you can't make it the Saturday *pasar malam.*

Puduraya Hawker Court (Map pp78-9; Puduraya Bus Station, Jln Cheng Lock; meals RM3-15; 🕑 7am-10pm) The cheapest place for hawker food is this bustling food centre inside the Puduraya Bus Station. A bowl of spicy *tom yam* (red-chilli–based hot-and-sour seafood soup) soup will set you back just RM5.

Mangrove Food Court (Map pp78-9; Central Market; meals RM5-25; 🕑 10am-10pm) Various Asian cuisines are showcased at this upmarket food court, upstairs at the souvenir market.

Two recommendations for something out of the ordinary are **Madam Tang's stall** (Map pp78-9; Jln Petaling; sweets RM2-5), run by an elderly lady who makes her own tasty *mochi* (Japanese-style fruit jellies with rice starch) and the **Hong Kee stall** (Map pp78-9; Jln Sultan; mains RM10-20) in front of the KK convenience store, which specialises in barbecued Portuguese-style seafood and chicken rice, slow-cooked in a clay pot.

CHINESE

Probably the most popular restaurants for travellers are the open-air cafés (open 11am to 11pm) on Jln Hang Lekir, which cuts across the Jln Petaling Market, where meals cost about RM10 to RM30. These places all serve cold beers at reasonable prices (around RM12 for a big bottle of Tiger) and Chinese and Malay staples of varying quality. Based on our experiences, the satay (grilled meat skewers) tends to be good while fried rice and noodles are less

HAWKER-STALL WORKER JOAN CHAN

Joan Chan works at the Hong Kee claypot chicken and Portuguese fish barbecue hawker stall (above) in Chinatown, run by three generations of the same family.

What is life like when you work on a hawker stall? Our stall is a family business – like most hawker stalls I think – but we've been here 25 years. My uncle and auntie work here, and so do my brothers. There are nine of us in total. It's hard work but it's nice to work with your family, and we only work in the afternoons when things start to cool down. Other people have to go to work in the mornings when the day is getting hotter and hotter. Why do we only cook these dishes? Well my grandfather tried claypot chicken and barbecued fish and decided it was so good we had to go out and cook it ourselves! It's not all work though. On my days off I do the same stuff as other people – I go to Times Square (p122) and Sungei Wang (p122) to buy clothes and go bowling with my friends, or sing karaoke. That's the great thing about KL – there's so much to do.

What are your tips for finding good street food in KL? Look for lots of people sitting around in the street and food being cooked fresh on the spot. Don't expect things to be toned down for foreigners though – we Malaysians like our food spicy!

successful. The main attraction is watching the crowds of tourists from as far afield as Sydney and Saudi Arabia haggling furiously over fake goods at the surrounding market stalls.

Sing Seng Nam (Map pp78-9; 2 Medan Pasar; mains RM5-10; 7am-5pm Mon-Sat) A popular workers' canteen specialising in inexpensive bowls of chicken rice and 'curry fish'.

Purple Cane Tea Restaurant (Map pp78-9; 2272 3090; 1 Jln Maharajalela; mains RM10-20; 11.30am-3pm & 6-9pm Mon-Fri, 11.30am-9.30pm Sat & Sun) Tucked behind the Chinese Assembly Hall, this laid-back place uses tea as an ingredient in most of its dishes. Intriguing specials include chicken soup with tea and ginseng, and beef simmered in lychee tea.

Restoran Oriental Bowl (Map pp78-9; 2032 5577; 5-7 Leboh Pudu; mains RM10-30; 10am-6pm Mon-Sat) Chinese office workers are lured to this health-food restaurant by the menu of Chinese dishes cooked with ginseng and medicinal herbs from the traditional Chinese pharmacy downstairs.

Chinatown also has a number of informal hawker-style restaurants, with various food stations serving classic Malay Chinese dishes. Almost all offer fried rice, fish curry, rice porridge, *mee* and tofu dishes – a meal should cost less than RM20. Recommendations include **Restoran Zhing Kong** (Map pp78-9; Jln Hang Kasturi; 7am-9pm), **Kedai Kopi Lai Foong** (Map pp78-9; Jln Cheng Lock; 6.30am-8pm) and **West Lake Restoran** (Map pp78-9; 15 Jln Sultan; 7am-2am).

EUROPEAN & FUSION

As well as the following restaurants, you can get decent Western meals at the Reggae Bar (see p116).

Coconut House (Map pp78-9; 2031 2830; 30 Jln Pudu Lama; pizzas RM15-30; noon-midnight, to 1am Fri&Sat) Hidden away on an alley north of Jln Pudu, this cheerfully bohemian restaurant serves great pizzas that have been prepared in a wood-fired oven.

Coliseum Café (Map pp78-9; 2692 6270; 100 Jln TAR; meals RM15-60; 10am-10pm) Resisting the passage of time, the café at the Coliseum still enjoys a good reputation for its sizzling steaks. Even if you don't come for dinner, it's worth stopping by for a cocktail at the atmospheric wood-panelled bar next door.

Café Café (Map pp78-9; 2141 8141; www.cafecafekl.com; 175 Jln Maharajalela; mains RM80-100; 6pm-midnight) Chinatown has a noticeable shortage of venues for a romantic dinner but Café Café is one of a kind. Flickering candles, crystal chandeliers and soft piano music conjure up exactly the right mood. The menu features a sophisticated selection of French and Italian dishes.

INDIAN

Capital Café (Map pp78-9; Jln TAR; satay sticks 50 sen; 7.30am-9pm) If you're wandering through Little India, drop into this hole-in-the-wall café for excellent Malay satay sticks (beef and chicken) with peanut sauce.

Lakshmi Vilas (Map pp78-9; 2072 2166; Lebuh Ampang; mains RM4-10; 5am-10.30pm) One of several good vegetarian curry houses on Lebuh Ampang serving tasty *thali* (plate meals) for just RM4. Leave some space for *barfi* (milk fudge) and other Indian sweets.

Bilal Restoran (Map pp78-9; 2078 0804; 33 Jln Ampang; mains RM4-10; 8am-9pm) This anonymous-looking canteen just east of Little India has a good reputation for South Indian Muslim food, served canteen-style with fresh roti and naan bread.

Sangeetha (Map pp78-9; 2032 3333; 65 Lebuh Ampang; mains RM5-20; 8am-midnight;) Tasty *thalis* and other South Indian dishes are sold at this restaurant that has the added bonus of powerful air-conditioning. The Friday lunch buffet (RM14) always pulls in a crowd.

MALAY & NONYA

our pick **Old China Café** (Map pp78-9; 2072 5915; www.oldchina.com.my; 11 Jln Balai Polis; mains RM20-60; 11.30am-10pm) Housed in the old guild hall of the Selangor & Federal Territory Laundry Association, this atmospheric café captures some of the charm of old KL. The walls are huge, and covered with old bric-a-brac, and the cook prepares Nonya dishes from Melaka and Penang, including a fine beef rendang (coconut and lime-leaf curry) with coconut rice and fiery Nonya laksa soup with seafood.

Precious (Map pp78-9; 2273 7372; 1st fl, Central Market; mains RM20-60; 11.30am-10pm) The owners of Old China Café also run this upmarket place in the Central Market, which manages to recreate the mood of mining-era KL despite the mall setting. The food is good and the art and antiques on display are mostly for sale.

THAI

Gin Ger (Map pp78-9; 2273 7371; 1st fl, Central Market; mains from RM30; noon-10pm) Wooden screens and Thai knick-knacks disguise the mall

MAMAK RESTAURANTS

A modern update to the traditional hawker stalls run by Indian Muslims, *mamak* restaurants have taken Kuala Lumpur (KL) by storm. These huge canteens offer some of the best food in KL, from spicy fish curries and fried rice to *dosa* (lentil flour pancakes), *roti canai* (flatbread with curry sauce) and fabulous tandoori chicken. There's no alcohol, but patrons wash down meals with huge mugs of Malay-style tea and coffee or fruit juices and lassi (Indian drinking yogurt). There are plenty of fruit and shaved ice desserts for pudding – ask for *ais kacang* ('ice ka-chang') or ABC (short for *air batu campur* meaning mixed ice). Best of all, most *mamak* restaurants are open 24 hours. Prices are a bargain – *roti canai* costs less than RM1 and a full meal of tandoori chicken, vegetable curry and naan bread shouldn't set you back more than RM15. Order your food by walking around the various food stations; a waiter will come to the table to take your drinks order and add up your bill, which is paid at the cashier when you finish. Try the following recommendations:

Devi's Corner (Map p94; cnr Jln Telawi 1 & Jln Telawi 3, Bangsar Baru; 6am-5am) A pavement-café mood prevails at this foliage-drenched canteen facing the Bangsar Village malls. The tray curries are excellent, with plenty of fish, prawns and other seafood.

Lotus Hotel (24hr) Chow Kit (Nasi Kandar Penang; Map p92; 1 Jln Medan Tuanku); KLCC (Map p92; Jln Binjai) Just north of Little India, Lotus is Chow Kit's favourite *nasi kandar* (Penang-style steamed rice) canteen. Expect huge trays of fish curry and lots of spicy fried meat and vegetables.

Nasi Kandar Bestari (off Map pp72-3; Jln 23/70a, Desa Sri Hartamas; 24hr) The most popular *mamak* house in Desa Sri Hartamas, serving tasty snack meals and rehydrating tea and coffee to people staggering home from pubs and bars.

Nasi Kandar Pelita (24hr) Bangsar Baru (Map p94; cnr Jln Telawi & Jln Telawi 5); KLCC (Map pp84-5; 149 Jln Ampang) Serves exquisite Indian Muslim food, including magnificent *roti canai* and *hariyali tikka* (spiced chicken with mint, cooked in the tandoor). The swish, fan-cooled pavilion near the KLCC is probably the flashiest of all the *mamak* canteens in KL.

Restoran Buharry (Map p92; 22-24 Jln Doriaswamy; 7am-2am Mon-Sat, 8.30am-10.30pm Sun) Giant fans blow cool, moist air around this popular hang-out for office workers on Asian Heritage Row. All the usual *mamak* favourites are on offer, plus excellent *tom yam* (red chilli–based hot-and-sour soup) and delicious mango smoothies.

Restoran Hameed's (Map pp78-9; Jln Sultan Mohamed; 5am-11pm) Conveniently located near Pasar Seni LRT station, Hameed's has steaming trays of hot curries, biryani and fried rice. Come at lunchtime for mouth-watering swimmer crabs and prawns, fried whole in chilli sauce.

Restoran Yusoof dan Zakhir (Map pp78-9; Jln Hang Kasturi; 24hr) A huge banana-yellow and palm tree–green canteen opposite Central Market serving huge portions of delicious *mamak* food. Fresh coconuts are chopped open at the entrance to provide a refreshing natural accompaniment to the spicy dishes served inside.

location at this upmarket Thai restaurant inside Central Market. It's a quiet place but the food is excellent. Try the Thai salads.

Golden Triangle & KLCC

HAWKER STALLS & FOOD COURTS

As well as the following options, be sure to visit Jln Alor food street (p106) for more top-notch hawker grub.

Signatures Food Court (Map pp84-5; Level 2, Suria KLCC; mains RM3-20; 10am-10pm) KLCC's best food court, showcasing a wide range of Asian cuisines. There's a smaller food court in the Ampang Wing on level Four.

Medan Selera Food Court (Map pp84-5; Lot 10, 50 Jln Sultan Ismail; mains RM3-20; 9am-1am) Extensive Asian food court on the lower level of Lot 10.

Avenue 10 Food Court (Map pp84-5; 10th fl, Berjaya Times Square, 1 Jln Imbi; mains RM3-20; 10am-10pm) Well stocked but slightly soulless food court in the Times Square mall.

CHINESE

Blue Boy Vegetarian Food Centre (Map pp84-5; ☎ 2144 9011; Jln Tong Shin; mains RM3-10; 7.30am-9.30pm) A cheerful hawker-style cafeteria that prepares vegetarian food so artfully that even hardened carnivores come back for another helping. It occupies the base of an apartment block, just past the end of Tingkat Tong Shin.

U Village (Map pp84-5; Jln Bulan 1; mains RM3-15; 9am-10pm) Locals pack into this bustling canteen throughout the day for Hong Kong–style Cantonese food at bargain prices, served in double-quick time. The barbecued pork rice is a treat. It's near the back door to Sungei Wang, opposite Plaza Chow Kit.

Restoran Dragon View (Map pp84-5; ☎ 2142 4111; Changkat Bukit Bintang; mains from RM10; 24hr) Diners are lured into this partly open-air Chinese restaurant by a kitchen window hung with crisp fresh vegetables. Food is prepared in a dozen different styles with a choice of beef, pork, fish, prawns, chicken, tofu or frog meat.

Crystal Jade La Mian Xiao Long Bao (Map pp84-5; ☎ 2148 2338; Annex Block, Lot 10, 50 Jln Sultan Ismail; mains RM15-40; 11am-10.30pm, from 10.30am Sat & Sun) A huge photographic menu makes ordering easy at this highly regarded Chinese restaurant at Lot 10. Specialities include steamed *xiao long bao* (Shanghai-style soup dumplings) and *la mian* (long hand-pulled noodles) fried or served in meaty soups.

Restoran Oversea (Map pp84-5; ☎ 2144 7567; www.restoranoveresea.com.my; 84-88 Jln Imbi; mains RM15-50) An unpretentious banquet restaurant that should feel comfortingly familiar to anyone who has spent time in mainland China. Specialities include pork belly, fish (cooked in various styles) and streaky bacon cooked in a pot with dried chillies.

Shang Palace (Map pp84-5; ☎ 2074 3904; Shangri-La Hotel, 11 Jln Sultan Ismail; mains RM20-300; 10.30am-2.30pm & 6.30-10.30pm) Seafood is the speciality at this gorgeously designed Chinese banquet restaurant. Topping the bill is 'Monk Jumps Over the Wall': shark fin, abalone, scallop and sea cucumber served in a monk's bowl (RM290). It's worth coming just to see the fabulous temple-style entrance.

Si Chuan Dou Hua (Map pp84-5; ☎ 2147 2303; Grand Plaza Parkroyal, Jln Sultan Ismail; mains from RM30) For a break from Cantonese seafood and dim sum, head to this sleek modern place in the Parkroyal hotel and try fiery Sichuan dishes from southwest China. Green tea flows freely from giant long-spouted teapots.

Tai Thong Grand Restaurant (Map pp84-5; ☎ 2162 4433; www.taithong.com.my; 2nd fl, North Block, Wisma Selangor Dredging, Jln Ampang; meals RM30-100) A popular lunchtime stop for dim sum, this upmarket Chinese banquet house switches to a Cantonese à la carte menu in the evening. Locals come here for the filling set meals.

EUROPEAN & FUSION

Palate Palette (Map pp84-5; ☎ 2142 2148; 21 Jln Mesui; mains RM10-30; noon-midnight Tue-Thu, noon-2am Fri & Sat) Picasso and Mondrian colours set the mood at this upbeat bar and restaurant just off Jln Nagansari. Arty locals come here for the broad fusion menu that features dishes as diverse as shepherds' pie and teriyaki salmon.

Bon Ton (Map pp84-5; ☎ 2141 3848; www.bontonkl.com; 8 Jln Conlay; mains RM20-70; noon-midnight Mon-Sat) Housed in an atmospheric Malay-style wooden pavilion just east of the Bukit Bintang tourist area, Bon Ton serves excellent Euro-Asian fusion food, plus a series of set menus showcasing cooking from around Malaysia. Sample such unusual dishes as *tom yam* carbonara, and black pepper and mango chicken.

Top Hat (Map pp84-5; ☎ 2142 8611; www.top-hat-restaurants.com; 7 Jln Kia Peng; mains RM30-70; closed Sun lunch) Set in an old mansion behind the KLCC, Top Hat offers more imaginative European and Asian cooking plus set menus of traditional Malay cooking. Whatever you order for mains, start with the house speciality, *pie tee* (crispy hat-shaped shells stuffed with shredded vegetables). Also check out the Top Room jazz bar (p120) upstairs at the weekends.

Frangipani (Map pp84-5; ☎ 2144 3001; 25 Changkat Bukit Bintang; mains RM30-100; 7.30pm-10.30pm Tue-Sun) Much feted for its innovative approach to European fusion cooking, Frangipani is leagues ahead of most of the competition. The décor is as slick as the menu, with a stunning dining room surrounding a reflecting pool, and there's an equally stylish bar upstairs.

Nerovivo (Map pp84-5; ☎ 2070 3120; www.nerovivo.com; 3A Jln Ceylon; mains RM50-100; noon-3pm & 6pm-midnight) Italian food all round at this refined, partly open-air restaurant uphill from Changkat Bukit Bintang. Pizza and pastas are sublime and there's a good value antipasti buffet lunch (RM20).

Le Bouchon (Map pp84-5; ☎ 2142 7633; www.lebouchonrestaurant.com; 14-16 Changkat Bukit Bintang; mains RM60-100; noon-2pm Tue-Fri, 7.30-10.30pm Tue-Sun) The dining room at this tasteful French-owned place could have been plucked straight from a Burgundy chateau. The wine list is extensive and the house bouillabaisse (seafood soup with saffron) is highly recommended.

Prego (Map pp84-5; ☎ 2773 8013; Westin Kuala Lumpur, 199 Jln Bukit Bintang; mains RM60-100) Arguably KL's finest Italian restaurant, Prego offers delectable Italian pizzas and pasta in chic but family-friendly surroundings. Come on Sunday for the free-flowing champagne brunch

(RM128/188 for three/five courses), with a balloon-twisting clown to entertain the kids.

Lafite (Map pp84-5; ☎ 2716 3111; Shangri-La Hotel, 11 Jln Sultan Ismail; mains RM60-200; noon-2.30pm Mon-Fri, 7-10.30pm Mon-Sat) The elegant French restaurant at the Shangri-La Hotel serves very fine food in very fine surroundings, with a wine cellar to match. The menu runs to foie gras, duck confit and Brittany oysters.

INDIAN & MIDDLE EASTERN

Srirekha (Map pp84-5; ☎ 2145 4339; 39 Jln Sultan Ismail; mains RM10-30; 11.30am-11.30pm) Probably the Golden Triangle's most authentic Indian restaurant, Srirekha pulls in huge crowds of Indian tourists (which can slow down the service). The Chettinad specialities are excellent and the house *thali* is cracking value at RM8/9 (veg/nonveg).

Restoran Sahara Tent (Map pp84-5; ☎ 2144 8310; Hotel Fortuna, 87 Jln Berangan; mains RM10-30; 11am-2am) Probably the most authentic of the new Middle Eastern restaurants opening up around Jln Bukit Bintang. Come here for Turkish coffee, meaty kebabs and couscous, then sit back with a bubbling shisha (RM15).

Spice of India (Map pp84-5; ☎ 2164 9221; Level 4, Suria KLCC; mains RM30-60; 11.20am-10.30pm) Don't be put off by the mall location – Spice of India offers some of the best North Indian food in the capital. Tandoori dishes are the house speciality, and the atmosphere is refreshingly informal.

Sagar (Map pp84-5; ☎ 2141 2532; Hotel Istana, 73 Jln Raja Chulan; mains RM30-100; lunch & dinner) The sophisticated restaurant at Hotel Istana enjoys an enviable reputation for spicy North Indian food. There's a branch in the One Bangsar food street (see p107).

JAPANESE

Most of the malls have fast-food sushi bars, but the following restaurants are worth a visit.

Kameya Restoran Jepun (Map pp84-5; ☎ 2142 0153; Federal Hotel Bldg, off Jln Bukit Bintang; mains RM20-50) A small, cosy and authentic Japanese restaurant situated near Plaza Low Yat. The menu covers everything from sushi and sashimi to tempura and *edamame* (boiled green soya beans).

Wa-Raku (Map pp84-5; ☎ 2145 0448; 3 Jln Stonor; mains RM50-200; lunch & dinner Mon-Sat) Japanese expats gather at this upmarket restaurant on the edge of the business district for authentic food and a sense of Zenlike calm. The sashimi is great and there are some good-value set menus.

MALAY & NONYA

Restoran de Kitaro (Map pp84-5; Jln Bulan 1, off Bukit Bintang; mains RM1-20; 7am-midnight) A busy open-air canteen next to BB Plaza serving possibly the cheapest *roti canai* (80 sen) and *nasi lemak* (RM1.50) in KL.

Restoran Nagansari Curry House (Map pp84-5; Jln Nagansari; meals RM5-10; 7am-midnight) This simple hawker-style restaurant serves a good selection of Malay dishes – soup *mee, tom yam* and so on – with a few Indian favourites thrown in for good measure. Fans blow moist air around the dining hall to keep diners cool.

Restoran Sakura (Map pp84-5; ☎ 2148 4315; 163-169 Jln Imbi; mains RM10-25; 11.30am-1am) Try this huge restaurant on the road behind the Ritz Carlton for Malay food in more upmarket surroundings. Look out for good-value late-lunch and early-supper specials.

Little Penang Kafé (Map pp84-5; ☎ 2163 0215; Level 4, Suria KLCC; mains from RM15; 11.30am-9.30pm) Probably the most enticing of the midrange restaurants on the 4th floor of Suria KLCC, this airy café serves authentic food from old Penang, including specialities such as curry *mee* (spicy soup noodles with prawns) and spicy Siamese *lemak laksa* (curry laksa).

Seri Melayu (Map pp84-5; ☎ 2145 1833; www.serimelayu.com; 1 Jln Conlay; set lunch/dinner RM35/60) Housed in a vast wooden pavilion, Seri Melayu firmly targets the coach-tour crowd, but the dinner show (starting at 8.30pm) is nevertheless good fun, the food is tasty and the buffet is all-you-can-eat.

our pick **Bijan** (Map pp84-5; ☎ 2031 3575; www.bijanrestaurant.com; 3 Jln Ceylon; mains RM60-100; noon-2.30pm & 6.30-10.30pm Mon-Sat, 4.30-10.30pm Sun) One of KL's best Malay restaurants, Bijan offers skilfully cooked traditional dishes in a sophisticated dining room that spills out into a tropical garden. Must-try dishes include *rendang daging* (dry beef curry with lemongrass), *masak lemak ikan* (Penang-style fish curry with turmeric) and *ikan panggang* (grilled skate with tamarind).

Seri Angkasa (Map pp84-5; ☎ 2020 5055; www.serimelayu.com; Menara KL, Jln Puncak; buffet lunch/dinner RM69/115) The owners of Seri Melayu also run this glitzy revolving restaurant atop the Menara KL tower (p88). As well as the lunch and dinner buffets, there are set meals for brunch and high tea at weekends, plus a full á la carte menu. There's a dress code so wear long trousers and shoes rather than sandals.

THAI & VIETNAMESE

Old Siam (Map pp84-5; ☎ 2148 3449; 23 Tingkat Tong Shin; mains RM20-60; 7.30pm-10.30pm) Part of a large Thai restaurant group, Old Siam still manages to feel cosy and inviting, partly because of the old-fashioned shophouse setting. The Thai food is competently prepared and there are happy-hour specials on drinks before 9pm.

our pick **Sao Nam** (Map pp84-5; ☎ 2144 1225; www.saonam.com.my; 25 Tingkat Tong Shin; mains RM30-70; noon-2.30pm & 7.30-10.30pm Tue-Sun) This excellent Vietnamese restaurant is decorated with colourful propaganda posters. The kitchen turns out huge plates of delicious Vietnamese food, garnished with basil, mint, lettuce and sweet dips. Despite being listed as a starter, the *banh xeo* (a huge Vietnamese pancake with meat, seafood or vegetables) is a meal all by itself.

Brickfields & KL Sentral

Gem Restaurant (Map p90; ☎ 2260 1373; 124 Jln Tun Sambanthan, Brickfields; mains RM5-20; 11.30am-11.30pm;) A Brickfields stalwart, this calm, air-conditioned restaurant serves good South Indian food, including specialities from Chettinad, Andhra Pradesh and the Malabar coast. The *thali* is great value.

Chynna (Map p90; ☎ 2264 2266; Hilton Kuala Lumpur, KL Sentral, Brickfields; mains RM60-150; noon-2.30pm & 6.30-10.30pm) The best of the Hilton's cutting-edge Studio restaurants, centred on Frank Woo's sculpture, *Dancing Shadow*. Shanghai-chic décor and lots of upmarket Cantonese and east-coast Chinese cooking.

Al Nafourah (Map p90; ☎ 2263 7888; 8th fl, Le Méridien, 2 Jln Stesen Sentral, Brickfields; mains from RM100; noon-3pm & 6.30-11pm) The opulent Ottoman-style décor at this Levantine restaurant at the Méridien is worth a visit all by itself. Happily, the food matches the ostentatious surroundings. There's even a resident belly dancer.

Brickfields also has a number of informal hawker-style restaurants serving tasty Malay Chinese dishes for RM2 to RM15. Try **Cheong Hua** (Map p90; 1A Jln Tun Sambanthan 4; 6am-10pm) for fish porridge and noodle soups or **Restoran Makanan Laut Lai Fatt Ikan Bakar** (Map p90; 25-29 Jln Thambapillai; 5pm-2am) for delicious fresh seafood and *ikan panggang* (grilled skate with tamarind paste).

Chow Kit

The best hawker food in Chow Kit is found inside the Bazaar Baru market (p93); the atmosphere is lively, the food tasty and cheap and you can pick up an astonishing variety of tropical fruit for dessert at the surrounding market stalls.

Pesona Food Court (Map p92; 2nd fl, Maju Junction mall, Jln TAR; 7am-7pm) This is a decent shopping-centre food court near the Tune Hotel.

Bangsar Baru & Mid Valley City

As well as the following suggestions, there are dozens of restaurants dotted around the

PUDU MARKET HAWKER COURT

Kuala Lumpur (KL) has dozens of intriguing, off-the-beaten-track places to eat – our favourite is the permanent hawker court at Pudu Market (p91), known locally as **Pusat Makanan Peng Hwa** (Map pp72-3; Jln Pasar Baru; mains RM3-15; 24hr). This congregation of cooks sprawls beneath a gigantic tin roof behind the wet and dry market. The pavilion is as big as an aircraft hangar – fans on the ceiling whir ineffectually, failing almost completely to drive away the tropical fug. Nevertheless, as the sun sets, this is *the* place to be. The hundred or so plastic tables and chairs fill suddenly with locals ordering big bottles of ice-cold Tiger beer and bags of Chinese marinated sunflower seeds. Waitresses in matching T-shirts fight their way through the crowds, crunching over the discarded sunflower husks with trays of beer and mugs of *teh tarik*. (tea with evaporated milk) Foreigners are a rarity here – diners at the surrounding tables cast curious looks but raise their glasses in greeting as soon as you make eye contact. Come with some friends and make a night of it.

The food stalls around the edge of the hangar serve excellent noodles, wanton soups, fried rice, stir-fries and grilled seafood, all at bargain prices. Finish with a huge mound of *ais kacang* (shaved ice, syrup, sweet beans and fruit) then jump on the last LRT train home.

city-sized Mid Valley Megamall (see p122) and more upmarket choices in One Bangsar (see p107).

HAWKER STALLS & FOOD COURTS

Held on Sunday evenings, the Bangsar Baru *pasar malam* on Jln Telawi is an institution; you'll find all manner of tempting take-away food stalls serving local treats such as *otak otak* (spicy fish paste grilled in banana leaves) and the crepelike *apam balik*. If you can't wait till Sunday, there's a permanent hawker court (open 8am to 10pm) at the junction of Jln Telawi 4 and Jln Maroof.

Food Junction (off Map p94; Level 3, Mid Valley Megamall, Mid Valley City; ⌚ 10.30am-10pm) Spic-and-span food court in the Mid Valley Megamall serving all sorts of Asian treats.

EUROPEAN & FUSION

Country Farm Organics (Map p94; ☎ 2284 2094; Ground fl, Bangsar Village I, 1 Jln Telawi 1, Bangsar Baru; snacks from RM6; ⌚ 10am-10pm) This place has lots of veggie options and everything is organic.

La Bodega (Map p94; ☎ 2287 8318; www.bodega.com.my; 14 & 16 Jln Telawi 2, Bangsar Baru; mains RM10-40; ⌚ 8am-1am) This popular, trendy place is four venues in one: an all-day deli-café serving good sandwiches; a chilled-out tapas bar; a formal dining room; and a lively lounge bar. Good wine and authentic tapas and paella complete the Spanish mood.

Alexis Bistro (Map p94; ☎ 2284 2880; www.alexis.com.my; 29 Jln Telawi 3, Bangsar Baru; mains from RM30; ⌚ noon-midnight, to 1am Fri & Sat) Consistently good food is delivered at this Bangsar stalwart where Asian favourites such as laksa mix it up with European fare. After your meal, move on to its ultrasmooth Bar Upstairs (see p118).

Delicious (Map p94; ☎ 2287 1554; Ground fl, Bangsar Village II, Jln Telawi 1, Bangsar Baru; mains from RM40; ⌚ 11am-midnight, to 1am Fri & Sat) Shoppers break for lunch to enjoy healthy salads, pasta, sandwiches and pies at this neat and contemporary place in the Bangsar Village II mall.

our pick **Telawi Street Bistro** (Map p94; ☎ 2284 3168; www.telawi.com.my; 1 Jln Telawi 3, Bangsar Baru; mains RM50; ⌚ noon-1am Mon-Fri, 10am-1am Sat & Sun) Bangsar's favourite bistro, with a fine menu of European and Asian fusion cooking (grilled meats and seared scallops set the tone) and a lively upstairs bar. You'll find that the best tables are on the balcony overlooking the street.

INDIAN

Annalakshmi (off Map p94; ☎ 2284 3799; Boulevard, Mid Valley Megamall, Mid Valley City; prices discretionary; ⌚ 11.30am-3pm & 6.30-10.30pm) Run by the charitable Temple of Fine Arts (p91), this Indian buffet restaurant serves hearty, spicy South Indian vegetarian food. Prices are discretionary – you pay what you think the meal was worth and proceeds help fund the charitable work of the foundation.

Kampung Baru

Saturday evening is the best time to eat in Kampung Baru, when dozens of hawker stalls set up around Jln Raja Muda Musa for the weekly *pasar malam*, which rolls through till early Sunday morning. You can find all sorts of Malay specialities here, from *ikan panggang* to *rojak* (spicy fruit-and-vegetable salad), and the night market positively crackles with energy.

Plenty of hawker-style restaurants stay open all week to cater to the crowds of city workers who descend on Kampung Baru every lunchtime in search of a cheap meal. The following places can furnish you with a tasty Malay meal for RM15 or less.

Warong Perasan (Map p92; Jln Raja Muda Musa; ⌚ 8am-4am) Good for *mee soto* (noodle soup), *nasi ayam* (chicken rice) and fried fish.

Ikan Bakar Berempah (Map p92; Gerak 21, Jln Raja Muda Musa; ⌚ 24hr) Well-known for its excellent barbecued fish.

Bujang Lapok (Map p92; cnr Jln Daud & Jln Raja Alang; ⌚ noon-midnight) This place serves similar food to Ikan Baka Berempah in a tiled, fan-cooled pavilion.

Chop 'n' Steak (Map p92; 16 Jln Daud; ⌚ 5pm-2am) A Malay-style steak and chicken restaurant arranged around mock-up of a fishing boat.

Desa Sri Hartamas

This happening drinking-and-dining area is awash with Japanese and Korean restaurants.

Hartamas Square (off Map pp72-3; Jln 23/70a; mains RM20-30; ⌚ 5pm-3am) A huge covered hawker court with sports on big TV screens, cold beers and a mass of hawker stalls serving excellent grilled fish, noodles, fried rice, curries and other Malay Chinese treats. The most fun place to dine in Desa Sri Hartamas.

Matsuba Japanese Restaurant (off Map pp72-3; ☎ 6201 1100; 1st fl, 19 Jln 19/70a; meals RM20-50; ⌚ noon-2pm & 6-10pm) An unpretentious Japanese place that attracts a younger crowd with good value bento box sets (including sushi, sashimi and teriyaki).

Restoran Edo Jo (off Map pp72-3; ☎ 6201 8212; 9 Jln 22a/70a; meals RM20-100; 6pm-midnight, to 1am Fri/Sat) Top-notch Japanese food served in a tasteful wooden dining room with raised banquet rooms hidden by paper screens. Japanese expats come to Edo Jo for a taste of home.

To reach Desa Sri Hartamas, take a taxi or pick up Rapid KL bus U7 from in front of the Pekeliling Bus Station in Titiwangsa (near Titiwangsa monorail station and LRT). In the reverse direction, hail a taxi on Jln 23/70a. The journey takes 20 to 40 minutes, depending on traffic.

Elsewhere

There are several other interesting restaurants and food courts dotted around the city.

Medan Hang Tuah (Map pp72-3; 4th fl, The Mall, Legend Hotel, Jln Putra; meals RM5-15; 10am-10pm) A Pudu-based re-creation of an old city street, complete with mock shophouses. The food stalls here serve excellent and cheap Malay, Chinese and Indian food.

D'Istana Jalamas Café (Map p92; ☎ 4025 3161; Jln Tun Razak, Titiwangsa; mains from RM10; 7.30am-8pm) The café at Istana Budaya serves *mamak* favourites such as fish-head curry in classier than average surroundings.

Yu Ri Tei (Map pp72-3; ☎ 4044 0422; Sentul Park Koi Centre, Jln Strachan; mains RM15; 11am-9pm) If you come up to KLPac (p121) to see a show, drop into this charming Japanese teahouse surrounded by ponds at the Sentul Park Koi breeding centre. The menu runs to ramen, tempura and various types of dumplings and fried rice. Jln Strachan is off Jln Ipoh.

Restoran Nelayan Titiwangsa (Map pp72-3; ☎ 4022 8400; www.nelayan.com.my; Taman Tasik Titiwangsa; mains RM15-60; 11am-2.30pm Sat-Thu. 6.30-10.30pm daily) Housed in a wooden pavilion at Taman Tasik Titiwangsa, Restoran Nelayan offers a popular Malaysian buffet (lunch/dinner from RM18/28). There's touristy but entertaining cultural shows (8.30pm daily except Monday), free with buffet supper.

DRINKING

The Golden Triangle is the epicentre of the drinking scene in KL, though party people are increasingly focusing their attention on Asian Heritage Row (Jln Doraisamy), close to the Medan Tuanku monorail station. Bangsar, south of the city centre, remains popular, though the bars here are losing out to the new pubs and clubs in Desa Sri Hartamas, a half-hour taxi ride west of the centre. Wear shoes rather than sandals if you want to visit the more upmarket bars in town. For a more peripatetic night out, see the Monorail Pub Crawl boxed text, below.

Coffee-drinkers are also well catered for in KL. As well as the ubiquitous Starbucks and Coffee Bean & Tea Leaf branches found all over the city (normally with free wi-fi internet access), there are several informal cafés where you can drink without contributing to the demise of small coffee shops around the world.

A MONORAIL PUB CRAWL

Many of the best drinking holes in Kuala Lumpur (KL) are accessible on the monorail, opening up the possibility of a pub crawl right across the city. Starting in Chinatown, wet your whistle at one of the streetside restaurants in the Petaling Street Market (p77) or the traveller-friendly Reggae Bar (see p116), or join the hardened Chinese drinkers for a tumbler of rice wine at the **Chinatown Liquor Shop** (Map pp78-9; Jln Sultan, Chinatown; 10am-9pm). Suitably refreshed, jump on the monorail at Maharajalela and ride the rails to Bukit Bintang.

Depending on the depth of your wallet, you can either sip with the beautiful people in the Village Bar (p117) or Tiffin Bay (p117) at Starhill Gallery, or join the chill-out crowd in the Green Man (p116), Finnegan's (p116) or the Ceylon Bar (p117). Either way, it pays to invest in some tasty street food on Jln Alor (p106) before jumping back on the monorail to Medan Tuanku.

Asian Heritage Row should be your final destination. For a late-night party, take your pick from SaVanh (p117) or Bed (p117), or enjoy a calmer drink in Brit-style pub the Ivy (p117). To go all out, make sure you are still presentable then continue to the Loft (p120), Cynna (p120) or Maison (p120) to dance till the wee hours. With any luck, Restoran Buharry (p110) should still be open for a rehydrating mango smoothie before you take a taxi home.

Chinatown & Around

CAFÉS

Old Town Kopitiam (Map pp78-9; Ground fl, Central Market; coffee & snacks from RM5; 10am-9.30pm) A convincing recreation of an old-fashioned *kopi tiam* (Malay Chinese coffee shop) serving *teh* (tea), *kopi* (coffee) and breakfast snacks such as eggs, toast and soup. There's another branch in Plaza Low Yat (p122).

Other venues for serious tea and coffee enthusiasts:

Purple Cane Tea House (Map pp78-9; 3rd fl, 6 Jln Panggong; 11am-8pm) Serves a broad range of Chinese green and jasmine teas.

Ikopi (Map pp78-9; 1st fl, 6 Jln Panggong; noon-10pm Wed-Mon) Coffees from around the world are brewed in contraptions that look like they were built by mad scientists.

BARS

Chinatown has few formal bars – Bukit Bintang is a much better area for nightlife. For an inexpensive night out, the Backpackers Travellers Inn (p101) has a grungy traveller bar on its roof. Lots of travellers sip beers at the open-air restaurants in the Petaling Street Market (p77).

Reggae Bar (Map pp78-9; 2272 2158; 158 Jln Tun HS Lee; 10.30am-3am) Travellers gather in droves at this laid-back bar near the Petaling Street Market. Bob Marley dominates the sound system most nights and there are beer promos, pool tables and pub grub, served till late.

Zeta Bar (Map p90; 2264 2264; www.kl-studio.com; Hilton Kuala Lumpur, 3 Jln Stesen Sentral, Brickfields; 6pm-1.30am, to 3am Fri & Sat) If you're down in Brickfields, the classy and expensive bar at the Hilton pulls in a well-to-do 30-something crowd. Big-name DJs and artists of the calibre of Blondie sometimes appear in the hotel ballroom.

Golden Triangle

CAFÉS

Olé Café (Map pp84-5; 2148 9007; 48 Changkat Bukit Bintang; tea & coffee from RM7; 11am-midnight) A roomy coffee shop with free wi-fi, blissful air-con and good tea, coffee and cakes.

Sixty Nine Bistro (Map pp84-5; 2144 3369; 14 Jln Kampung Dollah; noon-1.30am, from 2pm Fri & Sat) A very funky youth venue with junk-shop treasures on the walls and resident fortune tellers.

Wings (Map pp84-5; 2144 3309; www.wingsmusicafe.com; 16 Jln Kampung Dollah; 6.30am-1am, to 2am Fri & Sat) A few doors down from Sixty Nine Bistro, this cheerful student hang-out has regular live music, though most drinkers prefer to chill out on the front terrace.

PUBS

Finnegan's (Map pp84-5; 2145 1930; www.finneganspubs.com; 51 Jln Sultan Ismail; 10am-1am) This Irish chain-pub faithfully recreates the mood of a local boozer. It's a good place for a knees-up, with stout and bitter on tap and a decent pub-grub menu. Happy-hour prices apply before 8pm.

Green Man (Map pp84-5; 2141 9924; www.greenman.com.my; 40 Changkat Bukit Bintang; noon-1am, to 2am Fri-Sun) Another Irish-ish pub with Guinness and bitter on tap, plus a menu of stodgy British food and a pool table. It's calmer indoors than on the busy terrace.

BARS

There are two main districts for drinking in the Golden Triangle: Jln P Ramlee and the streets north of Jln Bukit Bintang.

Legends (Map pp84-5; 2166 6603; 20 Jln Sultan Ismail; 11am-2am) A bawdy, boisterous sports bar with big screens showing all the big rugby,

BREWS WITH A VIEW

With all of this city's towering skyscrapers, it would be unthinkable for there not to be some bars to enjoy the sky-high views from in Kuala Lumpur (KL). Some of KL's most exclusive nightspots are perched on top of cloud-busting towers, offering dizzy views over the whole of the city. Topping the bill is **Luna** (Map pp84-5; 2332 7777; Level 34, Menara PanGlobal, Jln Punchak; cover Fri & Sat RM50; 5pm-1am), which lords it over the city from the top floor of the Pacific Regency Suites. This is KL at its most chic – the bar coils around a swimming pool, and features giant, soft furnishings, screens of crystal beads and chill-out booths with glass walls and views that plummet to street level. Things can get very busy at weekends. Enter via the elevator on the 7th floor of the hotel.

The other elevated bar currently pulling in a crowd is the **Skybar** (Map pp84-5; 2332 9888; Level 33, Traders Hotel, KLCC; 7pm-1am, to 3am Fri & Sat) in the Traders Hotel, a lofty chill-out space overlooking the KLCC Park. It's chic, futuristic and exclusive. Dress to impress.

GAY & LESBIAN KL

The gay scene in Kuala Lumpur (KL) took a knock recently with the closure of Liquid, formerly KL's most relaxed and friendly gay venue. But don't worry – there are several other bars and clubs where the scene is still going strong. Visit www.princeworldkl.com and www.utopia-asia.com/klbars.htm for more listings of gay nights and special events in KL.

Blue Boy (Map p84-5; ☎ 2142 1067; 54 Jln Sultan Ismail; cover RM20; from 6pm) At the bottom of the heap is this grungy pick-up joint just off Jln Sultan Ismail behind the rebranded Millennium Hotel. Come before 11pm to sing karaoke with the winking lady boys; later it gets packed with a rent-boy crowd.

Frangipani Bar (Map p84-5; ☎ 2144 3001; 25 Changkat Bukit Bintang; cover RM30; 6pm-1am) On Friday nights, the seductive bar above the restaurant of the same name (p84-5) hosts a stylish and discrete gay crowd.

Garçon (Map p92; ☎ 2381 2088; www.maison.com.my; Maison, 8 Jln Yap Ah Shak; cover RM25-30; 9pm-3am Sun) This is the Sundaynight gay-friendly session at club Maison (p92) in Asian Heritage Row. It's a glam space that attracts a glam crowd, with the DJs from former gay haunt Bliss.

La Queen (Map p84-5; ☎ 017-325 9985; Nouvo, 5 Jln P Ramlee; cover RM20-35; 9pm-3am Fri & Sat) This unashamedly hedonistic gay venue at the Nouvo club is rapidly growing in popularity. It's big on theme parties with lots of events supporting local gay organisations.

cricket, American football and premiership soccer games.

our pick **Ceylon Bar** (Map pp84-5; ☎ 2145 7689; 20-2 Changkat Bukit Bintang; 4pm-1am, from 11am Sun) Big, comfy lounges, inexpensive drinks and a genuinely convivial mood make this one of the friendliest drinking holes in KL. Come early to bag one of terrace tables or the sofas inside.

No Black Tie (Map pp84-5; ☎ 2142 3737; 17 Jln Mesui; 6pm-1am Mon-Sat) Blink and you'd miss this discrete bar and bistro, hidden away on a residential street north of Jln Bukit Bintang. The bar was founded by Malaysian concert pianist Evelyn Hii and jazz bands and classical-music ensembles play from around 9.30pm.

Tiffin Bay/Tiff's Jazz Lounge (Map pp84-5; ☎ 2782 3870; 4th fl, Starhill Gallery, 181 Jln Bukit Bintang; noon-1am) Reminiscent of the Mad Hatter's tea party, the upstairs bar at Starhill Gallery features oversized polka-dot lounges and lamp stands made from piles of crockery. Jazz bands play from 9pm in front of a shimmering light display.

our pick **Village Bar** (Map pp84-5; ☎ 2782 3852; Feast Level, Starhill Gallery, 181 Jln Bukit Bintang; noon-1am) Columns of glasses and bottles and cascades of dangling lanterns lend an *Alice in Wonderland* quality to this bar on the Starhill Gallery food floor (p107). Prices are high, but the décor is rather spectacular.

SevenAteNine (Map pp84-5; ☎ 2167 7789; Ground fl, The Ascot, 9 Jln Pinang; 5pm-1am Mon-Fri, 6pm-1am Sat) White sheets hang over the tables and sofas at this sleek nightspot near the KLCC. There's a sophisticated dinner menu and acoustic bands play on Thursday.

Jln P Ramlee has numerous theme bars with live music or DJs and happy-hour specials. Unfortunately, these places tend to attract lots of sex workers and sexpats. **Beach Club Café** (Map pp84-5; ☎ 2166 9919; 97 Jln P Ramlee; 6pm-3am Tue-Sun) and **Rum Jungle** (Map pp84-5; ☎ 2148 0282; Jln P Ramlee; 5pm-3am) are the most popular places in this part of town.

Asian Heritage Row

SaVanh (Map p92; ☎ 2697 1181; 64 Jln Doriaswamy) The downstairs bar at CoChine (p108) is dark and moody, with trickling water features and Khmer temple carvings on the walls. A place for creatures of the night.

Ivy (Map p92; ☎ 2693 2260; 48 Jln Doraisamy; 11am-2am) The Ivy faithfully recreates the feel of a British gastro pub. The downstairs bar has draft beers (including Guinness) and bar snacks, while the upstairs restaurant showcases modern European cooking.

Bed (Map p92; ☎ 2693 1122; www.bed.com.my; 33 Jln Yap Ah Shak; cover Fri & Sat RM40; 9pm-3am Tue-Sat) The famous Bed concept has been imported from Bangkok to KL. The resulting bar is small but ubercool, with an upbeat DJ soundtrack and glowing neon furniture.

Bangsar Baru, Desa Sri Hartamas & Around

CAFÉS

Bakerzin (Map p94; Ground fl, Bangsar Village I, 1 Jln Telawi 1, Bangsar Baru; 8.30am-11pm) Delicious cakes

MANAGING EDITOR JOHN LIM

John Lim is managing editor of *KLue* (www.klue.com.my), the capital's leading lifestyle and entertainment magazine, which keeps his finger on the pulse of nightlife in Kuala Lumpur (KL).

How do you find the best places to eat in KL? I recommend Foodster at FriedChillies (www.friedchillies.com). It's a fantastic blog site run by people who are really passionate about food. The dining scene in KL is pretty dynamic. There are lots of new European and fusion places opening up, particularly around Changkat Bukit Bintang, but some of the best places to eat are small local restaurants that have no name. They never make it into the dining guides, but you'll find loads of reviews on FriedChillies.

What would be the perfect KL night out? I'd tell people to start off on Asian Heritage Rowp107 – just walk up and down and take your pick from the hip modern clubs and cool places to chill out. Then head on to Zouk (p120), KL's only superclub. At the end of the night, head to one of KL's *mamak* (Indian Muslim) restaurants for a delicious late-night snack. *Mamak* food grew out of Indian hawker stalls, but sit-down *mamak* restaurants (see p110) are springing up all over KL.

Who are the big Malaysian film makers to look out for? There are several directors making interesting arthouse films and documentaries, exploring the boundaries of religion and race. If you only see one Malaysian film, make it *Sepet* by Yasmin Ahmad. The word means 'slit eyes', a Malay nickname for Chinese Malaysians. The story is a bittersweet romance between a Chinese boy and a Malay girl. It's a story lots of Malaysians can relate to. James Lee is quite the local film auteur, although he's not as well known in his own country as he is abroad – his best-known pictures are *Room To Let* and *Beautiful Washing Machine*. Amir Muhammad is considered a 'controversial' film maker in Malaysia because his work pushes the boundaries when it comes to issues that the government won't allow to be discussed in the public arena. His movie *Lelaki Komunis Terakhir* (The Last Communist Man) was banned, along with his follow-up movie *Apa Khabar Orang Kampung* (Village People Radio Show).

and pastries are the stock in trade at Bakerzin. Come for breakfast or a naughty-but-nice treat after a hard afternoon's shopping.

PUBS & BARS

Bar Upstairs (Map p94; ☎ 2284 2880; www.alexis.com.my; 29 Jln Telawi 3, Bangsar Baru; 🕑 6pm-1am, to 2am Fri & Sat) The bar at this popular bistro is probably the most chilled-out drinking spot in Bangsar Baru. Comfortable chairs and soothing sounds on the decks.

Bar Flam (Map p94; ☎ 2284 6721; www.flams.com; 16 Jln Telawi 3, Bangsar Baru) This is a stylish, modernist lounge-bar and attracts design darlings and Bangsar trendies. Most people dine at the attached restaurant before they dance.

Black Hole (☎ 2300 1170; 22 Jln 25/70a, Desa Sri Hartamas; 🕑 5pm-2am) Older locals come to this big Desa Sri Hartamas party pub to wine and dine outside and dance upstairs. It's brash, boisterous and good honest, fun.

There is a popular branch of the Irish pub chain **Finnegan's** in Bangsar (Map p94; ☎ 2284 0476; 6 Jln Telawi 5). There's also a branch located in Desa Sri Hartamas (☎ 2300 0538; 70-72 Jln 27/70a, Desa Sri Hartamas). The upstairs bars at Telawi Street Bistro (p114) and La Bodega (see p114) are also excellent spots to dine and dance the night away, attracting a young professional crowd.

ENTERTAINMENT

KL has a remarkably upbeat nightlife for an Islamic country, though much of the credit for this goes to the Chinese and Indian communities and their relaxed attitudes to alcohol and dancing. Don't expect the all-out hedonism of Bangkok – drinking in KL tends to be more restrained, unless of course you visit Zouk (p120) or one of other clubs and dance bars dotted around the city. Attitudes to drinking are founded in religion – places catering to Chinese and Indian Malaysians and foreigners normally serve alcohol and places that target Malays stick to tea, coffee and juices.

As well as the pubs, bars and clubs, KL has numerous cinemas, karaoke bars and venues for live music, particularly jazz and local guitar-based rock.

Cinemas

Most of the big shopping centres have plush multiplexes showing international blockbusters, plus Malay, Chinese, Cantonese and Hindi films. Tickets range from RM6 to RM12, depending on the time of day. Most of KL's cultural centres (see p74) screen occasional arthouse films – contact them directly for details.

DiGi IMAX Theatre (Map pp84-5; ☎ 2117 3046; www.timessquarekl.com/imax.html; 10th fl, Berjaya Times Square, 1 Jln Imbi; adult/child RM15/10) Shows blockbusters as well as IMAX specials.

Golden Screen Cinemas Golden Triangle (Map pp84-5; ☎ 8312 3456; www.gsc.com.my; 3rd fl, Berjaya Times Square, 1 Jln Imbi); Mid Valley (off Map p94; ☎ 8312 3456; www.gsc.com.my; Mid Valley Megamall, Mid Valley City) Book a seat in Gold Class (RM40) for La-Z-boy–style reclining chairs and a drinks service.

Tanjung Golden Village (Map pp84-5; ☎ 7492 2929; www.tgv.com.my; Level 3, Suria KLCC)

Karaoke

Karaoke bars are everywhere in KL but, like elsewhere in Southeast Asia, some have a seedy side. One place you'll get no funny business is **Neway** (Map pp84-5; ☎ 2143 3999; 4th fl, Berjaya Times Square; cover RM12-32; 🕑 11am-4am), a futuristic karaoke complex in Berjaya Times Square that attracts hordes of teenagers and whole families at weekends. The price for sharing the gift of song (ahem) varies depending on the time of day.

Live Music

KL has a vibrant live music scene, with lots of local bands performing original compositions – a refreshing change from the ubiquitous covers bands in other Southeast Asian capitals. The jazz and indie scenes are particularly animated, and big international artists are increasingly adding KL to their Asia tours. A collective of KL bands and singers has created the website Troubadours (www.troubadourskl.blogspot.com) to publicise shows by local artists – a good resource for listings of upcoming gigs and other live events. It's also worth checking the line-up of indie bands at Laundry (p120). The Istana Budaya (p121) hosts regular classical-music concerts, particularly during the KL Festival (p100).

Hard Rock Café (Map pp84-5; ☎ 2715 5555; Hotel Concorde, 2 Jln Sultan Ismail; cover charge RM35 Fri & Sat; 🕑 11.30am-2am, to 3am Fri&Sat) Ok, so it's a tacky international chain, but it's worth swinging by for the impressive line-up of live bands. Weekends have the best live acts.

Planet Hollywood (Map pp84-5; ☎ 2144 6602; KL Plaza, 170 Jln Bukit Bintang; cover charge RM35; 🕑 11am-3am) A similar experience is offered by the

RESTAURANT & BAR OWNER-MANAGER MARIA DANKAR

Maria Dankar is the manager of Top Hat (p111), a popular restaurant and jazz bar in a handsome old Kuala Lumpur (KL) mansion. Maria moved to the capital in the 1950s so she's seen half a century of change in the Malaysian capital.

How has KL changed over the years? Oh my goodness! The city is changing so fast these days. It's best not to leave the house because the street will change as soon as you turn your back! I saw the Petronas Towers go up right in front of me. Now there are just a few old houses like ours left in the centre. The developers are always knocking at the door. If you live in one of these old houses, the maintenance is so high. We need three gardeners just to tend our grounds. And the developers can see the money in the sky – every new floor is more money in the bank. Some people even end up living in apartments in skyscrapers on the site of their old houses!

Is there a distinctive KL identity? I think our diversity *is* our identity. We all come from different ethnic groups but we've learned to work together to accommodate all these different religions and different ways of doing things. We're very conscious of each other's needs. And now Air Asia is bringing in people from right across Asia; it's making the city even more cosmopolitan.

What is the jazz scene like in KL? There are only about five proper jazz places in town, but we're all busy. Some places do the modern stuff, but we're not really a Hard Rock Café kind of place – we like that old-fashioned, New Orleans kind of jazz. But we're trying to start up a jazz association to get the next generation interested in our kind of music.

local branch of Planet Hollywood. Bands play from around 10pm.

Dewan Filharmonik Petronas (Map pp84-5; ☎ 2051 7007; www.malaysianphilharmonic.com; Box Office, Tower 2, Petronas Towers, KLCC; tickets from R20-210; box office 10am-6pm Mon-Sat) A state-of-the-art concert hall inside the Petronas Towers. The respected Malaysian Philharmonic Orchestra plays here (mostly at weekends) along with other local and international ensembles. Smart dress is required.

Jazz bands and singers do the rounds of the intimate stages at No Black Tie (p117) and Tiff's Jazz Lounge (p117).

Other jazz venues:

Top Room@Top Hat (Map pp84-5; 7 Jln Kia Peng; cover RM20-50; 10.30am-1am Fri & Sat, 5pm-late Sun) See boxed text, p119, for more on this venue.

Bangkok Jazz (Map pp84-5; ☎ 2145 8708; Chulan Sq, Jln Raja Chulan; 5pm-1am)

Clubs

KL's lively club scene is fast and frenetic – places go in and out of fashion overnight, so for the latest information check the pages of local street press listing (see p75) or visit www.nightspots.com.my. The following nightspots are all stalwarts of the scene. Most clubs impose charge a cover of RM20 toRM50 from Thursday to Saturday, which includes one drink.

ASIAN HERITAGE ROW

Maison (Map p92; ☎ 2381 2088; www.maison.com.my; 8 Jln Yap Ah Shak; 9pm-3am Wed-Sun) Just off Asian Heritage Row, five shophouses have been knocked together to form this huge bar and club complex. It's urban, trendy and very slick – dress your best to make it past the bouncers. If you need a break from the hip-hop and House beats inside, there's a streetside shisha bar out front.

A linked balcony that gets crammed with beautiful people in beautiful outfits at weekends, **Loft** (Map p92; ☎ 2692 5668; www.loftkl.com; 28-40 Jln Doriaswamy; 9pm-3am) and **Cynna** (Map p92; ☎ 2694 2888; www.loftkl.com; 28-40 Jln Doriaswamy; 6pm-3am) are two stylish clubs with separate entrances. Dress smartly to get past the clipboard nazis on the door.

GOLDEN TRIANGLE

Espanda (Map pp84-5; ☎ 2142 6666; 97 Jln Sultan Ismail; 6pm-3am Tue-Sun) A long-established club in the Jln P Ramlee entertainment district with resident DJs and regular theme nights. Zouk has stolen some of Espanda's thunder but it still gets busy at weekends.

Passion (Map pp84-5; ☎ 2141 8888; www.poppy-collection.com; 18-1 Jln P Ramlee; 4pm-2am, to 3am Fri & Sat) Part of the Poppy Collection – a group of bars, clubs and restaurants on Jln P Ramlee – Passion attracts trendy 30-somethings with an inclination towards R&B and House.

Ruums (Map pp84-5; ☎ 012-638 0666; www.ruumsclub.com; Jln Sultan Ismail; 4pm-3am) A huge dance club in the Life Centre complex, with hectares of floor space and a booming sound system playing straight-forward commercial club sounds.

our pick **Zouk** (Map pp84-5; ☎ 2171 1997; www.zoukclub.com.my; 113 Jln Ampang; 9pm-3am Tue-Sun) Housed in a striking amoeba-shaped complex located on Jln Ampang, the Malaysian branch of this famous Singapore superclub is the undisputed king of the KL club scene. (For many people Zouk *is* the KL club scene.) There are four separate venues under one roof. Filled with bulbous organic forms, the two-storey Zouk Mainroom hosts glitzy theme nights, big-name DJs and over-the-top dance parties with lots of competitions and freebies. Dance music connoisseurs head to the more sophisticated Velvet Underground or the smaller and edgier Loft, where leading Malaysian DJs road test personal projects. For a less frenetic night out, try the Terrace Bar (no cover; open 5pm to midnight Sunday to Tuesday, 5pm to 3am Wednesday to Saturday) by the main entrance. For an inside view, see p39 for a profile on Zouk's regular DJ, Gabriel.

DESA SRI HARTAMAS & PETALING JAYA

Several trendy club-bars have opened at the Curve complex (off Map pp72–3), west of Sri Hartamas in Petaling Jaya. Rapid KL bus U88 runs here from Bangsar LRT station, or you can take a taxi or bus from the Kelana Jaya LRT station.

Laundry (☎ 7728 1715; laundrybar.blogspot.com; The Curve, Mutiara Damansara; admission free; 5pm-2am) The first of the new breed of suburban club-bars in KL, Laundry has a reputation for slow service but brilliant live music. The attitude can be a bit overbearing but the bar does a commendable job of supporting local musical talent, particularly indie bands.

Sanctuary (☎ 7710 5033; Level 1, The Curve, Mutiara Damansara; admission free; noon-1am) A very slick concept nightspot, Sanctuary has indoor and outdoor bars, a Southeast Asia restaurant and an 'ice bar' serving chilled vodka in (dare we say it) chilled-out surroundings.

Soda Club (☎ 6201 3778; Jln 23/70a; cover RM35; 🕑 5pm-2am) A gigantic, flashing neon Sri Hartamas club. Dress up to get past the bouncers and expect lots of drinks promos, theme nights and fast-paced House.

Cultural Shows

Central Market (p77) hosts a regular programme of free events, including traditional Malay, Indian and Chinese dance and music from Borneo. Pick up a monthly calendar from the information desk. The Malaysian Tourism Centre (p76) hosts a song-and-dance extravaganza in its auditorium (adult/under 12 RM5/free) at 3pm on Tuesday, Thursday and weekends, probably the most professional show in town. There's also an evening dance show at 8.30pm daily in the attached restaurant **Saloma** (Map pp84-5; ☎ 2161 0122; evening buffet RM70; 🕑 11am-midnight).

Several tourist restaurants in KL offer stage shows based on traditional Malay dance. The shows are colourful and energetic, though the authenticity of some of the dances is debatable. Restoran Nelayan Titiwangsa (p115) has cultural shows at 8.30pm daily except Monday (free with the buffet supper). Seri Melayu (p112) runs traditional Malay music and dance performances from 8.30pm nightly, backed up by an extensive buffet (RM60 including show).

Spectator Sports

Malays follow football (soccer) and basketball enthusiastically, but the big spectator sport in Kuala Lumpur is motor racing. About 60km south of the centre, the **Sepang International Circuit** (off Map pp72-3; ☎ 8778 2222; www.malaysiangp.com.my; Jln Pekeliling, Sepang) hosts some of the biggest events in Asian motorsports, from the Malaysian Motorcycle Grand Prix (in October) to the Petronas Malaysian Formula One Grand Prix (in March/April). Events take place throughout the year so check the website for listings or visit the **office** (☎ 2273 9335; 🕑 10am-5pm Mon-Sat) in KL Sentral.

Footy fans can catch international matches at the **National Sports Complex** (Kompleks Sukan Negara; off Map pp72-3; ☎ 8994 4660; www.ksn.com.my; Sri Petaling, Bukit Jalil), accessible from the Bukit Jalil LRT station. For information on fixtures, contact the **Football Association of Malaysia** (☎ 7873 3100; www.fam.org.my). Basketball games run by the **Malaysia Amateur Basketball Association** (MABA; www.malaysia-basketball.com) take place at the **Stadium Bola Keranjang** (Map pp78-9; Jln Hang Jebat) in Chinatown.

Theatre

Actors Studio Bangsar (off Map p94; ☎ 2094 0400; www.theactorsstudio.com.my; Level 3, West Wing, Bangsar Shopping Centre, Jln Maarof) Theatre and comedy are staged at this studio located in a shopping centre a couple of kilometres north of Bangsar Baru. Prices depend on the performance.

Chinese Assembly Hall (Map pp78-9; ☎ 2274 6645; 1 Jln Maharajalela) Stages occasional shows of Chinese traditional dance and theatre, though no English translation is provided. Prices depend on the performance.

Istana Budaya (National Theatre; Map p92; ☎ 4026 5555; www.istanabudaya.gov.my; Jln Tun Razak, Titiwangsa; tickets RM100-300) The National Theatre is the setting for big-production music, dance and theatre shows. Keep an eye out in the local press for traditional musicals and shadow-puppet shows, and plays inspired by events in Malay history. The website has a listing of upcoming shows.

Kuala Lumpur Performing Arts Centre (KLPac; Map pp72-3; ☎ 4047 9000; www.klpac.com; Sentul Park, Jln Strachan; tickets RM20-300) Part of the Sentul West regeneration project, this modernist performing-arts complex puts on a wide range of progressive theatrical events. You can combine a night at the theatre with a stroll in peaceful Sentul Park and dinner at the Sentul Koi Carp Breeding Centre (see boxed text, p98).

Sutra Dance Theatre (Map pp72-3; ☎ 4021 1092; www.sutradancetheatre.com; 12 Persiaran Titiwangsa 3, Titiwangsa) Indian classical dance is showcased at this dance studio and cultural centre in Titiwangsa. See the calendar on the website for upcoming shows and prices.

Taman Budaya (Map pp78-9; ☎ 2078 1542; www.heritage.gov.my; Jln Tun HS Lee) A good venue for performances of traditional Malaysian theatre and dance. The building – an AC Norman construction from 1893 – used to be a school. Shows take place at weekends at 8.30pm; contact the centre for details of upcoming events and prices.

SHOPPING

When it comes to shopping for brand-name consumer goods, KL is nipping at the heels of

Hong Kong and Singapore. Prices for clothes are incredibly competitive, and cameras and electronics are also good value, though not quite as cheap as in Bangkok or Singapore. Malaysia also has one of the most prolific counterfeit industries in the world, producing everything from fake Calvin Klein jeans to pirate DVDs and computer software, but why waste money on fakes when you can buy the real thing for not much more in a department store sale?

The capital is the best place to find original handicrafts from all over the country, although many crafts are imported from Indonesia, Vietnam, Thailand, India or China.

Shopping Malls

You'll find most of what you need at these gigantic shopping malls.

Avenue K (Map pp84-5; Jln Ampang; 10am-9pm) A relatively new arrival, this slick mall is slowly filling up with exclusive designer boutiques (eg CK, Hugo Boss) and upmarket home-décor stores. It's above the KLCC LRT station.

Bangsar Village I & II (Map p94; cnr Jln Telawi 1 & Jln Telawi 2, Bangsar Baru; 10.30am-10.30pm) These twin malls offer upmarket fashions (including international brands such as Ted Baker and local Malay designers), plus some good stores for kids and a decent Western-style supermarket.

Berjaya Times Square (Map pp84-5; www.timesquarekl.com; 1 Jln Imbi; 10am-10pm) Teen fashions and toy stores abound at this youth-oriented mall just south of Bukit Bintang. The Metrojaya department store has good deals on clothes and there's a big branch of Borders bookstore. Regular kids' expos are held here, from comic fairs to pint-sized talent contests. The centre also has a bowling alley, karaoke, a cinema, an IMAX cinema and an indoor theme park with a looping roller coaster.

Curve (off Map pp72-3; 7710 6868; www.thecurve.com.my; Mutiara Damansara; 10am-10pm) The latest addition to the KL shopping scene, this uber-modern mall has loads of international names, including Ikea and Tesco. It's about 15km west of the centre in Petaling Jaya; a free shuttle bus runs three times a day between the mall and the Royale Bintang Hotel on Jln Bukit Bintang (see the website for details).

Imbi Plaza (Map pp84-5; 2148 7425; Jln Imbi; 11am-9pm) A good IT mall selling mainly parts, peripherals and blank digital media.

Lot 10 (Map pp84-5; 2716 8615; www.ytlcommunity.com/lot10; 50 Jln Bukit Bintang; 10am-9.30pm) Lots of genuine brand-name fashion stores and a branch of the reliable Isetan department store.

Mid Valley Megamall (off Map p94; 2938 3333; www.midvalleycity.com; Mid Valley City; 10am-10pm) Mega is the only way to describe this enormous mall, off Jln Syed Putra. The Megamall has 300 stores, two department stores (Metrojaya and Jusco), an 18-screen cinema, a bowling alley, a huge food court and a colourful Hindu temple. The IT World Zone on the 2nd floor is good for electronics. The new KL Komuter Mid Valley station makes getting here a cinch. There are also Rapid KL buses to Chinatown and a free shuttle bus to Bangsar LRT station.

Plaza Low Yat (Map pp84-5; 2148 3651; 7 Jln 1/77; 10am-10pm) KL's best IT mall, with laptops and digital cameras on the ground floor and mobile phones and computer peripherals and accessories upstairs. Digital camera memory cards, card-readers and portable hard drives are particularly good value. It's off Jln Bukit Bintang.

Starhill Gallery (Map pp84-5; 2782 3855; www.starhillgallery.com; 181 Jln Bukit Bintang; 10am-9.30pm) Pack the platinum charge card – this glitzy mall is packed with exclusive fashion brands including Louis Vuitton, Salvatore Ferragamo and Alfred Dunhill. The basement level is a virtual village of upmarket restaurants (see p107), while the 'Pamper' floor has some of KL's best spas (see boxed text, p95).

Sungei Wang Plaza (Map pp84-5; 2148 6109; www.sungeiwang.com; Jln Sultan Ismail; 9.30am-9.30pm) This mall, interlinked with BB Plaza (Map pp84–5; 2148 7411), is confusing to negotiate but jam-packed with youth-oriented fashions and accessories. There's a branch of the Parkson Grand department store, plus a post office and various fastfood restaurants.

Yet another reason for heading to the KLCC is the fine Suria KLCC (p86) shopping complex at the foot of the Petronas Towers. It's strong on both local and international brands and there's a huge branch of the Isetan department store.

Department Stores

The best places to buy clothes are the big shopping mall department stores (see above), particularly during the sales. You can also try the following independent department stores for inexpensive shirts, shorts and swimwear:

Sogo (Map pp78-9; 2698 2111; Jln TAR, Little India; 10am-9.30pm)

UO Superstore Chinatown (Map pp78-9; ☎ 2032 1201; Jln Sultan; 10.30am-10pm); Chow Kit (Map p92; ☎ 2691 9951; Jln TAR; 10.30am-10pm)

Craft & Souvenir Shops

House of Suzie Wong (Map pp84-5; ☎ 2143 3220; www.houseofsuziewong.com; Muse fl, Starhill Gallery, 181 Jln Bukit Bintang; 10am-9.30pm) Antiques from across Asia are gathered together in informal room settings at this eccentric Starhill Gallery store. Staff can tell you the individual history of where each item was found.

Kompleks Budaya Kraf (Map pp84-5; ☎ 2162 7533; www.kraftangan.gov.my; Jln Conlay; 10am-6pm) A government enterprise, this huge complex on the outskirts of the business district mainly caters to coach tours, but it's worth a visit to browse the shops and stalls selling batik, wood carvings, pewter, basketware, glassware and ceramics. You can see craftsmen and artists at work in the surrounding Art Colony (check www.artkoloni.com), and the complex runs informal craft classes.

Peter Hoe Evolution (Map pp78-9; ☎ 2026 0711; 2 Jln Hang Lekir; 10am-7pm) Peter Hoe's original batik designs on sarongs, shirts and dresses are the main draw, but the shop also has an impressive range of Asian home-décor items. There are several similar stores on the same block.

Pucuk Rebung (Map pp84-5; ☎ 3382 0769; www.pucukrebung.com; Level 3, Suria KLCC, cnr Jln Ampang & Jln P Ramlee; 10am-10pm) Half museum, half shop, this upmarket arts-and-craft store offers genuine antiques and Malay ethnological items. Only some of the items are for sale – it's worth popping in to see the cannons, carvings and old photos, even if you can't afford the hefty price tags on the things you can buy.

Royal Selangor Pewter Factory (off Map pp72-3; ☎ 4145 6122; visitorcentre.royalselangor.com; 4 Jln Usahawan Enam, Setapak Jaya; 9am-5pm) Located 8km northeast of the city centre, the world's largest pewter manufacturer offers some very appealing souvenirs made from this malleable alloy of lead and silver. You can try your own hand at creating a pewter dish at the School of Hard Knocks (p99). The factory has an interesting visitor centre (to get here, take the LRT to Wangsa Maju station and then a taxi) or you can visit the retail outlets in KL's malls.

Tenmoku Pottery (Map pp84-5; ☎ 6187 5898; www.tenmokupottery.com.my; Level 3, Suria KLCC, cnr Jln Ampang & Jln P Ramlee; 10am-9.30pm) Based near the Batu Caves, Tenmoku Pottery specialises in vases, bowls and other ceramics inspired by natural forms. There are branches at the Central Market and the Mid Valley Megamall.

Formerly held on the first Saturday of the month in front of the National Art Gallery (p93), the Kuala Lumpur Craft Market is on hold until the gallery reopens in 2008. Check with the gallery to see if the market is up and running again. Chinatown's Central Market (p77) is also a handy spot for handicrafts and fabric, and the gift shop at the Islamic Arts Museum (p83) is stacked with interesting arts and crafts from across the Islamic world.

Art Galleries

Kuala Lumpur is turning out some eye-catching modern art (often inspired by tribal and religious themes) and much of it is for sale in the art galleries dotted around the city. As well as the following high-brow galleries, you can commission oil portraits for as little as RM250 at the painters studios in the Central Market Annexe (Map pp78–9).

Art Seni (Map pp84-5; Muse fl, Starhill Gallery, 181 Jln Bukit Bintang; 10am-9.30pm) One of several upmarket galleries at the Art Colony in the Starhill Gallery mall, with lots of paintings and photos by up-and-coming Malaysian artists.

Galeri Tangsi (Map pp78-9; ☎ 2691 0805; PAM Centre, 6 Jln Tangsi; 10am-6.30pm Mon-Fri, 10am-1pm Sat) Interesting art space in a heritage building west of Merdeka Sq.

Sarawak Paradise in Borneo (Map pp84-5; ☎ 2142 6113; 25 Jln Bukit Bintang; 10am-10pm) Part tourist office for Malaysian Borneo, this government enterprise stocks paintings by popular Sarawak artist Ramsay Ong (see www.artrageouslyasia.com).

Valentine Willie Fine Art (Map p94; ☎ 2284 2348; www.artsasia.com.my; 1st fl, 17 Jln Telawi 3, Bangsar Baru; noon-8pm Mon-Fri, noon-6pm Sat) One of KL's best galleries, with frequent shows representing some of the country's top artists.

Specialist Stores

British India (off Map p94; ☎ 2938 3826; Mid Valley Megamall, Mid Valley City; 10am-9.30pm) The Mid Valley Megamall store of a flashy chain selling sophisticated fashions with an ethnic flavour. (There are branches of this store in most of KL's big malls.)

Jim Thompson Silk (Map pp84-5; ☎ 2141 8689; Explore fl, Starhill Gallery, 181 Jln Bukit Bintang; 10am-7pm) KL branch of the Thai silk company founded by Jim Thompson, who disappeared in 1967 in Malaysia's Cameron Highlands. You can buy sumptuous loose silk as well as ready-made clothes.

Mumbai Sé (Map p94; ☎ 2287 0810; Ground fl, Bangsar Village II, Jln Telawi 1; 🕑 10.30am-10.30pm) This is the first KL branch of this upmarket Singapore store selling iridescent Indian fashions and home bric-a-brac.

Purple Cane Tea Arts (Map pp78-9; ☎ 2031 1877; 11 Jln Sultan; 🕑 10am-10pm) One of several specialist tea shops in Chinatown where you can sample and buy exotic teas, plus all the tea-making paraphernalia to go with them. There's another branch in the Mid Valley Megamall.

Silk Street (Map pp78-9; ☎ 2694 0402; 136 Jln TAR; 🕑 10am-8pm) A huge multistorey silk store with reams of silk sold by the yard and a resident tailor.

Tear Proof (Map pp84-5; Level 3, Suria KLCC; 🕑 10am-10pm) Good for backpacks, rugged outdoor wear and camping equipment. There are branches in Berjaya Times Square, the Curve and the Mid Valley Megamall.

Teratai (Map pp84-5; ☎ 2144 8866; www.teratai.com.my; 4th fl, Lot 10, Jln Bukit Bintang; 🕑 10am-9.30pm) An upmarket Asian arts and crafts, tailored towards Western home décor.

Yogini Mystical Treasures (Map pp84-5; ☎ 2144 2889; www.yoginimystical.com; 4th fl, Lot 10, Jln Bukit Bintang; 🕑 10am-9.30pm) A treasure house of Tibetan Buddhist art imported from across the Himalaya.

If you plan to do any scuba diving or snorkelling in Malaysia, these stores can kit you out with everything you need:

Dive Station (off Map p94; ☎ 2282 1948; 3rd fl, Mid Valley Megamall, Mid Valley City; 🕑 10am-10pm)

Planet Scuba (Map p94; ☎ 2287 2822; Jln Telawi 5, Bangsar Baru; 🕑 11am-9pm Tue-Sat, 11am-6pm Sun)

Markets

There are several interesting daily markets, including the Petaling Street Market (p77) in Chinatown, the Bazaar Baru Market (p93) in Chow Kit and the Pudu Market (p91) in Pudu. Another useful market is the nightly **clothes market** (Map p92; Jln Haji Taib; 🕑 3pm-midnight) in Chow Kit, which sells similar goods to the Petaling Street Market at slightly lower prices.

See the boxed text, p91, for information on KL's *pasar malam*.

GETTING THERE & AWAY

KL is the main gateway to Malaysia, with numerous flight, train and bus routes fanning out across the country and Asia. Penang is easily accessible by bus, train and plane (including cheap flights on Air Asia), while Melaka is just two hours away by bus or long-distance taxi – close enough for a day trip.

Air

KL's main airport is **Kuala Lumpur International Airport** (KLIA; off Map pp72-3; ☎ 8777 8888; www.klia.com.my), 75km south of the city centre at Sepang. At the international arrivals hall there's a useful **Tourism Malaysia office** (☎ 8776 5651; 🕑 9am-midnight), a **Celcom stand** (🕑 7am-11pm) selling prepaid SIM cards for your mobile phone, and counters for all the main car-rental firms (see p234). Note that airline regulations are strictly enforced – only one carry-on bag is permitted and liquids can only be carried on board in bottles of less than 100mL, which must be presented for screening in a clear plastic bag.

All of Air Asia's flights are handled by the nearby **Low Cost Carrier-Terminal** (LCC-T; off Map pp72-3; ☎ 8777 8888; http://lcct.airasia.com). Air Asia tickets are best purchased online at www.airasia.com. You can get information and book (using online terminals) at their small **office** (Map p90; ☎ 1300-889 933; 🕑 9am-9pm) in KL Sentral station. See p227 for listings of other airlines with offices in KL.

Berjaya Air's flights arrive at **Sultan Abdul Aziz Shah Airport** (off Map pp72-3; ☎ 7845 8382) at Subang, around 20km west of the city centre.

Boat

Several private companies run ferries to Tanjung Balai and Dumai on Sumatra in Indonesia from Pelabuhan Klang (Port Klang), accessible by KTM Komuter train from KL Sentral or by public bus (RM3.50) from the small Klang bus stand by Pasar Seni LRT station in Chinatown. Ferries run to Tanjung Balai (RM100, 3½ hours) at 11am Monday to Saturday. Ferries to Dumai (RM100, 3½ hours) leave between 9am and 10am daily. Note that you need an Indonesian visa in advance for the crossing to Tanjung Balai.

Bus

KL has several bus stations. Chinatown's Puduraya Bus Station handles most long-distance buses to Peninsular Malaysia, Singapore and Thailand. However, buses to Kota Bahru, Kuala Terengganu and the jetty for the Perhentian Islands leave from the Putra Bus Station on Jln Tun Ismail, and buses to Kuala Lipis, Jerantut and Temerloh leave from the Pekeliling Bus Station at Titiwangsa.

If you're travelling to Singapore and want to avoid the stress of dealing with Puduraya, **Aeroline** (Map pp84-5; ☎ 6258 8800; www.aeroline.com.my) runs six services daily (adult/child from RM80/50, five hours) from outside the Corus Hotel on Jln Ampang, just east of KLCC, using comfortable, air-conditioned double-decker coaches. **Plusliner/NICE** (Map pp78-9; ☎ 2272 1586; www.plusliner.com) runs a similar upmarket service from outside the Old KL Train Station on Jln Sultan Hishamuddin. There are around eight daily buses to Singapore (adult/child RM80/60) and six daily buses to Penang (five hours) – NICE coaches cost RM27/13.50, Plusliner coaches cost RM58/43.

PEKELILING BUS STATION

Next to the Titiwangsa LRT and monorail stations on Jln Tun Razak, **Pekeliling Bus Station** (Hentian Bas Pekeliling; Map p92; ☎ 4042 7256) is in the north of the city, just off Jln Tun Razak next to Titiwangsa LRT and monorail stations. There's a left-luggage counter (RM3 per bag per day) open from 8am to 8pm.

Transnasional Express (☎ 4256 8218) has departures to Kuala Lipis (RM11.20, four hours, six daily) and Raub (RM8.30, 2½ hours, three daily). Several companies including **Plusliner** (☎ 4042 1256) run hourly services to Kuantan (RM16.90, four hours) till around 10.30pm; many go via Temerloh (RM8.60, 2½ hours). Buses to Jerantut (RM13, three hours, four daily) also go via Temerloh. Buses to Genting Highlands (RM5.60, one hour) leave half-hourly from 7am to 9pm.

PUDURAYA BUS STATION

Huge, hectic, crowded and invariably overheated, **Puduraya Bus Station** (Hentian Bus Puduraya; Map pp78-9; ☎ 2070 0145) is the kind of place you want to get in and out of quickly. The crowds provide plenty of cover for pickpockets and bag-snatchers, and agents for the bus companies will pounce on you as soon as you walk in the door with spiels to convince you that their company is the best choice for your destination. This said, buses run from here across Malaysia and further afield to Singapore and Thailand, and departures are fast and frequent throughout the day. Inside the main entrance on Jln Pudu, you'll find a small information counter and a booth for the **tourist police** (☎ 2115 9999). Head to the back of the station for the **left-luggage counter** (🕑 6am-midnight; per day per bag RM3) and the food court (see p108).

Buses depart from the basement level, but tickets are purchased from the ticket desks at the back of the main concourse. To find a bus, wander up and down the aisles checking the lists of departure times – staff will shout out their destinations as you walk past but make sure the departure time suits you, as agents sometimes sell tickets for buses that won't be leaving for several hours. Government-owned **Transnasional Express** (☎ 2070 3300) is the largest operator, with buses to most major destinations. To find your bus, look for the name of the bus company on the signboards by the steps that lead down to the basement. There are more private bus company offices over the road on Jln Pudu.

Services are so numerous that you can often turn up and get a seat on the next bus, but to be safe, book the day before, or a few days before during peak holiday periods. When taking night buses, check what time the bus arrives in the morning; if you arrive too early, you'll have to wait until the hotels open their doors before you can check in.

Typical adult fares and journey times from KL follow:

Destination	Fare (RM)	Duration (hr)
Alor Setar	30	6
Butterworth	24	5
Cameron Highlands	18-23	4
Had Yai (Thailand)	40	7
Ipoh	13-14	3
Johor Bahru	24	5
Kuantan	18	4½
Melaka	9-10	2
Penang	27	5
Singapore	30	5½

PUTRA BUS STATION

Several services to the east coast leave from the quieter and less intimidating **Putra Bus Station** (Hentian Bas Putra; Map pp72-3; ☎ 4042 9530) on Jln Tun Ismail, opposite the Putra World Trade Centre. To get here, take the LRT to PWTC station, or a KTM Komuter train to Putra station. There's a left-luggage counter (RM3 per bag per day) open from 7am till 10pm.

At around 9.30am and 9.30pm, there are buses to Kota Bahru (RM31 to RM35, eight hours), Kuala Terengganu (RM30, seven hours), and the jetty for boats to Pulau Perhentian (RM31, five to six hours).

Car

KL is probably the best place to hire a car for touring Peninsular Malaysia, though driving out of KL is complicated by a confusing one-way system and contradictory road signs that can throw off your sense of direction completely – see p233 for more on driving in Malaysia. All the major companies have offices at the airport. City offices – generally open from 9am to 6pm weekdays and 9am to 1pm Saturday – include the following:

Avis (Map pp84-5; ☎ 2144 4487; www.avis.com.my; Ground fl, Angkasa Raya Bldg)
Hertz (Map pp84-5; ☎ 2148 6433; www.hertz.com.my; Ground fl, Kompleks Antarabangsa, Jln Sultan Ismail)
Mayflower (Map pp84-5; ☎ 2144 1188; www.mayflowercarrental.com.my; 42 Jln Sultan Ismail)
Orix (Map pp84-5; ☎ 2142 3009; www.orixcarrentals.com.my; Mezzanine Level, Federal Hotel, Jln Bukit Bintang)

Long-Distance Taxi

With plenty of cheap flights and comfortable trains and buses, there is little reason to use long-distance taxis – they take just as long as buses but they cost more and they only leave when they have a full compliment of passengers, or when one passenger agrees to pay the whole-taxi fare. However, they are cheaper than ordinary taxis for long journeys.

If you feel inclined to take a shared taxi, whole-taxi fares from the depot on the 2nd floor of the Puduraya Bus Station include Melaka (RM140), Penang (RM360), Johor Bahru (RM300), Ipoh (RM200) and the Cameron Highlands (RM200). There's a smaller stand at the Pekeliling Bus Station serving Temerloh, Jerantut, Kuantan and Raub. Toll charges are normally included, though some unscrupulous drivers make passengers pay extra.

Train

KL Sentral station is the national hub of the **KTM** (Keretapi Tanah Melayu Berhad; Map p90; ☎ 2267 1200; www.ktmb.com.my; ⏲ info office 10am-7pm, ticket office 7am-10pm) railway system, which extends through Malaysia into Thailand and Singapore. You can buy tickets in advance at the station or get the handy **ticket delivery service** (☎ 2267 1200; ⏲ 8.30am-5pm Mon-Sat) to speed the ticket to your hotel room for RM4. Services run daily to Singapore, Butterworth (for Georgetown, Penang) and Hat Yai (connecting with trains to Bangkok and other parts of Thailand) – see p235 for more information.

The same company runs the KTM Komuter train service around KL (see p128).

GETTING AROUND

On paper, KL should have one of the best public transport systems around, with numerous bus routes and a sophisticated rail-based mass transit system made up of the KTM Komuter, KLIA Ekspres, KLIA Transit, LRT and monorail systems. Unfortunately the systems are poorly integrated. As a rule, you need a different ticket for each service and many of the 'interchange' stations are actually on different streets, linked by a series of walkways and overpasses.

This said, the monorail and Kelana Jaya/Terminal Putra line of the LRT provide access to most points of interest in the city centre, avoiding the traffic jams that plague the inner-city roads. The rechargeable Touch & Go stored value card (available at all LRT stations for an RM10 deposit) can be used at the electronic gates to the LRT, train and monorail systems.

See the transit network map, p127.

To/From the Airports

KLIA

The most hassle-free way to reach KL from KLIA is the **KLIA Ekspres** (☎ 2267 8000; www.kliaekspres.com; one-way adult/child RM35/15, return adult/child RM70/30). This comfortable express train departs every 15 to 20 minutes from 5.45am to 11.45pm and completes the journey to KL Sentral station in just 28 minutes. From KL Sentral, you can transfer to your final destination by monorail, LRT, KTM Komuter trains or by taxi. If you're flying from KL on Malaysia Airlines, you can check your baggage in at KL Sentral before making your way to KLIA. The half-hourly KL Transit service (adult/child one-way RM35/15) also connects KLIA with KL Sentral, but it stops at three other stations en route (Salak Tinggi, Putrajaya and Bandar Tasik Selatan) so the total journey takes about 35 minutes.

KL has a useful shuttle bus service between the airport and the city. The **Airport Coach** (☎ 8787 3894; one-way RM10) departs hourly from 5am until 10.30pm to KL Sentral (one hour) and from 6.30am to 12.30am to KLIA.

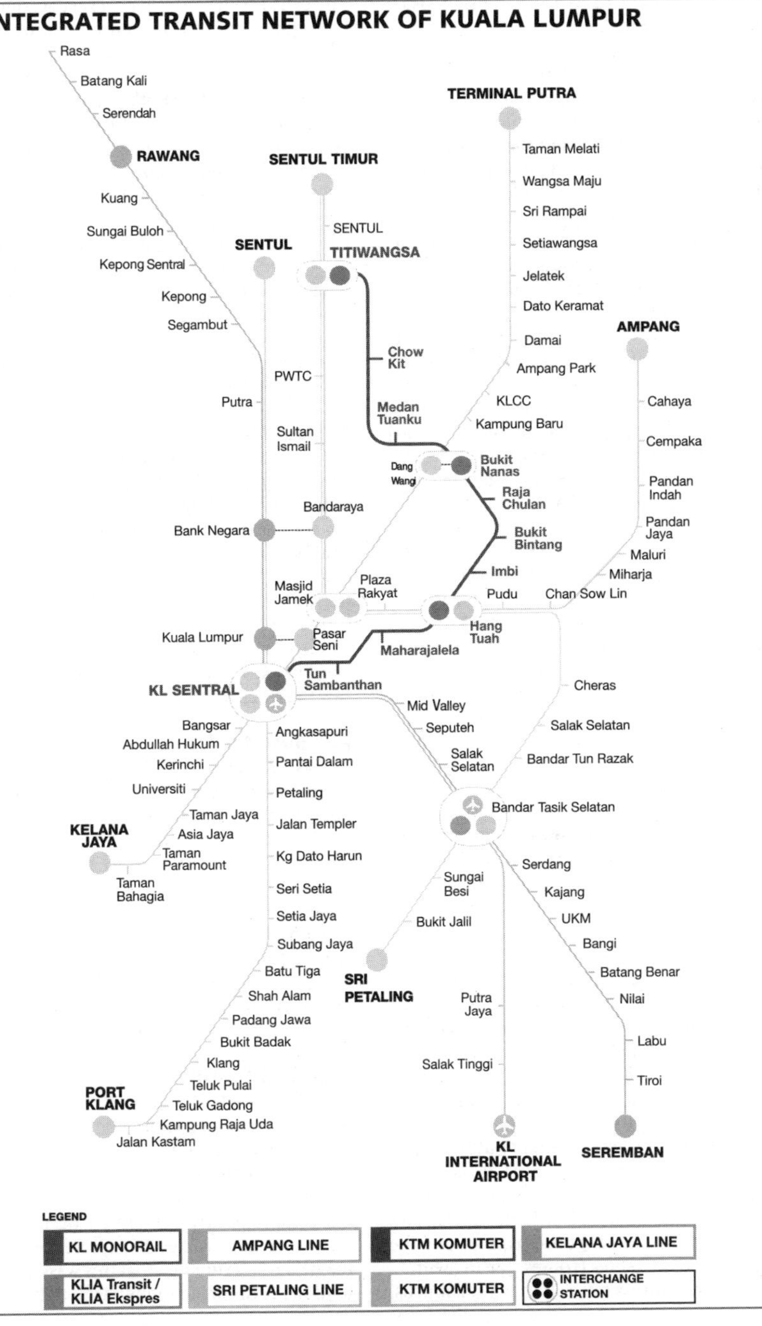
INTEGRATED TRANSIT NETWORK OF KUALA LUMPUR
Rasa
Batang Kali
Serendah
RAWANG
Kuang
Sungai Buloh
Kepong Sentral
Kepong
Segambut
Putra
SENTUL TIMUR
SENTUL
SENTUL
TITIWANGSA
PWTC
Sultan Ismail
Chow Kit
Medan Tuanku
TERMINAL PUTRA
Taman Melati
Wangsa Maju
Sri Rampai
Setiawangsa
Jelatek
Dato Keramat
Damai
Ampang Park
KLCC
Kampung Baru
AMPANG
Cahaya
Cempaka
Pandan Indah
Pandan Jaya
Maluri
Miharja
Chan Sow Lin
Dang Wangi
Bukit Nanas
Raja Chulan
Bukit Bintang
Imbi
Pudu
Hang Tuah
Bandaraya
Bank Negara
Masjid Jamek
Plaza Rakyat
Kuala Lumpur
Pasar Seni
Maharajalela
Tun Sambanthan
KL SENTRAL
Mid Valley
Seputeh
Salak Selatan
Cheras
Salak Selatan
Bandar Tun Razak
Bandar Tasik Selatan
Bangsar
Abdullah Hukum
Kerinchi
Universiti
Taman Jaya
Asia Jaya
Taman Paramount
KELANA JAYA
Taman Bahagia
Angkasapuri
Pantai Dalam
Petaling
Jalan Templer
Kg Dato Harun
Seri Setia
Setia Jaya
Subang Jaya
Batu Tiga
Shah Alam
Padang Jawa
Bukit Badak
Klang
Teluk Pulai
Teluk Gadong
Kampung Raja Uda
Jalan Kastam
PORT KLANG
Sungai Besi
Bukit Jalil
SRI PETALING
Putra Jaya
Salak Tinggi
KL INTERNATIONAL AIRPORT
Serdang
Kajang
UKM
Bangi
Batang Benar
Nilai
Labu
Tiroi
SEREMBAN
LEGEND
KL MONORAIL
AMPANG LINE
KTM KOMUTER
KELANA JAYA LINE
KLIA Transit / KLIA Ekspres
SRI PETALING LINE
KTM KOMUTER
INTERCHANGE STATION

The bus stand at KLIA is clearly signposted inside the terminal.

To reach central KL by taxi head to the taxi coupon desk inside the terminal (look for the yellow sign in arrivals). Standard taxis cost RM67 for up to three people, premier taxis for four people are RM93 and the journey takes around one hour. If you try to negotiate a fare directly with the taxi drivers waiting outside the arrivals hall, you'll pay hundreds of ringgit for the same ride. When going to the airport by taxi, make sure that the agreed fare includes tolls; expect to pay RM65 from Chinatown or Jln Bukit Bintang.

If you're changing to a flight on Air Asia, there's a useful shuttle bus between KLIA and the LCC-T – it runs every 20 minutes from 6am to midnight and the fare is RM1.50. Penny-pinchers can use this bus to get to Nilai (RM3.50) to connect with the KTM Komuter train to KL Sentral (RM4.70). A taxi between the two airports costs RM33.

LCC-T

To reach the LCC-T from KL Sentral, jump on the **Skybus** (www.skybus.com.my); buses run half-hourly from around 4.30am to 12.45am and the fare for the one-hour journey is RM9. Travelling from the LCC-T, prepaid taxis charge RM62 to Chinatown or Jln Bukit Bintang (50% more from midnight to 6am). Buy your coupon at the desk near the arrivals hall exit. A taxi from the city to LCC-T will cost around RM65.

SULTAN ABDUL AZIZ SHAH AIRPORT

The easiest way to reach the Sultan Abdul Aziz Shah Airport is to take a taxi (around RM40).

Bus

Although there are several smaller companies, most buses in KL are provided by either **Rapid KL** (☎ 1800-388 228; www.rapidkl.com.my) or **Metrobus** (☎ 5635 3070). Rapid KL buses are the easiest to use as destinations are clearly displayed. Its buses are divided into four classes, and tickets are valid all day on the same class of bus. Bas Bandar (routes starting with B, RM2) services run around the city centre. Bas Utama (routes starting with U, RM2) buses run from the centre to the suburbs. Bas Tempatan (routes starting with T, RM1) buses run around the suburbs. Bas Ekspres (routes starting with E, RM4) are express buses to distant suburbs.

You can also buy an all-day ticket covering all nonexpress buses (RM4) and a ticket covering all Rapid KL buses and trains (RM7). All the bus routes have recently been renumbered – there's an **information booth** (Map pp78-9; 🕑 7am to 9pm) in front of Pasar Seni LRT station where you can pick up a route map and information on various season tickets.

Local buses leave from half a dozen small bus stands around the city – useful stops in Chinatown include Jln Sultan Mohamed (by Pasar Seni), Klang Bus Station (south of Pasar Seni), Bangkok Bank (on Lebuh Pudu), Medan Pasar (on Lebuh Ampang), Central Market (on Jln Hang Kasturi) and the Kota Raya department store (on Jln Cheng Lock); see Map pp78–9.

KL Monorail

KL's air-conditioned **monorail** (☎ 2273 1888; www.monorail.com.my; RM1.20-2.50) zips from KL Sentral in the south to Titiwangsa in the north, linking up many of the city's sightseeing areas. Trains run from 6am to midnight. Useful stops include KL Sentral (for the train station and airport transport), Maharajalela (for Chinatown), Imbi and Bukit Bintang (for the Golden Triangle), Medan Tuanku (for Asian Heritage Row and Chow Kit) and Titiwangsa (for the Pekeliling Bus Station).

KTM Komuter Trains

The **KTM Komuter** (☎ 2267 1200; www.ktmb.com.my) service provides a suburban rail link using long-distance railway lines, with its main hub at KL Sentral. There are two lines: Rawang to Seremban and Sentul to Pelabuhan Klang. Useful stops include Mid Valley (for the Mid Valley Megamall), Subang Jaya (for Sunway Lagoon), Nilai (for the cheap local bus to the airports) and Pelabuhan Klang (for ferry services to Sumatra). Trains run every 15 to 20 minutes from approximately 6am to 11.45pm. Tickets start from RM1 for one stop.

Light Rail Transit

As well as the buses, **Rapid KL** (☎ 1800-388 228; www.rapidkl.com.my) runs the Light Rail Transit (LRT) system. There are three lines: Ampang–Sentul Timur, Sri Petaling–Sentul Timur and Kelana Jaya–Terminal Putra. However, the network is poorly integrated because the lines were constructed by different companies (there are rumours that this was done intentionally to spread money around between

KL's political elite). As a result, you need a new ticket to change from one line to another, and you may also have to follow a series of walkways, stairs and elevators, or walk several blocks down the street. See the table below for useful stops on the different lines.

An electronic control system checks tickets as you enter and exit via turnstiles. Single-journey fares range from RM1 to RM2.80, or you can buy an all-day pass for RM7, which also covers you for Rapid KL buses. You can buy tickets from the cashier or electronic ticket machines but, for some reason, these only accept a single note for each transaction – the rest of the ticket price must be made up in coins. Trains run every six to 10 minutes from 6am to 11.45pm. If you're going to be in KL for a while, consider investing in a monthly combined travel card (RM90 or RM125 including Rapid KL buses).

Station	Line	Use for
KL Sentral	Terminal Putra–Kelana Jaya	Brickfields, buses & trains to the airports
Pasar Seni	Terminal Putra–Kelana Jaya	Chinatown, Puduraya Bus Station
Masjid Jamek	All Lines	Interchange station; Masjid Jamek, Merdeka Sq
KLCC	Terminal Putra–Kelana Jaya	Petronas Towers, KLCC
Dang Wangi	Terminal Putra–Kelana Jaya	Asian Heritage Row
Kampung Baru	Terminal Putra–Kelana Jaya	Kampung Baru
Kelana Jaya	Terminal Putra–Kelana Jaya	Sunway Lagoon
PWTC	Ampang–Sentul Timur, Sri Petaling–Sentul Timur	Putra Bus Station
Titiwangsa	Ampang–Sentul Timur; Sri Petaling–Sentul Timur	Pekeliling Bus Station, Titiwangsa Park

Taxi

KL has plenty of air-conditioned taxis, which queue up at designed taxi stops across the city. You can also flag down moving taxis, but drivers will only stop if there is a convenient place to pull over. Fares start at RM2 for the first two minutes, with an additional 10 sen for each 45 seconds. From midnight to 6am there's a surcharge of 50% on the metered fare, and extra passengers (more than two) are charged 20 sen each. Luggage placed in the boot is an extra RM1 and there's an RM12 surcharge for taxis to KLIA.

Unfortunately, some drivers have a limited geographical knowledge of the city, and many are reluctant to use the meter, even though this is a legal requirement. Taxi drivers lingering outside luxury hotels are especially guilty of this behaviour, citing KL's traffic or the out-of-the-way location of your destination as a reason for an elevated cash fare. This is baloney. If a driver demands a fixed fare, bargain hard, or walk away and find another taxi. As a guide, you can get right across the centre of town for RM5 on the meter or RM10 after bargaining. Note that KL Sentral and some large malls have a coupon system for taxis where you pay in advance.

AROUND KUALA LUMPUR

You don't have to spend your whole trip confined to the city. There are easy transport links from KL to attractions like the Batu Caves, Zoo Negara and the theme parks at Genting Highlands and Sunway Lagoon. The following places can easily be visited as day trips from the city by taxi, train or bus.

SOUTH OF KUALA LUMPUR

Sunway Lagoon & Around

About 10km southwest of Kuala Lumpur in Petaling Jaya, **Sunway Lagoon** (off Map pp72-3; ☎ 5639 0000; www.sunway.com.my/lagoon; 3 Jln PJS 11/11, Bandar Sunway; wet & dry parks adult/child RM45/30, all parks RM65/50; 🕑 11am-6pm Mon-Fri, from 10am Sat & Sun) is Malaysia's best water park, with all sorts of splashtastic water slides and a surge pool with waves big enough to surf on. The park was built over an old tin mine and the theming is outrageous – some parts have a Wild West theme, some parts are African, faux waterfalls cascade on all sides and a 428m pedestrian suspension bridge stretches across the entire lagoon. On weekends, you can surf from 5pm to 6pm and body board from 3pm to 4pm. As well as the watery attractions, there's a dry amusement park with roller coasters and a log flume, an 'extreme park' with paintball and quad bikes, a slingshot G-force ride and a petting zoo for kids. Out of respect for Muslim sensibilities, there's a dress code:

one-piece swimsuits or leggings and a T-shirt are preferred attire for women, while speedos or tight shorts (à la Daniel Craig's James Bond) are preferred attire for men.

Looming over Sunway Lagoon is the equally wacky **Sunway Pyramid Mall** (☎ 7494 3000; www.sunway.com.my/pyramid; 3 Jln PJS 11/15, Bandar Sunway; 🕑 10am-10pm), styled like an Egyptian pyramid, complete with hieroglyphs and a looming fibreglass sphinx (it used to have a human face but it was remodelled as a lion after protests from the local mosque regarding the depiction of the human form, forbidden under some strict interpretations of the Quran). As well as the usual brand-name stores, there's a good selection of mall-restaurants, a bowling alley and a full-sized **ice rink** (☎ 7492 6800; weekday/weekend RM13/16; 🕑 9am-8pm, to 10pm Sat & 9pm Sun).

The easiest way to get to Sunway is take the Putra LRT to Kelana Jaya (RM2.10), then feeder bus T623 (RM1) or a taxi (RM11) to the Sunway Pyramid. Shuttle buses U63, U67 and U756 run here from Subang Jaya station on the KTM Komuter line. A taxi all the way from central KL will cost around RM21.

There are more waterslides and wave pools east of Sunway at **Desa Waterpark** (off Map pp72-3; ☎ 7118 8338; www.desawaterpark.com.my; Taman Danau Desa; adult/child RM18/12; 🕑 noon-6pm Mon-Fri, 10am-6pm Sat & Sun). It's smaller than Sunway Lagoon, but generally less crowded. The best way to get here is by taxi from Salak Selatan KTM Komuter station (on the Rawang–Seremban line).

Mines Resort City

About 10km south of KL, this **resort** (off Map pp72-3; www.mines.com.my; Seri Kembangan, Selangor Darul Ehsan) was built over the workings of the world's largest open-cast tin mine. This former wasteland has been reborn as a flashy leisure resort with lakes, shopping malls, amusements, a golf club, a convention centre and several luxury hotels, including the glitzy, Mughal-themed **Palace of the Golden Horses** (www.palaceofthegoldenhorses.com.my).

The main attraction for visitors is the **Mines Wonderland** (☎ 8942 5010; www.mineswonderland.com.my; adult/child RM32/21; 🕑 6pm-11pm Tue-Fri, 5pm-11pm Sat & Sun), an evening-only leisure park with an illuminated musical fountain, boat rides, an animal park with white tigers, a selection of mostly gentle rides, a sculpture park full of gaudily painted Chinese dragons and a winter wonderland where locals come to experience the thrill of getting cold. It's tacky as anything, but kids seem to love it.

To get here, charter a taxi or take the KTM Komuter train to Serdang station, cross the highway on the footbridge then walk for about 15 minutes to the park.

Putrajaya

The city that is destined to be the new capital of Malaysia is slowly taking shape about 20km south of KL, on the way to KLIA. Covering 4932 hectares of former rubber and palm-oil plantations, the planned city will one day house 320,000 civil servants and their families, forming the new epicentre of Malaysian politics and international relations. Monumental new buildings have already been constructed to house the judiciary and other government ministries, as well as the offices and new official residence of the prime minister. Several huge mosques have already appeared, but so far there are no religious monuments for any other ethnic groups – further fuel for claims of government bias against Indian and Chinese Malaysians. Thus far, there is no real commercial life to speak of, but it's worth visiting to see the striking modern architecture and explore some of the formal parks and gardens.

The main street in Putrajaya is Persiaran Perdana, which runs from the modernist **Putrajaya Convention Centre** (☎ 8887 6000; www.pcc.gov.my; Precinct 5) (worth visiting for the views) to **Dataran Putra** (Putra Square) and the imposing, mosquelike **Perdana Putra**, housing the offices of the prime minister. On the way, you'll cross two of Putrajaya's striking modernist bridges; there are nine in total, all built in different styles. Just before the Perdana Putra, the handsome **Putra Mosque** (Persiaran Perdana; 🕑 for non-Muslims 9am-1.30pm & 3-6pm Sat-Thu, 3-6pm Fri) has space for 15,000 worshippers and an ornate red-tile dome, influenced by Safavid architecture from Iran. Appropriately dressed non-Muslim visitors are welcome outside of prayer times.

North of Perdana Putra, near the prime minister's official residence, the **Taman Botani** (Botanic Gardens; ☎ 8888 9090; Precinct 1; admission free; 🕑 10am-7pm daily, visitors centre 10am-6pm Tue-Fri, 10am-7pm Sat & Sun) features attractive tropical gardens on the lakeshore. A tourist tram trundles between the flower beds and trestles, and you can hire bicycles for RM4 for two hours (RM4 for one hour on weekends). Further north is the serene **Wetland Park** (☎ 8889 4373; Precinct 13; admission free; 7am-7pm; visitors centre 10am-6pm Tue-Sat, 10am-7pm Sun), a contemplative space with peaceful nature trails, soothing birdsong, fluttering butterflies and picnic tables overlooking the lake. Canoeing and boating trips can be arranged from Tuesday to Sunday.

Cruise Tasik Putrajaya (☎ 8888 5539; www.cruisetasikputrajaya.com) offers 45-minute cruises around the lake (adult/child RM30/20) from the jetty near the Putra Mosque, plus more intimate half-hour trips in gondalalike *perahu* (RM20/10).

The easiest way to reach Putrajaya is on the KLIA Transit train from KL Sentral (RM9.50, every 30 minutes 5.30am to midnight). From the bus stand at Putrajaya Sentral, local Nadi Putra buses fan out around the compound, charging a flat fare of 50 sen. Taxis operate on a coupon system – it costs RM9 to reach any of the major sights in the park or RM30 for an hour of sightseeing. A new monorail system was under construction at the time of writing, but the project is likely to take several years to complete. A taxi to central KL or KLIA costs RM48.

NORTH OF KUALA LUMPUR

Batu Caves

The Hindu temples in downtown KL are just appetisers for this huge Hindu **cave complex** (off Map pp72-3; admission free; 8am-9pm), 13km north of the capital. The Batu Caves were first discovered around 120 years ago by American naturalist William Hornaday, but the Hindu community soon adopted the site as their principle place of worship. Today the caves are dotted with Hindu shrines and statues painted in outrageous colours. The central Temple Cave – open to the sky and dripping with stalactites – is reached by a flight of 272 steps, which ascends beside a 43m-tall golden statue of Muruga (Lord Subramaniam), the patron deity of the caves. Cheeky macaque monkeys use the caves as their own adventure playground, leaping from stalactite to stalagmite and soliciting snacks from pilgrims and tourists. The monkeys bite, so keep your distance. The caves are busy most days, but 1.3 million pilgrims descend on the complex every January/February for the Thaipusam festival, which features surreal acts of self-mortification – see the boxed text, p221, for more on this fascinating celebration.

About halfway up the steps, a path branches off to the smaller **Gua Gelap** cave system which you can explore with a head-torch on a half-hour guided tour (adult/child RM35/23). There are some dramatic limestone formations but the caves are damp and muddy and you may have to do some wriggling and crawling to squeeze through the narrow tunnels. At the bottom of the steps, another path leads to the **Art Gallery** (admission RM1; 8am-1pm & 4-8.30pm), a collection of statues and dioramas telling tales from Hindu legends.

Taxis from KL charge around RM12 on the meter, or about RM20 if you have to bargain. In the opposite direction, you'll always have to bargain. Alternatively, take Metrobus 11 (RM2; 45 minutes) from the Bangkok Bank bus stand in Chinatown.

Zoo Negara

About 13km northeast of KL, this **zoo** (☎ 4108 3422; www.zoonegara.org.my; Hulu Kelang; adult/child RM15/6; 9am-5pm Mon-Fri, 9am-10.30pm Sat & Sun) is one of Asia's better zoos. Although some of the enclosures could definitely be bigger, the animals seem mostly content. The zoo boasts an impressive range of beasties, from hippos and giraffes to elephants, lions and tigers. Animal shows take place throughout the day and there are several cafés and snack stands. See the boxed text, p132, for details on feeding the animals.

Taxis charge around RM30 from central KL or you can take Metrobus 16 (RM2) from in front of the Central Market in Chinatown.

Orang Asli Museum

In the sleepy village of Gombak, 25km north of KL, the this **museum** (off Map pp72-3; ☎ 6189 2113; www.jheoa.gov.my; Gombak; admission free; 8.30am-5pm Sat-Thu) is devoted to the history, rituals and customs of Malaysia's aboriginal people. More than 150,000 Orang Asli (Original People) are found in Peninsular Malaysia, divided into three sub-groups – the Negrito, Senoi and Proto-Malays.

Despite playing an important role in the development of modern Malaysia – the Orang Asli helped the colonial authorities discover all sorts of valuable natural resources in the rainforests and provided invaluable support for troops fighting the communists during the Emergency – the tribes are increasingly marginalised today. The museum is run as a social project by Jabatan Hal Ehwal Orang

FEEDING TIME AT ZOO NEGARA

There can't be many zoos where you get to feed the animals yourself. The vendors at Zoo Negara selling bags of carrot chips and bunches of green bamboo are not here to promote a new low protein diet – these veggie snacks are destined for the elephants, camels, deer and giraffes waiting eagerly at the low fences to their enclosures. As animal management strategies go, this has some merit. The foodstuffs on offer are selected to compliment the animals' natural diet and you'll see little of the heart-rending pacing found in many zoos in Asia. Even if you worry about the dignity of these magnificent beasts, you'd have to have a heart of stone to not feel some sense of childlike wonder while feeding strips of green bamboo to a snuffling jumbo.

Carnivore feeding time is something else. Do not be fooled into thinking that the live rats are anything other than crocodile food. The quick splash and sudden snap can be a little unsettling, but it's arguably closer to the natural feeding habits of predators than the sanitised feeding practices at many Western zoos. And the crocodiles seem to like it – Zoo Negara was the first zoo to successfully breed false gharials and African dwarf crocodiles in captivity.

Asli (JHEOA), the department of aboriginal affairs. Inside you can see some thought-provoking displays on the various tribes of the region, and there's a small shop selling the eye-catching wood carvings by the Mah Meri people and *tongkat ali* – a form of wild ginseng alleged to have Viagra-like properties!

You can get here on Metrobus 174 from Lebuh Ampang in Chinatown (RM2), but check locally to see if this has changed during the reshuffle of bus numbers. The museum entrance is hidden so ask the driver to let you know when you've arrived.

Forest Research Institute of Malaysia

Escape the crush of the city at this 600-hectare rainforest **reserve** (FRIM; Map pp72-3; ☎ 6279 7575; www.frim.gov.my; Selangor Darul Ehsan; admission RM5), around 16km northeast of KL. FRIM was established by the British in 1929 to conduct research into the sustainable management of Malaysia's rainforests. Its work has become increasingly important with the growing threats from logging and urban expansion. Numerous tours run here from KL (see p99), or you can make your way by public transport. The park has some interesting diversions for visitors who brave the humidity and mosquitoes.

As well as a network of nature trails, there's an excellent **information centre** (🕑 8am-5pm Mon-Fri, 9am-4pm Sat & Sun) and a **museum** (admission free; 🕑 8am-5pm Mon-Fri, 9am-4pm Sat & Sun) with displays on FRIM's conservation activities. The main attraction is a 200m **forest walkway** (adult/child RM5/1; 1🕑 0am-1.30pm Tue-Thu & Sat), suspended 30m above the forest floor. As well as inducing instant vertigo, the walkway will take you right into the canopy, offering great views of the rainforest, with the towers of KL rising behind. If you've ever imagined what life is like for monkeys, this could be your chance to find out.

A series of well-marked **nature trails** wind through the trees, passing scenic picnic spots and waterfalls you can splash around in. Hardcore mountain-bike enthusiasts head deep into the jungle on a series of rough forestry tracks (2.5km to 23km).

To get here, take the KTM Komuter train to Kepong (RM1.30) and then a taxi to FRIM (RM5). Ask the driver to come back and pick you up a few hours later. Most people bring a picnic but there's decent canteen serving Malay food. You can also camp here if you give the centre advance notice.

Templer Park

About 22km north of KL beside Hwy 1, this **nature park** (off Map pp72-3; 🕑 24hr) was once part of a rubber estate, but the Forestry Department took over in the 1980s, preserving 1200 hectares of primary jungle from the developers. Today it's a popular weekend retreat for nature-oriented locals, with walking and jogging trails (also good for mountain bikes), picnic tables and a series of ponds, streams and waterfalls where you can swim (modestly dressed of course). The park covers a huge area but there are no signs saying 'Templer Park' – look instead for the sign saying 'Hutan Lipur Kanching' which marks the path to the waterfalls area.

Metrobus 43 runs here every 15 minutes from the Bangkok Bank bus stand on Lebuh Pudu in Chinatown (RM2).

Genting Highlands

There are two reasons to come to the **Highlands** (☎ 2718 1118; www.genting.com.my; complex & casino admission free, other attractions extra; 24hr). One is the cool, mountain air. The other is the sheer spectacle of this huge, tacky casino-cum-theme-park-cum-resort-hotel-cum-shopping-centre-cum-entertainment-palace. Set on a lofty hilltop about 54km north of KL, Malaysia's answer to Las Vegas is completely over the top and you'll either love it or loath it. There are several casinos here (minimum age 21, closed to Malaysian Muslims), plus hotels, restaurants, bars, shops and venues, and two big theme parks.

The relentlessly commercial **indoor theme park** (adult/child RM21/19; 9am-midnight, from 8am Sat & Sun) is much less exciting than the **outdoor theme park** (adult/child RM33/22; 10am-7pm Mon-Fri, 8am-10pm Sat, 8am-8pm Sun), which has looping roller coasters, sudden-drop rides and a log flume. You can buy an all-day pass or pay for individual rides. Note that the outdoor park is sometimes shut down by swirling clouds during the monsoon. Nearby, the 6000-seater **Arena of Stars** is the place to come to see Malaysian crooners singing big production numbers on ice skates with backing singers dressed as St Bernards dogs. We're not kidding.

The **Genting Skyway** (one-way/return RM5/10; 7.30am-11pm, to midnight Sat) runs from the base of the hill to the casino complex, with dramatic views over the rainforest. Just downhill from the casino complex, you can connect with Malaysia's spiritual side at the **Chin Swee Caves Temple** (daylight hours). Dominated by a towering Chinese pagoda, this Taoist fantasy is dotted with Buddhist statues and ornate pavilions. The main shrine is dedicated to Chin Swee, a revered 11th-century monk from Fujian, China, and there's a monumental seated-Buddha statue in the gardens. Shuttle buses run here hourly from Genting (RM5 return) or you can take the Awana Skyway to the Temple stop.

GETTING THERE & AWAY

Whichever way you come to Genting, the journey from KL will take about an hour. The most convenient way to get here is to take the **Go Genting** (www.genting.com.my) bus from KL Sentral – package tickets cost RM26 (RM39 on weekends and public holidays) including entry to the theme parks and the ride on the Skyway. The bus leaves approximately hourly from 8am to 7pm; book at the ticket desk inside the station building. The fare for the bus transfer only is RM8.30/6.70 per adult/child. Shuttle buses also run between Genting and the Pekeliling Bus Station in Titiwangsa (RM5.60). Taxis flagged down in the street charge around RM70/150 one-way/return from central KL; slightly cheaper shared taxis (RM50) leave from the 2nd floor of the Puduraya Bus Station.

Melaka

Outlined to the west by sandy coastline and filled inland with waves of jungle-carpeted hills, the sultry city-state of Melaka is the cradle of modern Malaysia. While everything from international trade to the country's political system (based on the Malaccan sultanate) began here, the city and state have, for the most part, avoided becoming a congested metropolis and instead remain peaceful enclaves basking in the memory of a majestic past. It's said that the soul of the country can be glimpsed here. It's true, this is Malaysia's good side and it has become one of the county's most popular destinations. The variations on traditional cuisine, including the famed Malay-Chinese Nonya food, are reason enough to visit.

The road from past glory has been potholed even in recent history. Massive land reclamation projects, begun during the economic boom only to taper off during the ensuing economic downturn, pushed the historic waterfront so far inland that it endangered the traditional livelihood of the Portuguese fishing community. Today, Melaka's rich seam of heritage is under threat from those twin fruits of development: commercialisation and modernisation.

While the coastlines of Pulau Besar and Tanjung Bidara don't compare to the country's other beaches, they do make a relaxing getaway or day trip from the state's capital. Melaka is close enough to Kuala Lumpur (KL) for a day trip, but allow at least a couple of days to do justice to this fascinating historic enclave.

HIGHLIGHTS

- Browsing and grazing at Friday- and Saturday-night **Jonker's Walk Night Market** (p158) then stopping for a drink at an open-air café
- Indulging your tourist-tacky desires by taking a ride in one of Melaka city's uniquely kitsch **trishaws** (p151)
- Pondering *popiah* (spring roll), checking out chicken rice balls and lingering over *laksa lemak* (curry laksa) in Melaka city's **restaurants** (p156)
- Topping up your suitcase with spinning tops, creative clothing and perhaps an antique treasure after a day of **shopping** (p161) in Melaka city's Chinatown
- Getting an up-close tour of the Peranakan experience at the **Baba-Nonya Heritage Museum** (p144)
- Enjoying the views and the cool air of the sanctuary at **St Paul's Church** (p141)
- Driving through villages and farms to the coastline of the Strait of Melaka and its long white-sand beach, **Tanjung Bidara** (p166)

TELEPHONE CODE: 06 | POPULATION: 688,694 | AREA: 1652 SQ KM

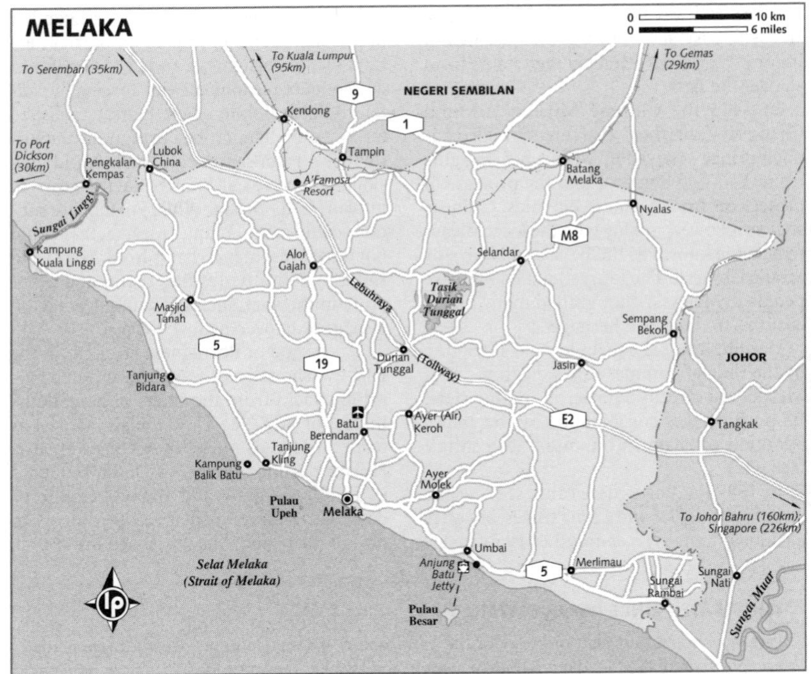

MELAKA CITY

Back when KL was a malaria-ridden swamp and Penang was yet to become the 'Pearl of the Orient', Melaka was already one of the greatest trading ports in Southeast Asia. Today the city is a sleepy backwater compared with its high-rolling cousins, but that's exactly where its charm lies. There isn't even a major airport or city rail station so the only way in or out from within Malaysia is by road. With the oldest functioning mosque, Catholic church and Buddhist temple in the country, the city's past has been preserved, nearly pickled in fact, around its Chinatown and colonial centre. Yet despite being exceedingly old, Melaka manages to entice visitors with its present-day personality, a quirky amalgam best represented by its resident artists, cooks, fortune-tellers and fabulously creative trishaws (bicycle rickshaws). The action blends effortlessly with the surrounding Peranakan, Portuguese and Dutch architecture; Buddhist, Taoist and Indian temples; and Islamic mosques.

And have we mentioned the food? If you're eating local dishes, it's unlikely you'll have a bad meal. From the distinct Peranakan dishes to Eurasian Portuguese cooking and Indian banana-leaf shops, the citywide restaurant aromas add further colour to the cultural mosaic that makes Melaka such an astonishing destination.

HISTORY

The history of the city-state of Melaka is a tale that begins with a legend then falls into the hands of battling colonial forces. However it's told, the story of the state is inseparable from that of the city for which it was named. Historians have not been able to pinpoint the exact year that Melaka was founded but most agree it was sometime in the late 14th century. Before this time, Melaka was a simple fishing village.

Parameswara, a Hindu prince from Sumatra, was the founder of Melaka (see the boxed text, p136). Under Parameswara, the city became a favoured port for waiting out monsoons and resupplying trading ships plying the strategic Selat Melaka (Strait of

Melaka). Halfway between China and India, and with easy access to the spice islands of Indonesia, Melaka attracted merchants from all over the East.

In 1405 the Chinese Muslim Admiral Cheng Ho (see p144), the 'three-jewelled eunuch prince', arrived in Melaka bearing gifts from the Ming emperor and the promise of protection from Siamese enemies. Chinese settlers followed, mixing with the local Malays to become known as the Baba and Nonya or Straits Chinese. The longest-settled Chinese people in Malaysia, they grafted many Malay customs to their own heritage.

Despite internal squabbles and intrigues, by the time of Parameswara's death in 1414, Melaka was already a powerful trading state. Its position was consolidated by the state's adoption of Islam in the mid-15th century (see p22).

In 1509 the Portuguese came seeking the wealth of the spice and China trades, but after an initially friendly reception, the Malaccans attacked the Portuguese fleet and took a number of prisoners. This prompted an outright assault by the Portuguese, and in 1511 Alfonso de Albuquerque took the city, forcing the sultan to flee to Johor, where he re-established his kingdom. Under the Portuguese, the fortress of A'Famosa was constructed, and missionaries such as St Francis Xavier strove to implant Catholicism. While Portuguese cannons could easily conquer Melaka, they could not force Muslim merchants from Arabia and India to continue trading there, and other ports in the area, such as Islamic Demak on Java, grew to overshadow Melaka.

The period of Portuguese strength in the East was short-lived, as Melaka suffered harrying attacks from the rulers of neighbouring Johor and Negeri Sembilan, as well as from the Islamic power of Aceh in Sumatra. Melaka declined further as Dutch influence in Indonesia grew and Batavia (modern-day Jakarta) developed as the key European port of the region. Melaka passed into Dutch

THE PIRATE PRINCE PARAMESWARA

Part legend and part fact, the story of the 14th-century Indonesian prince Parameswara is the accepted tale of the founding of both Singapore and Melaka. Known by many names in different cultures, Parameswara was said to be a direct descendent of Alexander the Great (also known as Raja Iskandar Zulkarnain), and he possessed many semimagical items, including a bejewelled crown thought to be part of the treasures of Solomon.

In different tellings, Parameswara either asks his father permission to colonise an island he saw in the distance (Temasek, the future Singapore) or was chased away from Indonesia by a Javanese enemy and fled to Temasek to hide. Either way, on route to the island Parameswara and his faithful crew sailed into a massive storm unlike any they had ever encountered. Just as everyone had accepted their fate to die, Parameswara threw his valuable crown into the sea as an offering to the sea god. The sea was calmed the instant the crown hit the water.

But their trials were far from over. When the stalwart sailers arrived on Temasek, they were met by a fierce lion. Parameswara drew his sword to slay the beast but just as he was about to strike, his eyes met those of the lion's. In an instant there was a communication of respect and understanding and the lion quietly absconded into the jungle. Parameswara named his new city Singapura, meaning the Lion City. Unfortunately, his piracy and other exploits provoked a Siamese attack, forcing him to flee once more, this time up the Malay peninsula to the town of Muar in the Johor province. While lions and rough seas had been but mere trifles for Parameswara, he and his men were driven from this new area by a particularly vicious band of monitor lizards. At another short stop, the refugees' freshly built fortress fell into ruins for no apparent reason, making them move on once more.

Not giving up, the group trudged further north and it was here that their luck would change. While hunting at the mouth of the Bertam River, Parameswara saw a white mouse-deer *(pelanduk)* kick one of his hunting dogs in its defence. The prince was so impressed by the valiant and courageous deer that he decided to build a new city on the spot. He asked one of his servants the name of the tree that was shading them and took the name to christen his town Melaka.

At the end of his life, Parameswara converted to Islam, opening the doors of the faith to the rest of the peninsula.

MELAKA IN...

Two Days

Melaka is small enough that you'll be able to soak up many of its charms in only two days. Start the first day at **Roti Canai Terbang** (p159) to enjoy a flaky pancake with tea or coffee and to get a taste of the cultural mix of the city by people-watching from your table. Next head towards the historic city centre where you can snap the requisite photo of yourself in front of **Porta de Santiago** (p142). Work off your breakfast with a climb up the long stairway to explore the ruins of **St Paul's Church** (p141) then backtrack down the hill to the **Sultanate Palace** (p143). Visit the museums of your choice along the pedestrian road towards the **Stadthuys** (see p142). Grab a trishaw here for a city tour and then lunch in Little India afterwards – wander around the sari shops around here. In the evening (if it's Friday or Saturday) don't miss the **Jonker's Walk Night Market** (p158) to snack and peruse, then finish the night at a pavement pub table where you could stay till all hours of the morning.

Sleep in if you need to on day two then have a traditional dim sum breakfast at **Low Yong Mow** (p157) before losing yourself for most of the day in Chinatown. Take an afternoon **riverboat cruise** (p152) then treat yourself to a **reflexology foot massage** (p148) at the end of the day. Dine at **Capitol Satay** (p159) for a meal to end all meals.

One Week

Follow the two-day schedule then sweat out the next morning on a bike tour with **Eco Bike Tour** (p152) before chilling in the air-con for the afternoon with a cooking class at the **Hotel Equatorial** (p155). Rent a car for days four and five to visit **Tanjung Bidara** (p166) and **Alor Gajah** (p164) and have fun getting lost along side roads where you'll find sleepy *kampung* (villages) unused to foreign visitors. On days six and seven visit the rest of Melaka city including **Medan Portugis** (p147), **Bukit China** (p146) and **Villa Sentosa** (see p147).

hands after an eight-month siege in 1641. The Dutch ruled Melaka for only about 150 years. Melaka again became the centre for peninsular trade, but the Dutch directed more energy into their possessions in Indonesia. In Melaka they built fine public buildings and churches, which remain the most solid suggestions of European presence, while Medan Portugis is still home to Portuguese Eurasians, many of whom are practising Catholics who speak Kristang (Cristão), a creole (see the boxed text, p147) littered with archaic Portuguese.

When the French occupied Holland in 1795, the British – Dutch allies –temporarily assumed administration of the Dutch colonies. The British administrators, essentially traders, were opposed to the Dutch policy of trade monopoly and saw the potential for fierce rivalry in Malaysia between themselves and the Dutch. Accordingly, in 1807 they began demolishing A'Famosa fortress and forcibly removing Melaka's Dutch population to Penang to prevent Melaka rivalling British Malayan centres if Dutch control was restored. Fortunately Sir Thomas Stamford Raffles, the far-sighted founder of Singapore, stepped in before these destructive policies went too far, and in 1824 Melaka was permanently ceded to the British in exchange for the Sumatran port of Bencoolen (Bengkulu today).

Melaka, together with Penang and Singapore, formed the Straits settlements, the three British territories that were the centres for later expansion into the peninsula. However, under British rule Melaka was eclipsed by other Straits settlements and was soon quickly superseded by the rapidly growing commercial importance of Singapore. Apart from a brief upturn in the early 20th century when rubber was an important crop, Melaka returned again to being a quiet backwater, awaiting its renaissance as a tourist drawcard.

ORIENTATION

Melaka is a medium-sized town that's easy to navigate and compact enough to explore on foot or trishaw. While the city is the perfect size for getting around by bike, the traffic, lack of a hard shoulder and an excessive quantity

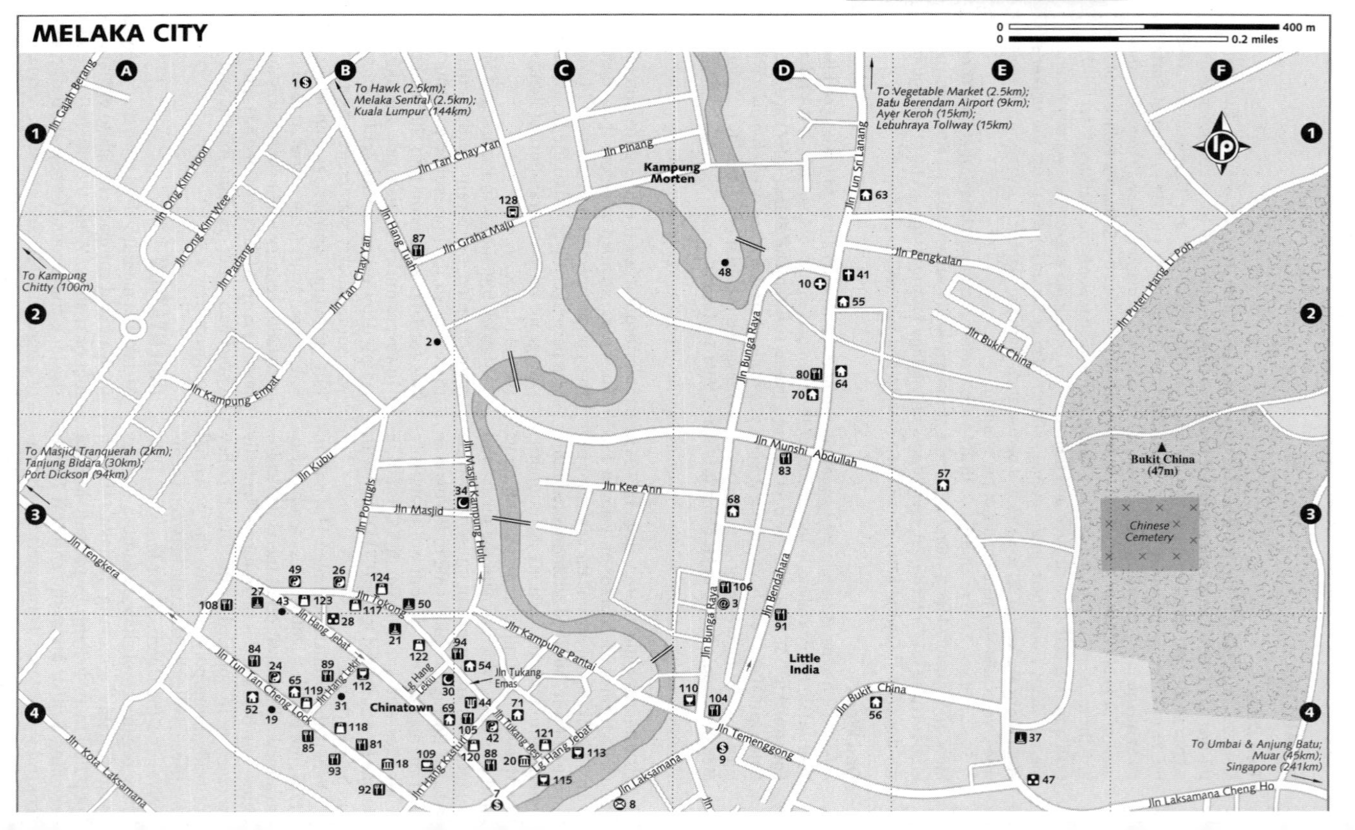
MELAKA CITY
0.2 miles
400 m
To Hawk (2.5km); Melaka Sentral (2.5km); Kuala Lumpur (144km)
To Vegetable Market (2.5km); Batu Berendam Airport (9km); Ayer Keroh (15km); Lebuhraya Tollway (15km)
To Kampung Chitty (100m)
To Masjid Tranquerah (2km); Tanjung Bidara (30km); Port Dickson (94km)
To Umbai & Anjung Batu; Muar (45km); Singapore (241km)
Bukit China (47m)
Chinese Cemetery
Kampung Morten
Little India
Chinatown
Jln Gajah Berang
Jln Ong Kim Hoon
Jln Ong Kim Wee
Jln Padang
Jln Kampung Empat
Jln Tan Chay Yan
Jln Hang Tuah
Jln Graha Maju
Jln Pinang
Jln Kubu
Jln Portugis
Jln Masjid
Jln Masjid Kampung Hulu
Jln Kee Ann
Jln Tokong
Jln Hang Jebat
Jln Hang Lekir
Lg Hang Lekiu
Jln Tun Tan Cheng Lock
Jln Tengkera
Jln Kota Laksamana
Jln Hang Kasturi
Jln Tukang Besi
Jln Tukang Emas
Jln Kampung Pantai
Jln Laksamana
Jln Temenggong
Jln Bunga Raya
Jln Bendahara
Jln Munshi Abdullah
Jln Tun Sri Lanang
Jln Pengkalan
Jln Bukit China
Jln Puteri Hang Li Poh
Jln Laksamana Cheng Ho

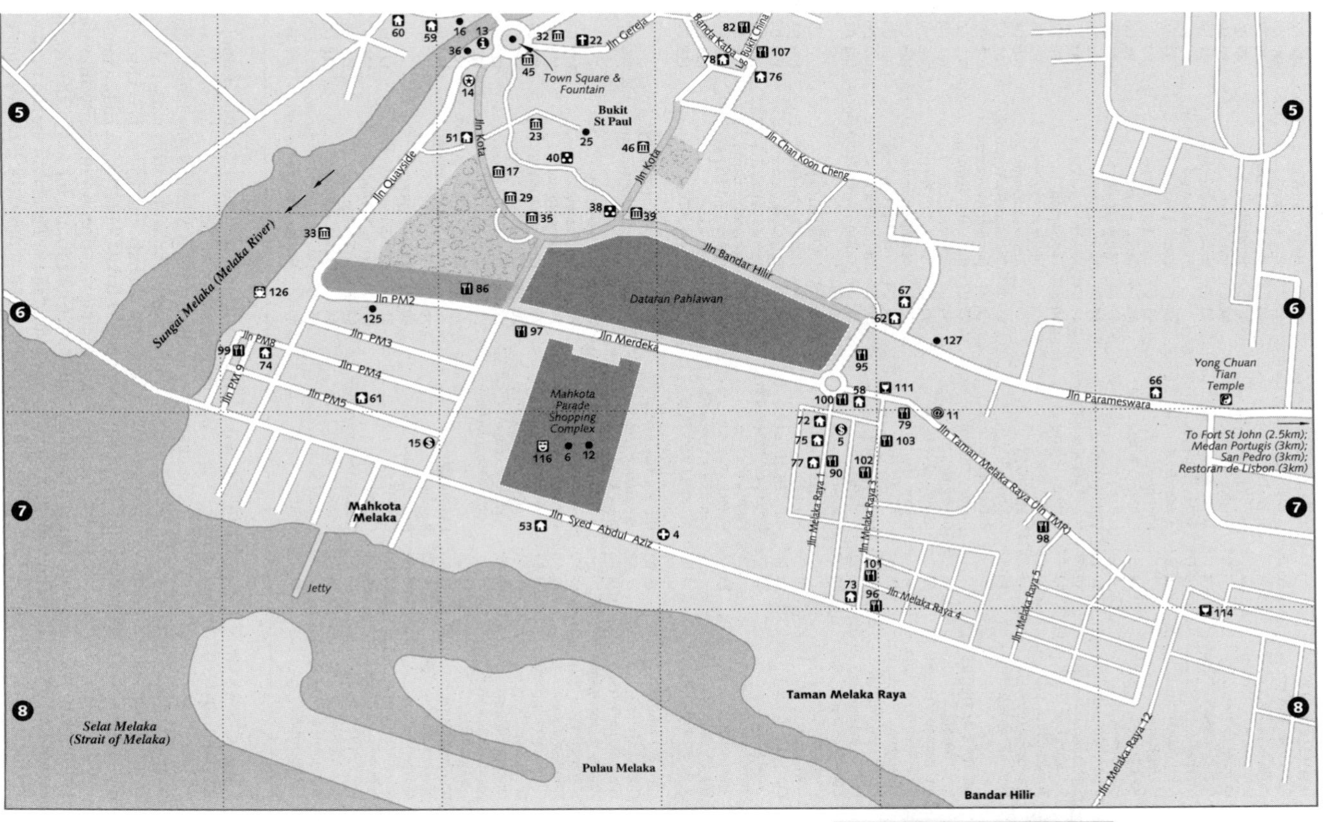
Town Square & Fountain
Bukit St Paul
Jln Gereja
Banda Kaba
Lg Bukit China
Jln Kota
Jln Quayside
Jln Chan Koon Cheng
Sungai Melaka (Melaka River)
Jln Bandar Hilir
Dataran Pahlawan
Jln PM2
Jln PM3
Jln PM4
Jln PM5
Jln PM8
Jln PM 9
Jln Merdeka
Mahkota Parade Shopping Complex
Jln Parameswara
Yong Chuan Tian Temple
To Fort St John (2.5km); Medan Portugis (3km); San Pedro (3km); Restoran de Lisbon (3km)
Jln Taman Melaka Raya (Jln TMR)
Jln Melaka Raya 1
Jln Melaka Raya 3
Jln Melaka Raya 4
Jln Melaka Raya 5
Jln Melaka Raya 12
Mahkota Melaka
Jln Syed Abdul Aziz
Jetty
Taman Melaka Raya
Selat Melaka (Strait of Melaka)
Pulau Melaka
Bandar Hilir
4
5
6
11
12
13
14
15
16
17
22
23
25
29
32
33
35
36
38
39
40
45
46
51
53
58
59
60
61
62
66
67
72
73
74
75
76
77
78
79
82
86
90
95
96
97
98
99
100
101
102
103
107
111
114
116
125
126
127
5
6
7
8

MELAKA

INFORMATION

Fenix Internet Centre ... (see 58)
HSBC ... **1** B1
Immigration Office ... **2** B2
Internet Centre ... **3** D3
Mahkota Medical Centre ... **4** D7
Maybank ... **5** D7
MPH Bookstores ... **6** C7
OCBC Bank ... **7** C4
Post Office ... **8** C4
Public Bank ... **9** D4
Southern Hospital ... **10** D2
Surf Zone ... **11** E7
Syarikat Buku Thai Kuang ... **12** C7
Tourist Office ... **13** C5
Tourist Police ... **14** C5
United Overseas Bank ... **15** B7

SIGHTS & ACTIVITIES

8 Heeren St ... **16** C5
Architecture Museum ... **17** C5
Baba-Nyonya Heritage Museum ... **18** B4
Biossentials Puri Spa ... (see 65)
Body in Balance ... (see 52)
Chee Mansion ... **19** B4
Cheng Ho Cultural Museum ... **20** C4
Cheng Hoon Teng Temple ... **21** B4
Christ Church ... **22** C5
Democratic Government Museum ... **23** C5
Eng Choon (Yong Chun) Association ... **24** B4
Governor's House ... **25** C5
Guangfu Temple ... **26** B3
Guanyin Temple ... **27** B3
Hang Kasturi's Tomb ... **28** B4
History & Ethnography Museum ... (see 45)
Islamic Museum ... **29** C5
Kampung Kling Mosque ... **30** B4
Leong San Thong ... **31** B4
Literature Museum ... (see 45)
Maritime Archaeological Museum ... **32** C5
Maritime Museum ... **33** B6
Masjid Kampung Hulu ... **34** C3
Muzium Rakyat ... **35** C6
Naval Museum ... (see 33)
Parameswara Tours ... **36** C5
Poh San Teng Temple ... **37** E4
Porta de Santiago ... **38** C5
Proclamation of Independence Memorial ... **39** C6
Putuo Traditional Chinese Medicine Therapy Centre ... (see 28)
St Paul's Church ... **40** C5
St Peter's Church ... **41** D2
Sanduo Temple ... **42** C4
Souvenir Menj ... **43** B3
Sri Poyyatha Vinayagar Moorthi Temple ... **44** C4
Stadthuys ... **45** C5
Sultanate Palace ... **46** C5
Sultan's Well ... **47** E4
Villa Sentosa ... **48** D2
Wah Teck Kiong Temple ... **49** B3
Xianglin Temple ... **50** B3

SLEEPING

Aldy Hotel ... **51** C5
Baba House ... **52** B4
Century Mahkota Hotel ... **53** C7
Chong Hoe Hotel ... **54** C4
City Bayview Hotel ... **55** D2
Eastern Heritage Guest House ... **56** D4
Emperor Hotel ... **57** E3
Fenix Inn ... **58** D6
Heeren House ... **59** B5
Heeren Inn ... **60** B5
Hollitel ... **61** B6
Hotel Equatorial ... **62** E6
Hotel Grand Continental ... **63** D1
Hotel Orkid ... **64** D2
Hotel Puri ... **65** B4
Kancil Guest House ... **66** F6
Malacca Straits Hotel ... **67** E6
Mimosa Hotel ... **68** D3
Number Twenty Guesthouse ... **69** B4
Renaissance Melaka Hotel ... **70** D2
Sama-Sama Guest House ... **71** C4
Samudera Backpacker's Hostel ... **72** D7
Samudra Inn ... **73** D7
Seri Costa Hotel ... **74** B6
Shirah's Guest House ... **75** D7
Tony's Guesthouse ... **76** D5
Travellers' Lodge ... **77** D7
Yellow Mansion Hotel ... **78** D5

EATING

Bayonya ... **79** E7
Bulldog Café ... **80** D2
Cafe 1511 ... **81** B4
Capitol Satay ... **82** D5
Centrepoint Food Court ... **83** D3
Coconut House ... **84** B4
Donald & Lily's ... **85** B4
Glutton's Corner ... **86** C6
Hang Tuah Mall ... **87** B2
Heeren House ... (see 59)
Hoe Kee Chicken Rice ... **88** C4
Howard's ... **89** B4
Ind Ori ... **90** D7
Indian Hawker Stalls ... **91** D4
Kenny's Nonya Delights ... **92** B4
Limau-Limau Café ... **93** B4
Low Yong Mow ... **94** C4
Malay Food Stalls ... **95** D6
Malay Hawker Stalls ... **96** D7
Nancy's Kitchen ... (see 89)
Newton Food Court ... **97** C6
Ole Sayang ... **98** E7
Restoran Amituofoh ... **99** B6
Restoran Banya ... **100** D6
Restoran Sek Yow Fook ... **101** D7
Restoran Wuguzhan ... **102** D7
Roti Canai Terbang ... **103** E7
Selvam ... **104** D4
Tart & Tart Bakery ... (see 20)
Teachew Cuisine ... **105** C4
Teck Ann Pharmacy ... **106** D3
UE Tea House ... **107** D5
Vegan Salad & Herbs House ... **108** A3

DRINKING

Calanthe Art Café ... **109** B4
Discovery Café ... **110** D4
Friends Café ... **111** E6
Geographér Café ... **112** B4
Honky Tonk Haven ... **113** C4
Pure Bar ... **114** F8
Voyager Travellers Lounge ... **115** C4

ENTERTAINMENT

Golden Screen Cinemas ... **116** C7

SHOPPING

Lim Trading ... **117** B3
Malaqa House ... **118** B4
Orangutan House ... **119** B4
Orangutan House ... **120** C4
Orangutan House ... **121** C4
Tile Shop ... **122** B4
Top Spinning Academy ... **123** B3
Wan Aik Shoemaker ... **124** B3

TRANSPORT

Dumai Ferry Service ... **125** B6
Ferries to Dumai ... **126** B6
Jin Fu Shin ... **127** E6
Local Bus Station ... **128** C1
Luxury Buses to Singapore ... (see 53)
Malaysia Airlines ... (see 53)

of parked cars could make this option too adrenalin-charged for some people.

The city is cleaved in two by the Sungai Melaka (Melaka River). The colonial, historic centre of Melaka is situated on the eastern side of the river, focussed around Town Sq (also known as Dutch Sq) where the old Stadthuys (town hall) and Christ Church are standout physical reminders of the Dutch presence. Bukit St Paul (St Paul's Hill), site of the original Portuguese fort of A'Famosa, rises above Town Sq.

Further north is Melaka's tiny Little India, with its night-time hawker stalls and sari shops. This area spreads east where it is abruptly stopped by Bukit China (China Hill), a tomb-laden bump that rises incongruously from the city flats. Chinatown to the west of the river is lined with Chinese Peranakan shophouses and antique shops, atmospheric Buddhist temples and ancient mosques. The centre of Chinatown is Jln Hang Jebat, which is more commonly called 'Jonker's Walk', meaning 'junk walk', for the many antique shops found here.

South of Melaka's old historical quarter are Mahkota Melaka and Taman Melaka Raya, two areas built on reclaimed land. While much of this area is bustling with shops and cheap places to stay, the southeastern region of Taman Melaka Raya, has become deserted after a short-lived economic boom; it's now home mostly to bird hotels, set up for collecting bird's nests for birds-nest soup. Bridging Mahkota Melaka to the historic quarter is the Dataran Pahlawan, a dwarfing new mall and shopping/restaurant complex.

INFORMATION

Bookshops

MPH Bookstores (☎ 283 3050; G73B, ground fl, Mahkota Parade Shopping Complex, Jln Merdeka; ⏰ 9am-10pm) Has the city's best selection of English-language titles.

Syarikat Buku Thai Kuang (☎ 282 0511; F59 & 60, 1st fl, Mahkota Parade Shopping Complex, Jln Merdeka; ⏰ 10am-10pm) Mostly textbooks plus some dusty English titles.

Emergency

Melaka Police Hotline (☎ 285 1999; Jln Kota)

Immigration Office

Immigration office (☎ 282 4958; 2nd fl, Wisma Persekutuan, Jln Hang Tuah)

Internet Access

Several cafés in Chinatown have a computer for clients and charge around RM3 per hour.

Fenix Internet Centre (Fenix Hotel,156 Jln Taman Melaka Raya; per hr RM2.5) Also has fax and full business services.

Internet Centre (54 Jln Bunga Raya; per hr RM3.50)

Surf Zone (120 Jln Taman Melaka Raya; per hr RM2.50)

Medical Services

Mahkota Medical Centre (☎ 281 3333, 284 8222; Jln Merdeka) A private hospital offering a full range of services.

Southern Hospital (☎ 283 5888; 16 Jln Bendahara) Private hospital with a 24-hour clinic.

Money

Moneychangers are scattered about, mainly in Chinatown and near the bus stations.

HSBC (Jln Hang Tuah) Has 24-hour ATMs (MasterCard, Visa, Maestro, Cirrus and Plus).

Maybank (Jln Melaka Raya 2)

OCBC Bank (Lorong Hang Jebat) Just over the bridge in Chinatown, it has a 24-hour ATM that takes Visa and Plus.

Public Bank (Jln Laksmana)

United Overseas Bank (Jln PM5) Has a 24-hour ATM (Mastercard, Visa, Maestro, Cirrus and Plus)

Post

Post office (Jln Laksamana; ⏰ 8.30am-5pm Mon-Sat) Off Town Sq.

Tourist information

Tourist office (☎ 281 4803, 1800-889483; www.melaka.gov.my; Jln Kota; ⏰ 9am-1pm & 2-5.30pm) Free maps of Melaka and other bumph. It's opposite Christ Church.

Tourist police (☎ 281 4803; Jln Kota; ⏰ 8am-11pm)

SIGHTS

Melaka's sights veer unmistakably towards the historical. While several of the listings following (with the exception of museums) could be seen in a 30-second glance, there is a remarkable richness of stories surrounding each edifice that increases its charm exponentially. Most central sights can be visited on the walking tour (p148).

Historic Town Centre

Melaka has a ridiculous number of museums clustered along Jln Kota. Notables include the dusty **Islamic Museum** (admission RM2; ⏰ 9am-5.30pm Tue-Sun) and the small but worthwhile **Architecture Museum** (admission RM2; ⏰ 9.30am-5pm Tue-Sun) that focuses on local housing design. Most of the other superfluous institutions use a bland diorama format where visitors walk through a maze of wordy displays. Anyone without the attention span of a law student is advised to sprint past this area and hop into the nearest technicolour trishaw. If you're going to visit any museum here, make it the **Muzium Rakyat** (People's Museum; adult RM2; ⏰ 9am-6pm Wed-Mon), with its lengthy descriptions of the local sports of *gasing uri* (top-spinning) and *silat* (a martial art) downstairs, a meagre kite display on the 2nd floor and a creepy yet compelling 'Beauty Museum' on the 3rd floor which explores how different cultures mutilate themselves in order to look good (Western plastic surgery hasn't made it in yet).

ST PAUL'S CHURCH

This church is a wonderfully breezy sanctuary reached after a steep and sweaty climb

VOICES FROM THE STREET

We began by listening to the voices of ordinary Malaccans. We listened to the city's streets, as we searched out hidden corners and abandoned alleyways. Listened to houses and temples, ruins and cemeteries. Even to the murmurs and whispers of empty spaces. We listened at every turn, at every step. To the living and the dead. The past and the present. In the hope that the story of an extraordinary place and its people would be told. And we heard them speak.

Extract from Malacca: Voices from the Street by Lim Huck Chin and Fernando Jorge (2005)

Lim Huck Chin and Fernando Jorge are two architects who worked on the restoration of a Dutch period shophouse (8 Heeren St) and have since produced *Malacca: Voices from the Street,* a gorgeous book of photos and stories about the town. You can learn about their work by visiting the website www.malaccavoices.com or by visiting the house at **8 Heeren Street** (admission free; 11am-4pm Tue-Sat). Note that although this building is called 8 Hereen St, the street name today is Jln Tun Tan Cheng Lock.

Lim and Jorge's words and pictures capture the magic of Melaka that many residents fear is under threat in the rush to paint heritage buildings in garish colours in the name of conservation.

up a flight of stairs. Originally built by a Portuguese captain in 1521 as the small Our Lady of the Hill chapel, St Paul's Church is a sublime testament to Catholicism in East Asia and offers bright views over Melaka from the summit of knobby Bukit St Paul. Inside the decaying stone interior are hefty, intricately engraved tombstones (of the Dutch nobility that are buried here) that lend an eerie air to an otherwise light atmosphere. The church was regularly visited by St Francis Xavier, who performed several 'miracles' in the church (see the boxed text, p154), and following his death in China the saint's body was temporarily interred here for nine months before being transferred to Goa, where it remains today. Visitors can now look into his ancient tomb (surrounded by a wire fence) in the centre of the church, and a marble statue of the saint gazes wistfully over his beloved city.

In 1556 St Paul's was enlarged to two storeys, and a tower was added to the front in 1590. The church was renamed following the Dutch takeover, but when the Dutch completed their own Christ Church at the base of the hill, it fell into disuse. Under the British it lost the tower, although a lighthouse was built, and the church eventually ended up as a storehouse for gunpowder. It has been in ruins for more than 150 years.

PORTA DE SANTIAGO (A'FAMOSA)

A quick photo stop but a must for anyone visiting Melaka, Porta de Santiago was built by the Portuguese as a fortress in 1511. The Dutch were busy destroying the bulk of the fort when forward-thinking Sir Stamford Raffles came by in 1810 and saved what remains today. Look for the 'VOC' inscription of the Dutch East India Company on the arch; ironically, this part of the fort was used by the Dutch after their takeover in 1670.

In November 2006, work on a highly controversial 110m revolving tower at a site near the tourist office, uncovered another part of the famous wall, thus halting further tower construction. Locals are thrilled that the sure-bet eyesore will be relocated, presumably further away from the city's historic centre, and the archaeological site will be excavated and turned into yet another of Melaka's historical sites. Check with the miniscule **Maritime Archaeological Museum** (Jln Laksamana; admission free; 9am-5.30pm Wed-Sun) near the clock tower for the most authoritative and up-to-date news of the recently discovered wall.

STADTHUYS

Melaka's most unmistakable landmark and favourite trishaw pick-up spot is the **Stadthuys** (282 6526; Town Sq; admission adult/child RM5/2; 9am-5.30pm Sat-Thu, 9am-12.15pm & 2.45-5.30pm Fri), the imposing salmon-pink town hall and governor's residence. It's believed to be the oldest Dutch building in the East, built shortly after Melaka was captured by the Dutch in 1641, and is a reproduction of the former Stadhuis (town hall) of the Frisian town of Hoorn in the Netherlands. With substantial solid doors and louvred windows, it is typical of Dutch colonial architecture. Its red paint job is thanks to the British, who brightened it up from a sombre Dutch white in 1911, 87 years after they were ceded the colony. Numerous scenarios have been proposed as to why the British painted the building this colour, but the most likely theory is that the red laterite stone used to build the Stadthuys showed through the whitewashed plastering, and/or heavy tropical rain splashed red soil up the white walls – the thrifty Brits decided to paint it all red to save on maintenance costs. The vivid colour theme extends to the other buildings around Town Sq and the old clock tower.

Housed inside the Stadthuys is the informative **History & Ethnography Museum** (🕑 guided tours 10.30am & 2.30pm Sat & Sun), which has a re-created 17th-century Dutch dining room as well as displays of Chinese and Malay weapons and ceramics. Upstairs there's a room on Melaka's history. Unfortunately there's very little information about the building, which is what intrigues most people who visit the site. Up the hill is the mildly interesting **Literature Museum**, focusing on Malaysian writers. Admission to both museums (as well as the **Governor's House** and the **Democratic Government Museum**) is included in the admission price to Stadthuys.

SULTANATE PALACE

Housing a cultural museum, this wooden replica of the **palace of Mansur Shah** (Jln Kota; admission RM2; 🕑 9am-6pm Tue-Sun) of Mansur Shah, the famous sultan who ruled Melaka from 1456 to 1477, is based on descriptions from the *Malay Annals* of the original palace, and is built entirely without nails. The three-storey building is divided into eight chambers and three galleries containing a mishmash of artefacts, photographs and drawings depicting the sultan and the Malay communities of this period.

Chinatown

Now you're talking. This is Melaka's most vibrant area, where you could easily entertain yourself for a few days simply by strolling through the teeter-tottering lanes. Surreptitiously peer into small shops where you might see a painter at work, an old man fabricating bicycle parts with a blow-torch or a stout woman plucking chickens for the restaurant next door. When your feet get sore

HANG TUAH & MELAKA'S STREET-NAME MUSKETEERS

If you start looking around at Melaka's street names you'll notice that several begin with the word 'Hang', which was an honorary title in ancient times. The Hang of Melaka's street signs were in fact some of the region's greatest *laksmana* (admirals) of the 15th century – Hang Tuah and his friends Hang Kasturi, Hang Jebat, Hang Lekir and Hang Lekiu. Their stories are some of the most beloved in Malaysia and are chronicled in both the *Malay Annals* (see p36) and the *Hikayat Hang Tua*, a romantic collection of tales involving Hang Tuah.

The undisputed leader of the band of buddies was Hang Tuah who, with his friends, mastered techniques of *silat* (a martial art) and meditation. The group was recognised early on by the sultan of the day, Tun Perak, when it managed to fight off a band of pirates that were attacking a village. Hang Tuah soon became inseparable from the sultan to whom he pledged his absolute loyalty.

While there are many heroic tales of Hang Tuah, the most famous is his battle with near-brother Hang Jebat (or according to some versions, Hang Kasturi). A rumour had circulated that Hang Tuah was having an affair with one of the sultan's concubines. The sultan unfairly sentenced Hang Tuah to death without a trial but the executioner disobeyed the sultan's orders and secretly hid the admiral in a remote corner of Melaka. Believing that Hang Tuah had been killed for a crime he didn't commit, Hang Jebat went on a kung-fu-blockbuster-style killing spree in the palace and the sultan and his army found themselves in a losing battle. Word reached the sultan that Hang Tuah was still alive, so the sultan called his faithful servant back knowing that he was the only man alive who could defeat Hang Jebat. It took seven days, but Hang Tuah finally killed his old friend who had been fighting for his name.

The story is still highly discussed today as it represents a paradox in the Malay psyche between loyalty and justice. It has also been adapted into several major Malay films including, most recently, *Puteri Gunung Ledang* (2004) starring M Nasir.

just pop in for a half-hour of foot reflexology or a massage.

BABA-NONYA HERITAGE MUSEUM

Touring this traditional Peranakan townhouse brings you back to a time when women hid behind elaborate partitions when guests dropped by, and every social situation had its specific location within the house. The captivating **museum** (☎ 283 1273; 48-50 Jln Tun Tan Cheng Lock; adult/child RM8/4; 🕑 10am-12.30pm & 2-4.30pm Wed-Mon) is arranged to look like a typical 19th-century Baba-Nonya residence. Furniture consists of Chinese hardwoods fashioned in a mixture of Chinese, Victorian and Dutch designs with mother-of-pearl inlay. Displays of 'Nonya ware', multicoloured ceramic designs from Jiāngxī and Guǎngdōng provinces in China and made for Straits Chinese, add to the presentation. The highlight is the tour guides, who tell tales of the past with a distinctly Peranakan sense of humour. The admission price includes a tour if there are enough people.

CHENG HO CULTURAL MUSEUM

A lengthy paeon to Ming Admiral Cheng Ho (Zhenghe), this extensive **museum** (☎ 283 1135; 51 Lorong Hang Jebat; adult/child RM20/10; 🕑 9am-6pm Mon-Thu, 9am-7pm Fri-Sun) charts the tremendous voyages of the intrepid Chinese Muslim seafarer. At the age of 13, Cheng Ho was castrated and became a eunuch servant to the Chinese emperor's fourth son, Prince Zhu Di. He proved an exceptional servant, and later became an army officer and ultimately the admiral of China's 'Treasure Fleet', a convoy that solidified China's control over most of Asia during the 15th century. The admiral visited Melaka at least five times during his extraordinary voyages and set up a warehouse complex somewhere along the northern side of the Sungai Melaka (Melaka River) – the exact location is unknown. Photographs of Chinese descendents in Africa are intriguing while the puppet show is entertaining (despite its gruesome side). It's a great stop for history buffs although there's too much information here for anyone expecting to casually visit. The ticket price includes a 15-minute film presentation on Cheng Ho.

CHENG HOON TENG TEMPLE

Malaysia's oldest traditional Chinese temple (dating from 1646) remains a central place of worship for the Buddhist community in Melaka. Notable for its carved woodwork, the **temple** (Qing Yun Ting or Green Clouds Temple; 25 Jln Tokong; 🕑 7am-7pm) is dedicated to Kuan Yin, the

BABA-NONYA'S LAST STAND

It's impossible to be in Melaka for even a day without hearing about the Baba-Nonya, also called the Peranakans. In Malay the word 'Peranakan' means 'descendant', and nowadays this word usually refers to the Chinese descendants who intermarried with Malays. Men are called Baba and the women Nonya; this creates the second name for the culture, the Baba-Nonya.

While the history of Chinese descendents in Melaka has recently become more questioned, the common story is that the mix of cultures began with the arrival of Hang Li Po, daughter of the 15th-century emperor of China, who brought an entourage of 500 family members and servants with her to her new home in Melaka. The Straits-born Chinese descendants retained their religion (Buddhism and ancestor worship) and ethical beliefs but absorbed the Malay language and some cultural habits. The food, commonly called Nonya food, in honour of the women who did most of the cooking, is another delicious story entirely (see p46).

While some Straits-born Chinese intermarried with local Malays, many families imported Chinese brides or sent daughters to China to find husbands; in this way, the culture stayed ethnically predominantly Chinese. Because of their mixed cultural background, the Peranakans flourished during the British colonial era when they became British educated and usually filled important civil service and administration posts. This led to them frequently being called the 'King's Chinese'. While some converted to Christianity, many still retained their ancestral religion. Once the British departed, the special treatment from being cultural go-betweens for the Europeans to both the Chinese and Malay communities ended and the Peranakans gradually began to become absorbed by the newer Chinese community. Melaka is the stronghold of what remains of the culture, and the tourism that this attracts has helped strengthen and prolong the graceful nuances of the dying culture.

WHAT'S THAT SMELL?

Sungai Melaka (Melaka River) winds romantically past the banks of Chinatown and the Stadthuys, carrying with it colourful wooden ships, fishermen in small boats and a disconcerting amount of industrial waste. Starting in 2005 the city invested about RM100 million to clean up the sludgy river and build grassy areas and walking paths along its shores. A catamaran designed to clean up oil slicks was employed to remove rubbish then compress it into a material that could be used to reinforce the banks. The next step, underway in 2007, was the beautification of the banks followed by domestic wastewater and cesspool treatment; reservoirs were built to trap scum, oil and refuse.

Unfortunately, these measures are not enough for a community that has become used to throwing its waste, such as greasy residue from restaurants and plastic bags, into the river. Industrial waste from agriculture (including pesticides and herbicides) and factories accounts for approximately 45% of the slime, much of which, even after the river's cleanup and new reservoirs, will make its way to the sea. The odour rises with the falling tides.

goddess of mercy. All building materials for the temple were imported from China, along with the artisans involved in its construction. More recently (in 2003), the structure won a Unesco award for outstanding architectural restoration. A robed effigy of Kuan Yin can be found within the main temple hall, itself an explosion of black, gold and red. Worshippers also pray to the altar of Tianhou, goddess of seafarers, to the left of Kuan Yin. Across the street from the main temple is a traditional opera theatre.

MASJID KAMPUNG HULU

Yet another aged superlative, **Masjid Kampung Hulu** (Jln Masjid Kampung Hulu) is the oldest functioning mosque in Malaysia and was, surprisingly, commissioned by the Dutch in 1728. The Portuguese had destroyed all non-Christian establishments during their occupation, including Melaka's first mosque, which had reputedly stood across from where the Stadthuys stands today. Aiming for a kinder, gentler form of colonisation involving cultural and religious pluralism, the Dutch decided to help the locals re-build their places of worship instead of smashing them to bits. The resulting mosque is made up of predominantly Javanese architecture with a multitiered roof in place of the standard dome; at the time of construction, domes and minarets had not yet come into fashion. Chinese touches include the crownlike pinnacle surmounting the roofs and the curved eaves and ceramic roof and floor tiles that were imported from China.

MASJID TRANQUERAH

Masjid Tranquerah (Masjid Tengkera; Jln Tengkera) takes a back seat to Masjid Kampung Hulu in terms of age but is still one of the oldest mosques in Malaysia (over 150 years old). In its graveyard is the tomb of Sultan Hussein of Johor, who signed over the island of Singapore to Stamford Raffles in 1819. The sultan later retired to Melaka, where he died in 1853. The mosque is out of Chinatown about 2km towards Port Dickson along Jln Tun Tan Cheng Lock, which turns into Jln Tengkera.

Avoid visiting this and any Malaysian mosque during prayer times, always remove your shoes and dress conservatively (knees to elbows covered). Although not required, women should wear a headscarf if possible.

Around the City Centre

KAMPUNG CHITTY

As well as the Baba-Nonya, Melaka also has a small community of Chitty – Straits-born Indians, offspring of the Indian traders who intermarried with Malay women. Having arrived in the 1400s, the Chitties are regarded as older than the Chinese-Malay Peranakan community (see the boxed text, opposite). Their area of town, known as Kampung Chitty, lies west of Jl Gajah Berang, about 1km northwest of Chinatown; look for the archway with elephant sculptures beside the Mutamariman Temple. It's a pretty district in which to wander and see traditional Malay-style houses. The tiny **Chitty Museum** (☎ 281 1289; 🕑 9.30am-5pm Tue-Sun) makes a great excuse to stroll to Kampung Chitty. It's a community effort with a collection of colourful artefacts such as traditional water-pots, multitiered brass oil lamps, serving trays, sculptures, handicrafts and photographs.

The best time to visit is in May, during the Mariamman Festival (Pesta Datuk Charchar), a Hindu celebration when you might also be fortunate enough to witness a traditional Indian wedding ceremony.

LITTLE INDIA

Heading east from Kampung Chitty, past Chinatown and across the river, is Melaka's surprisingly plain Little India. While it's not nearly as charming as the historic centre or Chinatown, this busy area along Jln Bendahara and Jln Temenggong is a worthwhile place for soaking in some Indian influence and grabbing an excellent banana-leaf meal. During Deepavali (see p220) a section of Jln Temenggong closes to traffic to make way for Indian cultural performances and street-food vendors.

BUKIT CHINA

Further east is Bukit China, which, besides being the largest Chinese graveyard outside of China, is also Melaka's best jogging track (see opposite). More than 12,500 graves, including about 20 Muslim tombs, cover the 25 grassy hectares. Since the times of British rule until today there have been several attempts to acquire Bukit China for road widening, land reclamation or development purposes. Fortunately, Cheng Hoon Teng Temple (p144), along with strong community support, has thwarted these attempts.

In the middle of the 15th century the sultan of Melaka imported the Ming emperor's daughter from China as his bride, in a move to seal relations between the two countries. She brought with her a vast retinue, including 500 handmaidens, and Bukit China was chosen to be their residence. It has been a Chinese area ever since, along with the two adjoining hills and eventually became the burial ground for Chinese traders. Chinese graveyards are often built on hillsides to maximise positive feng shui. At the foot of Bukit China, called San Bao Shan (Three Treasures Mount) in Mandarin, **Poh San Teng Temple** was built in 1795 and contains images of Kuan Yin and the Taoist entity Dabo Gong. To the right of the temple is the **Sultan's Well**, a 15th-century well built by Sultan Mansor Shah for his Chinese wife, Princess Hang Li Poh. It was an important source of water for Melaka and a prime target for opposition forces wanting to take the city.

ST PETER'S CHURCH

Melaka has Malaysia's oldest traditional Chinese temple (p144) and functioning mosque (p145), so it's no surprise that **St Peter's Church** (Jln Bendahara) is the oldest functioning Catholic church in Malaysia, built in 1710 by descendants of early Portuguese settlers. The church has a striking white façade, stained-glass windows, the Latin words 'Tu es Petrus' (You are the Rock) above the altar and a bell cast in Goa (India) in 1608. On Good Friday the church comes alive when Malaccan Christians flock here, many of them making it the occasion for a trip home from far-flung parts of the country.

FORT ST JOHN

Although the British demolished most of Porta de Santiago (p142), they spared this small Dutch **fort** (Bukit Senjuang) off Jln Bukit Senjuang. Originally a Portuguese chapel dedicated to St John the Baptist (until the Dutch rebuilt it in the 18th century), it stands on a hilltop to the east of town just before the turn-off to Medan Portugis. Only a few walls and cannon emplacements of the fort remain, but there are fine views from the hilltop. In the mornings a group of locals practice t'ai chi on the grassy field next to the fort.

The Riverfront

MARITIME MUSEUM & NAVAL MUSEUM

Housed in a huge re-creation of the *Flor de la Mar*, a Portuguese ship that sank off the coast of Melaka (see the boxed text, below),

SUNKEN TREASURE OF THE FLOR DE LA MAR

The Portuguese takeover of Melaka in 1511 was no peaceful affair. After 40 days of fighting the city fell to the European forces and about two months later it was sacked for its treasures for three days. The spoils were taken and stored on the *Flor de la Mar* and three other vessels bound for Portugal. Admiral Alfonso de Albuquerque claimed that the booty, including 60 tonnes of gold, the sultan's throne, 200 chests of diamonds and two bronze lion sculptures that had been a gift to the sultan from the emperor of China, were the finest treasures he had ever seen.

No sooner had the ships set sail than they encountered a storm off the coast of Sumatra. The three ships sank and have never been recovered.

KRISTANG

The creole language of Kristang (also called Papiah Kristang, Cristão or Cristan – derived from the word Christian) has survived in Melaka for half a millennium. Spoken by descendents of the Portuguese who first came to Melaka, Kristang employs a grammatical structure similar to Malay although its vocabulary is largely extracted from archaic Portuguese, making it partially comprehensible to visitors from Portugal. Most speakers of the creole live in Melaka, but small populations lie scattered in Singapore and elsewhere in Malaysia. Its shrinking population of speakers and an increasing preference for English among the younger generations is endangering the language, but many speakers of Kristang are fighting for its preservation. Some Kristang expressions include *bong pamiang* (good morning), *mutu merseh* (thank you) and *teng bong*? (how are you?). For further information on the Kristang language, go to www.joanmarbeck.net.

the **Maritime Museum** (admission RM2; ⌚ 9am-5.30pm) merits a visit. Clamber up for a detailed examination of Melaka's history picked out by rather faded and dated props. The museum continues in the building next door with more absorbing exhibits featuring local vessels, including the striking *Kepala Burung* (a boat carved like a feathered bird) plus an assortment of nautical devices.

VILLA SENTOSA

While not an official museum, this 1920s Malay *kampung* (village) house called **Villa Sentosa** (Peaceful Villa; ☎ 282 3988; www.travel.to/villa sentosa; entry by donation; ⌚ 9am-1pm & 2-5pm Sat-Thu, 2.45-5pm Fri), on the Melaka River in Kampung Morten, is well worth a visit. A member of the family will show you around the house, accessed via a bridge, introducing a varied collection of objects, including Ming dynasty ceramics, a 100-year-old copy of the Quran and a certificate of honour awarded by King George V to the late Tuan Haji Hashim Bin Dato Demang Haji Abdul Ghani (who lived here). Most of all, it's an opportunity to wander through a genuine *kampung* house. You can also add to the visitors' book, copious volumes of which record congratulatory remarks from legions of visitors, some well known. Afterwards, stroll around Kampung Morten and its other traditional *kampung* houses.

Medan Portugis

Roughly 3km east of the city centre on the coast is **Medan Portugis** (Portuguese Sq). The small *kampung* centred on the square is the heart of Melaka's Eurasian community, descended from marriages between the colonial Portuguese and Malays 400 years ago, many of whom speak Kristang (see the boxed text, above). A French missionary first proposed the settlement to the British colonial government in the 1920s, but the square, styled after a typical Portuguese *mercado* (markets) and lending the settlement a cultural focus, wasn't completed until the late 1980s.

In the open square area, the Portuguese community office bulletin board displays advertisements for cultural events and news articles, some relating to how Melaka's land reclamation has damaged local family-run fisheries.

The *kampung* is unexceptional, however, and the square is often empty, except on Saturday evenings when cultural events are staged. But the sea breeze is lovely while enjoying a relaxing beer or meal at the many restaurants in and around the square. Town bus 17 from the local bus station will get you here; see p163.

ACTIVITIES

Walking & Jogging

If you're searching for a patch of green in the city centre head straight to Bukit China (opposite). Of course, this is historical Melaka, so the popular walking and jogging hill also happens to be a major Chinese cemetery.

To walk or jog Bukit China, take Jln Puteri Hang Li Po from the Poh San Teng Temple on the corner of Jln Munshi and take the first right into the driveway of SJKC Pay Fong III School. The steps leading to the trail can be seen from here. The well-marked path winds up and down for about 3km, passing many ancient graves. The huge horseshoe-shaped tombs are those of the Kapitan China, the heads of the Chinese community in colonial times. Two 15th-century Malay chieftains are buried on Bukit Tempurong Plain at the south of the trail, and several *kermat* (sacred Muslim graves) are found on the northeast foot of the hill. The oldest tomb (located near the basketball court of SRJK Pay Fong III School) is a double burial of Mr and Mrs Huang Wei-Hung and was built in 1622. In 1933 the Cheng Hoon Teng Temple (p144) restored the headstones; the aging tomb was brought back to life a second time (so to speak) in 2001. From the top of the hill, there is a full-circle panorama of the city across paddy fields and to Pulau Besar.

Reflexology & Massage

You're probably not going to be developing any stress headaches from visiting laid-back Melaka, but just to melt you even more there are several reflexology and traditional massage therapy centres around the city.

Putuo Traditional Chinese Medical Therapy Centre (☎ 286 1052; 134 Jln Hang Jebat; 1hr reflexology RM38, 1hr chi body massage RM60; 10am-10pm Mon-Thu, 10am-midnight Fri-Sun) The women here know their stuff and offer straightforward, excellent-value services. Get your feet expertly massaged while watching Chinese soap operas with the giggling staff or get a full body chi massage in a quieter back room. If you have specific ailments, anything from migraines to water retention, the owner will create a special treatment for you. There are also ear candles, fire cupping, body scrubs and more. The centre's ambience is no-frills Chinese institutional.

Body in Balance (☎ 13 23 10512; 123 Jln Tun Tan Cheng; 30min/1hr massage RM30/60) Attached to Baba House (p153); traditional Malay, Thai and aromatherapy massages are offered here. Sweet, soothing smells emanate from the curtained hutlike room that would look quite at home on a tropical beach. It's a simple set-up but charmingly Malay.

Biossentials Puri Spa (☎ 282 5588; www.hotelpuri.com; Hotel Puri, 118 Jln Tun Tan Cheng Lock; spa services from RM50; Thu-Mon) This international calibre spa in a sensual garden has a delicious menu of treatments including steams, body wraps, scrubs, facials and a variety of massage. There are several packages available including the sublime two-hour Vitality Purification (RM265) which includes a Thai herbal steam bath, skin tapping for circulation, detoxifying marine body mask, herbal bath and a deep-tissue massage. Bliss!

WALKING TOUR

Melaka's Chinatown is a compact area packed to the brim with interesting edifices and museums. This tour takes you to the principal sights but you'll find plenty of other ones on your own to entertain you along the way.

Start at the delightful Town Sq, Melaka's historic hub. The most imposing relic of the Dutch period in Melaka is the **Stadthuys (1**; p142). Exit the Stadthuys and contemplate **Christ Church (2)**, constructed from pink laterite bricks brought from Zeeland in Holland. Dutch and Armenian tombstones still lie in the floor of the church's interior, while the massive 15m-long ceiling beams overhead were each cut from a single tree. Sit down and admire the marvellous **fountain (3)** in Town Sq, emblazoned with four bas-relief images of Queen Victoria's face in profile and affixed with an inscribed plaque reading: 'Victoria Regina 1837–1901. Erected by the people of Malacca in memory of a Great Queen 1904.'

Walk west across the bridge over the Melaka River (for information on riverboat cruises see p152). On the far shore, turn left and stroll along Jln Tun Tan Cheng Lock, but watch out for racing traffic. Formerly called Heeren St, this narrow thoroughfare was the preferred address for wealthy Baba (Straits-born Chinese; see the boxed text, p144) traders who were most active during the short-lived

> **WALK FACTS**
>
> **Start** Town Sq
> **Finish** Melaka River
> **Distance** 2.5km
> **Duration** Three hours

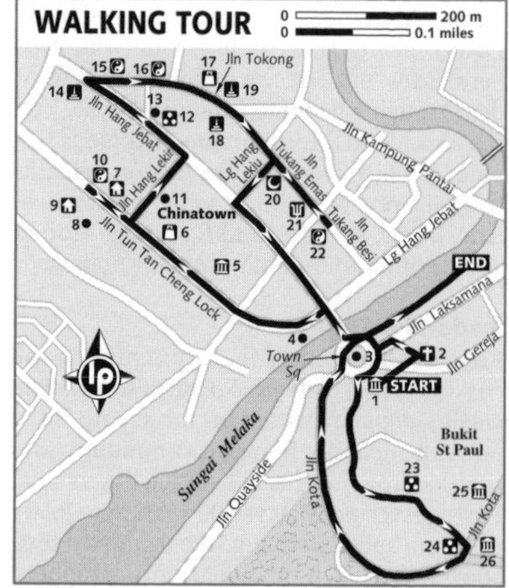

rubber boom of the early 20th century. These typical Peranakan houses, with their intricate tiles and plasterwork, fuse Chinese, Dutch and British influences in a style that has been described as Chinese Palladian and Chinese baroque. The interiors open into airy courtyards that admit sun and rain – similar to Chinese courtyard houses. A finely restored example of this architectural style can be found at **8 Heeren St (4)**, a 1700s Dutch period shophouse. Thanks to a RM57,000 grant from the US Department of State's Ambassador's Fund for Cultural Preservation, the Badan Warisan (Heritage Trust of Malaysia) was able to revive the building while retaining its original features as much as possible. The project was partially chronicled by Lim Huck Chin and Fernando Jorge in their beautifully designed coffee-table book *Malacca: Voices from the Street* (see the boxed text, p142).

An intriguing insight into the local vernacular can be gleaned from the **Baba-Nonya Heritage Museum** (**5**; p143). Pop into **Malaqa House** (**6**; p161) and pick over its horde of antiques before continuing to the elegant **Hotel Puri** (**7**; p153); the Chinese characters emblazoned on the door literally mean 'Longevity Mountain, Fortuitous Sea'. The impressive classical-style building set back from the street opposite is the **Chee Mansion** (**8**; 115-117 Jln Tun Tan Cheng Lock), a Chinese family shrine not open to the public.

Another traditional house now serving as a hotel, **Baba House** (**9**; p153), is just ahead. The **Eng Choon (Yong Chun) Association** (**10**; 122 Jln Tun Tan Cheng Lock) is an impressively well-kept Chinese guildhall, containing a small shrine to two Taoist deities. Admire the painted gods on the doors and the carved dragons adorning the stone pillars. Chinese characters written on the building mean 'Peace to the country and the people' – which you see elsewhere in Chinatown.

Backtrack along Jln Tun Tan Cheng Lock and walk north up Jln HangLekir (Third Cross St), past a string of restaurants and antique shops. Opposite Howard's restaurant (p158) is the dignified **Leong San Thong** (**11**; Dragon Hill Hall; 8 Jln Hang Lekir), built in 1928. At the junction, turn left onto Jln Hang Jebat, formerly known as Jonker's St (or Junk St Melaka), famed for its antique and craft shops (browse at will, but bargains can be elusive). On Friday and Saturday nights, the street is for pedestrians only and is transformed into a market of stalls.

Continuing west, you'll approach the all-white **Hang Kasturi's Tomb** (**12**; boxed text, p143) on your right; there is no historical evidence that the tomb is the final resting place of the great warrior. Beyond here is the tempting **Putuo Traditional Chinese Medicine Therapy Centre** (**13**; opposite) – just the spot for a revitalising foot massage and doses of reflexology. Further along on your left is the small, modern and pink **Guanyin Temple** (**14**; Guanyin Tang) dedicated to the Buddhist goddess of compassion. Seated in the second hall is the Taoist Jade Emperor, flanked by two attendants. The central effigy of Kuan Yin is a modern Qianshou (1000-arm) version.

Turn right here and head up Jln Tokong (Temple St) and past a couple of small Chinese shrines, the **Wah Teck Kiong Temple (15)** and the **Guangfu Temple** (**16**; Guangfu Gong). Ahead is the **Wan Aik Shoemaker** (**17**; p161) shop on your left – the specialist manufacturer crafts doll-like shoes for bound feet, once the height of gruesome fashion for well-to-do Chinese women in Melaka.

Chinatown's most elaborate and celebrated Chinese temple, the **Cheng Hoon Teng Temple** (**18**; p144), is opposite the more recently constructed **Xianglin (Fragrant Forest) Temple (19)**, which endeavours to follow the layout of a traditional Chinese Buddhist temple. Adding splashes of colour to Jln Tokong are the Chinese shops selling red and gold lanterns, paper money and funerary preparations. The street used to be famed for its goldsmiths, but most have moved to other areas.

Continue east to the **Kampung Kling Mosque (20)**. This hoary mosque has a multitiered *meru* roof (a stacked form similar to that seen in Balinese Hindu architecture), which owes its inspiration to Hindu temples, and a Moorish watchtower minaret typical of early mosques in Sumatra. Further along is the **Sri Poyyatha Vinayagar Moorthi Temple (21)**, one of the first Hindu temples built in the country. It was built in 1781 on the plot given by the religiously tolerant Dutch and dedicated to the Hindu deity Vinayagar. Slightly further ahead is the **Sanduo Temple** (**22**; Sanduo Miao), another Chinese shrine encapsulating effigies of Dabo Gong, Jinhua Niangniang (who women entreat for children) and Kuan Yin.

Backtrack and turn left along the exterior wall of the mosque back along Lorong Hang Lekiu (Fourth Cross St) to Jln Hang Jebat. Stroll back to Lorong Hang Jebat

TOP 10 WAYS TO ENJOY MELAKA'S CHINATOWN

- Start the day with a traditional dim sum breakfast
- Hunt for antiques in creaky old shops
- Buy a pair of bright Nonya clogs then clack your way around town
- Buy knick-knacks such as spinning tops, Chinese good-luck charms and chopsticks
- Peruse quiet artist's studios
- Slurp an icy science-experiment-gone-wrong-looking *cendol* (mung-bean-flour noodles and shaved ice doused in coconut milk, palm-sugar syrup and condensed milk) in the day's heat
- Cure tired, hot feet, blistered by your new clogs, with a reflexology foot massage
- Enjoy the local's favourite meal of chicken rice ball
- Have your fortune read at the Jonker's Walk Night Market
- Chill to live music at a streetside bar on a balmy Friday or Saturday night

(First Cross St) and the bridge, noting the decorative touches along the way – mosaics, tiling, inlaid coloured stones, carvings, Western-style balustrades, balconies, shutters and ornamentations.

Traverse the bridge, cross Town Sq back to the Stadthuys and clamber up the steps leading to the top of Bukit St Paul, topped by the fabulous ruins of **St Paul's Church** (**23**; p141).

There are steps from St Paul's Church down the hill to **Porta de Santiago** (**24**; p142), once the main gate of the Portuguese fortress A'Famosa, originally constructed by Alfonso de Albuquerque in 1512.

To the east, at the base of Bukit St Paul, is the **Sultanate Palace** (**25**; p143). Across the way, in a British villa dating from 1911 is the **Proclamation of Independence Memorial** (**26**; admission free; 9am-6pm Sat-Thu, 9am-noon & 3-6pm Fri), a museum charting the history of Malaysia's progression to independence. There's too much to read and perhaps not enough to look at (although the Japanese officer's sword from occupation days is noteworthy). Ironically, this grand building topped by Mogul-inspired domes was once the Melaka Club, a bastion of colonialism.

Follow Jln Kota around the base of Bukit St Paul and head back to Town Sq. Conclude your walk by ambling along the short brick promenade on the eastern bank of the Melaka River (parallel with Jln Laksamana), and take in riverine views, bars, the occasional barber and walls of distinctive Dutch bricks.

COURSES

The best souvenir you can bring home from Melaka is the cuisine. The **Hotel Equatorial** (p155) runs the only cookery course in town, which is available both as part of a hotel package and as an independent course. Instruction in Nonya cooking is given at the hotel's Seri Peranakan Restaurant by its head chef, Bong Geok Choo. The hotel package, the **'Wok & Walk'** (per person sharing a double RM265), includes a one-night stay in a 'superior' room, one buffet breakfast, one Nonya set lunch, one buffet dinner, two cooking workshop sessions, a walking tour of historical Melaka and a souvenir cookbook. It's quite a bargain when you consider that the published price of a one-night stay in a superior room without all the extras is nearly twice this amount.

If you'd rather take the course à la carte, two-hour classes are given for either **lunch** (RM55; 10.30am-12.30pm) or **dinner** (RM60; 4.40-6.30pm) and include a set meal and a certificate of completion. You'll cook three Nonya dishes, including specialities such as *ayam pong teh* (miso soy chicken) or *udang lemak nenas* (prawns with pineapple and spicy coconut), hands-on with the chef.

It's advised to book these courses at least one month in advance to secure the availability of the chef, but if you're running late you could always contact the hotel to see if there's space available on an already scheduled course.

Those interested in learning the beadwork techniques for Nonya shoes should inquire at **Souvenir Menj** (☎ 676 1926; 111 Jln Hang Jebat; closed Tue), a huge shoe shop that can help organise private courses. Since there aren't too many inquiries, prices aren't set and are up for discussion – also be warned that teachers aren't always available. Of course if more people ask, classes will become more regular. Ask for Dawn Tan.

MELAKA FOR CHILDREN

Melaka is a popular family destination although most of the child-friendly activities are found out of town in Ayer Keroh (p163) and at the A'Famosa Resort (p165) in Alor Gajah. The city of Melaka is mellow enough for walking around with kids, particularly around the pedestrian promenade at the historic centre (where there is also a small playground), but, as in most Malay towns, traffic can be a problem midcity and crossing the road means bolting ahead at full speed while dodging cars. Chinatown lacks sidewalks but the traffic is light. Trishaw rides are sure to be a favourite activity and the Jonker's Walk Night Market (p158), with its street performers, endless snacks and trinkets, is sure to please. Kids will want to go into the Maritime Museum (p146) because it's in a great big, cartoonlike ship, but know that the interior isn't nearly as fun as the exterior.

Check out the Mahkota Parade Shopping Complex (p162) for scheduled children's events such as dance performances or even paint-ball (for bigger kids). The cinema in the same complex occasionally shows big-name children's films, and just about every fast-food chain in existence has an outlet in this mall. To entice children to eat local food, try a food court where kids can see what they are getting before they order and have a wide range of choices. Newton Food Court (p159) is the best for kids, with lots of open spaces, an adjacent grassy area and a playground. Don't forget to make a stop for an ice *cendol* (shaved ice with syrup, coconut milk, strange jellies, beans and sometimes sweet corn)!

WACKY MELAKA

Melaka is an atypical Malay town, not only for its historical importance, but for its cre_ative, off-beat residents who add spice to more than their laksa.

You can't miss Melaka's **trishaws**. Nowhere else in Malaysia will you find such a wild and crazy collection of trishaws. These guys seem to be competing for who can bedeck their vehicles in the most outrageously kitsch plastic flowers, semimacabre baby-doll heads, religious paraphernalia and tinsel. Add some flashing Christmas lights, a satin parasol and a sound system and you've got one proud peddler. While taking a ride in one of these things is the most high-profile 'I'm a tourist' things you might ever do outside of Disneyland, it's an unabashed hoot and is great support for an industry that is dying nearly everywhere else in the country. As a spectator, keep an eye out for big tourist groups hiring out trishaws en masse: the effect, with several '80s dance hits blaring at the same time, cameras snapping and all that glitzy decoration, turns the streets of Melaka into a giant circuslike parade. Main trishaw pick-up spots include the Hotel Equatorial, Porta de Santiago and the Stadthuys; a 20-minute ride should cost RM10 to RM15.

Uncover your destiny at one of several little Chinese **fortune-teller booths** along Jonker's Walk on Friday and Saturday nights. The local Chinese in Malaysia frequently consult these mystics to ask for advice or to find out the most auspicious times of the year for certain occasions (such as weddings, financial investments, travel etc). Techniques range from card reading to fortune sticks, palm reading and Chinese astrology.

Dr Ho Eng Hui eats fire and throws knives, but the real reason to stick around and watch this Jonker's Walk Night Market kung fu master is to see him pummel his index finger into a coconut. If you're not familiar with the strength of a coconut's husk, think back to Tom Hanks in the film *Castaway*. Remember how he spends hours hurling a coconut on the rocks trying to break the damn thing open? Now a soft little human finger just shouldn't be able to pierce through a coconut's husk, let alone the interior nut – but this guy really does it and has been entertaining folks by doing so for more than 35 years. With the slogan 'Malaysia Boleh!' (literally 'Malaysia can do!') Dr Ho Eng Hui is in fact a doctor, and the purpose of his performance is to sell a miracle oil (RM10) that cures aches and pains. Find him at the southern end of Jln Hang Jebat between about 6.30pm and 9pm on Friday and Saturday.

TOURS

A handful of local tour guides hang out at the **Discovery Café** (3 Jln Bunga Raya) and charge RM70 to RM100 for a half-day of guiding. Particularly recommended is party-loving Nonya guide **Peck Choo** (☎ 13 208 0024; wickedpch@yahoo.com), who knows every nook and cranny of Melaka better than just about anyone. She

MELAKA

can lead tours on anything from short historic walks to several-day jaunts around the province and beyond. She is buddies with most of the other guides and can help set potential clients up with another guide or a specialist if need be. For tours originating from KL see p99.

Parameswara Tours (☎ 286 5468; RM10; ⏰ every hr 11am-3pm) This company has daily riverboat cruises along the Melaka River from the quay behind the tourist office on Jln Kota. The trip takes 40 minutes, and at least eight people are needed for a trip. The boat travels to Kampung Morten, where Villa Sentosa is located, past old *godown* (river warehouses). You can also charter a minimum 12-person boat to Pulau Besar (return adult/child RM25/15, departs 9am and returns 5pm). For regularly scheduled ferries to Pulau Besar, see p163.

Eco Bike Tour (☎ 019-652 5029; www.melakaonbike.com; per person RM50) For something different and to explore the fascinating landscape around Melaka, join Alias for his popular three-hour bike ride through 20km of oil-palm and rubber-tree plantations and delightful *kampung* communities surrounding town. Pick-up is from the Travellers' Lodge (p155). The tour changes depending on local events or festivals in the area; some may stop at a local wedding ceremony (only when available, of course). The tour can leave at either 8am or 3pm any day of the week as long as there are at least two people. There aren't any big hills and water is supplied.

FESTIVALS & EVENTS

Melaka celebrates all the major Malaysian holidays, including Chinese New Year, Thaipusam and National Day (see p219). While the festivals here might not be as big as in KL or Penang, they are more manageable and intimate.

Masimugam Festival A Malaccan version of Thaipusam, just as gory but without the crowds, takes place shortly after Chinese New Year in Kampong Cheng, about 15km outside of Melaka city in February/March.

Easter Good Friday and Easter Sunday processions are held outside at St Peter's Church in March/April.

Melaka Historical City Day Public holiday on 15 April in celebration of the founding of Melaka.

Vesak Day Parade Celebrates the birth, death and enlightenment of Buddha on the first full moon of the fourth month of the Chinese calendar (May). In Melaka there is a big and colourful parade.

Festa San Juan In late June, just before the Festa San Pedro, Melaka's Eurasian community hosts this festival at the chapel on top of St John's Hill.

Festa San Pedro Honouring this patron saint of the Portuguese fishing community, celebrations take place at St Peter's Church in late June and normally include a float procession from the Porta de Santiago to Medan Portugis, with cooking, fishing, handicraft and carnival festivities.

Dragon Boat Festival This Chinese festival, marked by a dragon boat race in the Strait of Melaka in June/July, commemorates the death by drowning of 3rd-century BC Chinese poet and statesman Qu Yuan.

Hungry Ghosts (Phor Thor) Festival Smaller than the same festival in Penang, the Melaka version in August is still worthwhile. Offerings and prayers are given to dead relatives who are temporarily released to roam the earth.

Festa Santa Cruz This festival in mid-September finishes with a candlelight procession of Malaccan and Singaporean Catholics to Malim chapel.

Christmas Malaccans descend on Medan Portugis to view the brightly decorated homes.

SLEEPING

Melaka has an exceptional selection of budget options, many of which exceed the quality of the lesser midrange choices. Jln Melaka

ISLAM'S JOURNEY TO MELAKA

Islam was introduced to Malaysia from the same source as Hinduism – Indian traders. The earliest Indian visitors came from the southeast peninsula (which is Hindu) while later Indian businessmen arrived from northeast India and were Muslim. The traders were very influential and those Malaccans who converted to Islam found it bettered business relations. It's no wonder that the upper classes and rulers such as Prince Parameswara, tantalised by Indian prosperity, who first converted to the new religion. Once the rulers became faithful, the trickle down was rapid.

While Parameswara was the first sultan of Melaka and also the first to embrace Islam, not all of the following sultans were Muslim. Once converted, the Malay names inevitably would change; Parameswara became Raja Iskandar Shah. His son Raja Ibrahim kept the name Parameswara although he did keep to the Persian trend of adding 'Shah' to his name to highlight the fact that he was a ruler.

Raya has become a sort of tourist ghetto, in a low-key Malaccan sort of way, and is only a short walk from Chinatown – midrange in this area tends to be geared towards Malay family and business travellers. The few top-end establishments in Melaka are in high-rises that are nearly all clustered along or near busy Jln Bendahara in Little India. While this might be convenient for folks coming to Melaka on business, Chinatown and areas around the historic centre are much more pleasant for the casual tourist. Some midrange and top-end hotels raise their tariff from Friday to Sunday; the weekday rate is quoted here.

Chinatown

If you have the option of staying in Chinatown, do it. Staying here elevates the Melaka experience.

Sama-Sama Guest House (☎ 305 1980; www.sama-sama-guesthouse.com; 26 Jl Tukang Besi; dm RM10, d RM15-30) Reggae music softly sings from the entrance/common area while cats (and the odd human) snooze through the afternoon. This place is so mellow that it feels like you should be on a beach somewhere but in fact you're very much in central Melaka. The rooms and building are just as quirky as their hippy-ish Swiss-Chinese owners, with a courtyard overflowing with potted plants, miniponds, wind chimes and wooden statues. Some rooms open up to the courtyard while others overlook the street, but they all feel intimately linked by the creaky wood floors and the breezes that run through the wide walkways. The whole place, including the shared toilets and showers, is kept sparkling clean.

Chong Hoe Hotel (☎ 282 6102; 26 Jln Tukang Emas; s/d RM25/43;) In an enviable location in Chinatown just up the street from Sama-Sama, this standard Chinese cheapy is no-nonsense good value and, although it's worn, it's clean.

Baba House (☎ 281 1216; thebabahouse@pd.jaring.my; 125-127 Jln Tun Tan Cheng Lock; s/d/f RM59/75/190;) In a row of restored Peranakan shophouses, this elegant Baba building is beautifully arranged with tilework, carved panels and a cool interior courtyard. Rooms, many windowless, aren't nearly as glitzy as the lobby and are dark, drab and worn. Some claim the hotel is haunted but the spooks appear to be friendly in nature.

Heeren Inn (☎ 288 3600; heerenin@streamyx.com; 23 Jln Tun Tan Cheng Lock; d RM78-145;) While this place is housed in an attractive and deep Chinatown building that seemingly goes on forever, the motel-like, windowless rooms here lack the ancient flair of the building. Rooms bordering the light-filled central courtyard (complete with water garden) are the brightest of the bunch. The sinks are little bigger than soap dishes, but shower rooms are otherwise new and clean and the family-run atmosphere throughout is comforting.

our pick **Number Twenty Guesthouse** (☎/fax 281 9761; www.selesalifestyle.com; 20 Jln Hang Jebat; d incl breakfast RM96;) A 1673 Dutch mansion meets urban-Zen chic at Melaka's most stylish digs. This place maintains a perfect balance of old and new with its dark wood beam construction and high ceilings, a touch of Chinese art, low opium beds and modern lighting. The common area has elongated windows that look over Jln Hang Jebat (and hence the Jonker's Walk Night Market on Friday and Saturday nights) and you can kick back on plush soft couches and watch DVDs on the plasma TV. Not all rooms have windows, but you can always get a little air on the rooftop garden, which is ideal for taking in the sunset. To conform with Melaka city's preservation standards, the guesthouse wasn't allowed to build en-suite bathrooms so all rooms here have shared bathrooms. It's gay friendly.

Hotel Puri (☎ 282 5588; www.hotelpuri.com; 118 Jln Tun Tan Cheng Lock; d/f RM110/305;) One of Chinatown's gems, Hotel Puri is an elegant creation in a superb old renovated Peranakan manor house. Its elaborate lobby, decked out with beautiful old cane and inlaid furniture, opens to a gorgeous courtyard garden (a wi-fi area) which leads to a 'history room' where guests can peruse Melaka's past through books and photographs. Standard rooms have butter-yellow walls, crisp sheets, satellite TV, wi-fi and shuttered windows. There's an on-site spa (p148), and breakfast, taken in the courtyard or air-conditioned dining area, is included.

Aldy Hotel (☎ 283 3232; www.aldyhotel.com.my; 27 Jln Kota; d RM118-280, tr/f RM220/260;) Standing out like a red, sore thumb atop a bistro opposite the foot of Bukit St Paul, this boutique-style hotel has a location to die for and is a great choice for families. Old grey carpet and decades-old décor darken the halls but things perk up again in the rooms, which are newly remodelled, modern and equipped with satellite TV. Wi-fi, rooftop Jacuzzi and barbecues

CREEPY MELAKA

Melaka is really, really old so it's no wonder there are some strange tales floating around town. Ask a local for a ghost story and you're sure to get several.

- Ghosts – sightings of a white figure next to a tombstone are common throughout the city.
- Vampires – in ancient Melaka there were reports of *pontianak,* beautiful female vampire-like creatures that would lurk in the trees waiting for their next victim. Their piercing laughter would sometimes wail through the night.
- The would-be-saint Francis performed a number of miracles during his time in Melaka but his most famous was bringing a young girl back to life after she had been dead and buried for three days.
- In 1948 the Dutch freighter *Orang Medan* sent out an SOS from the Strait of Melaka. When the ship was found drifting, all the crew members, including the radio operator with his finger still on the button, were found dead. No wounds were found on the sailors, but soon after the boat was boarded by its hopeful saviours it burst into flames.

on Thursday nights add to the package. There's no additional charge for children under 12 sharing a room with parents but room rates go up during holidays and peak season. Prices includes a set breakfast.

Heeren House (☎ 281 4241; www.melaka.net/heerenhouse; 1 Jln Tun Tan Cheng Lock; s RM129, d RM119-139; ❄) Lodging here positions you right in the heart of Chinatown, on the waterfront and within range of top local restaurants and sights. The airy, clean and lovely rooms (six in all) in this former warehouse largely overlook the river, with polished floorboards, traditional furniture (some with four-post beds) and clean showers. The least expensive room (with twin beds and no river view) on the ground floor is the best choice when the weather is very hot; it stays cool in the shade of a mango tree right outside. A popular café is in the foyer and breakfast comes with the price of the room.

Jalan Taman Melaka Raya & Around

Shirah's Guest House (☎ 286 1041; shirahgh@tm.ent.my; 2nd fl, 207-209 Jln Melaka Raya 1; dm/s RM10/15, d RM20-45; ❄ 💻) Brightly painted walls and a gentle Malay welcome make this place sit somewhere between a backpackers and a homestay. There's an inviting common room, a rooftop garden, informative bulletin boards, bike hire, internet access and kitchen facilities. Some rooms have balconies (one with a four-post bed) and all have high ceilings. Humane dorms are single-sex and have only four beds apiece. Add a small library and free movies and you have a real winner.

Samudra Inn (☎ 282 7441; samudrainn@hotmail.com; 348b Jln Melaka Raya 3; dm RM12, s RM18-35, d RM24-45; ❄) A short walk from the historic centre, this charming place is for lovers of peace and quiet. Caged birds chirp softly in the courtyard area but other than that, you won't hear a peep out of anyone. TV time (satellite) is till 10pm and there are kitchen facilities if you want to cook. The ex-teacher owners take extra steps to make sure their guests are comfortable such as taking lone visitors out to dinner and giving great advice about where to eat and shop. You won't find a more secure or wholesome place. Pricier rooms have a shower, and balcony and laundry service is available.

Samudera Backpacker's Hostel (☎ 283 4231; 205b Jln Melaka Raya 1; s RM18-30, d RM25-35, tr RM55; ❄) Not to be confused with the much more cosy Samudra Inn, this backpackers isn't a bad choice. The cheaper rooms are windowless boxes but the higher-priced room with air-con and private bathroom have arty exposed-brick walls and are more comfortable. The place is new, clean and well looked after – it hasn't drawn in much of backpacker crowd yet so you might just have the place to yourself.

Kancil Guesthouse (☎ 281 4044; www.machinta.com.sg/kancil; 177 Jln Parameswara; s/tw/d RM18/28/30; 💻) West of the small Taoist Yong Chuan Tian Temple, quite a way from the city centre, this pleasant guesthouse offers spacious, secure lodgings along a road studded with picturesque Malaccan houses. The road itself is lethal with traffic, but the house is lovely and deep, with a gorgeous garden out back, and the owners are pleasant and helpful. There's also bike rental (per day RM10) and internet access (per hour RM3.50). Bus 17 from Melaka Sentral passes by here.

Travellers' Lodge (☎ 226 5709; 214b Jln Melaka Raya 1; d RM26-46;) This is one of the more social and deservedly popular backpacker places in town. The kick-up-your-feet common area has an elevated-platform TV lounge with cushions and mats strewn about – perfect for lounging. Rooms are all clean, with windows and tiled floors, and a handful of them span two levels making a sort of miniloft; pricier air-con rooms have showers. The sheltered roof terrace up the vertigo-inducing steps is a boon, dotted with flowers and plants, and the lodge runs to a café (alcohol-free). Management is friendly, helpful and is further enlivened by Alias, who runs Melaka's only bike tour (p152).

Hollitel (☎ 286 0607; mollykoo@yahoo.com; G-20K Jln PM 5, Plaza Mahkota; d RM50-120;) In the grid of blocks southwest of Jln Merdeka, this place, one of the better of a cluster down here, offers clean rooms with electric showers (except in the cheapest rooms), TV and air-con (no phones), internet access (RM3 per hour) and free drinking water in the foyer. It's really just a crash pad designed for low-budget Malaysian business travellers and families.

Fenix Inn (☎ 281 5511; www.fenixinn.com; 156 Jln Taman Melaka Raya; d RM128-168;) Efficiency is the name and business is the game at this crisp, new hotel. Rooms are small and characterless but have new carpet and coffee- and tea-making appliances; most have a window. Polite management, drinking water on each floor and the business centre with a particularly good crop of terminals for internet access (RM2.5 per hour) make this a good choice for anyone who has to work on the road. Discounts offered.

Malacca Straits Hotel (☎ 286 1888; www.malaccastraitshotel.com.my; 27 Jln Chan Koon Cheng; r/ste RM128/188;) Smack up against the Hotel Equatorial, this hotel calls itself a 'batik boutique' hotel, and it's not a bad description. While the hotel opened in 2007, it's a remodel of an older building so the hallways and lobby area still have an air of old funk. The spacious rooms however have been given greater attention and are furnished to the hilt with some exquisite teak furniture including four-post beds in every room and batik fabrics everywhere. While standard rooms all have bathtubs, an upgrade to a suite adds a Jacuzzi. Don't overlook the authentic *songket* (gold-and-silver-threaded-fabric) that lines the hallways and, of course, the smiling service. Wi-fi is available at the on-site café.

Seri Costa Hotel (☎ 281 6666; fax 286 4931; Jln PM 8, Plaza Mahkota; r RM145;) This is a modern, clean and smart three-star hotel southwest of Jln Merdeka catering mainly to Malaysian guests. Rooms are fully equipped with satellite TV and coffee- and tea-making facilities, and come with teakwood beds and furniture. Good promotional rates are offered.

Century Mahkota Hotel (☎ 281 2828; www.melaka.net/centurymahkota; Jln Syed Abdul Aziz; 1-bed apt Sun-Thu RM178, Fri & Sat RM198, 2-bed apt Sun-Thu RM298, Fri & Sat RM318;) Filling a huge section of reclaimed waterfront south of the Mahkota Parade Shopping Complex, this resort-style hotel has a range of suites and apartments, plus an ample range of facilities including two large swimming pools, restaurants, bars and tennis and squash courts. It's very popular with Singaporean and Malaysian families. We've heard complaints about the cleanliness and service for short stays, but the long-stay apartments can be an OK deal if you get an apartment with a good view. Apartment prices rise further during holiday periods.

Hotel Equatorial (☎ 282 8333; www.equatorial.com; Jln Parameswara; d RM420-500;) The Hotel Equatorial can't be beat for its location near the historic centre. While it's a bit frayed around the edges, this somehow just adds to the colonial charm of the hotel. Good discounts online can cut prices nearly in half, making this elegant choice (weekday and promotional rates usually start at around RM248) excellent value. Service is well mannered and the overall presentation is crisp. There's a swimming pool, ladies-only pool, a quality fitness centre, tennis court and wi-fi access. It's worth upgrading to one of the deluxe rooms (RM500), which have either balconies or heaps of extra room space. Special packages are available through the hotel, including tours and specials such as cookery courses (see p150). Room price includes RM88 meal credit at any of the hotel's four restaurants.

Little India to Bukit China

Eastern Heritage Guest House (☎ 283 3026; 8 Jln Bukit China; dm/s/d/tr RM8/22/26/33) This well-located guesthouse (the neighbourhood has one foot in Chinatown and the other in Little India) has an authentic antique feel – as in maybe the walls haven't been pained in a few decades. Yet that's part of the charm of the superb old Melaka building dating from 1918, with Peranakan tiling, impressive carved panelling and lots of wide open spaces with plenty of natural light. There's a dipping pool, sunroof area, a downstairs common room, reception doubles as a bar, and breakfast is thrown in. The upstairs dorm is airless and bland but double and single rooms are brightened up by original murals on the walls. Angle for the RM26 double with balcony.

Tony's Guesthouse (☎ 688 0119; 24 Jln Banda Kaba; d/tr RM20/27) Backpacker-friendly, with some long-stayers clinging to cheap rooms, Tony's has been nurtured to popularity by its travel-minded namesake mentor. The lobby, hung with images of Che Guevara, Marilyn Monroe and Elvis, has a café.

Yellow Mansion Hotel (☎ 283 8885; www.yellowmansion.com; 45 Jln Banda Kaba; s/tw/tr/f RM50/60/90/130;) This Malay-run hotel is very clean with polite staff. Some doubles (all with shower) are windowless, so check them first, but the family room offers tremendous space.

Mimosa Hotel (☎ 282 1113; www.mimosahotel.com; 108 Jln Bunga Raya; r incl breakfast RM98-166;) You can tell this place caters to a local clientele from the 'No Durian' signs on the elevator. It's somewhat bland and functional, but it's also clean, modern and fully equipped. The hotel is in a great location in a bustling Chinese area, with good discounts on rates found online, but there's not much in the way of a view.

Hotel Grand Continental (☎ 284 0088; www.ghihotels.com.my; 20 Jln Tun Sri Lanang; d incl breakfast RM210) It's in the characterless north and there's a lack of charm, but promotional rates make it good value.

Hotel Orkid (☎ 282 5555; www.hotelorkidmelaka.com; 138 Jln Bendahara; r incl breakfast RM250;) A centrally located modern high-rise hotel, all rooms here have in-house video, coffee- and tea-making facilities and minibar. Blankets on the beds (no bedspreads) are a little ratty, but the place is clean and many rooms have fabulous views. Bathrooms are the size of a small closet. There's a health spa, restaurant and lounge with live music.

Emperor Hotel (☎ 284 0777; www.theemperorhotel.com; 123 Jln Munshi Abdullah; r incl breakfast RM250;) This is probably the least appealing of the hotels in this category, but excellent promotional rates (around RM80 to RM100 for a double) make it a better option – despite the deserted carbuncular eyesore attached. Upper floors have good views, all rooms come with bathroom, fridge and TV with in-house video, and there's a fitness centre and restaurants.

City Bayview Hotel (☎ 283 9888; www.bayviewintl.com; Jln Bendahara; r RM398;) This hotel was newly renovated in 2006 and complete with a fresh and invigorating edge, it has a sports bar, smallish kidney-shaped pool, dance club and breakfast included in the room price. Sheets and all bedding are new and crisp, and the views over the old town from some rooms are quite spectacular. This is a favourite with families, and kids will enjoy the rather weird computerised speaking lift. The glass lobby is refreshingly modern for such a historically oriented town. Fish for promotional prices.

Renaissance Melaka Hotel (☎ 284 8888; infomkz@po.jaring.my; Jln Bendahara; d RM470;) By far the ritziest of Melaka's top-end hotels, the Renaissance offers five-star service and old-school luxury. Large windows in the rooms take advantage of views that sweep over Melaka in all directions, while the spacious rooms, equipped with comfy Renaissance beds, are modern and chic while incorporating classic Chinese touches. You can relax in the tasteful Famosa Lounge off the lobby (open 11am to midnight), build up a sweat in the squash courts or at a yoga class then sink a drink in the pub (with regular live music).

EATING

Melaka's food mirrors the city's eclectic, multicultural DNA. Nonya cuisine (prepared here with a salty Indonesian influence) is a celebrated school of cooking with the classic dish of Melaka, laksa. It's also the home of Portuguese Eurasian food: hunt down Portuguese-influenced Kristang cuisine in the Medan Portugis – it's mostly seafood and rice, but the fiery 'devil curry' is worth an encounter. Melaka's Chinese speciality is chicken rice ball, a Hokkien-style chicken served with rice that's been rolled up into savoury ping-pong-ball-sized dumplings.

Eats on the streets include *youtiao* (fried bread sticks; 40 sen), *rougan* (dried meat strips; RM26 for 250gms) and Nonya pineapple tarts. For drinks, quaff sugarcane juice (RM1) or soy milk (RM1), or stop by Chinese street vendors for sweet water-chestnut tea (RM1) – hot or cold, it's a real thirst-quencher. Also look out for Chinese pharmacies such as **Teck Ann Pharmacy** (58 Jln Bunga Raya) serving tall glasses of chrysanthemum tea (RM1).

The Mahkota Parade Shopping Complex is mostly a centre for Western fast food, though

DON'T LEAVE MELAKA WITHOUT TRYING...

- Laksa – the regional version is distinguished by its broth infused with coconut milk and lemongrass.
- *Popiah* – an uber–spring roll stuffed with shredded turnip, carrots, prawns, chilli, garlic, palm sugar and much, much more.
- *Cendol* – shaved-ice monstrosity with jellies, syrup and coconut milk – looks gross, tastes great.
- Nonya pineapple tarts – buttery pastries with a chewy pineapple-jam filling.
- Chicken rice ball – self-explanatory dish with Hokkien-style chicken and balled-up rice dumplings.
- *Asam* fish heads – spicy tamarind fish-head stew.
- Satay *celup* – like fondue but better – dunk tofu, prawns and more into bubbling soup to cook it to your liking.
- Selvam's Friday vegetarian special – 10 different Indian vegetarian dishes let you sample the many flavours of Melaka's Indian heritage (see p159).

the food court on the 1st floor has the usual Malaysian hawker favourites. Just across the street, the colossal Dataran Pahlawan on Jln Merdeka is a vast complex of shops, salons, cafés, restaurant and entertainment and cultural facilities.

Most restaurants are open from 11.30am to 10pm, while more simple cafés open around 10am and close at about 5pm.

Chinatown

our pick **Low Yong Mow** (☎ 282 1235; Jln Tokong; dim sum RM1-6; 🕐 5am-noon, closed Tue) Famous Malaysia-wide for large and delectably well-stuffed *pao* (steamed pork buns), this place is Chinatown's biggest breakfast treat. With high ceilings, plenty of fans running and a view of Masjid Kampung Kling, the atmosphere oozes all the charms of Chinatown. Take your pick from the endless variety of dumplings, sticky rice dishes and mysterious treats that are wheeled to your table. It's great for early-bus-departure breakfasts and is usually packed with talkative, newspaper-reading locals by around 7am.

Tart & Tart Bakery (☎ 282 1181; 45 Lorong Hang Jebat; snacks from RM2.50) This simple, relaxing Malay-run Chinatown snack shop does a small range of bite-size snacks, from blueberry and cheese tarts (RM2.50) to pineapple pies (RM3.50), apple pies (RM3.50) and *kaya* (RM2.50) – coconut cream that you spread on bread.

Kenny's Nonya Delights (Jln Tun Tang Heng Lock; mains RM2.50-5; 🕐 8am-5pm, closed Mon) It's a hole-in-the-wall café, but this friendly little place, right near the junction of Jln Hang Kasturi, serves up some of the best Nonya food bargains in Melaka. This is an excellent place to have a quick snack of Nonya-style laksa (RM3), *popiah* (spring roll; RM4) or a *nasi lemak* breakfast (curry laksa; RM1.50). The restaurant bottles its sauces, which make delicious (albeit heavy) souvenirs.

Donald & Lily's (☎ 284 8907; snacks RM3; 🕐 9.30am-4pm, closed Tue) Just finding this place is an adventure. Take the alleyway across from Malaqa House to the west until you reach another alley on your left that leads behind the buildings of Jln Tun Tan Cheng Lock. You'll see what looks like a few hawker stalls selling *cendol* but if you look closer there's a little stairway behind 31 Jln Tun Tan Chen Lockleading to hidden, but very popular Donald & Lily's. Why bother looking? This is Melaka locals' favourite stop for the regional-style laksa (RM3) and Nonya *cendol* (RM1.20). The setting is like being in someone's living room and the service is beaming.

Limau-Limau Café (☎ 698 4917; 89 Jln Tun Tan Cheng Lock; cappuccinos RM6.90; 💻) Decorated with dark-coloured ceramics and an arty twist, this quiet café extends through several rooms and a pleasant interior courtyard. Take a seat for salads, sandwiches (RM3.90 to RM6.90), fruit juices (RM4 to RM5), milk shakes (RM6.50 to RM7.50) or internet access (RM3 per half-hour). Its second location on Jln Hang Jebat has similar décor and the same menu.

Cafe 1511 (☎ 286 0151; www.cafe1511.com; 52 Jln Tun Tan Cheng Lock; meals RM8; 🕐 10am-6pm, closed

Wed; 💻) Next to the Baba-Nonya Heritage Museum is this high-ceilinged Peranakan café, with original tiles along the wall, lovely carved screens, a mishmash of decorative objects from Southeast Asia and a Nonya menu. There's free 15-minute internet for guests and this is one of the few places in Chinatown where you'll find a Western set breakfast (RM5).

Heeren House (☎ 281 4241; sandwiches RM9; ⏰ 11am-6pm) In the hotel of the same name: make this a lunch slot for a light meal of sandwiches on fresh baked bread, salads (from RM11) and yummy brownies (RM4). You can browse the integrated shop for a wonderful selection of upscale batik and other crafts from all around Southeast Asia, while you wait for your food to arrive.

Nancy's Kitchen (15 Jln Hang Lekir; meals RM10; ⏰ 11am-5.30pm, closed Tue) In a town already known for its graciousness, this home-cooking Nonya restaurant is our favourite for friendly service. If you want an intimate meal, head elsewhere. The server is as chatty and full of suggestions as they come, and will have you making conversation with the other handful of customers in no time. It's like a happy dinner (or lunch) party with particularly good food. Try the house speciality, chicken candlenut (RM10).

Vegan Salad & Herbs House (☎ 282 9466; 22 Jln Kubu; meals RM10; ⏰ 10am-4pm Fri-Wed) Around the corner from the Buddhist Guanyin Temple, this health-conscious spot offers a range of healthy uncooked, crisp vegetables, brown rice set lunches and wholemeal bread buns.

Hoe Kee Chicken Rice (☎ 283 34751; 4 Jln Hang Jebat; meals RM11; ⏰ 8.30am-3pm, closed last Wed of month) Just look for the queue along the street past the peanut vendor to find Melaka's busiest restaurant, serving the local speciality of chicken rice ball and *asam* fish head (fish heads in a spicy tamarind gravy; price depends on market value). You'll need to arrive here off-hours (try around 10am) or expect to wait – for a long time. Is it worth it? What's already good tastes better after you've been smelling it in anticipation for 45 minutes, and the restaurant's setting, with wood floors and ceiling fans, seems to further bring out the exotic flavours.

Teachew Cuisine (☎ 282 2353; 55 Jln Hang Kasturi; meals RM20; ⏰ 11.30am-2.30pm & 6-11.30pm, closed Mon) We walked past this place for about a week before we realised there was a restaurant here, and yet it's Melaka's claim to *haute cuisine*. Duck past mum, who washes the dishes on the pavement and spends all day chopping veggies and dismembering chickens. Smile at uncle who runs the rickety soup stall that efficiently covers the restaurant's doorway, and then you're in for a surprise. The secret interior room is air-conditioned, the tables are set with China's finest and the walls are decorated with an impressive collection of hard liquor bottles and odd landscape paintings. There's no menu but everyone knows that you're supposed to order the soft-shell crab or the prawns. The chef, a northern China native, has apparently cooked for the president of Singapore, and Malaysian notables have their visits documented with pictures on the walls. It's expensive, we found the food just OK, but the experience of eating here is worth every sen.

Coconut House (☎ 282 9128; 128 Jln Tun Tan Cheng Lock; meals RM30; ⏰ 2pm-midnight Mon-Thu, 2pm-1am Fri, 11am-midnight Sat & Sun) It's a cheesy name, but there's oodles of inviting space and atmosphere upstairs and down at this bar-restaurant. The menu boasts a popular pizza selection, rosemary roast chicken (RM22), slow-roasted shoulder of pork (RM25) and other tasty offerings. The namesake coconut tree rises proudly into sunlight from an interior courtyard.

Howard's (☎ 286 8727; 5 Jln Hang Lekir; meals RM40; ⏰ lunch & dinner Wed-Mon) A finely crafted ambience of creaseless linen, elegant furniture, black-and-white check tile floor, flavoursome international cuisine (lobster bisque, roast rack of lamb) and unobtrusive service, Howard's is a thoroughly unhurried and intimate experience and a top romantic dining choice. Topped off with an impressive wine list, this is definitely Chinatown's swankiest choice.

On Friday and Saturday nights, Jln Hang Jebat turns into the not-to-be-missed Jonker's Walk Night Market. Here you'll find heaps of snacks and hawkers stalls where you can graze and nibble to make a satisfying meal. For self-catering or curiosity, there's a local **vegetable market** (Taman Laksmana) on Saturday night from around 5.30pm.

Jalan Melaka Raya & Around

Restoran Amituofoh (☎ 292 6426; 2-20 Jln PM9, Plaza Mahkota, Bandar Hilir; meals free, contributions welcome; ⏰ breakfast, lunch & dinner) Conventional wisdom dictates that there's no such thing as a free meal. This Buddhist vegetarian restaurant – the gift of a Chinese philanthropist – generously breaks the rules by providing food on the house. You may make a contribution (and we highly advise you do), otherwise there are few conditions: you must wash your own plates and cutlery, and taking food away is not permitted.

Roti Canai Terbang (Jln Melaka Raya 3; 70 sen-RM3; breakfast) Get excellent *roti canai* (flaky flatbread) either plain or stuffed with your choice of onion, egg, cheese or all three. This is the biggest *roti canai* establishment we've ever seen and it packs with locals. Wash down your pancake with a thick, sweet milky coffee or tea.

Ind Ori (282 4777; 236 Jln Melaka Raya 1; dishes RM1-15; 8am-midnight) Mmm, Indonesian Pedang food, fresh and heated in a point-and-ask buffet. It's just like the real thing but without the flies and dubious sanitation issues. House specialities include delicious avocado juice with chocolate sauce (RM4.50) and *sekotang* (sweet cream and peanut dumplings with green beans and hot ginger; RM5.80).

Restoran Sek Yow Fook (284 0452; cnr Jln Melaka Raya 3 & Jln Melaka Raya 4; meals RM3-6; breakfast, lunch & dinner) There's a little of everything at this hodge-podge Chinese place but it's all surprisingly good. English cooked breakfasts (RM5) are available from 8am or there's a little *congee* (rice porridge) stall for those wanting to start the day local-style. For lunch dive into the excellent Chinese buffet (around RM4), but don't arrive past around 2.30pm when the dregs have been sitting out *sans* refrigeration for hours. For kids (or fussy grown-ups) there's an 'Elvis Presley' peanut-butter-and-banana sandwich (RM1.50) on offer. A bar in the back serves beer.

Restoran Banya (282 8297; 154 Jln Taman Melaka Raya; meals RM9; 10am-10pm, closed Thu) Friendly staff will help you decode the menu at this centrally located place. The reputation here isn't as strong as some of the other Nonya restaurants in town but we found the food delicious.

Ole Sayang (283 1966; 198 Jln Taman Melaka Raya; meals RM13; 10am-10pm, closed Wed) Go here for ambient Nonya atmosphere, decorated with old wooden furniture and dim lighting. While this place is one of the best known in Melaka, we found that the food wasn't of a higher standard than the other Nonya places around town.

Bayonya (292 2192; 164 Jln Taman Melaka Raya; meals RM15; 10am-10pm, closed Tue) This authentic eatery is a locals' favourite for its excellent and inexpensive home-cooked Peranakan cuisine. One of the must-tries here is the durian *cendol* (RM5).

Restoran Wuguzhan (282 1918; 256-257 Jln Melaka Raya 3; meals RM15) This Chinese organic vegetarian health-food eatery was temporarily closed when we passed, but it's got a good reputation for delivering carrion-free calories in the form of inexpensive Chinese-style veggie dishes. Handy for the local guesthouses, the menu runs to sweet-and-sour 'veggie chicken' (RM8), seaweed wholemeal bread roll (RM3), veggie duck noodle soup (RM4) and beyond.

Two **Malay hawker centres** (meals around RM4) are in the eastern region of this area, one near the Jln TMR roundabout and the other just east of the base of Jln Melaka Raya 3 on Jln Sayed Abdul Aziz. The former is the larger of the two in a covered area and serves everything from fresh juices to fish-head curry and Nonya food.

Serving a wider range of fare with Chinese in the main hall and halal food at the back, **Newton Food Court** (Jln Merdeka), just west of Mahkota Parade Shopping Complex, is Melaka's newest and most attractive hawker centre. It's under an immense, sweeping thatched roof and is bordered by palms. Little dessert stalls set up along the adjoining grassy area perfect for picnicking.

Further west, also on Jln Merdeka, is Glutton's Corner, which is more of a group of restaurants than stalls. Prices are higher than at other hawker centres and the clientele more upscale.

Little India to Bukit China

OUR PICK **Capitol Satay** (283 5508; 41 Lorong Bukit China; meals RM8) Famous for its satay *celup* (a Melaka adaptation of satay steamboat), this place is usually packed to the gills and is one of the cheapest outfits in town. Stainless-steel tables have bubbling vats of soup in the middle where you dunk skewers of okra stuffed with tofu, sausages, chicken, prawns and bok choy. Side dishes include pickled eggs and ginger. Dining here is not only satisfying to the gut and palate, but great fun and a chance for some gregarious feasting.

Selvam (281 9223; 3 Jln Temenggong; meals RM8) This is a classic banana-leaf restaurant always busy with its loyal band of local patrons ordering tasty and cheap curries, roti and tandoori chicken sets (RM5.50). Even devout carnivores will second-guess their food preferences after trying the Friday-afternoon vegetarian special with 10 varieties of veg for only RM6.

UE Tea House (20 Lorong Bukit China; meals RM8) Another dim sum place, more simple than Chinatown's Low Yong Mow, but very tasty just the same. Sip Chinese tea and gorge yourself on the impressive array of steamed dumplings.

Bulldog Café (☎ 292 1920; 145 Jln Bendahara; meals RM10) Nonya, Chinese, Thai and Western dishes. For cheap snacks, sample the Nonya *popiah* – lettuce, bean sprouts, egg and chilli paste in a soft sleeve (RM2) or the *pai tee* (crispy cone-shaped morsels of rice flour, stuffed with vegetables; RM3).

Follow the sounds of a chopping meat cleaver to **Medan Makan Bunga Raya** (Hungry Lane; btwn Jln Bendahara & Jln Bunga Raya) where you can feast on Indian-style curry-pork rice in the very busy evenings or try the local speciality of *gula melaka* (palm sugar) during the day. The **Centrepoint food court** (Jln Munshi Abdullah) is a recommended place to seek out Indian and Malay treats for lunch. Further north, **Hang Tuah Mall** (Jln Hang Tuah), a pedestrian walk, swarms with open-air food stalls every evening.

Medan Portugis

There's really not much reason to head out to this nondescript neighbourhood other than to eat. On Friday and Saturday evenings, head to **Restoran de Lisbon** (Medan Portugis; meals RM30), where you can sample Malay-Portuguese dishes at outdoor tables. Try the delicious local specialities of chilli crabs (RM20) or the distinctly Eurasian devil curry (RM10). Also visit **San Pedro** (4 Jln D'Aranjo), on the street immediately behind the square, with a cosy, local atmosphere for Malay-Portuguese meals. Any other time of the week, Medan Portugis has food stalls, serving similar dishes to those found at restaurants at seaside tables.

DRINKING & ENTERTAINMENT

Bars often open midday and, although they technically close at 1am, will stay open longer if there's enough fun still going on.

Unfortunately Melaka's beloved and long-running Sound and Light Show had closed at the time of writing due to the exorbitant amount of light that emanates from the new Dataran Pahlawan shopping centre into the now defunct theatre. No immediate plans have been made to relocate the show. For a darkened cinema experience head to the four-screen **Golden Screen Cinemas** in the Mahkota Parade Shopping Complex, which usually shows a few blockbusters as well as the standard Malay and Bollywood flicks.

Melaka is studded with watering holes, and your best bet for anything from a mellow night out to a late night of drinking is in Chinatown. The Friday and Saturday night Jonker's Walk Night Market (p158) closes down Jln Heng Lekir to traffic and the handful of bars along the lane become a mini street party with tables oozing beyond the sidewalks, live music and plenty of good-natured revelry.

Geographér Café (☎ 281 6813; www.geographer.com.my; 83 Jln Hang Jebat; large Tiger beers RM17.20; 🕙 10am-1am Wed-Sun) This ventilated, breezy bar with outside seating and late hours in a prewar corner shophouse is a godsend. Seat yourself with a beer amid the throngs and applaud resident artist-musician Mr Burns as he eases through gnarled classics from Chuck Berry to JJ Cale. A tasty choice of local and Western dishes and laid-back but professional service round it all off. The apple pie (RM8) is to die for.

our pick **Calanthe Art Café** (☎ 292 2960; 11 Hang Kasturi; coffees RM2.50; 🕙 noon-11pm Tue-Thu, noon-midnight Fri-Sun; 💻) The Zen water garden atmosphere of this light- and plant-filled café is like reflexology for the travel-weary soul. Try coffees from each of the 13 Malaysian states, either hot or cold or in a RM12 coffee cocktail. There are also smoothies (RM8), espresso drinks (from RM4.50) and light Malaysian and Western meals from RM4.50. A quiet internet terminal at the back will cost you RM3 per hour.

GAY & LESBIAN MELAKA

Although it's not what you'd call a thriving gay scene, Melaka's proximity to Kuala Lumpur (KL) and eclectic population make it a popular stop for both foreign and local gay travellers. The atmosphere is relaxed and uncommonly open for Malaysia.

Try **Pure Bar** (591a Jln Taman Melaka Raya), a former gay-friendly guesthouse that has become a fun bar-nightclub, popular with locals and welcoming to visiting gay and lesbian travellers.

Honky Tonk Haven (68 Lorong Hang Jebat; ⏲ 11am-1am Wed-Mon, 4pm-1am Tue) A great new addition to the Melaka drinking scene, this music bar is run by Kiwi jazz pianist Joe 'Itchy Fingers' Webster and his singing wife Jill. Jazz memorabilia photos line the walls and spontaneous sessions of live music are performed by Joe, Jill and their collection of talented friends. It's a place to make fast friends, grab a quick meal (including real New Zealand–style burgers for RM8, and RM7 all-day breakfasts) and find out how funky you really are.

Voyager Travellers Lounge (☎ 281 5216; 40 Lorong Hang Jebat; 💻) It'll draw you in with promises of free internet and its 9.30pm Wednesday movie nights, but you'll keep coming back to this place for the mellow and surprisingly local vibe. Ease back into a wicker chair and order a cold beer from the glowing bar built out of recycled bottles. The young owner can help arrange activities throughout Melaka.

Friends Café (Jln TMR; ⏲ noon-2am) Buzzing with everyone from businessmen to young and hip locals, this convivial spot serves espresso drinks (RM5.50 to RM10) in the day and becomes a lively bar at night. It's a hard-to-miss spot right where Jln Melaka Raya 3 meets Jln Taman Melaka Raya. There are light meals including sandwiches (RM10) and *tom yam* (red chilli–based hot-and-sour soup; RM8) and the whole place is a wi-fi zone.

Discovery Café (3 Jln Bunga Raya; 💻) The staff take things at a serious stroll and the food is mediocre, but the location near the Melaka River, the late hours and the outside seating maintain a somewhat shaky allure. Stop by if you're looking for a tour guide (see p151).

SHOPPING

Taking time to browse Chinatown's eclectic mix of shops is an activity in itself, even if you hate shopping. Start with the antique shops along Jln Hang Jebat (Jonker's Walk) and Jln Tun Tan Cheng Lock where you'll see dusty old junk, polished ancient relics and everything in between. Unless you really know your antiques, be very cautious about spending money in these shops. Prices are high and haggling is essential.

Other Malaccan favourites are Nonya beaded shoes which, depending on the quality and intricacy of the beadwork, can cost from RM70 to RM2000. A cheaper alternative is Nonya 'clogs', colourful slap-arounds with a wooden base and a single plastic-strip upper. Browse other shops for funky Southeast Asian and Indian clothing, shoulder bags, incense, hand-made tiles, charms and crystals, cheap jewellery and more. Peek into the growing array of silent artists studios where you might see a painter busy at work in a back room.

The following Chinatown shops are real standouts.

Top Spinning Academy (79 Jln Tokong; ⏲ 10am-4pm) If you enter this shop, be prepared for a very enthusiastic traditional top-spinning lesson by *gasing uri* extraordinaire Simpson Wong. You aren't expected to purchase anything although you probably will if you get the hang of the spin – a top is only RM2. Mr Wong is a charming fellow who genuinely appears to just want people to play tops with him. Go in and make his day.

Tile Shop (☎ 283 1815; 31 Jln Tokong) Intricately beautiful minireplicas of the fine European tiles that grace some of Melaka's fine colonial buildings can be found here. You'll also find flat ceramic pictures of teapots and Chinese household items in stylish frames. A tile or art piece will cost around RM30. While here, peep into the shop next door that makes papier-mâché temple offerings.

Wan Aik Shoemaker (56 Jln Tokong) Raymond Yeo continues the tradition began by his grandfather in the same little shoemaker's shop that has been in his family for generations. The beaded Nonya shoes here are considered Melaka's finest and begin at a steep, but merited RM300. Tiny silk-bound-feet shoes (from RM90) are also available, although nowadays they are just a curiosity rather than a necessity.

Lim Trading (☎ 292 6812; 63 Jln Tokong) Across from Wan Aik, busy Mr Lim is a second-generation craftsman (his apprenticeship began at the age of six) who also fashions gorgeous handmade Nonya bead slippers (from RM180).

Malaqa House (☎ 281 4770; 70 Jln Tun Tan Cheng Lock; ⏲ 10am-6pm Mon-Fri, 10am-7pm Sat & Sun) This is a huge museum-like shop in an elegant building stuffed to the gills with antiques and replicas – it's not cheap, but it bursts with character.

Orangutan House (59 Lorong Hang Jebat; ⏲ 10am-6pm Thu-Tue) Having mushroomed to an impressive three outlets, this hip and brightly painted T-shirt shop adds its own brand of zest and colour to Chinatown's multifaceted personality. All shirts are the work of local artist Charles Cham (see the boxed text, p162)

ARTIST CHARLES CHAM

Charles Cham (www.charlescham.com) is a Melaka-born artist whose bright Orangutan art and T-shirt shops have become Melaka institutions.

What is the best thing about being an artist in Melaka? Melaka is small, old, colourful and sandwiched between Kuala Lumpur and Singapore. This makes it a popular tourist destination and many artists make a living here. More and more artists from other towns and new art graduates are moving in. Being an artist in Melaka means you can work in a 'living museum'. The face of the city is changing but the feeling remains the same.

If your best friend were coming to town where would you go? I'd bring them to Jln Hang in the day to hunt for some bargains then we'd take a sunset riverboat cruise. On weekend nights we'd check out Jonker's Walk Night Market (p158) and end up at the watering holes between Jln Hang Jebat and Jln Hang Lekir – some are open till 4am!

and have themes spanning from Chinese astrology animals to rather edgy topics (at least for Malaysia) such as 'Use Malaysian Rubber' above a sketch of a condom. Other branches are at 96 Jln Tun Tan Cheng Lok (closed Tuesday) and 12 Jln Hang Jebat (closed Thursday).

Dataran Pahlawan (Jln Merdeka) is Melaka's largest mall, with a collection of upscale designer shops and restaurants in the western half and an odd, nearly underground-feeling craft and souvenir market in the eastern portion. For practical needs such as camera shops, a pharmacy or electronics store, head to **Mahkota Parade Shopping Complex** (☎ 282 6151; Lot B02, Jln Merdeka), which is invariably packed with locals and often has some sort of performance or event going on.

GETTING THERE & AWAY

Melaka is 144km from Kuala Lumpur, 224km from Johor Bahru and just 94km from Port Dickson. The North–South Hwy (Lebuhraya), linking Johor Bahru and Kuala Lumpur, is the main route through the state. Most travellers arrive and depart from Melaka overland, as the airport outside town does not handle domestic flights. Express buses to KL and Singapore are plentiful and bus connections link with other peninsular destinations. Trains do not stop at Melaka but at Tampin, 38km north of town. Daily boats connect with Dumai in Sumatra.

Boat

High-speed **ferries** (☎ 281 6766) make the trip from Melaka to Dumai in Sumatra twice daily at 9am and 3pm (one-way/return RM80/150, two hours). Boats return from Dumai at 10.30am and 1pm. Dumai is a visa-free entry port into Indonesia for citizens of most countries. Ferries also run to Pekan Baru (one-way/return RM120/210, six hours) in Sumatra. Tickets are available at the **Dumai Ferry Service** (☎ 286 1811; G35 Jln PM2, Plaza Mahkota) and other ticket offices near the wharf. Same-day tickets are on sale after 8.30am, but it's best to book the day before.

Bus

Melaka Sentral, the well-designed modern long-distance bus station, is inconveniently located on Jln Cempaka, off Jln Tun Razak in the north of town. A taxi into town should cost around RM20, or you can take bus 17 (which leaves about every 15 minutes) to Chinatown. Frequent buses head to Kuala Lumpur (RM9 to RM10, two hours) and further afield to Singapore (RM18, 4½ hours, departures approximately hourly) and Johor Bahru (RM16, 3½ hours). There are also less frequent departures for Georgetown (RM35, eight hours), Jerantut (RM17, five hours), Mersing (RM17.50, 4½ hours) and Kota Bharu (RM42, 10 hours). Luggage deposit at Melaka Sentral is RM2 per bag. There is also an accommodation reservation counter for hotels in Melaka, a money changer and restaurants. **Luxury buses** (☎ 645 3218) also depart once daily (RM22, 4½ hours) to Singapore from the Century Mahkota Hotel (p155).

Car

Car-hire prices begin at around RM145 per day (RM2000 per month) for a Proton Wira 1.5L automatic; prices are inclusive of insurance and tax. If you're driving, Melaka's one-way traffic system and scattered traffic requires patience. Try **Hawk** (☎ 283 7878; 52 Jln Cempaka, Taman Seri Cempaka, Peringgit Jaya) opposite Melaka Sentral.

Taxi

Long-distance taxis leave from Melaka Sentral. Whole-taxi rates include KL (RM155), Kuala Lumpur International Airport (RM140), Johor Bahru (RM250) and Mersing (RM250).

Train

The nearest train station is 38km north of Melaka at **Tampin** (☎ 441 1034) on the main north–south line from KL to Singapore. Taxis from Melaka cost around RM50.

GETTING AROUND

Melaka is easily explored on foot, but a useful service is town bus 17, which runs every 15 minutes from Melaka Sentral to the centre of town, past the huge Mahkota Parade Shopping Complex, to Taman Melaka Raya (40 sen) and on to Medan Portugis (80 sen).

Bicycles can be hired at some guesthouses and hotels for around RM10 a day; there are also a few bike-hire outfits around town, including **Jin Fu Shin** (55 Jln Parameswara; per day RM6; 9.30am-7pm).

Taking to Melaka's streets by trishaw is a popular tourist option. Competition among the old drivers is keen and their vehicles are becoming increasingly kitsch, festooned with flashing lights, plastic garlands of flowers, gaudy parasols and bells – a bit like aging mods. See p151 for more. By the hour they should cost about RM35 to RM40, or RM15 for any one-way trip within the town, but you'll have to bargain.

Taxis should cost around RM10 to RM12 for a trip anywhere around town with a 50% surcharge between 1am and 6am.

AROUND MELAKA

Melaka state sits demurely in the shadow of its namesake city and consists of some peaceful off-the-beaten track *kampung* as well as two fabricated and arguably tacky resort areas popular with Malaysian and Singaporean tourists. Most of the sights outside Melaka city can be visited on a day trip from town although staying in Alor Gajah or at Tanjung Bidara will introduce you to a sleepy, village Melaka unavailable in the capital.

AYER KEROH

About 15km northeast of Melaka, Ayer Keroh (also spelled Air Keroh) has several contrived tourist attractions that are largely deserted on weekdays. Kids will like the lushly landscaped **Melaka Zoo** (adult/child RM7/4, night zoo adult/child RM10/5; 9am-6pm daily, night zoo 8-11pm Fri & Sat) with plenty of shady, open spaces and a playground close to the entrance. It's the second-largest zoo in the country (with 200 different species) and the animals' conditions aren't bad compared with many Asian zoos. The best time to go is at night when the nocturnal animals awaken; take the Friday- and Saturday-night shuttle bus (RM12) that picks up at larger hotels in Melaka city. It's also possible to volunteer at the zoo by cleaning cages and helping out with educational activities; those curious should contact the education unit at education@zoomelaka.org.my.

Just across from the zoo is the **Butterfly & Reptile Sanctuary** (adult/child RM5/3; 9am-6pm), which has a collection of exotic creepy crawlies, snakes and some sad crocodiles at the reptile park. The highlight are the free-flying local butterflies that flutter about the gardens.

But the main attraction in Ayer Keroh is the **Taman Mini Malaysia/Asean** (adult/child RM4/2; 9am-6pm), a large theme park that has examples of traditional houses from all 13 Malaysian states, as well as neighbouring Asian countries. Also here is **Hutan Rekreasi Air Keroh** (Air Keroh Recreational Forest; admission free), part secondary jungle and part landscaped park with paved trails, a 250m canopy walk, picnic areas and a forestry museum.

It's a pricey decision to stay in Ayer Keroh. The best of the area's resorts is **INB Resort** (☎ 553 3023; www.inbresort.com; d/f RM90/160;), which has tidy air-con villas arranged on pleasant grounds with a good pool. Prices go up during weekends, holidays and high season.

Ayer Keroh can be reached on town bus 19 from Melaka (RM1, 30 minutes), or a taxi will cost around RM30.

PULAU BESAR

The small island of Pulau Besar, southeast of Melaka and 5km off the coast, is a popular weekend getaway, with a few historic graves and reminders of the Japanese occupation during WWII, but the main reason to come here is for the clean white-sand beaches. The water is a little clearer than on the mainland (but remember this is still the polluted Strait of Melaka) and the hilly island is cloaked in greenery with jungle walks.

A HAVEN FOR HAWKSBILLS

Environmentalists went into a tizzy when it was announced that Pulau Upeh, a 2.8-hectare island 3.2km off of the coast of Melaka, was for sale. The weed-covered island might not be a beach-laden beauty, but it's the second most important nesting ground for the hawksbill turtle on the Malay peninsula. The good news is that the Malaysian government wants to buy Pulau Upeh and turn it into a turtle sanctuary; the bad news is that all the bureaucratic red tape to buy the island could take years. During this time poachers could decimate the easy-to-reach, unprotected island's turtle population.

While Peninsular Malaysia has lost nearly all of its once-numerous leatherback turtles (recorded nestings in the region now hover around 10 per year), hope remains for the hawksbill turtle. With only 15,000 female hawksbill turtles left worldwide (according to the US Fish & Wildlife Service), about 1000 hawksbills nest in Malaysia, one-third of which lay on beaches around Melaka.

The intrepid voyagers make a perilous journey year after year through the debris, oil spills and ship traffic of the Strait of Melaka, yet their real enemy awaits on the beach. The Malaccan people have been harvesting turtle eggs throughout known memory and they believe that eating them increases male virility and can protect the health of a fetus in utero. A recent study concluded that over 70% of Malaccan children living near turtle beaches had tasted turtle eggs. The World Wide Fund for Nature Malaysia has begun community projects sensitising local communities to the turtle's plight but also offering cash (RM1.30 per egg) to harvesters if they bring eggs to their hatchery. It's asked that only half the eggs are brought in while the other half can be consumed by the population.

Turtle tourism is not practised as yet in Melaka. If by chance you are offered a chance to watch nesting turtles, go in very small groups, be very still and quiet, keep at least 2m away from the animals, don't use flash cameras or lights, and remain behind the turtles where they can't see you. Use the same precautions during hatchings.

To find out how you can help with hawksbill turtle projects, go to the website for the World Wide Fund for Nature Malaysia at www.wwfmalaysia.org.

At the time of research the island's only hotel, **Chandek Kura Resort** (☎ 295 5899; d/tr RM118/138;), had closed down with unclear plans for the future. The only available lodging option nowadays is in a tent, which you can pitch at the **camp site** (☎ 281 8007; per person with tent rental RM20) next to the resort; call before arrival to secure a site. A handful of basic *kedai kopi* (coffee shops) can be found nearby.

Boats (adult/child RM12/9, 25 minutes) depart from the jetty at **Anjung Batu** (☎ 261 0492) at 8am, 10am, noon, 2.30pm, 5pm and 6.30pm (last boat returns at 7pm). The jetty is several kilometres past the old pier at Umbai, southeast of Melaka city.

Pulau Besar can also be reached by chartering a boat from the jetty behind the tourist office on Jln Kota in Melaka city. From Umbai you'll need to charter a boat from enterprises such as **Azrin Boat Services** (☎ 019-307 7775) for RM100 return; service is 24 hours. You can reach either jetty in less than an hour by the local bus 2 from Melaka.

ALOR GAJAH

Just off the road to KL, 24km north of Melaka, is the crisp, countryside town of Alor Gajah. In the town centre is peaceful and grassy Alor Gajah Sq, which is bordered by a charming array of gaily painted and aging shophouses. It's hard to believe that only 10 minutes' drive from this honest Malay town is A'Famosa Resort, a place Malaysia Tourism loves to tout as the region's foremost leisure and holiday stop; if you're into man-made and cleaned-up versions of the natural world, don't miss it. Most Melaka–KL buses stop in Alor Gajah so it's possible to make a short stop here if you're willing to change buses. A taxi to A'Famosa from the bus station should cost around RM15.

Sights

Right in Alor Gajah Sq is the **Museum of Custom & Tradition** (admission RM1; 9am-5.30pm Wed-Thu, Sat & Sun, 9am-12.15pm & 2.45-5.30pm Fri), which exhibits a modest collection of Malay wedding customs, bridal gifts and ceremonial rites. Ask in the museum about the tombs of British soldiers killed in 1832 situated in the primary school just off the square, and someone may escort you over for a quick inspection.

Half an hour away from historic Melaka and one hour from KL, the 520-hectare **A'Famosa Resort** (www.afamosa.com) is an all-encompassing resort popular with Malay and Singaporean tourists. Even though the whole place is contrived and cheesy, you'd be hard pressed not to have fun at the 8-hectare **Water World** (adult/child RM30/23; 11am-7pm Mon & Wed-Fri, 9am-8pm Sat & Sun), which has two seven-story-high speed slides, a tube ride and even a man-made beach with a wave pool. Less adrenalin-oriented activities for families include a tot's activity pool and a giant family raft ride. **Animal World Safari** (admission with all rides & shows adult/child RM59/49; 9am-6pm) spreads over another 61 hectares. The animal shows have an array of critters dressed in human clothing and doing human activities (for example an orang-utan that plays golf) and are not something that animal lovers will enjoy; the safari bus ride only takes half an hour but is fun for kids. A special rate of adult/child RM73/59 gets you into both the Animal World Safari and Water World. Also within the resort is a 27-hole **golf course** that is rated in the country's top 10.

Sleeping & Eating

You can stay at **A'Famosa Resort** (522 0777; www.afamosa.com; hotel r from RM158, villas from RM488, condotel from RM198) in either the standard hotel, large villas (three to five bedrooms) designed for groups and families, or 'condotels' (one to three bedrooms) with sweeping views over the resort. Prices go up on weekends, holidays and during peak season.

A more authentic way to visit Alor Gajah is with a visit or stay at the upscale antitheses of A'Famosa, the over-the-top lush **Desa Paku House & Garden** (556 2639; mush@tm.net.my; Alor Gajah; d incl 4 meals per day RM750) about 2km from the village of Alor Gajah. Retired Royal Malaysian Air Force officer Mushlim Musa has turned his attention away from the sky and very deeply into plants, to the point that his spiritual philosophies have become intertwined with his garden. His endless work on and passion for the fruits, rare flowers, blooming heliconias (200 of the world's 500 varieties are represented here), graceful palms and lazy water gardens make the entire jungle beam with health. The house is no less grand and contains some spectacular antiques and fascinating painted tiles within its distinctly Malaccan hardwood walls. Rooms are available in the main house or in a secluded bungalow bordering one of

SPICES TO OIL: MODERN-DAY PIRACY IN THE STRAIT OF MELAKA

Piracy has been rife in the Strait of Melaka since before legendary Prince Parameswara (see the boxed text, p136) founded Melaka with his faithful pirate crew in the late 1400s. The geography of the Strait of Melaka, which creates a shipping bottleneck among thousands of islands, makes the region perfect for piracy – bandits can simply disappear beyond the sea. Today, the strait's importance is no less than it was in the day of the spice trade and is considered as economically significant as the Suez or Panama Canals. Linking three of the world's most populous nations (India, Indonesia and China), the 805km-long route carries between one fifth and one quarter of the world's sea trade including one quarter of all sea-transported oil; in 2003 there were an estimated 11 million barrels per day passing through the Strait of Melaka. Traffic is expected to expand as oil consumption rises in China.

While pirate attacks in the strait have been dropping recently (50 attacks in 2006 down from 79 in 2005), the figures had been steadily climbing in previous years (from only 25 in 1994 to 220 in the year 2000). By mid-2007, 42 acts of piracy had already been documented. The pirates are estimated to hail primarily from Indonesia and the often-violent attacks are aimed at petty theft of ship's stores, cash, motor parts and the crew's personal items. While these attacks stem from the poor economic conditions in Indonesia, more rare, organised attacks that target the ships' cargo are now considered acts of terrorism.

In 2004, Malaysia, Singapore and Indonesia began to coordinate their naval patrols of the area. More recently, antipiracy patrols have gone high-tech with security systems, which include real-time ship-locator devices, now required for vessels over 500 gross tons.

Most pirate attacks take place in Indonesian waters, and they are never a threat to visitors to Melaka.

the garden's many lotus-filled ponds. A garden and house tour (per person RM50; 9am to noon or 3pm to 6pm, by reservation) is available for a minimum of 10 people and includes morning or afternoon tea with a selection of Malay cakes. If the rest of the food here is on par with the delicately perfect Malay cake we tried, it wouldn't be hard eating the four meals a day that are included in the room rate. Remember that this is a homestay in the middle of a tamed jungle, so don't expect an insect-free, hotel-like experience. There is no public transport to Desa Paku so you'll need to have your own means of transportation or else organise a taxi. To get there from Melaka, go through Alor Gajah town, straight through the roundabout, and then take a right at the Masjid Tanah junction. After about a kilometre, turn right at the sign for Kampung Paku. After about 600m turn left into a gate, then take your first right.

TANJUNG BIDARA

To really get away from it all, head to lovely white-sand Tanjung Bidara, about 30km northwest of Melaka. It's well away from the main highway, requiring you to take back roads through rice paddies and farms to get to the shore. While this is a popular weekend trip for Malaccan families, it's deserted midweek except for maybe one or two fishermen casting from the beach. There's a large food court at the main entrance to the beach but only one valiant stall is open outside of Saturday and Sunday. The water lapping on the fine sand is brown with sediment and pollution so it's not the best place for swimming, but it is fun to sit against the jungle and watch the massive freighters head down the famous Strait of Melaka.

The main beach area is at **Tanjung Bidara Beach Resort** (☎ 384 2990; fax 384 2995; tw Sun-Thu RM70, Fri & Sat RM100, chalets Thu-Sun RM130, Fri & Sat RM150;), a quiet, relaxing but musty resort with a small swimming pool and restaurant.

Further budget accommodation is strung out over several kilometres along the beach, broken only by a large military camp. In the colourful, friendly Malay village of Kampung Balik Batu, about 20km south of Tanjung Bidara, are several simple beachside chalet guesthouses.

Buses 42 and 47 from Melaka go to Masjid Tanah, from where a taxi to Tanjung Bidara Beach Resort or Kampung Balik Batu costs RM7.

Penang

Affectionately known as the Pearl of the Orient, Penang, like the finest of its namesake gem has layers of multihued depth. Georgetown attracts tourists with its eclectic colonial architecture, temples and museums, lively Chinese culture, nonstop shopping and array of food. But don't forget the rest of the island where you'll find Penang National Park, Malaysia's newest and smallest national park with its secluded monkey beaches, a mainstream resort town on the northern coast, Penang Hill with its funicular railway and colonial hill station, and the crowded, brightly painted Kek Lok Si Temple – the largest Buddhist shrine in the country.

If you take a ride around the island, you'll go through sprawling urban mediocrity that suddenly gives way to primary rainforests, rocky coastline dotted with white-sand beaches, fruit plantations and rickety fishing villages. You could choose a tour where you'll be led through all the major sights or spend a day or two meandering through forgotten corners with your own transport. The beaches aren't as spectacular as on Malaysia's east-coast islands or even just north on Pulau Langkawi, but they do offer a peaceful respite from the city.

The strip of mainland coast known as Seberang Perai (or Province Wellesley) is the mainland portion of the state that many people don't even know is Penang. There's little to do other than hop on an onward train or catch the few sights of Butterworth – unless you take the local fishermen's ferry to Penang Island, a Malay side of Penang that few tourists ever see.

Fast and frequent flights make it possible to make a day trip to Penang from Kuala Lumpur (KL), but you'd miss much of what the island has to offer. For a more leisurely trip, come by bus or train and spend a few days soaking up the refreshingly unhurried island atmosphere.

HIGHLIGHTS

- Eating at Georgetown's myriad **hawker stalls** (p194)
- Hiking to white-sand monkey beaches in **Penang National Park** (p207) and enjoying the rainforest in **Teluk Bahang Forest Reserve** (p206)
- Grooving to Bollywood tunes, dining on banana-leaf meals or shopping for saris in Georgetown's **Little India** (p183)
- Exploring the baroque **Khoo Kongsi** (p181)
- Joining the mob of tourists visiting **Kek Lok Si Temple** (p202) and taking the cable car to the statue of Kuan Yin
- Touring Chinatown's **Cheong Fatt Tze Mansion** (p181) to learn about its original Chinese merchant-owner
- Taking a drive through Penang Island's sleepy southern **fishing villages** (p204)

Penang National Park
Teluk Bahang Forest Preserve
Georgetown
Kek Lok Si Temple
Southern Fishing Villages

TELEPHONE CODE: 04	POPULATION: 1.31 MILLION	AREA: 1031 SQ KM

HISTORY

Little is known of Penang's early history. Chinese seafarers were aware of the island, which they called Betelnut Island, as far back as the 15th century, but it appears to have been uninhabited. An English merchant-adventurer called Captain James Lancaster, swung by in 1593 and at this time Penang was still an unpopulated jungly wilderness. It wasn't until the early 1700s that colonists arrived from Sumatra and established settlements at Batu Uban and the area now covered by southern Georgetown. The island came under the control of the sultan of Kedah, but in 1771 the sultan signed the first agreement with the British East India Company handing them trading rights in exchange for military assistance against Siam.

Fifteen years later Captain Francis Light, on behalf of the East India Company, took possession of Penang which was formally signed over in 1791. Light renamed it Prince of Wales Island, as the acquisition date fell on the prince's birthday. It's said that Light fired silver dollars from his ship's cannons into the jungle to encourage his labourers to hack back the undergrowth for settlement.

Unbeknownst to the sultan of Kedah, Light had promised military protection without getting the OK from the East India Company. When Kedah was later attacked by Siam, no aid was given. The sultan tried to take back the island but was unsuccessful. His fumbled attempt only resulted in more land, a strip of the mainland now called Seberang Perai, being ceded to Light in 1800. The sultan did however manage to bargain for rental fees; the East India company agreed to an annual honorarium of 10,000 Spanish dollars payable to the sultan of Kedah. Through the years the amount has increased and today the state of Penang still pays the sultan of Kedah RM18,800 per year.

Light permitted new arrivals to claim as much land as they could clear, and this, together with a duty-free port and an atmosphere of liberal tolerance, quickly attracted settlers from all over Asia. By the turn of the 18th century Penang was home to over 10,000 people.

The local economy was slow to develop, as mostly European planters set up spice plantations – slow-growing crops requiring a high initial outlay. Although the planters later turned to sugar and coconut, agriculture was hindered by a limited labour force.

In 1805 Penang became a presidency government, on a par with the cities of Madras and Bombay in India, and so gained a much more sophisticated administrative structure.

Penang briefly became the capital of the Straits Settlements (which included Melaka and Singapore) in 1826, until it was superseded by the more thriving Singapore. By the middle of the 19th century, Penang

TURNING JAPANESE?

The Japanese began bombing the island of Penang on 8 December 1941; after nine days of nonstop air raids the island surrendered. When the schools reopened, they taught only in Japanese, cinemas played only Japanese films and amusement parks were reborn as gambling halls. Many public buildings and private houses were taken over and rice was rationed. Soon consumer goods became hard to come by and the Japanese declared that Penang's currency was no longer legal. The new currency brought inflation and the development of a black market. Many Penang residents fended off starvation by growing their own fruits and vegetables and keeping chickens.

But all this was nothing compared to the terror that the new regime instilled in the people of Penang. The Japanese were accused of attempting to purge the island of its Chinese population, and the rigidity and militancy of the regime was difficult for everyone. In the early days rape was commonplace, and officers would spontaneously order beheadings as well as a slew of horrific tortures. Men were sent away to do forced labour on the Burma Railway in Thailand (also called the Death Railway) where many died of starvation, disease and overwork.

While the reign of terror was meant to scare the populace into accepting Japanese rule and culture, it had the opposite affect. An underground resistance, made up primarily of Chinese and Malay members of the communist party, quietly flourished. The shattered economy was no aid to the Japanese war effort. With the bombing of Hiroshima and Nagasaki in 1945, the Japanese surrendered and the British limped back to re-establish their shaken authority.

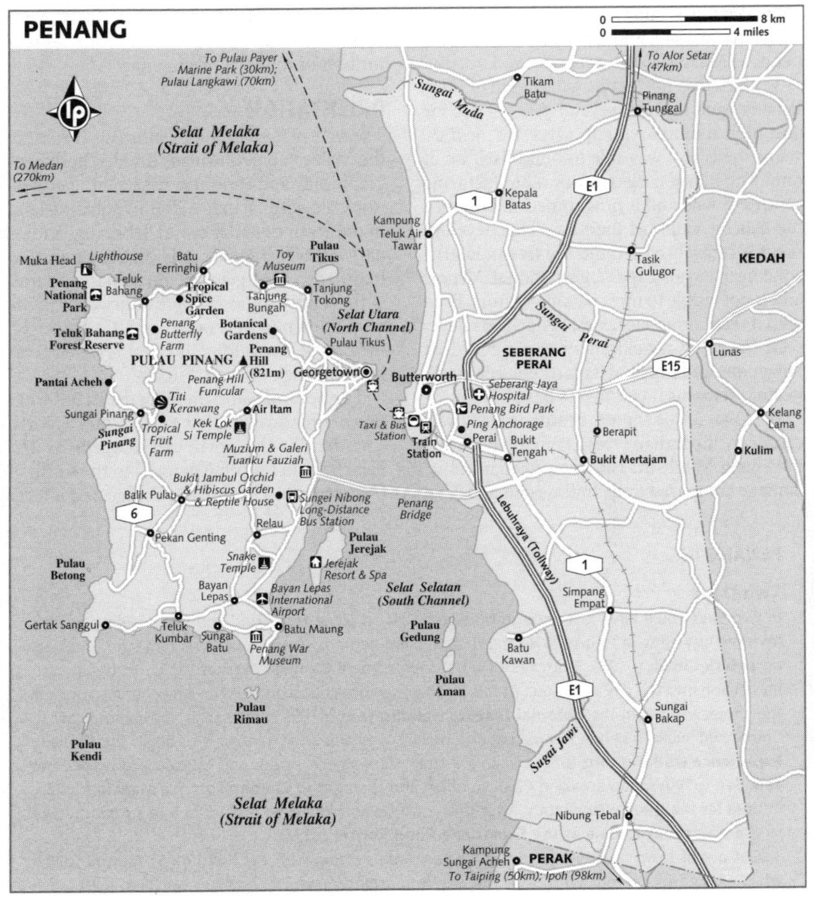

had become a major player in the Chinese opium trade, which provided more than half of the colony's revenue. It was a dangerous, rough-edged place, notorious for its brothels and gambling dens, all run by Chinese secret societies.

In 1867 the simmering violence came to a head when large-scale rioting broke out between two rival Chinese secret societies: the Cantonese-speaking Ghee Hin and the Hakka-speaking Hai San, who had each allied themselves with similar Malay groups. Today's Cannon St is so-named from the holes in the ground from cannon balls that had been fired from Khoo Kongsi (p181).

During the early 20th century the romance of Penang attracted visits by Somerset Maugham, Joseph Conrad, Rudyard Kipling and Herman Hesse.

There was little action in Penang during WWI, but WWII was a different story. When it became evident that the Japanese would attack, Penang's Europeans were immediately evacuated leaving behind a largely defenceless population. Japan took over the island on 19 December 1941, only 12 days after the attack on Pearl Harbour in the US. The following three and a half years were the darkest of Penang's history (see opposite).

Things were not the same after the war. The local impression of the invincibility of the British had been irrevocably tainted and the end of British imperialism seemed imminent. The Straits Settlements were dissolved in

1946, Penang became a state of the Federation of Malaya in 1948, and it became one of independent Malaysia's 13 states in 1963.

With its free-port status withdrawn in 1969, Penang went through several years of decline and high unemployment. Over the next 20 years, the island was able to build itself up as one of the largest electronics manufacturing centres of Asia and is now sometimes dubbed the 'Silicon Valley of the East'. This development is centralised around the free industrial zone near Bayan Lapas International Airport and is not visible to most passing visitors. Even with its economic successes, Penang has never seen the rapid development experienced by Singapore, and much of its early colonial architecture remains intact to this day.

In 2004, 33 of the 68 deaths in Malaysia caused by the Indian Ocean tsunami occurred in Penang. While the island received minimal damage compared to its Indonesian and Thai neighbours, it's estimated that the disaster cost the island's agriculture and fisheries sector tens of millions of ringgit.

ORIENTATION

The state of Penang, on the northwest coast of the Malaysian peninsula is divided both geographically and administratively into two sections: Penang Island, a 293km square island in the Strait of Melaka, and Seberang Perai, a narrow 760km square strip on the peninsular mainland. Georgetown, on Penang Island, is the state capital, while Butterworth is the largest town in Seberang Perai. Confusingly, the city of Geogetown is often referred to as just 'Penang', or even 'Pinang'.

The body of water dividing the island from the mainland is called Selat Utara (North Channel) to the north of Georgetown and Selat Selatan (South Channel) to the south of Georgetown. The Penang Bridge and a ferry

PENANG IN...

Two Days

In two days you'll have just enough time to fill up on some tasty food and get a feeling for this textured city. Stay in Georgetown the first day and begin by fuelling up on a dim sum breakfast on **Lebuh Cintra** (p195). From here walk through **Kuala Kangsar Market** (p195) to begin your immersion into the city's clamour. At this point you might choose to head up Jln Penang to browse the shops and begin the **Colonial District walking tour** (p185) in reverse. If you'd rather get to Chinatown, walk to Lebuh Pitt via Lebuh Chulia, Love Lane and Lg Stewart to begin the **Chinese Experience walking tour** (p186). Take a trishaw from wherever you end up to arrive by noon at **Teik Sen** (p196) for an amazing Chinese lunch and then get to **Cheong Fatt Tze Mansion** (p181) in time for the three o'clock tour. After this you'll be knackered, so rest up before strolling down to the waterfront to dine at the **Esplanade Food Centre** (p194).

Get out of town on day two to the Air Itam area starting with the **Kek Lok Si Temple** (p202) which you can lose yourself in for most of the morning. Have lunch at the excellent vegetarian restaurant on the premises. Next take a taxi (recommended) or take the hot and sticky 3km walk to the base of **Penang Hill** (p202) to ride the funicular railway to the top. Spend the rest of the afternoon strolling the trails in the cool air and watch the sunset from the top of the hill. That night walk around boisterous **Little India** (p183) and gorge yourself on spicy curries.

One Week

One week gives you much more time to savour Georgetown and to get out to see the rest of the island. Follow the two-day itinerary then stay in Georgetown again on the third day to do whichever walking tour you missed on day one. Have a tiffin lunch at **Sarkies Corner** (p198) then visit the **Pinang Peranakan Mansion** (p183) in the afternoon. For dinner head out to **Gurney Drive** (p194) to eat hawker food and shop the night away. For the next three days explore the rest of the island including **Penang National Park** (p207), **Batu Ferringhi** (p209) and the **southern fishing villages** (p204). Consider spending a night or two in Batu Ferringhi during this time. On your last day spend the morning at the **Botanical Gardens** (p203) then shop all afternoon along Jln Penang or at any of the city's many **shopping malls** (p201). Finish your trip with a luxurious dinner at **Thirty Two** (p198) or eat on the street with the locals at **Restoran Sup Hameed** (p197).

TOO BIG FOR ITS BRIDGES

Before 14 September 1985 Penang's only link to the mainland was an overcrowded ferry. Today an average of 70,000 people cross the 13.5km Penang Bridge, one of the longest bridges in the world. With its maximum capacity of 100,000 people per day being exceeded regularly, the bridge is now being expanded from four lanes to six and the work is expected to be completed by June 2008. Twelve new toll booths will be built to make sure traffic flows just as quickly.

Even though this increases the bridge's capacity by 50%, those in the know say this won't be enough to meet Penang's rapid development needs. Plans are already underway to build a second bridge linking Batu Maung at the southeastern tip of the island to Batu Kawan on the mainland. Construction was expected to begin in late 2007 and take five years.

link the 3km stretch between Butterworth and Georgetown.

Penang Island is a somewhat turtle-shaped island with a mostly forested interior, its highest point being the western peak of Penang Hill (821m). The coastal plains are narrow, the most extensive part forming a triangular peninsula in the northeast where Georgetown, the state capital is located. Many of Penang's sights such as the Botanical Gardens and Kek Lok Si Temple are located in this flat area between Georgetown and Penang Hill.

The coastal area around the island heading east from Georgetown is mostly urban, past the Penang Bridge and towards Bayan Lepas International Airport at the island's southeastern corner. From here, pass fishing villages and rural towns up to the island's northwestern point, where you'll find the walkable Teluk Bahang Forest Reserve and the 2300 hectare Penang National Park. Penang's best beaches are along the north coast at the resort town of Batu Ferringhi, only 13km from Georgetown.

There are a number of small islets off the coast of Penang, the biggest being Pulau Jerejak which is located in the narrow channel between Penang Island and the mainland.

FESTIVALS & EVENTS

All the Malay festivals are celebrated in Penang, but with this island's extraordinary enthusiasm. Current events are listed in the *Penang Tourist Newspaper*. For more on festivals and events, see p219.

January–February

Thaipusam This masochistic festival is celebrated as fervently as in Singapore and KL, but without quite the same crowds. The Sri Mariamman temple (p183) and Nattukotai Chettiar and Waterfall Hilltop temples (p184) are the main centres of activity in Penang.

Chinese New Year Celebrated with particular gusto in Penang. The Khoo Kongsi is done up for the event, and dance troupes and Chinese-opera groups perform all over the city. On the night before the 15th day of the new year, a fire ceremony takes place at Tua Pek Kong temple (p184).

Chap Goh Meh The 15th day of the new year celebrations, during which local girls throw oranges into the sea; see the boxed text p172. Traditionally the girls would chant 'throw a good orange, get a good husband' while local boys watched and later contacted their dream girl through matchmakers. The new year is also one of the only times to see Baba-Nonya performances of *dondang sayang* (spontaneous and traditional love ballads).

May–August

Penang International Floral Festival Held when many of the trees are flowering; experts show keen horticulturalists around (May/June).

Penang International Dragon Boat Festival A colourful and popular regatta (May/June) featuring traditional dragon boats.

Penang Beach Carnival In Batu Ferringhi (June); this carnival is highlighted by traditional sporting events such as *gas uri* (top spinning) and *sepak takraw* (a ball game played over a net, much like badminton but with the players using their feet).

Penang Food & Cultural Festivals Highlights the best of Penang's multi-ethnic heritage (August).

Hungry Ghosts Festival (Phor Thor) The gates of hell are said to be opened every year on the 15th day of the seventh month of the Chinese lunar calendar. To appease the hungry ghosts, Penangites set out food offerings and endeavour to entertain them with puppet shows and streetside Chinese-opera performances. This is a magical time to be in the city (August).

September–December

Lantern Festival Celebrated by eating moon cakes, the Chinese sweets once used to carry secret messages for underground rebellions in ancient China (mid-September).

Deepavali The Hindu Festival of Lights is celebrated with music and dancing at venues in Little India (October).

HOLY ORANGES *Celeste Brash*

Penang might be renowned for its festivals but that doesn't mean that events are the same as they were in ancient times. Case in point: on the 15th day of the Chinese New Year (Chap Goh Meh) it's the tradition for unmarried maidens to throw oranges into the sea so that they'll have luck finding a good husband (see p171). Feeling lucky to be in town researching the area at this time, I thought this would be the perfect chance to catch a glorious Penang cultural moment. It didn't turn out exactly as I expected.

By the time I reached Pitt St it was a chaotic mass of bodies. A tour bus covered with cartoon cut outs, feather-like garlands and sparkles, and blasting cheesy techno music, arrived on the scene and a group of beautiful young Chinese women dressed in glittering dresses descended into the crowd. The girls pressed their way through a group doing a dragon dance and I let myself be moved towards the sea with the human tide of photosnappers and babbling families.

Suddenly a group of older Chinese men dressed in sombre grey suits appeared from out of nowhere with military escorts. The crowd went nuts and cleared a red carpet–sized avenue for them to pass. Eventually we all stopped around a humble tent that had a funnel of netting strung across the top and a bunch of big blue buckets filled with water in the middle.

With the elegant women sidelined as onlookers, the old men began throwing oranges into the funnel net on the tent – the oranges would fall through the middle and, if tosser was lucky, it would plunk into a bucket. It looked just like one of those carnival games where you can win a giant stuffed St Bernard. When the men had gotten their share of oranges into the buckets, some boys passed fruit around to onlookers and everyone bombarded the tent, as if it were an oncoming flu bug, with citrus. Then everyone left. So much for beautiful maidens (who I don't think even got any oranges), but I could only laugh about never knowing what to expect from Southeast Asia.

Penang Island Jazz Festival Features local and international artists at Batu Ferringhi (November–December).

Pesta Pulau Penang (Penang Island Festival) This annual festival (November–December) features various cultural events, parades and a funfair.

GETTING THERE & AWAY

The mainland strip of Seberang Perai is easily accessed by road and rail from other parts of the peninsula. Butterworth is the transport hub, and the departure point for ferries to Penang Island, which is also linked to the mainland by road-bridge. Buses to all major towns on the peninsula leave from both Penang Island and Butterworth. Georgetown also has ferry links to Langkawi and to Medan in Indonesia, and an airport with regular flights to KL, Singapore, Johor Bahru and Langkawi.

Air

DOMESTIC FLIGHTS

There are several daily connections between Penang and KL (one-way from RM60) – Malaysia Airlines has more flights but Air Asia is far cheaper, particularly if you book ahead. There are also flights to Langkawi (one-way from RM99).

Domestic flights to/from Penang are available through:

Air Asia (☎ 644 8701; www.airasia.com; ground fl, Kompleks Komtar)

Firefly (☎ 03-7845 4543; www.fireflyz.com.my; Bayan Lepas International Airport)

Malaysia Airlines (☎ 262 0011; www.malaysiaairlines.com; Menara KWSP, Jl Sultan Ahmad Shah)

INTERNATIONAL FLIGHTS

Penang is a major centre for cheap airline tickets, although international air fares are less competitive than they used to be. Sample fares: Singapore Airlines to Singapore RM393, Thai Airways to Bangkok RM900, and Malaysia Airlines to Sydney RM2650. Fares change from day to day so check locally for the latest prices – Air Asia has bargain flights to Bangkok from just RM186 online if you book well in advance.

Airline offices that have international connections to Penang Island are:

Air Asia (☎ 644 8701; www.airasia.com; ground fl, Kompleks Komtar)

Cathay Pacific (☎ 226 0411; www.cathaypacific.com; Menara Boustead, 39 Jln Sultan Ahmad Shaw)
Firefly (☎ 03-7845 4543; www.fireflyz.com.my; Bayan Lepas International Airport)
Malaysia Airlines (☎ 262 0011; www.malaysiaairlines.com; Menara KWSP, Jl Sultan Ahmad Shah)
Singapore Airlines (☎ 226 6211; www.singaporeair.com; Wisma Penang Gardens, Jl Sultan Ahmad Shah)
Thai Airways International (THAI; ☎ 226 6000; www.thaiair.com; Wisma Central, 41 Jl Macalister)

Boat

Travellers can skip over to the Indonesian island of Sumatra from Penang Island via ferry. There are ferries each way in the morning, and times can change, but generally ferries depart Georgetown at 8.30am and return at 10.30am (one-way/return RM150/250); the trip takes 4½ to five hours. The boats leave from Georgetown's Swettenham jetty and land in Belawan where the remaining journey to Medan is completed by bus (included in the price). Buy tickets the day before to verify departure times. Upon arriving at Belawan port, most nationalities will need to pay a fee of US$25 per person for a month-long Indonesian visa.

Langkawi Ferry Service (LFS; Map p176; ☎ 264 3088; 8 Lebuh King, Georgetown) has offices near the Tourism Malaysia office in Georgetown. It runs daily ferries from Georgetown to Kuah on Langkawi (one-way/return RM50/90, two to 2½ hours). Boats leave at 8am and 8.30am; the second service takes slightly longer and calls in at Pulau Payer first, but you won't be able to disembark unless you're on a diving or snorkelling package (see p185). Boats return from Langkawi at 2.30pm and 5.30pm. Try to book a few days in advance to ensure a seat.

If you're arriving by sailboat, Penang's old Church Street Pier has been completely overhauled to become the **Tanjong City Marina** (www.tgctmarina.com.my), a lovely full-service docking area, including immigration services, with 102 berths and good security.

Bus

Long-distance bus services leave Georgetown from the express bus station on Jln Sungei Nibong, just to the south of Penang Bridge. While it may be more convenient to buy your tickets from travel agents on Lebuh Chulia or some guesthouses and hotels, it's a safer bet to buy your ticket in person at the bus-company offices at the station.

From Sungei Nibong there are several daily buses to KL (RM27, five hours), as well as less frequent buses to Melaka (RM35, seven hours, two daily), Kota Bharu (RM36, seven and a half hours; one daily), Kuala Terengganu (RM39, 10 hours, two daily) and elsewhere – book well in advance. There are five daily buses to Tanah Rata (RM30) in the Cameron Highlands.

Minibus 25 runs regularly between the more central Komtar bus station and Sungei Nibong.

Many more buses leave from next to the mainland ferry terminal in Butterworth, and a few long-distance buses also leave from other parts of Georgetown. **Newsia Tours & Travel** (☎ 261 7933; 35-36 Pengkalan Weld) is a major agent.

SINGAPORE

From the Komtar Bus Station: Singapore (RM50, 10 hours, two daily), to Johor Bharu's Larkin Bus Station (RM40, nine hours, one daily)

THAILAND

From the bus station at Komtar, there are also bus and minibus services to Thailand, including Hat Yai (RM22), Phuket (RM60), Ko Phi-Phi (including boat, RM68), Ko Samui (including boat, RM55) and even Bangkok (RM90), though it's a long haul. The minibuses usually don't go directly to some destinations; you'll probably be dumped for a change of vehicle in Hat Yai or Surat Thani, sometimes with significant waiting times. It can be better to buy your ticket from a Thai guesthouse that contracts directly with a minibus agency, instead of from bucket shops on Lebuh Chulia. Then, in the case of your minibus showing up two hours late, or not at all, you have someone to hold responsible. However, you might be able to get cheaper tickets if you buy directly at the bus station.

Taxi

Long-distance taxis operate from a depot beside the Butterworth ferry terminal on the mainland. Typical whole-taxi fares are higher than anywhere else in Peninsular Malaysia, and include such rip-offs as KL RM300, Ipoh

RM180, Kota Bharu RM300, Lumut RM200 and Taiping RM180.

Train

The **train station** (Map p169; ☎ 323 7962) is next to the jetty and bus station in Butterworth, on the mainland. There is a nightly train to KL (economy/2nd class/berth RM17/38/48), arriving the next morning. In the opposite direction there is a daily train to Hat Yai, Thailand (economy/2nd class/berth RM19/27/68) early in the morning which arrives mid-morning Thai time (Thailand's one hour behind). There is also an international express train leaving Butterworth in the early afternoon which arrives in Hat Yai in the evening and in Bangkok around noon the next day. Fares and timetables change rapidly, so check with the station or the railway company website (www.ktmb.com.my) before you travel.

Advance bookings on long-distance trains can be made at the **Railway Booking Office** (Pengkalan Weld), near the Weld Quay terminal – see below for details of how to get to Butterworth; for more information on train services in Malaysia see p235.

GETTING AROUND

Seberang Perai and Penang Island are linked by road-bridge and a 24-hour ferry service. For information about getting around in Georgetown see p201.

Boat

There's a 24-hour ferry service between Georgetown and Butterworth. Ferries take passengers and cars every eight minutes from 6.20am to 9.30pm, every 20 minutes until 11.15pm, and hourly after that until 6.20am. The journey takes 15 minutes. Fares are charged only for the journey from Butterworth to Penang; returning to the mainland is free. The adult fare is RM1.20; cars cost RM7.70 (depending on the size).

Bus

All buses leave from Georgetown (see p201) and go as far as the Bayan Lepas International Airport on the east coast and to Teluk Bahang on the north coast. There are no buses on the west coast of the island.

Buses from Georgetown to other parts of the island are frequent but if you want to stop in several places in one day it's easiest to have your own transport. This is also convenient since the main road does not run along the coast except on the northern side, and you have to leave the main road to get to the small fishing villages and isolated beaches.

USEFUL PENANG BUSES

Penang has streamlined its bus system. In Georgetown, buses can be caught at the Pengkalan Weld stop (Map p176), near the Weld Quay terminal or at Komtar. Most of the buses also have stops along Lebuh Chulia. Useful buses:

- Air Itam U201, U202 or U203
- Batu Ferringhi U105 or U101
- Bayan Lepas Airport U307 and U401
- Penang Hill U204
- Snake Temple U302
- Teluk Bahang U101

CAR

Penang Bridge is one of the longest bridges in Asia at 13.5km. If you drive across to the island there's a RM7.70 toll payable at the toll plaza on the mainland, but no charge to return.

RENTAL

Penang's a good place to rent a car, but you'll probably have to reserve in advance, especially for weekends and holidays or if you need an automatic car. Rates start at around RM100 per day plus insurance but drop for longer rentals. Good deals can be found at smaller agents, though the main companies are also worth trying for special deals.

There are many car-hire companies in Georgetown:

Avis (☎ 643 9633; www.avis.com; Bayan Lepas International Airport)
Budget (☎ 643 6025; www.budget.com; Bayan Lepas International Airport)
Hawk (☎ 881 3886; www.hawkrentacar.com; Bayan Lepas International Airport)
Hertz (Map p176; ☎ 263 5914; www.hertz.com; 38 Lebuh Farquhar)

Motorcycle & Bicycle

You can hire bicycles and motorcycles from many places, including travellers' guesthouses and shops along Lebuh Chulia or out at Batu Ferringhi. It costs RM10 to rent a bicycle, and motorcycles start at RM30 per day. Before heading off on a motorbike just remember that if you don't have a motorcycle licence your travel insurance in all likelihood won't cover you.

Taxi

Outlying sights serviced by taxi from Georgetown include Batu Ferringhi (RM30), Penang Hill/Kek Lok Si Temple (RM20), Pulau Tikus (RM14), the Botanical Gardens (RM20), the Snake Temple (RM30) and Bayan Lepas International Airport (RM38).

GEORGETOWN

It's full of car exhaust and has a marked lack of sidewalks, but Georgetown is able to woo even the most acute cityphobe with its never-ending cultural surprises. Dodge traffic while strolling past Chinese shophouses where folks might be roasting coffee over a fire or sculpting giant incense for a ceremony. Trishaws, peddling tourists and the occasional local, cruise around the maze of chaotic streets and narrow lanes past scenes that look like they've been created for a movie set. Outside the historic centre, soaring skyscrapers and massive shopping complexes gleam high above.

Just when you get the gist of Chinatown, you enter Little India, which is like a street party at night with its twinkling lights, blaring Bollywood music and countless shops with a rainbow of silk saris in the windows and on the streetsides. Blocks away the serious white buildings of the Colonial District sit mutely along the waterfront.

Though each district is distinct, they do overlap; you'll find Chinese temples in Little India and mosques in Chinatown. Along certain streets you'll have your pick of delicious Indian curries, spicy Malay specialities or local Chinese noodle creations all lined up one after the other. Arrive on an empty stomach and graze at will. Between the city's outrageous hawker food and fine restaurants this is the food capital of Malaysia.

HISTORY

Georgetown officially became a city in 1957 (with the status granted by Queen Elizabeth II), making it the first official city in the Federation of Malaya – KL wasn't official until 1972. Ironically, the town's citydom has come into question since Georgetown merged with rural Penang in 1974 to form the Municipal Council of Penang Island. Technically, some argue, the city of Georgetown no longer exists. The debate continues, creating quite a spark among locals, but no conclusion has been reached.

Whatever the documents state, it's fairly obvious that Georgetown is an important dot on the map. The city's (if you care to call it that) true creation was when Captain Francis Light established Georgetown as a fort in 1786; he named the settlement after the Prince of Wales who later became King George IV. While the site was ideal for a port, the terrain (a swamp) was not, so Light and his economically driven men cleared, levelled and filled the area. The fort soon became a trading nexus and the island's population reached 12,000 by 1804.

The town's original boundaries were Lebuh Light, Lebuh Chulia (originally called Malabar St), Lebuh Pitt (now officially called Jln Masjid Kapitan Keling but still referred to as Pitt St) and Lebuh Bishop; for more on confusing street names see Orientation, p177. The warehouses and godowns extended from Lebuh Pantai (Beach St) to the sea. The land around Beach St began to erode away into the 1800s and thus Weld Quay, the new waterfront, was built in the 1880s; commercial buildings sprang up like mushrooms. Today, historical Beach St is dominated by the old buildings of shipping companies, import/exporters and bankers that have been working with port activities for generations.

Thanks to some strict rent controls, Georgetown retained many colonial-era shophouses that make the city such an architectural gem. Unfortunately, the controls were repealed in 2000 and many prewar buildings have given way to generic high-rises. While the city is full of enthusiasts bent on saving its heritage, the local government has few preservation rules or guidelines and risks losing many of its gorgeous old buildings to big business. Even so, the city still has enough ambience to have been voted the most liveable city in Asia by Employment Conditions Abroad Limited (ECA International) in 2007.

In 2006 the federal government announced a plan to build a monorail transit system connecting Georgetown to Tanjung Tokong in the north and Bayan Lepas International Airport in the south. No date has been projected for the completion.

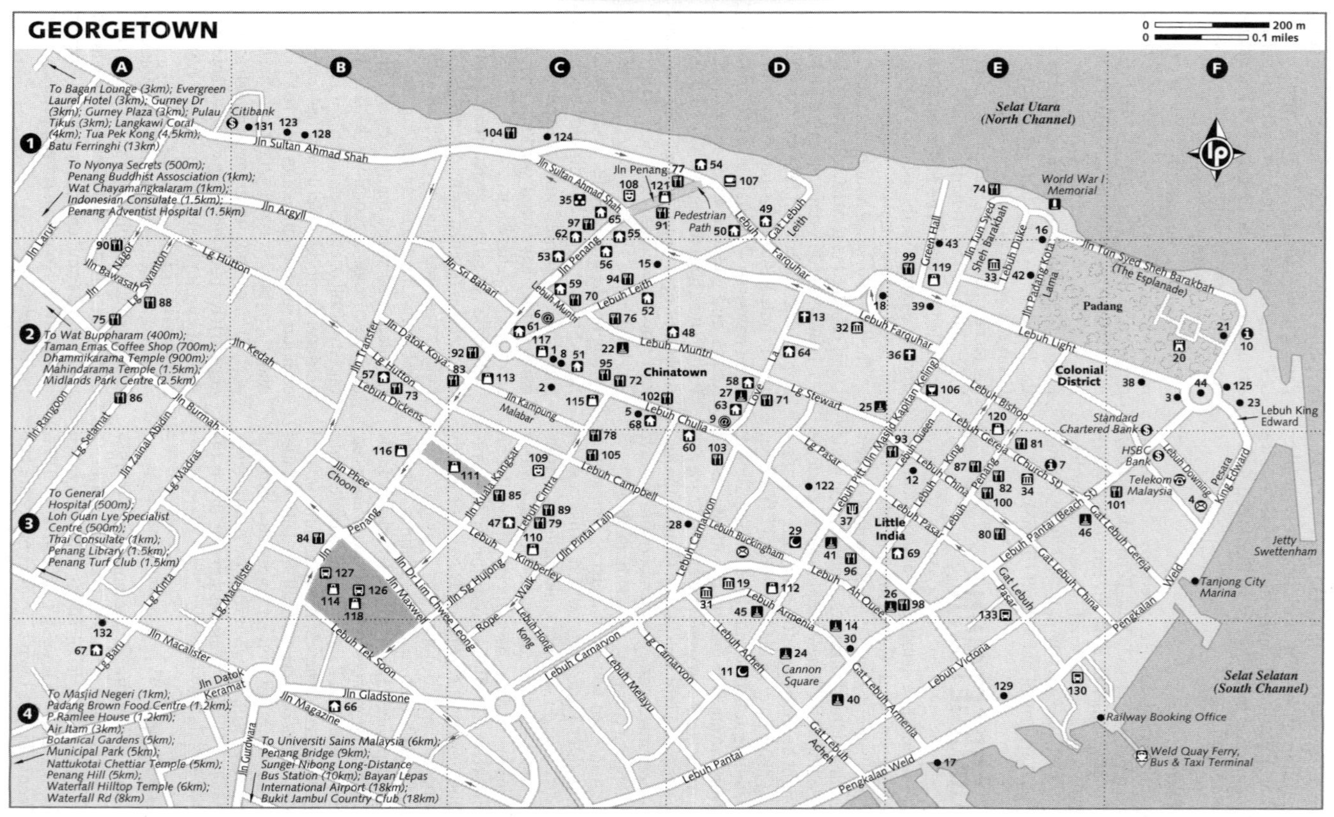
GEORGETOWN
0 200 m
0 0.1 miles
Selat Utara (North Channel)
Selat Selatan (South Channel)
Padang
Colonial District
Chinatown
Little India
World War I Memorial
Jln Tun Syed Sheh Barakbah (The Esplanade)
Jln Padang Kota Lama
Lebuh Light
Lebuh Farquhar
Lebuh Leith
Lebuh Muntri
Lebuh Chulia
Lebuh Campbell
Lebuh Cintra
Lebuh Pantai (Beach St)
Lebuh Gereja (Church St)
Lebuh Bishop
Lebuh China
Lebuh Pasar
Lebuh Armenia
Lebuh Acheh
Lebuh Carnarvon
Lebuh Buckingham
Lebuh Pitt (Jln Masjid Kapitan Keling)
Jln Penang
Jln Sultan Ahmad Shah
Jln Dr Lim Chwee Leong
Jln Maxwell
Jln Magazine
Jln Burmah
Jln Transfer
Jln Argyll
Lebuh King Edward
Pengkalan Weld
Lebuh Downing
HSBC Bank
Standard Chartered Bank
Telekom Malaysia
Citibank
Cannon Square
Tanjong City Marina
Jetty Swettenham
Railway Booking Office
Weld Quay Ferry, Bus & Taxi Terminal
Pedestrian Path
To Bagan Lounge (3km); Evergreen Laurel Hotel (3km); Gurney Dr (3km); Gurney Plaza (3km); Pulau Tikus (3km); Langkawi Coral (4km); Tua Pek Kong (4.5km); Batu Ferringhi (13km)
To Nyonya Secrets (500m); Penang Buddhist Association (1km); Wat Chayamangkalaram (1km); Indonesian Consulate (1.5km); Penang Adventist Hospital (1.5km)
To Wat Buppharam (400m); Taman Emas Coffee Shop (700m); Dhammikarama Temple (900m); Mahindarama Temple (1.5km); Midlands Park Centre (2.5km)
To General Hospital (500m); Loh Guan Lye Specialist Centre (500m); Thai Consulate (1km); Penang Library (1.5km); Penang Turf Club (1.5km)
To Masjid Negeri (1km); Padang Brown Food Centre (1.2km); P.Ramlee House (1.2km); Air Itam (3km); Botanical Gardens (5km); Municipal Park (5km); Nattukotai Chettiar Temple (5km); Penang Hill (5km); Waterfall Hilltop Temple (6km); Waterfall Rd (8km)
To Universiti Sains Malaysia (6km); Penang Bridge (9km); Sungei Nibong Long-Distance Bus Station (10km); Bayan Lepas International Airport (18km); Bukit Jambul Country Club (18km)

INFORMATION
100 Cintra Street....................(see 47)
Forestry Department.............(see 114)
Happy Holidays..........................1 C2
HS Sam Book Store.....................2 C2
Immigration Office.....................3 F2
Main Post Office........................4 F3
NJ Books Centre.........................5 C2
Omegatec...................................6 C2
Penang Heritage Trust................7 E3
Penang Tourist Guide Association.......................(see 114)
Popular Bookshop.................(see 114)
Silver-Econ Travel.......................8 C2
Spider Web Internet...................9 D2
Tourism Malaysia......................10 F2

SIGHTS & ACTIVITIES
Acheen St Mosque.................. 11 D4
Alpha Utara Gallery..................12 E3
Cathedral of the Assumption.... 13 D2
Cheah Kongsi.......................... 14 D4
Cheong Fatt Tze Mansion.........15 C2
City Hall....................................16 E1
Clan Jetties...............................17 E4
Convent Lebuh Light................ 18 D2
Dr Sun Yat Sen's Penang Base.. 19 D3
Fort Cornwallis.........................20 F2
Fort Cornwallis Chapel............(see 20)
Fort Cornwallis Lighthouse.......21 F2
Hainan Temple.........................22 C2
Hawaii Travel & Tours..............23 F2
Khoo Kongsi.............................24 D4
Kuan Yin Teng..........................25 D2
Lim Kongsi...............................26 E3
Loo Pun Hong..........................27 D2
Market 28 D3
Masjid Kapitan Keling...............29 D3
Nonya Shoe Maker...................30 D4
Penang Islamic Museum...........31 D3
Penang Museum......................32 D2
Peranakan Museum................(see 47)
Pinang Gallery.........................33 E2
Pinang Peranakan Mansion......34 E3
Protestant Cemetery................35 C1
St George's Church..................36 E2
Seri Rambai..........................(see 20)
Sri Mariamman Temple............ 37 D3
State Assembly Building...........38 F2
Supreme Court.........................39 E2
Tan Kongsi............................... 40 D4
Teochew Temple......................41 D3
Town Hall.................................42 E2
Trisula Yoga.............................43 E2
Victoria Memorial Clock Tower.........................44 F2
Yap Kongsi............................... 45 D3
Yeoh Kongsi.............................46 E3

SLEEPING
100 Cintra Street......................47 C3
75 Traveller's Lodge.................48 D2
Bayview Hotel (New Wing).......49 D1
Bayview Hotel (Old Wing)........50 D1
Blue Diamond Hotel.................51 C2
Cathay Hotel............................52 C2
Cheong Fatt Tze Mansion............................(see 15)
Cititel Hotel.............................53 C2
Eastern & Oriental Hotel...........54 D1
Hotel Continental.....................55 C1
Hotel Malaysia.........................56 C2
Hutton Lodge...........................57 B2
Love Lane Inn...........................58 D2
Merchant Hotel........................59 C2
New Banana Guesthouse..........60 D3
Oriental Hotel..........................61 C2
Peking Hotel............................62 C1
Pin Seng Hotel.........................63 D2
SD Guesthouse.........................64 D2
Segara Ninda...........................65 C1
Shangri-La Traders Hotel..........66 B4
Sunway Hotel...........................67 A4
Swiss Hotel..............................68 C2
Vintage Coral Shine Hostel........69 E3

EATING
1885.......................................(see 54)
Bake 'n' Take...........................70 C2
East Xiamen Delicacies.............71 D2
Ecco..72 C2
Ee Beng Vegetarian Food..........73 B2
Esplanade Food Centre.............74 E1
Food Stalls...............................75 A2
Green Hut................................76 C2
Hana Shima..............................77 D1
Hong Kong Restaurant.............78 C3
Hsiang Yang Fast Food.............79 C3
Hui Sin Vegetarian Restaurant..80 E3
Kafeteria Eng Loh.....................81 E3
Kaliammans..............................82 E3
Kayu Nasi Kandar.....................83 C2
Kek Seng Café..........................84 B3
Kirishima................................(see 53)
Kuala Kangsar Market...............85 C3
Lorong Selamat Food Stalls.......86 A2
Madras New Woodlands Restaurant..........................87 E3
New World Park Food Court.....88 A2
Ng Kee Cake Shop....................89 C3
Nyonya Baba Cuisine................90 A2
Opera......................................91 C1
Passage Thru India....................92 C2
Peace & Joy.............................93 E3
Red Garden Food Paradise & Night Market........................94 C2
Restoran Ali Selamat.................95 C2
Restoran Kapitan......................96 D3
Restoran Sup Hameed...............97 C1
Restoran Tomyam.....................98 E3
Revolving Restaurant.............(see 49)
Sarkies Corner........................(see 54)
Spice & Rice.............................99 E2
Sri Ananda Bahwan.................100 E3
Sri Weld Food Court................101 F3
Stardust.................................102 C2
Teik Sen.................................. 103 D3
Thirty Two..............................104 C1
Tho Yuen Restaurant.............. 105 C3

DRINKING
Beach Blanket Babylon...........(see 77)
Coco Island Traveller's Corner..(see 51)
Farquhar's Bar........................(see 54)
Pitt Street Corner....................106 E2
Segafredo Espresso.................107 D1
Soho Free House....................(see 62)

ENTERTAINMENT
Club Momo............................108 C1
Glo..(see 77)
R&B Pub................................(see 59)
Rock World............................109 C3
Slippery Senoritas...................(see 77)

SHOPPING
Bee Chin Heong......................110 C3
Chowraster Bazaar..................111 C3
Fuan Wong.............................112 D3
Hong Giap Hang......................113 C2
Komtar...................................114 B3
Lean Giap Trading.................. 115 C2
Mydin's Wholesale Emporium............................116 B3
Oriental Arts & Antiques......... 117 C2
Penang Pewter.......................(see 77)
Prangin Mall...........................118 B3
Renaissance Pewter................(see 77)
Royal Selangor Pewter.............119 E2
Siddhi Gifts and Crafts............120 E2
Street Market..........................121 C1

TRANSPORT
Air Asia..................................122 D3
Cathay Pacific.........................123 B1
Hertz.....................................124 C1
Langkawi Ferry Service............125 F2
Local Bus Station....................126 B3
Long Distance Bus Departures..127 B3
Malaysia Airlines.....................128 B1
Newsia Tours & Travel............129 E4
Pengkalan Weld Bus Stop........130 E4
Singapore Airlines...................131 B1
Thai Airways International...... 132 A4
TransitLink City Bus Station.....133 E3

PENANG

ORIENTATION

Georgetown is on the northeastern corner of the island, where the channel between island and mainland is narrowest. This city centre is fairly compact and most places can easily be reached on foot or by trishaw. The old colonial district centres on Fort Cornwallis. Lebuh Pantai is the main street of the 'city', a financial district crammed with banks and stately buildings that once housed the colonial administration. After dark, be cautious about personal safety as this area becomes eerily deserted.

You'll find many of Georgetown's budget hotels and hostels along Lebuh Chulia in

CLAN JETTY LEGACY AT WELD QUAY

During the late 18th century and early 19th century, Weld Quay in Georgetown was the centre for one of the world's most thriving ports and provided plentiful work for local people and the never-ending influx of immigrants. Soon a community of Chinese grew up around the quay, with floating and stilt houses along rickety docks; these docking and home areas became known as the clan jetties. Six of the seven jetties that developed were owned by the individual clans: Lim, Chew, Tan, Lee, Yeoh and Koay; the seventh jetty was a mixed-clan dock known as Chap Seh Keo.

It's a wonderful image: a port full of Chinese junks unloading their cargo onto the docks, where a human chain of workers carry the sacks across the gangplank out to the port clerk. *Sampan* (small boats) would row to the larger ships to unload passengers (often new immigrants) and more cargo.

The first setback to this ocean-based way of life came with the Japanese occupation in WWII (see p168) when the Lim Jetty was entirely destroyed during the bombing and the Yeoh jetty had its bridge wrecked. At the beginning of the occupation, trading nearly came to a halt and the only trade that managed to continue were small smuggling operations from Indonesia and Thailand. Soon the jetty folk became peddlers for contraband and the women, who had previously stayed at home, went out to sell the goods. The jetties began to get a reputation as an area for thugs and thieves.

After the war, port activity picked up again and peaked in the late '50s. Unfortunately the era was shortlived and when the port reorganised in the '60s, many of the jetty residents had to leave their way of life for more inland city areas to find work.

Today the clan jetties have become a low-income area with a jumble of dilapidated floating houses and planks. The only jetty that retains any communal clan-based activity is the Chew jetty whose people come together once a year to worship their temple deity. Many of Penang's heritage enthusiasts are pressing for preservation of the area. On the forefront is Dr Chan Lean Heng who wrote an indepth report on the jetties entitled *The Case of the Clan Jetties,* which was presented at the Penang Story International Conference in 2002; it can be read at www.asiaexplorers.com.

Chinatown, where backpackers congregate in the cheap restaurants and bars. At the western end of Lebuh Chulia, Jln Penang is a main thoroughfare and a popular shopping street. In this area are a number of midrange hotels, and, at the waterfront end of the street, the venerable Eastern & Oriental Hotel (E&O); see p193 for the hotel's story.

If you follow Jln Penang south, you'll pass the modern multipurpose Kompleks Tun Abdul Razak (Komtar) shopping mall, and eventually leave town and continue towards Bayan Lepas International Airport. If you turn west at the waterfront end of Jln Penang you'll follow the coastline and eventually come to the northern beaches, including Batu Ferringhi. This road runs right around the island back into town, via the airport.

Finding your way around Georgetown can be slightly complicated. Jln Penang may also be referred to as Jln Pinang or as Penang Rd – but there's also a Penang St, which may also be called Lebuh Pinang! Similarly, Chulia St is Lebuh Chulia; Pitt St is sometimes Lebuh Pitt, but is also Jln Masjid Kapitan Keling. Many streets are still referred to locally by their English names: Lebuh Gereja, for example, is Church St, and Lebuh Pantai is Beach St. Fortunately, since June 2007, the street signs started to be replaced with ones that have both the current Malay name and the old English name. Maps are sold at bookshops (see below).

Trishaws are the ideal way of getting around Georgetown, particularly at night when travelling this way takes on an almost magical quality.

INFORMATION

Bookshops

For secondhand books, check out the small shops along Lebuh Chulia.

HS Sam Book Store (☎ 262 2705; 473 Lebuh Chulia) One of the best, the self-proclaimed 'most organised used-book shop in town' has a fair range of popular paperbacks.

NJ Books Centre (☎ 261 6113; 425 Lebuh Chulia) Also buys and sells secondhand books.

Popular Bookshop (Komtar, Jln Penang) Stocks novels, travel books, maps and a selection of books on Penang and Malaysia.

Immigration offices

Immigration Office (☎ 261 5122; 29A Lebuh Pantai)

Internet Access

Internet cafés have a lifespan slightly longer than a housefly, so don't count on these listings being there forever. Loads of internet places can be found along Lebuh Chulia.

Omegatec (☎ 629 9901; 50 Lebuh Leith; per hr RM4; 11am-2pm & 5-9pm Mon-Sat)

Spider Web Internet (☎ 263 3335; 322 Lebuh Chulia; per hr RM3.50)

Internet Resources

www.asiaexplorers.com A phenomenally good website with indepth information about the sights and heritage of Penang, as well as other points around Malaysia and Asia.

www.globalethicpenang.net Information on the Penang Global Ethic Project, a local interfaith group which organises talks and exhibitions on religions and peace issues.

www.tourismpenang.gov.my Details of sights and restaurants in Penang, not updated too often.

Libraries

Penang Library (☎ 229 3555; 2936 Jln Scotland; 9am-5pm Tue-Sat, 9am-1pm Sun)

Medical Services

The Community Directory put out by the Penang Heritage Trust (right) has listings of traditional and modern healthcare centres.

General Hospital (☎ 229 3333; Jln Hospital)

Loh Guan Lye Specialist Centre (☎ 228 8501; 19 Jln Logan)

Penang Adventist Hospital (☎ 222 7200; www.pah.com.my; 465 Jln Burma)

Money

Branches of major banks are on Lebuh Pantai and Lebuh Downing, near the main post office, and most have 24-hour ATMs. At the northwestern end of Lebuh Chulia there are numerous moneychangers open longer hours than the banks and with more competitive rates. Moneychangers are also scattered around the banks on Lebuh Pantai and at the ferry terminal, although you'll probably get better rates on the mainland from the moneychangers at the Butterworth bus station.

Post

Post Office (Lebuh Buckingham)

Tourist Information

The extremely useful monthly **Penang Tourist Newspaper** (RM3) has comprehensive listings of shops, tourist attractions and hotel promotions, as well as detailed pull-out maps. It's usually available free from tourist offices and some hotels.

Forestry Department (☎ 262 5272; 20th fl, Komtar, Jln Penang) Provides pamphlets and information about Penang's parks and forests.

Penang Heritage Trust (☎ 264 2631; www.pht.org.my; 26 Lebuh Gereja; 9.30am-2.30pm & 2.30-4.30pm Mon-Fri) Information on the history of Penang, conservation projects and heritage walking trails.

Penang Tourist Guide Association (☎ 261 4461; www.ptga.org.my; 3rd fl, Komtar, Jln Penang; 10am-6pm Mon-Sat) Hard to find but much better than the official tourist office. Look for signs near the McDonald's on the 3rd floor.

Tourism Malaysia (☎ 262 0066; 10 Jln Tun Syed Sheh Barakbah; 8am-5pm Mon-Fri) Georgetown's main tourist information office gives out maps and bus schedules but little else.

Travel Agencies

Most, but not all, of the agencies in Georgetown are trustworthy. Reliable operators that many travellers use to purchase discounted airline tickets:

Happy Holidays (☎ 262 9222; 432 Lebuh Chulia)

Silver-Econ Travel (☎ 262 9882; 436 Lebuh Chulia)

PENANG

DANGERS & ANNOYANCES

Although a reasonably safe place to wander around in, Georgetown, like any big city, does have its seamy side. Foreign tourists have been attacked and mugged in Love Lane and other dimly lit sidestreets at night, and it's unwise to linger in these areas alone after dark. Lone women have a particularly rough time of it and can expect some hoots, leering and occasional rude gestures. Dressing appropriately by wearing loose (not see-through) clothing that covers shoulders to knees helps, but doesn't entirely alleviate the problem. Violence is rare but do be cautious.

Robberies have occurred in some backpacker hostels, so you should never leave valuables, especially your passport, unattended. Meanwhile, drug dealing still occurs in Georgetown, despite Malaysia's very stiff antidrug laws; don't get involved.

SIGHTS

Colonial District

As the oldest British settlement in Malaysia, many grand colonial buildings can still be found in Penang and many of the buildings are marked with signs explaining their history and significance. You can follow the Heritage Trail walking tours that also take in temples and mosques in Chinatown – pick up a pamphlet of the routes at the tourist offices or the Penang Heritage Trust (p179). There's also a free bus shuttle (7am to 7pm Monday to Friday, to 2pm Saturday), which runs between the jetty and Komtar, winding its way through the colonial core of Georgetown. It's a good way to get a quick overview of the town, and you can get on and off again at various numbered stops. A map of the route is in the *Penang Tourist Newspaper*.

FORT CORNWALLIS

Among Penang's oldest sights are the time-worn walls of **Fort Cornwallis** (☎ 261 0262; Lebuh Light; adult/child RM3/2; 🕑 9am-6.30pm). It was here that Captain Light first set foot on the virtually uninhabited island in 1786 and established the free port where trade would, he hoped, be lured from Britain's Dutch rivals. At first a wooden fort was built, but between 1808 and 1810 convict labour replaced it with the present stone structure.

Today only the outer walls of the fort are standing, and the area within is now a park. A bronze statue of Captain Light stands near the entrance, although as no pictures of him could be found, it was modelled on the likeness of his son, William, who founded Adelaide in Australia. The small **chapel** in the southwest corner was the first to be built in Penang; ironically, the first recorded service was the 1799 marriage of Francis Light's widow, Martina, to a certain John Timmers. There are exhibitions on the history of Penang in a series of cells on the south flank of the fort, and you can also wander around the battlements, which are liberally studded with old cannons.

Seri Rambai, the most important and largest cannon, faces the north coast and was cast in 1603. It has a chequered history: the Dutch gave it to the sultan of Johor, after which it fell into the hands of the Acehnese. It was later given to the sultan of Selangor and then stolen by pirates before ending up at the fort.

PENANG MUSEUM

Penang Museum (☎ 261 3144; Lebuh Farquhar; admission RM1; 🕑 9am-5pm Sat-Thu) is one of the best presented museums in Malaysia. There are engaging exhibits on the customs and traditions of Penang's various ethnic groups, with photos, documents, costumes, furniture and other well labelled displays. Look out for the beautifully carved opium beds, inlaid with mother-of-pearl.

Upstairs is the history gallery, with a collection of early-19th-century watercolours by Captain Robert Smith, an engineer with the East India Company, and prints showing landscapes of old Penang. You can also play some videos of Penang's many cultural festivals.

Outside, one of the original Penang Hill funicular railcars is now a kiosk selling an unusual array of souvenirs including antique costume jewellery and coins; all proceeds benefit the Penang Heritage Trust.

PROTESTANT CEMETERY

Here on Jln Sultan Ahmad Shah, the mouldering tombs of colonial officials huddle together under a canopy of magnolia trees. Here you'll find the graves of Captain Francis Light and many others, including governors, merchants, sailors and Chinese Christians who had fled the Boxer Rebellion only to die of fever in Penang. Also here is the tomb of Thomas Leonowens, the young officer who married Anna – the schoolmistress to the King of Siam made famous by Deborah Kerr in the *King and I*. The 1999 remake, *Anna and the King*, was filmed in Malaysia, including some scenes in Penang.

Chinatown

Inland from the old colonial district lie the twisting streets of the old city, dotted with temples, mosques and traditional businesses. The large Chinatown stretches from Lebuh Pantai to Jln Penang. It's centred on Lebuh Chulia, which is still the lively heart of Georgetown, although pockets of Indian and Malay areas remain within and around it.

Chinatown is a delight to wander around any time of day. Set off in any direction and you're certain to find plenty of interest, whether it's the beautiful old Chinese shophouses, an early morning vegetable market, a temple ceremony, the crowded antique shops or a late *pasar malam* (night market).

All the usual Chinese events are likely to be taking place: colourful parades at festival times or elderly women setting up their stalls for a day's business. All around you'll hear those distinctively Chinese noises – the whining, high-pitched music of TVs inside houses, the trilling of caged songbirds and excited conversations at numerous coffeeshop tables.

STALWART SIKHS

You'll notice that the steps of the decadent Khoo Kongsi (below) clan house are guarded by two, life-sized granite Sikh sentinels. While this might seem strange for a Chinese edifice, the guards are a testament to an important ingredient in Penang's melting pot background: the Sikhs from the Punjab region of India.

Brought from India in the 19th century by the British, the Sikhs were employed as guards due to their reputation as honest and reliable people. The fact that one of the country's greatest temples would use Sikhs as symbolic protectors shows how deep the confidence was in these people.

Today's Penang is home to some 2,000 Sikh families but very few still work in their traditional profession of guardians. Many still speak Punjabi and hold high-placed jobs in several areas of Penang business.

The Sikhs' shrine was once housed inside Fort Cornwallis because most of the first Sikh arrivals were with the British military. Eventually this location proved impractical and the government allotted the Sikhs land on Brick Kiln Rd for a new temple. While most of the Sikh's religious activity revolves around the new shrine, their annual festival of Vaisakhi, the traditional harvest festival held on 14 April every year, still takes place inside of the walls of ancient Fort Cornwallis. Visitors can expect plenty of Sikh folk dancing (including the lively traditional Punjabi *bhangra*), music and art.

KHOO KONGSI

Near the end of Lebuh Pitt (Jln Masjid Kapitan Keling) is the **Khoo Kongsi** (☎ 261 4609; 18 Cannon Sq; adult/child RM5/free; 9am-5pm). A *kongsi* is a clan house, a building that's partly a temple and partly a meeting hall for Chinese of the same clan or surname.

Penang has many *kongsi*, but the clan house of the Khoo is by far the finest and is not to be missed. Work began in the 1890s, and the clan house was so magnificent and elaborate that nobody was surprised when the roof caught fire on the night it was completed in 1901; the misfortune was put down to divine jealousy of the ostentatious design, so the Khoo clan rebuilt it in a marginally less extravagant style.

The present *kongsi*, which dates from 1906, is also known as the Dragon Mountain Hall. It's a wildly colourful mix of dragons, carved columns, lanterns, paintings and ceramic tiles, while at ground level there is an exhibition on the lineage of the Khoo clan. Facing the *kongsi* is a permanent stage for Chinese opera.

KUAN YIN TENG

On Lebuh Pitt (Jln Masjid Kapitan Keling) is the temple of Kuan Yin – the goddess of mercy, good fortune, peace and fertility. Built in the early 19th century by the first Hokkien and Cantonese settlers in Penang, the temple is not impressive, but it's very central and popular with the Chinese community. It seems to be forever swathed in smoke from the outside furnaces, where worshippers burn paper money, and from the incense sticks waved around inside. It's a very active place, and Chinese-theatre shows take place on the goddess' birthday, celebrated on the 19th day of the second, sixth and ninth lunar months (see festivals and events listings on p219).

CHEONG FATT TZE MANSION

Built in the 1880s, the magnificent 38-room, 220-window **Cheong Fatt Tze Mansion** (☎ 262 0006; 14 Lebuh Leith; admission RM10) was commissioned by Cheong Fatt Tze, a local Hakka merchant-trader. The future entrepreneur left China as a penniless teenager and eventually established a vast financial empire throughout east Asia, earning himself the dual sobriquets 'Rockefeller of the East' and the 'last Mandarin'.

The mansion blends Eastern and Western designs, with louvred windows, Art Nouveau stained glass and beautiful floor tiles, and is a rare surviving example of the eclectic architectural style preferred by wealthy Straits Chinese of the time. The house sits on the 'dragon's throne', meaning that there is a mountain (Penang Hill) behind and water (the channel) in front – the site was chosen for its excellent feng shui. Walking into this house, you feel like you could stay here forever. A tour (11am and 3pm Monday to Saturday) is the only way you can see the house (unless you stay here) – the best way to linger and learn about the

CLAN RIVALS

Between the mid-1800s and the mid-1900s Penang welcomed a huge influx of Chinese immigrants primarily from the Fujian province of China. In order to help introduce uncles, aunties, cousins, 10th cousins, old neighbourhood buddies and so on to their new home, the Chinese formed clan associations and built clan houses to create a sense of community, provide lodging, help find employment, and more, for newcomers. In the associated temples the clan would worship patron deities.

As time went on, many clan associations became extremely prosperous and their buildings grew to be more and more ornate. Clans began to compete with each other over the decadence and number of their temples. Thanks to this rivalry, today's Penang has a one of the densest concentrations of clan architecture found outside of China.

These are the houses of the five great Hokkein clans that formed the backbone of early Penang:

Cheah Kongsi (8 Lebuh Armenia) A simple but welcoming house that retains its community feel.

Khoo Kongsi (18 Cannon Sq) This is Penang's most famous and ornate clan house; see p181.

Yeoh Kongsi (3 Gat Lebuh Chulia) Apparently unchanged since WWII, this 1841 building is gracefully authentic.

Lim Kongsi (234 Lebuh Pantai) Set up in 1860, this house is currently under restoration and is known as Kew Leong Tong, which means Hall of Nine Dragons. The association is open to anyone with the surname Lim, no matter their origin, and is the only clan house in Penang with a female patron deity. At the entrance to the shrine, look for the well of Mar Chor Poh, the patron saint of sailors, who also happens to be a Lim.

Tan Kongsi (Seah Tan Crt, off Lebuh Pantai) Built in 1878, the ornate interior of this temple of the Tan clan is reminiscent of Khoo Kongsi. Today, Tan is one of Penang's most common surnames.

Cheah and Khoo Kongsi can be visited on the Chinese Experience walking tour, p186.

mansion's quirks. Note that it's not allowed to take pictures in the interior of the mansion.

The building was rescued from ruin in the 1990s and is currently run as an exclusive homestay hotel (see p192). You may have seen the house shortly after its restoration in the 1992 Catherine Deneuve film *Indochine*.

DR SUN YAT SEN'S PENANG BASE

The leader of the 1911 Chinese revolution (which overturned the Ching dynasty and established China as the first republic in Asia) Dr Sun Yat Sen, had his **headquarters** (120 Lebuh Armenia; admission free; hours vary) in this building from 1909–11. It was here the 1910 Canton uprising was planned – although unsuccessful, the uprising was a turning point for the revolution's success. The shophouse is a humble building, chosen in this obscure area of town for its low profile.

Dr Sun Yat Sen lived in Penang with his family for about six months in 1910. This house was not his residence but was the central meeting place for his political party, and some members did live here. His office on Dato Keramat Rd was demolished.

Today the house has been restored in a refreshingly low-key way, in fact it almost feels as if you're walking into someone's home. Take time to browse the interesting paraphernalia about and from the doctor's life. There are no set opening hours so you have to ring the bell and hope that someone is in (which is often the case).

ACHEEN ST MOSQUE

A short walk from Khoo Kongsi, the **Acheen St Mosque** (Lebuh Acheh) is unusual for its Egyptian-style minaret (most Malay mosques have Moorish minarets). Built in 1808 by a wealthy Arab trader, the mosque was the focal point for the Malay and Arab traders in this quarter – the oldest Malay *kampung* (village) in Georgetown. It's open to visitors but all the usual mosque etiquette should be exercised: conservative clothing, take your shoes off, avoid prayer times and be respectfully quiet.

PENANG ISLAMIC MUSEUM

The **Penang Islamic Museum** (☎ 262 0172; 128 Lebuh Armenia; adult/child RM3/1; 9.30am-6pm Wed-Mon) is housed in a restored villa that was once the residence of Syed Alatas, a powerful Acehnese merchant of Arab descent who led the local Acehnese community during the Penang riots of 1867. Today it holds a wordy exhibition on the history of Islam in Malaysia, along with some 19th-century furniture and a life-sized diorama of a dock scene upstairs.

HAINAN TEMPLE

This small gem demands a closer look. Dedicated to Mar Chor Poh, the patron saint of seafarers, the **Hainan Temple** (Lebuh Muntri) was founded in 1866 but not completed until 1895. A thorough remodelling for its centenary in 1995 refreshed its distinctive swirling dragon pillars and brightened up the ornate carvings. The compound is usually buzzing with activity.

LOO PUN HONG

The tiny **Loo Pun Hong** (70 Love Lane) is one of the most unobtrusive of Penang's many Chinese temples. This one, built in the 1880s, is dedicated to Lo Pan, the legendary inventor of carpentry tools, and is Malaysia's oldest carpenters' guild house. Set back from the lane, it has an ornate altar inside, along with a giant drum and bell.

100 CINTRA STREET

Dating from 1881 and restored a century later, this old house at **100 Cintra Street** (☎ 264 3581; adult/child RM5/2.50; ⏰ 11am-6pm Tue-Sun) contains the tiny Peranakan Museum celebrating Penang's rich Baba-Nonya heritage. Furniture, costumes, porcelain and household items are displayed in recreations of late-19th-century interiors. There's a small antiques bazaar and a café downstairs. While the museum was closed when we passed, it was scheduled to reopen. See also sleeping review, p190.

Little India

Centred on Lebuh Pasar, Little India is a bustling enclave suffused with the scents of sandalwood and spices and alive with the sounds of Hindi music blaring from numerous Bollywood video stores. It's an area full of sari shops, elaborate temples and restaurants, and although relatively small, it has a distinct atmosphere and is an inviting place to wander around.

SRI MARIAMMAN TEMPLE

About midway between Kuan Yin Teng and the Kapitan Keling Mosque you'll find this Hindu temple, another example of Penang's religious diversity. The **Sri Mariamman Temple** (Lebuh Pitt) is typically South Indian; an elaborately sculpted and painted superstructure representing Mt Meru (the cosmic mountain that supports the heavens) rises above its shrine. Built in 1883, it's Georgetown's oldest Hindu temple and a testimony to the strong Indian influence you'll find in this otherwise most Chinese of towns. Penang's Thaipusam (p221) procession begins here, and in October a wooden chariot takes the temple's deity for a spin around the neighbourhood during Vijayadasami festivities. It's open from 8am to12pm and from 4pm to 9pm daily. It's polite to ask permission from the staff to enter and be sure to take your shoes off.

PINANG PERANAKAN MANSION

The beautifully restored **Pinang Peranankan Mansion** (☎ 264 2929; www.pinangperanakanmansion.com; 29 Lebuh Gereja; adult/child RM10/free; ⏰ 9am-5pm Mon-Sat) re-creates the typically ornate home of a wealthy Baba-Nonya family of the late 19th century. It's filled with antiques and furniture of the period, and architectural features such as the colourful tiled floors and ironwork have been preserved. There's also an exhibition on Nonya customs, and guided tours take place at 11.30am and 3.30pm.

MASJID KAPITAN KELING

Penang's first Indian Muslim settlers (East India Company troops) built **Masjid Kapitan Keling** (cnr Lebuh Buckingham & Lebuh Pitt) in 1801; Lebuh Pitt is now also known as Jln Masjid Kapitan Keling. The mosque's domes are yellow, in a typically Indian-influenced Islamic style, and it has a single minaret. It looks sublime at sunset. All the usual mosque etiquette applies: conservative dress, avoid prayer times, take your shoes off and be respectfully quiet. Also, ask permission from the mosque officials before entering.

ALPHA UTARA GALLERY

Housed in an attractively renovated traditional town house, the **Alpha Utara Gallery** (☎ 262 6840; www.alpha-utara.com; 83 Lebuh China; admission free; ⏰ 10am-6pm Mon-Sat, noon-5pm Sun) was opened in 2005 as an exhibition space for paintings by contemporary local artists, based around the works of Penang-born artist Khoo Sui Hoe. There are temporary exhibitions spread over two floors, and a bookshop downstairs.

Other Sights

P RAMLEE HOUSE

Who would have guessed that this humble, and now thoroughly restored *kampung* **house**

BUDDHISM IN PENANG

While Malaysia is officially and predominantly Muslim, the Chinese population has remained mostly Buddhist. As one of Malaysia's most Chinese states, Penang has an uncommonly diverse and burgeoning Buddhist community that embraces not only traditional Chinese Buddhism, but also the Thai, Burmese, Sinhalese and Tibetan schools of Buddhist philosophy.

Kuan Yin Teng (Goddess of Mercy; p181) was built in the early 1800s, making it the oldest Chinese temple in Penang and the second oldest in the country; **Cheng Hoon Teng Temple** (p144), in Melaka, grabs the first place title by a hundred years or so. Later in the century the venerable Miao Lian came from China to construct the **Kek Lok Si Monastery** (p202), near Penang Hill, which would become Malaysia's biggest Buddhist temple, and in 1925 the **Penang Buddhist Association** (below) was founded.

Several Thai temples around the island attract Chinese worshippers, in addition to members of the local Thai community, and Malaysia's only Burmese temple, **Dhammikarama Temple** (below), is in central Georgetown. A Sinhalese temple **Mahindarama Temple** (☎ 282 5944; 2 Kampar Rd) attracts an English-educated crowd. Zen Buddhism has yet to make much of an impact, while Tibetan Buddhism is becoming increasingly popular since the Dalai Lama's much publicised visit to Malaysia in 1981.

(4A Jln P Ramlee; admission free; 🕑 9am-6pm Tue-Sun, closed from noon-3pm Fri) was the birthplace of Malaysia's biggest megastar, P Ramlee. Ramlee was particularly known for his singing voice and acted in and directed 66 films in his lifetime. No other Malaysian celebrity has ever reached the same iconic status. He died of a heart attack at the age of 44 in 1973. Artefacts and photos are displayed in the main room, while the other areas of the house are furnished as they would have been when Ramlee grew up and are scattered with his personal items.

WAT CHAYAMANGKALARAM & DHAMMIKARAMA

Just off Jln Burma, the main road to Batu Ferringhi, is this **wat** (Temple of the Reclining Buddha; Lorong Burma). This brightly painted Thai temple houses a 33m-long reclining Buddha, draped in a gold-leafed saffron robe. The claim that it's the third longest in the world is a dubious one, but it's a colourful temple and worth a visit.

The **Dhammikarama Burmese Buddhist Temple** (☎ 226 95755; 24 Jln Burma) stands opposite, with two large stone elephants flanking the gates. Penang's first Buddhist temple, built in 1805, it has been significantly added to over the years.

You can get to both temples on the Teluk Bahang-bound bus U101 from Weld Quay or Komtar.

PENANG BUDDHIST ASSOCIATION

Completed in 1931, this unusual Buddhist **temple** (Jln Anson) is about 1km west of town. Instead of the typical colourful design of most Chinese temples, this one shows Art Deco influences and looks like a frosted cake, all white and pastel. Interior Buddha figures are carved from Italian marble, and glass chandeliers hang above. Penang's Buddhist community gathers here on Wesak Day (April/May) to celebrate the triple holy-day of the Buddha's birthday, attainment of enlightenment and death.

OTHER MOSQUES & TEMPLES

The glossy, modern **Masjid Negeri** (State Mosque) is at Air Itam, about 5km west of town. It's the biggest in Penang with a striking 50m-high minaret,

Nattukotai Chettiar Temple on Waterfall Rd, near the Botanical Gardens, is the largest Hindu temple in Penang and is dedicated to Bala Subramaniam. Further along on the left side is a gate leading up to the **Waterfall Hilltop Temple**, the destination of the Thaipusam procession from Little India's Sri Mariamman Temple.

Northwest of Georgetown, past Gurney Dr out at Tanjung Tokong, **Tua Pek Kong** is dedicated to the god of prosperity and dates from 1837.

ACTIVITIES

Malaysia is becoming a popular golfing destination and Penang has some exceptionally affordable international-standard golf courses – Japanese businessmen fly in for just a day or two to take advantage of them. The island's premier course is located at **Bukit Jambul Country Club** (☎ 644 2255; 2 Jln Bukit Jambul; 18 holes from RM50) near Bayan Lepas International Airport. Golf Malaysia rated it the second-most-beautiful course in Malaysia, and the stunning and very challenging 18 holes were carved straight out of the rocky jungle terrain.

At the **Penang Turf Club** (☎ 229 3233; www.penangturfclub.com; Batu Gantong) horse-racing events take place on two consecutive weekends every two months. Seats are cheap, but gambling on the race outcome is illegal. **Horse riding** is sometimes offered Monday to Friday.

Diving and snorkelling excursions to tiny, uninhabited Pulau Payer, 32 nautical miles north of Penang, are run by **Langkawi Coral** (☎ 899 8822; www.langkawicoral.com; 64 Jln Tanjung Tokong; snorkelling/diving RM260/350). The trips include a buffet lunch and time for sunbathing and fish-feeding. It also does day trips and overnight sojourns to the resort area of Pulau Langkawi (day trip adult/child RM300/200, overnight adult/child RM550/350) which include a set lunch, tours to islands around Langkawi and lodging where applicable – the set snack is at McDonald's.

WALKING TOURS

Colonial District

With so much traffic, Georgetown isn't the most pedestrian-friendly city. This tour takes you through one of the more relaxing, less traffic-filled areas of the city where you'll find most of the main colonial landmarks. It could take up to three hours depending on how long you stop at Fort Cornwallis and the museums.

Start off at the eastern end of Lebuh Light, at the neoclassical **State Assembly Building** (**1**; Dewan Undangan Negeri), where it's a short stroll to the **Victoria Memorial Clocktower (2)**. This gleaming white tower topped by a Moorish dome was donated by a local Chinese millionaire to honour Queen Victoria's Diamond Jubilee in 1897, it stands 18m (60ft) tall – one foot for each year of her reign. Walk northwards along Jln Tun Syed Sheh Barakbah, past the tourist information centre to the **Fort Cornwallis Lighthouse** (**3**; admission RM1) on your left. The 21m-high lighthouse was opened in 2007 and serves no navigational purposes but about half the city can be seen from the top. Continue up the street towards the waterfront where the sidewalk veers to the left. Follow the walls of **Fort Cornwallis** (**4**; p180), where Captain Francis Light first set up what would become the city you are visiting today. Enter through the main gate, read about the fort's history in the air-con display rooms and check out the cannon. Exit from the same main gate and continue west along the waterfront. On your left is Georgetown's *padang*, an open playing

WALK FACTS

Start State Assembly Building
Finish Eastern & Oriental Hotel (E&O)
Distance 2km
Duration Two hours

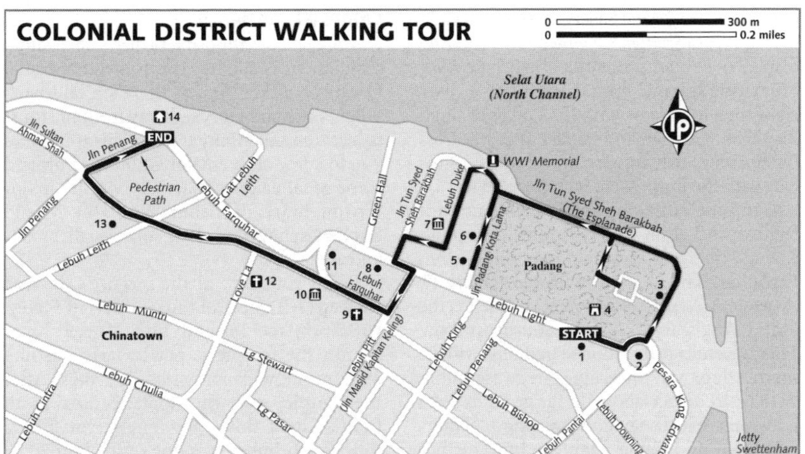

AUTHOR KHOO SALMA

Khoo Salma is the respected author of several books on Penang's cultural heritage and history. Find out more about her work at www.lestariheritage.net.

Where is your favourite area to wander in Penang? The 'Street of Harmony' (also called Pitt Street or Jln Masjid Kapitan Keling) where we have a church, three Confucian-Buddhist-Taoist temples, two mosques and a Hindu temple. You can savour the relaxed multicultural and multilingual environment. At the southern end is the 'Secret Society' enclave, where sociopolitical organisations carved out their territories in the 19th century. They fought not along ethnic lines, but rather formed cross-cultural alliances to gain control over territory, manpower, opium and other concessions. Today, it is a marvellous neighbourhood of mosques and Chinese clan temples, with clandestine gateways and hidden passageways leading to courtyards. We can literally retrace the covert trails and escape routes of the days of the 'wild, wild east'.

field surrounded by public buildings, which is a typical feature of Malaysian colonial cities. On your right is the Esplanade promenade which borders Selat Utara (North Channel). When you reach the end of the *padang*, turn left down Jln Padang Kota Lama, admiring the grandiose architecture of the **Town Hall (5)** and **City Hall (6)**, two of Penang's most imposing buildings, with fine porticos. The Town Hall, completed in 1880, is Penang's oldest municipal building and was once a venue for performances, including a group of Filipino musicians who played here from 1890 to 1954. The courtroom segment of the 1999 film *Anna and the King* was filmed here also but, at the time of writing, the building was closed and its future unsure.

Backtrack up Jln Padang Kota Lama to the seafront, then turn left; there's a WW1 memorial here on the water side of the road. Continue on, taking a left onto Lebuh Duke to the modern **Pinang Gallery** (**7**; Lebuh Duke; admission free; 9am-5pm Mon-Sat) which has a rotating display of contemporary local art. Take a left on exiting the museum. Lebuh Duke veers right then intersects with Jln Tun Syed Sheh Barakbah. Turn left and watch out as you cross the horrendously busy road to come face-to-face with the impressive **Supreme Court (8)**.

Continue east along Lebuh Light and turn right onto Lebuh Pitt (Jln Masjid Kapitan Keling), then take your first right onto Lebuh Farquhar. The elegant **St George's Church** (**9**; services 8.30am & 10.30am Sun) on your left is the oldest Anglican church in Southeast Asia. This gracefully proportioned building, with its marble floor and towering spire, was built in 1818 with convict labour. In the grounds there is an elegant little pavilion, housing a memorial plaque to Francis Light. A little further on is the **Penang Museum** (**10**; p180) which is worth a visit. At the corner of Lebuh Light you will see **Convent Lebuh Light (11)**, a girls' school established in 1852. The building was the office of the Penang government in the early 19th century. Continuing on Lebuh Farquhar you'll pass the double-spired **Cathedral of the Assumption (12)**, named for the feast day on which its Catholic founders landed here from Kedah.

Keep going west, where, at the corner of Lebuh Leith, you'll come upon the deep-blue façade of the **Cheong Fatt Tze Mansion** (**13**; p181) where, if your timing is right you can take a tour, before moving onto Jln Penang. Turn right (north) up the pedestrianised section of this street, finally reaching the majestic **Eastern & Oriental Hotel** (**14**; p193) where you can reward yourself with tiffin or a cocktail on the lawn.

Chinese Experience

One of the most atmospheric parts of Penang's Chinatown is slightly south of Little India. On these rickety lanes, there's a laid-back neighbourhood vibe, set away from the tourist centres and stinky traffic. This tour takes you to a few of the major Chinese sights and some smaller ones, partially via the major thoroughfare of Lebuh Pitt (Jln Masjid Kapitan Keling) and along some smaller roads and alleyways.

Begin your tour at the incense-clad **Kuan Yin Teng** (**1**; Temple of the Goddess of Mercy; p181); on the 1st and 15th of each lunar month the temple is particularly bustling and smoky with joss-stick offerings. After the temple, start the hoof heading south (don't worry, this is the longest you'll have to walk). Lebuh Pitt is one of the borders of

WALK FACTS
Start Kuan Yin Teng
Finish Khoo Kongsi
Distance 1.2km
Duration 1½ hours

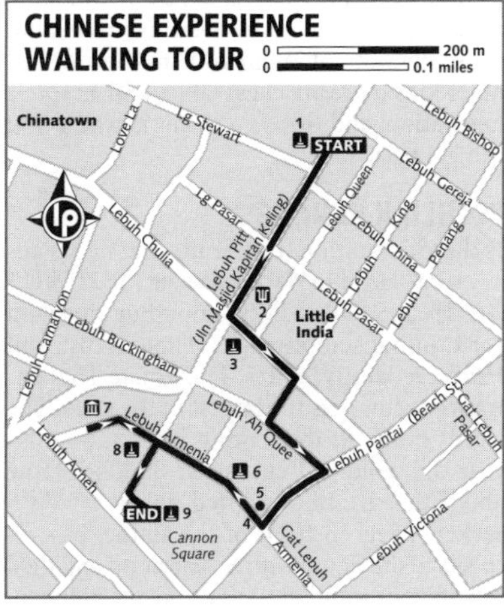

Little India; if you wish to mix in a little Indian with your Chinese, cross the road at Lebuh Pasar and continue down Lebuh Pitt to the **Sri Mariamman Temple** (**2**; p183), Georgetown's oldest Hindu temple, which holds a magnificent diamond-and-emerald encrusted statue of Lord Subramanium. Turn left at Lebuh Chulia and walk to the peaceful refuge of the **Teochew Temple (3)** on the right hand side of the road. Browse the diorama explaining the impressive restoration of this 1870 building that was built by Penang's Teochew (Chaozhou) community, which orginated from southern China. Ask the attendant if any Teochew opera or music performances are scheduled. Continue down Lebuh Chulia, turning right on Lebuh King, left on Lebuh Ah Quee then right onto Lebuh Pantai (Beach St). Take your next right onto **Lebuh Armenia (4)**, which was turned into a 19th-century Bangkok street (including elephants) for the 1999 film *Anna and the King*. Although the street is named for Penang's Armenian population (such as the famous Sarkies who established the Eastern & Oriental Hotel, see p193), there's no evidence that any Armenians actually ever lived here. In the early 1800s the street was known as Malay Lane from a *kampung* settlement here, and later the Chinese named it *pak thang-ah kay* (copper worker's street) because this is where brass- and copperwares were sold. It later became a centre for Chinese secret societies and was one of the main fighting stages of the 1867 Penang riots (see p168). There are some benches here so take a little break if you need to. Just across the street from the benches is the **Nonya shoe maker** (**5**; 4 Lebuh Armenia), which has no sign. No English is spoken but there's a paper on the wall explaining the Nonya shoe beading technique. Enjoy your stroll down Lebuh Armenia, passing dusty barber shops and private homes till you reach the **Cheah Kongsi Temple (6)** on the right side of the road, home to the oldest Straits Chinese clan association in Penang. It's a down-home sort of place, with some displays of old newspaper clippings and photos and a re-creation of a Nonya kitchen c 1910–50. Continue down Lebuh Armenia to **Dr Sun Yat Sen's Penang Base** (**7**; p182). The *Kwong Wah Jit Poh* newspaper was started here by Dr Sun and his followers; today it is one of the oldest Chinese-language newspapers in the world. Knock on the door and hope that someone's home.

Cross the street and backtrack to the corner of Lebuh Pitt to the small 1924 Hokkien clan house **Yap Kongsi (8)** with its outer altar decorated in symbols from the *Tao Teh Ching*. Visitors are welcome inside but you have to get permission at the kongsi's office first, located on the premises of the clan house. Turn right on Lebuh Pitt, which is very quiet down this end, with many older Chinese homes. Go left onto Cannon Sq, which brings you straight to the magnificently ornate **Khoo Kongsi** (**9**; p181). From here you can catch a trishaw to explore farther a field.

COURSES

Penang has no organised cookery courses but you can contact the **Chef Association** (www.campg.org; ☎ 226 8659) to see if any of their chefs would be interested in giving a lesson or two. The earlier you get in touch with the association, the more likely you are to find an instructor. Prices are not set and will need to be agreed upon by you and the chef and will depend on the venue, menu, group number and number of lessons.

Yogis and yoginis come from all over the world to get their teacher training and certification at **Trisula Yoga** (☎ 263 7155; www.trisulayoga

.com; 22 Jln Green Hall), as it's one of only four yoga schools in Malaysia that is a registered yoga school (RSA) with Yoga Alliance USA and Asia Yoga Alliance India. Certification is in 'nondenominational' hatha yoga and generally takes six weeks. Occasionally the school also runs reiki training courses so check the website if you're interested. For regular lay-person classes, call or email for times (which change regularly); pilates is also available.

For pewter-making workshops, see the review of the Royal Selangor Pewter outlet, p200.

GEORGETOWN FOR CHILDREN

Inner-city Georgetown with its busy streets and lack of sidewalks isn't the greatest place to stroll with kids but there are plenty of diversions to entertain. Trishaw rides are always fun, the *padang* next to Fort Cornwallis, along the waterfront esplanade, is a relaxing place with lots of open spaces, and eating at food courts offer some kid-friendly options. Along with the beaches of Batu Ferringhi (good for little kids to play in the sand and the gentle surf) and the available watersports (p209), the Butterfly Park (p207) in Titi Kerawang and the Botanical Gardens (p203), the following are family favourites:

If your kids have seen *Toy Story 2*, they might feel bad for the more than 100,000 toys locked up in the **Toy Museum** (☎ 460 2096; Jln Tanjung Bungah; admission adult/child RM10/6; ⏰ 9am-9pm) with nobody to really love them; no one has tried to break Woody free yet. Don't miss the Chamber of Horrors (not suitable for very young or sensitive kids), Chamber of Monsters, Cave of Dinosaurs, Hall of Cartoons, Chamber of Comic Book Heroes and Hall of Beauties (for lovers of Barbie). Some displays have voiceovers and sound effects but other than that there's not much action. Still it's a fun kitsch place to visit; chances are that everyone will see some old friends in the collection. The most expensive toy is a RM9000, 1.8m tall Gundam Robot from Japan – but we're betting even a Stinky Pete original would garner more than that.

The huge shopping-cum-recreation complex **Midlands Park Centre** (☎ 226 8588; Jln Burma) has everything from myriad shops and fast-food places, to a bowling alley and Adventure Island – a water theme park on the roof of the 8-storey building. The water park is the main draw. It has a giant pool, plenty of thrill rides and views of Pulau Tikus and the northern beaches.

Near the Botanical gardens, and signposted as Taman Perbandaran, the well-maintained, landscaped **Municipal Park** (Jln Burma), formerly known as Youth Park, has good playgrounds, some splash pools, basketball courts, walking trails, biking and roller-blading trails and, generally, lots of room to run around. For older kids there are chess tables and an internet station, and there's a cafeteria where you can get basic fare.

PECULIAR PENANG

Is there a question in your life that needs answering? Head to **Wat Buppharam** (☎ 227 7430; 8 Perak Rd), a 1942 Buddhist temple bursting with cartoonlike sculptures of Thai, Taoist and Hindu religious figures. The ornate Thai entrance archway is the largest in the state. The wat is home to the 'Lifting Buddha', a 100-year-old, gold-leaf encrusted Buddha statue about the size of a well-fed house cat. As a seeker, kneel in front of the statue, pay respects to the figure with a clear mind and then ask, in your mind, the yes or no question you wish to have answered; ask also that you wish for the figure to become light for an affirmative answer. Try to lift the statue. To verify the answer, ask your question again, only this time ask that the statue become heavy. Lift again. We tried this and got a very firm 'no' answer while a friend received a 'yes'. Months down the line it ended up that the statue was right in both cases. When the statue is heavy it won't budge and when it's light it lifts off the platform like a butterfly. You can decide for yourself if there's something cosmic going on.

TOURS

Most sights on the island are easily reached independently but only expect to see one or two in a day if you're taking local transport, perhaps three or four if you're getting lost in traffic with your own car. For folks on a small-time budget, taking a tour can be a wise choice. Several agents around town book a range of tours at similar prices. **Happy Holidays** (☎ 262 9222; 432 Lebuh Chulia), **Ping Anchorage** (Map p169; ☎ 397 7993; www.pinganchorage.com.my; 25B Jln Todok 2, Seberang Jaya, Seberang Perai) and **Hawaii Travel & Tours** (☎ 262 6755; 1 Jln Tun Syed Sheh Barakbah), a few doors from the Tourism Malaysia office, sell tickets for a half-day Round-Island Tour (RM69) which includes a visit to a fishing village, and a Georgetown by Night trishaw tour (RM69), among others.

For more indepth coverage of Georgetown, go with the highly recommended Penang Heritage Trust (see p179) which organises a few walking tours, including the Little India Experience and the Heritage Trail walks, (which takes in the Cheong Fatt Tze Mansion). Both last around three hours, and cost RM60, including entry fees. Penang Heritage Trust also has free brochures with details of self-guided walks such as the World Religions Walk and Historic Georgetown Trails.

The **Penang Tourist Guide Association** (p179) can also get you in touch with excellent guides who lead themed tours on everything from food to symbology. These tours are the most economical option in town (RM50 to RM60, minimum two people, three hours). Member Joann Khaw, who leads many of the tours through the Cheong Fatt Tze Mansion (p181), leads architecture tours (particularly recommended) through the city and tours to the clan jetties (see boxed text, p178), as well as several others.

VOLUNTEERING

There is no end of volunteering opportunities in Penang. The **Penang Heritage Trust** (☎ 264 2631; www.pht.org.my; 26 Lebuh Gereja; 🕑 9.30am-2.30pm & 2.30-4.30pm Mon-Fri) puts out a free community directory which provides contact information for nonprofit organisations, including those dealing with environmental, social and cultural issues. Of course monetary donations to any of these grassroots organisations is another great way to help out.

The Christian-oriented **Eden Handicap Centre** (☎ 228 2758; www.edenhandicap.org; Kompleks Masyarakat Penyayang, Jln Utama) always needs volunteers, for any length of time. Activities might include helping with sports, chaperoning outings with disabled children, gardening, teaching computer skills and so on. Call Mr Lee Sin Kok to arrange times.

Most volunteering at the **Penang SPCA** (☎ 281 6559; www.spca-penang.net; Jln Jeti Jelutong) will involve bathing dogs or just socialising with the animals in the pound. If you're staying longer you might help with fundraising projects or you could even foster a kitten or puppy (although most hotels won't allow this!) until it can be vaccinated and find a permanent home.

SLEEPING

Georgetown has all the accommodation possibilities you would expect in a big, bustling tourist city, from the grungiest hostels to the swankiest hotels. Midrange options are mostly found along Jln Penang, consisting of a string of high-rises. Cacaphonic Lebuh Chulia and quieter Love Lane make up the heart of Penang's backpacker-land, crammed with cheap hostels and hotels where it pays to check a few out before parting with your cash. There are some pretty ropey dives here, and some are fronts for brothels; back rooms full of scantily clad ladies and

CAUSTIC RIVER

Winding and farting through the heart of Georgetown before spewing into Selat Selatan (South Channel), Sungai Pinang is considered the filthiest river in Malaysia. Over the years it's become a drain for a 50km urban spread of factories, markets and tightly quartered residents who have freely dumped whatever they've wanted into the flowing sludge. Today it not-so-proudly bears a Class V classification, which means it is unable to sustain life and contact with the water is dangerous for humans.

In December 2005 a clean-up project began with goals of turning what many consider to be a sewer into a clean Class II river for swimming and boating. Optimists imagined fish fluttering through clear waters, and a tourist jetty was built in hopes of offering scenic river tours. As the 2007 projected completion date approached, it became obvious that it wasn't that easy. The river still stinks, no one in their right mind would go picnicking on the banks and the jetty has been happily claimed by local fishermen.

A new study of the river has been implemented by the government and it's now estimated that clean up will cost another RM2 billion, on top of the RM21 million that's already been spent. While residents hope to see the river return to a reasonable state, few are confident that the measures will work, let alone be sustainable.

ladyboys in the lobby offering massages might arouse your suspicions. There are a handful of top-end hotels in Georgetown, but most are strung out along Gurney Dr and Batu Ferringhi, and tend to be of the gargantuan chain-resort persuasion.

Be warned that during holidays, most notably Chinese New Year, hotels tend to fill up very quickly and prices can become ridiculously inflated; if you intend to stay at this time, book well in advance.

Budget

75 Travellers' Lodge (☎ 262 3378; 75 Lebuh Muntri; dm RM7, s RM15-18, d RM18-40;) In a great location away from the hullabaloo of Lebuh Chulia, but still in the heart of Chinatown, the 75 doesn't have much character but is an OK place to crash. Rooms are the standard backpacker box, but are among some of the few budget ones in town that have windows. Mr Low is a friendly and helpful owner and it's easy to be social over a beer or coffee on the balcony. It was spic and span when we passed but we've received the odd grumble about the cleanliness of this place.

Blue Diamond Hotel (☎ 261 1089; 422 Lebuh Chulia; dm/s/d from RM8/20/30;) The staff have stiff drinks in hand by 11am, and the party continues into the wee hours of the night at the popular beer garden, Coco Island Traveller's Corner (p199), which dominates this hotel. Rooms are in a potentially gorgeous old Chinese mansion. There's plenty of light pouring in, but carved panels are paint-chipped, there's an unfortunate coating of dust everywhere and tubs are rust-stained; the whole place is crying out for a dose of TLC. It's a very social hub with a busy internet area at the back. Air-con rooms with private showers cost RM45.

100 Cintra Street (☎ 264 3581; 100 Lebuh Cintra; dm/s/d RM9.50/25/38) Upstairs, in a wonderful old Peranakan house which incorporates a café and a small sometimes-open museum (p183) is this collection of very simple but striking budget rooms. Open the sliding iron door to your room and step into the past (thankfully a cleaned-up version). You get a mattress on a wooden platform with a mosquito net and fan for that colonial Eastern experience. The dorm, though, is less private, with five beds arranged on an open landing. A proper dorm room has been in the planning for ages but doesn't look likely in the near future.

Love Lane Inn (☎ 412 9002; 54 Love Lane; s/d/t RM16/30/40;) Pastel colours brighten the dim corridors opening up to the tiny courtyards and sitting areas of this basic hostel. Singles are boxy and windowless but doubles are bigger and usually have three beds. The entire establishment is sparkling clean. While owner Jimmy gets good reviews from travellers, we've heard complaints about some rude staff. There's a little on-site café and travel centre where you can book travel or organise tours.

Swiss Hotel (☎ 262 0133; 431F Lebuh Chulia; s/d without bathroom RM17/21, s/d RM19/24) Depending on your attitude, you could find this very un-Swiss place either depressingly bleak or sparked with grungy character. It has a distinctly Chinese institutional style and the management is very insistent that it's a hotel and not a guesthouse. The rooms upstairs are bigger than those downstairs and all are dark but clean; a bathroom means a toilet and a *mandi* (the local style bath where you scoop water out of a tub and pour it on yourself to bathe). You might have to turn sideways, or lose weight to fit up the skinny back stairway.

SD Guesthouse (☎ 264 3763; www.sdguesthouse.com.my; 16 Love Lane; s/d 18/25) Clean, modern, windowless rooms line bright corridors and a sweet little garden. Baths get all the proper scrubbing. This would be one of the quietest places in town were it not for the 'bird hotel' (for collecting nests for birds-nest soup) next door. Luckily the squawkers are slumbering by around 9pm.

Pin Seng Hotel (☎ 261 9004; 82 Love Lane; s/d RM20/25) This small hotel tucked down a little alley has the usual bottom budget set-up with slightly shabby fan rooms and shirtless locals snoozing in the foyer. It's friendly and a decent place to try if you're looking for an 'authentic' experience. Although in the heart of backpacker-land, it caters to a more local crowd.

Vintage Coral Shine Hostel (☎ 261 8407; 99 Lebuh King; s/d from RM20/30;) The main draw of this place is its location in the heart of bustling Little India. The fan rooms are very simple, with thin mattresses and no windows; it's worth paying the extra RM10 for a larger air-con room. The shared bathrooms are very modern. Staff aren't super-friendly at first but warm up once you're booked in.

New Banana Guesthouse (☎ 262 6171; 355 Lebuh Chulia; d with air-con RM25-30;) Hey this place really is new! While it lacks the rickety charm of the competition, there's a lot to be said for a coat of fresh paint, unmouldy carpeting and no scum caked in the corners. Attached bathrooms are equally spotless but all rooms are windowless. Take a drink in the downstairs restaurant-bar that promises to become a popular travellers' hang-out.

Peking Hotel (☎ 263 6191; 50A Jln Penang; r RM57-69;) While the architecture here is technically Art Deco, it's descended irretrievably into what might be called 'retro-hospital', with baby blue–and-white walls, lots of light pouring in and tiled floors. The upside is that the building materials of this place age much less noticeably than the darkly carpeted competition. It's good value, institutionally clean and quite friendly. There's a pub in the same building that is popular with local Chinese, so bring ear-plugs if you're a light sleeper.

Oriental Hotel (☎ 263 4211; www.oriental.com.my; 105 Jln Penang; r from RM69;) It's just like the disco days of 1977 at the Oriental, although the flashy look is obviously a hangover rather than a modern re-creation. Still, it's remarkably clean and well kept, especially when you consider that those technicolour curtains could only be vintage. There are good views (most rooms overlook the city) and the location, on the corner of Jln Penang and Lebuh Chulia, couldn't be more central. Try out your best Donna Summer impersonation in the karaoke lounge downstairs.

our pick **Hutton Lodge** (☎ 263 6003; www.huttonlodge.com; 175 Lorong Hutton; dm/s/d/t without bathroom RM20/40/55/75, s/d/t RM50/70/90;) Opened in 2007, this hotel in a refurbished colonial home is much better value than many midrange options. The butter-yellow building with hardwood detail has an airy patio lined with potted palms and an entrance/common area with high ceilings and internet stations. Unfortunately the rest of the house was gutted for the renovation and has been rebuilt into a plain, but well-lit and ventilated, lodge. Shared bathrooms are deluxe-hotel standard, the entire place is immaculate and the staff are friendly and eager to make the place a hit; we have no doubt that they'll succeed. All rooms have air-con, the showers are hot and a basic continental breakfast is included in the price. It's a gay-friendly establishment.

Midrange

Cathay Hotel (☎ 262 6271; 15 Lebuh Leith; s/d RM69/92;) It's trying hard to be as bland as the bigger hotels, but the spacious colonial Chinese building of this place, with it's light-infused courtyard, high ceilings and latticed windows, can't help but remain atmospheric. Everything from the grand entrance to the massive carved wooden doors on the rooms give hints of an era when this must have been an elegant beauty. Today it's faded, decorated with shabby furniture and the tiles are permanently stained from who knows what. Friendly Chinese caretakers can be found reading the paper, an old lady seems to endlessly sweep around the lobby and there's a pervasive sense of peace. You may remember seeing the hotel in the 1995 film *Beyond Rangoon*.

Segara Ninda (☎ 262 8748; www.segaraninda.com; 20 Jln Penang; s & d RM70-100;) This elegant century-old villa was once the town residence of Ku Din Ku Meh, a wealthy timber merchant and colonial administrator in what is now southern Thailand. His home has been tastefully renovated, incorporating original features such as the carved wooden ventilation panels and staircase and tiled floors. A courtyard with fountains and plants is a midcity oasis and the homestay atmosphere is soothing. There are 14 simply but elegantly furnished rooms of varying sizes; the cheaper ones are very 'compact' and room price increases with room size. This place books up very fast so be sure to reserve in advance.

Merchant Hotel (☎ 263 2828; 55 Jln Penang; s & d from RM78, tr from RM98;) The rather dark, spooky lobby is hardly inviting, but this hotel has clean and well-lit, though somewhat tatty, rooms, all with TV and fridge. However, there's the R&B Pub (p199) on the 1st floor which goes on till the early hours.

Hotel Continental (☎ 263 6388; www.hotelcontinental.com.my; 5 Jln Penang; r/ste from RM80.50/172.50;) Another accidentally retro place, the Continental brings us into the bright-geometric-print '80s. It's a gigantic hotel with 200 comfortable midrange rooms with fridges and TV. As the price indicates, this is a slight step up from some other midrange choices in town. There are some nice touches such as wooden, louvered closets, turned-down sheets and a small rooftop pool. Standard rooms don't have windows, which makes them airless and cave-like, so be sure to upgrade to a superior if you can. Prices vary throughout the year.

Hotel Malaysia (☎ 263 3311; www.hotelmalaysia.com.my; 7 Jln Penang; r from RM99;) At the high end of this price category, Hotel Malaysia is slightly more luxurious than the other standard hotel-style places in this range. Standout features include new crisp sheets, professional service and views over the Cheong Fatt Tze mansion to the Penang Bridge. With TVs, both baths and showers in all rooms and a great location, this place is a winner in the bland category. A buffet breakfast is included in the price.

Bayview Hotel (263 3161; www.bayviewhotels.com; 25A Lebuh Farquhar; r RM150-185;) A plush and sparkling high-rise chain hotel, topped by a revolving restaurant (p198) with 360-degree views of Georgetown, this is a fun and central place to stay. Standard rooms are in the dark and musty 'old wing', while uncommonly spacious deluxe rooms and above maximise the waterfront views of the 'new wing'. There are a couple of other restaurants in the hotel, as well as a 'fun pub' with regular live music.

Sunway Hotel (229 9988; www.sh.com.my; 33 Lorong Baru; d RM180;) Near Komtar, which could be convenient for those visiting Penang on business, this efficient hotel has clean, modern rooms which more or less resemble a Western Holiday Inn. The surrounding area is particularly traffic clogged, noisy and rubbish laden but you are isolated from all that once inside the hotel. All the amenities of a top-end hotel are available including a spa, gym, baby-sitting services and wi-fi.

Top End

our pick **Cheong Fatt Tze Mansion** (262 5289; www.cheongfatttzemansion.com; 14 Lebuh Leith; r from RM250;) Stay in the world-famous Blue Mansion for the ultimate Eastern colonial experience; as the hotel staff will tell you, this option is an 'heirloom with rooms'. The house has near perfect feng shui that draws you in, pampers the senses and makes you want to nest here – even if you don't have a clue what feng shui is, by the time you leave you'll realise it's powerful stuff. The house is arranged around a plant-filled central courtyard from which the greatest *chi* energy emanates. This 'heart' of the house was specially chosen by a feng shui master; the rest of the house, with its twin wings of rooms, evolved from here. What can't be seen is gold that has been auspiciously buried in special corners of the house – don't go digging for it though since it's encrusted somewhere in the foundation. Each room is uniquely themed and has dreamy names like 'fragrant poem' and 'jolie', and represent a moment of Cheong Fatt Tze's life – the particularly beautiful 'old kitchen' room for example has artefacts and documentation of the original owner's interest in wine. A delicious breakfast is included in the price and is served in the courtyard which is also a wi-fi area. Some guests say they have trouble sleeping here despite the wonderful energy, peace and quiet; old folks say it's the ghosts. The mansion is also a tourist attraction (see review, p181) and is gay-friendly.

Cititel Hotel (370 1188; www.cititelpenang.com; 66 Jln Penang; s/d from RM255/300;) Don't bring any mangosteens to this concrete giant lording over Jln Penang. While durians are usually the offending fruit, this hotel puts a second fruit on the forbidden list in order avoid staining its fluffy white duvets. The views from the large modern rooms are particularly lovely, especially from the ones that overlook the sea. It's brightly lit, always busy and offers regulation business-traveller comforts, along with a few restaurants. Discounts are normally available.

Shangri-La Traders Hotel (262 2622; www.shangri-la.com; Jln Magazine; r from RM285;) Right near the Komtar shopping centre in an area swarming with traffic but little charm, this massive, shiny hotel rides the line between very classy and old-fashioned. Rooms are spacious, with comfy beds and views of the city, but could do with a remodel. Guests are encouraged by the staff to stay on the more pricey Trader's Club floor (rooms from RM335) where there is greater security as well as other perks like wi-fi, free breakfast and an exclusive cocktail bar; however, all the top-end facilities you could expect, including a gym, several restaurants and a mediocre outdoor pool, are available to everyone. Guests can also enjoy the facilities of the much more upscale Shangri-La Resort in Batu Ferringhi at no extra charge, with a free shuttle bus between the two.

Evergreen Laurel Hotel (226 9988; www.evergreen-hotels.com; 58 Gurney Dr; s & d from RM485;) One of several five-star high-rises strung out along the shoreline on Gurney Dr, 4km west of the city centre, this hotel has reliably good service although, for the price, rooms are getting to be on the old side. It has tennis courts, a gym, business centre, all the other top-end facilities, and rooms at the front have great sea views. The area around the hotel is great for taking a stroll and at night hawker's stalls abound. Wi-fi is in the lobby only, but the staff can give you a cable for room connection. Breakfasts here get rave reviews from travellers.

Eastern & Oriental Hotel (E&O; ☎ 222 2000; www.e-o-hotel.com; 10 Lebuh Farquhar; ste from RM485;) This is one of the rare hotels in the world where historic opulence has gracefully moved into the present (see boxed text, below). It's undoubtedly Penang's and, arguably, Malaysia's most grand hotel, established by the Sarkies brothers in 1884. Rooms (which are all suites) were completely refurbished in 2001, and seamlessly blend European comfort with Malaysian style using hardwood antiques and sumptuous linens; those with a sea view (RM574) are worth the extra outlay. The sea-facing, British-manicured lawn, is shaded by the biggest and oldest Java tree in Penang and conjures images of colonial suit-clad gentlemen and parasol-wielding ladies picnicking. If you ever wanted to foray into the lives of the rich and famous, this is the place to do it.

EATING

People come to Penang just to eat. Even if you thought you came here for another reason, your goals might change dramatically once you start digging into the Indian, Chinese, Malay, Thai and various hybrid treats available. Days revolve around where and what to eat, and three meals a day starts to sounds depressingly scant. It's the same for locals for whom eating out is a daily event. Any restaurant worth it's salt (or chilli as the case may be) will be swarming with customers from opening to closing.

Don't leave town without trying *asam* laksa (Penang laksa). Locals are very opinionated about which places serve the best laksa – a fun

THE EASTERN & ORIENTAL HOTEL

Dominating the seafront end of Jln Penang is the historic **Eastern & Oriental Hotel** (E&O; 10 Lebuh Farquhar). Originally built in 1884 as the Eastern Hotel, it became so popular that the following year it was expanded and renamed the Eastern & Oriental Hotel. The stylish E&O was the archetypal 19th-century colonial grand hotel, established by two of the famous Armenian Sarkies brothers, Tigram and Martin, the most famous hoteliers in the East, who later founded Raffles Hotel in Singapore.

In the 1920s the Sarkies promoted the E&O as 'The Premier Hotel East of Suez' (a catchy phrase the brothers later used to advertise *all* their hotels) which supposedly had the 'longest seafront of any hotel' in the world, at 842ft. High-ranking colonial officials and wealthy planters and merchants filed through its grand lobby, and the E&O became firmly established as a centre for Penang's social elite. Rudyard Kipling, Noel Coward and Somerset Maugham were just some of the famous faces who passed through its doors.

The Sarkies almost closed the E&O when the rent was raised from £200 to £350 a month. Arshak Sarkies, a third brother (a gambler by nature), convinced the family to open the Raffles Hotel instead. Arshak's generosity was legendary: he often paid the £50 to £60 passage back to England for broken-hearted (and empty-pocketed) rubber planters and tin miners. Some observers said that Arshak ran the E&O not to make money, but to entertain: he seemed more keen on waltzing around the ballroom with a whisky-and-soda balanced on his head than in adding up a balance sheet. Shortly before his death, Arshak began lavish renovations to the E&O. This expense, coupled with loans to friends that were conveniently forgotten, finally bankrupted the family business in 1931. Still, Arshak's funeral was one of the grandest Penang had ever seen.

In the 1990s the E&O closed and fell into disrepair, but a huge renovation programme was begun to rescue one of Georgetown's most prominent and glamorous landmarks. In 2001 it once again opened for business, as a luxury, all-suite grand hotel with elegant, spacious rooms decorated with the best of colonial style. Today, the E&O offers some fine dining, and the colonial Penang experience isn't complete until you've taken tiffin on its grand lawn (p198).

The E&O features in several stories by Somerset Maugham, who was a regular (and often difficult) guest. For more on dashing Arshak Sarkies, read George Bilainikin's entertaining *Hail Penang! Being the Narrative of Comedies and Tragedies in a Tropical Outpost Among Europeans, Chinese, Malays and Indians.*

See also the hotel review, above.

experiment is to ask around and try everyone's favourite till you find your own, otherwise the hawker stalls on Gurney Dr are a good hunting ground. Laksa lemak is a coconut milk–laden version of the dish; originally a Thai dish, it's been wholeheartedly adopted by Penang.

Like Melaka, Penang is also a place to try Nonya (Straits Chinese) cuisine, but it's not nearly as easy to find here and even when you do it's not as authentic as its southern cousin. Seafood is found all over and there are many restaurants that specialise in fresh fish, crabs and prawns.

Despite its Chinese character, Penang has a strong Indian presence which adds another fantastic dimension to the dining scene. A popular speciality to sample is Curry Kapitan, a chicken curry that is supposed to have been named when a Dutch sea captain asked his Indonesian mess boy what was to eat that night. The answer was 'curry, Kapitan' and it's been on the menu ever since.

Opening hours are flexible but you can expect most places to be open from 8-10am for breakfast, 12-2pm for lunch and 6-10pm for dinner.

Hawker Centres & Food Courts

Penang is known as the hawker capital of Malaysia and most of Georgetown's specialities – claiming mixed Malay and Chinese extraction – are best fetched from a portable cart or food centre. Each area has its own personality, and often a speciality, and the settings range from slap-up umbrella markets, to modern covered buildings. At night, the seaside venues bring out all the sultriness of the island, delicious smells linger in the air and snacking becomes paramount. Eating like a queen (or king) at these places is so cheap it's nearly free.

Esplanade Food Centre (Jln Tun Syed Sheh Barakbah; dinner) You can't beat the seaside setting of this food centre that's nestled right in the heart of Penang's colonial district. One side is called 'Islam' and serves halal Malay food and the other is called 'Cina' and serves Chinese and Malay specialities including delicious *rojak* (a fruit-and-vegetable salad) and fresh fruit-juices. If you're sitting on the heathen's side you can also enjoy some of the cheapest beer in town (a small Tiger costs RM5.50). When you're done with your meal, stroll along the breezy seafront esplanade with the city's budding couples.

Gurney Drive (Gurney Dr; dinner) Penang's most famous food area was once known as North Beach but was later named for Sir Henry Gurney, a British High Commissioner who was assassinated by Malayan communist guerrillas in 1951. Today it's a mish-mash of the city's most modern high-rises and some of the grandest colonial mansions on the island. It's posh for a hawker area so the food is a bit more pricey here than elsewhere but it's worth that few extra ringgit to have a table facing the sea. You'll find absolutely everything from Malay to Western food, and it's known for its laksa stalls and good people-watching. For the best *rojak* try the Penang-famous Aye Chye stall. The area around is also home to the Gurney Plaza shopping centre (p201) where you can grab a coffee at Coffee Bean or

PENANG MUST EATS

Char kway teow Medium-width rice noodles are stir-fried with egg, vegetables, shrimp and Chinese sausage in a dark soy sauce.

Chee cheong fun A popular dim sum dish, these are broad, paper-thin rice noodles that are steamed and rolled around a filling of prawns served with an oily, chilli dipping sauce.

Curry mee *Mee* (curly egg noodles) are served in a spicy coconut-curry soup, garnished with bean sprouts, prawn, cuttlefish, cockles, beancurd and mint.

Hokkien mee A busy and spicy pork-broth soup crowded with egg noodles, prawns, bean sprouts, *kangkong* (water convolvulus), egg and pork.

Asam laksa Also known as Penang laksa, this is a fish-broth soup spiked with a sour tang from *asam* (tamarind paste) and a mint garnish; it comes with thick, white, rice noodles.

Rojak A fruit-and-vegetable salad tossed in a sweet-tamarind-and-palm-sugar sauce and garnished with crushed peanuts, sesame seeds and chillies.

Won ton mee This is a Cantonese clear-broth soup of wheat-and-egg noodles swimming with wontons (rice-paper dumplings stuffed with shrimp), vegetables and *char siew* (barbecued pork); the regional twist adds *belacan* (fermented shrimp paste).

Starbucks (which will cost far more than your meal) or shop the night away.

Kuala Kangsar Market (Jln Kuala Kangsar; 6am-noon) Here you'll find vendors dexterously folding and stuffing slippery *chee cheong fun* (broad rice noodles filled with prawns or meat); watching the creation of the dish is much easier than wrestling the noodles into your mouth (good luck). Wander through the lush veggie-and-fish market to snack on fruit and Chinese baked goods.

Padang Brown Food Court (Jln Pantai; lunch & dinner) Everyone in town knows that this is the spot for delectable *popiah* (spring rolls) although the *won ton mee* (egg vermicelli served with pork dumplings or sliced roast pork) and *bubur caca* (it's pronounced *cha cha* – don't be so childish – and it's a delicious dessert porridge made with coconut milk and banana) is another good reason to try the food in this area. In the afternoons try the *yong tau foo* (clear Chinese soup with fish balls, lettuce, crab sticks, cuttlefish and more).

Lorong Selamat Food Stalls (off Jln Burma; dinner) This is the place to go for the city's best *char kway teow*, but you'll also find lip-smacking *won ton mee* and other Chinese Penang favourites. The setting, on a dingy lane off one of Penang's busiest streets isn't spectacular but the locals' enthusiasm for the food here creates a lively ambiance.

New World Park Food Court (Lorong Swanton; lunch & dinner) Every stall serves something different (as opposed to the centre having a particular speciality) at this ultramodern, covered food court with mist-blowing fans and shiny industrial décor. It's new, spotlessly clean and garnering a good reputation among Penangites. The *ais kacang* (shaved-ice desert with syrup, jellies, beans and, sometimes, even corn on top) here gets particularly good reviews.

Sri Weld Food Court (Lebuh Pantai; lunch & dinner) A good hunting ground for *nasi lemak* (coconut rice with a variety of accompaniments) wrapped up in a banana-leaf packet.

Red Garden Food Paradise & Night Market (Lebuh Leith; breakfast, lunch & dinner) Groove to '80s hits in this red-themed courtyard – the chairs and tables are red and the walls are white and red. This place has yet to win over the locals, but it has an excellent location in the heart of Chinatown and has a wide selection of food including most local specialities, dim sum (for breakfast), pizza and even sushi. Green Hut (p198) has an outlet here, selling its outrageous Australian desserts. It's not a bad choice for families looking for something low-key, and is one of the few hawker centres with plenty of parking.

Chinese

There are so many Chinese restaurants in Georgetown that it is difficult to give recommendations. A wander down any street in Chinatown is likely to turn up hidden gems and there are very basic coffee shops all over the city. A classic Penang breakfast is dim sum – search around Lebuh Cintra for the best options.

Ng Kee Cake Shop (☎ 261 2229; 61 Lebuh Cintra; cakes 60 sen-RM3; 9am-9pm, closed Sun) A great place for a snack; pick up some delicious nut brittle or a pastry filled with slightly sweet bean-paste. The egg-custard tarts aren't so bad either.

Tho Yuen Restaurant (☎ 261 4672; 92 Lebuh Campbell; dim sum 90 sen-RM5; breakfast & lunch, closed Tue) Our favourite place in town for dim sum. It's packed with newspaper-reading loners and chattering groups of locals all morning long, but you can usually squeeze in somewhere. Servers speak minimal English but do their best to explain the contents of their carts to the clueless round-eye. Do try the steamed sticky rice with mushrooms but remember not to take too much from the first cart that comes by, although you'll be tempted – save room because there's more to come.

Hsiang Yang Fast Food (97 Lebuh Cintra; meals RM2-6; breakfast & lunch) Chinatown is full of coffee shops and this is one of the most popular with an inexpensive Chinese buffet serving seafood, meat and vegetarian dishes in stainless-steel trays. There are also a collection minivendors peddling noodles, satay and *popiah* (spring rolls). It's best to arrive around noon for the buffet, when the food is still fresh.

Kafeteria Eng Loh (cnr Jln Gereja & Lebuh Penang; mains from RM2.50; breakfast, lunch & dinner) Another very simple, and rather frayed, coffee-shop set-up, always full of locals chatting over bowls of *kway teow* and chicken rice.

Hui Sin Vegetarian Restaurant (☎ 262 1443; 11 Lebuh China; meals around RM4; 8am-4pm Mon-Sat) This excellent-value buffet restaurant is the place to go for a filling meat-free lunch. Take what you want from the selection of vege_tables, curries and variety of different beancurds on offer, and you'll be charged accordingly. Wash it down with a glass of Chinese tea.

Peace & Joy (87 Lebuh China; mains from RM4; breakfast, lunch & dinner) Basic and ever-busy Chinese coffee shop serving up cheap roast pork and rice dishes.

Ee Beng Vegetarian Food (262 9161; 20 Lebuh Dickens; meals around RM5; breakfast, lunch & dinner) Popular self-service place for cheap, mostly vegetarian food, of the tofu and green vegetables variety. It also offers fish curry for those craving something more meat-like.

East Xiamen Delicacies (53 Love Lane; lunch set RM5.40; lunch & dinner, closed Mon) With tables made from antique sewing-machine stands, ageing tiled floors, overhead fans and scrolls for menus, this quaint little café is one of Penang's most atmospheric. The food is equally interesting with tasty homestyle recipes such as *teochew lor ark* (stewed duck; RM6) eaten with rice or congee, *mangkuang* (vegetarian dumplings stuffed with shredded yam-bean and chives, also known as *kuchai kueh*; RM5) and *kuang cheang Teluk Anson* (yam blended with groundnuts, wrapped in soya bean skin and deep fried; RM4).

Hong Kong Restaurant (264 4375; 29 Lebuh Cintra; mains from RM6; lunch & dinner) Very popular seafood and dim sum restaurant with an extensive menu.

our pick **Teik Sen** (Lebuh Carnavon; meals around RM10; noon-2.30pm & 5.30-8.30pm) Located just steps away from Lebuh Chulia, at first glance this open café looks like any other popular Chinatown establishment. On closer look you'll notice that patrons are dressed up – button shirts and high heels. Once you try the food you'll understand. This is a step up from the everyday delicacies of Chinatown – just when you thought it couldn't get better, it did. There's a menu translated into English but chances are you'll be the only one among the tightly packed throngs who needs it. Try the curry prawns (RM12), crispy chicken with plum sauce (RM12) or fried eggplant with bean paste (RM8). The adventurous can try other specialities like the braised sea cucumber and fish maws (RM20 to RM24). Arrive by noon for lunch and 6.30pm for dinner, unless you want to wrestle a local for a table.

Indian

Finding good Indian food in Penang is a no-brainer. Little India is replete with cheap eating places, especially along Lebuh Pasar and Lebuh Penang, serving up curries, roti, tandoori and biryani – you'll find restaurants usually specialise in either southern or northern Indian fare. Other places are scattered all around town. While eating in a restaurant offers a greater selection of dishes and more refined atmosphere, the food at streetside cafés is often just as good.

Madras New Woodlands Restaurant (263 9764; 60 Lebuh Penang; mains from RM3; breakfast, lunch & dinner) It draws you in with its display of Indian sweets outside, but once you try the food you might not have room for dessert. Tasty banana-leaf meals and North Indian specialities are served, as well as the best mango lassi in town.

Sri Ananda Bahwan (264 4204; 55 Lebuh Penang; mains from RM3; breakfast, lunch & dinner) Basic Indian eatery, seemingly forever full of chatting locals, serving up tandoori chicken, *roti canai* (unleavened flaky flat bread served with curry dhal) and *murtabak* (*roti canai* filled with meat or vegetables). There's an air-con dining hall if you prefer more comfort.

Restoran Kapitan (264 1191; 93 Lebuh Chulia; mains from RM3; 24hr) Very busy restaurant specialising in tandoori chicken and biryani, along with fish and mutton curries. It also serves some excellent masala tea.

Kaliammans (262 8953; 43 Lebuh Penang; mains from RM4; lunch & dinner) Smart, air-con restaurant serving North and South Indian cuisine, as well as Western food such as pizza. It's regarded as one of the better Indian budget places in town. The best value is the tasty banana-leaf set meals, but the garlic naan with *palak paneer* (spinach and cottage cheese) is to die for.

Spice & Rice (261 8585; 1 Green Hall; mains from RM10; noon-1am) Southern Indian food is served with class on crisp white table clothes laden with wine glasses and candles. There's an OK (but good for Penang) wine list, cocktails are on offer and the service is excellent. Goanese fish curry, chicken tikka and, ahem, goat-brain masala are just some of the menu items. There's live jazz on Thursday and Friday nights from 8.30pm; otherwise you'll have to suffer through the pseudo-soft rock and country and western music that's pumped through the stereo. If you're cold, ask the staff to turn down the air-con.

Passage Thru India (262 0263; 132 Lebuh Penang; mains RM12; lunch & dinner) The ambiance here is nearly as enjoyable as the food: swirly Indian frescoes liven up the walls, sparkly sheer curtains drape effortlessly about and the collection of eclectic light fixtures inspires creative ideas of what to do with your own place when you return home. Soothing Indian music tops of the experience. Specialities from all over India are on offer, served on a banana leaf. The tandoori and fish dishes are particularly recommended. A great place but a bit overpriced.

Malay

Hovering somewhere between Indian and Malay is *roti canai* (unleavened, flaky flat bread served with curry dhal) that is an all-time breakfast favourite. You'll find most stalls and restaurants serving this around Jln Penang.

Taman Emas Coffee Shop (1W Jln Gottlieb; laksa RM3; breakfast & lunch, closed Mon) A complete pain to find (you'll need the help of a local or a particularly friendly taxi driver), but this is our choice for Penang's best laksa. There are also a few minivendors here selling *popiah* (spring rolls) and other treats.

Kek Seng Café (Jln Penang; breakfast, lunch & dinner; from RM3) Other folks argue that this place serves the best laksa in town. It's between Jln Burma and Jln Macalister. You decide.

Restoran Ali Selamat (262 6794; 416 Lebuh Chulia; mains from RM3; 24hr) This typical *nasi kandar* (mixed dishes to go with rice) café specialises in fish and chicken curries. It's a busy place, and you serve yourself.

Restoran Sup Hameed (261 8007; 48 Jln Penang; mains from RM3; 24hr) With sprawling tables well beyond the actual restaurant like a trail of busy, dining ants down the sidewalk this ultrapopular smorgasbord at the north end of Jln Penang has everything from spicy *sup* (soup!) and *nasi kandar* to *roti canai*. Curried squid is the house speciality.

Kayu Nasi Kandar (264 4767; 216 Jln Penang; mains from RM4; 24hr) Popular food court–style place serving cheap and tasty Malay and Indian dishes, including fish curry, tandoori chicken and vegetarian options.

Nonya

Penang, like Melaka and Singapore, was the home of the Straits-born Chinese, or Baba-Nonya, who combined Chinese and Malay traditions, especially in their kitchens. Penang's Nonya (or Nyonya) cuisine is a tad more fiery due to the island's proximity to Thailand. These days, though, true Nonya cuisine is becoming harder to find and restaurants are a bit out of the way. The best hunting ground is on Jln Nagor where a line of Chinese shophouses have been converted to house chic restaurants and bars.

Nyonya Baba Cuisine (227 8035; 44 Jln Nagor; mains from RM6; lunch & dinner Thu-Tue) Near Nyonya Secrets, this is another great place to sample authentic Nonya food – try the deep-fried fish or *hong bak* (pork in thick gravy).

Nyonya Secrets (227 5289; 32 Jln Service; mains from RM8; noon-3pm & 6-10pm Wed-Mon) This tiny place hidden down a nondescript side street offers a menu of spicy Nonya favourites such as *otak-otak* (fish wrapped in banana leaves) and sweet-and-spicy *kerabu* (flavoured with lemongrass, chillies and coconut) prawns. It does excellent-value set lunches for RM12.

Thai & Japanese

Restoran Tomyam (632 592; 21 Lebuh Chulia; mains from RM6; lunch & dinner) A hole-in-the-wall place serving interesting spicy combinations from Islamic southern Thailand, like steamed fish with garlic and sour plum. The green mango salad (RM4) is particularly delicious, the staff uncommonly friendly.

Hana Shima (263 1819; The Garage, 2 Jln Penang; mains from RM15; lunch & dinner) Good-quality Japanese restaurant offering sushi and sashimi set menus (RM15 to RM29). Right next door is the associated Hana K Bar, which is a popular after-work hang-out for locals, and not a bad choice for a drink.

Kirishima (370 0108; Cititel Hotel, 66 Jln Penang; meals from RM28; lunch & dinner) Japanese living in or visiting Penang head straight here, and many foreigners cite it the best sushi they've ever had. The setting is dark Japanese chic, with saki bottles lining the walls. As well as sushi there is also excellent seafood. Reserve in advance for peak hours.

Western

There's a concentration of smart Western restaurants and coffee bars on the short pedestrianised section of Jln Penang leading up towards the E&O Hotel. Komtar has a supermarket and numerous fast-food outlets.

Bake 'n' Take (263 8323; Lebuh Muntri; mains from RM5; 8.15am-8.30pm Mon-Sat) Small bakery with a sit-down café serving light snacks, rolls, sandwiches and cakes.

Stardust (263 5723; 370D Lebuh Chulia; mains from RM5; breakfast, lunch & dinner) Busy backpacker café serving up economical breakfasts and light meals, with films showing in the even_ ings. There are also a few fan-only rooms upstairs (RM25) if you want to stay.

Ecco (☎ 262 3178; 402 Lebuh Chulia; mains around RM9; ⏲ lunch & dinner, closed Sun) Those craving Mediterranean-inspired fare will find this place a godsend. It's extremely popular with locals but draws in its share of hungry Lebuh Chulia backpackers as well. The speciality is pizza, but dishes like Cajun spiced chicken and roasted aubergine sandwiches on focca-cia will keep you coming back. The chef is so concerned about quality that he purportedly grows his own basil for the pesto.

Green Hut (102 Lebuh Muntri; daily specials RM10; ⏲ breakfast & lunch, Wed-Sun) Any homesick Westerners should head straight here where the Australian expat owners do a great stand-in for mum and dad, as well as offering heaps of travel advice and comfort foods like shepherds pie (RM12). Coffees, pizzas, quiches and sandwiches are good but the desserts, such as the now Penang-renowned sticky date pudding (RM5), are what makes the place tick. The hut also has a small outlet selling only desserts at the Red Garden Food Paradise & Night Market (p195).

PENANG

Opera (☎ 263 2893; 3E Jln Penang; mains from RM18; ⏲ lunch & dinner) This place is all about fusion with steel-grey walls, black-and-white table cloths, all accented with Asian hardwoods. Cool jazz murmurs in the background. The food mixes things up even more with some interesting Western and Asian dishes including 'hazelnut fish and chips' and stir-fried ostrich.

Sarkies Corner (☎ 222 2000; 10 Lebuh Farquahar; tiffin lunch RM19) The colonial Penang experience isn't complete without sitting down to a fine tiffin lunch at the Eastern & Oriental Hotel. Served between noon and 2pm from Monday to Friday in elegant surroundings, lunch is a filling and surprisingly inexpensive meal consisting of various items such as mussels, curried chicken and lamb, with a view out onto the lawn and the sea beyond. Try a pot of Prince of Wales tea afterwards. The staff say they don't care if you're dressed like a vagabond, but after checking out the other diners you might. For other dining options at the hotel see 1885, right.

Revolving Restaurant (☎ 262 9493; Bayview Hotel, Lebuh Farquhar; buffet adult/child RM38/22; ⏲ dinner) Get your city bearings while filling your belly at this restaurant-cum–tourist attraction. It takes an hour for the disc to make a complete rota-tion during which you can fill your plate as often as you like from the well-spread buffet of Western dishes (such as roast lamb) to Malay and even Japanese specialities. There's live music from 8.30pm.

Thirty Two (☎ 262 2232; 32 Jln Sultan Ahmad Shah; mains from RM40; ⏲ dinner) Genteel restaurant in an elegant seaside mansion with a small garden and nice little alcoves. Dishes like six-spice marinated barbecue chicken, lobster, steaks and Osso Bucco lamb are on the menu but the house speciality is the crab laksa. There's a cocktail bar, and live jazz on Friday and Saturday evenings. Dress code is smart casual.

1885 (☎ 261 8333; 10 Lebuh Farquahar; mains from RM45; ⏲ dinner) It doesn't get more elegant than a candlelit table at the E&O Hotel's main restaurant. The menu is ever-evolving, but you can always count on excellent Western cuisine such as sea bass with truffle sauce and roast duck. Service is top of the line. Open for dinner only, there's a smart-casual dress code (no T-shirts, shorts or sandals). While this is just about as posh as it gets in Malaysia, convert the price into your home currency and you'll see what phenomenal value this is.

DRINKING

You can get a beer at most Chinese restaurants although not anywhere Malay. Food courts with Chinese vendors have the cheapest drinks prices in town and the bill goes up exponentially once you get to a restaurant or bar. Wine is available mostly by the bottle at finer restaurants, although the selection is poor and the prices exorbitant – the house wines available by the glass have usually been sitting in the fridge for a long while and are mostly of the syrupy sweet variety. One of the nicest areas for a drink is along the pedestrian section of Jln Penang, where a handful of chic bars spread out along the sidewalk and Penang's beautiful people came out in the evening to stroll and mingle. Foodcourt beer starts at RM5.50 but usually costs from RM6 to RM7. At a bar or restaurant expect to pay from RM8 to RM10 and cocktails often start at RM15. Most bars are open from around 5pm to1am.

Pitt Street Corner (94 Lebuh Pitt) The Wild West meets Little India at this saloon-style bar complete with swinging doors. It's a friendly, atmospheric place to sit down with a cold beer on a hot day and watch Indian musicals on the wall-mounted TV.

Soho Free House (50 Jln Penang; ⏲ noon-midnight) This place starts rocking out early ('80s music

GAY & LESBIAN PENANG

Penang is second only to KL for its gay and lesbian scene, which doesn't have to stay quite as hushed up as in many of Malaysia's more conservative cities. Popular hang-outs include Batu Ferringhi (p209) and the Midlands Park Centre (p201).

Bagan Lounge (☎ 226 4977; 18 Jln Bagan Jermal) A restaurant, as well as a bar, this cosy, secluded place is popular with hip under-thirties and expats. There's a sultry jazz diva who enhances the décor of cushy couches, giant mirrors, fairy lights and ceiling fans. Not much goes on till the music starts around 10pm. This is also a great place for a romantic dinner.

Beach Blanket Babylon (The Garage, 2 Jln Penang) Another stylish bar run by the owners of Bagan, Sunday night is men's night with half price on standard pours and a discount on beer for anyone male.

Club Momo A short jaunt from Beach Blanket Babylon, bar-hop here on Sunday for the locally dubbed 'Gentlemen Prefer Longs' night. See full review, below.

anyone?) with a mostly Chinese clientele who nosh bangers and mash (RM13.50) and swill pints like good Brits. The main postwork party happens downstairs, while the quieter upstairs area has a few pool tables and windowside tables overlooking Jln Penang. It shows live sports on satellite TV on Saturday.

Coco Island Traveller's Corner (☎ 264 3608; 273 Lebuh Chulia) A true traveller hang-out that fronts the Blue Diamond Hotel (p190), you'll find plenty of long-haulers, lonely souls and locals looking for foreign friends in this beer garden. Besides beer and hard liquor there are noodles, rice and steaks on the menu – mains hover around the RM5 mark.

Farquhar's Bar (10 Lebuh Farquhar) Colonial British-style bar inside the E&O Hotel, serving beer, traditional pub food and cocktails; try its signature drink, the Eastern & Oriental Sling (RM16.50) brought to you by a white-coated barman.

Segafredo Espresso (cnr Lebuh Farquhar & Jln Penang; 10.30am-2.30am) This place is trying to decide if it's a coffeehouse or a bar. OK espresso drinks are available, as well as cocktails (from RM19). It's a franchise, and feels like it with '80s hits showing on the TV screen; the cigarette smoking locals turn up after 10pm.

ENTERTAINMENT

Clubs

Penang's best dancing venues are along stylish upper end of Jln Penang and are set up for drinking as much as, if not more than, for dancing. Karaoke can be found in several hotels along Jln Penang including the Oriental Hotel (p191).

R&B Pub (1st fl, Merchant Hotel, 55 Jln Penang; 9.30pm-2.45am) Inside the Merchant Hotel, this lively club features live music most nights. There's also a dart board and pool table, but shorts and sandals are no-nos here.

Rock World (☎ 261 3168; off Lebuh Campbell) One of Penang's oldest venues, definitely looking its age. It still gets lively on weekends though, and features local Chinese bands. You can't miss the gargantuan neon spider web hanging over the front.

Glo (☎ 261 1066; The Garage, 2 Jln Penang) A glitzy club with thumping house music and a packed weekly programme. There's cabaret on Friday, game shows on Saturday and dance shows and talent competitions on other days. Ladies get free drinks all night long on Wednesday.

Slippery Senoritas (The Garage, 2 Jln Penang) Come to this see-and-be-seen Latin club for live music, salsa dancing and a Tom Cruise *Cocktail*-esque show, put on by the bar staff, involving flames, fruit and cards among other things. This is a place for dressing to the hilt, so don't show up in your flip flops. It's popular with Western expats, and the adjoining restaurant serves tasty Western and Mexican fare.

Club Momo (☎ 262 3030; The Bungalow, Upper Penang) This place has a Middle Eastern and Mediterranean theme going, complete with a Harem Club with sofas and Moroccan tents. There's a special dance floor and alcoves for VIPs, live music and theme-music nights. On Wednesday women get in free. Alfresco Asian-fusion dining is on a leafy patio.

Cinemas

Golden Screen Cinemas (Gurney Plaza, Gurney Dr) Penang's biggest cinema complex with 12 screens and THX sound is in the Gurney Plaza shopping complex (p201). Tickets generally cost from RM7 to RM10 depending on the time of day and day of the week. Thus, it is RM7 before 6pm and RM10 on Fri night and all day Sat and Sun but only RM8 on week nights.

SHOPPING

Penang is a fun place to shop with plenty of outlets for local crafts and antiques, as well as cameras and electronics at competitive prices (although Kuala Lumpur has a wider range). Bargaining is usually required, except in department stores. Jln Penang is the best shopping street in Georgetown including several outlets selling creative and exotic women's clothing. Along this same road you'll also find **Mydin's Wholesale Emporium** (☎ 262 9915; Jln Penang), part of a nationwide chain that sells everything from toothpaste to watches and DVDs at rock-bottom, no-need-to-bargain prices.

A good souvenir is items of Penang Pewter (below), a rather more affordable version of the better-known Royal Selangor Pewter, though of equal quality.

Antiques

Fine Chinese and European china are what's most readily available around town.

Lean Giap Trading (☎ 262 0520; 443 Lebuh Chulia; 10.30am-6.30pm Mon-Sat) This jumbled-up little store sells a miscellany of goods including silverware, Oriental furniture, porcelain and glass.

Oriental Arts & Antiques (☎ 261 2748; 440 Lebuh Chulia; 11am-6pm Mon-Sat) Anything old seems to end up in this place, which has a selection of porcelain, furniture, jewellery, toys and general bric-a-brac.

Arts & Crafts

Penang is brimming with shops selling similar, primarily Chinese, trinkets like calligraphy, watercolour paintings, good-luck charms and placemats. There are also a few shops along Jln Penang selling batik and some fabulous Indian embroidered silk and cotton clothing. On the last Sunday of every month, the pedestrian section of Jln Penang hosts a **street market** (10am-6pm) selling Malaysian arts and crafts such as dolls, batik, pottery, T-shirts and painted tiles, as well as items like bottled chutney.

Bee Chin Heong (☎ 261 9346; 58 Lebuh Kimberley; 10am-8.30pm) This interesting outlet sells a colourful, bewildering assortment of religious statues, furniture and temple supplies; if you're after a huge Chinese couch, a household shrine or have RM55,000 to spend on a 2m-tall carved-wood Buddha, this is the place to come. Even if you're not buying, it's still worth a look round.

Fuan Wong (☎ 262 9079; www.fuanwong.com; 88 Lebuh Armenia; 11am-6pm Mon-Sat) This small gallery showcases the exquisite fused-glass creations of Penang artist Wong Keng Fuan. Colourful bowls and quirky sculptures are for sale.

Hong Giap Hang (☎ 261 3288; 193-195 Jln Penang; 10am-8pm Mon-Sat, 11am-5pm Sun) If you're looking for pewter products, this place has one of the best ranges in town, selling all the different varieties. It also sells woodcarvings, jewellery, porcelain, crystal and batik.

Penang Pewter (The Garage, Jln Penang; 11am-10pm) It's a small shop but has a large array of Penang Pewter direct from the factory.

Renaissance Pewter (☎ 264 5410; The Garage, 2 Jln Penang; 10.30am-7pm Mon-Sat) Locally made Renaissance pewter is another, much cheaper, alternative to Royal Selangor. Decorative tankards, tea caddies, vases and keyrings can be had here.

Royal Selangor Pewter (☎ 263 6742; 30 Lebuh Light) The top name in Malaysian pewter. This outlet

PENANG PEWTER

Something you'll see in many shops, particularly along Jln Penang, is Penang Pewter. Malaysia was once one of the world's largest tin producers and today Royal Selangor, which was founded in 1885, is one of the most renowned pewter companies in the world. With Royal Selangor's haughty reputation comes a hefty price tag for its pewter. Penang Pewter, as Malaysia's second-name Pewter company, can be a real bargain compared to the picture frames, goblets, vases and the like produced by its upscale compatriots. The company's newest claim to fame is its gold-plated pewterware, which it happily adds to its 600 or so available items.

If you're not fussed about great quality or brand names, even cheaper pewter items, many of which you can get custom engraved, are available in small shops around Komtar shopping complex. Pewter was once made with lead, but today's varieties are not and are comprised primarily of tin with a hint of copper. The soft metal is easily handcrafted with intricate designs.

stocks its current range, and pewter-making workshops can be arranged here, costing RM50 for about one hour. Book at least two days in advance.

Siddhi Gifts & Crafts (☎ 264 1005; 34 Lebuh Penang) Indian woodcarvings, incense sticks and pewter souvenirs are sold at this little shop.

Shopping Centres

There are dozens of malls in Georgetown but most hover in locations away from the colonial centre.

Chowraster Bazaar (Jln Penang) This shabby old market hall is full of food stalls downstairs, with lots of fruit on display. Upstairs there are clothes stalls, secondhand book stalls and simple cafés.

Komtar (Jln Penang) Penang's oldest mall is housed in a 64-storey landmark tower. There are hundreds of shops in a place with the feel of an ageing bazaar. Here you'll find everything from clothes, shoes and electronics to everyday goods. The Penang Tourist Guide Association has a desk on the 3rd floor, there's a Tesco Hypermarket, and you can take an elevator ride (RM5) from the ground floor to the 58th floor where there's a tourist viewing-area with amazing views over the island.

Prangin Mall (Jln Penang) Adjoining Komtar, the biggest mall in Penang houses a huge number of shops and restaurants, including smarter chain stores such as Parkson Grand which has a wide range of clothes, cosmetics, household goods and such. There's also a cinema showing the odd Western blockbuster.

Gurney Plaza (Gurney Dr) The most chic mall, with international chain stores like The Body Shop and Esprit. Mac users will find an Apple store here, and there's a massive music store, bookstore and several electronics outlets. The state's biggest cineplex, Golden Screen Cinemas (p199) is here, as well as a mini theme park, fitness centre and a health spa. Shop all day, then dine at the colourful hawker centre (p194) in the evening.

Midlands Park Centre (☎ 226 8588; Jln Burma) This is like a scaled down version of Prangin Mall, with an attached hotel and a rooftop water park (see p188).

GETTING THERE & AWAY

See the Getting There & Away (p172) and Getting Around (p174) sections for information on transport to and from Georgetown.

GETTING AROUND

To/From the Airport

Penang's Bayan Lepas International Airport (☎ 643 4411) is 18km south of Georgetown. There's a coupon system for taxis from the airport. The fare to Georgetown is RM30.

Taxis take about 45 minutes from the centre of town, while the bus takes at least an hour. Buses U307 and U401 run to and from the airport (RM3) every half hour between 6am and 11pm daily and stop at Komtar and Weld Quay.

Bus

Buses around Penang are run by the government-owned Rapid Penang and the entire system was entirely revamped in July 2007. Bus routes are divided into Utama (U), or Trunk routes that leave Georgetown to destinations around the island, and Tempatan (T), or local routes that do shorter circuits. All U routes originate at Weld Quay and most also stop at Komtar. Most buses have stops along Lebuh Chulia. For a full list and a map of the routes go to www.wikipedia.org/wiki/rapidpenang.

Fares around town start at RM1 and only the farthest flung destinations, like Teluk Bahang, will cost RM3. Some handy routes are set out in the Useful Penang Bus routes table, p174.

Taxi

Penang's taxis all have meters, which drivers flatly refuse to use, so negotiate the fare before you set off. Typical fares around town cost around RM5 to RM15. For rates around the island see p175.

Trishaw

Bicycle rickshaws are an ideal way to negotiate Georgetown's backstreets and cost around RM30 per hour – as with taxis, it's important to agree on the fare before departure. You won't have any trouble finding one – more often than not, the drivers will hail you! From the ferry terminal, a trishaw to the hotel area around Lebuh Chulia costs from RM10 to RM15 (or you can walk there in about 15 minutes).

THE REST OF THE ISLAND

It's not all Georgetown you know. When exploring the rest of the island, you'll find the same cultural mix but in smaller, easier to swallow doses and with a lackadaisical, paradisiacal backdrop. You can make a circuit of the island by car, motorcycle, or if you're really fit, bicycle, but it's not possible to circle the whole island by bus. If travelling by motorcycle or car, plan to spend a minimum of five hours, including plenty of sightseeing and refreshment stops. If you're on a bicycle allow all day or maybe even stop in Teluk Bahang for the night to rehydrate and rest the thighs.

It's 70km all the way round, but only the north-coast road runs beside the beaches. The route takes you from Georgetown around the island clockwise. The road to Bayan Lepas and the airport is congested and built up, but it gets much quieter further around on the island's western side.

PENANG HILL

☎ 04

Rising 821m above Georgetown, the top of Penang Hill provides a cool retreat from the sticky heat below, being generally about 5°C cooler than at sea level. From the summit there's a spectacular view over the island and across to the mainland. There are some gardens, a simple food court (with one of the original cable cars kept on show outside), a hotel, police station and post office. At the top is an exuberantly decorated **Hindu temple** and a **mosque**. Penang Hill is wonderful at dusk as Georgetown, far below, starts to light up.

Penang Hill was first cleared by Captain Light, soon after British settlement, in order to grow strawberries (it was originally known as Strawberry Hill). A trail to the top was opened from the Botanical Gardens waterfall and access was by foot, packhorse or sedan chair. The official name of the hill was Flagstaff Hill (now translated as Bukit Bendera), but it is universally known as Penang Hill.

Efforts to make it a popular hill resort were thwarted by difficult access, and the first attempt at a mountain railway, begun in 1897, proved to be a failure. In 1923 a Swiss-built **funicular** was completed (one-way/return RM3/4; runs every 30 minutes from 6.30am to 9.30pm Sunday to Friday, till 11.30pm Saturday). A tiny **museum** (admission free) inside the station displays some photographs and oddments from those early days. The trip takes a crawling 30 minutes, with a change of carriages at the halfway point. On the way, you pass the bungalows originally built for British officials and other wealthy citizens. Queues on weekends and public holidays can be horrendously long, with waits of up to 30 minutes but on weekdays queues are minimal.

A number of roads and **walking trails** traverse the hill. From the trail near the upper funicular station you can walk the 5.5km to the Botanical Gardens (Moon Gate) in about three hours. The easier 5.1km tarred jeep track from the top also leads to the gardens, just beyond the Moon Gate. There are a couple of numbered pitstops, with views, along the trails, and you might be lucky enough to find someone stationed there to serve you a cup of tea.

Penang's longest forest trail, the Penang Hill Forest Challenge (p206) runs from the upper funicular station to Teluk Bahang 6.6km away. This is a challenging trail taking the jeep track from the top to station 1 (Western Hill), a forest trail to station 10, then continuing on a forest track towards Teluk Bahang. Trees along the trail are marked with white paint and reflectors at 10m intervals. Expect a minimum of four hours to hike this trail if you are fit, and it's recommended by the Penang Forestry Department that hikers go in groups of at least four people, inform someone of where they are going before setting out, and that each person carries at least 2L of water.

The 11-room **Bellevue Hotel** (☎ 829 9500; penbell@streamyx.com; s & d RM132, f RM154) is the only place to stay on Penang Hill, but while the garden offers some splendid views over Georgetown, the hotel is a little frayed at the edges and overpriced. It has a restaurant and a small **aviary garden** (adult/child RM4/2; 🕑 9am-6pm) featuring exotic birds. You can get a drink or snack in the hotel restaurant to take in the view but be warned that this might be one of your more expensive food purchases in Malaysia.

Getting There & Away

From Weld Quay, Komtar or Lebuh Chulia, you can catch one of the frequent bus U204.

The energetic can take one of the walking trails (see above) to/from the Botanical Gardens or from Teluk Bahang.

KEK LOK SI TEMPLE

The largest Buddhist temple in Malaysia stands on a hilltop at Air Itam, near Penang Hill. Founded by an immigrant Chinese Buddhist, construction started in 1890, took more than 20 years to complete and was largely funded by donations from Penang's Baba-Nonya (Straits Chinese) elite. The temple is still being added to.

To reach the entrance, walk through a maze of souvenir stalls, past a tightly packed turtle pond and murky fish ponds, until you reach **Ban Po Thar** (Ten Thousand Buddhas Pagoda; admission RM2) a seven-tier, 30m-high tower. The design is said to be Burmese at the top, Chinese at the bottom and Thai in between. In another three-storey shrine, there's a large Thai Buddha image that was donated by King Bhumibol of Thailand. There are several other temples here, as well as shops and a **vegetarian restaurant** (☎ 828 8142; mains from RM5; 🕑 10am-7pm Tue-Sun), while a **cable-car** (one-way/return RM4/2) whisks you to the highest level, presided over by an awesome 120ft-high bronze **statue of Kuan Yin**, goddess of mercy. Sixteen highly decorated bronze columns (still under construction) will eventually support a roof over the statue, and 1000 2m-high statues of the goddess are planned to surround this area.

Also up here are a couple more temples, a fish pool and statues of the 12 animals of the Chinese zodiac.

It's an impressive complex, though crowded with tourists and shoppers as much as worshippers. The temple is about a 3km walk from Penang Hill station, or you can hop on bus U204 to Air Itam. Tell the driver you want to get off near the temple.

BOTANICAL GARDENS

Don't join the throngs of Penang visitors that miss the 30-hectare **Botanical Gardens** (☎ 227 0328; www.jkb.penang.gov.my; Waterfall Rd; admission free; 🕑 5am-8pm). The area has been called a 'green lung' for the busy city and it has become a place to safe keep the unique flora and some fauna of the island. Also known as the Waterfall Gardens, after the stream that cascades through from Penang Hill, they've also been dubbed the Monkey Gardens for the many long-tailed macaques that scamper around. Don't be tempted to feed them: monkeys do bite, and there's a RM500 fine if you're caught. Walking with food or a plastic bag that looks like it contains food might also make you prone to attacks, and we're not kidding. You'll also see dusky leaf monkeys, black giant squirrels and a myriad of giant bugs and velvety butterflies, which are all considerably more docile.

Once a granite quarry, the gardens were founded in 1884 by Charles Curtis, a tireless British plant lover who collected the first specimens and became the first curator. At first the gardens were primarily used for the commercial cultivation of spices including cloves, pepper and nutmeg. Today Penangites love their garden and you'll find groups practising Tai Chi, jogging, picnicking and even line-dancing throughout the week. Weekends see more families in the gardens, and evenings belong to the lovebirds. The best time to visit is during the Penang International Floral Festival (see p171) around late May or early June.

Within the grounds are an orchid house, palm house, bromeliad house, cactus garden and numerous tropical trees, all labelled in English. The most famous tree in the gardens is the cannonball tree, which produces large pink flowers that eventually give off stinking fruits about the size and shape of a human head. Continuing the human body-part theme is the Palm of Buddha tree that gives off fruits resembling human hands. On weekdays only, you can get all your kooky horticultural questions answered at the **Plant Information Kiosk** (🕑 8am-4.30pm).

To get here, take bus U102. There's also a path that leads to/from the top of Penang Hill (see opposite).

MUZIUM & GALERI TUANKU FAUZIAH

Six kilometres south of Georgetown, on the sprawling campus of Universiti Sains Malaysia, is the **Muzium & Galeri Tuanku Fauziah** (☎ 657 7888; admission free; 🕑 10am-5pm Sun-Thu, 10am-12.15pm & 2.45-5pm Fri, 10am-1pm Sat), previously known as the USM Museum & Art Gallery. It holds a collection of traditional Malaysian and Indonesian musical instruments – including several full *gamelan* (traditional) orchestras, aboriginal and Baba-Nonya pieces, and fascinating contemporary Malaysian art and photography. The university campus is on an old spice plantation with a few colonial buildings.

Take bus U302 or U704. If you take the U704, be sure to get off at the university stop before the bus turns onto the Penang Bridge and carries you away to the mainland.

BUKIT JAMBUL ORCHID & HIBISCUS GARDEN & REPTILE HOUSE

Heading inland from the University is the 2 hectare, descriptively named **Bukit Jambul Orchid & Hibiscus Garden & Reptile House** (☎ 644 8863; admission adult/child RM4/1; 🕑 9.30am-5.30pm).

The flower gardens which include a cactus garden, a waterfall, a Japanese pond, tea house and plenty of tropical flowers beyond orchids and hibiscus are pleasant to visit. Be warned that there is a mini-zoo which includes two caged Bengal tigers. There is also a collection of flightless birds, two turtle species and some giant Amazonian aparaima fish. If you're around in September you'll get to see the blooms of the world's largest tiger orchid, which grows to 7.6cm.

The reptile house has about 50 tanks filled with snakes and skinks plus a pair of saltwater crocodiles. The snake show is on weekends and holidays at 11.30am and 3.30pm.

PULAU JEREJAK

Lying 1.5 nautical miles off Penang's southeast coast, thickly forested Pulau Jerejak is an island that until recently served as a dumping ground for Penang's unwanted residents. Sir Francis Light actually arrived on Pulau Jerejak before setting foot on Penang and the island was at that time already called Jerejak by local fishermen. There was talk of building Fort Cornwallis on the site but a malaria outbreak, which was probably due to land clearing on Penang, quickly made Georgetown look like a better option.

At the end of the 19th century Pulau Jerejak served as a leper colony and, later, as a quarantine area for contagious diseases until WWII when there were rumours it was used as a German submarine base. After the war Penang had a severe tuberculosis outbreak and the sufferers were once again sent to Jerejak. If that wasn't enough, the island became a penal colony and then a rehabilitation centre for the country's worst criminals and drug offenders.

Today ecotourism has brightened things up and the island is now private property, occupied by the **Jerejak Resort & Spa** (☎ 658 7111; www.jerejakresort.com; 1-night packages per person from RM148;) which is located on the site of the old leper colony. Packages available through the website, which usually include transport, breakfast and a massage, make staying here good value.

The new chalets are beautifully furnished and the Asian-chic spa offers massage, body scrubs and steam baths. The less luxurious 'adventure village' complex has simple doubles (RM150) and dorms (four/six beds RM230/330), though you will need to book the whole dorm room. Camping, including tent rental, is RM80 for two people or RM100 for four people.

The resort has its own jetty, and day trippers are welcome. Boats leave roughly every two hours (adult/child RM25/16). There are several activities on the island including jungle trekking (one hour, RM20); wall climbing (RM10); mountain biking (RM15) and a suspension bridge trail (RM15). No buses run past the jetty; a taxi from Georgetown will cost around RM40.

SNAKE TEMPLE

Three kilometres before the airport, you'll see Penang's **Snake Temple** (Temple of the Azure Cloud; 9am-6pm) on the western side of the road. The temple is dedicated to Chor Soo Kong, a Buddhist priest and healer, and was built in 1850 by a grateful patient. The several resident, venomous Wagler's pit vipers and green tree snakes are said to be slightly doped by the incense smoke drifting around the temple during the day, but at night slither down to eat the offerings. There's a small **snake exhibition** (adult/child RM5/3) with tanks containing various snakes, including pythons and cobras. Persistent snake handlers will charge RM30 for taking a photo of you holding a snake. While interesting, it's not really worth coming all the way out here unless you're doing a tour of the island or going to other nearby sights as well.

Bus U302 runs every 30 minutes from Weld Quay and Komtar and passes the temple.

SOUTHERN FISHING VILLAGES

Batu Maung

About 3km after the snake temple, at the end of the Bayan Lepas Expressway, you reach the turnoff to the Chinese fishing village of Batu Maung. Once home to a biodiverse mangrove swamp, encroaching development from the Bayan Lepas Industrial Zone has resulted in extensive clearing. Development here is expected to skyrocket with the building of the new bridge linking Penang to the mainland (see boxed text, p171). It's Penang's deep-sea fishing port so there are plenty of dilapidated, brightly painted boats along the coast.

The renovated seaside temple here, **Sam Poh Temple**, has a shrine dedicated to the legendary Admiral Cheng Ho (see p144) who was also known as Sam Poh. The temple sanctifies a huge 'footprint' on the rock that's reputed to belong to the famous navigator. Devotees pray before his statue here and drop coins into the water-filled footprint.

Perched on top of the steep Bukit Batu Maung is the **Penang War Museum** (☎ 626 5142; Bukit Batu Maung; adult/child RM25/12.50; 🕑 9am-7pm). The former British fort, built in the 1930s, was used as a prison and torture camp by the Japanese during WWII. Today, the crumbling buildings have been restored as a memorial to those dark days. Barracks, ammunition stores, cookhouses, gun emplacements and other structures can be explored in this eerie, atmospheric place, and there are information boards in English all over the site.

Also in town is the **Penang Aquarium** (admission adult/child RM5/2; 🕑 10am-5pm, closed Wed) which houses 25 tanks filled with colourful fish and some not-so colourful stonefish; there is a tactile tank with a young green turtle, and visitors can also feed koi. Next door to the aquarium is the World Fish Centre, a research institute funded by Unesco.

Batu Muang is a fishing port so of course there are plenty of opportunities to sample fresh fish. **The Beginning of the World** (from RM5; 🕑 breakfast & lunch) and **Best View Seafood** (from RM5; 🕑 breakfast & lunch) are recommended. Batu Muang bus U307 leaves every half hour from Weld Quay and Komtar.

Sungai Batu

This is a beach village utterly off the beaten track and unaccustomed to foreigners, be on your best behaviour and cover up if you're going to visit. While the beach isn't as stunning as some others, the surroundings of delightful *kampung* houses, flowers and picket fences make this one of the more scenic spots on the island. On the way to the beach you pass a small green lake created by sand mining that's now filled with lotus flowers.

You need a car to get to Sungai Batu. To get there coming from Batu Muang, turn left at the mosque on the left-hand side on the way to Teluk Kumbar. From here follow Jln Sungai Batu and you'll be able to find your way from there. The road here can get muddy after a rain.

Teluk Kumbar

Penangites come here with one thing in mind: seafood. While some housing estates have sprung up recently – which is probably linked to plans for the new bridge in nearby Batu Muang (see p171) – the village is still a calm and beautiful stretch of sugary sands. Stop at one of the Malay food stalls for some *mee udang* (spicy noodles with prawns) or at the well-known Chinese restaurant **Good Friend Seafood** (from RM3; 🕑 lunch & dinner) which is known for its seafood and its meat satay.

Detour from Teluk Kumbar to **Gertak Sanggul**, which has gorgeous beaches, brightly painted fishing boats swaying in the sea and stalls on the shore selling fresh goodies. As enticing as it may look, don't swim here; pollution from the area's many pig farms make it a very bad idea. From the shore you can glimpse **Pulau Kendi** which is the most distant island in the state of Penang.

BALIK PULAU

Balik Pulau is the main town on the island circuit, with a population of 120,000. There are a number of restaurants, food stalls and a daily market here, but no accommodation. It's a good place for lunch and the local speciality, laksa *balik pulau*, is a must. It's a tasty rice-noodle concoction with a thick fish-broth, mint leaves, pineapple slivers, onions and fresh chillies, best sampled at the **Balik Pulau Market**.

Balik's Catholic **Holy Name of Jesus Church** was built in 1854 and its twin spires stand impressively against the jungle behind. The town's other claim to fame is its hill orchards of clove and nutmeg trees which fruit during the month of July and between November and January. From late May to July, this is the place to come for durians.

A new town centre, expected to be completed in August 2007, will house the island's biggest wet and dry market as well as a huge new food court.

Balik Pulau is the terminus of bus U401 from Georgetown.

SUNGAI PINANG TO PANTAI ACHEH

After Balik Pulau you pass through an area of Malay *kampung* and clove, nutmeg, rubber, even durian, plantations. Sungai Pinang, a busy Chinese village built along a stagnant river (it's a different tributary from the Sungai Pinang in the boxed text on p189), is worth a peek. Further on is the turnoff to Pantai Acheh, another small, isolated fishing village.

About 2km further north along the road to Teluk Bahang is the hillside 10-hectare **Tropical Fruit Farm** (☎ 227 6223; 🕑 9am-6pm), which cultivates over 250 types of tropical and subtropical fruit trees, native and hybrid. Its two-hour tours (adult/child RM25/17) are very educational, and include fruit tastings and a glass of fresh juice. The farm endeavours to use only organic fertilisers, some of which it produces itself; although not completely chemical-free, it's a good start. On Saturday and Sunday there's a **barbecue lunch** (adult/child RM35/28; noon-3pm), which includes salads made with garden veggies, all-you-can-drink fresh fruit juice and, of course, plenty of tropical garden fruit for dessert. If you get lunch, the farm's tour costs RM10. Most visitors come on organised trips but it's no problem showing up on your own. The hourly T501 bus runs between Balik Pulau and Teluk Bahang four times a day, passing Sungai Pinang and the fruit farm.

TITI KERAWANG

After the turnoff to Pantai Acheh, the road starts to climb and twist, offering glimpses of the coast and the sea far below. During durian season stalls are set up along the road selling the spiky orbs, and you can see nets strung below the trees to protect the precious fruit when they fall.

The jungle becomes denser here and soon you reach Titi Kerawang. Until recently, a waterfall flowed into a natural swimming pool just off the road, but the nearby dam has left the stream a trickle.

TELUK BAHANG & AROUND

The village of Teluk Bahang marks the western end of the island's northern beach strip. It's a sleepy fishing village with very little going on and locals have dubbed the area 'the end of the world'. While it is in fact the end of the paved road and human civilisation, it's only the beginning for hikers, who will revel in the numerous forest trails of Teluk Bahang Forest Reserve and Penang National Park. Those coming from the mainland or Borneo will be very pleased to know that Penang's forests are the only ones in Malaysia that are leech-free; no such luck with the mosquitoes though. For those not wanting to dirty their boots, even without the bloodsuckers, there's a handful of manmade flora- and fauna-based sights near the village.

Visitors are encouraged to dress conservatively in and around this rural village and use discretion with wearing swimming costumes on beaches near the town – if everyone on the beach is fully clothed, it's best to do the same. When in the park, it's usually OK to get into your togs for a swim. If you do go in the water, watch out for jellyfish.

If you're on a tour, you might visit the **Pinang Cultural Centre** (☎ 885 1175) which only opens for large, pre-arranged tour groups. Local handicraft exhibitions, cultural shows and buffets are held here. Your hotel should have the latest details and costs. Just outside Teluk Bahang is the **Craft Batik** factory and shop, a somewhat touristy and overpriced outlet for sarongs and the like.

To get here from Georgetown, use the northern coastal road passing through Tanjung Tokong, Tanjung Bungah and Batu Ferringhi.

Sights

TELUK BAHANG FOREST RESERVE

The 873-hectare **Teluk Bahang Forest Reserve** (☎ Ranger's Office 885 1280; admission free) contains a buzzing chunk of Penang's virgin rainforests. Guides are rarely available, so pick up a hiking leaflet, available at the ranger's office at the park entrance or at the **Forestry Department** (Map p176; ☎ 262 5272; 20th fl, Komtar, Jln Penang) in Georgetown; the leaflets have trail maps and some information on plant identification. Also ask at either of these offices about **camping** in the reserve.

To get to the park entrance from Batu Ferringhi, get off the bus U101 at the Teluk Bahang roundabout, turn left and walk 15 minutes. The park entrance will be on your left just past the Penang Butterfly Farm.

Trails

There are only five mapped trails in the park, the most well known being the **Penang Hill Forest Challenge**, the longest trail in Penang that leads all the way to the top of 821m Penang Hill. This walk is obviously less strenuous in the downhill direction and is covered in the Penang Hill section (p202); from the Teluk Bahang end, expect the trek to take at least eight hours. One of the better walks is the easy 800m **Monkey-Cup Forest Trail** where you can search for carnivorous 'monkey-cups', more commonly known as pitcher plants. The 'flower' of this strangely beautiful plant is actually a modified leaf that traps insects then digests them with secreted liquids. The plant is not poisonous and is reportedly used

as rice-cooking containers in Sarawak, as well as having innumerable medicinal qualities. Intermediate trails are the 1.2km **Simpoh Gajah Trail** that passes through virgin jungle, the 2.9km **Charcoal Kiln Trail** which has some gnarly uphill bits through lovely forest to an old 1950s charcoal kiln; and the much more difficult 4.2km **Ridge Top Trail** that branches off from the Charcoal Kiln Trail to reach a ridge 400m above sea level. This last trail has some fantastic views over Telok Bahang, as well as pitcher plants to look out for along the way – if you don't have too much blinding sweat stinging your eyes.

Forestry Museum

It's best to visit the **Forestry Museum** (☎ 885 2388; admission RM1; 9am-5pm Tue-Thu, Sat & Sun, 9am-noon & 2.45-5pm Fri) before you take off on a hike so you'll know what to look for on the trail. While of most interest to plant and insect nerds (and we love 'em!), the museum does offer plenty of information to anyone who's willing to spend the time browsing. The most dramatic features are an 11m-high tree trunk and some insect and butterfly displays.

PENANG BUTTERFLY FARM

A little nearer the coast is the **Penang Butterfly Farm** (☎ 885 1253; 830 Jln Teluk Bahang; adult/child RM15/7.50; 9am-5pm Mon-Fri, 9am-6pm Sat & Sun) with several thousand live butterflies, representing over 150 species. You can also see some fascinating beetles, lizards and spiders.

PENANG NATIONAL PARK

At just 2300ha, **Penang National Park** is the smallest in Malaysia; it's also one of the newest, attaining national park status in 2003. It has some interesting and challenging trails through the jungle, as well as some of Penang's finest and quietest beaches.

The small **Penang National Park office** (☎ 881 3500; Jln Hassan Abbas; 8am-4.30pm Mon-Fri, 8am-noon & 2-4pm Sat & Sun) is near the park entrance in Teluk Bahang. It has a few maps and leaflets and can help organise guides (full day RM100), although they may be hard to find on weekdays. There are toilet facilities and **camping grounds** at Teluk Bahang Beach (close to the town and amenities), Pantai Kerachut (about a two-hour walk from the park entrance) and Teluk Tukun (20 minutes from the park entrance); check at the park office for availability of camp sites.

The park entrance, located at the park office, is at the end of the road after passing through Teluk Bahang town.

Trails

From Teluk Bahang follow the trail to the suspension bridge. Here you have the choice of turning right towards Teluk Tukun and Muka Head or left to Pantai Kerachut. The easiest walk is to the right and it's a 20-minute stroll to **Teluk Tukun** beach where Sungai Tukun flows into the ocean. There are some little pools to swim in here. Following this trail along the coast about 25 minutes more brings you to the private **University of Malaysia Marine Research Station**, where there is a supply jetty, as well as **Tanjung Aling**, a nice beach to stop at for a rest. From here it's another 45 minutes or so down the beach to **Teluk Duyung**, also called Monkey Beach, after the numerous primates who scamper about here on the beach, on **Muka Head**, the isolated rocky promontory at the extreme northwestern corner of the island. On the peak of the head, another 15 minutes along, is an off-limits 1883 **lighthouse** and an Achenese-style **graveyard**. The views of the surrounding islands from up here are worth the sweaty uphill jaunt.

A longer and more difficult trail heads left from the suspension bridge, towards **Pantai Kerachut**, a beautiful white-sand beach which is a popular spot for picnics and is a green turtle nesting-ground. Count on about two hours to walk to the beach on the well-used trail. On your way is the unusual **meromictic lake**, a rare natural feature composed of two separate layers of unmixed freshwater on top and seawater below, supporting a unique mini-ecosystem. From Pantai Kerachut beach you can walk about two hours onward to further-flung and isolated **Teluk Kampi**, which is the longest beach in the park; look for **trenches** along the coast that are remnants of the Japanese occupation in WWII.

PENANG

TROPICAL SPICE GARDEN

Along the road from Teluk Bahang to Batu Ferringhi is the **Tropical Spice Garden** (☎ 881 1797; www.tropicalspicegarden.com; Jln Teluk Bahang; admission adult/child RM13/5, adult/child incl tour RM20/5; 🕒 9am-6pm), a tranquil botanical garden planted with more than 500 species of flora, with an emphasis on spices. Ferns, bamboo, ginger and heliconias are among the lush vegetation and you might spot a giant monitor lizard or two. Walk up to the small café to sample fruit juices mixed with garden spices and enjoy the panoramic view through the trees from the terrace. Tours are by appointment only. To get here by bus, take any Teluk Bahang bus and let the driver know that you want to get off here. There's a beautiful roadside white-sand beach just across the road from the gardens.

Sleeping

Teluk Bahang is only 4km from Batu Ferringhi so if the few options here don't suit you, there are plenty more over there.

Miss Loh's Guest House (☎ 885 1227; 159 Jln Teluk Bahang; dm/s/d from RM8/15/30; ❄) This peaceful, ramshackle place is set in a large garden away from the seafront, with several cats and dogs wandering about. The accommodation is about as basic as you can get, but travellers keep returning, and some stay for months on end. Rates are negotiable for longer stays, but Miss Loh won't accept telephone reservations.

Hotbay Motel (☎ 016 4559062; Jln Teluk Bahang; r RM75-85; ❄) In the main shopping area east of the roundabout, Hotbay offers fair motel-style rooms, with a communal TV lounge at the front. Rooms with five and seven beds are also available (RM150/210).

Previously called the Penang Mutiara Beach Resort, the **Intercontinental Penang Resort** (www.intercontinental.com) was closed for remodelling at the time of writing but was expected to open around July 2008. It's a huge resort on a good stretch of white beach.

Eating

With all those fishing boats in the harbour, fresh and tasty seafood is guaranteed. A group of busy hawker stalls congregate at the final bus stop after the roundabout. Sadly, Teluk Bahang's famous End of the World Restaurant was destroyed in the 26 December 2004 tsunami.

Restoran Khaleel (Jln Teluk Bahang; mains from RM4; 🕒 24hr) is a good-value little food court next to the Hotbay Motel. The usual Malay specialities such as *nasi goreng* (fried rice) and fish-head curry are available.

The main shopping area along the road heading east to Batu Ferringhi also has a few coffee shops where you'll find cheaper Chinese dishes and seafood, as well as a couple of good

South Indian places which sell *murtabak* and *dosa* (savoury Indian pancakes).

Getting There & Away

Bus U101 runs from Georgetown every half-hour all the way along the north coast of the island as far as the roundabout in Teluk Bahang.

BATU FERRINGHI

The road from Teluk Bahang that winds along the coast to Batu Ferringhi is a picturesque stretch of small coves and more beaches. The quaintness abruptly stops at Batu Ferringhi (Foreigner's Rock), a concrete-clad resort strip. Stretching along the main drag of Jln Batu Ferringhi, the road is lined with big hotels, Malay restaurants and tourist shops flogging neon kiddie floats and cheesy postcards. While many resorts line the beach, the most gentle and ambient area in town is the jumble of cheap backpacker places and beachfront cafés that form a small community along the western portion of the sugary white beach.

Batu Ferringhi takes its name from a small rocky island just off the eastern end of the beach. Once, this island served as a landmark for passing sailors who would stop here to fill up on water from a nearby river. Local Malay called the sailors *ferringi,* which comes from an Indian term meaning Europeans. Eventually the village took on the name for itself and the rocky mound is now known as Lover's Isle.

The sand of Batu Ferringhi is fine for sunbathing, but doesn't compare to Malaysia's best; the water isn't as clear as you might expect, and often swimming means battling jellyfish. The beach itself can be dirty, especially on weekends when hordes of day trippers visit. Still, it's the best easy-access beach stop on the island.

There's a good night market and the **Yahong Art Gallery** (☎ 881 1251; 58-D Jln Batu Ferringhi) sells a vast range of Asian antiques and art, including jewellery, pewter, batik paintings, woodcarvings, and, less appealingly, ivory.

Activities

There are a few companies offering watersport activities on the beach. **Wave Runner Watersport** (☎ 881 4753) operates from the Waverunner

PENANG

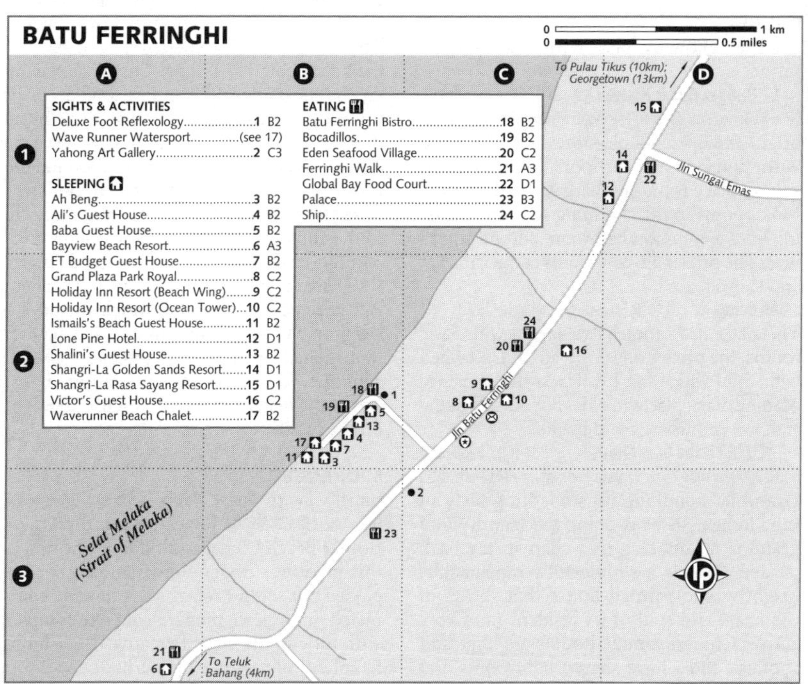

Beach Chalet (opposite). Among the activities on offer are jet-skiing (30 minutes, RM100), water-skiing (15 minutes, RM60) and parasailing (15 minutes, RM50). You can also book a deep-sea fishing trip (three hours, RM250). All hotels and guesthouses will be more than happy to set you up with their affiliated tour companies as well.

After that you might need a relaxing massage. Try the beachfront **Deluxe Foot Reflexology** (☎ 017 429 0722) which offers a 45-minute foot massage for RM40.

Sleeping

Batu Ferringhi, along with Teluk Bahang, was once a favourite stopover on the budget traveller's trail, and although there's still a clutch of backpacker hostels near the beach, these days the place is dominated by huge luxury developments. There are very few midrange options out here but the budget places are good value, big discounts are often available at the resorts outside the high season (roughly December to February). Staying out here is a completely different, more relaxing, experience from the city digs of Georgetown.

PENANG

BUDGET

All the following places provide laundry services.

ET Budget Guest House (☎ 881 1553; etguesthouse2006@yahoo.com; 47 Batu Ferringhi; r RM25-60; ❄) In a bright and open double-storey Chinese home with polished wood floors, this friendly, snoozy place is the best bargain on the beach. Most rooms in the charming old-time building have a common bathroom and mosquito nets. The pricier air-con rooms come with TV and shower.

Ah Beng (☎ 881 1036; 54C Batu Ferringhi; r RM25-70; ❄) This place has a motel-style layout with basic rooms, the pricier ones with air con, attached bath, mini-fridge and TV. It lacks the ambience of some of the places in older buildings, but the staff are enthusiastic and helpful.

our pick **Baba Guest House** (☎ 881 1686; babaguesthouse2000@yahoo.com; 52 Batu Ferringhi; r RM35-60; ❄) Grandma's cooking up something tasty in the kitchen, sister is doing the laundry and grandpa is snoozing in a chair in the back garden. This is a wonderfully ramshackle, brightly blue-painted house that shows of the heart and soul of its resident (and very active) Chinese family. Rooms are large and spotless, most have shared bathrooms and the dearer air-con rooms come with a fridge and shower. Grab your book, put up your feet on the colonial wood terrace and relax the day away. The beach is only about five steps away. When you're ready, the family can help arrange onward transport.

Shalini's Guest House (☎ 881 1859; ahlooi@pc.jaring.my; 56 Batu Ferringhi; r RM35-60; ❄) This old, two-storey wooden house on the beach has an Indian family atmosphere; although not every_one in the family is outwardly friendly, they do warm up eventually. Rooms are basic but neat and some have balconies. The priciest ones have private bathrooms.

Victor's Guest House (☎ 881 1005; 399 Jln Batu Ferringhi; r RM35-60; ❄) Down a dusty lane, off the main road and away from the beach, Victor's is a friendly Indian guesthouse with large and clean – but frayed –rooms upstairs and down. The bare brick walls are a bit cheerless, but it's OK value and in a quiet, very secure, location with chickens pecking about outside. Only the air-con rooms have attached bathrooms, and are much more spacious than those without air-con.

Ali's Guest House (☎ 881 1316; www.alisferringhiguesthouse.enetmyne.com; 53 Batu Ferringhi; tent RM10, r RM50-140, ❄) With a courtyard overflowing with tree ferns and a wooden terrace that just nails that colonial feeling, this place has by far the most appealing and eclectic décor in the budget range. The simple rooms aren't as interesting as the common areas but most have air-con, attached bathrooms and TVs, and the room price includes breakfast. Room sizes range from singles to family rooms sleeping four people. The downstairs, bamboo-and-cushion-clad common area has a good library, DVD area and wi-fi. An unusual option here is a beachside tent rental, which includes a sleeping bag and bathroom use. The helpful management can arrange transport and all activities. An associated bar-restaurant is just across the road from the guesthouse and right on the beach.

MIDRANGE

Ismail's Beach Guest House (☎ 881 2569; Batu Ferringhi; r RM70-80; ❄) Back behind the Wave-runner Beach Chalet and right on the beach, this place was under construction when we passed but several rooms were already completed. It's a clean, modern concrete complex with little in the way of creative décor but it has plenty of new-place perks like crisp sheets and little dust. All rooms have air-con, attached bath and TV.

Waverunner Beach Chalet (☎ 019 472 7789; 54 Batu Ferringhi; r RM80;) Right on the sand, this is a brick chalet block with just five rooms, so it's often full. Rooms are clean, with tiled floors, two double beds, TVs, kettles and private showers; but the are signs of wear and tear. There are a few food stalls on the doorstep. Wave Runner Watersport (p209) operates from here.

TOP END

Lone Pine Hotel (☎ 881 1511; www.lonepinehotel.com; 97 Jln Batu Ferringhi; r from RM275;) Batu Ferringhi's original hotel, established in 1948 still feels like a 1950s holiday camp (remember *Dirty Dancing*?). In contrast to the nearby mega-resorts, it's a relatively small, low-rise hotel, with only 50 rooms; even though it does retain old world ambience, it's been completely renovated. Rooms are enormous but have an institutional feel, mostly due to the greying, speckled tiles. Bathrooms are a step up from a standard public restroom. A big draw are the balconies or terraces with seaviews and the shady, pine-forested lawn just off the excellent stretch of beach. There's a pool but it's L-shaped, so not much good for anything besides lazy laps.

Holiday Inn Resort (☎ 881 1601; www.penang.holiday-inn.com; 72 Jln Batu Ferringhi; r from RM420;) Big, family-friendly resort with accommodation blocks on either side of the main road; rooms in the sea-facing Beach Wing are more expensive (from RM530). There's a wide range of rooms to choose from, including themed 'kidsuites', which come with TV, video and playstation. There's also a well-equipped kids' club, tennis courts and a gym.

Bayview Beach Resort (☎ 881 2123; www.bayviewbeach.com; Batu Ferringhi; r/ste from RM475/770;) At the southern, and quieter, end of the beach, this is a gigantic place set in lovely palm-filled gardens. The hotel is built like a shopping mall, with the many levels of rooms encircling a skylit courtyard. A glass elevator jets you up and down through the middle. Rooms are fraying and staff are less friendly than at some of the other resorts but everything you could wish for is here, including a watersports centre, gym, squash courts, shops and bars – there's a bar in the middle of the large swimming pool too.

Shangri-La Golden Sands Resort (☎ 886 1191; www.shangri-la.com; r RM490-575;) In the same Shangri-La family as the high-class Rasa Sayang (below) this hotel is more like the group's big-haired, cheesy-grinned little sister. If you could just imagine Julie the Loveboat cruise director leading you through the orderly array of blue, rubber woven lawn chairs, sprawling cement walkways and mushroom-like thatched hut shaded areas to the rattan lobby, you could have a lot of fun here. Rooms move into the modern age and are spacious with marble bathrooms. Staff are a little brusque but get the job done.

Grand Plaza Park Royal (☎ 881 1133; www.penang.parkroyalhotels.com; Batu Ferringhi; s/d/ste from RM520/550/1200;) With 324 rooms this place isn't the biggest resort here, but it's comfy, modern and a great choice. The lobby lounge, with its squashy sofas and piano bar, leads out onto a clean and attractive stretch of beach and a sparkling swimming pool. Rooms are large and have some nice touches, such as interesting shell art in the bathrooms. Sea views are preferable of course, but cost more. Nonguests can use the gardens and pools for RM25 per day, including lunch.

our pick Shangri-La Rasa Sayang Resort (☎ 881 1966; www.shangri-la.com; Jln Batu Ferringhi; r from RM600;) Outclassing every other resort on the island, this vast and luxurious establishment feels like something out of a South Sea dream. The newly renovated complex is unpretentiously chic and liveable. Rooms are large and decorated with fine hardwood furniture, and cloud-like white duvets float on the beds; all have balconies and many have sea views. The exclusive Rasa wing takes high-end to another elevation with its decadent suites – while the rest of the resort welcomes children, this area is adults-only. And did we mention the gardens? Palms, plumeria and bird of paradise create a lush enclave for the winding, partially shaded naturalistic swimming pool. A thin stretch of beach borders the gardens. As you'd expect, the hotel's Chi Spa is the most posh on Penang Island and is housed in 11 serene villas surrounded by lush plants. There's a yoga studio with regular yoga and meditation classes as well as a spa shop where you can shop for bath goodies to bring home. There are also tennis courts, a putting green and several restaurants. The service is the perfect balance of professionalism and easygoing friendliness.

Eating & Drinking

Batu Ferringhi Bistro (Batu Ferringhi; mains from RM6; 6pm-4am) This is a basic beach bar with a small menu of Chinese and Western dishes. There are tables on the sand and it's a pleasant place to relax with an evening beer.

Bocadillos (Batu Ferringhi; mains RM8; breakfast & lunch daily, till sunset Sat & Sun) Amongst the little local-style cafés around the budget guesthouses is this gem of a place serving some of the best Western breakfasts and snacks in Penang. It's a Mediterranean menu with pizzas, burgers and fresh-baked pita sandwiches stuffed with creative salads. Enjoy a fresh fruit juice and homemade baked goods while gazing across the beach out to sea.

Palace (☎ 881 1313; 78 Jln Batu Ferringhi; mains from RM12; 2-11pm) Very gaudily decorated Indian restaurant specialising in tandoori dishes, though it also serves Italian and Arabic cuisine.

Ship (☎ 881 2142; 69B Jln Batu Ferringhi; mains from RM15; noon-midnight) You can't miss this one; it's a full-size replica of a wooden sailing ship, specialising in hefty steaks and seafood. Escargot and oysters are also on the somewhat overpriced menu. It's quite smart inside, but rather dark.

Ferringhi Walk (☎ 881 3325; 16 Jln Batu Ferringhi; mains from RM16; 4-11pm) At the southern end of the beach, this place has an outside seating area and a varied menu featuring lots of Chinese dishes, seafood and grills.

Eden Seafood Village (☎ 881 1236; 69A Jln Batu Ferringhi; mains from RM20; 3.30-10.30pm) Huge barn-like place serving seafood plucked from aquariums at the entrance. Oysters, crab, lobster and countless kinds of fish are available. There's a free dance show every evening at 8.30pm.

There are some basic foodstalls on the beachfront near the budget guesthouses, where you can enjoy some fresh fish, while **Global Bay Food Court** (cnr Jln Batu Ferringhi & Jln Sungai Emas) is a good place for inexpensive Western and Chinese meals.

Getting There & Away

Buses U101 and U105 run from Weld Quay and from Komtar, in Georgetown, and take around 30 minutes to reach Batu Ferringhi.

TANJUNG TOKONG

Once a small fishing village, this area has experienced rapid development since the 1980s, mostly of the highrise variety. The town is known for its temple, **Tua Pek Kong** which is dedicated to the Taoist god of prosperity. While the temple looks rather ordinary, it hosts an annual ritual, Chneah Hoay, on the 14th night of the Chinese New Year that draws folks in from around the island. During the ceremony, the year's fortune is divined from flames that are fanned inside a special, ceremonial urn.

Facing the temple is a sitting area that was funded by the famous Tiger Balm guy, Aw Boon Haw. The nearby open-air seafood restaurant is renowned throughout Penang and the town is also known for its chicken rice.

TANJUNG BUNGAH & PULAU TIKUS

Heading back into Georgetown from Batu Ferringhi, you'll pass **Tanjung Bungah** (Cape of Flowers), the first real beach town close to the city – but it's not good for swimming. Inexplicably, big hotels and apartment blocks are cropping up everywhere, but Batu Ferringhi is still a better option.

After Tanjung Bungah, you'll enter the Pulau Tikus (Midlands) suburbs, full of discos, wining-and-dining venues, cinemas, and megamalls like Midlands Park Centre (p188) and Island Plaza. Georgetown has encroached enough that this area could nearly be considered a neighbourhood, rather than a separate town. A taxi from Georgetown's Lebuh Chulia to Midlands costs RM15.

Pulau Tikus is also the beginning of scenic Gurney Dr with its great sea views and hawker food (see p194); see p201 for Gurney Plaza. Eventually it intersects with Jln Sultan Ahmad Shah, formerly Millionaire's Row, where nouveau riche Chinese in the early 20th century competed to see who could build the most impressive mansion. Many of the homes have now been demolished and abandoned, taken over by squatters, fronted by office space or even converted into fast-food outlets. Keep moving in this direction and you'll have made it back to central Georgetown.

SEBERANG PERAI

Living in the shadow of the tourist megalith of Penang Island, Seberang Perai has become the forgotten half of the state. While it doesn't hold much to entice visitors, Butterworth has one or two interesting places to visit if you're passing through, and the friendly island of Pulau Aman is the perfect place to go for an immersion into the Malay side of life. The province was previously called Wellesley Province named for Richard Wellesley, the governor-general of Bengal from 1797–1805.

BUTTERWORTH

You probably won't spend much time in the industrial town of Butterworth, which lacks the historic points of interest and charm found on Penang Island. The main reason most travellers come here is to pass through and cross the channel to visit Penang. The town has a large ferry port and an air force base.

The only major point of interest is the **Penang Bird Park** (Taman Burung Pinang; ☎ 399 1899; Jln Todak; adult/child RM15/7.50; 9am-7.30pm), 7km east of the ferry terminal across the river. This landscaped park has more than 300 species of birds, mostly from Southeast Asia, including parrots, hornbills and hawks. There's a walk-in aviary, lily pond, a playground and a large collection of orchids, hibiscus and palms. To get there, take one of the frequent buses from Butterworth bus station to Seberang Jaya (RM1).

Right next to the Penang Bird Park is **Arulmigu Karumariamman Temple**, a South Indian Hindu temple with the largest and tallest (22m) *rajagopuram* (main temple tower) in Malaysia. The entrance to the *rajagopuram* is also the largest in the country at nearly 6.5m. The temple was completed in 1997.

If you're a Chinese-temple freak, it's worth checking out **Rumah Berhala Tow Boo Kong** (Nine Emperor Gods Temple) which began its existence as a shed on a rented piece of land in 1971. The temple blossomed little by little and was completed in its final form in the year 2000. It's exceedingly ornate for a modern edifice, with a dramatic roof swarming with curving pagodas and golden dragons. It's home to a Taoist group who worship the Nine Emperor Gods, the nine sons of the Queen of Heaven, who are the patron deities of, among other things, prosperity and health. Their festival, called none other than the **Nine Emperor Gods Festival**, is held on the ninth day of the ninth lunar month each year when the Nine Emperor Gods are believed to descend to Earth from the stars. For nine days devotes show off their religious fervour and the temple becomes a hive of followers. Vegetarian food and snacks are prepared and sold at stalls during this time. The temple is north of the Jln Raja Uda and the Butterworth-Kulim Expressway. Look out for the temple on the right side of the road after the Butterworth Outer Ring Rd intersection.

Sleeping & Eating

There's little to detain you in Butterworth for the night, but there are several hotels if you do wish to stay.

Ambassadress Hotel (☎ 332 7788; 4425 Jln Bagan Luar; r from RM45;) This sleepy Chinese hotel above a cheap *kedai kopi* (coffee shop) of the same name is a fair, if rather timeworn, budget option. Air-con rooms cost RM63, and all have attached bathrooms.

Hotel Berlin (☎ 332 1701; 4802 Jln Bagan Luar; s/d from RM100/120;) A few doors down from the Ambassadress, the Berlin offers a bit more comfort, and discounts are normally available. There's a gym and sauna, and breakfast is included in the price.

Sunway Hotel (☎ 370 7788; www.sh.com.my; 11 Lebuh Tenggiri Dua, Seberang Jaya; s/d RM180/200;) This modern tower, close to the Penang Bird Park, in the suburb of Seberang Jaya is aimed primarily at business travellers, with the usual smart international setup. Rooms sport 'oversized beds' and you can even get 'karaoke on demand' through your TV.

There are numerous cheap Chinese cafes scattered around the town centre though one of the better places is **Sri Ananda Bahwan Restaurant** (☎ 323 6228; 2982 Jln Bagar Luar; mains from RM3; 6.30am-midnight), a popular Indian place which serves vegetarian/nonvegetarian set lunches for RM3.50/5. It has a particularly good selection of colourful, handmade Indian sweets, which you can have boxed to take away.

Getting There & Away

Most of the land transport (buses, trains, taxis) between Penang and other places in peninsular Malaysia and Thailand leaves from Butterworth, not far from the train station and next to the terminal for ferries going to or from Georgetown. See the Getting There & Away (p172) and Getting Around (p174) sections for information on transport services to/from Butterworth.

PULAU AMAN

For anyone really wanting to get off the beaten track, head to the tiny fishing island of **Pulau Aman** (Peace Island; population 300), southeast of Penang Island, and 4.5km off the coast of Bukit Tambun in Seberang Perai The whole island can be covered on foot in about an hour; trees are labelled with scientific and local names, making the walk a bit educational as well. The oldest known *sukun* (breadfruit tree) in Malaysia can be found in the village, and is said to have been planted in 1891; it's marked with a basic cement sign. Other elegant *sukun* are found all over the island. There is one small **beach** at the north, but don't even consider exposing your knees or shoulders, let alone your midriff, to sunbathe here. Several paths lead through the village and a cement path goes partway around the island. At the end of the cement path on the waterside is **Telaga Emas Well** (Golden Well) that was purportedly dug in 1879 and is now covered with a modern shelter to protect it from decay; the well is also special because it never runs dry. Don't forget mosquito repellent if you walk around the island.

Off the north coast of Pulau Aman is **Pulau Gedung**, a deserted island that was once the tramping ground for the region's numerous pirates (see p21). Everything of interest on the forested island revolves around pirates: there's **Gua Lanun** (Pirate's Cave, where the sailors stashed their loot) and **Batu Perompak** (Pirate Rock) which is also the tomb of local pirate captain Panglima Garang. You'll have to bargain with a local Pulau Aman fisherman for transport to the island or you can prearrange the voyage by contacting the **Seberang Perai Fishermen Association** (☎ 397 9796).

To get to Pulau Aman take the ferry (one-way adult/child RM4/2), filled with fishermen and their families, that leaves the Bukit Tambun pier (departures 10am, 1pm, 4pm and 7pm; 30 minutes) for the fishing village on the northeast side of the island. The return trips to Bukit Tambun are at 8am, 12pm, 3pm and 6pm.

Directory

CONTENTS

ACCOMMODATION

Accommodation in Kuala Lumpur (KL), Melaka and Penang ranges from sky-scraping five-star hotels to grungy backpacker dives that scrape the bottom of the barrel. The good news is that accommodation is refreshingly inexpensive, even at the top end of the market. Outside of public holidays (around major festivals such as Chinese New Year in January/February) most midrange and top-end hotels offer big discounts – always ask about special offers.

For the purposes of this book, we have divided accommodation up into the following categories: budget is for rooms under RM70; midrange from RM71 to RM200 per room and top end at RM201 and above per room.

> **BOOK YOUR STAY ONLINE**
>
> For more accommodation reviews and recommendations by Lonely Planet authors, check out the online booking service at www.lonelyplanet.com/hotels. You'll find the true, insider lowdown on the best places to stay. Reviews are thorough and independent. Best of all, you can book online.

Promotional rates can bring rooms at many top-end hotels into the midrange category. A 5% government tax applies to all hotel rooms (including at cheaper hotels) and almost all top-end hotels levy an additional 10% service charge. Credit cards are widely accepted at midrange and top-end hotels; cash payment is expected at cheaper places.

As a rule, budget hotels offer poky boxy rooms, often with thin plywood partition walls and no windows; you normally have a choice of private or shared bathrooms and fan or air-conditioning. At midrange hotels air-con is standard, and rooms typically have TVs, phones, proper wardrobes and other appealing mod cons. Some offer full top-end facilities – restaurants, business centres and swimming pools – at midrange prices.

Top-end hotels in Malaysia pull out all the stops. Rooms have every conceivable amenity, from in-room internet access (typically over a LAN cable), to safes, minibars, slippers and robes, and even prayer mats for Muslim guests. Top-end hotels typically quote prices as ++ (called plus-plus), which means the 10% service charge and 5% government tax haven't been included in the price. We quote net prices for all budget and midrange places.

Camping

Camping is possible on Pulau Besar near Melaka (see p163) and in Penang National Park (p207), Teluk Bahang Forest Reserve (p206) and Pulau Jerejak (p204) near Penang. The **Forest Research Institute of Malaysia** (FRIM; Map pp72-3; ☎ 6279 7575; www.frim.gov.my; Selangor Darul Ehsan; admission RM5) also allows camping if you get permission in advance. Most sites are fairly

PRACTICALITIES

- The electricity supply (220–240V, 50 cycles) is highly reliable – sockets take a UK-type three-square-pin plug.
- English-language newspapers include the *New Straits Times*, the *Star* and the *Malay Mail*.
- Radio Malaysia has three main radio stations (KL frequencies given): HITZ FM (92.9 FM; top 40), MIX FM (94.5 FM; adult contemporary) and Light & Easy FM (105.7 FM; easy listening). Check locally for frequencies in Melaka and Penang. See www.bbc.co.uk/worldservice for details of local frequencies for BBC Radio World Service.
- Malaysia has two terrestrial government television channels, TV1 and TV2, and three commercial stations, TV3, NTV7 and TV9, plus a host of satellite channels on the Astro network.
- Malaysia follows the metric system for weights and measures.

simple – just flat spaces for tents and sometimes a toilet block (usually with non-potable water). Bring your own tent, preferably with a mosquito net; see p132.

Homestays

Homestays with Malaysian families are becoming increasingly popular. Options in this book include the cheerful Ben Soo Homestay (p103) in KL, and Desa Paku House & Garden (p165) at Alor Gajah. Penang also has some beautifully converted mansions that offer a homestay-type experience. Contact local offices of Tourism Malaysia (p225) for more information on local homestay programmes.

Hostels & Guesthouses

Kuala Lumpur, Melaka and Penang all have cheap hostels and guesthouses, ranging from clusters of box rooms in city towers to informal huts on the beach. Most offer dorm beds (from as little as RM9) as well as basic rooms with shared or private bathrooms and a choice of fan or air-con. Seek out the smaller, family-owned places for a more relaxed, homestay-like experience. Many of these places do not provide a top sheet; bring a towel, blanket or sleeping bag–liner to keep the air-con chill at bay.

Hotels

All the cities in this book have numerous hotels, ranging from cheap Chinese-run places that target locals to five-star palaces that attract global high-fliers. Rooms almost always have telephones, air-con and private bathrooms, and extras such as TVs and fridges are usually available. In cheaper hotels, 'single' normally means one double bed, and 'double' means two double beds – so four people can easily share a double room. To aid ventilation, the walls of cheaper rooms may not meet the ceiling, which is terrible for acoustics and privacy – bring earplugs.

In more upmarket hotels, 'superior' rooms are normally standard rooms, while 'deluxe' or 'club' rooms have better facilities. In many midrange hotels only the deluxe rooms have windows. Top-end hotels offer the same luxuries found worldwide – TVs, bathtubs, safes, minibars, hairdryers, tea- and coffee-making facilities and, off course, slippers and monogrammed terry robes.

Resorts

Penang Island and several other islands on the west coast have Asian-style beach resorts of varying standards, from simple huts to international-style resort hotels. Posher resorts have restaurants, swimming pools, evening entertainment and family-friendly beach activities.

BUSINESS HOURS

Most of Peninsular Malaysia works Monday to Friday, with Saturday a half day. Government offices are usually open from 8am to 4.15pm Monday to Friday. Most close for lunch from 12.45pm to 2pm (12.15pm to 2.45pm on Friday for Muslim prayers). Banks generally open 9.30am to 4.30pm on weekdays and 9.30am to noon on Saturday, though smaller branches may keep shorter hours.

Shop hours are variable – most are open from around 9.30am to 7pm from Monday to Saturday. Major department stores and shopping malls are open from around 10am until 9pm or 10pm, seven days a week.

CHILDREN

Practicalities

KL, Melaka and Penang are great places to travel with children. Hygiene standards are high and you should be able to steer clear of stomach bugs by sticking to purified water, washing fruit, eating at more upmarket restaurants and making sure children wash their hands regularly (alcohol handwash is available from most pharmacies). Keep children away from animals, even friendly cats and dogs – rabies (p241) is a risk and even pets can carry skin diseases. For more on health issues, see p237.

There are discounts for children at most tourist attractions and for most transport options. Many beach resorts have special family chalets and hotels can often provide an extra bed, either free or for a small charge. However, cots are not widely available. Public transport is comfortable and relatively well organised, but pushing a stroller around can be a hassle with the high kerbs, bumpy pavements and missing drain covers.

Baby formula, baby food and nappies (diapers) are easily available; though it makes sense to stock up on these items before heading to remote destinations or islands. Créche facilities are available at some large malls. Note that few taxis have car seats or seatbelts in the back seat – if you bring a child seat from home, the only place you can secure it is up front by the driver, although this is generally regarded as the most risky seat in the event of a crash.

Lonely Planet's *Travel with Children* by Cathy Lanigan and others contains useful advice on how to cope with kids on the road and what to bring along to make things go more smoothly, with special attention paid to travelling in developing countries. Also useful for general advice is www.travelwithyourkids.com.

Sights & Activities

KL is the easiest place to keep small travellers amused. The big shopping malls are awash with kid-friendly entertainments – bowling, ice-skating, cinemas, comic book and toy shops – and there are numerous educational museums and family-focused theme parks and water-parks. KL also has a good zoo and aquarium. Other options include splashing around in jungle pools at forest reserves and some excellent parks and adventure playgrounds in KL, Melaka and Penang. For more on these options, see the sections on activities for children in KL (p99), Melaka (p151) and Penang (p188).

CLIMATE

Lying just 2° to 7° north of the equator, Peninsular Malaysia is as hot and steamy as Tom Jones in a greenhouse. Temperatures and humidity are high year round, with temperatures rarely dropping below 20°C, even at night. In the cities, you can normally find somewhere with air-conditioning to escape to when the heat gets too much. The heat can feel even more oppressive in the jungle because of the increase in humidity.

Although Malaysia is monsoonal, only the east coast of the peninsula has a real rainy season – elsewhere there is just a little more rain than usual. Rain tends to arrive in brief torrential downpours, providing a welcome relief from the heat. During the monsoon

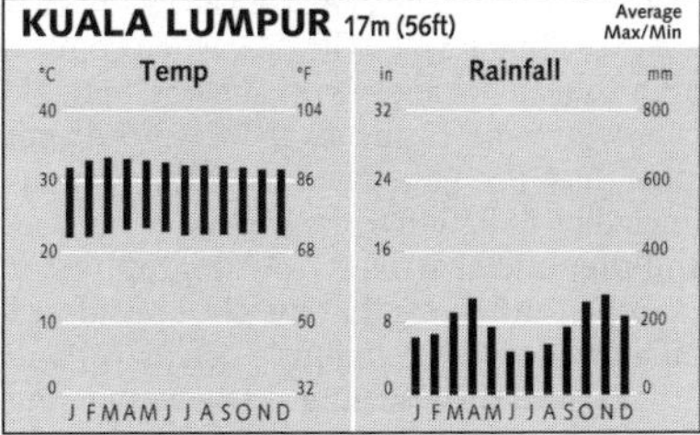

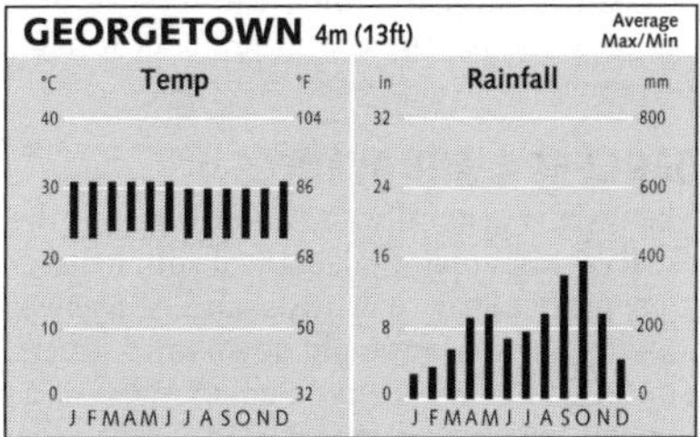

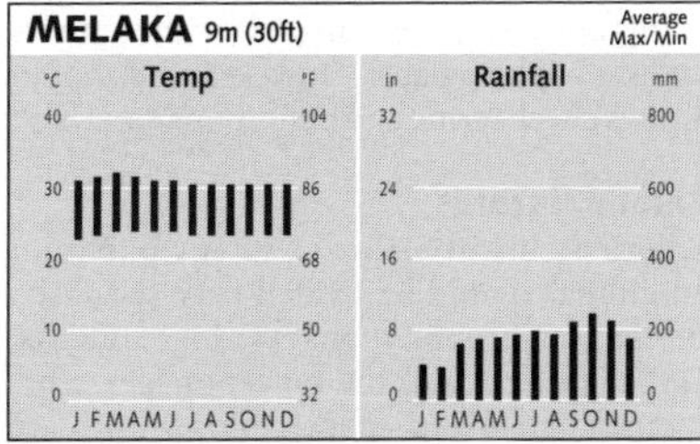

it may rain every day, but it rarely rains all day. Humidity tends to hover around the 90% mark, but you can always escape the clammy heat by retreating to the cooler hills.

For current weather forecasts check the website of the **Malaysian Meteorological Department** (www.kjc.gov.my/english/weather/weather.html).

For tips on the best times to visit the region, see p17.

COURSES

Numerous courses are possible in KL, Melaka and Penang, from Malay and Nonya cookery to language and art courses and lessons in traditional music, song and dance. KL has the widest selection of courses (see p98), but there are also some interesting options in Melaka (p150) and Penang (p187).

CUSTOMS REGULATIONS

The following can be brought into Malaysia duty free: 1L of alcohol, 225g of tobacco (200 cigarettes or 50 cigars) and souvenirs and gifts not exceeding RM200 (RM500 when coming from Labuan or Langkawi). Cameras, portable radios, perfume, cosmetics and watches do not incur duty. Prohibited items include weapons (including imitations), fireworks and 'obscene and prejudicial articles' (pornography, for example, and items that may be considered inflammatory, or religiously offensive) and drugs. Heed this warning – drug smuggling carries the death penalty in Malaysia.

Visitors can carry only RM1000 in and out of Malaysia; there's no limit on foreign currency.

DANGERS & ANNOYANCES

Malaysia is generally a safe country but the usual caveats apply – take care of your belongings, particularly in crowds, and be wary of walking alone late at night down unlit streets. Touting is not as big a problem in Malaysia as in neighbouring nations, but there are a few scams to look out for. Operators mentioned in this book have been checked by the authors and should be reliable. However, you should always check terms and conditions carefully.

Animal Hazards

Rabies occurs in Malaysia, so any bite from an animal should be treated very seriously. Be cautious around monkeys, dogs and cats. On jungle treks look out for centipedes, scorpions, spiders and snakes. Mosquitoes are likely to be the biggest menace. The risk of malaria is low and anti-malarial tablets are rarely recommended but dengue fever (p240) is a growing problem, so take precautions to avoid mosquito bites by covering up exposed skin or wearing a strong repellent containing DEET. See p243 for advice on how to deal with bites, including snake bites, and stings.

Scams

The most common scams involve seemingly friendly locals who invite you to join rigged card games, or shops who trick travellers into buying large amounts of gold jewellery or gems at elevated prices. You can normally identify people who do not have your best interests at heart by their manner. Anyone who accosts you in the street asking 'where you come from' or claiming to have a 'relative studying abroad' may be setting you up for a scam – the best option is not to reply at all. At the Malaysia-Thailand border, don't believe anyone who claims that you are legally required to change sums of money into ringgit or baht before crossing the border – no such regulation exists.

Theft & Violence

Malaysia is not particularly prone to theft or violence. Nevertheless it pays to keep a close eye on your belongings, especially your travel documents (passport, travellers cheques etc). Muggings do happen, particularly afterhours and in the poorer, run-down areas of cities. Be wary of demonstrations, particularly over religious or ethnic issues, as these can turn violent.

Credit-card fraud is a growing problem in Malaysia. Use your cards only at established businesses and guard your credit-card numbers closely. See p223 for more hassles involving credit cards in Malaysia.

It's worth carrying a small, sturdy padlock for cheap hotel-room doors and hostel lockers and to keep prying fingers out of your bags in left-luggage rooms.

DISCOUNT CARDS

A Hostelling International (HI) card can be used to waive the small initial membership fee at some hostels, YMCAs and YWCAs. An international student identity card (ISIC) offers some useful discounts, though many student discounts, such as for train travel, are available only for Malaysian students. Seniors qualify for many discounts with proof of age.

EMBASSIES & CONSULATES

The following countries are among nations with diplomatic representation in Malaysia. Unless mentioned otherwise, all are in Kuala Lumpur (☎ 03).

Australia (Map pp84-5; ☎ 2146 5555; www.australia.org.my; 6 Jln Yap Kwan Seng)
Brunei (Map pp72-3; ☎ 2161 2800; Level 19, Menara Tan & Tan, 207 Jln Tun Razak)
Canada (Map pp72-3; ☎ 2718 3333; kualalumpur.gc.ca; Level 17, Menara Tan & Tan, 207 Jln Tun Razak)
Cambodia (off Map pp72-3; ☎ 4257 1150; reckl@tm.net.my; 83/JKR 2809 Lingkungan U Thant)
China (Map pp72-3; ☎ 2163 6815; my.chineseembassy.org; 229 Jln Ampang)
France (Map p92; ☎ 2053 5500; www.ambafrance-my.org; 192-6 Jln Ampang)
Germany (Map pp72-3; ☎ 2170 9666; www.kuala-lumpur.diplo.de; Level 26, Menara Tan & Tan, 207 Jln Tun Razak)
India (off Map pp72-3; ☎ 2093 3510; www.indianhighcommission.com.my; 2 Jln Taman Duta)
Indonesia Kuala Lumpur (Map pp72-3; ☎ 2116 4000; www.kbrikl.org.my; 233 Jln Tun Razak, Kuala Lumpur) Georgetown (off Map p176; ☎ 04-227 5141; 467 Jln Burma, Georgetown, Penang)
Ireland (Map pp72-3; ☎ 2161 2963; www.ireland-embassy.com.my; 5th fl, South Blk, Ampang Walk, 218 Jln Ampang)
Italy (off Map pp72-3; ☎ 4256 5122; www.ambkualalumpur.esteri.it; 99 Jln U Thant)
Japan (Map pp72-3; ☎ 2142 7044; www.my.emb-japan.go.jp; 11 Persiaran Stonor)
Laos (Map pp72-3; ☎ 4251 1118; 12a Persiaran Madge)
Myanmar (Map pp72-3; ☎ 2442 4085; 5 Taman U Thant 1)
Nepal (Map pp84-5; ☎ 2164 5934; www.nepalembassy.com.my; 13th fl, Wisma MCA, 163 Jln Ampang)
Netherlands (Map pp72-3; ☎ 2168 6200; www.netherlands.org.my; 7th fl, South Block, Ampang Walk, 218 Jln Ampang)
New Zealand (Map pp84-5; ☎ 2078 2533; www.nzembassy.com/malaysia; Level 21 Menara IMC, 8 Jln Sultan Ismail)

TRAVEL ADVISORIES

For latest travel advisories check the following websites:

Australia (www.smartraveller.gov.au)
Canada (www.voyage.gc.ca)
New Zealand (www.safetravel.govt.nz)
UK (www.fco.gov.uk/travel)
US (http://travel.state.gov/travel)

Philippines (Map pp84-5; ☎ 2148 9989; www.philembassykl.org.my; 1 Changkat Kia Peng)
Singapore (Map pp72-3; ☎ 2161 6277; www.mfa.gov.sg/kl; 209 Jln Tun Razak)
Spain (Map pp72-3; ☎ 2148 4868; emb.kualalumpur@mae.es; 200 Jln Ampang)
Thailand Kuala Lumpur (Map pp72-3; ☎ 2148 8222; thaikul@mfa.go.th; 206 Jln Ampang, Kuala Lumpur) Georgetown (off Map p176; ☎ 04-226 8029; 1 Jln Tunku Abdul Rahman, Georgetown, Penang)
UK (Map p92; ☎ 2170 2200; www.britain.org.my; 185 Jln Ampang)
USA (Map pp72-3; ☎ 2168 5000; http://usembassymalaysia.org.my; 376 Jln Tun Razak)
Vietnam (Map pp84-5; ☎ 2148 3270; www.mofa.gov.vn/vnemb.my; 4 Persiaran Stonor)

FESTIVALS & EVENTS

Malaysia has a huge number of religious holidays and celebrations, as well as sporting spectaculars, like the Malaysian Grand Prix, and special events laid on by Tourism Malaysia and the government. Some festivals have a fixed date, but Hindus, Muslims and Chinese all follow a lunar calendar, so the dates for many religious festivals vary each year (Muslim holidays move forward 11 days each year, while Hindu and Chinese festivals change dates but fall roughly within the same months). **Tourism Malaysia** (www.tourism.gov.my) has listings of festivals and events on its website, or pick up a calendar of events pamphlet from any tourist office.

See the destination chapters for details of events specific to particular towns and cities.

January–February

Thai Pongal A Hindu harvest festival marking the beginning of the Hindu month of Thai, considered the luckiest month of the year. Celebrated by Tamils.
Chinese New Year Dragon dances and pedestrian parades mark the start of the new year. Celebrations last 15 days; children receive *ang pow* (money in red packets), businesses traditionally clear their debts and everybody wishes you *kong hee fatt choy* (a happy and prosperous New Year).
Thaipusam One of the most dramatic Hindu festivals (now banned in India), in which devotees honour Lord Subramaniam with acts of self-mortification; see boxed text, p221.

March–April

Malaysian Grand Prix Formula 1's big outing in Southeast Asia is held at the Sepang International Circuit near KL; see p100.

Birthday of the Goddess of Mercy Offerings are made to the very popular Kuan Yin at temples across the region.
Birthday of the Monkey God The birthday of T'se Tien Tai Seng Yeh is celebrated twice a year. Mediums pierce their cheeks and tongues with skewers and go into trances, writing special charms in blood.

April–May

Chithirai Vishu The start of the Hindu new year.
Wesak Day (Vesak Day) Buddha's birth, enlightenment and death are celebrated with various events, including the release of caged birds to symbolise the setting free of captive souls.

June

Festa de San Pedro Christian celebration on 29 June in honour of the patron saint of the fishing community, particularly celebrated by the Eurasian-Portuguese community of Melaka.
Birthday of the God of War Kuan Ti, who has the ability to avert war and to protect people during war, is honoured on his birthday.
Dragon Boat Festival Commemorates the Malay legend of the fishermen who paddled out to sea to prevent the drowning of a Chinese saint, beating drums to scare away any fish that might attack him. The festival is celebrated from June to August, with boat races in Penang (see p171).

July–August

Birthday of Kuan Yin The goddess of mercy has another birthday!
Sri Krishna Jayanti A 10-day Hindu festival celebrating popular events in the life of Krishna.

August–September

Festival of the Hungry Ghosts The souls of the dead are released for one day of feasting and entertainment on earth. Chinese Malaysians perform operas and lay out food for their ancestors. The ghosts eat the spirit of the food, but thoughtfully leave the substance for mortal celebrants. Mainly celebrated in Penang (see p171).
National Day (Hari Kebangsaan) Malaysia celebrates its independence on 31 August with parades and events all over the country, but particularly in KL.
Vinayagar Chaturthi During the Tamil month of Avani (around August and September), prayers are offered to Vinayagar, another name for the popular elephant-headed god Ganesh.
Lantern Festival The overthrow of the Mongol warlords in ancient China is celebrated by eating moon cakes and lighting colourful paper lanterns. Moon cakes are filled with bean paste, lotus seeds and sometimes a duck egg–yolk.

September–October

Navarathri In the Tamil month of Purattasi, the Hindu festival of 'Nine Nights' is dedicated to the wives of Shiva, Vishnu and Brahma. Young girls are dressed as the goddess Kali.
Festival of the Nine Emperor Gods Nine days of Chinese operas, processions and other events honour the nine emperor gods.

October–November

Thimithi (Fire-Walking Ceremony) Hindu devotees prove their faith by walking across glowing coals at temples in Melaka.
Deepavali Rama's victory over the demon king Ravana is celebrated with the Festival of Lights, when tiny oil-lamps

ISLAMIC FESTIVALS

The major Islamic events each year are connected with Ramadan, when Muslims fast from sunrise to sunset. Fifteen days before the start of Ramadan, on Nisfu Night, it is believed the souls of the dead visit their homes. During Ramadan Lailatul Qadar (Night of Grandeur), Muslims celebrate the arrival of the Quran on earth, before its revelation by the Prophet Mohammed. Hari Raya Puasa (also known as Hari Raya Aidilfitri) marks the end of the month-long fast, with two days of joyful celebration and feasting. Hari Raya Puasa is the major holiday of the Muslim calendar and it can be difficult to find accommodation, particularly on the coast. The start of Ramadan moves forward 11 days every year in line with the Muslim lunar calendar – the fast is set to begin on 2 September 2008 and 22 August 2009, but dates can vary as the exact phases of the lunar cycle are open to interpretation.

Apart from Ramadan, the other major Islamic festival is Hari Raya Haji, a two-day festival marking the successful completion of the hajj (pilgrimage to Mecca) and commemorating the willingness of Abraham to sacrifice his son. Many shops, offices and tourist attractions close and locals consume large amounts of cakes and sweets. The festival takes place in on 8 December 2008 and 28 November 2009. Malaysian Muslims also celebrate the birth of the prophet Mohammed with the festival of Mawlid al-Nabi, which takes place on 20 March 2008 and 9 March 2009. Awal Muharram (Muslim New Year) falls on 10 January and 29 December 2008, 18 December 2009 and 7 December 2010.

THAIPUSAM

After Deepavali, the most important event in the Hindu calendar is the festival of Thaipusam, held every year during January or February. Marking the birthday of Murugan (Subramaniam), son of Shiva, the festival takes place when the Pusam constellation is at its highest point during the Hindu month of Thai, hence the name. Thaipusam is celebrated with riotous processions at Batu Caves (p131) near Kuala Lumpur (KL) and the Nattukotai Chettiar Temple and Waterfall Hilltop Temple in Penang (see p184). The Batu Caves celebrations alone attracted 1.3 million devotees in 2007.

The greatest spectacle of Thaipusam is the procession of *kavadi* carriers, devotees who subject themselves to seemingly masochistic acts to give thanks for answered prayers. Many of the devotees carry offerings of milk in *paal kudam* (milk pots), often connected to their skin by hooks. Even more striking are the *vel kavadi* (great cages of spikes that pierce the skin of the carrier and are decorated with peacock feathers, pictures of deities and flowers). Some penitents pierce their tongues and cheeks with hooks, skewers and tridents hung with objects like limes and unripe coconuts. Couples whose prayers for children have been answered carry their babies on their shoulders in saffron cradles made of sugar-cane stalks.

Before engaging in these ritual acts, pilgrims devote a month to prayer, abstaining from sex and following a strict vegetarian diet. The physical piercings are carried out while in a trance and participants claim to feel no pain; later the wounds are treated with lemon juice and holy ash to prevent scarring. A few foreigners join the procession and even participate in acts of self-mortification but, like firewalking, these rituals are best left to the faithful – every year doctors treat dozens of poorly prepared devotees for skin lacerations or exhaustion after the rigours of Thaipusam.

are lit outside Hindu homes to guide Rama back from exile. The lights also attract Lakshmi, the goddess of wealth, who will not enter an unlit home. Indian businesses start the new financial year, and families take a predawn oil bath, put on new clothes and share sweets.

Birthday of Kuan Yin This popular goddess of mercy gets to celebrate her birthday for the third time in the year.

Guru Nanak's Birthday The birthday of Guru Nanak, founder of the Sikh religion, is celebrated on 22 November.

December

Winter Solstice Festival A Chinese festival to offer thanks for a good harvest.

FOOD

Malaysia is foodie heaven, with a breathtaking array of dishes and cuisines, from local Malay, Nonya, Chinese and Indian food to dishes drawn from across the globe. For a complete description, see the eating listings in the regional chapters and browse the Food & Drink chapter (p42).

Many restaurants in Malaysia close between lunch and dinner and few places stay open later than 10.30pm. Standard dining hours in Kuala Lumpur, Melaka and Penang are as follows: breakfast from 8am to 11am, lunch from noon to 2.30pm, and dinner from 6pm to 10.30pm.

GAY & LESBIAN TRAVELLERS

Malaysia is a predominantly Muslim country and the level of tolerance for homosexuality is vastly different from its neighbours. Sex between men is illegal at any age and *syariah* Islamic laws (which apply only to Muslims) forbid sodomy and cross-dressing. Fortunately outright persecution of gays and lesbians is rare, the trumped-up case against the former deputy prime minister Anwar Ibrahim (see p28) being a notable exception.

Nonetheless, gay and lesbian travellers should avoid behaviour that attracts unwanted attention. Malaysians are quite conservative about displays of public affection. Although same-sex handholding is quite common for men and women, this is rarely an indication of sexuality; an overtly gay couple doing the same would attract attention, though there is little risk of vocal or aggressive homophobia.

There's actually a fairly active gay scene in KL (see boxed text, p117). The lesbian scene is more discreet, but it exists for those willing to seek it out. Start looking for information on www.utopia-asia.com or www.fridae.com, both of which provide good coverage of gay and lesbian events and activities across Asia.

The **PT Foundation** (www.ptfmalaysia.org) is a voluntary nonprofit organisation providing HIV/AIDS and sexuality education, care and support programs for marginalised communities in Malaysia.

HOLIDAYS

As well as fixed secular holidays, various religious festivals (which change dates annually) are national holidays. These include Chinese New Year (in January/February), the Hindu festival of Deepavali (in October/November), the Buddhist festival of Wesak (April/May) and the Muslim festivals of Hari Raya Haji, Hari Raya Puasa, Mawlid al-Nabi and Awal Muharram (Muslim New Year); see p219 for dates. There are also a number of state holidays, usually associated with the local sultan's birthday or a Muslim celebration.

Public Holidays

Fixed annual holidays include the following:

New Year's Day 1 January
Federal Territory Day 1 February (in Kuala Lumpur and Putrajaya only)
Labour Day 1 May
Wesak Day Variable
Yang di-Pertuan Agong's (King's) Birthday 1st Saturday in June
National Day (Hari Kebangsaan) 31 August
Christmas Day 25 December

School Holidays

Schools in Malaysia break for holidays five times a year. The actual dates vary from state to state but are generally in January (one week), March (two weeks), May (three weeks), August (one week) and October (four weeks).

INSURANCE

We strongly recommend taking out travel insurance – if you can't afford insurance, you definitely can't afford the consequences if anything does go wrong. Check the small print to see if the policy covers potentially dangerous sporting activities, such as diving or trekking. For medical treatment, some policies pay doctors or hospitals directly but most require you to pay on the spot and claim later (keep all receipts and documentation). Check that the policy covers ambulances or an emergency flight home.

For information on health insurance see p237 and for car insurance see p234.

Worldwide travel insurance is available at www.lonelyplanet.com/travel_services. You can buy, extend and claim online anytime – even if you're already on the road.

INTERNET ACCESS

Internet cafés (charging RM3 to RM8 per hour) are found everywhere and many hotels offer free (or discounted) access for guests. Some top-end hotels offer in-room internet-access over a LAN Ethernet cable. Wi-fi is also becoming increasingly common at hotels (usually in the lobby) and in chain coffeeshops like Starbucks, often for free (registration may be required). The website www.wi-fihotspotlist.com/browse/intl/2000032 has a good list of hotspots. However, you should be aware of the security risk of sending sensitive information over a wireless connection. Bring a three-pronged, square-pin adaptor (as used in the UK) for your laptop power cable.

If you don't have wi-fi, you can arrange dial-up internet in Malaysia using prepaid cards. Major internet providers include **Jaring** (www.jaring.my) and **Telekom Malaysia** (www.tm.com.my). Check that your laptop modem is enabled to work outside your home country.

LEGAL MATTERS

In any dealings with the local police forces it will pay to be deferential. You're most likely to come into contact with them either through reporting a crime (some of the big cities in Malaysia have tourist police stations for this purpose) or while driving. Minor misdemeanours may be overlooked, but don't count on it. Be careful about offering anyone a bribe – you never know how officials will respond and you could make things worse rather than better.

Drug trafficking carries a mandatory death penalty. A number of foreigners have been executed in Malaysia, some of them for possession of amazingly small quantities of heroin.

COMING OF AGE IN MALAYSIA

- The legal age for voting is 21.
- You can drive legally at 18.
- Heterosexual sex is legal at 16.
- To legally buy alcohol you need to be 21 (this is rarely enforced).

Even possession can bring down a lengthy jail sentence and a beating with the *rotan* (cane). You only get one life – don't blow it by gambling with drugs in Malaysia.

MAPS

Periplus (www.periplus.com) produces useful maps of Malaysia, Peninsular Malaysia and KL, but the free maps available from Tourism Malaysia are also pretty good – particularly the pocket-sized KL and Georgetown city maps.

MONEY

See the Quick Reference page (inside the front cover) for currency exchange rates.

ATMs & Credit Cards

International credit and debit cards backed by Visa, Mastercard, Cirrus or Plus are widely accepted in Malaysian shops, hotels and restaurants and you can use them in many ATMs. Make sure you know your PIN number – many shops require you to enter your PIN *and* provide a signature. And a word of warning: credit-card fraud is so widespread in Malaysia that many banks block foreign cards as soon as they are used in a Malaysian ATM – even if you notify your bank that you are travelling to Malaysia. If this happens, you'll need to call the bank and verify your identity to get the card unlocked.

If you have any questions about whether your cards will be accepted in Malaysia, ask your home bank about its reciprocal relationships with Malaysian banks. Branches of **Maybank** (www.maybank2u.com.my), and other major banks can arrange credit-card advances over the counter with a passport as ID.

Contact details for credit-card companies in Malaysia:

American Express (☎ 2050 0000; www.americanexpress.com/malaysia)
MasterCard (☎ 1800 804 594)
Visa (☎ 1800 800 159)

Currency

The Malaysian ringgit (RM) is made up of 100 sen. Coins in use are 1 sen, 5 sen, 10 sen, 20 sen and 50 sen; notes come in RM1, RM5, RM10, RM50 and RM100 (RM2 notes are being phased out). Previously fixed against the US dollar, the ringgit now floats against an undisclosed basket of currencies.

Malaysians sometimes refer to the ringgit as 'dollars', the old name for the country's currency – if in doubt, ask if people mean US dollars of 'Malaysian dollars' (ie ringgit). Be sure to carry plenty of small bills with you when venturing outside cities – people often cannot change bills larger than RM10.

Taxes & Refunds

There is no general sales tax but there is a government tax of 5%, plus a service tax of 10% at larger hotels and restaurants.

Travellers Cheques & Cash

Banks in the region are efficient and there are plenty of private moneychangers, open longer hours and sometimes with better rates. Banks usually charge a commission for cash and cheques (around RM10 per transaction, with a possible extra fee for each cheque), whereas moneychangers offer free transactions. However, moneychangers in rural areas may not accept travellers cheques.

All major brands of travellers cheques are accepted across the region. Cash in major currencies is also readily exchanged, though like everywhere else in the world the US dollar has a slight edge.

PHOTOGRAPHY

Malaysians are generally relaxed about having their picture taken, though it's still polite to ask permission first. To avoid causing offence, always ask before taking pictures in mosques or temples. For advice on taking better photos, Lonely Planet's *Travel Photography: A Guide to Taking Better Pictures* is written by travel photographer Richard I'Anson.

Print film is widely available – a 36-exposure roll of Kodak or Fuji print film costs around RM10 for 100 or 200ASA and RM13 for 400ASA. Slide film is much harder to find – where available, a 36-exposure roll of 100ASA Kodak or Fuji slide film costs around RM22. Expect to pay around RM20 to process and print a 36-exposure roll of print film (4in by 6in prints). There are photo-processing shops in all the big malls.

Digital memory cards are available everywhere and at bargain prices – internet cafés and photo-processing centres can burn your digital pictures to CD or DVD for around RM15.

POST

Pos Malaysia Berhad (www.pos.com.my) runs a fast and efficient postal system with good poste restante services at major post offices. As a rule, post offices are open from 8am to 5pm from Monday to Saturday, but closed on the first Saturday of the month and on public holidays.

Aerograms and postcards cost 50 sen to send to any destination. Letters weighing 20g or less cost 90 sen to Asia, RM1.40 to Australia or New Zealand, RM1.50 to the UK and Europe, and RM1.80 to North America. A 1kg parcel to most destinations will cost RM30 to RM35 by sea and RM60 to RM70 by air. Registered mail costs an extra RM3.90 (letters and parcels up to 2kg only).

Main post offices in larger cities sell packaging materials and stationery.

TELEPHONE

Telephone numbers in KL have eight digits; in Penang and Melaka they have seven digits. Mobile phone numbers generally have 10 digits, starting with 012, 013, 016, 017 or 019.

Area Codes

The telephone area codes for cities covered in this book are KL (☎ 03), Penang (☎ 04) and Melaka (☎ 06). Phone calls to Singapore are STD (long-distance) rather than international calls – the code is ☎ 02.

Fax

Fax facilities are available at Telekom offices in the cities and at some main post offices. If you can't find one of these try a travel agency or large hotel. As a rough indication, international faxes cost around RM12 to send and RM5 per page to receive.

International Calls

The easiest and cheapest way to make international calls is to buy a local SIM card for your cellular phone. Calls made from hotel phones are extremely expensive and only certain payphones permit international calls. Most budget hotels provide an international-enabled payphone in the lobby. You can make operator-assisted international calls from local Telekom offices. To save money on landline calls, buy a prepaid international calling card (available from convenience stores).

To call overseas from Malaysia, dial ☎ 00, then the country code. Call ☎ 108 for the international operator and ☎ 103 for directory inquiries. To call Malaysia from overseas dial the international access code, then ☎ 60, the Malaysian area code (minus the first zero), then the number.

Local Calls

Making domestic telephone calls in Malaysia is usually a simple matter, provided you can find a working payphone (try train stations, shopping malls and big hotels). Local calls cost 10 sen for three minutes. Payphones take coins or prepaid cards which are available from Telekom offices and convenience stores. Some also take international credit cards. You'll also find a range of discount calling cards at convenience stores and mobile-phone counters.

Mobile Phones

As long as you have arranged global-roaming with your home provider, your GSM digital phone will automatically tune into one of the region's digital networks. If not, buy a prepaid SIM card for one of the local networks on arrival. The initial SIM card will cost RM10 and you can buy extra credit at mobile-phone desks across the country (in units of RM10, RM20, RM40 and RM60). The rates for a local call is around 40 sen per minute. There are three big cell phone companies, all with similar call rates and prepaid packages – **Celcom** (www.celcom.com.my), **DiGi** (www.digi.com.my), and **Hotlink/Maxis** (www.maxis.com.my).

If your phone is locked into a particular network at home, you must get it unlocked first for this to work. If may be easier to pick up a cheap phone in Malaysia – new and secondhand 'handphones' (as mobile phones are called) are sold everywhere.

TIME

Peninsular Malaysia is eight hours ahead of GMT/UTC (London). Thus, noon in Kuala Lumpur is 8pm in Los Angeles and 11pm in New York, 4am in London, and 2pm in Sydney and Melbourne. See the World Map (p266) for international time zones.

TOILETS

Although there are some places with Asian squat-style toilets, Western-style sit-down loos are becoming the norm. Toilet paper is not usually provided; instead, you will find a hose or a spout on the toilet seat which you are supposed to use as a bidet. Or a bucket of water and a tap. Public toilets in malls usually charge an entry fee, but this often includes toilet paper. If you're not comfortable with the 'hand-and-water' technique, carry packets of tissues or toilet paper wherever you go.

TOURIST INFORMATION

Tourism Malaysia (Map pp72-3; ☎ 03-2615 8188; www.tourismmalaysia.gov.my; 17th fl, Putra World Trade Centre, 45 Jln Tun Ismail, Kuala Lumpur) has an efficient network of domestic offices, which tend to be good for brochures and free maps but rather weak on hard factual information. Its overseas offices are useful for predeparture planning – follow the 'Contact Us' link on the website for listings. For regional offices see Kuala Lumpur (p76), Melaka (p141) and Penang (p179).

TRAVELLERS WITH DISABILITIES

Although it's not the worst country in Asia in terms of disability access, Malaysia makes very few concessions for the mobility impaired. Kuala Lumpur is better than most towns, with pavement ramps and lots of lifts, including in malls and at commuter train stations. However, road crossings are few and far between and poorly covered manholes mean wheelchair-users are often better off on the road. The new RapidKL buses usually have a wheelchair ramp, though drivers may be reluctant to use it. On the upside, taxis are cheap and both Malaysia Airlines and KTM (the national rail service) offer 50% discounts on travel for travellers with disabilities.

Before setting off get in touch with your national support organisation (preferably with the travel officer, if there is one). The following organisations offer general travel advice:

Accessible Journeys (☎ 610-521-0339; www.disabilitytravel.com) In the US.

Holiday Care Service (☎ 0845-124 9971; www.holidaycare.org.uk) In the UK.

Mobility International USA (☎ 541-343 1284; www.miusa.org)

Nican (☎ 02-6241 1220; www.nican.com.au) In Australia

VISAS

Visitors to Malaysia must have a passport valid for at least six months beyond the date of entry, and travellers are occasionally asked to provide proof of a ticket for onward travel and sufficient funds to cover their stay. The following gives a brief overview of the visa requirements – full details are available on the website www.kln.gov.my.

Citizens of the UK, USA, Australia, New Zealand, South Africa and most nations in western Europe (including Scandinavia and new EU member states) are granted permission to stay for up to three months without a visa. However, extensions of stay are only permissible for citizens of approved nations (generally prosperous nations like Australia, America and the UK). Citizens of most other countries either qualify for a one month visa-free stay or can apply for a one-month visa on arrival at approved international airports and seaports in Malaysia. Citizens of Israel can only enter Malaysia with a visa – which is granted at the discretion of the Malaysian embassy in the country where you apply.

Sabah and Sarawak are treated like separate countries with additional permit conditions; more comprehensive information on Malaysian Borneo can be found in Lonely Planet's *Malaysia, Singapore & Brunei* and *Borneo.*

Visa Extensions

Depending on your nationality, it may be possible to extend your visa at an immigration office in Malaysia for an additional one or two months. Extensions tend to be granted only for genuine emergencies. It's normally easier to hop across the border to Thailand, Singapore or Indonesia and re-enter the country – this counts as a new visit, even if you re-enter the same day.

If you do need to extend your visa, head to the immigration offices in KL (p74), Melaka (p141) or Penang (p178) before your existing visa expires, with evidence of a confirmed ticket back to your home country.

VOLUNTEERING

There are lots of opportunities for volunteers in Malaysia, but these tend to focus on rural areas rather than KL, Melaka and Penang. Most people arrange a placement with a volunteer agency in their home country before they travel, but you can try contacting local organisations – see p100 of the KL chapter, and p189 in Penang for some recommendations in KL and Penang. Melaka Zoo (p163) also accepts volunteers, with advance notice.

WOMEN TRAVELLERS

The key to travelling with minimum hassle in Malaysia is to blend in with the locals, which means dressing modestly and being respectful, especially in areas of stronger Muslim religious sensibilities. Regardless of what local non-Muslim women wear, it's better to be safe than sorry – we've had reports of attacks on women ranging from minor verbal aggravation to physical assault. Hard as it is to say, the truth is that women are much more likely to have problems in Malay-dominated areas, where attitudes are more conservative.

In Malay-dominated areas, you can halve your hassles just by tying a bandanna over your hair (a minimal concession to the headscarf worn by most Muslim women). When visiting mosques, cover your head and limbs with a headscarf and sarong (many mosques lend these out at the entrance). At the beach, most Malaysian women swim fully clothed in T-shirts and shorts, so don't even think about going topless.

Be proactive about your own safety. Treat overly friendly strangers, both male and female, with a good deal of caution. In cheap hotels check for small peepholes in the walls and doors; when you have a choice, stay in a Chinese-operated hotel. On island resorts, stick to crowded beaches, and choose a chalet close to reception and other travellers. Take taxis after dark and avoid walking alone at night in quiet or seedy parts of town.

Tampons and pads are widely available in Malaysia, especially in the big cities, and over-the-counter medications for common gynaecological health problems (like yeast infections) are also fairly easy to find.

WORK

It is possible to find work in Malaysia, but the company that employs you normally has to help sort out the immigration paperwork. Malaysia is clamping down on illegal workers and this is not the time to get caught working on the sly. Some guesthouses and dive centres in popular resort areas take on foreigners, and international resort chains may have openings for reps and other staff – contact these companies in your home country.

Teaching English is another option if you have the right credentials (a TEFL certificate is the bare minimum). Would-be teachers should check some of the many TEFL and ESL sites: www.tefl.com and www.eslcafe.com are good sites.

Depending on the nature of your job, you'll need either an Expatriate Personnel Visa or Temporary Employment Visa. For details and requirements, check the website of the **Immigration Department of Malaysia** (www.imi.gov.my).

Transport

CONTENTS

GETTING THERE & AWAY

ENTERING MALAYSIA

The main requirement for entry to Malaysia is a passport that is valid for at least six months after the date of entry and proof of an onward ticket and adequate funds for your stay. In practice, you'll rarely be asked to prove this. There are no restrictions on entering Malaysia by air and leaving by land or sea, or vice versa. For details of visa and other entry requirements, see p225. Note that Sabah and Sarawak are treated as separate entities from Peninsular Malaysia, with additional entry procedures, even if you are arriving from Peninsular Malaysia.

Flights, tours and rail tickets can be booked online at www.lonelyplanet.com/travel_services.

AIR

Airports & Airlines

The main gateway to Malaysia is **Kuala Lumpur International Airport** (KLIA; off Map pp72-3; www.klia.com.my), 75km south of KL at Sepang. It shares its runways with the new Low Cost Carrier Terminal (LCC-T), the Malaysian hub for Air Asia. Penang also handles a number of international flights, including a convenient Air Asia hop to Bangkok.

See below for the main airline offices in KL (the websites have listings for offices in other cities).

Air Asia (Map p90; airline code AK; ☎ 8775 4000; www.airasia.com; 1st fl, KL Sentral Station; hub Low Cost Carrier Terminal, Sepang, Kuala Lumpur)
Air China (Map pp84-5; airline code CA; ☎ 2166 1999; www.airchina.com.cn; Level 7, Plaza OSK, Jln Ampang; hub Beijing Capital International Airport)
Air India (Map pp84-5; airline code AI; ☎ 2142 0323; www.airindia.com; 14th fl, Angkasa Raya Bldg, 123 Jln Ampang; hub New Delhi International Airport)
Air France (Map pp84-5; airline code AF; ☎ 7712 4545; www.airfrance.com; 1st fl, Grand Plaza Parkroyal, Jln Sultan Ismail; hub Paris Charles de Gaulle International Airport)
All Nippon Airways (ANA; Map pp84-5; airline code NH; ☎ 2032 1331; www.ana.co.jp; 11th fl, Wisma Goldhill, 67 Jln Raja Chulan; hub Narita International Airport, Tokyo)
Berjaya Air (Map pp84-5; airline code J8; ☎ 2145 2828; berjaya-air.com; Level 6, Berjaya Times Sq, 1 Jln Imbi; hub Sultan Abdul Aziz Shah Airport, Subang)
British Airways (Map pp84-5; airline code BA; www.britishairways.com; Agent: Holiday Tours & Travel, ☎ 7712 4747, Level 5, Wisma UOA II, Jln Pinang; hub Heathrow International Airport, London)
Cathay Pacific Airways (Map pp84-5; airline code CX; ☎ 2035 2777; www.cathaypacific.com; Suite 22, Level 1, Menara IMC, 8 Jln Sultan Ismail; hub Hong Kong International Airport, Hong Kong)
China Airlines (Map pp84-5; airline code CI; ☎ 2142 7458; www.china-airlines.com; Ground fl, Amoda Bldg, 22 Jln Imbi; hub Taoyuan International Airport, Taipei)
China Eastern (Map pp84-5; airline code MU; ☎ 2166 1666; www.ce-air.com; Level 2, Plaza OSK, Jln Ampang; hub Pudong International Airport, Shanghai)

THINGS CHANGE...

The information in this chapter is particularly vulnerable to change. Check directly with the airline or a travel agent to make sure you understand how a fare (and ticket you may buy) works and be aware of the current security requirements for international air travel. Shop carefully. The details given in this chapter should be regarded as pointers and are not a substitute for your own careful, up-to-date research.

CLIMATE CHANGE & TRAVEL

Climate change is a serious threat to the ecosystems that humans rely upon. While air travel is not the only contributing factor, it is the fastest-growing generator of the gases thought to cause climate change. Lonely Planet regards travel, overall, as a global benefit, but believes we all have a responsibility to limit our personal impact on global warming.

Flying and Climate Change

Pretty much every form of motorised travel generates CO2 (the main cause of human-induced climate change) but planes are far and away the worst offenders, not just because of the sheer distances they allow us to travel, but because they release greenhouse gases high into the atmosphere. The statistics are alarming: two people taking a return flight between Europe and the US can produce as much CO2 as an average household's gas and electricity consumption over a whole year.

Carbon Offset Schemes

Climatecare.org and other websites use 'carbon calculators' that allow travellers to offset the level of greenhouse gases they are responsible for with financial contributions to sustainable travel schemes that reduce global warming – including projects in India, Honduras, Kazakhstan and Uganda. Lonely Planet, together with Rough Guides and other concerned partners in the travel industry, support the carbon offset scheme run by climatecare.org. Lonely Planet offsets all of its staff and author travel. For more information check out our website: www.lonelyplanet.com.

Emirates (Map pp84-5; ☎ 2058 5888; www.emirates.com; 1st fl, Shangri-La Hotel Annexe, UBN Tower, Jln P Ramlee; hub Dubai International Airport)
Etihad (Map pp84-5; airline code EY; ☎ 2687 2222; www.etihadairways.com; Level 32, Menara Standard Chartered, Jalan Sultan Ismail; hub Abu Dhabi International Airport)
EVA Air (Map pp84-5; airline code BR; ☎ 2163 2978; www.evaair.com; 12th fl, Kenanga International Bldg, Jln Sultan Ismail; hub Taiwan Taoyuan International Airport, Taipei)
Garuda Indonesian Airlines (Map pp84-5; airline code GA; ☎ 2162 2811; www.garuda-indonesia.com; Level 19, Menara Citibank, 165 Jln Ampang; hub Soekarno-Hatta Jakarta International Airport)
Indian Airlines (Map pp78-9; airline code IA; ☎ 2692 5954; indian-airlines.nic.in; 2nd fl, Wisma Paradise, Jln Bunus; hub New Delhi International Airport)
Jet Airways (Map pp84-5; airline code 9W; ☎ 2148 9020; www.jetairways.com; 2nd fl, Angkasa Raya Bldg, Jln Ampang; hub New Delhi International Airport)
Japan Airlines (JAL; Map pp84-5; airline code JL; ☎ 2161 1740; www.japanair.com; Level 20, Menara Citibank, 165 Jln Ampang; hub Narita International Airport, Tokyo)
KLM Royal Dutch Airlines (Map pp84-5; airline code KL; ☎ 7712 4555; www.klm.com; 1st fl, Grand Plaza Parkroyal, Jln Sultan Ismail; hub Amsterdam Schipol Airport)
Kuwait Airways (Map pp84-5; airline code KU; ☎ 2031 6033; www.kuwait-airways.com; 7th fl, UBN Tower, 10 Jln P Ramlee; hub Kuwait International Airport)
Lufthansa (Map pp84-5; airline code LH; ☎ 2052 3428; www.lufthansa.com; 18th fl, Kenanga International Bldg, Jln Sultan Ismail; hub Frankfurt International Airport)
Malaysia Airlines (Map pp84-5; airline code MA; ☎ 7843 3000, from outside Malaysia 1300 883 000; www.malaysiaairlines.com; Bangunan MAS, Jln Sultan Ismail; hub Kuala Lumpur International Airport)
Myanmar International Airways (MIA; Map pp84-5; airline code UB; www.maiair.com; Agent: Worldwide Aviation Agencies, ☎ 2143 3755, 13th fl, Central Plaza, 34 Jln Sultan Ismail; hub Yangon International Airport)
Philippine Airlines (Map pp84-5; airline code PR; www.philippineairlines.com; Agent: Pacific World Travel, ☎ 2141 0767, 2nd fl, Angkasa Raya Bldg, Jln Ampang; hub Ninoy Aquino International Airport, Manila)
Qatar Airways (Map pp84-5; airline code QR; ☎ 2141 8281; www.qatarairways.com; 18th fl, Central Plaza, 34 Jln Sultan Ismail; hub Doha International Airport)
Royal Brunei Airlines (Map pp84-5; airline code BI; ☎ 2070 7166; www.bruneiair.com; 2nd fl, Menara UBN, 10 Jln P Ramlee; hub Brunei International Airport, Bandar Seri Begawan)
Royal Nepal Airlines (Map pp78-9; airline code RA; ☎ 2692 4858; www.royalnepal-airlines.com; 2nd fl, Wisma Paradise, Jln Bunus; hub Tribhuvan International Airport, Kathmandu)
Singapore Airlines (Map pp78-9; airline code SQ; ☎ 2692 3122; www.singaporeair.com; 10th fl, Menara Multi-Purpose, Capital Sq, 8 Jln Munshi Abdullah; hub Singapore Changi Airport, Singapore)

Sri Lankan Airlines (Map pp84-5; airline code UL; ☎ 2143 3353; www.srilankan.aero; 1st fl, Kompleks Antarabangsa, Jln Sultan Ismail; hub Bandaranaike International Airport, Colombo)

Thai Airways International (Map pp84-5; airline code TG; ☎ 2034 6900; www.thaiair.com; 30th fl, Wisma Goldhill, 67 Jln Raja Chulan; hub Suvarnabhumi International Airport, Bangkok)

Vietnam Airlines (Map pp84-5; airline code VN; ☎ 2141 2416; www.vietnamairlines.com.vn; 1st fl, Wisma MPL, Jln Raja Chulan; hub Tan Son Nhat International Airport, Saigon and Noi Bai International Airport, Hanoi)

Tickets

KL is a busy international hub and there are numerous flights from Europe, Australia and further afield with most large European, Asian and Middle Eastern carriers. Flights to KL are normally cheaper than flights to Penang and KL is a good place to pick up tickets to other destinations in Asia, particularly now that Air Asia offers budget flights across the region.

Australia

Discounted return fares from Melbourne or Sydney to KL start at around A$700 in the low season, rising to A$1200 in the high season (December to February). Malaysia Airlines, Singapore Airlines and Qantas Airways all offer good deals; also check some of the Middle Eastern airlines that fly between Europe and Australia. Malaysia Airlines flies to Brisbane, Adelaide and Perth, and Cathay Pacific offers connections through Hong Kong to Cairns. You can also connect to Penang with Malaysian Airlines and other carriers.

Brunei

Royal Brunei Airlines and Malaysia Airlines have direct flights between Bandar Seri Begawan and KL – full-fare tickets cost around RM1500, but promotional fares go as low as RM900 return.

Canada

There are no direct flights between Canada and Malaysia; the cheapest fares involve connections through Asia. Eva Air often has good deals via Taiwan. For flights to Malaysia, low-season return fares from Vancouver start at C$1300; from Toronto C$1400.

DEPARTURE TAX

There's a RM40 airport tax on international flights out of Malaysia and a RM5 tax on domestic flights, included in the ticket price.

Continental Europe

There's not much variation in air fares from the main European cities. Lufthansa, Air France and KLM have direct flights to KL from their European hubs and Malaysia Airlines has flights across the region, or you can connect cheaply with one of the big Asian or Middle Eastern carriers. From Frankfurt, Paris, Amsterdam, Stockholm and other European capitals, expect to pay around €650 return (or equivalent).

Hong Kong & China

Return flights from KL to Hong Kong with Malaysia Airlines or Cathay Pacific start from RM1500/HK$4500. There are also direct flights from Hong Kong to Penang. Malaysia Airlines, Air China, China Southeastern and several other airlines offer flights between KL and Beijing, Shanghai and other cities in mainland China from around RM2000.

Indonesia

Air Asia has direct connections between KL and various Indonesian islands – fares include Jakarta (one-way from RM145), Medan (from RM140), Padang (from RM105), Bandung (from RM165), and Denpasar (Bali) and Surabaya (from RM165). Fares from Indonesia to Malaysia are broadly equivalent in Indonesian rupiahs. Malaysia Airlines and Garuda service similar routes but fares are much higher than Air Asia. Note that Garuda has been added to the European blacklist of unsafe airlines.

Japan

Malaysia Airlines, ANA and JAL are the main carriers flying between KL and Japan. Return flights to KL start at around ¥47,000. It's usually slightly cheaper to fly to/from Tokyo Narita, rather than Osaka/Kansai International Airport.

New Zealand

Low-season return tickets start at NZ$1300 between Auckland and KL on Malaysia Airlines, Emirates and others; add around NZ$400 for high-season fares.

Singapore
Malaysia Airlines has hourly flights between KL and Singapore (return from RM800/SG$400), around half of them code-sharing with Singapore Airlines. Malaysia Airlines connects Singapore to Penang for a similar fare. It's slightly cheaper to buy tickets in Malaysia.

South Asia
Air India, Jet and Indian Airlines offer regular flights between KL and Delhi, Mumbai, Hyderabad, Chennai and Bengaluru – return fares range from RM1200 to RM1400. Royal Nepal Airlines has five flights per week between KL and Kathmandu; fares start at RM1700. Sri Lankan Airlines offers connections to Colombo from around RM1200.

Thailand
Round-trip flights between Bangkok and KL or Penang with Thai Airways or Malaysia Airlines cost around RM1290/11,000B. It's much cheaper to fly with Air Asia – starting fares from KL: Bangkok RM70, Chiang Mai RM140, Krabi RM60 and Phuket RM70. Berjaya Air flies between KL's Sultan Abdul Aziz Shah Airport and Koh Samui one-way for RM380.

The Rest of Southeast Asia
Air Asia has direct flights between KL and Phnom Penh (from RM170/US$55) and Siem Reap (from RM220/US$60). For the Philippines, Air Asia offers cheap flights from KL to Clark Airport (just north of Manila) from around RM160/P2370, or you can fly with Malaysia Airlines or Philippine Airlines to Manila (around RM900/P11,800) or Cebu (around RM1100/P14,400).

Vietnam Airlines flies daily between KL and Ho Chi Minh City for around RM1100/US$320, while Myanmar International Airways flies direct between KL and Yangon for around RM1000/US$290; for both routes, it's much cheaper to connect through Bangkok on Air Asia.

UK
London has the best deals for flights to Malaysia. The cheapest fares are normally on Middle Eastern carriers like Qatar Airways, Emirates or Eithad, or Sri Lankan Airlines via Colombo. Fares start from UK£400 in the low season and UK£550 in the high season.

USA
Malaysia Airlines flies to KL from New York (Newark) and Los Angeles, or you can connect through Europe or other hub cities in Southeast Asia. Fares are similar from either the east coast or the west coast – bank on US$800 upwards.

LAND
Peninsular Malaysia shares land borders with Thailand and Singapore (via the Singapore-Johor Bahru Causeway). There are also sea crossings from Peninsular Malaysia to Sumatra in Indonesia. Malaysian Borneo shares a land border with Brunei and Indonesia – more detailed information on these crossings are in Lonely Planet's *Indonesia* and *Malaysia, Singapore & Brunei* guidebooks.

Brunei
The main overland route into Brunei is via bus from Miri in Sarawak; it's also possible to travel overland between Limbang and Lawas in Sarawak and Bangar in the eastern part of Brunei. Many nationalities are permitted to visit Brunei without a visa for tourism – check with Bruneian embassies overseas to confirm details.

Indonesia
To travel by land between Sarawak in Malaysia and Kalimantan in Indonesia, you can take the daily bus from Pontianak to Kuching in Sarawak, crossing at the Tebedu/Entikong border. This border does not provide visas on arrival so if you need a visa to enter Indonesia, you'll have to obtain one in advance before boarding the bus (Kuching has the nearest embassy to the border).

Singapore
BUS
The Causeway linking Johor Bahru with Singapore handles most traffic between the two countries. Trains and buses run from all over Malaysia straight through to Singapore, or you can take a bus to Johor Bahru and get a taxi or one of the frequent buses from Johor Bahru to Singapore. Direct buses between Singapore and KL cost between S$30/RM30 and S$50/RM80 depending on the level of comfort – the journey takes around five hours; for further details see p124. Buses from KL to Johor Bahru cost RM24; you can then take the Singapore-Johor Bahru Express (RM2.40/

S$2.10) or SBS bus 170 (RM1.70/S$1.30) across the Causeway to downtown Singapore. There are also direct buses to Singapore and Johor Bahru from Melaka (see p162) and Butterworth, near Penang.

There is a second causeway linking Tuas, in western Singapore, with Geylang Patah in Johor Bahru. This is known as the Second Link, and some bus services to Melaka and up the west coast head this way. If you have a car, tolls on the Second Link are much higher than the charge on the main Causeway. A good website with details of express buses between Singapore, Malaysia and Thailand is the **Express Bus Travel Guide** (www.myexpressbus.com).

TRAIN

KTM Komuter (☎ 2267 1200; www.ktmb.com.my) trains run three times a day between Singapore and KL Sentral station and the journey takes seven to nine hours; seats cost from RM21 and ordinary/deluxe berths cost from RM38/111.80. In the opposite direction fares are the same, but in Singapore dollars – a rip-off considering the difference in the exchange rates. To get around this, either start your journey in Johor Bahru (in which case the train ride counts as a domestic trip) or buy the outbound and return ticket separately, saving money on the return leg from Malaysia. Fares to KL from Johor Bahru start at RM20 for a seat and RM37 for a berth.

Immigration officers at the Malaysia–Singapore border do not always stamp your passport, which can cause problems when you leave Malaysia. Keep your immigration card and train ticket to present to officials on departure.

Thailand

There are regular trains, buses and boats between Malaysia and Thailand. However, the political situation in the far south of Thailand is highly volatile, particularly in the Yala, Pattani, Songkhla and Narathiwat provinces along the Malaysian border. Muslim separatists have carried out hundreds of murders and bombings in the area – check the security situation carefully before travelling overland through southern Thailand. Note that Malaysia is an hour ahead of Thailand.

BUS & CAR

The most popular land route between Thailand and Malaysia is the bus or train from Hat Yai in Thailand to Butterworth in Malaysia (crossing the border at Padang Besar or Bukit Kayu Hitam). You can also cross via the Rantau Panjang–Sungai Golok and Pengkalan Kubor–Tak Bai crossings on the east coast. Direct buses between KL's Puduraya bus station and Hat Yai cost RM40 (seven hours). Coming from Thailand, various travel agencies and guesthouses in Southern Thailand offer minibus transfers across the border to Penang.

TRAIN

Trains from Singapore to Kuala Lumpur connect with northbound **KTM Komuter** (☎ 03-2267 1200; www.ktmb.com.my) trains to Hat Yai via Butterworth (near Penang). From KL Sentral Station, the *Ekspres Senandung Langkawi* leaves at 9pm daily, reaching Butterworth at 5.50am and Hat Yai at 10.20am (local time). In the opposite direction, the train leaves Hat Yai at 3.50pm, reaching Butterworth at 10pm and KL at 6.45am. For the trip from KL to Hat Yai, seats/berths start from RM44/52.

Another useful train is the daily *International Express* from Butterworth all the way to Bangkok, which connects with trains from KL and Singapore. The train leaves Butterworth at 2.20pm, reaching Bangkok at 10.50am the next day. In the opposite direction, the train leaves Bangkok at 2.45pm, reaching Butterworth at 1.45pm. Upper/lower berths cost RM103.90/111.90. You can also use this train to reach Hat Yai, which has frequent train and bus connections to other parts of Thailand.

The Asian sector of the opulent **Eastern & Oriental Express** (www.orient-express.com) also connects Singapore, KL and Bangkok. This luxuriously equipped train runs on set dates monthly (check the website for the schedule) and takes 42 hours to complete the 1943km journey from Singapore to Bangkok. From KL to Bangkok, the fare is US$1740 per person in a double compartment in the Pullman coach; meals, tea and coffee are included, gin and tonics are extra. You can travel in even more unashamed luxury in the 'state' and 'suite' coaches.

SEA

Brunei

Boats connect Brunei to Lawas and Limbang in Sarawak, and to Pulau Labuan, from where boats go to Sabah. With the exception of speedboats for Limbang, all international boats now depart from Muara, 25km north-east of Bandar Seri Begawan.

Indonesia

There are numerous ferry routes between Indonesia and Malaysia. From Peninsular Malaysia, all boats go to Sumatra – the most useful routes are from Medan to Penang; from Dumai to Melaka (see p162); and from Tanjung Balai and Dumai to Pelabuhan Klang, the seaport for Kuala Lumpur (see p124).

Singapore

A number of ferry companies operate across the narrow Straits of Singapore to Malaysia. As well as the popular cruises from Singapore's HarbourFront Ferry Terminal (see www.singaporecruise.com), there are frequent passenger ferries from the Changi Ferry Terminal to the small jetties at Tanjung Belungkor and Pengerang (one-way S$18, 45 minutes). You'll have to take connecting buses on the far side to reach Johor Bahru and buses north to Melaka, Penang or KL.

Thailand

For an interesting and little-used back route into Thailand, consider taking the ferry from Penang to Pulau Langkawi (see p173) and a second ferry from Kuah jetty to Satun on the Thai coast (RM25, one hour). From the port you can take a taxi to Satun town or join the ferry to the idyllic Tarutao Islands. Make sure you get your passport stamped going in either direction.

The Philippines

Several companies run passenger ferries between Sabah and Zamboanga on Mindanao in the Philippines, but security can be an issue on this route – check locally before you travel.

GETTING AROUND

AIR

Domestic Air Services

The national carrier **Malaysia Airlines** (☎ 1300 883 000, from outside Malaysia 7843 3000; www.malaysiaairlines.com) has delegated many of its domestic routes to budget carrier **Air Asia** (☎ 8775 4000; www.airasia.com), cutting the cost of domestic travel considerably. Flights on Air Asia should be booked online and prices are cheaper the earlier you book – the flight from KL to Penang can cost as little as RM60 if you book far enough ahead. Both airlines also offer numerous international routes (see p227).

Tiny **Berjaya Air** (Map pp84-5; airline code J8; ☎ 2145 2828; berjaya-air.com; Level 6, Berjaya Times Sq, 1 Jln Imbi) flies from the Sultan Abdul Aziz Shah Airport at Subang to the islands of Pulau Tioman, Pulau Pangkor and Pulau Redang in Peninsular Malaysia, as well as Koh Samui in Thailand. Many domestic flights within Borneo are operated by **Fly Asian Express** (www.flyasianxpress.com).

There are no ferries between Peninsular Malaysia and Borneo so flying is the only option – Malaysia Airlines and Air Asia serve the regional airports at Kuching, Sibu, Bintulu and Miru in Sarawak and Pulau Labuan, Kota Kinabalu, Sandakan and Tawau in Sabah. Note that local flights in Malaysian Borneo are often cancelled or delayed during the monsoon and flights are often completely booked during school holidays. At other times it's easier to get a seat at a few days' notice, but always book as far in advance as possible.

Discounts & Special Flights

Discounts of 25% to 50% are available for flights around Malaysia on Malaysia Airlines, including for families and groups of three or more. Student discounts are reserved for students enrolled in institutions in Malaysia. Air Asia flights are heavily discounted if you book well in advance over the internet.

Air Passes

Malaysia Airlines' Discover Malaysia pass costs US$199 for five flights anywhere in Malaysia within a 28-day period. You must have flown into Malaysia on a Malaysia Airlines flight to qualify for this pass, and you must apply within 14 days of arriving in the country. Taxes are extra and each sector counts as one flight, including transit flights.

BICYCLE

Rural Malaysia is well set up for long-distance bicycle touring, but cycling in the cities is more tricky. To get anywhere in KL, you must negotiate busy highways, braving the erratic city traffic. Most cyclist ride on the hard shoulder on major roads – a rear-view mirror is a valuable asset for occasions when you need to pull into the carriageway to avoid obstacles. Road signs are normally in English, or comprehensible Bahasa Malaysia, and you can get by with a racer in the cities and on major roads in the peninsula (a mountain bike is recommended for trips to backwaters, particularly national parks).

There are good jungle trails for off-roading at Templer Park (p132) and the Forest Research Institute of Malaysia (FRIM; p132). **KL Bike Hash** (www.bikehash.freeservers.com) runs monthly mountain-bike forays around the capital (visitors are welcome to ride along for an RM10 donation). The website has loads of useful general information on cycling in Malaysia and dozens of links to other cycling sites.

Kuala Lumpur is the best place to buy or find spares for bicycles – elsewhere, motorcycle mechanics can help with minor repairs. International-quality bicycles and components can be bought in bigger cities, but top-spec machines and fittings are hard to find. Bringing your own is the best bet. Bicycles can be transported on most international flights if packed correctly; check with the airline about extra charges and shipment specifications.

BOAT

There are no services connecting Peninsular Malaysia with Malaysian Borneo, but ferries run from Peninsular Malaysia to Sumatra and local boat services connect the mainland to offshore islands. See the transport sections in the regional chapters for details. As elsewhere in Southeast Asia, boat operators take crazy risks: overloading boats and sailing in dangerous conditions. The authorities do little to enforce the safety rules – if a boat looks overloaded or otherwise unsafe, *do not board*. On any boat trip, try to sit near the emergency exits and consider your escape route in an emergency.

BUS

Bus travel in Malaysia is fast, comfortable and economical. However, drivers are notorious for speeding and risky overtaking and accidents are depressingly common. Some travellers prefer to avoid night buses as accidents are much less common during the day. **Transnasional Express** (☎ 03-4047 7878; www.nadi.com.my/transportation_home.asp) is Malaysia's largest bus operator, with services all over the country, but there are dozens of other companies offering services around Peninsular Malaysia, and further afield to Singapore and Thailand. Buses generally leave from big intercity bus stands, which may be some distance from the centre. The buses run by **Plusliner** (www.plusliner.com) and **Aeroline** (www.aeroline.com.my) tend to stop at convenient locations in town centres. You can reserve seats in advance on most intercity routes.

Air-con and ordinary buses service most major routes, but there isn't a huge difference in fares. If you travel in an air-conditioned bus, always wear sufficient clothing and bring a blanket if you really feel the cold – some buses are virtual ice-boxes on wheels. Ekspres (express) buses cost slightly more but make fewer stops, cutting journey times.

Small towns and *kampung* (villages) all over the country are serviced by public buses, usually rattlers without air-con. These buses are invariably dirt cheap and are great for sampling rural life. In most towns there are no ticket offices, so ask local people where to find the correct bus and buy your ticket from the conductor after you board.

CAR & MOTORCYCLE

Driving in Malaysia is a breeze compared to most Asian countries. The government has invested heavily in the roads – influenced perhaps by the success of Petronas, the state petroleum and gas company, and the Proton Saga, the first Malaysian-built motorcar. Road surfaces are generally of a high quality and motorway services are very similar to what you would find in the West. Leaded and unleaded petrol are widely available for around RM1.90 per litre and hire companies offer self-drive services at the international airports in KL and Penang. Traffic is fairly light out on the highways, and there's a 110km per hour speed limit, so you can cover long distances quickly. Small motorcycles can be hired in Georgetown for exploring Penang Island, but they are not really up to long-distance touring.

That's the good news. The bad news is that drivers in Malaysia have the same devil-may-care attitude as drivers elsewhere in Asia. This means inconsiderate tailgating, risky overtaking, dangerous speeding and sudden unsignalled turns. Crashes are not uncommon – the mountain highway from KL to Genting Highlands sees minor collisions almost daily. Always drive defensively and be ready for unexpected manoeuvres from drivers around you. A further hassle for drivers is the confusing layout of Malaysian road junctions.

Although well-signposted, exits appear with little notice, giving you a narrow window of time to get into the right lane. Assuming you make the turn, exits spiral off other exits like fettuccine curled around a fork – if you're not careful, you can end up back on the highway driving back the way you came.

To help you orientate yourself, the Lebuhraya (North-South Hwy), is a six-lane expressway that runs for 966km along the length of the peninsula from the Thai border in the north to Johor Bahru in the south, stopping near the Causeway to Singapore. Toll charges for using the expressway vary according to the distance travelled, which keeps the traffic light. Many locals prefer the free, but more crowded, ordinary highways.

Bring Your Own Vehicle

It is technically possible to bring your vehicle into Malaysia, but there are reams of red tape and the costs are prohibitively expensive – a hire car is a much better proposition.

Driving Licence

A valid overseas licence is needed to rent a car. An International Driving Permit is usually not required but it is recommended that you bring one, just to be safe. Most rental companies also require that drivers are at least 23 years old (and less than 65), with at least one year of driving experience.

Hire

Kuala Lumpur is the easiest place to rent a car (see p126), but there are also several car rental companies in Penang (p174). Most of the big international rental companies have airport desks and downtown offices. The big advantage of dealing with the international chains is their countrywide network of offices – you can often pick up in one city and drop off in another for a RM50 surcharge.

Unlimited-distance rates for a 1.3L Proton Saga, the cheapest and most popular car in Malaysia, start per day/week at RM150/900. There's a 5% tax on top of this and you'll pay an extra daily fee of RM15 for insurance against theft and RM30 for a collision-damage waiver, which reduces the excess in the event of accident to RM500. It's worth taking both these options – if you have an accident without this cover, you may be required to pay for both the damage to the other vehicle and any medical bills for the passengers. Rates drop substantially for longer rentals – it is often possible to get a Proton Saga for as little as RM2000 per month, including unlimited kilometres and insurance.

Reliable car-rental companies include **Avis** (www.avis.com.my), **Hertz** (www.hertz.com.my), **Mayflower** (www.mayflowercarrental.com.my), and **Orix** (www.orixcarrentals.com.my). Small (100cc to 125cc) motorcycles can be hired in Penang for around RM30 per day. However, you are unlikely to be covered by insurance if you don't have a motorcycle license.

Insurance

Rental companies will provide insurance when you hire a car, but always check what the extent of your coverage will be, particularly if you're involved in an accident. Make sure you are covered for damage to other vehicles and third-party medical treatment in the event of a crash. You might want to take out your own insurance or pay the rental company an extra premium for an insurance excess reduction.

Road Rules

Driving in Malaysia broadly follows the same rules as in Britain and Australia – cars are right-hand drive and you drive on the left side of the road. However, locals bend the rules, and sometimes break them completely. Always try to predict problems ahead of time. Be aware of possible road hazards, particularly stray animals, wandering pedestrians and the large number of motorcyclists. The speed limit is 110km per hour on expressways but it can slow to as little as 50km per hour on *kampung* (village) back roads, so take it easy. Wearing safety belts is compulsory and a very sensible idea, though they are only fitted to front seats.

Malaysian drivers show remarkable common sense compared to other countries in the region. However, there are still plenty of drivers who take dangerous risks. Lane-drift is a big problem and signalling, when used at all, is often unclear. A flashing left indicator can mean 'you are safe to overtake', or 'I'm about to turn off', or 'I've forgotten to turn my indicator off', or 'look out, I'm about to do something totally unpredictable'. Giving a quick blast of the horn when you're overtaking a slower vehicle is common practice, and helps alert otherwise sleepy drivers to your presence.

HITCHING

Keep in mind that hitching is never entirely safe in any country in the world, and we don't recommend it. Travellers who decide to hitch, particularly single women, should understand that they are taking a small but potentially serious risk. People who do choose to hitch will be safer if they travel in pairs and let someone know where they are planning to go. Nevertheless, hitching is comparatively easy in Malaysia, though buses are so cheap that few people bother. Note that hitchers are banned from the Lebuhraya.

LOCAL TRANSPORT

Local transport varies widely from place to place. Taxis are found in most large cities and most have meters – government-set rates are as follows: flagfall (first 2km) is RM2; 10 sen for each 200m or 45 seconds thereafter; 20 sen for each additional passenger over two passengers; RM1 for each piece of luggage in the boot (trunk); plus 50% between midnight and 6am. Although drivers are legally obliged to use the meter, many prefer to make up a (usually elevated) fare on the spot, particularly in Penang. If a driver refuses to use the meter, either find another cab or bargain hard. Taxis also provide long-distance transport – see below.

Bicycle rickshaws (trishaws) supplement the taxi service in Georgetown, Melaka and some other cities, providing an atmospheric, if bumpy, means of exploring the backstreets. Bigger cities also have cheap and frequent buses and KL has commuter trains (p128), and a Light Rail Transit (LRT; p128) and monorail (p128) system.

Long-Distance Taxi

Long-distance taxis cover similar routes to the buses, but few people use them to travel from KL to Melaka or Penang as buses are cheaper and much more frequent. Long haul taxi services operate on a shared basis and taxis leave from fixed depots – look for the 'Teksi' signs. There is space for four passengers and you can either charter the whole taxi or just pay for one seat (a quarter of the whole-taxi fare) and share the cost with three other passengers. Taxis leave when there are four passengers, or when one passenger pays the whole taxi fare, which can mean a long wait. Early morning is generally the best time to find people to share a taxi.

Taxi rates to specific destinations are fixed by the government and the whole-taxi fare is usually posted at the taxi stand. Air-con taxis cost a few more ringgit than those without air-con, and fares are generally about twice the comparable bus fares. If you want to charter a taxi to an obscure destination, or by the hour, you'll probably have to do some negotiating. As a rule of thumb, you should pay around 50 sen per kilometre.

TOURS

Getting around Peninsular Malaysia under your own steam is rarely difficult, but there are numerous tour companies who will make all the arrangements for you. Tour agents in KL offer day tours to Melaka and other attractions around KL, as well as Taman Negara National Park in the north of the peninsula. See Kuala Lumpur (p99), Melaka (p151) and Penang (p188) for listings of local operators and tours.

TRAIN

Trains in Malaysia are run by the privatised national railway company **KTM** (Keretapi Tanah Melayu Berhad; ☎ 03-2267 1200; www.ktmb.com.my), which also runs the commuter train service in KL. Although slow, the trains are modern, comfortable and inexpensive and travelling long-distance by train in Asia has a certain charm. There are basically two lines – one up the east coast, and one up the west coast, connecting with Singapore in the south (see p231) and the Thai city of Hat Yai in the north (see p231).

As well as long-haul trips to Thailand and Singapore, you can use the train to get from KL to Butterworth and Penang. The *Ekspres Senandung Langkawi* train leaves KL at 9pm daily, reaching Butterworth at 5.50am the next morning; the return trip leaves Butterworth at 10pm, reaching KL at 6.45am. Seats cost from RM30 and berths from RM38. There's also the *Sinaran Express*, which leaves KL at 8.25am, reaching Butterworth at 4.10pm; the return services leaves Butterworth at 2pm, reaching KL at 9.50pm. Economy/superior seats cost RM19/30.

Services & Classes

There are two main types of rail services: express and local trains. Express trains are air-conditioned and have a mixture of 'premier' (1st class), 'superior' (2nd class) and sometimes 'economy' seats (3rd class). On overnight trains you'll find 'premier night deluxe' cabins (upper/lower berth cost RM50/70 on top of the standard fare), 'premier night standard cabins' (upper/lower berths cost RM18/26 on top of the standard fare), and 'standard night' cabins (upper/lower berths cost RM12/17 on top of the standard fare). Express trains stop only at main stations, while local services stop everywhere, including the middle of the jungle – it's a fascinating if somewhat slow way to explore the country.

Train schedules are reviewed biannually, so check on KTM's website for the latest situation before you make detailed plans.

Health

Dr Trish Batchelor

CONTENTS

Health issues and the quality of medical facilities vary enormously depending on where and how you travel in Southeast Asia. Many of the major cities are now very well developed, although travel to rural areas can expose you to a variety of health risks and inadequate medical care.

Travellers tend to worry about contracting infectious diseases when in the tropics, but infections are a rare cause of serious illness or death in travellers. Pre-existing medical conditions such as heart disease, and accidental injury (especially traffic accidents), account for most life-threatening problems. Becoming ill in some way, however, is relatively common. Fortunately most common illnesses can either be prevented with some common-sense behaviour or be treated easily with a well-stocked traveller's medical kit.

The following advice is a general guide only and does not replace the advice of a doctor trained in travel medicine.

BEFORE YOU GO

Pack medications in their original, clearly labelled containers. A signed and dated letter from your physician describing your medical conditions and medications, including their generic names, is also a good idea. If carrying syringes or needles, be sure to have a physician's letter documenting their medical necessity. If you have a heart condition bring a copy of your ECG taken just prior to travelling.

If you happen to take any regular medication bring a double supply in case of loss or theft. You can buy many medications over the counter without a doctor's prescription, but it can be difficult to find some of the newer drugs, particularly the latest antidepressant drugs, blood pressure medications and contraceptive pills.

HEALTH ADVISORIES

It's a good idea to consult your government's website on health and travel before departure, if one is available:

Australia (www.dfat.gov.au/travel)
Canada (www.hc-sc.gc.ca/english/index.html)
New Zealand (www.safetravel.govt.nz)
South Africa (www.dfa.gov.za/consular/travel_advice.htm)
UK (www.dh.gov.uk/en/Policyandguidance/Healthadvicefortravellers)
US (www.cdc.gov/travel)

INSURANCE

Even if you are fit and healthy, don't travel without health insurance – accidents do happen. Declare any existing medical conditions you have – the insurance company *will* check if your problem is pre-existing and will not cover you if it is undeclared. You may require extra cover for adventure activities such as rock climbing. If your health insurance doesn't cover you for medical expenses abroad, consider getting extra insurance. If you're uninsured, emergency evacuation is expensive –bills of over US$100,000 are not uncommon. See p222 for more on travel insurance.

VACCINATIONS

Specialised travel-medicine clinics are your best source of information; they stock all available vaccines and will be able to give specific recommendations for you and your trip. The doctors will take into account factors such as your vaccination history, the length of your trip, activities you may be undertaking and underlying medical conditions, such as pregnancy.

Most vaccines don't produce immunity until at least two weeks after they're given, so visit a doctor four to eight weeks before departure. Ask your doctor for an International Certificate of Vaccination (otherwise known as the yellow booklet), which will list all the vaccinations you've received.

Recommended Vaccinations

The World Health Organization (WHO) recommends the following vaccinations for travellers to Malaysia:

Adult diphtheria and tetanus Single booster recommended if none in the previous 10 years. Side effects include sore arm and fever.

Hepatitis A Provides almost 100% protection for up to a year. A booster after 12 months provides at least another 20 years' protection. Mild side effects such as headaches and a sore arm occur in 5% to 10% of people.

Hepatitis B Now considered routine for most travellers. Given as three shots over six months. A rapid schedule is also available, as is a combined vaccination with Hepatitis A. Side effects are mild and uncommon, usually a headache and a sore arm. Lifetime protection occurs in 95% of people.

Measles, mumps and rubella (MMR) Two doses of MMR are required unless you have had the diseases. Occasionally a rash and flulike illness can develop a week after receiving the vaccine. Many young adults require a booster.

Polio There have been no reported cases of polio in Malaysia in recent years. Only one booster is required as an adult for lifetime protection. Inactivated polio vaccine is safe during pregnancy.

Typhoid Recommended unless your trip is less than a week and only to developed cities. The vaccine offers around 70% protection, lasts for two to three years and comes as a single shot. Tablets are also available. However the injection is usually recommended as it has fewer side effects. A sore arm and a fever may occur.

Varicella If you haven't had chickenpox, discuss this vaccination with your doctor.

These immunisations are recommended for long-term travellers (more than one month) or those at particular risk:

Japanese B Encephalitis Three injections in all. Booster recommended after two years. A sore arm and a headache are the most common side effects, although a rare allergic reaction comprising hives and swelling can occur up to 10 days after any of the three doses.

Meningitis Single injection. There are two types of vaccination: the quadrivalent vaccine gives two to three years' protection, while the meningitis group C vaccine gives around 10 years' protection. Recommended for long-term backpackers aged under 25.

Rabies Three injections in all. A booster after one year will then provide 10 years' protection. Side effects are rare – occasionally a headache and a sore arm.

Tuberculosis (TB) A complex issue. Adult long-term travellers are usually recommended to have a TB skin test before and after travel, rather than a vaccination. Only one vaccine is given in a lifetime.

SARS

In March 2003 the world's attention was drawn to the outbreak of an apparently new and serious respiratory illness in China and Southeast Asia that became known as SARS (Severe Acute Respiratory Syndrome). Although the disease resulted in 800 deaths, there have been no new reported cases since 2004. However, there are still fundamental questions to be answered about SARS – where did it come from, will it come back and can we develop a rapid test or treatment for it? It is a sensible precaution to check the local press and seek immediate advice from your embassy in the event of any new outbreaks – see p219 for a list of embassies in Kuala Lumpur.

Required Vaccinations

Proof of yellow fever vaccination will be required if you have visited a country in the yellow-fever zone (ie Africa or South America) within the six days prior to entering Malaysia.

MEDICAL CHECKLIST

Recommended items for a personal medical kit:

- antibacterial cream, eg Muciprocin
- antibiotics for diarrhoea, eg Norfloxacin or Ciprofloxacin; Azithromycin for bacterial diarrhoea; and Tinidazole for giardiasis or amoebic dysentery
- antibiotics for skin infections, eg Amoxicillin/Clavulanate or Cephalexin
- antifungal cream, eg Clotrimazole
- antihistamines for allergies, eg Cetrizine for daytime and Promethazine for night
- anti-inflammatory, eg Ibuprofen

HEALTH

- antinausea medication, eg Prochlorperazine
- antiseptic for cuts and scrapes, eg Betadine
- antispasmodic for stomach cramps, eg Buscopan
- contraceptives
- decongestant for colds and flus, eg Pseudoephedrine
- DEET-based insect repellent
- diarrhoea 'stopper', eg Loperamide
- first-aid items such as scissors, plasters, bandages, gauze, thermometer (electronic, not mercury), sterile needles and syringes and tweezers
- indigestion medication, eg Quick Eze or Mylanta
- iodine tablets (unless you are pregnant or have a thyroid problem) to purify water
- laxative, eg Coloxyl
- migraine medication (your personal brand), if a migraine sufferer
- oral-rehydration solution for diarrhoea, eg Gastrolyte
- paracetamol for pain
- permethrin (to impregnate clothing and mosquito nets) for repelling insects
- steroid cream for allergic/itchy rashes, eg 1% to 2% hydrocortisone
- sunscreen and hat
- throat lozenges
- thrush (vaginal yeast infection) treatment, eg Clotrimazole pessaries or Diflucan tablet
- urine alkalisation agent, eg Ural, if you're prone to urinary tract infections.

INTERNET RESOURCES

There is a wealth of travel health advice on the internet. For further information, **Lonely Planet** (www.lonelyplanet.com) is a good place to start. The **World Health Organization** (WHO; www.who.int/ith) publishes a superb book called *International Travel & Health,* which is revised annually and is available free online. Another website of general interest is **MD Travel Health** (www.mdtravelhealth.com), which provides complete travel health recommendations for every country and is updated daily. The **Centers for Disease Control & Prevention** (CDC; www.cdc.gov) website also has good general information.

FURTHER READING

Lonely Planet's *Healthy Travel – Asia & India* is a handy pocket-size book packed with useful information including pretrip planning, emergency first aid, immunisation and disease information and what to do if you get sick on the road. Other recommended references include *Traveller's Health* by Dr Richard Dawood and *Travelling Well* by Dr Deborah Mills – check out the website www.travellingwell.com.au.

IN TRANSIT

DEEP VEIN THROMBOSIS (DVT)

Deep vein thrombosis (DVT) occurs when blood clots form in the legs during plane flights, chiefly because of prolonged immobility. The longer the flight, the greater the risk. Though most blood clots are reabsorbed uneventfully, some may break off and travel through the blood vessels to the lungs, where they may cause life-threatening complications.

The chief symptom of DVT is swelling or pain in the foot, ankle or calf, usually but not always on just one side. If a blood clot travels to the lungs it may cause chest pain and difficulty in breathing. Travellers with any of these symptoms should immediately seek medical attention.

To prevent the development of DVT on long flights you should walk about the cabin, perform isometric compressions of the leg muscles (ie contract the leg muscles while sitting), drink plenty of fluids and avoid alcohol.

JET LAG & MOTION SICKNESS

Jet lag is common when crossing more than five time zones. It causes symptoms including insomnia, fatigue, malaise or nausea. To help avoid jet lag try drinking plenty of fluids (nonalcoholic) and eating light meals. Upon arrival, seek exposure to natural sunlight and readjust your schedule (for meals, sleep etc) as soon as possible.

Antihistamines such as dimenhydrinate (Dramamine) and meclizine (Antivert, Bonine) are usually the first choice for treating motion sickness. Their main side effect is drowsiness. A herbal alternative is ginger, which works like a charm for some people.

IN MALAYSIA

AVAILABILITY OF HEALTHCARE

Kuala Lumpur and Penang have clinics catering specifically to travellers and expats and there are international-standard hospitals in

Melaka. Private clinics are marginally more expensive than local medical facilities, but they tend to offer a superior standard of care and they can also liaise with insurance companies should you require evacuation. Recommended clinics are listed under Information in the capital city sections of country chapters in this book. Your embassy and insurance company are also good contacts.

Self-treatment may be appropriate if your problem is minor (eg traveller's diarrhoea), you are carrying the appropriate medication and you cannot attend a recommended clinic. If you think you may have a serious disease, do not waste time – travel to the nearest quality facility to receive attention. It is always better to be assessed by a doctor than to rely on self-treatment. Over-the-counter medicines and prescription drugs are widely available from reputable pharmacies across Malaysia.

INFECTIOUS DISEASES

Cutaneous Larva Migrans

This disease, caused by dog hookworm, is common on some beaches. The rash starts as a small lump, then slowly spreads in a linear fashion, and is intensely itchy, especially at night. It is easily treated with medications and should not be cut out or frozen.

Dengue Fever

This mosquito-borne disease is becoming increasingly common in Malaysia, especially in cities. As there is no vaccine available it can only be prevented by avoiding mosquito bites. The mosquito that carries dengue bites day and night, so use insect avoidance measures at all times. Symptoms include high fever, severe headache and body ache. Some people develop a rash and experience diarrhoea. There is no specific treatment, just rest and paracetamol – do not take aspirin as it increases the likelihood of hemorrhaging. See a doctor to be diagnosed and monitored.

Filariasis

A mosquito-borne disease that is very common in the local population, yet very rare in travellers. Mosquito-avoidance measures are the best way to prevent this disease.

Hepatitis A

This food- and water-borne virus infects the liver, causing jaundice (yellow skin and eyes), nausea and lethargy. There is no specific treatment for hepatitis A, you just need to allow time for the liver to heal. All travellers to Malaysia should be vaccinated against hepatitis A.

Hepatitis B

The only sexually transmitted disease (STD) that can be prevented by vaccination, hepatitis B is spread by body fluids, including sexual contact. In Malaysia, 3.5% of the population are carriers of hepatitis B, and usually are unaware of this. The long-term consequences can include liver cancer and cirrhosis.

Hepatitis E

Hepatitis E is transmitted through contaminated food and water and has similar symptoms to hepatitis A, but is far less common. It is a severe problem in pregnant women and can result in the death of both mother and baby. There is currently no vaccine, and prevention is by following safe eating and drinking guidelines.

HIV

HIV is a growing problem in Malaysia and unprotected heterosexual sex is the main method of transmission. There is no cure and treatment with antiretroviral drugs just delays the onset of symptoms. Practising safe sex or avoiding sex with untested partners is the only means of prevention.

Influenza

Present year-round in the tropics, influenza (flu) symptoms include high fever, muscle aches, runny nose, cough and sore throat. It can be very severe in people over the age of 65 or in those with underlying medical conditions such as heart disease or diabetes; vaccination is recommended for these individuals. There is no specific treatment, just rest and paracetamol.

Japanese B Encephalitis

This viral disease is transmitted by mosquitoes, but most cases occur in rural areas and vaccination is usually only recommended for travellers spending more than one month outside of cities. There is no treatment, and a third of infected people will die while another third will suffer permanent brain damage.

Leptospirosis

Leptospirosis is most commonly contracted after river rafting or canyoning. Early symptoms are very similar to the flu and include headache and fever. It can vary from a very mild to a fatal disease. Diagnosis is through blood tests and it is easily treated with Doxycycline.

Malaria

Malaria is uncommon in Peninsular Malaysia and antimalarial drugs are rarely recommended for travellers. However, there may be a small risk in rural areas. Remember that malaria can be fatal. Before you travel, seek medical advice on the right medication and dosage for you.

Malaria is caused by a parasite transmitted by the bite of an infected mosquito. The most important symptom of malaria is fever, but general symptoms such as headache, diarrhoea, cough or chills may also occur. Diagnosis can only be made by taking a blood sample.

Two strategies should be combined to prevent malaria – mosquito avoidance, and antimalarial medications. Most people who catch malaria are taking inadequate or no antimalarial medication.

Travellers are advised to prevent mosquito bites by taking these steps:

- Use a DEET-containing insect repellent on exposed skin. Wash this off at night, as long as you are sleeping under a mosquito net. Natural repellents such as Citronella can be effective, but must be applied more frequently than products containing DEET.
- Sleep under a mosquito net impregnated with Permethrin.
- Choose accommodation with screens and fans (if not air-conditioned).
- Impregnate clothing with Permethrin in high-risk areas.
- Wear long sleeves and trousers in light colours.
- Use mosquito coils.
- Spray your room with insect repellent before going out for your evening meal.

There are a variety of medications available:

Artesunate Derivatives of Artesunate are not suitable as a preventive medication. They are useful treatments under medical supervision.

Chloroquine and Paludrine The effectiveness of this combination is now limited. Common side effects include nausea (40% of people) and mouth ulcers. Generally not recommended.

Doxycycline This daily tablet is a broad-spectrum antibiotic that has the added benefit of helping to prevent a variety of tropical diseases, including leptospirosis, tick-borne disease, typhus and meliodosis. The potential side effects include photosensitivity (a tendency to sunburn), thrush in women, indigestion, heartburn, nausea and interference with the contraceptive pill. More serious side effects include ulceration of the oesophagus – you can help prevent this by taking your tablet with a meal and a large glass of water, and never lying down within half an hour of taking it. Must be taken for four weeks after leaving the risk area.

Lariam (Mefloquine) This weekly tablet suits some people but serious side effects can include depression, anxiety, psychosis and fits. Anyone with a history of depression, anxiety, other psychological disorder, or epilepsy should not take Lariam. It is considered safe in the second and third trimesters of pregnancy. It is around 90% effective but tablets must be taken for four weeks after leaving the risk area.

Malarone This new drug is a combination of Atovaquone and Proguanil. Side effects are uncommon and mild, most commonly nausea and headache. It is the best tablet for scuba divers and for those on short trips to high-risk areas. It must be taken for one week after leaving the risk area.

A final option is to take no preventive medication but to have a supply of emergency medication should you develop the symptoms of malaria. This is less than ideal, and you'll need to get to a good medical facility within 24 hours of developing a fever. If you choose this option the most effective and safest treatment is Malarone (four tablets once daily for three days). Other options include Mefloquine and Quinine but the side effects of these drugs at treatment doses make them less desirable. Fansidar is no longer recommended.

Measles

This highly contagious bacterial infection is spread via coughing and sneezing. Most people born before 1966 are immune as they had the disease in childhood. Measles starts with a high fever and rash and can be complicated by pneumonia and brain disease. There is no specific treatment.

Rabies

Rabies is a potential risk in Malaysia and the disease is invariably fatal if untreated. Rabies is spread by the bite or lick of an infected animal – most commonly a dog or monkey. You should seek medical advice immediately after any animal bite and commence postexposure treatment. Having pretravel vaccination means the postbite treatment is greatly simplified. If an animal bites you, gently wash the wound with soap and water, and apply iodine based antiseptic. If you are not prevaccinated you will need to receive rabies immunoglobulin as soon as possible.

STDs

The most common STDs in Malaysia include herpes, warts, syphilis, gonorrhea and chlamydia. People carrying these diseases often have no signs of infection. Condoms will prevent gonorrhea and chlamydia but not warts or herpes. If after a sexual encounter you develop any rash, lumps, discharge or pain when passing urine seek immediate medical attention. If you have been sexually active during your travels have an STD check on your return home.

Tuberculosis

While TB is rare in travellers, those who have had significant contact with the local population (such as medical and aid workers and long-term travellers) should take precautions. Vaccination is usually only given to children under the age of five; it's recommended adults at risk are tested both before and after travel. The main symptoms are fever, cough, weight loss, night sweats and tiredness.

Typhoid

This serious bacterial infection is also spread via food and water. It gives a high and slowly progressive fever, headache and may be accompanied by a dry cough and stomach pain. It is diagnosed by blood tests and treated with antibiotics. Vaccination is recommended for all travellers spending more than a week in Malaysia, or travelling outside of the major cities. Be aware that vaccination is not 100% effective so you must still be careful with what you eat and drink.

Typhus

Murine typhus is spread by the bite of a flea whereas scrub typhus is spread by mites. These diseases are rare in travellers. Symptoms include fever, muscle pains and a rash. You can avoid these diseases by following general insect-avoidance measures. Doxycycline will also prevent them.

TRAVELLER'S DIARRHOEA

Traveller's diarrhoea is by far the most common problem affecting travellers. In over 80% of cases, traveller's diarrhoea is caused by a bacteria (there are numerous potential culprits), and therefore responds promptly to treatment with antibiotics. Treatment with antibiotics will depend on your situation – how sick you are, how quickly you need to get better, where you are etc.

Traveller's diarrhoea is defined as the passage of more than three watery bowel actions within 24 hours, plus at least one other symptom such as fever, cramps, nausea, vomiting or feeling generally unwell.

Treatment consists of staying well-hydrated; rehydration solutions such as Gastrolyte are the best for this. Antibiotics such as Norfloxacin, Ciprofloxacin or Azithromycin will kill the bacteria quickly.

Loperamide is just a 'stopper' and doesn't get to the cause of the problem, but it can be helpful in certain situtation, eg if you have to go on a long bus ride. Don't take Loperamide if you have a fever, or blood in your stools. Seek medical attention quickly if you do not respond to an appropriate antibiotic.

Amoebic Dysentery

Amoebic dysentery is very rare in travellers but is often misdiagnosed by poor-quality labs. Symptoms are similar to bacterial diarrhoea, ie fever, bloody diarrhoea and generally feeling unwell. You should always seek reliable medical care if you have blood in your

DRINKING WATER

- Never drink tap water.
- Bottled water is generally safe – check the seal is intact at purchase.
- Avoid ice unless you are sure it is safe.
- Avoid fresh juices – they may have been watered down.
- Boiling water is the most efficient method of purifying it.
- The best chemical purifier is iodine. It should not be used by pregnant women or those who suffer with thyroid problems.
- Water filters should also clear out viruses. Ensure your filter has a chemical barrier such as iodine and a small pore size, ie less than four microns.

diarrhoea. Treatment involves two drugs: Tinidazole or Metroniadzole to kill the parasite in your gut, and then a second drug to kill the cysts. If left untreated complications such as liver or gut abscesses can occur.

Giardiasis

Giardia lamblia is a parasite that is relatively common in travellers. Symptoms include nausea, bloating, excess gas (including 'eggy' burps), fatigue and intermittent diarrhoea. The parasite will eventually go away if left untreated but this can take months. The treatment of choice is Tinidazole, with Metroniadzole being a second option.

ENVIRONMENTAL HAZARDS

Air Pollution

Air pollution, particularly vehicle pollution, is an increasing problem in most of Southeast Asia's major cities. If you have severe respiratory problems speak with your doctor before travelling to any heavily polluted urban centres. This pollution also causes minor respiratory problems such as sinusitis, dry throat and irritated eyes. If you're troubled by the pollution leave the city for a few days and get some fresh air.

Diving

Divers and surfers should seek specialised advice before they travel to ensure their medical kit contains treatment for coral cuts and tropical ear infections, as well as the standard problems. Divers should ensure their insurance covers them for decompression illness – get specialised dive insurance through an organisation such as **Divers Alert Network** (DAN; www.danseap.org). Have a dive medical before you leave your home country – there are certain medical conditions that are incompatible with diving and economic considerations may override health considerations for some dive operators.

Food

Eating in unhygienic restaurants is the biggest risk factor for contracting traveller's diarrhoea. Ways to prevent it include eating only freshly cooked food, avoiding shellfish and food that has been sitting around in buffets. Peel all fruit, cook vegetables, and soak salads in iodine water for at least 20 minutes. Eat in busy restaurants with a high turnover of customers.

Heat

Malaysia is hot and humid throughout the year. For most people it takes at least two weeks to adapt to the hot climate. Swelling of the feet and ankles is common, as are muscle cramps caused by excessive sweating. Prevent these by avoiding dehydration and excessive activity in the heat. Don't eat salt tablets (they aggravate the gut); drinking rehydration solution or eating salty food helps. Treat cramps by stopping activity, resting, rehydrating with double-strength rehydration solution and gently stretching.

Dehydration is the main contributor to heat exhaustion. Symptoms include feeling weak; headache; irritability; nausea or vomiting; sweaty skin; a fast, weak pulse; and a normal or slightly elevated body temperature. Treatment involves getting out of the heat and/or sun, fanning the victim and applying cool wet cloths to the skin, laying the victim flat with their legs raised and rehydrating with water containing a quarter of a teaspoon of salt per litre. Recovery is usually rapid and it is common to feel weak for some days afterwards.

Heat stroke is a serious medical emergency. Symptoms come on suddenly and include weakness, nausea, a hot dry body with a body temperature of over 41°C, dizziness, confusion, loss of coordination, fits and eventually collapse and loss of consciousness. Seek medical help and commence cooling by getting the person out of the heat, removing their clothes, fanning them and applying cool wet cloths or ice to their body, especially to the groin and armpits.

Prickly heat is a common skin rash in the tropics, caused by sweat being trapped under the skin. The result is an itchy rash of tiny lumps. Treat by moving out of the heat and into an air-conditioned area for a few hours and by having cool showers. Creams and ointments clog the skin so they should be avoided. Locally bought prickly-heat powder can be helpful.

Tropical fatigue is common in long-term expats based in the tropics. It's rarely due to disease and is caused by the climate, inadequate mental rest, excessive alcohol intake and the demands of daily work in a different culture.

Insect Bites & Stings

Bedbugs don't carry disease but their bites are very itchy. They live in the cracks of furniture and walls and then migrate to the bed at night to feed on you. You can treat the itch with an antihistamine.

Lice inhabit various parts of your body but most commonly your head and pubic area. Transmission is via close contact with an infected person. They can be difficult to treat and you may need numerous applications of an antilice shampoo such as Permethrin. Pubic lice are usually contracted from sexual contact.

Ticks are contracted after walking in rural areas. They are commonly found behind the ears, on the belly and in armpits. If you have had a tick bite and experience symptoms such as a rash at the site of the bite or elsewhere, fever, or muscle aches you should see a doctor. Doxycycline prevents tick-borne diseases.

Leeches are found in humid rainforest areas. They do not transmit any disease but their bites are often intensely itchy for weeks afterwards and can easily become infected. Apply an iodine-based antiseptic to any leech bite to help prevent infection.

Bee and wasp stings mainly cause problems for people who are allergic to them. Anyone with a serious bee or wasp allergy should carry an injection of adrenaline (eg an Epipen) for emergency treatment. For others pain is the main problem – apply ice to the sting and take painkillers.

Most jellyfish in Malaysian waters are not dangerous, just irritating. First-aid for jellyfish stings involves pouring vinegar onto the affected area to neutralise the poison. Do not rub sand or water onto the stings. Take painkillers, and if you feel ill in any way after being stung you should seek medical advice. Take local advice if there are dangerous jellyfish around and keep out of the water.

Parasites

Numerous parasites are found among locals in Malaysia; however, most are rare in travellers. To avoid parasitic infections, wear shoes and avoid eating raw food, especially fish, pork and vegetables. A number of parasites are transmitted via the skin by walking barefoot including strongyloides, hookworm and cutaneous *Larva migrans*.

Skin Problems

Fungal rashes are common in humid climates. There are two common fungal rashes that affect travellers. The first occurs in moist areas that get less air such as the groin, armpits and between the toes. It starts as a red patch that slowly spreads and is usually itchy. Treatment involves keeping the skin dry, avoiding chafing and using an antifungal cream such as Clotrimazole or Lamisil. *Tinea versicolor* is also common – this fungus causes small, light-coloured patches, most commonly on the back, chest and shoulders. Consult a doctor.

Cuts and scratches become easily infected in humid climates. Take meticulous care of any cuts and scratches to prevent complications such as abscesses. Immediately wash all wounds in clean water and apply antiseptic. If you develop signs of infection (increasing pain and redness) see a doctor. Divers and surfers should be particularly careful with coral cuts as they become easily infected.

Snakes

Poisonous and harmless snakes are found in many rural areas in Malaysia. Assume all snakes are poisonous and never try to catch one. Always wear boots and long pants if walking in an area that may have snakes. First aid in the event of a snakebite involves pressure immobilisation via an elastic bandage firmly wrapped around the affected limb, starting at the bite site and working up towards the chest. The bandage should not be so tight that the circulation is cut off, and the fingers or toes should be kept free so the circulation can be checked. Immobilise the limb with a splint and carry the victim to medical attention. Do not use tourniquets or try to suck the venom out. Antivenin is available for most species.

Sunburn

Even on a cloudy day sunburn can occur rapidly. Always use a strong sunscreen (at least factor 30), making sure to reapply after a swim, and always wear a wide-brimmed hat and sunglasses outdoors. Avoid lying in the sun during the hottest part of the day (10am to 2pm). If you become sunburnt stay out of the sun until you have recovered, apply cool compresses and take painkillers for the discomfort. One percent hydrocortisone cream applied twice daily is also helpful.

WOMEN'S HEALTH

Pregnant women should receive specialised advice before travelling. The ideal time to travel is in the second trimester (between 16 and 28 weeks), when the risk of pregnancy-related problems are at their lowest and pregnant women generally feel at their best. During the first trimester there is a risk of miscarriage and in the third trimester complications such as premature labour and high blood pressure are possible. It's wise to travel with a companion. Always carry a list of quality medical facilities available at your destination and ensure you continue your standard antenatal care at these facilities. Most of all, ensure travel insurance covers all pregnancy-related possibilities, including premature labour.

None of the more effective antimalarial drugs are completely safe in pregnancy. WHO recommends that pregnant women do *not* travel to areas with Chloroquine-resistant malaria.

Traveller's diarrhoea can quickly lead to dehydration and result in inadequate blood flow to the placenta. Many of the drugs used to treat various diarrhoea bugs are not recommended in pregnancy. Azithromycin is considered safe.

In Kuala Lumpur, Melaka and Penang, supplies of sanitary products are readily available. Birth control options may be limited so bring adequate supplies of your own form of contraception. Heat, humidity and antibiotics can all contribute to thrush. Treatment is with antifungal creams and pessaries such as Clotrimazole. A practical alternative is a single tablet of fluconazole (Diflucan). Urinary tract infections can be precipitated by dehydration or long bus journeys without toilet stops; bring suitable antibiotics.

TRADITIONAL MEDICINE

Traditional medical systems are widely practised in Malaysia. There is a big difference between these traditional healing systems and 'folk' medicine. Folk remedies should be avoided, as they often involve rather dubious procedures with potential complications. In comparison, traditional healing systems such as traditional Chinese medicine are well respected, and aspects of them are being increasingly utilised by Western medical practitioners.

All traditional Asian medical systems identify a vital life force, and see blockage or imbalance as causing disease. Techniques such as herbal medicines, massage, and acupuncture are utilised to bring this vital force back into balance, or to maintain balance. These therapies are best used for treating chronic diseases such as chronic fatigue, arthritis, irritable bowel syndrome and some chronic skin conditions. Traditional medicines should be avoided for treating serious acute infections.

Be aware that 'natural' doesn't always mean 'safe', and there can be drug interactions between herbal medicines and Western medicines. If you are utilising both systems ensure you inform both practitioners what the other has prescribed.

Language

CONTENTS

The official language of Kuala Lumpur, Melaka and Penang is Bahasa Malaysia, and it is spoken almost universally, not least because it is compulsory to pass it in order to attain the high school certificate. English is also quite widely understood, but the difference in accent between Westerners and Malays can be a struggle for both parties. If you come across locals who don't understand English there will usually be someone around willing to pitch in and translate.

Along with Malay and English, there are several Indian and Chinese languages spoken in the region, such as Hokkien, Cantonese, Tamil and Malayalam.

BAHASA MALAYSIA

In its most basic form, Malay is very simple. Verbs aren't conjugated for tense; the notion of time is indicated by the use of adverbs such as 'yesterday' or 'tomorrow'. For example, you can change any sentence into the past tense by simply adding *sudah* (already). Many nouns are pluralised by simply saying them twice – thus *buku* is 'book', *buku-buku* is 'books', *anak* is 'child', *anak-anak* is 'children'. There are no articles (a, an, the). Thus 'a good book' or 'the good book' is simply *buku baik*. There is no verb 'to be', so again it would be *buku baik* rather than 'the book is good'. Malay is also a very poetic and evocative language – 'the sun', for example, is *matahari*, or 'the eye of the day'.

For a more comprehensive guide to the language, get hold of Lonely Planet's handy pocket-sized *Malay Phrasebook*.

PRONUNCIATION

Most letters are pronounced the same as their English counterparts, although a few vowels and consonants differ.

Vowels

a	as the 'u' in 'hut'
e	a neutral vowel like the 'a' in 'ago' when unstressed, eg *besar* (big); when the stress falls on **e** it's more like the 'a' in 'may', eg *meja* (table).
i	as in 'hit'
o	as in 'note'
u	as in 'flute'
ai	as in 'aisle'
au	a drawn out 'ow', as in 'cow'
ua	each vowel is pronounced, as 'oo-a'

Consonants

c	always as the 'ch' in 'chair'
g	always hard, as in 'go'
ng	as the 'ng' in 'singer'
ngg	as 'ng' + 'g' (as in 'anger')
j	as in 'join'
r	pronounced clearly and distinctly
h	as the English 'h' but slightly stronger (like a sigh); at the end of a word it's almost silent
k	as English 'k', except at the end of the word, when it's more like a glottal stop (ie the 'nonsound' created by the momentary closing of the throat before each syllable in the expression 'oh-oh!')
ny	as in 'canyon'

Word Stress

In Malay words, most syllables carry equal emphasis, but a good rule of thumb is to put stress on the second-last syllable. The main exception is the unstressed **e** in words such as *besar* (big), pronounced 'be-*sar*'. Unfortunately, there's no single rule to determine whether **e** is stressed or unstressed.

ACCOMMODATION

I'm looking for a ...	*Saya mencari ...*
guesthouse	*rumah tetamu*
hotel	*hotel*
youth hostel	*asrama belia*
bed	*katil*

MAKING A RESERVATION

(for phone or written inquiries)

To ...	*Ke ...*
From ...	*Daripada ...*
I'd like to book ...	*Saya nak tempah ...* (see the list on this page for bed and room options)
for the nights of ...	*untuk malam ...*
in the name of ...	*atas nama ...*
credit card	*kad kredit*
type	*jenis*
number	*nombor*
expiry date	*tempoh tamat*
Please confirm availability and price.	*Tolong sahkan tempahan dan harga.*

Where is a cheap hotel?
Di mana ada hotel yang murah?
What is the address?
Apakah alamatnya?
Could you write the address, please?
Tolong tuliskan alamat itu?
Do you have any rooms available?
Ada bilik kosong?
I'd like to share a dorm.
Saya nak berkongsi (bilik hostel/asrama).

I'd like a ...	*Saya hendakkan ...*
single room	*bilik untuk satu orang*
double room	*bilik untuk dua orang*
room with two beds	*bilik yang ada dua katil*
room with air-con	*bilik dengan alat hawa dingin*
room with a fan	*bilik dengan kipas*
room with a bathroom	*bilik dengan bilik mandi*

How much is it ...?	*Berapa harga ...?*
per night	*satu malam*
per week	*satu seminggu*
per person	*satu orang*

May I see it?
Boleh saya lihat biliknya?
Where is the bathroom?
Bilik mandi di mana?
I (don't) like this room.
Saya (tidak) suka bilik ini.
I'm/We're leaving today.
Saya/Kami nak mendaftar keluar hari ini.

CONVERSATION & ESSENTIALS

Addressing people

In Malaysia, *kamu* is an egalitarian second-person pronoun, equivalent to 'you' in English. The polite pronoun for the equivalent of English 'I/we' is *kami*. In polite speech, you wouldn't normally use first-person pronouns, but would refer to yourself by name or form of address, eg *Makcik nak pergi ke pasar* (Auntie wants to go to the market).

When a ddressing a man or a woman old enough to be your parent, use *pakcik* (uncle) or *makcik* (aunt). For someone only slightly older, use *abang* or *bang* (older brother) and *kakak* or *kak* (older sister). For people old enough to be your grandparents, *datuk* and *nenek* (grandfather and grandmother) are used. For a man or woman you meet on the street you can also use *encik* or *cik* respectively.

Hello.	*Helo.*
Good morning.	*Selamat pagi.*
Good day. (said around midday)	*Selamat tengah hari.*
Good afternoon.	*Selamat petang.*
Good night.	*Selamat malam.*
Goodbye. (said by person leaving)	*Selamat tinggal.*
Goodbye. (said by person staying)	*Selamat jalan.*
Yes.	*Ya.*
No.	*Tidak.*
Please.	*Tolong/Silakan.*
Thank you (very much).	*Terima kasih (banyak).*
That's fine/ You're welcome.	*Boleh/Sama-sama.*
Excuse me, ...	*Maaf, ...*
Sorry/Pardon.	*Maaf.*
I'm sorry. (forgive me)	*Minta maaf.*
How are you?	*Apa khabar?*
Fine thanks.	*Khabar baik.*
What's your name?	*Siapa nama kamu?*
My name is ...	*Nama saya ...*
Where are you from?	*Dari mana asal saudara?*
I'm from ...	*Saya dari ...*
How old are you?	*Berapa umur saudara?*
I'm (20 years old).	*Umur saya (dua puluh tahun).*

SIGNS

Masuk	Entrance
Keluar	Exit
Pertanyaan	Information
Buka	Open
Tutup	Closed
Dilarang	Prohibited
Di Larang Merokok	No Smoking
Bahaya	Danger
Ada Bilik Kosong	Rooms Available
Penuh/Tak Ada Bilik Kosong	Full/No Vacancies
Polis	Police
Balai Polis	Police Station
Tandas	Toilets
Lelaki	Men
Perempuan	Women
Panas	Hot
Sejuk	Cold
Tarik	Pull
Tolak	Push

I like ...	*Saya suka ...*
I don't like ...	*Saya tidak suka ...*
Just a minute.	*Sebentar/Sekejap.*
Good/Very nice.	*Bagus.*
Good/Fine.	*Baik.*
No good.	*Tidak baik.*

DIRECTIONS

Where is ...?	*Di mana ...*
Which way?	*Ke mana?*
Go straight ahead.	*Jalan terus.*
Turn left.	*Belok kiri.*
Turn right.	*Belok kanan.*
at the corner	*di simpang*
at the traffic lights	*di tempat lampu isyarat*
at the T-junction	*di simpang tiga*
behind	*di belakang*
in front of	*di hadapan*
next to	*di samping/di sebelah*
opposite	*berhadapan dengan*
near	*dekat*
far	*jauh*
here	*di sini*
there	*di sana*
north	*utara*
south	*selatan*
east	*timur*
west	*barat*
beach	*pantai*
bridge	*jambatan*
island	*pulau*
mosque	*masjid*
museum	*muzium*
sea	*laut*
square	*dataran*

EMERGENCIES

Help!	*Tolong!*
There's been an accident!	*Ada kemalangan!*
I'm lost.	*Saya sesat.*
Go away!	*Pergi!*
Stop!	*Berhenti!*
I've been robbed!	*Saya dirompak!*
Call ...!	*Panggil ...!*
a doctor	*doktor*
an ambulance	*ambulans*

HEALTH

Where is a ...	*Di mana ada ...*
chemist/pharmacy	*apotik/farmasi*
dentist	*doktor gigi*
doctor	*doktor*
hospital	*hospital*
I'm ill.	*Saya sakit.*
It hurts here.	*Sini sakit.*
I'm allergic to ...	*Saya alergik kepada ...*
antibiotics	*antibiotik*
aspirin	*aspirin*
bees	*lebah*
nuts	*kacang*
penicillin	*penisilin*
peanuts	*kacang putih*
I'm ...	*Saya ...*
asthmatic	*sakit lelah*
diabetic	*sakit kencing manis*
epileptic	*sakit gila babi*
pregnant	*hamil*
antiseptic	*antiseptik*
condoms	*kondom*
contraceptive	*kontraseptif* or *pencegah hamil*
diarrhoea	*cirit-birit*
fever	*demam panas*
headache	*sakit kepala*
medicine	*ubat*
sunblock cream	*krim pelindung cahaya matahari*
pill/tablet	*pil/tablet*
quinine	*kina/kuinin*
sanitary napkins	*tuala wanita*

sleeping pills	*pil tidur*
tampons	*tampon*

LANGUAGE DIFFICULTIES

Do you speak English?
Bolehkah anda berbicara Bahasa Inggeris?
Does anyone here speak English?
Ada orang yang berbahasa Inggeris di sini?
How do you say ... in Malay?
Macam mana cakap ... dalam Bahasa Melayu?
What does ... mean?
Apa ertinya ...?
I understand.
Saya faham.
I don't understand.
Saya tidak faham.
Please write it down.
Tolong tuliskan.
Please repeat it.
Tolong ulangi.
Can you show me (on the map)?
Tolong tunjukkan (di peta)?

NUMBERS

0	*kosong/sifar*
1	*satu*
2	*dua*
3	*tiga*
4	*empat*
5	*lima*
6	*enam*
7	*tujuh*
8	*delapan/lapan*
9	*sembilan*
10	*sepuluh*
11	*sebelas*
12	*dua belas*
13	*tiga belas*
14	*empat belas*
15	*lima belas*
16	*enam belas*
17	*tujuh belas*
18	*lapan belas*
19	*sembilan belas*
20	*dua puluh*
21	*dua puluh satu*
22	*dua puluh dua*
30	*tiga puluh*
40	*empat puluh*
50	*lima puluh*
60	*enam puluh*
70	*tujuh puluh*
80	*lapan puluh*
90	*sembilan puluh*
100	*seratus*
200	*dua ratus*
1000	*seribu*
2000	*dua ribu*

PAPERWORK

name	*nama*
nationality	*bangsa*
date of birth	*tarikh lahir*
place of birth	*tempat kelahiran tempat lahir*
sex/gender	*jantina*
passport	*pasport*
visa	*visa*

QUESTION WORDS

Who?	*Siapakah?*
What?	*Apa?*
When?	*Bilakah?*
Where?	*Di mana?*
How?	*Berapa?*
Which?	*Yang mana?*

SHOPPING & SERVICES

I'd like to buy ...	*Saya nak beli ...*
How much (is it)?	*Berapa (harganya)?*
I don't like it.	*Saya tak suka ini.*
May I look at it?	*Boleh saya lihat barang itu?*
I'm just looking.	*Saya nak tengok saja.*
It's cheap.	*Murah.*
It's too expensive.	*Mahalnya.*
Can you lower the price?	*Boleh kurang sedikit?*
No more than ...	*Tak lebih daripada ...*
That's a good price.	*Harganya dah murah.*
I'll take it.	*Saya nak beli ini.*

Do you accept ...?	*Boleh bayar dengan ...?*
credit cards	*kad kredit*
travellers cheques	*cek kembara*

more	*lebih banyak*
less	*kurang*
big	*besar*
bigger	*lebih besar*
small	*kecil*
smaller	*lebih kecil*
this	*ini*
that	*itu*

I'm looking for a/the ...	*Saya nak cari ...*
bank	*bank*
barber	*tukang cukur*
bookshop	*kedai buku*
city centre	*pusat bandar*
chemist/pharmacy	*apotik/farmasi*
... embassy	*kedutaan besar ...*

grocery	*kedai makanan*
market	*pasar*
night market	*pasar malam*
police station	*stesen polis*
post office	*pejabat pos*
public telephone	*telepon umum*
public toilet	*tandas awam*
shop	*kedai*
shopping centre	*pusat membeli-belah*
telephone centre	*pusat telefon*
tourist office	*pejabat pelancong*

I want to change ...	*Saya nak tukar wang ...*
money (cash)	*wang tunai*
travellers cheques	*cek kembara*

What time does it open/close?
Pukul berapa buka/tutup?
I want to call ...
Saya mau menelefon ...

TIME & DATES

What time is it?	*Pukul berapa?*
(It's) 7 o'clock.	*Pukul tujuh.*
When?	*Bila?*
in the morning	*pagi*
in the afternoon	*tengahari*
in the evening	*petang*
at night	*malam*
today	*hari ini*
tomorrow	*besok/esok*
yesterday	*semalam*
How long?	*Berapa lama?*
hour	*jam*
week	*minggu*
year	*tahun*

Monday	*hari Isnin*
Tuesday	*hari Selasa*
Wednesday	*hari Rabu*
Thursday	*hari Khamis*
Friday	*hari Jumaat*
Saturday	*hari Sabtu*
Sunday	*hari Minggu*

January	*Januari*
February	*Februari*
March	*Mac*
April	*April*
May	*Mei*
June	*Jun*
July	*Julai*
August	*Ogos*
September	*September*
October	*Oktober*
November	*November*
December	*Disember*

TRANSPORT
Public Transport

What time does the ... leave?	*Pukul berapakah ... berangkat?*
boat	*bot*
bus	*bas*
plane	*kapal terbang*
ship	*kapal*
train	*keretapi*

I'd like a ... ticket.	*Saya nak tiket ...*
one-way	*sehala*
return	*pergi-balik*

I want to go to ...
Saya nak ke ...
How can I get to ...?
Bagaimana saya pergi ke ...?
How many kilometres?
Berapa kilometer?
The (train/bus) has been delayed.
Kereta api/bas itu telah terlambat.
The (train/bus) has been cancelled.
Kereta api/bas itu telah dibatalkan.

the first (bus)	*(bas) pertama*
the last (train)	*keretapi terakhir*
airport	*lapangan terbang*
bus station	*stesen bas*
bus stop	*perhentian bas*
platform number	*nombor platform*
rickshaw/trishaw	*beca*
ticket office	*pejabat tiket*
ticket window	*(tempat/kaunter) tikit*
timetable	*jadual*
train station	*stesen keretapi*

Private Transport

I'd like to hire a/an ...	*Saya nak menyewa ...*
car	*kereta*
motorbike	*motosikal*
bicycle	*basikal*

Is this the road to ...?	*Inikah jalan ke ...?*
Where's a service station?	*Stesen minyak di mana?*
Please fill it up.	*Tolong penuhkan tangki.*
I'd like (30) litres.	*Saya nak (30) liter.*
diesel	*disel*
leaded petrol	*petrol plumbum*
unleaded petrol	*petrol tanpa plumbum*

ROAD SIGNS

Beri Jalan	Give Way
Lencongan	Detour
Dilarang Masuk	No Entry
Tidak Boleh Memotong	No Overtaking
Dilarang Letak Kereta	No Parking
Masuk	Entrance
Kosongkan	Keep Clear
Jalan Tol	Toll Way
Bahaya	Danger
Perlahan-Perlahan	Slow Down
Jalan Sehala	One Way
Keluar	Exit

(How long) Can I park here?
(Beberapa lama) Boleh saya letak kereta di sini?
Where do I pay?
Di mana tempat membayar?
I need a mechanic.
Kami memerlukan mekanik.
The car/motorbike has broken down (at ...)
Kereta/motosikal saya telah rosak (di ...)
The car/motorbike won't start.
Kereta/motosikal saya tidak dapat dihidupkan.
I have a flat tyre.
Tayarnya kempis.
I've run out of petrol.
Minyak sudah habis.
I've had an accident.
Saya terlibat dalam kemalangan.

TRAVEL WITH CHILDREN

Do you have a/an ...?	*Ada ...?*
I need a/an ...	*Saya perlukan ...*
baby change room	*bilik salin bayi*
car baby seat	*tempat duduk bayi*
child-minding service	*penjagaan anak*
children's menu	*menu kanak-kanak*
(disposable) nappies/diapers	*(pakai buang) kain lampin*
formula (milk)	*(susu) rumusan bayi*
(English-speaking) babysitter	*penjaga anak (yang tahu bercakap dalam Bahasa Inggeris)*
highchair	*kerusi tinggi*
potty	*bekas najis*
stroller	*kereta tolak bayi*

Are children allowed?
Adakah kanak-kanak dibenarkan masuk?

Glossary

See p50 for culinary terms.

adat – Malay customary law
adat temenggong – Malay law with Indian modifications, governing the customs and ceremonies of the sultans
air – water
air terjun – waterfall
alor – groove; furrow; main channel of a river
ampang – dam
ang pow – red packets of money used as offerings, payment or gifts
APEC – Asia-Pacific Economic Cooperation
arak – Malay local alcohol
Asean – Association of Southeast Asian Nations
atap – roof thatching

Baba-Nonya – descendants of Chinese immigrants to Melaka and Penang who intermarried with Malays and adopted many Malay customs; also known as Peranakan, or Straits Chinese; sometimes spelt Nyonya
Bahasa Malaysia – Malay language; also known as Bahasa Melayu
bandar – seaport; town
baru – new; common in placenames
batang – stem; tree trunk; the main branch of a river
batik – technique of imprinting cloth with dye to produce multicoloured patterns
batu – stone; rock; milepost
bendahara – chief minister
bomoh – spiritual healer
British Resident – chief British representative during the colonial era
bukit – hill
bumiputra – literally, sons of the soil; indigenous Malays
bunga raya – hibiscus flower (national flower of Malaysia)

dadah – drugs
dato' – see *datuk*
datuk – literally, grandfather; general male nonroyal title of distinction
dipterocarp – family of trees, native to Malaysia, that have two-winged fruits
dusun – small town; orchard; fruit grove

Emergency – the guerrilla war between communist rebels and the Malaysian government

genting – mountain pass
godown – river warehouse
gopuram – Hindu temple tower
gua – cave
gunung – mountain

hilir – lower reaches of a river
hutan – jungle; forest

imam – keeper of Islamic knowledge and leader of prayer
Islam Hadhari – policy of progressive Islamic government, promoted by prime minister Abdullah Badawi
istana – palace

jalan – road

kain songket – traditional Malay handwoven fabric with gold threads
kampung – village; also spelt kampong
kangkar – Chinese village
karst – characteristic scenery of a limestone region, including features such as underground streams and caverns
kedai kopi – coffee shop, often used for rustic restaurants
khalwat – literally, close proximity; exhibition of public affection between the sexes which is prohibited for unmarried Muslim couples
kongsi – Chinese clan organisations, also known as ritual brotherhoods, heaven-man-earth societies, triads or secret societies; meeting house for Chinese of the same clan
kopi tiam – traditional coffee shop
kota – fort; city
kramat – Malay shrine
kris – traditional Malay wavy-bladed dagger
KTM – Keretapi Tanah Melayu; Malaysian railway organisation
kuala – river mouth; place where a tributary joins a larger river

laksamana – admiral
langur – slender, dark-faced monkey
laut – sea
lebuh – street
Lebuhraya – expressway or freeway; usually refers to the North-South Highway, which runs from Johor Bahru to the Thai border
lorong – narrow street; alley
LRT – Light Rail Transit (Kuala Lumpur)
lubuk – deep pool

macaque – stocky monkey, often found at temples
mamak – Indian Muslim
mandi – bathe; Southeast Asian wash basin

masjid – mosque
MCP – Malayan Communist Party
merdeka – independence
muara – river mouth
muezzin – mosque official who calls the faithful to prayer

negara – country
negeri – state
Negrito – a dark-skinned indigenous tribal people
nonya – see *Baba-Nonya*

orang asing – foreigner
Orang Asli – literally, Original People; Malaysian aborigines
Orang Laut – literally, Coastal People
Orang Ulu – literally, Upriver People

padang – grassy area; field; also the city square
pantai – beach
parang – long jungle knife
PAS – Parti Islam SeMalaysia
pasar – market
pasar malam – night market
pawang – see *bomoh*
Pejabat Residen – Resident's Office
pekan – market place; town
pelabuhan – port
pencak silat – see *silat*
penghulu – chief or village head
pengkalan – quay
perahu – Malay-style sampan
Peranakan – refers to the *Baba-Nonya* or Straits Chinese
Proto-Malays – an indigenous tribal group; ancestors of the modern Malays
pua kumbu – traditional finely woven cloth
pulau – island
puteri – princess

raja – prince; ruler
raja muda – crown prince; heir apparent
rakyat – common people
rama rama – butterfly
rantau – straight coastline
rattan – stems from climbing palms used for wickerwork and canes
rimba – jungle
rotan – cane used to punish miscreants
roti – bread

sampan – small boat
samsu – Malay alcohol
sarung – all-purpose cloth, often sewn into a tube, and worn by women, men and children; also spelt sarong
seberang – opposite side of road; far bank of a river
selat – strait
semenanjung – peninsula
Senoi – one of Malaysia's indigenous tribal groups
silat – martial-arts dance form
simpang – crossing; junction
songkok – traditional Malay headdress worn by Muslim men
Straits Chinese – see *Baba-Nonya*
sultan – ruler of one of Malaysia's nine states
sungai – river
syariah – Islamic system of law

tambang – river ferry; fare
tamu – weekly market
tanah – land
tanjung – headland
tasik – lake
teluk – bay; sometimes spelt *telok*
temenggong – Malay administrator
towkang – Chinese junk
tunku – prince

ujung – cape
UMNO – United Malays National Organisation

warung – small eating stalls
wayang – Chinese opera
wayang kulit – shadow-puppet theatre
wisma – office block or shopping centre

yang di-pertuan agong – Malaysia's head of state, or 'king'
yang di-pertuan muda – under-king
yang di-pertuan negeri – governor

The Authors

JOE BINDLOSS

Coordinating Author, Kuala Lumpur

Joe first got hooked on Malaysia on long stopovers between London and Melbourne. Kuala Lumpur was where he ate his first bowl of *tom yam* soup and Penang where he first discovered the joys of laksa. Since then, he's been back numerous times, drawn by the easy pace of life, the energising cultural mix and the siren song of *roti canai*. Joe was born in Cyprus but now lives in London, where he writes about travel, education and city life for various newspapers, guidebooks and magazines.

CELESTE BRASH

Melaka & Penang

After attending Chiang Mai University in Thailand for a semester, Celeste Brash made her first foray into Malaysia and quickly fell in love with the ease of travel, the food and the cultural treats. She's come back several times since on long-haul trips through Southeast Asia and has always gone out of her way to spend time in Penang, one of her favourite cities. When not desensitising her taste buds with *sambal*, she and her family live in Tahiti, where the food is comparably bland and where some unaccustomed locals who have tried her cooking call her 'Spice Girl'.

CONTRIBUTING AUTHORS

Dr Trish Batchelor wrote the Health chapter. Trish is a general practitioner and travel medicine specialist who works at the CIWEC Clinic in Kathmandu, Nepal, and is a medical advisor to the Travel Doctor New Zealand clinics. She has travelled extensively through Southeast and East Asia.

Robyn Eckhardt wrote the Food & Drink chapter. Robyn has collaborated with photographer David Hagerman on food-focused articles for publications such as *Saveur*, *Olive*, *Travel + Leisure*, the *Chicago Tribune* and the *Wall Street Journal Asia*. After living in Asia for over 12 years she feels qualified to judge Malaysia the region's tastiest destination.

LONELY PLANET AUTHORS

Why is our travel information the best in the world? It's simple: our authors are independent, dedicated travellers. They don't research using just the internet or phone, and they don't take freebies in exchange for positive coverage. They travel widely, to all the popular spots and off the beaten track. They personally visit thousands of hotels, restaurants, cafés, bars, galleries, palaces, museums and more – and they take pride in getting all the details right, and telling it how it is. Think you can do it? Find out how at lonelyplanet.com.

Behind the Scenes

THIS BOOK

This first edition was written by Joe Bindloss and Celeste Brash. The book was commissioned in Lonely Planet's Melbourne office and produced by the following:

Commissioning Editors Holly Alexander, Tashi Wheeler
Coordinating Editors Maryanne Netto, Jeanette Wall
Coordinating Cartographer Corey Hutchison
Coordinating Layout Designer Carol Jackson
Managing Editors Geoff Howard, Katie Lynch
Managing Cartographer David Connolly
Managing Layout Designer Celia Wood
Assisting Editors Daniel Corbett, Kate Evans, Kate James, Robyn Loughnane, Alison Ridgway, Averil Robertson
Assisting Layout Designer Jacqui Saunders
Cover Designer Rebecca Dandens
Language Content Coordinator Quentin Frayne
Project Manager Chris Love

Thanks to Judith Bamber, Sin Choo, Eoin Dunlevy, Ryan Evans, Mark Germanchis, Nicole Hansen, Laura Jane, Yvonne Kirk, Lisa Knights, Adriana Mammarella, John Mazzocchi

THANKS

JOE BINDLOSS

This book is for my kid brothers Peter and Eddie – hopefully some of it will still be current when they go off on their own big round-the-world trips. In Kuala Lumpur, thanks to the helpful staff of Malaysia Tourism and the chefs who cooked up such brilliant food at Nasi Kandar Pelita and the other mamak restaurants around KL. Special thanks are due to Piers Benatar, Alan Maishman and Nadia Lobach for coming out to help road-test the KL nightlife and dining sections. Credit also to John Lim, Maria Danker, DJ Gabriel, Zulkifli Razali and Joan Chan for taking time out to contribute to Local Voices. Last up, thanks to Yean Ng and DJ Didjital at Zouk, and to Simon Richmond for his helpful text in *Malaysia, Singapore & Brunei*.

CELESTE BRASH

Thanks to my mom, Jan, for exploring Penang with me and to my husband, Josh, and kids Jasmine and Tevai for making the trip more insect-oriented. Joann Khaw is my hero history buff and

THE LONELY PLANET STORY

Fresh from an epic journey across Europe, Asia and Australia in 1972, Tony and Maureen Wheeler sat at their kitchen table stapling together notes. The first Lonely Planet guidebook, *Across Asia on the Cheap,* was born.

Travellers snapped up the guides. Inspired by their success, the Wheelers began publishing books to Southeast Asia, India and beyond. Demand was prodigious, and the Wheelers expanded the business rapidly to keep up. Over the years, Lonely Planet extended its coverage to every country and into the virtual world via lonelyplanet.com and the Thorn Tree message board.

As Lonely Planet became a globally loved brand, Tony and Maureen received several offers for the company. But it wasn't until 2007 that they found a partner whom they trusted to remain true to the company's principles of travelling widely, treading lightly and giving sustainably. In October of that year, BBC Worldwide acquired a 75% share in the company, pledging to uphold Lonely Planet's commitment to independent travel, trustworthy advice and editorial independence.

Today, Lonely Planet has offices in Melbourne, London and Oakland, with over 500 staff members and 300 authors. Tony and Maureen are still actively involved with Lonely Planet. They're travelling more often than ever, and they're devoting their spare time to charitable projects. And the company is still driven by the philosophy of *Across Asia on the Cheap*: 'All you've got to do is decide to go and the hardest part is over. So go!'

Peck Choo is one wild and crazy woman. The folks at Samudra Inn, Melaka, saved my gut and a lot of work hours by getting me to a good doctor on a Sunday. Special thanks to local-voice victims Khoo Salma and Charles Cham.

ACKNOWLEDGMENTS

Many thanks to the following for the use of their content:

Globe on title page ©Mountain High Maps 1993 Digital Wisdom, Inc.

Integrated Transit Network of Kuala Lumpur © KL Monorail System Sdn Bhd

Extract from *Malacca: Voices from the Street* © Lim Huck Chin and Fernando Jorge (2005).

SEND US YOUR FEEDBACK

We love to hear from travellers – your comments keep us on our toes and help make our books better. Our well-travelled team reads every word on what you loved or loathed about this book. Although we cannot reply individually to postal submissions, we always guarantee that your feedback goes straight to the appropriate authors, in time for the next edition. Each person who sends us information is thanked in the next edition – and the most useful submissions are rewarded with a free book.

To send us your updates – and find out about Lonely Planet events, newsletters and travel news – visit our award-winning website: **www.lonelyplanet.com/contact**.

Note: we may edit, reproduce and incorporate your comments in Lonely Planet products such as guidebooks, websites and digital products, so let us know if you don't want your comments reproduced or your name acknowledged. For a copy of our privacy policy visit www.lonelyplanet.com/privacy.

Index

000 Map pages
000 Photograph pages

INDEX

000 Map pages
000 Photograph pages

Y

Z

12am
1am
2am
3am
4am
5am
6am
7am
8am
9am
10am
11am
12pm
Mon
Sun
International Date Line
ARCTIC OCEAN
Queen Elizabeth Is (Can)
Ellesmere Is (Can)
Greenland (Denmark)
GREENLAND SEA
NORWEGIAN SEA
CHUKCHI SEA
BEAUFORT SEA
Banks Is (Can)
Victoria Is (Can)
BAFFIN BAY
Baffin Is (Can)
Russia
Alaska (US)
Iceland
NORTH SEA
BERING SEA
HUDSON BAY
LABRADOR SEA
United Kingdom
GULF OF ALASKA
Canada
Ireland
NORTH ATLANTIC OCEAN
8.30am
United States
Azores (Port)
Portugal
Spain
Morocco
NORTH PACIFIC OCEAN
Midway Is (US)
Bermuda (UK)
Canary Is (Sp)
GULF OF MEXICO
Mexico
The Bahamas
Cuba
Haiti
Mauritania
Mali
Hawaii (US)
Eastern Caribbean Islands
Cape Verde
Guatemala
Nicaragua
CARIBBEAN SEA
Senegal
Burkina Faso
Guinea
Panama
Venezuela
Guyana
Liberia
Ghana
Galapagos Is (Ecuador)
Colombia
Suriname
GULF OF GUINEA
EQUATOR
Kiribati
Ecuador
Samoa
2.30am
Ascension (UK)
Peru
Brazil
Tahiti
French Polynesia (Fr)
Tonga
Cook Is (NZ)
Bolivia
SOUTH ATLANTIC OCEAN
Pitcairn Is (UK)
Easter Is (Chile)
Paraguay
Chile
Uruguay
New Zealand
Argentina
Tristan da Cunha (UK)
12.45am
Gough Is (UK)
Chatham Is (NZ)
SOUTH PACIFIC OCEAN
Falkland Is (UK)
South Georgia & South Sandwich Is (UK)
Bouvet Is (Norway)

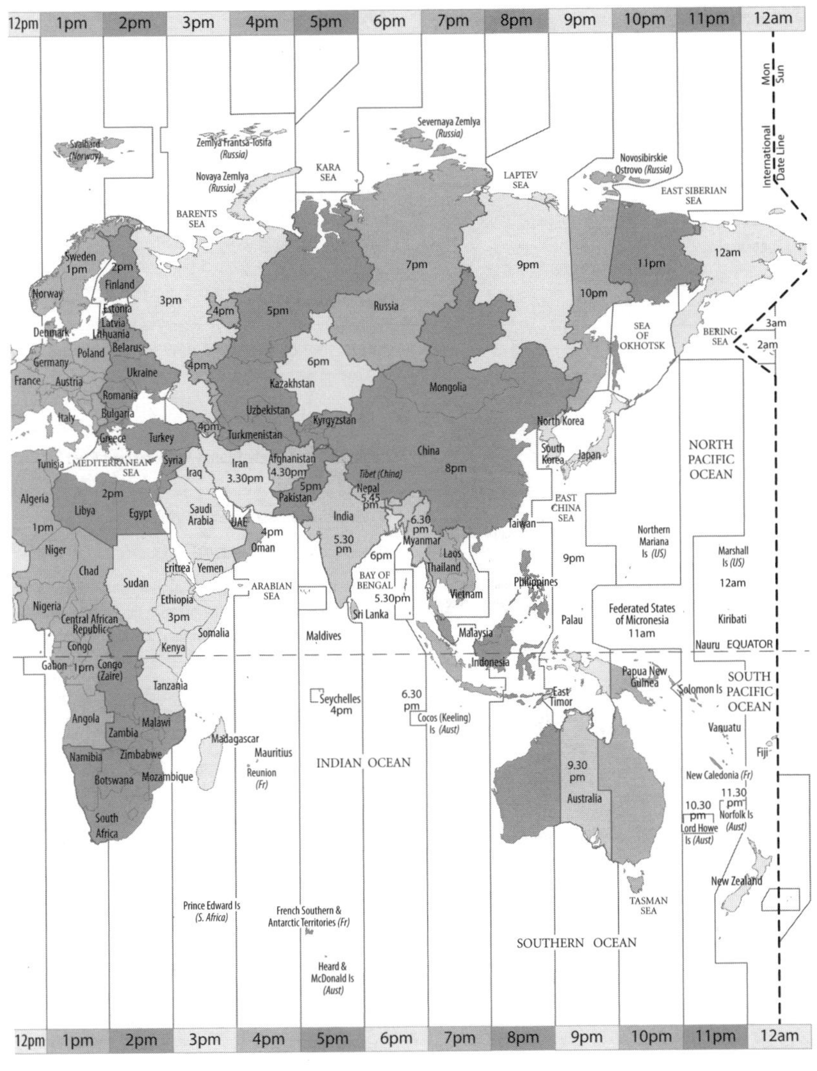
12pm
1pm
2pm
3pm
4pm
5pm
6pm
7pm
8pm
9pm
10pm
11pm
12am
Mon
Sun
International Date Line
Svalbard (Norway)
Zemlya Frantsa-Iosifa (Russia)
Novaya Zemlya (Russia)
Severnaya Zemlya (Russia)
KARA SEA
BARENTS SEA
LAPTEV SEA
Novosibirskie Ostrovo (Russia)
EAST SIBERIAN SEA
Sweden 1pm
Finland
Norway
Estonia
Latvia
Lithuania
Denmark
Belarus
Poland
Germany
Ukraine
France
Austria
Romania
Bulgaria
Italy
Greece
Turkey
Tunisia
MEDITERRANEAN SEA
Syria
Iraq
Iran 3.30pm
Algeria
Libya
Egypt
Saudi Arabia
UAE
Oman
Yemen
Eritrea
Sudan
Ethiopia 3pm
Somalia
Kenya
Tanzania
Niger
Chad
Nigeria
Central African Republic
Congo
Gabon
Congo (Zaire)
Angola
Zambia
Malawi
Namibia
Zimbabwe
Botswana
Mozambique
South Africa
Madagascar
Mauritius
Reunion (Fr)
Russia
Kazakhstan
Uzbekistan
Turkmenistan
Kyrgyzstan
Afghanistan 4.30pm
Pakistan
Mongolia
China
Tibet (China)
Nepal 5.45 pm
India 5.30 pm
6.30 pm Myanmar
Laos
Thailand
Vietnam
Sri Lanka
BAY OF BENGAL
5.30pm
ARABIAN SEA
Maldives
Seychelles 4pm
6.30 pm
Cocos (Keeling) Is (Aust)
INDIAN OCEAN
Malaysia
Indonesia
Philippines
Taiwan
North Korea
South Korea
Japan
EAST CHINA SEA
SEA OF OKHOTSK
BERING SEA
3am
2am
NORTH PACIFIC OCEAN
Northern Mariana Is (US)
Marshall Is (US)
Palau
Federated States of Micronesia 11am
Kiribati
Nauru EQUATOR
Papua New Guinea
Solomon Is
SOUTH PACIFIC OCEAN
East Timor
Vanuatu
Fiji
New Caledonia (Fr)
9.30 pm
Australia
10.30 pm
Lord Howe Is (Aust)
11.30 pm
Norfolk Is (Aust)
New Zealand
TASMAN SEA
SOUTHERN OCEAN
Prince Edward Is (S. Africa)
French Southern & Antarctic Territories (Fr)
Heard & McDonald Is (Aust)

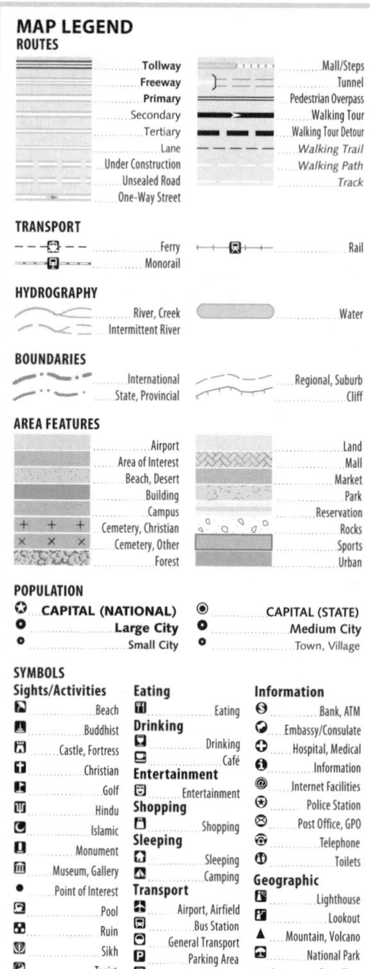

LONELY PLANET OFFICES

Australia

Head Office
Locked Bag 1, Footscray, Victoria 3011
☎ 03 8379 8000, fax 03 8379 8111
talk2us@lonelyplanet.com.au

USA

150 Linden St, Oakland, CA 94607
☎ 510 250-6400, toll free 800 275 8555
fax 510 893 8572
info@lonelyplanet.com

UK

2nd Fl, 186 City Rd,
London EC1V 2NT
☎ 020 7106 2100, fax 020 7106 2101
go@lonelyplanet.co.uk

Published by Lonely Planet Publications Pty Ltd
ABN 36 005 607 983

Cover photograph: Chinese blue house door with rickshaw/Mario Savola/Shutterstock. Many of the images in this guide are available for licensing from Lonely Planet Images: www.lonelyplanetimages.com.

Printed through Colorcraft Ltd, Hong Kong.
Printed in China.